TRAVELS IN THE MOGUL EMPIRE
1656 TO 1668

Travels in the Mogul Empire

1656 to 1668

FRANÇOIS BERNIER

A Revised and Improved Edition Based Upon Irving Brock's Translation by

ARCHIBALD CONSTABLE

MANOHAR

2026

First published 1891
Reprinted 2026

ISBN 978-81-19139-44-6

Published by
Ajay Kumar Jain *for*
Manohar Publishers & Distributors
4753/23 Ansari Road, Daryaganj
New Delhi 110 002

Printed and bound in India

TRAVELS

IN THE

MOGUL EMPIRE

A·D 1656-1668

BY

FRANÇOIS BERNIER

M·D OF THE FACULTY OF MONTPELLIER

A REVISED AND IMPROVED EDITION BASED
UPON IRVING BROCK'S TRANSLATION

BY

ARCHIBALD CONSTABLE

Westminster

ARCHIBALD CONSTABLE AND COMPANY

14 PARLIAMENT STREET S·W

MDCCCXCI

TABLE OF CONTENTS

LIST OF ILLUSTRATIONS

Figs 1-12 *reproduced by Messrs. Walker and Boutall, London.*

MAPS

Maps reproduced by John Bartholomew and Co., Edinburgh.

PREFACE

I WAS led to select *Bernier's Travels* as the opening volume of my ORIENTAL MISCELLANY Series for two reasons. An edition of this book had been promised, but never actually issued, by my Grandfather as one of the works to be included in that MISCELLANY, which may be regarded as the precursor of all the healthy, cheap, and popular literature of the present day; and, further, it was a book which I had ever admired, even before I was able, from actual experience, to fully appreciate its very remarkable accuracy.

Strange to say, although frequently reprinted and translated, there does not exist, so far as I am aware, any satisfactory edition as to general editing, notes, and so forth, and this has, I hope, proved of advantage to me. For all that, I cannot claim to have approached, even partially, an ideally perfect edition; but, to quote Bernier's own words as applied to his map of *The Mogol Empire,* I prefer to hope that I have produced a work 'not absolutely correct, but merely less incorrect than others that I have seen.' For instance, a copy of the Urdú translation made in 1875 by Colonel Henry Moore, and lithographed in two volumes 8vo, at Umritsur and Moradabad in 1886 and 1888 respectively, only reached my hands after the Bibliography had been printed off. Nor have I been able as yet to find any copy of a Lucknow reprint of the Delhi edition, No. 22 of the list.

In my treatment of Indian proper names, and Indian and Persian words generally, in my notes and elsewhere, I have availed myself very liberally of the 'time-honoured spelling' proviso or clause, laid down by authority, in the rules which govern the transliteration of such words.

In the matter of type, ornament, and printing generally, I have endeavoured to retain the old-time flavour of the early French and English editions, but I have never aimed at a facsimile reprint; and I need hardly add that in the text I have preserved the transliterations, admirably phonetic as they all are, to be found in the first French editions, and have avoided attempting any work that might be open to the charge of 'restoration' in the manner too often practised in the art of Architecture at the present day.

In accordance with these general principles I have given a translation of Bernier's Dedication to the French King, and of his Address to the Reader, both of which have been hitherto omitted from every edition except the first. They contain, as was generally the case at the period, a great deal of valuable personal history not to be found elsewhere, and all worthy of preservation.

The letter from M. de Monceaux the younger, to Mr. *H. O.*, given in the first English translation, and omitted in most of the subsequent reprints or new editions, has also been included, and containing as it does very pleasant testimony to the high esteem ('the most knowing Company on Earth') in which our own Royal Society was held by Foreign *savants* thus early in its history, I trust that it will prove of general interest, taken in connection with the identification of Mr. *H. O.* with the first indefatigable secretary of that illustrious body, which it has been my privilege to establish.

As will be seen from Appendix I., it is to the first English edition of Bernier that we are indebted for Dryden's masterpiece of *Aureng-Zebe*, a tragedy (first acted, it is believed, in the Spring of the year 1675, and printed in 1676) of which Dr. Johnson was moved to say that, founded on the actions of a great Prince then reigning, it was fortunate that his dominion was over nations not likely to employ their critics upon the transactions of the English stage; otherwise, 'if he had known and disliked his own character, our trade was not in those times secure from his resentment. His country is at such a distance, that the manners might be safely falsified, and the incidents feigned: for the remoteness of the place is remarked, by Racine, to afford the same conveniencies to a poet as length of time.' However, as may be gathered from Appendix I., the poetic licence allowed to himself by Dryden has enabled him to portray the character of Aurangzeb in a much more favourable light than the stern facts of history would warrant, and strange to say this seems to have been generally overlooked by those writers who have hitherto quoted Dr. Johnson's criticism.

An implicit believer in Professor J. R. Seeley's dictum—to be found in his work, *The Expansion of England*—that 'history, while it should be scientific in its method, should pursue a practical object; that is, it should not merely gratify the reader's curiosity about the past, but modify his view of the present and his forecast of the future,' I have endeavoured to illustrate several passages,—such as the Emperor Aurangzeb's distrust of a merely *mechanical* classical education, and Bernier's letter to Colbert concerning the absorption of gold in India,—by some comments applicable to them, as they are still 'burning questions' of the present hour; and I have thus, I hope, shown how I trust to be able at all times to justify my adoption of a recent utterance by Professor Max Müller as the *leit motiv* of my ORIENTAL MISCELLANY Series. I venture to draw the attention of all students of the origin of portrait-painting among the Moslem artists of India in the Mogul period, to the composition of the portraits I have reproduced as illustrations to Bernier's text. This is a subject I hope to treat of elsewhere, and thus endeavour to utilise the extensive collections I made in India during a series of years, with this object in view.

To my friend of bygone days in Lucknow,—and of the present too, I rejoice to think,—General Sir Martin Dillon, K.C.B., C.S.I., I am indebted for invaluable encouragement and help of all kinds. To the President and Council of the Royal Society I offer my sincere thanks for permission to examine the Oldenburg MS. correspondence in their archives. To Colonel Hanna I am grateful for his liberality in communicating to me the valuable original paintings which have added so much to the enrichment of this volume; and to Dr. V. Ball, F.R.S. of Dublin, for his aid with regard to Appendix II. My thanks are also due to Mr. George Scharf, C.B., and his assistant Mr. L. G. Holland, for their kind aid in the matter of the description of the Oldenburg portrait. To my kinsman, Archibald [David] Constable, I can never sufficiently express my obligation and sense of the valuable suggestions his oft-tried literary judgment so freely placed at my disposal at all times.

Following the traditions of my forefathers, I have done my utmost to enlist the skill and knowledge of craftsmen of our own country, as an aid to my project; and I believe that whatever may be the literary defects of this edition, only too well known to myself, its mechanical production does credit to my friends and fellow-workers, Mr. Allan Wyon, F.S.A., Chief Engraver of HER MAJESTY'S seals; Messrs. T. and A. Constable, HER MAJESTY'S Printers for Scotland; Messrs. McLagan and Cumming, Lithographic Artists, of Edinburgh; Messrs. Walker and Boutall, Automatic and Photographic Engravers, of London; Messrs. J. Bartholomew and Company, Geographers, of Edinburgh; and, finally, to my binders, Messrs. Matthew Bell, Colley, and Company, of London, who have received all my suggestions, and given effect to them, in a spirit which has largely aided me in elaborating my designs for the standard binding of this Series. Messrs. Bell and Colley have also, I am comforted to think, long since forgiven me for suggesting the punning device on the binder's ticket, which has been prepared for use throughout my Publications.

A. C.

BRONDESBURY,
11*th November* 1891.

CHRONICLE

CHRONICLE

OF

SOME OF THE PRINCIPAL EVENTS

IN THE

LIFE AND TIMES

OF

FRANÇOIS BERNIER

Louis XIII., King of France.
James Stuart, VI. of Scotland and I. of England, reigns in England.
Jáhangír, Emperor of Hindostan.

Born at Joué, near Gonnord, in Anjou. His parents, cultivators of the soil, were leaseholders, in the Barony of Etiau, of land belonging to the Canonry of St. Maurice at Angers. **1620. September 25th or 26th.**

Baptized. **September 26th.**

> Aujourd'hui vingt-sixiesme jour de septambre mil six cent vingt, a esté baptizé par moy curé soubsigné François fils de honnorable homme Pierre Bernier et de Andrée Grimault; fut parrain vénérable et discret Messire François Bernier curé de Chantzaux, et marraine honneste fille Julliesne Bonnin, laquelle ma déclarer ne sçavoir signer.
>
> F. Bernier. Guytton.

—(*Register of the Parish of Joué, preserved in the Archives of the Commune of Joué-Etiau.*)

Charles I., King of England, begins to reign, 27th March 1625.
Louis XIV. succeeds to the throne of France, 14th May 1643.
Sháh Jahán, Emperor of Hindostan, 4th February 1628.
Commonwealth proclaimed in England, 30th January 1648-9.

Travels in Northern Germany, Poland, Switzerland and Italy. **1647-1650.**

1652. May 5th. Having passed an examination in physiology, for which he had been prepared by the philosopher Gassendi, in Provence, he matriculates at the University of Montpellier.

July 18th. Passes his examination as licentiate in medicine.

August 26th. Takes his degree as Doctor of Medicine, and subsequently goes to Paris.

1654. Visits Palestine and Syria.

1655. October 24th. Tends, together with Antoine de la Potherie, amanuensis, the philosopher Gassendi in his last illness, and is present at his death.

Bernier undoubtedly owed his great powers of accurate observation to his training under Gassendi, and he has warmly recorded his sense of gratitude to M. Chapelle (who first introduced him to that philosopher) in the last paragraph of his letter to M. Chapelain, on the Gentiles of Hindostan, see p. 349.

Admirable testimony to the genius of Gassendi has been borne by Henry Rogers as follows: 'The character of Gassendi's intellect is everywhere indicated by his works;—it was *critical* rather than inventive. . . . Gassendi's powers of acquisition must have been singularly active; nor was his logical acuteness, or the liveliness of his imagination, much inferior to the promptness and retentiveness of his memory. His learning is never mere learning; like that of many of his erudite contemporaries, it ministers to his intellect, but does not oppress it. The vivacity of his mind animates and penetrates the mass; and the acuteness of his reasoning and the exuberance of his illustrations relieve of much of their tedium discussions in themselves often uninviting enough.' *Encyc. Brit.* Eighth edition, 1856.

Aurangzeb proclaims himself Emperor of Hindostan, under the title of Alamgir, 21st July 1658.

1656-1658. Goes to Egypt. Has 'the plague' at Rosetta. Lives at Cairo for upwards of a year. Embarks at Suez for Jedda, where he is detained for nearly five weeks. Sails thence for Moka, where he arrives after a passage of fifteen days. Is compelled to abandon his intention of visiting Abyssinia, and sets sail in an Indian vessel for Surat, which he reaches in twenty-two days, most probably towards the end of 1658 or early in 1659.

1659. March-April. After the battle fought at Deorá near Ajmere, between the Princes Aurangzeb and Dárá, on the 12th-13th March 1659, Bernier, then on his way from Surat to Agra, is compelled by Dárá, whom he meets near Ahmedabad, to accompany him as his physician. Dárá being obliged to fly towards Sind, Bernier is harassed by robbers; but eventually reaches Ahmedabad, where he falls in with a Mogul Noble who was travelling to Delhi, and places himself under his protection.

Charles II. of England enters London, 29th May 1660. Restoration.

Is in Delhi, whence he dates his letter to M. de la Mothe le Vayer, see p. 239. **1663. July 1st.**

At Delhi, Aurangzeb about to start for Kashmír. **1664. December 14th.**

At Lahore, Aurangzeb having arrived there. **1665. February 25th.**

After travelling in Kashmír, he voyages to Bengal with Tavernier, who left Agra on the 25th November. On the 6th December they are at Alum Chand, about eighteen miles west of Allahabad. **December 6th.**

Tavernier and Bernier part company near Rájmahál. Bernier proceeding to Kásimbázár (Tavernier's *Travels.* Edited by Dr. Ball, London, 1889), afterwards travelling from Bengal to Masulipatam (see my text, p. 113) and Golkonda, where he heard of the death of the Sháh Jahán (p. 198), which event happened on the 22d January 1666. **1666. January 6th.**

In this year he was still in Golkonda (text, p. 195), and it is probable that in the early part of it he embarked at Surat, where he saw Chardin the traveller, see page 312. **1667.**

He is at Sheraz in Persia, see p. 300. **October 4th.**

Is at Taduan near Sheraz, whence he addresses a letter to M. Chapelain at Paris, received there on the 15th February 1669. **1668. June 4th.**

M. Chapelain addresses a letter on the 26th April from Paris to Bernier at Marseilles. **1669. April-May.**

Bernier is still at Marseilles, as would appear from a letter addressed to him there by M. Chapelain. It is probable that shortly after this date he was in Paris arranging for the publication of his Travels. **September 25th.**

Date of the French King's Licence for the printing and publishing of his book. **1670. April 25th.**

The transfer of all his rights in the publication, to Claude Barbin, is registered in the book of the Booksellers and Printers of Paris. **August 13th**

James II. succeeds to the Crown of England, 6th February 1685.

Visits England. **1685.**

Dies at Paris. **1688. September 22d.**

Extrait du Registre des sépultures faites en l'église paroissiale de St. Barthélemy à Paris de septembre 1677 *à mars* 1692.

Année 1688.—Le jeudi vingt-troisième septembre a été inhumé dans cette église Me François Bernier, docteur en médecine de la Faculté de Montpellier, âgé de soixante et treize ans, décédé le vingt-deuxième du dit mois en la maison place Dauphine, à la Renommée, de cette paroisse. Ont assisté au convoy Philippe Bourigault, aussi docteur en médecine de la dite Faculté, demeurant de présent susdite place Dauphine, et Martin Barthelemy d'Herbelot, escuyer, demeurant rue de Touraine, paroisse St. Sulpice.

B. D'HERBELOT. P. BOURIGAULT.

His friend D'Herbelot, the Orientalist, and his nephew Philippe Bourigault, who arranged for his burial, would appear to have given his age inexactly as seventy-three, whereas he was then a few days short of sixty-eight years.

Bernier does not appear to have been long ill, and it is said that his death resulted from an apoplectic fit, the effect of excitement caused by some rude bantering he had been subjected to when in the company of M. le Procureur-général de Harlay. He had made his will on the 18th September, bequeathing his property to his nephew Philippe Bourigault, charged with legacies to Antoine de la Potherie, his man of business, formerly secretary to Gassendi, to the Prior of Saint-Marc-lès-Vendôme, his two female servants, and another.

For the facts contained in the foregoing Chronicle I am mainly indebted to the researches of Drs. E. Farge and Pompée Mabille, and M. L. De Lens; see *Biographies and Miscellanea*, No. 12-16, p. xlii.

BIBLIOGRAPHY

A BIBLIOGRAPHY[1] OF THE WRITINGS OF FRANÇOIS BERNIER.

TRAVELS IN THE MOGOL EMPIRE.

Issues in the Author's Lifetime.

I.—AS A SEPARATE PUBLICATION.

HISTOIRE | DE LA DERNIERE | REVOLUTION | DES ETATS | DU GRAND MOGOL, | *Dediée AV ROY,* | *Par le Sieur F. BERNIER* | *Medecin de la Faculté de* | *Montpellier.* | [Ornament] | A PARIS, | Chez CLAUDE BARBIN, | au Palais, | ſur le Perron de la ſainte Chapelle. | M.DC.LXX. | *Avec Privilege du Roy.* | I **Paris 1670 2 vols. 12mo.**

[Frontispiece, Map of the Empire of the Great Mogul ; title-page ; Dedication to the King, two leaves ; Address to the Reader, one leaf ; pages 268. The map (reproduced at p. 238 of this volume) is interesting, and the position of many of the places tolerably accurate, others are very far out. For a translation of the Dedication to the King, and the Address to the Reader, see pp. xlv.-xlvii.]

EVENEMENS | PARTICULIERS, | Ou ce qui s'est passé de plus | considerable aprés la guerre | pendant cinq ans, ou en- | viron, dans les Etats du | grand Mogol. | *Avec vne Lettre de l'étenduë de* | *l'Hindoustan, Circulation de l'or* | *& de l'argent pour venir s'y abî-* | *mer, Richesses, Forces, Iustice,* | *& Cause principale de la Deca-* | *dence des Etats d'Asie.* | TOME II. | [Ornament] | A PARIS, | Chez CLAUDE BARBIN, au Palais, | ſur le Perron de la Ste Chapelle. | M.DC. LXX. | *Avec Privilege du Roy.* |

[Title-page. Pages 294. Abridgment of the Letters-Patent of the King, authorising the printing and publication of the book ; one leaf. This authority is dated Paris, 5th April 1670, and ends by stating that the Sieur Bernier had made over to Claude Barbin the right of printing, publishing, and selling the said work.]

N.B. In the British Museum Library Catalogue there is an entry—

[1] For much valuable aid in the preparation of this Bibliography I am indebted to Mr. John P. Anderson of the British Museum.

Pressmark 1434. *a.*—of the issue of Tome II. as a separate work in the same year, viz. 1670. A careful examination and measurement of the volume in question (which was at one time in the possession of Henri Ternaux—afterwards Ternaux-Compans—the well-known historian and bibliographer of books of early travel, each of the outside covers bearing his well-known crest, a ram's head, with his initials H. T. in Gothic letters, all stamped in gold), has convinced the writer that there is an error in the entry. The mistake has arisen from the fact that some owner of the volume has erased the words 'TOME II.' from the title-page. The British Museum cataloguer has thus been led to suppose that he had a copy of a 'reissue' in his hands; this belief being strengthened, perhaps, by the fact of the volume having the leaf with the *Extrait du Privilege du Roy* at the end, following page 294, as in the copy with 'TOME II.' on the title-page described above. The volume in question is half-bound in calf, gilt tooling and ornaments in the Ternaux-Compans style, and is lettered at the back EVENEMENTS | DES ETATS | DU MOGUL | PARIS 1670. |

2 **Paris 1671. 2 vols. 12mo.** SVITE | DES | MEMOIRES | DV S[R] BERNIER, | SVR | L'EMPIRE | DV GRAND MOGOL. | *DEDIEZ AV ROY* | [Ornament] | A PARIS, | Chez CLAVDE BARBIN, au Palais, | fur le Peron de la Sainte | Chapelle. | M.DC. LXXI | AVEC PRIVILEGE DV ROY. |

[Title-page. Pages 3-178. Letter to Monsieur de la Mothe le Vayer, written at Dehli 1st July 1663, descriptive of Dehli and Agra etc. Blank leaf. Pages 1-137, Letter to Monsieur Chapelain, despatched from Chiras in Persia, 4th October 1667, concerning the superstitions etc. of the Indous or Gentiles of Hindoustan. Pages 1-69, Letter to Monsieur Chapelle, despatched from Chiras in Persia, 10th June 1668, regarding his intention of resuming his studies of some points relating to the atomic theory, and the nature of the human understanding.]

SVITE | DES | MEMOIRES | DV S[R] BERNIER, | SVR | L'EMPIRE | DV GRAND MOGOL. | *DEDIEZ AV ROY.* | [Ornament] | A PARIS, | Chez CLAVDE BARBIN, au Palais, | fur le Perron de la Sainte | Chapelle. | M.DC. LXXI. | *AVEC PRIVILEGE DV ROY.* |

[Title-page. General title to the series of letters descriptive of the journey to Kashmír made in 1664 in the suite of the *Great Mogol*, one leaf. Pages 5-285. The series of nine letters to Monsieur de Merveilles, the first being written from Dehli on the 14th December 1664, Aurengzebe being then about to start. Pages 286-293. 'Some particulars omitted to be inserted in my first work, which will serve to improve the map of Hindoustan, and afford details concerning the Revenue of the Great Mogol.' On *verso* of page 293 an abstract of the King's Licence (for a translation, see p. 461 of this volume) given in Tome

II. of 1670, to which is appended the certificate of registration of the publication as follows :—

Registré ſur le Livre de la Communauté des Libraires & Imprimeurs de Paris, le 13. *Aouſt* 1670. *Signé* LOVIS SEVESTRE, *Syndic.*

THE | HISTORY | OF | The Late Revolution | OF | The EMPIRE of the | *GREAT MOGOL* : | TOGETHER WITH | The moſt considerable Passages, | for 5 years following in that *Empire.* | *To which is added,* | A LETTER to the Lord *COLBERT,* | touching the extent of *Indostan* | the | Circulation of the Gold and Silver of | the World, to diſcharge it ſelf there ; | as also the *Riches, Forces,* and *Justice* | of the ſame : And the Principal Cauſe | of the Decay of the States of *Aſia.* | By Monsr *F. BERNIER,* | Phyſitian of the Faculty of *Montpelier.* | *Engliſh'd out of French.* | *LONDON* | Printed, and sold by *Moſes Pitt* | at the *White Hart* in *Little Britain, Simon Miller* | at the *Star* in *St. Paul's* Church-Yard, and *John* | *Starkey* at the *Miter* near *Temple-Bar,* 1671. | 3 London 1671. 2 vols. 8vo.

[Title-page. Seven pages, an extract of a letter written to Mr. H[ENRY] O[LDENBURG] from Monsr *de Monceaux* the younger, giving a character of the book here *Englished,* and its Author. Six pages, *The Heads of the Principal Contents of this History, Added by the* English *Interpreter.* One page, Errata of Tome I. and Tome II. Pages 1-258, The history of the late Revolution of the Dominions of the Great *Mogol.*]

Particular Events; | OR THE | Most Considerable | PASSAGES | After the War of Five Years, or | thereabout, in the Empire of the GREAT MOGOL. | Together with a Letter concern-| ing the Extent of *INDOSTAN* ; the | Circulation of the Gold and Silver at | laſt ſwallow'd up there ; the Riches, Forces, Justice, and the Principal Cause of the Decay of the States of *ASIA.* | TOM. II. | *London,* Printed by S. G. for *Moses Pitt* at | the *White Hart* in *Little Britain,* 1671.

[Title-page as above. Pages 1-176, Particular events etc. Pages 1-102, Letter to Colbert. Map of The EMPIRE of the *Great* MOGOL. This map has been copied from the one in the First French edition, Paris, 1670, some of the names have been Anglicized, and, although not quite so well engraved, it is printed on better paper. One leaf, Advertisement of the publication by *M. Pitt* of an English translation, price 1s. 6d. in 8vo. of the voyage of *Roland Frejus* of *Marſeilles* to *Mauritania* in *Africk,* in 1666, by the *French* King's Order.]

A CONTINUATION | OF THE | MEMOIRES | OF | Monſieur BERNIER, | Concerning the | *Empire* of the *Great Mogol* : | *Wherein is contained* | I. An exact Deſcription of DEHLI | and AGRA, the Capital Cities of 4 London 1672. 2 vols. 8vo.

the Em- | pire of the Great MOGOL; together with | some particulars, making known the COURT | and GENIUS of the *Mogols* and *Indians*; | as alſo the Doctrine, and Extravagant Super | -ſtitions and Customs of the Heathen of | *INDOSTAN.* | 2. The Emperour of *Mogol's* Voyage to the | Kingdom of *Kachemire,* in the year 1664. | 3. A LETTER, written by the Author to | *M. Chapelle,* touching his Deſign of returning, after | all his Peregrinations, to his Studies; where he ta- | keth occaſion to discourse of | the Doctrine of | ATOMS, and the Nature of the Understanding of MAN, | TOME III. and IV. | English'd out of *French* by H. O. | *LONDON* | Printed, and are to be sold by *Moſes Pitt,* at | the *White Hart* in *Little Britain.* 1672. |

[Title-page. Four pages, The Heads of the Chief Contents of the *Third Tome.* Five pages, The Heads of the *Fourth Tome.* Three pages, List of books '*to be ſold by* Moses Pitt *at the* White Hart *in* Little Britain.' One Leaf, Licence for printing and publishing 'this Continuation of the *Memoires* of *Mons. Bernier,*' dated, *Whitehall, April* 24, 1671, and signed, *JOHN COOKE.* Pages 1-173, Letter to Monsieur de la Mothe le Vayer.]

A | CONTINUATION | OF THE | HISTORIE | OF | *Monsieur Bernier* Concerning the EMPIRE of | the GREAT MOGOL. | PARTICULARLY | A Relation of the Voyage made *A.* 1664 | by the great Mogol *Aurenge Zebe,* mar- | ching with his Army from *Dehly* to *La* | *hor,* from *Lahor* to *Bember,* and from | *Bember* to the Kingdom of *Kachemire,* by | the Mogols called the *Paradise of the* | *Indies.* | TOME IV. | London, Printed by S. G., and sold by *Moſes* | *Pitt* at the Signe of the White Hart in | *Little Britain.*

[Title-page. General title to the series of letters, one leaf. Pages 2-174, The series of nine letters to Monsieur de Merveilles. Pages 175-178, '*Some particulars forgotten to be inſerted in my firſt Book, to perfect the* Map *of* Indoſtan, *and to know the Revenue of the* Great Mogol.' Pages 1-39, Letter to Monsieur Chapelle. One page, List of books to be sold by *Moſes Pitt.* This is the earliest English translation of the Editio Princeps.]

5
Amsterdam
1672.
4 vols. in one.
12mo.

OPROER | int | RYCK VAN MOGOL, | t'Amſterdam, | *By Joannes Janſsonius van* | *Waeſberge. Anno* 1672. | [At foot of a copperplate engraving representing a Mogul executioner, sword in right hand, and holding up the head of a man whose body lies at his feet. In background a general scrimmage or uproar.]

VERHAEL | Van der laetſten | OPROER | Inden Staet des | GROOTEN | MOGOLS. | Tegelijck oock vervattende veeler- | ley ſeldſaeme Voorvallen. | Beſchreven | Door de Heer F. BERNIER, | Medicijn in de Faculteyt van | Montpellier | En nu Vertaeldt door | SIMON DE VRIES. | [Printer's mark, Spreading olive-tree with vine round trunk, aged man to right, with NON SOLUS to left.] | t'AMSTELDAM, | By JOHANNES JANSSONIUS van | WAESBERGE. 1672. |

[Engraved title-page, as above. Printed title-page, as above. Two pages, the Translator to the Reader, dated Utrecht, 1st May 1672, and signed SIMON de VRIES. Map IMPERII | MAGNI MOGOLIS | *Novis-sima Descriptio.* | Pages 1-140, History of the late Revolution, etc. Title-page to vol. ii. Pages 3-162, Occurrences after the war and the letter to Colbert. Title-page to vol. iii. Pages 3-94, Letter to Monsieur De la Mothe le Vayer. Pages 95-168, Letter to Monsieur Chappelain (*sic*). Pages 169-200, Letter to Monsieur Chapelle. Title-page to vol. iv. Pages 3-146, The series of nine letters to Monsieur de Merveilles on the journey to Kashmír, etc. Pages 147-151, Some particulars forgotten to be inserted in the first volume, etc. The Translator has taken the trouble to verify the figures, but has himself fallen into an error. His words are 'De reghte reeckeningh is: Over de 230. *Millionen Roupies*, of meer als 345. *Millionen* guldens sijnde 3450. Tonnen Gouds.' Which may be English'd thus: 'The correct amount of this statement is above 230 *millions* of rupees, or more than 345 millions of gulders which would amount to 3450 *tons* of gold.[1]

A very choicely printed edition, and the first with any pictorial illustrations. There are no notes of any kind, but here and there the French equivalent for the Dutch is given. The map of the Mogul Empire, which has been compiled from various sources, is in many ways superior to the one in the first French edition, and is reproduced at page 454 of my edition. Bombay, titled *Bombaja*, is shown, an early mention of the name of that city and territory ceded to Charles II. by the Portuguese in 1661.

The illustrations, all copperplate engravings, some of them rather weak in their mechanical execution, are as follows: Vol. i. facing page 12, to illustrate the incident recorded at page 13 of my edition, Begum Sahib and her Khansaman (Steward), a mere fancy sketch; Begum Sahib with an ostrich plume headdress, but with a very chubby, honest Dutch face, and so forth. Page 58, The battle of Samúgarh.

Vol. ii. page 10, The Tartar Princess shooting arrows into a band of Mogul soldiery, who are falling fast; see pp. 122, 123 of my edition. Page 22, Didar Khan and the wife of the Gentile Scrivener.

Vol. iii. page 33, The Great Mogul riding in state, several of the details correct, according to Bernier's text, as a whole a mere fancy sketch. Page 44, An outriding (*Suwarí*) of the Great Mogul. At page 61 is an interesting map of the Kingdom of Kashmír, a new and accurate delineation (REGNI KACHEMIRE *Nova et Accurata de-*

[1] A *ton* of gold = one hundred thousand gulders (Picard's *Dutch Dictionary*). Tavernier constantly talks of this measure of account. The gulder may be here taken as worth about 1s. 9d. to 1s. 9½d.

scriptio). This has been compiled from the text of Bernier's account, and is curiously incorrect. The royal elephants falling from the *Pire Penjale* (see page 408 of my edition, where this map is reproduced), are shown thereon. At the back of the map is inserted an engraving of an elephant fight; see page 276, *et seq.*, also a mere fancy sketch.]

6 [Edition not seen.]

La Haye
1671-72.
? vols.
12mo.

7 [Edition not seen. It is a German translation by Johann Wilhelm Serlin, who was also its publisher, of the first French editions, Nos. 1 and 2.]

Frankfort A/M.
1672-73.
4 vols.
12mo.

8 Istoria della ultima revoluzione delli Stati del Gran Mogor dell Sr. Bernier tradotta in Italiano. [Edition not seen.]

Milan 1675.
? vols.
12mo.

9 Vol. i. has the same title-page as in the 1671 edition (No. 3), with the addition of the words THE SECOND EDITION above the imprint.

London 1676.
2 vols.
8vo.

Vol. ii. the same title-page as in the first edition, but printed by William Godbid. Both these volumes are in smaller type than the first edition, but otherwise it has been followed. The third and fourth volumes of the first edition (No. 4) do not appear to have been reprinted for the second edition, but copies of the complete work, made up with vols. i. and ii. second edition, and iii. and iv. of the first, bound up together, are not uncommon. Probably vols. iii. and iv. did not sell as well as vols. i. and ii.

II.—WITH OTHER WORKS.

10 Collections of travels through Turkey into Persia and the East Indies, giving an account of the present state of those countries. . . . Being the travels of Monsieur Tavernier, Bernier, and other great men. . . . The second volume, London, Printed for Moses Pitt at the Angel in St. Paul's Churchyard, M.DC.LXXXIV.

London 1684.
Folio.

[A reprint of the four volumes of Bernier's History of the late Revolution, etc., London, 1671-2, is contained in pages 1-154. We learn from the copy of the letter from Monsieur de Monceaux the younger, as given in this edition, that the Translator's name was Mr. H[enry] Ouldinburgh. This name is also spelt Oldenburg, see Appendix V.]

Issues since the Author's Death.

I.—AS A SEPARATE PUBLICATION.

Voyages de François Bernier, Docteur en Medecine de la Faculté de Montpellier, contenant la Description des Etats du Grand Mogol, de l'Hindoustan, du Royaume de Kachemire, etc., . . . Le tout enrichi de Cartes et de Figures . . A Amsterdam, Chez Paul Marret, Marchand Libraire dans le Beurs-straet, à la Renommée. M.DC.XCIX. **11 Amsterdam 1699. 2 vols. 12mo.**

[Frontispieces to both volumes the same, the Great Mogul riding in state, a mere fancy sketch.

Vol. i., Map of the Mogol Empire, copied from the one in the first French edition, facing p. 5.

Vol. ii. The illustrations are as follows:—Engraving of Inhabitants of Agra, facing page 5, some of the details from authentic Eastern sources, but not applicable to Agra. Folding plate of The Court of the Great Mogul, facing page 40, compiled from the text of Bernier and various other writers, curious, here and there an authentic detail. This plate has been used to illustrate various other accounts of the Mogul Court. The Great Mogul being weighed against coin, folding plate, facing page 55, a mere fancy sketch. Two elephants fighting, folding plate facing page 63, copied in part from the engraving at page 61, vol. iii., of edition No. 5. Folding plate, facing page 97, background, hilly landscape with a representation of a Hindoo idol, of the Satyr type usually met with in books of travel of that period; to the left a Moslem Fakir playing on a *meerdung* (species of drum worn round the neck, and played on with the fingers of both hands); to the right, a female figure, intended, I believe, to represent a woman on the way to consult a devotee of some sort. Both of these figures have been copied from drawings after nature, and are undoubtedly quite authentic. Opposite page 113, folding plate of a Suttee ceremony; to the left two figures in Western dress looking on, a mere fancy sketch. At page 123, a Hindoo Fakir, with his arms above his head, from nature. Folding plate opposite page 236, the Great Mogul riding in state, copied from the engraving at page 33, vol. iii., edition No. 5. Several of the details of arms, musical instrument in hand of mounted figure in the foreground, etc., have been copied from an early MS. copy of the Ain-i-Akbari, in which there are drawings of these and other objects to illustrate the text, and after which the plates in Blochmann's[1] edition have been compiled. Other details, such as the trappings of the elephant, etc., incorrect and of no value. This plate (or modifications of it) has often been used for illustrating early books on India. At page 269, Carte nouvelle du ROYAVME DE KACHEMIRE, a French translation of the map at page 61, vol. iii., of edition No. 5, fairly well engraved. Facing page 343, a map of the sources of the river Nile, curious as an illustration to Bernier's text, and typical of the delineation of the sources of the Nile, and 'adjacent country' (!) that lingered on all maps until comparatively modern times.]

12
Amsterdam 1710 and 1709. (*sic.*) 2 vols. 12mo.

Voyages de François Bernier, etc. [A reprint of No. 11. Vol. ii. has M.DCC.IX. as imprint,—a mistake, I take it, for M.DCCXI., or it may be that vol. ii. is from another edition of 1709,—the ornaments on the title-pages of 1710 and 1709 differing.]

13
Amsterdam 1711. 2 vols. 12mo.

Voyages de François Bernier, etc. [A reprint of No. 11. The plates for the maps and illustrations wearing out, and showing great signs of having been 'touched up.']

14
Amsterdam 1723. 2 vols. 12mo.

Voyages de François Bernier, etc. [A reprint of No. 11., with the same maps and plates.]

15
Amsterdam 1724 and 1723. (*sic.*) 2 vols. 12mo.

Voyages de François Bernier, etc. [A reprint of No. 11, with a few errors corrected in vol. i., which has on the title-page *Nouvelle Edition revûe & corrigée*, but this is the only vol. of the new edition. Vol. ii. is of the 1723 edition, and bears on title-page M.DCCXXIII. The map of the Mogul Empire does not appear to have been issued with vol. i.]

16
Amsterdam 1725. 2 vols. 12mo.

Voyages de François Bernier, etc. [Edition not seen.]

17
London 1826. 2 vols. 8vo.

Travels in the Mogul Empire, by Francis Bernier. Translated from the French by Irving Brock. In two volumes. London: William Pickering, Chancery-Lane. 1826.

[1] Calcutta. Asiatic Society of Bengal, 1873, vol. i. All published as yet.

[An exceedingly well printed book. Valuable appendices, considering the period when published, and a preface that practically contains all that was then known about Bernier. The translator was handicapped by an evident want of any acquaintance with the East, and has therefore failed to bring out the extreme accuracy of much that Bernier records. Monsieur de Monceaux's letter to Mr. H. O., and the valuable statement regarding the Mogul Revenues (see pages 455-460 of my edition), have been omitted. As stated elsewhere, I have used Mr. Brock's translation to some extent as the basis for my own.]

In a prospectus, dated Edinburgh, 20th June 1825, *The travels of Francis Bernier, and his Account of the Court of the Great Mogul, 2 vols.*, is announced as a work under preparation for *Constable's Miscellany*. This book was never included in that series, and it is possible that the edition described above, No. 17, was originally prepared for it. At present I have not been able to verify this.

Bernier's Travels: comprehending a description of the Mogol 18
Empire including the Kingdom of Kashmir, etc. etc. etc. Translated **Calcutta 1826.**
from the French by John Steuart. Condo et compono quae mox **1 vol.**
depromere possim. Calcutta: Printed at the Baptist Mission Press, **8vo.**
11 Circular Road, 1826.

[Title-page. One leaf, dedication, dated Calcutta, 1st January 1826, to Captain George Anderson Vetch, of the Bengal Army.[1] Pages i.-iii, Translator's Preface. Page iv., blank. Pages v.-vi., Advertisement, which contains many mistakes relating to Bernier's career and other editions of his works. Pages vii.-viii, Contents. Pages 1-58, Letter to Monsieur Chapelain. The series of nine letters to Monsieur de Merveilles pages 59-143, from which the concluding six paragraphs as well as the answers to the five questions put by M. Thévenot have been omitted. Pages 144-213, Letter to Monsieur de la Mothe le Vayer, containing the description of Dehli and Agra, etc. At the end six pages of correspondence, being reprints of a series of letters signed 'Oscar,' 'Censorious,' and 'A Subscriber,' which appeared in the *India Gazette*, ranging in date from 12th January 1826 to 18th February 1826, relating to the forthcoming publication. 'Censorious' appears to have seen the MS., or perhaps proof-sheets, as he condemns the book from every point of view. 'Oscar,' who was perhaps Captain Vetch, replies, appealing for fair play: 'Most critics, Mr. Editor, have the grace to wait at least till the game is fairly started, and then give the *vieu holla*; but this poacher in the fields of criticism takes a pot-shot at his prey in its seat, while with palpitating breast it is about to open on the public view.'

[1] Fifty-fourth Regiment Native Infantry, in charge of the construction of the road from Benares to Allahabad. *Bengal Army List* for 1826.

Judging from the style of the translation, the intimate acquaintance with India apparent all through, and the endings, such as,

'I remain,
My dear Sir,
Your ever faithful and affectionate,
FRANCIS BERNIER'

which are, without any warrant, appended to many of the letters, Mr. Steuart was probably an East Indian clerk in some Government office, who had a knowledge of French. 'A Subscriber,' in the correspondence quoted above, states that on seeing the letters he was glad to observe that a translation of Bernier's travels was about to appear, and mentions that he has heard that the translator had already issued an English version of a 'most useful French work, in which, I understand, are to be found beautiful models of familiar letters.']

19
Paris 1830.
2 vols.
8vo.

Voyages de François Bernier, Docteur en médecine de la Faculté de Montpellier. . . . . Paris. Imprimé aux frais du Gouvernement pour procurer du travail aux ouvriers typographes, Aout, 1830.

[A mere reprint of edition No. 11, without the maps and illustrations. All the old typographical errors are repeated, and several new ones have crept in. In the words of M. L. de Lens (*Les correspondants de François Bernier pendant son voyage dans l'Inde* . . . Angers, 1872): 'C'est une simple réimpression, à laquelle aucun homme de lettres n'a donné ses soins. L'ouvrage fut publié aux frais du Gouvernement, dans le but indiqué ci-dessus [pour procurer du travail aux ouvriers typographes], sur un crédit de 40,000f. voté par la Chambre de députés.']

20
Bombay 1830.
1 vol.
8vo.

The history of the late Revolution, etc., Bombay: Re-printed at the Summachar Press, 1830.

[A verbatim, and to some extent facsimile, reprint of vols. i. and ii. of the first English edition, No. 3. The Editor, probably the proprietor of the Summachar Press, dedicates the book, by permission, to Sir John Malcolm, G.C.B., Governor of Bombay. Following the text, at the end of the book, is an announcement, which, as it contains much curious information worthy of record, and is an interesting specimen of quaint Indo-English composition, is here reprinted :—

PROSPECTUS.

Literature of India.

The Literati in *general* and the Lovers of Oriental Literature in *particular*, are hereby informed that it is intended to reprint

The History of the Revolution in the Empire of the GREAT MOGUL by Monsr: F. BERNIER, Physician of the Faculty of Montpellier (about A.D. 1656)—a work, the very name of which avows its importance, and its known scarcity, its value, and hence so highly and desirable as a record of Indian Affairs, as the most important Historical event that has engaged either Scholar or Historian;—a work so important in itself and written by an Eye-witness of that important transaction which forms the great Era of Hindoostanee reference as the foundation of another Dynasty,—claims the first place in the estimation, and search—and would do if as easily attainable, as it is now scarce—in the Library of every Indian Antiquarian,—a work that is not more known to, than it is prized by, every lover of ORIENTAL LITERATURE,—while at the same time, it is now so scarce,—that even a transient and hasty sight of it is a treat hardly obtainable—as a volume that requires (as it did in the present instance) years of patient and persevering search to procure. Forming as it does the basis of every document that relates to the celebrated AURUNGZEBE,—it is by this alone, self-avowed to be of the greatest importance.

Every attempt that is made by scientific research or literary labour to elucidate the history and establish the truth of any record regarding Hindoostan—this mighty aggregate of former kingdoms; must derive its materials from and refer to this work, because—it is the only authentic source of that information which an Eye-witness (and an eye-witness alone) can afford—as well as being the testimony of an European. By birth an European who had every advantage of time and place, under most favourable circumstances. By Education of a liberal profession—by Situation a Physician—and as such occupying the first of all possible opportunities for observation—unsuspected, and peaceably allowed access to every attainable particular—attending the ROYAL FAMILY, who were the contending parties—he would hear, and see, and know, All that was to be, or heard, or seen or known, and more than probably was he also consulted and confidently entrusted with all the PRIVATE reasons and resources which publicly influenced the Great contending BELLIGERENTS—while his situation thus placed for so long a time put him in possession of every information of the native character, under all its various and varying modifications, at such an eventful period—who then could possess greater or so great advantages!—as if Providentially placed there to record by simple historical detail, the passing events he witnessed as they occurred.

It is therefore proposed to reprint the London Edition ('Englished out of French') of 1671. And it is further proposed to do this *unaltered*, that a work so scarce, so valuable and so desirable may be easily procurable (as easy as it has hitherto been difficult) by every person who wishes to possess it, either as a depository in the Library, or a companion for the sitting-room: For the contemplation of the Philosopher, or the instruction of Youth.

It shews at once the Native Spirit of the Country and the manner in which their revolutions are accomplished : while the mighty and sudden effects that are produced—changeable or lasting—shew at once that overruling power which directs and disposes the wills and affections of men ! by results as unexpected as they were undesigned. While at the same time it exhibits the powerful contrast of European and Christian clemency in the present rule of England, throughout—her immense possessions, and almost boundless Empire in the same Land ; on the one hand Fire and Sword, Blood and Carnage, Desolation and Havoc, Robbery and Destruction mark the path of the NATIVE conqueror in every way ; while on the other hand Peace and Plenty—Forbearance and Security unite the Olive Branch with the Laurel to crown the CHRISTIAN Victories and make them the means of dispensing every advantage to soothe, to comfort and reward Native sufferings. The native victories succeed but to destroy—the English conqueror only to preserve and improve—the Native and the Christian therefore are alike interested in every event recorded in this History (of the MOGAL REVOLUTION) both in its cause and effect—and the influence it has produced on the character and Country at large : that character and Country which is being enlightened with all that the Native can receive, or the European bestow in whatever is useful, or attainable in the present state of human intellect.

ELEVEN YEARS of continued solicitude have been employed in searching for the Copy of a work now obtained and at last by accident :—a perseverance only stimulated by the known judgement of that enlightened friend who first named and of another who lately recommended it—the conviction of its importance, the pleasure of making its possession general—and the Hope that it would meet with that encouragement which it deserves ! It is then presumed, that those laudable intentions are not over-rated in fixing the price of the volume at 15 Rupees for Subscribers only: and 20 for non Subscribers, on or after the 15th February next, on which day it is intended that the work shall appear well printed in a large Type, on fine paper and occupying about 300 pages 8vo neatly half bound and Lettered.

Bombay, 15*th January* 1830.]

21 **Calcutta** **[1866.] 2 vols.** **8vo.**

Travels in the Mogul Empire by Francis Bernier. Translated from the French by Irving Brock. Calcutta, R. C. Lepage and Co., Printers and Publisher.

[A reprint of the edition No. 17, with the addition of several typographical errors. It is not edited in any sense, and the title-page is undated.]

22 **Delhi 1872.** **1 vol.** **12mo.**

A description of Dehli and Agra. The capital cities of the Empire of the Great Mogol, by Monsieur Bernier, Physician and companion of Danishmand Khan. Written at Dehli, 1st July 1663.

[This is a reprint, in 102 pages, of the letter to Monsieur de la Mothe le Vayer, from the third volume of the London edition of 1672. All the old errors are reproduced ; at page 77 the amusing one about the 'toothpick,' see page 214 of the present edition. No imprint or date, but a preface of three pages, signed W. H. T., and dated The Camp, Dehli, January 1st, 1872, which however gives no new facts, and is based upon the information contained in Bernier's own narrative. Outside cover, white paper, bearing a crescent and star in red, and half-title ; DEHLI AND AGRA in the time of AURANGZIB.
Price one rupee.]

II.—WITH OTHER WORKS.

Relacion de el Estado presente de el Gran Mogol segun la que imprimio el Doctor en Medecina FRANCESCO BERNIER año de 99. — 23 Brusselas 1701. 8vo.
[In don Sebastian Fernandez de Medrano's *Relaciones Modernas.* Pages 68-85. A mere abstract, but cleverly done.]

Mr. F. Bernier's Voyage to Surat : containing the History of the late Revolution of the Empire of the Great Mogol ; together with the most considerable Passages for five years following in that Empire. To which is added a letter to the Lord Colbert, etc. etc. Forming pages 102-236, vol. ii., of 'A Collection of Voyages and Travels . . . compiled from the curious and valuable library of the Earl of Oxford. . . . London, Thomas Osborne, 1745.' — 24 London 1745. Folio.
[A modernised reprint of the English editions of 1671-72, with various additional errors and misprints.]

Reise des Herrn Bernier in das Königreich Kachemir. Forming chapter xxiv. (pp. 99-128) of vol. xi. of Allgemeine Historie der Reisen zu Wasser und zu Lande . . Leipzig, bey Arkstee und Merkus, 1753. — 25 Leipzig 1753. Quarto.
[A useful compilation. More especially devoted to the Kashmir journey and description of that country. A few notes and references to other travellers, such as Roe. At page 106, a full-page engraving, titled *Rauchenara Begum*, a fancy picture, but founded upon authentic details. The engravings in Valentyn's *Beschryving . . . van de Levens der Groote Mogols*, 1726, having been utilised for this and other similar pictures, such as 'Begum Saheb,' 'Chah Jehan,' etc., inserted in other parts of the same volume as illustrations to abridgments of other Eastern travellers. The map of India in two sheets, which forms a frontispiece to this volume, compiled from the latest maps by *M. Bellin, Ing. de la Marine* 1752, is valuable.]

26
La Haye 1755.
Quarto.

Voyage de Bernier au Royaume de Kachemire. Pages 179-210 of vol. xiii. of Prévost d'Exiles' Histoire Générale des Voyages, ou Nouvelle Collection de toutes les relations de voyages par mer et par terre . . A La Haye, chez Pierre de Houdt, 1755.

[A French translation of No. 25. Copy of the engraving of Rauchenara Begum at page 188. French edition of Bellin's map, and in addition a French translation of Valentyn's Map of the Kingdom of Bengal. Engraving of Begum Saheb inserted at back of plate of Rauchenara, not as in the German edition.]

27
London 1811.
Quarto.

Bernier's voyage to the East Indies; containing the history of the late revolution of the empire of the Great Mogol, etc. etc. Pages 57-234 of vol. viii. of John Pinkerton's general collection of the best and most interesting voyages and travels in all parts of the world; many of which are now first translated into English. Digested on a new plan.

[A reprint of No. 24, with a few minor alterations. At page 64, a full-page engraving of Fort Gwalior from the North-west, after the view by Hodges. At page 150, N.E. view of the Cotsea Bhaug [Kudsia Bagh] on the river Jumna at Dehli, after Daniell.]

28
Paris 1816.
Octavo.

Voyage de Bernier à Cachemire. Chapter x., pages 169-232 of vol. v. of Abrégé de l'Histoire générale des voyages . . . Par J. F. Laharpe. Paris, Ledoux et Tenré, 1816.

[A tolerably full abridgment of Bernier's Journey to Kashmir.]

29
Paris 1833.
Octavo.

Bernier. Voyage à Cachemire (1638 (*sic*)—1670). Pages 84-108 of vol. xxxi. of 'Histoire universelle des voyages effectués par mer et par terre dans les cinq parties du Monde, sur les divers points du Globe. . . Revus ou Traduits par M. Albert Montémont. Paris, Armand-Aubrée.' [1833.]

[A cleverly written *précis* from a literary point of view. The date 1638 is evidently a misprint for 1658.]

Other Works by François Bernier.

1. Anatomia ridiculi Muris, hoc est, dissertatiunculæ J. B. Morini adversus expositam à P. Gassendi philosophiam, etc. Lutetiae, 1651, 4°.

2. Favilla ridiculi Muris, hoc est, dissertatiunculæ, ridicule defensæ a J. B. Morino, astrologo, adversus expositam à Petro Gassendi, Epicuri Philosophiam, etc. Lutetiæ, 1653, 4°.

3. Abrégé de la Philosophie de Gassendi en viii. tomes. Lyon, 1678, 8°.

[This is the first complete edition. Separate parts of the work were published, first at Paris in 1674 and 1675, and at Lyon in 1676.]

4. Seconde édition, reveüe et augmentée per l'autheur. 7 tom. Lyon, 1684, 12°.

5. Three Discourses of Happiness, Virtue, and Liberty. Collected from the works of the learn'd Gassendi, by Monsieur Bernier. Translated out of French. London: Printed for Awnsham and John Churchil [*sic*], at the Black Swan in Pater-Noster-Row, 1699, 8°.

6. Requeste des maîtres ès-arts, professeurs et régents de l'Université de Paris, présentée à la Cour souveraine du Parnasse, ensemble l'Arrest intervenu sur la dite requeste contre tous ceux qui prétendent faire enseigner ou croire de nouvelles découvertes qui ne soient pas dans Aristote.

[This is entirely distinct from Boileau's L'Arret burlesque. It was circulated in sheets during 1671. Both pieces are mentioned in the Letters of Mme. de Sévigné, 6th and 20th Sept. 1671, and they were published by Gabriel Guéret at La Haye the same year, in a volume entitled, 'La Guerre des Auteurs anciens et modernes,' pages 179-201. The two pieces were also published in 24 pages, 12° at Libreville in 1702, and they also appear in the editions of 'Menagiana' of 1713 and 1715.]

7. Eclaircissement sur le livre de M. de la Ville (le père Le Valois, jésuite) intitulé: Sentimens de M. Descartes touchant l'essence et les propriétés des corps, etc.

[This is included in Bayle's 'Recueil de quelques pièces concernant la philosophie de M. Descartes, 1684. In his preface he states that a few copies had been printed for private circulation some years before, probably either in 1680 or 1681.]

8. Doutes de Mr Bernier sur quelquesuns des principaux Chapitres de son Abrégé de la Philosophie de Gassendi. Paris, 1682, 12°.

9. Nouvelle division de la terre par les différentes espèces d'hommes qui l'habitent, envoyée par un fameux voyageux à M. l'abbé de la****.

[This appeared in the *Journal des Savants*, April 1684, and in the *Mercure de France* of 1722.]

10. Traité du Libre, et du Volontaire (Doute i.-iii. Extrait d'un livre de la Providence et du Destin par Hierocles.) Amsterdam, 1685, 12°.

11. Lettre sur le Café.

[Addressed to Philippe Sylvestre Dufour and printed at pp. 207-216, in his work entitled 'Traitez Nouveaux e curieux du Café, du Thé, et du Chocolate,' pages 207-216. Lyon, 1685, 12°.

12. Extrait de diverses pièces envoyées pour éstreines à Mme. de la Sablière.

[This appeared in the *Journal des Savants*, the 7th and 14th June 1688. It comprises the following articles: *Introduction à la lecture de Confucius; Description du canal de jonction des deux mers; Combat des vents; Maximes touchant le mouvement; Des Réfractions; Epitaphe de Chapelle; Observations médicales communiquées par un professeur de Montpellier.* The *Description du canal* du Languedoc appeared originally in the 'Mercure Galant,' February 1688.]

13. Copie des Etrenes envoyées à Madame de la Sablière. [Montpellier, 1688] 4°.

14. Mémoire de Mr Bernier sur le Quiétisme des Indes.

[This appeared in the 'Histoire des ouvrages des Sçavans,' Sept. 1688, pages 47-52.]

Biographies and Miscellanea.

1. Vincentii Panvrgi Epistola de tribus impostoribus, ad Clarissimum virum Ioan. Baptistam Morinvm, etc. Parisiis, 1654, 4°.

[In this violent attack upon Gassendi the author informs us: 'Hanc autem epistolam inscripsi titulo DE TRIBUS IMPOSTORIBUS, scilicet Petro Gassendo Epicureo Philosopho, Francisco Bernerio, Anatomista murium, et Neuraeo Pictone, Archipaedogo: Titulo quidem famoso, sed in his hominibus minime falso.' For an exhaustive account of the many polemical treatises which appeared under the same title about the beginning of the 17th century, see *De Tribus Impostoribus* M.D. IIC. *texte Latin, collationné sur l'exemplaire du Duc de la Vallière . . . Augmenté de variantes de plusieurs manuscrits, etc., et d'une notice philologique et bibliographique par Philomneste Junior. Paris. Gay* 1861.]

2. Io. Bapt. Morini docloris medici, et regii mathematvm professoris Defensio svæ dissertationis de Atomis et Vacuo; aduersus Petri Gassendi Philosophiam Epicuream, contra Francisci Bernerii, Andegaui Anatomiam ridiculi muris, etc. Parisiis, 1657, 4°.

3. François Bernier: In Niceron's 'Mémoires pour servir à l'histoire des Hommes Illustrés,' etc., vol. xxiii. pp. 364-370. Paris, 1733, 12°.

[This article, which contains many facts correctly stated, all doubtful dates, etc., being avoided, has formed the basis of many subsequent biographical articles until the appearance of the Angevin literature; see Nos. 12-16 below.]

4. François Bernier: In vol. i. of Eloy's *Dictionnaire historique de la Médecine.* Liége and Francfort, 1755, 2 vols. 8°.

[Short, but correct as far as it extends. In the second edition of Eloy, Mons, 1778, 4 vols. 4to, this notice is much extended, and in it will be found the earliest exact mention of Bernier's birthplace, 'Jouar près de Gonnord en Anjou.' M. Eloy concludes by a kindly reference to Bernier's observations on the medical science of the 'Brachmanes,' which he styles the earliest account of any philosophical value.]

5. François Bernier: In the 'Biographie Universelle,' vol. iv. pp. 304-306. Paris, 1811, 8°.

[Signed W[alckenae]r. A valuable article, based upon No. 3.]

6. In *The Edinburgh Review* for October 1815, in an article on certain accounts of parts of Western Asia, Elphinstone's *Account of the Kingdom of Caubul*, then just published, is criticised. The Reviewer characterises that work as being more of a treatise on the country visited, than a narrative of travels, and, quoting Elphinstone's eulogium on M. Volney's book on Syria and Egypt says (p. 417): 'But though the systematic fulness and method with which information is conveyed be an indisputable advantage of that mode of writing chosen by M. Volney and imposed upon Mr. Elphinstone by his situation, yet the reader must regret the absence of the picturesque and dramatic qualities of narrative, which, combined with the greatest accuracy and extent of knowledge, render Bernier the first of travellers, and which, without these substantial merits, bestow a powerful interest on the romantic adventures and relations of Bruce.'

7. Review of the 'Voyages of François Bernier,' in *The Retrospective Review*, vol. i., sec. ser., London 1827, pp. 245-268. [The Amsterdam editions of 1699 and 1710 are those reviewed. Extracts are given from Brock's translation, which is characterised as 'very good . . . Although we could have wished that more copious notes had brought the work to a level with the Oriental knowledge of the present day.']

8. In *The Quarterly Review* for January 1828, in an article on Bishop Heber's *Indian Journals*, etc., mention is made in a footnote, pp. 126-7, of Mr. Brock's translation of Bernier's Travels in the Mogol Empire, which is styled 'good.' The writer of the article further states that, 'If any of our readers are unacquainted with this excellent old traveller, we beg leave to tell them that his account of India is the most picturesque of all that have preceded Heber's; nor can we imagine anything more interesting than to compare his descriptions of the barbaric splendour of the court of Aurengzebe with the Bishop's account of his visit to his descendant, the present pageant-king of Dehli. We are sorry our limits prevent us from quoting the parallel passages. The mutability of human fortunes was never more strikingly pourtrayed.'

9. François Bernier: In 'Vies de plusieurs personnages célèbres, etc., by C. A. Walckenaer, vol. ii., pp. 74-77. Laon, 1830, 8°.

[A reprint of No. 5, with corrections and additions.]

10. François Bernier: In vol. i. of *The lives of celebrated travellers. By James Augustus St. John*, forming vol. ii. of Colburn and Bentley's National Library, London, 1831. [An abstract of Bernier's travels, with an account of his life founded upon the preceding article (No. 9) by Walckenaer, covering pages 192-220; well done, all the salient features being adequately brought forward.]

11. François Bernier: In 'Biographie Universelle (Michaud) ancienne et moderne . . nouvelle édition . . Paris, 1854 [*et seq.*]' Vol. iv. pp. 78, 79. [Signed W[alckenae]r, a mere reprint of No. 5.]

12. Éloge de François Bernier. Rapport de la Commission. Par Dr. E. Farge.

[In the 'Annales de la Société Linnéenne du Département de Maine et Loire, 3e Année, 1858, pp. 338-353.]

13. François Bernier, philosophe, médecin, et voyageur, par Dr. Pompée Mabille. Cosnier et Lachèse: Angers, 1864, 8°.

14. Les Correspondants de François Bernier, pendant son voyage dans l'Inde, par L. De Lens.

[In the 'Mémoires de la Société Nationale d'Agriculture, Sciences, et Arts d'Angers,' 1872, vol. xv., pp. 129-176. Angers, 1872. Reprinted in book form at Angers the same year.]

15. Documents inédits ou peu connus sur François Bernier, par L. De Lens.

[In the 'Revue Historique, Littéraire, et Archéologique de l'Anjou,' for 1872-73, vol. i. (Nouvelle série, illustrée), pp. 161-177, 332-348; vol. ii. pp. 75, 92.]

16. François Bernier, by L. De Lens. [In Célestine Port's 'Dictionnaire Historique,' vol. i., pp. 325-328. Paris, 1874, 8°.]

[It would be impossible to overstate the value of all that is contained in Nos. 12-16. The original and authentic material there made known for the first time must for ever form the basis of all succeeding Bernier Literature.]

DEDICATION, ETC.

TO THE KING

SIRE,

The Indians *maintain that the mind of a man cannot always be occupied with serious affairs, and that he remains forever a child in this respect: that, to develop what is good in him, almost as much care must be taken to amuse him as to cause him to study. This may be true with regard to the natives of Asia, but judging by all the great things I hear said everywhere regarding* FRANCE *and her* MONARCH, *from the Ganges and the Indus, the Tigris, and the Euphrates, unto the Seine, I have some difficulty in believing this to be a saying capable of universal application. Nevertheless I will still venture to offer* HIM *this History, because it seems to me capable of affording some hours of amusement to a* KING, *who might wish to find occasional relaxation from weighty affairs of State; not only because it is a Tragedy which I have just seen acted in one of the largest Theatres in the World, but from the fact of its being varied by several great and extraordinary incidents, affecting one of the most illustrious of the Royal Families of Asia. I cannot, however, doubt that it is written in a style devoid of elegance, and somewhat badly arranged, but I hope that* HIS MAJESTY *will chiefly take into* HIS *consideration the subject, and that* HE *will consider it nothing very extraordinary that during my long absence, whether wandering about the World, or attached to a Foreign Court, my language may have become semi-barbarous. Moreover, I am well pleased to return from such a distance, not quite empty-handed before* HIS MAJESTY, *and lay claim by this means to render* HIM *some account of so many years of my life, spent in absence from* HIS *Kingdom, for I have always remembered, no matter how far away I may have been, that I had a Master to whom I was accountable, being,*

HIS MAJESTY'S

Most humble and most obedient
Subject and Servant,
F. BERNIER.

TO THE READER.

I will not recount to you in a formal manner the Manners and Customs, the Learning and the Pursuits of the Mogols and the Indians, but will endeavour to make them known to you through Facts and actual Occurrences, by describing in the first place a Civil War and Revolution in which all the leading Statesmen of that nation took a part, adding thereto, that you may the better understand my narrative, a Map of the Country, which however I do not desire to put forth as absolutely correct, but merely as less incorrect than others that I have seen. Secondly, by relating some of the most important events which took place between the end of the War and my leaving the country; and thirdly, by means of Correspondence, which appears to me necessary to accomplish my purpose.

Should I be so fortunate as to succeed, I shall feel encouraged to publish other Letters concerning my Travels, and to translate from the Persian an Abridgment of an Ancient and Important History of the Kings of Kachmire,[1] which was compiled by order of King Jehan-Guyre, the son of that great Ekbar who so skilfully contrived to possess himself of that Kingdom.

[1] See p. 393, footnote [2].

An Extract of a LETTER Written to Mr. *H. O.*[1]

FROM

Monsr. *de Monceaux* the Younger, Giving a Character of the Book here *Englished*, and its Author.

Vertue sometimes is *no less interessed than Affection: Both, Sir, are glad to receive from time to time pledges mutually answering for those that have united themselves in a close correspondence. Yours indeed should demand of me such, as might be a security to you for the advance, you have been pleased to make me of your Friendship. But since at present I have nothing worth presenting you with; and yet am unwilling to give you any leisure to be diffident of my realness, or to repent for having so easily given me a share in your esteem, I here send you a* Relation *of* INDOSTAN, *in which you will find such considerable occurrences, as will make you confess I could not convey to you a more acceptable present, and that Monsieur* Bernier *who hath written it, is a very Gallant man, and of a mould, I wish all Travellers were made of. We ordinarily travel more out of* Unsetledness *than* Curiosity, *with a designe to* see *Towns and Countries rather than to* know *their Inhabitants and Productions; and we stay not long enough in a place to inform ourselves well of the Government, Policy, Interests, and Manners of its People.*

[1] Mr. Henry Ouldinburgh; see entry No. 10 of the *Bibliography*, p. xxx *ante*.

Monsieur Bernier, *after he had benefited himself for the space of many years by the converse of the famous* Gassendi; *seen him expire in his arms, succeeded him in his Knowledge, and inherited his Opinions and Discoveries, embarqued for* Ægypt, *stay'd above a whole year at* Cairo, *and then took the occasion of some* Indian *Vessels that trade in the Ports of the* Red Sea, *to pass to* Suratte; *and after twelve years abode at the Court of the* Great Mogol, *is at last come to seek his rest in his native Countrey, there to give an Accompt of his Observations and Discoveries, and to poure out into the bosome of* France, *what he had amassed in* India.

Sir, I shall say nothing to you of his Adventures which you will find in the Relations that are to follow hereafter, which he abandons to the greediness of the Curious, who prefer their satisfaction to his quiet, and do already persecute him to have the sequel of this History. Neither shall I mention to you the hazards he did run, by being in the neighbourhood of Mecca; *nor of his prudent conduct, which made him merit the esteem of his Generous* Fazelkan, *who since is become the first Minister of that Great Empire, whom he taught the principle Languages of* Europe, *after he had translated for him the whole Philosophy of* Gassendi *in Latin,*[1] *and whose leave he could not obtain to go home, till he had got for him a select number of our best* European *Books, thereby to supply the loss he should suffer of his Person. This, at least, I can assure you of,* that *never a Traveller went from home more capable to observe, nor hath written with more knowledge, candour, and integrity; that I knew him at* Constantinople, *and in some Towns of* Greece, *of so excellent a conduct, that I propossed him to myself for a Pattern in the designe I then had to carry my curiosity as far as the place where the Sun riseth;* that *I have often drowned in the sweetness of his entertainment the bitternesses, which else I must have swallowed all alone in such irksome and unpleasant passages, as are those of* Asia.

[1] *Petri Gassendi . . . opera omnia in sex tomos divisa . . . Lugduni sumptibus Laurentii Anisson, & Ioan. Bapt. Devenet M.DC. lviii,* is the edition here referred to.

Sir, you will do me a pleasure to let me know the sentiment your Illustrious Society[1] *hath of this Piece. Their approbation begets much emulation among the Intelligent, who all have no other Ambition than to please them. I my self must avow to you, that if I thought I could merit so much, I should not so stiffly oppose as I do, the publication of the Observations and Notes I have made in the* Levant. *I should suffer my friends to take them out of my Cabinet, where from the slight value I have for them, they are like to lie imprisoned, except the King my Master, by whose order I undertook those Voyages, should absolutely command me to set them at liberty, and to let them take their course in the world. Mean time, Sir, you will oblige me to assure those Great Men, who this day compose the most knowing Company on Earth, of the Veneration I have for the Oracles that come from their Mouth, and that I prefer their* Lyceum *before that of* Athens ; *and lastly, that of all their Admirers there is none, that hath a greater Concern for their Glory, than*

Paris, *Julij* 16,
1670.

De Monceaux.

---

[1] The Royal Society, of which Henry Ouldinburgh was the first Secretary; see Appendix v.

THE HISTORY

OF

THE LATE REBELLION

THE HISTORY OF THE LATE REBELLION IN THE STATES OF THE GREAT MOGOL

THE desire of seeing the world, which had induced me to visit *Palestine* and *Egypt,* still prompted me to extend my travels, and I formed the design of exploring the *Red Sea* from one end to the other. In pursuance of this plan, I quitted *Grand Cairo,* where I had resided more than a year, and in two-and-thirty hours (travelling at a *Caravan*-rate) reached the town of *Suez.* Here I embarked in a galley, and was conveyed in seventeen days, always hugging the coast, from *Suez* to the port of *Gidda,* half a day's journey from *Mecca.* Contrary to my expectation, and in violation of a promise which I had received from the *Beig*[1] of the *Red Sea,* I was constrained to land on this so-called holy territory of *Mahomet,* where no Christian, who is not a slave, dares set his foot. After a detention of nearly five weeks, I took my passage on board a small

[1] The Bey of the Red Sea was an important official who, among other duties, had control of the pilgrim traffic to Mecca, through Jeddah.

vessel, which, sailing along the shores of *Arabia Felix*, brought me in fifteen days to *Moka*, near the straits of *Bab-el-mandel*. It was now my intention to pass over to the island of *Masowa*, and *Arkiko*, on my way to *Gonder*,[1] the capital of *Habech*,[2] or Kingdom of *Ethiopia*; but I was informed that Catholics were not safe in that country, since the period when, through the intrigues of the Queen-Mother, the *Portuguese* were slaughtered, or expelled, with the Jesuit Patriarch whom they had brought thither from *Goa*; and that, in fact, an unhappy Capuchin had been recently beheaded at *Suaken*,[3] for having attempted to enter the kingdom. It seemed, indeed, that less risk would be incurred if I adopted the disguise of a *Greek* or an *Armenian*; and that when the King knew I could be of service to him, he would probably make me a grant of land, which might be cultivated by slaves, if I possessed the means of purchasing them; but that I should, at the same time, be compelled to marry immediately, as a monk, who had assumed the character of a *Greek* physician, had already been obliged to do; and that I could never hope to obtain permission to quit the country.

These considerations, among others which may be mentioned in the sequel, induced me to abandon my intention of visiting *Gonder*. I embarked, therefore, in

[1] Gondar, more correctly *Guendar*, formerly the capital of the Amharic kingdom of Abyssinia, with which there was a considerable trade to India. In the erection of its Fort—a massive building, designed on the plan of a mediæval stronghold, and built in the 16th century—Indian workmen were employed. It contained many Christian churches, and Venetian artists are said to have had a hand in the decoration of some of them. Bernier proposed to visit it, *viâ* Massowah, the well-known town on an island of the same name on the Abyssinian coast of the Red Sea, from thence crossing over to the mainland at the town of Arkiko, or Ercico.

[2] From the Arabic *Habash*, the country of Abyssinia, or Ethiopia. The *Abash* of Marco Polo. *Hubshee* is the modern Hindostanee term for all negroes.

[3] Suakin, or more correctly Sawákin, was then, as it still is, the chief port of the Soudan on the Red Sea.

an Indian vessel, passed the straits of *Bab-el-mandel,* and in two-and-twenty days arrived at *Sourate,* in *Hindoustan,* the empire of the *Great Mogol.* I found that the reigning prince was named *Chah-Jehan,* or King of the World. According to the annals of the country, he was the son of *Jehan-Guyre,* or Conqueror of the World, and grandson of *Ekbar,* or the Great: so that in tracing his genealogy upwards to *Houmayon,* or the Fortunate, the father of *Ekbar,* and to *Houmayon's* predecessors, *Chah-Jehan* was proved to be the tenth, in regular descent, from *Timur-Lengue,* the Lame Lord or Prince, whom we commonly, but corruptly, call *Tamerlan.*[1] This *Tamerlan,* so celebrated for his conquests, married a kinswoman, the only daughter of the prince who then reigned over the people of *Great Tartary* called *Mogols*; a name which they have communicated to the foreigners who now govern *Indoustan,* the country of the *Indous,* or *Indians.* It must not, however, be inferred that offices of trust and dignity are exclusively held by those of the *Mogol* race, or that they alone obtain rank in the army. These situations are filled indifferently by them and strangers from all countries; the greater part by *Persians,* some by *Arabs,* and others by *Turks.* To be considered a *Mogol,* it is enough if a foreigner have a white face and profess Mahometanism;[2] in contradistinction to the Christians of Europe, who are called *Franguis,*[3] and to the *Indous,* whose complexion is brown, and who are *Genitles.*[4]

[1] Amír Timúr, styled Sáhib Kirán, because he reigned more than thirty years, was born in 1336, and died in 1405. Called Timúr Lang (*Timúr i Leng*) from some defect in his feet. He married the sister of Amír Husain, the ruler of Balkh, the capital of Khurásán, whom he had deposed and put to death.

[2] See pp. 212, 404.

[3] Firinghees, from the Persian *Farangí, i.e.* a Frank, a European.

[4] In the original 'Gentils,' which throughout this edition will be rendered by the word Gentiles, in preference to using the old Anglo-Indian slang word 'Gentoo,' derived from the Portuguese *Gentio,* a gentile, a heathen, a term which was applied to the Hindoos in contradistinction to the *Moros* (old Anglo-Indian 'Moors'), or Muhammadans.

I learnt also on my arrival that this King of the World, *Chah-Jehan*,[1] who was about seventy years of age, was the father of four sons and two daughters; that some years had elapsed since he elevated his sons to the vice-royalty of his four most considerable provinces or kingdoms; and that he had been afflicted, for about the space of a twelvemonth, with a disorder which it was apprehended would terminate fatally. The situation of the father having inspired the sons with projects of ambition, each laid claim to the empire, and a war was kindled among them which continued about five years.

This war, as I witnessed some of the most important of its events, I shall endeavour to describe. During a period of eight years I was closely attached to the court; for the state of penury to which I had been reduced by various adventures with robbers, and by the heavy expenses incurred on a journey of nearly seven weeks, from Sourate to *Agra* and *Dehli*, the chief towns of the empire, had induced me to accept a salary from the *Great Mogol*, in the capacity of physician; and soon afterwards, by chance, I procured another from *Danechmend-Kan*,[2] the most learned man of Asia, formerly *Bakchis*, or Grand Master of the Horse, and one of the most powerful and distinguished *Omrahs*,[3] or Lords of the Court.

The eldest son of the *Great Mogol* was named *Dara*, or

[1] Sháh Jahán, the third son of the Emperor Jáhángír, was born at Lahore in 1593, and died in prison at Agra in 1666. He had four daughters, but Bernier mentions the eldest and the youngest only.

[2] A Persian merchant, by name Muhammad Shafí, or Mullá Shafí. He came to Surat about the year 1646, from which place he was sent for by the Emperor Sháh Jahán, who conferred upon him the command of 3000 men, and made him paymaster of the army (Bakhshí) with the title of Daníshmand Khán (Learned Knight). In the reign of Alamgír he received still further promotion, and was appointed Governor of Sháhjahánábád or New Delhi, where he died in 1670.

[3] Omrah, from *Umará*, the plural of the Arabic word *Amír*, a commander, a chief, a lord. The old travellers use the word Omrah as a singular for a lord or grandee, although properly speaking it should be applied collectively.

Darius: the second *Sultan Sujah,* or the Valiant Prince: the third was *Aureng-Zebe,* or the Throne's Ornament; and the name of the youngest was *Morad-Bakche,* or the Desire Accomplished. Of the two daughters, the elder was called *Begum-Saheb,* or the Chief Princess; and the younger *Rauchenara-Begum,* the Light of Princesses, or Princess of the Enlightened Mind.[1]

It is usual in this country to give similar names to the members of the reigning family. Thus the wife of *Chah-Jehan*—so renowned for her beauty, and whose splendid mausoleum is more worthy of a place among the wonders of the world than the unshapen masses and heaps of stones in Egypt—was named *Tage Mehalle,*[2] or the Crown of the Seraglio; and the wife of *Jehan-Guyre,* who so long wielded the sceptre, while her husband abandoned himself to drunkenness and dissipation, was known first by the appellation of *Nour-Mehalle,* the Light of the Seraglio, and afterwards by that of *Nour-Jehan-Begum,* the Light of the World.

The reason why such names are given to the great, instead of titles derived from domains and seigniories, as usual in *Europe,* is this: as the land throughout the whole empire is considered the property of the sovereign, there can be no earldoms, marquisates or duchies. The royal grants consist only of pensions, either in land or money, which the king gives, augments, retrenches or takes away at pleasure.

[1] Dárá Shikoh was born in 1615, and murdered by order of his brother Aurangzeb in 1659. Sultan Shujáh, born in 1616, is said to have been drowned with all his family in Arakan by the Rájá of that country in 1660, but see pp. 111-114.

Aurangzeb, who ascended the throne in 1658 under the title of Alamgír (Conqueror of the World), was born in 1619, and died in 1707. Murád Bakhsh, born in 1624, and murdered by order of Aurangzeb in 1662.

[2] Properly, Mumtáz Mahál, daughter of Asaf Khán, wazír, the brother of Núr Jahán Begum, wife of the Emperor Jáhángír. She was born in 1592, married in 1612, and died in child-bed a few hours after the birth of her daughter Raushan Ará Begum, in the year 1631.

It will not, therefore, appear surprising, that even the *Omrahs* are distinguished only by this kind of title. One, for instance, calling himself *Raz-Andaze-Kan*, another *Safe-Cheken-Kan*, a third *Barc-Andaze-Kan*; and others *Dianet-Kan* or *Danechmend-Kan*, or *Fazel-Kan*: which terms respectively signify The Disposer of Thunder, The Destroyer of Ranks, The Hurler of the Thunderbolt, The Faithful Lord, The Learned, and The Perfect; and so it is with others.

Dara was not deficient in good qualities: he was courteous in conversation, quick at repartee, polite, and extremely liberal: but he entertained too exalted an opinion of himself; believed he could accomplish everything by the powers of his own mind, and imagined that there existed no man from whose counsel he could derive benefit. He spoke disdainfully of those who ventured to advise him, and thus deterred his sincerest friends from disclosing the secret machinations of his brothers. He was also very irascible; apt to menace; abusive and insulting even to the greatest *Omrahs*; but his anger was seldom more than momentary. Born a *Mahometan*, he continued to join in the exercises of that religion; but although thus publicly professing his adherence to its faith, *Dara* was in private a *Gentile* with *Gentiles*, and a Christian with Christians. He had constantly about him some of the Pendets, or Gentile Doctors, on whom he bestowed large pensions, and from these it is thought he imbibed opinions in no wise accordant with the religion of the land: but upon this subject I shall make a few observations when I treat of the religious worship of the *Indous* or *Gentiles*. He had, moreover, for some time lent a willing ear to the suggestions of the Reverend Father *Buzée*, a Jesuit, in the truth and propriety of which he began to acquiesce.[1] There are persons, however, who

[1] Catrou in his *History of the Mogul Dynasty in India*, Paris, 1715, which is largely based upon the materials collected by Signor Manouchi, a Venetian, who was for forty-eight years a Physician at the Courts of

say that *Dara* was in reality destitute of all religion, and that these appearances were assumed only from motives of curiosity, and for the sake of amusement; while, according to others, he became by turns a Christian and a Gentile from political considerations; wishing to ingratiate himself with the Christians who were pretty numerous in his corps of artillery, and also hoping to gain the affection of the *Rajas*, or *Gentile* Princes tributary to the empire; as it was most essential to be on good terms with these personages, that he might, as occasion arose, secure their co-operation. *Dara's* false pretences to this or that mode of worship, did not, however, promote the success of his plans; on the contrary, it will be found in the course of this narrative, that the reason assigned by *Aureng-Zebe* for causing him to be beheaded was, that he had turned *Kafer*, that is to say an infidel, without religion, an idolater.

Sultan Sujah, the second son of the *Great Mogol*, resembled in many characteristic traits his brother *Dara*; but he was more discreet, firmer of purpose, and excelled him in conduct and address. He was sufficiently dexterous in the management of an intrigue; and by means of repeated largesses, bestowed secretly, knew how to acquire the friendship of the great *Omrahs*, and, in particular, of the most powerful *Rajas*, such as *Jessomseingue*[1] and others. He was, nevertheless, too much a slave to his pleasures; and once surrounded by his women, who were exceedingly numerous, he would pass whole days

Delhi and Agra, and for some time attached to Dárá's person, says that 'no sooner had Dara begun to possess authority, than he became disdainful and inaccessible. A small number of Europeans alone shared his confidence. The Jesuits, especially, were in the highest consideration with him. These were the Fathers . . . and Henry Busée, a Fleming. This last had much influence over the mind of the prince, and had his counsels been followed, it is probable that Christianity would have mounted the throne with Dara.'

[1] The Mahárájá Jaswant Singh, of Jodhpur, who was one of Alamgír's best generals, holding the rank of commander of 7000. He died near Kabul in 1678.

and nights in dancing, singing, and drinking wine. He presented his favourites with rich robes, and increased or diminished their allowances as the passing fancy of the moment prompted. No courtier, who consulted his own interest, would attempt to detach him from this mode of life: the business of government therefore often languished, and the affections of his subjects were in a great measure alienated.

Sultan Sujah declared himself of the religion of the *Persians*, although his father and brothers professed that of the *Turks*. *Mahometanism* is divided into various sects, which occasioned the following distich from the pen of the famous *Cheik-Sady*, author of the *Goulistan*.

> I am a drinking Derviche ; I am apparently without religion ;
> I am known by the seventy-two sects.[1]

Among all these sects there are two leading ones whose respective partisans are mortal enemies to each other. The one is that of the *Turks*, called by the *Persians* *Osmanlous*, or Followers of *Osman*, whom the *Turks* believe to have been the true and legitimate successor of *Mahomet*, the Great Caliph, or Sovereign Pontiff, to whom alone it belonged to interpret the *Koran*, and to decide the controversies that occur in the law. The other is that of the *Persians*, called by the Turks, *Chias*, *Rafezys* and *Aly-Merdans*; that is, Sectaries, Heretics, and Partisans of *Aly*; because the *Persians* believe that this succession and pontifical authority, of which I have just spoken, belonged only to *Aly* the son-in-law of *Mahomet*.

When he avowed himself one of the latter sect, *Sultan Sujah* was evidently actuated by motives of policy; for as

[1] By this he meant that he was to be numbered among the lost, alluding to the saying of the Prophet Muhammad, 'It shall come to pass that my people shall be divided into three-and-seventy sects, all of which, save only one, shall have their portion in the fire.' 'Tis said that the reason why the Prophet pitched on the number seventy-three was, that the Magians were divided into seventy sects, the Jews into seventy-one, and the Christians into seventy-two.

FIG. 1.—Prince Aurangzeb.

the *Persians* were in possession of the most important offices in the kingdom, and exercised the largest share of influence at the Court of the *Mogol*, he hoped thus to secure interest and support, whenever the tide of events should render them necessary.

Aureng-Zebe, the third brother, was devoid of that urbanity and engaging presence, so much admired in *Dara*: but he possessed a sounder judgment, and was more skilful in selecting for confidants such persons as were best qualified to serve him with faithfulness and ability. He distributed his presents with a liberal but discriminating hand among those whose goodwill it was essential to preserve or cultivate. He was reserved, subtle, and a complete master of the art of dissimulation. When in his father's court, he feigned a devotion which he never felt, and affected contempt for worldly grandeur while clandestinely endeavouring to pave the way to future elevation. Even when nominated Viceroy of the *Decan*, he caused it to be believed that his feelings would be better gratified if permitted to turn *Fakire*, that is to say, a beggar, a *Derviche* or one who has renounced the World; that the wish nearest his heart was to pass the rest of his days in prayer or in offices of piety, and that he shrank from the cares and responsibility of government. Still his life had been one of undeviating intrigue and contrivance; conducted, however, with such admirable skill, that every person in the court, excepting only his brother, *Dara*, seemed to form an erroneous estimate of his character. The high opinion expressed by *Chah-Jehan* of his son *Aureng-Zebe*, provoked the envy of *Dara*, and he would sometimes say to his intimate friends, that, of all his brothers, the only one who excited his suspicion, and filled him with alarm was that *Nemazi*—or, as we should say, 'that *Bigot*,' that ever-prayerful one.

Morad-Bakche, the youngest of the *Mogol's* sons, was inferior to his three brothers in judgment and address. His constant thought was how he might enjoy himself, and the pleasures of the table and of the field engaged his undivided attention. He was, however, generous and polite. He used to boast that he had no secrets: he despised cabinet intrigues, and wished it to be known that he trusted only to his sword and to the strength of his arm. He was indeed full of courage; and if that courage had been under the guidance of a little more discretion, it is probable, as we shall see, that he would have prevailed over his three brothers, and remained the undisputed master of *Hindoustan*.

Begum-Saheb, the elder daughter of *Chah-Jehan*, was very handsome, of lively parts, and passionately beloved by her father. Rumour has it that his attachment reached a point which it is difficult to believe,[1] the justification of which he rested on the decision of the *Mullahs*, or doctors of their law. According to them, it would have been unjust to deny the King the privilege of gathering fruit from the tree he had himself planted. *Chah-Jehan* reposed unbounded confidence in this his favourite child; she watched over his safety, and was so cautiously observant, that no dish was permitted to appear upon the royal table which had not been prepared under her superintendence.[2] It is not surprising, therefore, that her ascendency in the court of the *Mogol* should have been nearly unlimited; that she should always have regulated the humours of her father, and exercised a powerful influence on the most weighty concerns. This Princess accumulated great riches by means

[1] This statement is repeated by Valentyn, in his *Beschryving . . . van de Levens der Groote Mogols*, Dordrecht and Amsterdam, 1726, in these words:—'*Begum Saheb*, die om haare schoonheit van haaren Vader zeer, ja te veel, bemind wierd.'

Catrou says, 'To a great share of beauty Begóm-Saëb united a mind endued with much artifice. The attachment she always had for her father, and the profusion of the avaricious Cha-Jaham (*sic*) towards his daughter, caused a suspicion, that crime might be blended with their mutual affection. This was a popular rumour, which never had any other foundation than in the malice of the courtiers.'

[2] See p. 16 text, and footnote [1].

of her large allowances, and of the costly presents which flowed in from all quarters, in consideration of numberless negotiations intrusted to her sole management. The affairs of her brother *Dara* prospered, and he retained the friendship of the King, because she attached herself steadily to his interest, and declared openly in favour of his party. He cultivated with assiduous attention the goodwill of this valuable coadjutor, and it is thought promised that, on his accession to the throne, he would grant her permission to marry. This pledge was a remarkable one, the marriage of a Princess being of rare occurrence in *Hindoustan,* no man being considered worthy of royal alliance; an apprehension being entertained that the husband might thereby be rendered powerful, and induced perhaps to aspire to the crown.

I shall introduce two anecdotes connected with the amours of this Princess, and hope I shall not be suspected of a wish to supply subjects for romance. What I am writing is matter of history, and my object is to present a faithful account of the manners of this people. Love adventures are not attended with the same danger in *Europe* as in *Asia.* In *France* they excite only merriment; they create a laugh, and are forgotten: but in this part of the world, few are the instances in which they are not followed by some dreadful and tragical catastrophe.

It is said, then, that *Begum-Saheb,* although confined in a *Seraglio,* and guarded like other women, received the visits of a young man of no very exalted rank, but of an agreeable person. It was scarcely possible, surrounded as she was on all sides by those of her own sex whose envy she had long provoked, that her conduct should escape detection. *Chah-Jehan* was apprised of her guilt, and resolved to enter her apartments at an unusual and unexpected hour. The intimation of his approach was too sudden to allow her the choice of more than one place of concealment. The affrighted gallant sought refuge in the capacious cauldron used for the baths. The King's countenance denoted neither surprise nor displeasure ; he discoursed with his daughter on ordinary topics, but finished the conversation by observing that the state of her skin indicated a neglect of her customary ablutions, and that it was proper she should bathe. He then commanded the *Eunuchs* to light a fire under the cauldron, and did not retire until they gave him to understand that his wretched victim was no more.

At a subsequent period, *Begum-Saheb* formed another attachment, which also had a tragical termination. She chose for her *Kane-Saman,* or steward, a *Persian*, named *Nazerkan,* a young nobleman remarkable for grace and mental accomplishments, full of spirit and ambition, and the favourite of the whole court. *Chah-Hestkan,*[1] the uncle of *Aureng-Zebe,* greatly esteemed this young *Persian,* and ventured to propose him for *Begum-Saheb's* husband ; a proposition which was very ill received by the *Mogol.* He had indeed already entertained some suspicion of an improper intercourse between the favoured Nobleman and the Princess and did not long deliberate on the course he should pursue. As a mark of distinguished favour the King presented the *betel,*[2] in the presence of the whole court, to the unsuspecting youth, which he was obliged immediately to masticate, agreeably to the custom of the country. Betel is a small parcel made of aromatic leaves

[1] Sháista Khán, who, when Governor of Bengal, provoked a war with Job Charnock, Governor of the Factory of the East India Company at Golághát near Hughlí. He died in 1694, aged 93 years, after having filled many important offices of State under Sháh Jahán, and Alamgír.

[2] In the original 'un Betlay,' the leaf of the *Piper betel,* Lin., chewed with the dried areca-nut, thence improperly called *betel-nut* ; a very old mistake. Betel is from the Portuguese *betle,* derived from the Malayalim *vettila*=simple or mere leaf. Familiar to Anglo-Indians as Pawn, in Hindostanee Pán, from the Sanskrit *parna* a leaf. 'Pawn-sooparie' (*supárí,* the areca-nut in Urdú) is the well-known name in Northern India at the present day for the combination, as detailed by Bernier, offered to visitors with *itr* (otto) of roses, or other scents, which politely intimates the close of an entertainment, a friendly visit, or an official interview.

and other ingredients mixed up with a little of the lime made from sea-shells, this colours the lips and mouth red and agreeably perfumes the breath. Little did the unhappy lover imagine that he had received poison from the hand of the smiling Monarch, but indulging in dreams of future bliss, he withdrew from the palace, and ascended his *paleky*.[1] Such, however, was the activity of the poison, that he died before he could reach home.

Rauchenara-Begum, the *Mogol's* younger daughter, was less beautiful than her sister, neither was she so remarkable for understanding; she was nevertheless possessed of the same vivacity, and equally the votary of pleasure. She became the ardent partisan of *Aureng-Zebe,* and made no secret of her enmity to *Begum-Saheb* and *Dara.* This might be the reason why she amassed but little wealth, and took but an inconsiderable part in public affairs. Still, as she was an inmate of the *Seraglio,* and not deficient in artifice, she succeeded in conveying, by means of spies, much valuable intelligence to *Aureng-Zebe.*

Some years previous to the war, the turbulent disposition of his four sons had filled *Chah-Jehan* with perplexity and alarm. They were all married and of adult age; but, in utter disregard of the ties of consanguinity, each, animated by deadly hatred toward the others, had set up his pretensions to the crown, so that the court was divided into separate factions. The King, who trembled for his personal safety, and was tormented by sad forebodings of the events which actually befel him, would gladly have confined his refractory children in *Goüaleor,* a fortress which had often received members of the royal family within its walls, and considered impregnable, situated as it is on an inaccessible rock and containing within its walls good water and sufficient wherewithal to support its

[1] The Hindostanee word *pálkí,* from the Sanskrit *palyanka,* a bed, a palankin (Portuguese, *palanchino*), the well-known closed-in litter, with a pole projecting before and behind, which is borne on the shoulders of four or six men.

garrison; but he justly considered that they had become too powerful to be dealt with in so summary a manner. He was indeed in perpetual apprehension of their having recourse to arms, and either erecting independent principalities, or converting the seat of government into a bloody arena, in which to settle their personal differences. To save himself, therefore, from some impending and overwhelming calamity, *Chah-Jehan* resolved to bestow upon his sons the government of four distant provinces. *Sultan Sujah* was appointed to *Bengale*; *Aureng-Zebe* to the *Decan*; *Morad-Bakche* to *Guzarate*; and *Dara* to *Caboul* and *Moultan*. The three first-mentioned Princes repaired to their respective provinces without delay, and soon betrayed the spirit by which they were animated. They acted in every respect as independent sovereigns, appropriated the revenues to their own use, and levied formidable armies under pretence of maintaining tranquillity at home, and commanding respect abroad. *Dara*, because he was the eldest son and expected to succeed to the crown, did not quit the court of his father. *Chah-Jehan*, appearing to encourage that expectation, authorised his son to issue orders, and permitted him to occupy an inferior throne, placed among the *Omrahs*, beneath his own;[1] so that two kings seemed to reign with almost equal power;[2] but there is reason to believe that the *Mogol* practised much duplicity, and that, notwithstanding the respectful and affectionate

[1] Catrou says that the influence of Dárá grew to an astonishing height during the absence of his brothers. 'His eldest son ruled the empire with absolute power. A sopha had been prepared for him, lower, indeed, than the throne of his father; but he is the only instance of a prince of the Mogol race being allowed to be seated in the presence of the Emperor. He had the power to command a combat of elephants whenever he pleased; a distinction reserved only for the sovereign.'

[2] Bernier appears to have had in his mind the saying of S'adí contained in the chapter of the *Gulistán* on the Manners of Kings: 'It has been observed that ten Darweshes may sleep upon one blanket, but that one kingdom cannot contain two Kings.

demeanour of *Dara,* his father was never cordially attached to him. The old monarch lived in continual dread of being poisoned,[1] and carried on, it is supposed, a secret correspondence with *Aureng-Zebe,* of whose talents for government he always entertained a high opinion.

I have thought a slight sketch of *Chah-Jehan* and his sons a proper introduction to this history, and necessary to the right understanding of what is to follow. Nor could I well avoid adding a few particulars concerning his two daughters, who play so prominent a part in the tragedy. In the *Indies,* as well as in *Constantinople* and other places, the most momentous events are too often caused by the influence of the sex, although the people may be ignorant of this fact, and may indulge in vain speculations as to the cause of the agitation they deplore.

It may also elucidate my narrative to revert to the proceedings of *Aureng-Zebe,* of the King of *Golkonda,* and of his Vizier *Emir-Jemla* a short time before the war broke out: this may give my readers an insight into the character and genius of *Aureng-Zebe,* the hero of this history, and the future King of the *Indies.*

We shall first see in what manner *Emir-Jemla* laid the foundation of the power and supremacy of *Chah-Jehan's* third son.

During the time that *Aureng-Zebe* was intrusted with the government of the *Decan* the King of *Golkonda* had for his Vizier and general of his armies this *Emir-Jemla,* a *Persian* by birth,[2] and celebrated throughout *Hindoustan.* The Vizier's lineage was not noble, but his talents were of the first order: he was an accomplished soldier, and deeply

[1] In the original 'craignant sur tout le Boucon,' a curious fact not commonly known, also see *ante,* p. 11, where it is stated that the Emperor's food was prepared under the superintendence of the Begum Sáhib.

[2] Mír Muhammad Sàíd Ardástaní, surnamed Mír Jumla and afterwards entitled Mu'azzam Khán, Khán Khánán Sipah Sálár, was born in Ardistan near Ispahan, and came to India as the personal attendant of a Persian merchant. It was in 1656 that he threw himself on the

versed in business. His wealth, which was prodigious, he had acquired, not only by the opportunities afforded him as chief minister of an opulent kingdom, but likewise by means of his extensive commerce with various parts of the world, as well as by the diamond mines which he farmed under feigned names. These mines were worked with indefatigable industry, and it was usual to count his diamonds by the sacks-full.[1] His political influence, it may readily be imagined, was also very great, commanding as he did not only the armies of the king, but keeping in his own pay a formidable body of troops, with a corps of artillery composed principally of Franks or Christians. It ought likewise to be mentioned that the Vizier having found a pretext for the invasion of the *Karnatic*,[2] pillaged the whole of its ancient idol-temples, and thus increased his pecuniary resources to an incredible amount.[3]

protection of Sháh Jahán. On the accession of Aurangzeb he was appointed Governor of Bengal and died at Khizarpúr in Kúch Behár in 1663 after his return from an expedition against the kingdom of Assam. Amír Jumla is called, by Catrou, Mirza Mulla. See footnote [3], *below*. Tavernier also makes use of this name when writing of him.

[1] Thévenot says that he possessed 20 *mans*, or 408 Dutch *livres*, weight of diamonds. The *man* (Surat) of Thévenot may be taken as 40 seers, or 35·5 English pounds avoirdupois.

[2] 'Le Royaume de Karnates' in the original, which is a very correct definition of the country, which then had its northern limit at Bídar, and may be said to have embraced the Canarese-speaking people of southern India.

[3] Catrou bears out Bernier's narrative, and says that Amír Jumla was in the habit of selling the best diamonds to the Portuguese. 'Dom Philippes Mascarenhas, sent as Viceroy of the Indies for the Portuguese at Goa, was his principal correspondent. The object of Mirza Mulla [so Catrou calls Amír Jumla] was to secure to himself the protection of the Portuguese, in the event of a change of fortune. The Persian who found himself supported no longer placed any limits to his peculations. He plundered the temples of their idols; he seized upon all precious stones with which the statues were ornamented; he compelled the inhabitants of the Karnatic to surrender to him whatever they possessed of gold and jewels; and he caused those who, according to the custom of the country, had buried their treasures, to expire under the severity

The jealousy of the King of *Golkonda*[1] was naturally awakened: and he eagerly, but silently, sought an opportunity to destroy, or remove from his presence, one whom he regarded as a dangerous rival rather than an obedient subject. Surrounded by persons devoted to the interest of the minister, he felt the prudence of concealing his intentions; but in an unguarded moment, when informed for the first time of the improper intimacy subsisting between *Emir-Jemla* and the queen-mother, who still retained much beauty, he gave utterance to the feelings by which he had so long been oppressed, and denounced vengeance against this powerful offender.

The Vizier was at this time in the *Karnatic*; but, every important office at court being filled by his own and his wife's relations and friends, he was soon made acquainted with the danger which awaited him. This crafty man's first step was to write to his only son *Mahmet Emir-Kan*,[2]

of the lash. So many cruelties rendered him hateful in his Province; and such great wealth created him envy at Court.'

Tavernier in his *Travels in India* makes frequent mention of Dom Philippe de Mascarenhas, the Viceroy of Goa, who had formerly been the Governor of the Portuguese possessions in Ceylon. He first saw him at Goa on the 22d January 1648 and says of him—'He possessed a quantity of diamonds—all stones of great weight from 10 to 40 carats; two notably, which he showed me when I was at Goa. One of them was a thick stone, weighing 57, and the other 67½ carats, both being fairly clear, of good water and Indian cut.' Dr. V. Ball, in his exceedingly valuable edition of Tavernier's *Travels*, London 1889, has proved that the carat used by Tavernier was the Florentine, equal to 3·04 grs. troy, which is 4 per cent. lighter than the English carat of 3·17 grs. troy. The great Mascarenhas diamond would therefore have weighed 64⅝ carats English. The Dom was immensely wealthy, but he did not live to return to Europe with his ill-gotten gains, having died on board the vessel on which he was returning from Goa to Portugal. Tavernier states that the report was that he was poisoned and that it was held to be a just punishment for his having made away with many persons in the same manner, especially when he was Governor in the island of Ceylon.

[1] Abdullah Kutb-Sháh, the sixth Sultan of the Kutb-Sháhí dynasty of Golkonda; he died in 1674.

[2] Mír Muhammad Amín.

then with the King, to urge his immediate departure from court, under any false pretext, and to represent the necessity of his joining him in the *Karnatic*: but he found it impossible to elude the vigilance with which he was guarded. Disappointed in this, the Vizier's next measure was at once bold and original, and it brought the King of *Golkonda* to the very verge of destruction: so true it is that he who cannot keep his own counsel cannot preserve his crown. *Jemla* addressed a letter to *Aureng-Zebe*, at this time in Daulet-Abad,[1] the metropolis of the *Decan*, to the following effect:

'I have rendered, as all the world knows, essential services to the King of *Golkonda*, and he owes me a heavy debt of gratitude. Nevertheless, he is plotting my ruin and that of my family. May I be permitted, therefore, to throw myself under your protection? In acknowledgment of the kindness I anticipate at your hands, I suggest a plan by which you may easily obtain possession both of the King's person and kingdom. Confide in my integrity, and the enterprise will neither be difficult nor dangerous: assemble four or five thousand of your choicest cavalry, and proceed by forced marches towards *Golkonda*, which may be reached in sixteen days, spreading a rumour that this body of horse is escorting an ambassador from *Chah-Jehan*, who has affairs of moment to negotiate with the King at *Bagnaguer*.[2]

[1] The Fort of Daulatábád, anciently called Deogarh, was from a remote period the stronghold of the rulers of the Deccan. After Aurangzeb's death in 1707 this fortress and other Mogul territory in the Deccan passed into the hands of Asaph Jah, a distinguished general in Aurangzeb's service, the founder of the Nizam's dynasty, in whose family they have remained ever since.

[2] Bhágnagar, the 'Fortunate City,' called after Bhágmatí the favourite mistress of Kutb Sháh Muhammad Kulí, who founded it in 1589, removing his seat of government from Golkonda, about 7 miles distant, on account of its want of water and general unhealthiness. The historian Kháfí Khán states that some time after the death of Bhágmatí the name was changed to Haidarábád (Hyderabad), but that in the vernacular language of the people it continued to be called Bhágnagar. It is now the chief city and capital of the Haidarábád State.

'The *Dabir*,[1] through whose medium the first communication is always made to the King, is my relation—my creature—and entirely in my confidence: you have only to advance with rapidity, and I promise so to order it, that you shall arrive at the gate of *Bag-naguer* without exciting a suspicion that you are any other than an ambassador from *Chah-Jehan.* When the King advances, according to custom, to receive the credentials, you may easily secure his person, then his whole family, and dispose of him in the manner you may deem fit, inasmuch as his palace of Bag-naguer where he usually lives is unwalled, and without a ditch or fortifications of any sort. Meanwhile I will defray the whole expense of the expedition, and engage to pay fifty thousand rupees daily during the time it may be in progress.'

Aureng-Zebe, ever intent upon projects of ambition, immediately adopted the measures proposed in this letter. He proceeded at once towards the territory of the King of *Golkonda,* and with such address was the plot conducted, that when the Prince reached *Bag-naguer,* no one doubted that this formidable body of horse accompanied an embassy from the *Great Mogol.* The King, as is usual on similar occasions, repaired to his garden for the purpose of receiving the pretended ambassador with appropriate ceremony and honour; and while unsuspiciously approaching his perfidious enemy, he was about to be seized by ten or twelve slaves—*Georgians*—as had been projected, when an *Omrah,* who was in the conspiracy, touched with sudden remorse and compassion, exclaimed, 'Your majesty is lost if you do not instantly fly; this is *Aureng-Zebe,* and no ambassador.' It would be superfluous to describe the King's consternation: he fled from the spot, and, mounting the first horse he could find, rode at full speed to

[1] The *Dabir-ul-Mulk,* who exercises the functions of a Secretary of State for Foreign Affairs, is still a very important official at the Afghan and other Oriental courts.

the fortress of *Golkonda*,[1] distant only a league from *Bagnaguer*.

Although disappointed of his prey, *Aureng-Zebe* felt that that there was no occasion for alarm, and that he might securely prosecute his endeavours to obtain possession of the King's person. The entire spoliation of the palace was his next act. He stript it of all its costly contents, but sent the women to the King, according to a custom most scrupulously observed amongst Eastern despots. He then determined to besiege the King in his fortress, but as he was without a supply of the necessary munitions of war the siege was protracted, and *Chah-Jehan*, two months after its commencement, peremptorily commanded his son to relinquish his enterprise, and return without delay to the *Decan*; so that, although the fortress had been reduced to the last extremities from the want of provisions and war material, he was obliged to retire.

Aureng-Zebe was aware that in issuing these orders, the *Mogol* was influenced by *Dara* and *Begum* [*Saheb*], who foresaw that if permitted to pursue his designs against the King of *Golkonda*, he would become too powerful. The Prince, however, betrayed no resentment, but acknowledged the duty of implicit obedience to his father's commands. Before he retired he received ample indemnification for the expense of the armament, and stipulated that *Emir-Jemla* should have free permission to remove with his family, property, and troops, and that the silver coin of the realm should in future bear the arms of *Chah-Jehan*. Moreover, he married his son *Sultan Mahmoud*[2] to the King's eldest daughter, exacted a promise that the young Prince should be nominated successor to the throne of *Golkonda*, and received, as the Princess's

[1] Situated in a commanding position on a granite ridge. It is now used as the Nizam's treasury and a State prison.

[2] Sultán Muhammad, who died in 1676, in the State prison of Gwalior, where he had been confined by his father.

dowry, the fortress of *Ram-guyre*,[1] with the whole of its appurtenances.

These two great men, *Emir-Jemla* and *Aureng-Zebe*, were not long together before they planned great enterprises, and while returning to the *Decan*, they besieged and captured *Bider*,[2] one of the strongest places in *Visapour*.[3] They then proceeded to *Daulet-Abad*, in which city they lived upon terms of the closest intimacy, forming gigantic plans of future aggrandizement. Their union may be remembered as an important epoch in the history of *Hindoustan*: it prepared the way for the greatness and renown of *Aureng-Zebe*.

Jemla, who had by his address contrived to obtain frequent invitations to the court of *Chah-Jehan*, repaired at length to *Agra*, and carried the most magnificent presents, in the hope of inducing the *Mogol* to declare war against the Kings of *Golkonda* and *Visapour*, and against the *Portuguese*. On this occasion it was that he presented *Chah-Jehan* with that celebrated diamond which has been generally deemed unparalleled in size and beauty.[4] He dilated with earnestness on the benefits which would accrue from the conquest of *Golkonda*, whose precious stones were surely more deserving of his consideration than the rocks of *Kandahar*, whither the *Mogol* was about

[1] Rámgirí, about 113 miles to the north-east of the town of Hyderabad.

[2] Bídar, about 75 miles to the north-west of the town of Haidarábád (Hyderabad). Noted for the metal ware, bídarí (bidree) work, to which it has given its name.

[3] Bijápur, the great Moslem State, founded by a son of Murad II., the Ottoman Emperor who succeeded to the throne in 1422. Bernier follows the Hindoo form of the name, Vijayapura.

[4] Not the least valuable part of Dr. Ball's edition of Tavernier's *Travels*, is his identification of this diamond with the world-renowned gem the *Koh-i-núr*, or 'Mountain of Lustre,' which he has been able to do by a comparison of Tavernier's drawing of the Great Mogul's diamond with models of the *Koh-i-núr* as it was when brought to England in 1850, and by a scientific sifting of other evidence. For an abstract of Dr. Ball's account, which he has kindly sanctioned and revised, together with extracts from Catrou, relating to Amír Jumla, see Appendix II.

to lead an army: his military operations in that kingdom ought not to cease, he said, until the conquest of his arms extended to Cape *Comory*.[1]

The diamonds may have produced their effect upon the mind of *Chah-Jehan*; but it is the more received opinion that he was glad of a pretext for raising an army which should restrain the growing insolence of his eldest son and that it was for this reason he entered into the views of *Jemla*.

Whatever were his motives, he resolved to send an army towards the *Decan* under the *Emir's* command.

Dara had incurred his father's displeasure by his recent and undisguised attempts to become paramount in power and authority: but there was one act of his which *Chah-Jehan* regarded with peculiar horror and indignation, and which he was least disposed to forgive,—the murder of Vizier *Sadullah-Kan*,[2] a nobleman whom the *Mogol* considered the most accomplished statesman of *Asia*, and for whom he felt a warmth of friendship that became quite proverbial. What was the offence which *Dara* judged worthy of death is not ascertained. Perhaps he apprehended that in the event of the King's demise, the powerful ascendency of the Vizier might leave the crown at his disposal, and that he would place it on the head of *Sultan Sujah*, whose party he seemed to favour: or it is possible *Dara* may have been influenced by the reports promulgated respecting the intentions of *Sadullah-Kan*, who, from being an *Indian* [Hindoo] by birth, had excited the jealousy of the *Persians* at court. One of these rumours was, that

[1] The ancient and correct name of that Cape, the most southern point of India, Comorin being a Portuguese corruption of Kumárí ('a virgin').

[2] In the *Sháh Jahán-náma* of Ináyat Khán, it is stated that Sádullah Khán, 'Allamí, died from the effects of a severe and painful attack of colic. The Wazír, who was considered the most able and upright minister that ever appeared in India, died in 1656. Catrou also records that Dárá was accused of having caused Sádullah Khán to be poisoned.

after the death of *Chah-Jehan*, the Vizier designed to exclude the *Mogols* from the throne, and either to restore the royal race of the *Patans*,[1] or usurp the crown for himself or his son. His wife was a *Patan*; and it was pretended that he kept a well-appointed army of that people, cantoned in various parts, to aid him in accomplishing his project.

It was evident to *Dara* that to send troops to the *Decan* was in effect to increase, by so many men, the strength of *Aureng-Zebe*. He opposed the measure, therefore, with many arguments and entreaties, and by every art he could devise. Finding it, however, impossible to move *Chah-Jehan* from his purpose, he persuaded him to impose certain conditions, by which *Aureng-Zebe* should engage to abstain from all interference in the conduct of the war; fix his residence at *Daulet-Abad*; confine his attention to the government of the *Decan*; and also that the *Emir* should retain the absolute and undivided command of the army: leaving the whole of his family at court, as hostages for his fidelity. This last clause was extremely offensive to *Jemla*; but *Chah-Jehan* prevailed with him to yield compliance, assuring him that this stipulation was intended only to satisfy the caprice of his son, *Dara*, and that he should soon be followed by his wife and children. The *Emir* put himself at the head of a fine army, with which he marched into the *Decan*: and without tarrying in that country, entered *Visapour*, commencing his operations with the siege of *Kaliane*,[2] a place of considerable strength.

Such was the state of *Hindoustan* when the *Mogol*, who had passed his seventieth year, was seized with a disorder, the nature of which it were unbecoming to describe. Suffice it to state that it was disgraceful to a man of

[1] The Lódí Pathán dynasty of Delhi having been crushed by the Mogul invasion of Babar Sháh in 1526.

[2] *Káliání*, about 30 miles to the west of Bídar, in what is now par of the Haidarábád (Hyderabad) State.

his age, who, instead of wasting, ought to have been careful to preserve the remaining vigour of his constitution.[1]

The *Mogol's* illness filled the whole extent of his dominions with agitation and alarm. *Dara* collected powerful armies in *Dehli* and *Agra*, the principal cities of the kingdom. In *Bengale*, *Sultan Sujah* made the same vigorous preparations for war. *Aureng-Zebe* in the *Decan*, and *Morad-Bakche* in *Guzarate*, also levied such forces as evinced a determination to contend for empire. The four brothers gathered around them their friends and allies; all wrote letters, made large promises, and entered into a variety of intrigues. *Dara*, having intercepted some of these letters, showed them to his father, inveighing bitterly against his brothers; and *Begum* [*Saheb*], his sister, availed herself of so advantageous an opportunity to prejudice the *Mogol* against his three rebellious sons: but *Chah-Jehan* placed no confidence in *Dara*, and suspecting he had a design to poison him, swallowed no food without the utmost fear and caution. It is even thought that he corresponded at this time with *Aureng-Zebe*, and that *Dara*, being apprised of the circumstance, was transported with rage to such a degree as to threaten his father. Meanwhile, the King's distemper increased, and it was reported that he was dead: the whole court was in confusion; the population of *Agra* was panic-stricken; the shops were closed for many days, and the four Princes openly declared their settled purpose of making the sword the sole arbiter of their lofty pretensions. It was, in fact, too late to recede: not only was the crown to be gained by victory alone, but in case of defeat life was certain to be forfeited. There was now no choice between a kingdom and death: as *Chah-Jehan* had ascended the throne by imbruing his hands in the blood of his own brothers, so the unsuccessful candidates on the present

[1] This illness was in September 1657, when Sháh Jahán was upwards of 64 years of age.

occasion were sure to be sacrificed to the jealousy of the conqueror.

Sultan Sujah was the first who took the field. He had filled his coffers in the rich country of *Bengale* by utterly ruining some of the *Rajas* or *Kinglets* of that region, and by plundering others. He was therefore enabled to raise a numerous army: and confiding in the support of the *Persian* omrahs, whose religious views he had embraced, advanced rapidly on *Agra*. He issued a proclamation which set forth the death of his father by poison from the hand of *Dara*, and declared his determination both to avenge so foul a murder, and to occupy the vacant throne. *Chah-Jehan*, at the instance of *Dara*, hastened to undeceive him in regard to the rumour of his decease; the malady was giving way, he said, to the power of medicine, and he expressly commanded him to return forthwith to his government of *Bengale*. But as *Sultan Sujah's* friends at court represented the *Emperor's* disorder as incurable, he continued his march toward the capital, pretending that he was too well convinced of the death of his revered parent, and that if, contrary to his expectation, he should be yet alive, he was desirous of kissing his feet, and receiving his commands.

Aureng-Zebe also published his proclamations, and put his forces in motion, much at the same time as *Sultan Sujah*. He, too, was meditating an advance on *Agra* when he received a similar prohibition, both from the King and from *Dara*; the latter of whom menaced him with punishment if he quitted the *Decan*. He dissembled, however, like his brother of *Bengale*, and returned a similar answer; but as his finances were not abundant, and his army was comparatively small, he endeavoured to obtain by fraud what he could not hope to gain by arms. The immediate dupes of his artifice were *Morad-Bakche* and *Emir-Jemla*. In a letter to the former he said :—

'I need not remind you, my brother, how repugnant to my real disposition are the toils of government. While

Dara and *Sultan Sujah* are tormented with a thirst for dominion, I sigh only for the life of a *Fakire.* But, although renouncing all claim to the kingdom, I nevertheless consider myself bound to impart my sentiments to you, my friend, whom I have always tenderly loved. *Dara* is not only incapable of reigning, but is utterly unworthy of the throne, inasmuch as he is a *Kafer*—an idolater—and held in abhorrence by all the great *Omrahs. Sultan Sujah* is equally undeserving the crown ; for being avowedly a *Rafezy*—an heretic—he is of course an enemy to *Hindoustan.* Will you then permit me to say that in you alone are to be found the qualifications for ruling a mighty empire ? This opinion is not adopted by myself only ; it is likewise entertained by the leading nobles, who esteem you for your matchless valour, and are anxious for your arrival in the capital. With respect to myself, if I can exact a solemn promise from you that, when king, you will suffer me to pass my life in some sequestered spot of your dominions, where I may offer up my constant prayers to heaven in peace, and without molestation, I am prepared immediately to make common cause with you, to aid you with my counsel and my friends, and to place the whole of my army at your disposal. I send you one hundred thousand *roupies,* of which I entreat your acceptance, as an earnest of my best wishes. The time is critical : you should, therefore, not lose one moment in taking possession of the castle of *Sourate,* where I know the vast treasure of the State to be deposited.'

Morad-Bakche, whose wealth and power were comparatively limited, received his brother's proposals, accompanied as they were by so large a sum, with great delight, and was beyond measure elated at the prospect which now presented itself to him. The letter was everywhere exhibited, in expectation that the young men would be induced by its contents to enter with cheerfulness into his army, and that it might dispose the opulent merchants more willingly to lend the large sums he was exacting with undeviating rigour. He now assumed all the consequence and authority of a king; was profuse in his promises, and contrived everything so successfully that he soon collected a pretty numerous army. From this army it was his first care to detach three thousand men, under the command of *Chah-Abas,* a eunuch,[1] but a valiant soldier, to lay siege to the castle of *Sourate.*

Aureng-Zebe next turned his thoughts on *Emir-Jemla.* He sent to him his eldest son *Sultan Mahmoud* (whom he had married to the King of *Golkonda's* daughter)[2] with a request that he would come to him at *Daulet-Abad,* as he had intelligence of the greatest importance to impart. The *Emir* was at no loss to divine the nature of this intelligence, and refused to quit his army which was still engaged in the siege of *Kaliane*;[3] alleging that he had recently received tidings from *Agra,* and could assure *Sultan Mahmoud* that *Chah-Jehan* was not dead. In no case, however, could he think of co-operating with *Aureng-Zebe,* while his wife and children were in *Dara's* power: his determination was fixed; he would not be a party in the present quarrel.

Finding it impossible to accomplish the object of his mission, *Sultan Mahmoud* returned to *Daulet-Abad,* extremely displeased with the *Emir*; but *Aureng-Zebe,* no way discouraged, sent another message by his second son, *Sultan Mazum,*[4] who conducted his mission with so much address and urbanity, and made such protestations of friendship, that *Emir-Jemla* could not withstand the force of his solicitations. He vigorously prosecuted the siege of *Kaliane,* and having forced the garrison to capitulate, hastened to *Daulet-Abad* with the flower of his army.

[1] The Khwája Sháhbáz of Kháfí Khán, who, in his history, says that after the fort of Surat was reduced, a ransom of fifteen lakhs of rupees was demanded from the merchants of the place, who eventually agreed to pay six.

[2] See p. 21. [3] See p. 24.

[4] Muhammad Mu'azzam, who succeeded his father, Aurangzeb, with the title of Sháh Álam Bahádur Sháh, was born at Burhánpur in 1643, and died at Lahore in 1712.

Aureng-Zebe received *Emir-Jemla* with the strongest professions of kindness, calling him '*Baba*' and '*Babagy*' [Bábá Jí]—'Father,' and 'My Lord Father.' He embraced his welcome visitor a hundred times; and taking him aside, addressed him thus:—'I acknowledge the force of the objection made by you to *Sultan Mahmoud*, and it is the opinion of my friends at court, who are men of judgment, that it would be extremely imprudent, while your family are in the hands of *Dara*, to stir openly in my favour, or even to manifest the slightest disposition to promote the interest of my cause. But it is not for me to inform you that there are few difficulties which may not be overcome. A scheme has occurred to my mind, which, though at first it may surprise you, will, I doubt not, on reflection, appear to you well calculated to ensure the safety of your family. Suffer yourself to be confined in prison; it will have the effect of imposing upon the world, and we shall reap all the success we can desire from this plan: for who will ever imagine that a person of your rank could tamely submit to incarceration? In the mean time, I can employ a part of your troops in any manner you think fit; and you will not perhaps refuse, in furtherance of our project, to supply me with a sum of money, according to the offer you have so repeatedly made. With these troops, and this money, I may safely try my fortune. Allow me, therefore, to conduct you to the fortress of *Daulet-Abad* where you will be guarded by one of my sons; we may then deliberate upon the means to be pursued, and I cannot conceive how any suspicion should arise in the mind of *Dara*, or how he can reasonably ill-treat the wife and children of one who is apparently my enemy.'

I have authority for stating that such was substantially the language used by *Aureng-Zebe*. The considerations which dictated the *Emir's* answer to these strange propositions are not now so well known. It is certain, however, that he complied with them, that he consented to place the troops under *Aureng-Zebe's* orders, to lend him money, and, what is even more extraordinary, to be conducted to the fortress of *Daulet-Abad*. Some have thought that *Emir-Jemla* was really allured by the solemn assurance of advantages to be derived from his acquiescence, and that he was likewise influenced by the recollection of those vows of ardent and indissoluble friendship which had been so frequently interchanged between him and *Aureng-Zebe*. Others there are who, perhaps with more reason, believe that fear forbade him to withhold his assent, as the two sons of *Aureng-Zebe, Sultan Mazum* and *Sultan Mahmoud,* were present at the conference; the former completely armed, and assuming a look that could not be mistaken; the latter indulging in unseemly grimaces, after having raised his arm in a manner which implied an intention of proceeding to violence: for the pride of this Prince was mortified because his brother's mission had been attended with better success than his own, and he was at no pains to conceal his resentment.

When the imprisonment of *Emir-Jemla* became known that portion of the army which had been brought from *Visapour* demanded aloud the release of their commander, and would soon have opened the door of his prison, if they had not been appeased by the arts of *Aureng-Zebe,* who intimated to the superior officers that the *Emir's* confinement was quite voluntary, and a part, in fact, of a scheme understood between themselves. He was, besides, lavish of his presents: he promised advancement to the officers, and increased the pay of the private soldiers; giving them at once three months' advance as a pledge of his liberal intentions.

In this manner the troops lately under *Jemla's* command were persuaded to take part in the campaign meditated by *Aureng-Zebe,* who thus soon found himself in a condition to take the field. He first marched in the direction of *Sourate* for the purpose of accelerating the fall of that place, which persevered in a vigorous and unexpected resistance; but a few days after his army had been put in motion he received news of the surrender of that town.[1] He then despatched a congratulatory letter to *Morad-Bakche*; made him acquainted with all that had passed with *Emir-Jemla*; told him he was now at the head of a formidable force; that he possessed abundance of money, that his understanding with the principal courtiers was complete; and that he was fully prepared to proceed towards *Brampour*[2] and *Agra*. He then urged him to hasten his march, and he fixed the place for the junction of the two armies.

Morad-Bakche was disappointed in the amount of treasure found in *Sourate*; perhaps it had been exaggerated by report; or the governor, as was generally suspected, had appropriated a large portion of it to his own use. The money of which he came into possession only sufficed to pay the soldiers, who had been induced to enlist by the expectation of the immense wealth which the walls of *Sourate* were believed to enclose. Nor ought the capture of the town to have increased the military reputation of this Prince; for, although destitute of regular fortifications, it yet baffled his utmost endeavours for more than a month: and he had made no progress in the siege until the *Dutch* instructed him, for the first time, in the art of mining. The blowing up of a considerable part of the wall spread consternation in the garrison, and terms of capitulation were immediately proposed.[3]

The fall of *Sourate* facilitated the future operations of *Morad-Bakche*. It procured him a great name; mining is yet imperfectly known among the Indians, and nothing could have inspired them with more astonishment than the

[1] In January 1658.

[2] Burhánpur, called Brampore and sometimes Bramport by the old travellers, on the river Taptí, in the Nimár District, Central Provinces. Founded about 1400, and held by independent Muhammadan Princes until 1600, when it was annexed to the Mogul Empire by Akbar. It was the seat of the government of the Deccan until 1635 when Aurangábád took its place.

[3] See p. 28, footnote [1].

efficacious method in which this new art had been employed by *Morad-Bakche*. It was moreover universally believed that vast riches had fallen into his hands. But notwithstanding the fame acquired by this event, and all the flattering promises of *Aureng-Zebe*, the eunuch *Chah-Abas* urged him to disregard the extravagant declarations of his brother, and not rashly to throw himself into his hands. 'Listen,' he said, 'while it is yet time, to my advice; amuse him with fair words, if you please; but do not think of joining him with your forces. Let him advance alone toward *Agra*. We shall by and by receive positive intelligence of your father's state of health, and see the course that events may take. In the mean time you may fortify *Sourate*, a most important post, which will secure to you the dominion of an extensive country producing a rich revenue, and with a little management you may become master of *Brampour*, also a town in a commanding situation, and the key, as it were, of the *Decan*.'

But the letters daily received from *Aureng-Zebe* determined *Morad-Bakche* not to relax his exertions, and the wise counsel of the eunuch *Chah-Abas* was rejected. This acute statesman had a warm and affectionate heart, and was sincerely attached to the interests of his master. Happy would it have been for the young prince if he had listened to his sage advice; but *Morad* was blinded by an inordinate thirst for dominion: his brother's letters were more and more expressive of his entire devotedness to his cause, and he considered that, if left to his own resources, he should never be able to realise those schemes of greatness that continually haunted his imagination. He therefore broke up from his encampment at *Amed-Abad*, abandoned *Guzarate*, and made the best of his way, over mountains and through forests, to the rendezvous where *Aureng-Zebe* had halted some days in expectation of his arrival.

The junction of the armies was celebrated by great rejoicings and much festivity. The two brothers were inseparable, and *Aureng-Zebe* renewed his professions of unalterable affection and his protestations of complete disinterestedness. Of the kingdom, he repeated that he most assuredly entertained no thought; he had placed himself at the head of an army for the sole purpose of combating *Dara,* their common foe, and of seating *Morad* on the vacant throne. During the march of the armies toward the capital, *Aureng-Zebe* spoke in the same tone, and never omitted, either in private or public, to address his brother with the reverence and humility due from a subject to his sovereign, calling him *Hazaret,* 'King,' and 'Your Majesty.' Strange that *Morad* should never have suspected his honesty of intention, or that the late nefarious transactions in *Golkonda* should have made so slight an impression on his mind! but this Prince was blinded by a wild ambition for empire, and incapable of perceiving that he who had recently incurred so much infamy by his attempt to usurp a kingdom could feel little inclination to live and die a *Fakire.*

The combined armies formed an imposing force, and their approach created a great sensation at the seat of government. Nothing could exceed the uneasiness of *Dara,* and *Chah-Jehan* was appalled at the threatening aspect of affairs. Whatever scope he permitted to his imagination, he could conceive no event, however momentous and fraught with evil consequences, which might not be brought to pass by the talents of *Aureng-Zebe* and the intrepidity of *Morad-Bakche.* In vain did he despatch courier after courier announcing his convalescence, and assuring the two brothers that the whole of their proceedings should be buried in oblivion if they immediately returned to their respective governments: the united armies continued to advance, and as the King's malady was really considered mortal, the Princes had recourse to their usual dissimulation, affirming that the letters purporting to bear the King's sign-annual were forgeries by *Dara*; that *Chah-Jehan* was either dead or on the point of death; and that if he should happily be alive, they were desirous of prostrating themselves at his feet, and delivering him from the thraldom in which he was held by *Dara.*

Chah-Jehan's situation was indeed distressing:—afflicted with disease, and almost a prisoner in the hands of *Dara,* who, guided by a furious resentment, breathed nothing but war, and was unwearied in preparations for conducting it with vigour;—while his other children, regardless of repeated injunctions, accelerated their march toward *Agra.* But what a sad alternative was left him in this extremity! his treasures, he saw, must be dissipated, abandoned to his sons, and squandered at their pleasure; he was compelled to summon around him his faithful and veteran captains, who were generally unfavourable to *Dara,* and whom nevertheless he must command to espouse his cause, and take the field against the other Princes, though in his heart the old monarch felt more affection for them than for *Dara.* The danger being most pressing on the side whence *Sultan Sujah* was advancing, an army was immediately sent against that prince, while another was assembled in order to encounter the combined forces of *Aureng-Zebe* and *Morad-Bakche.*

Soliman-Chekouh,[1] *Dara's* eldest son, was the general nominated to the command of the corps sent to oppose *Sultan Sujah's* progress. He was about five-and-twenty years of age, of a fine person, not without ability, generous and popular. He was a favourite with *Chah-Jehan,* from whom he had already received great riches, and who intended him for his successor in preference to *Dara.* As the *Mogol's* chief anxiety was to avoid the effusion of blood in this unnatural contest, he appointed an old *Raja,* named *Jesseingue,*[2] to be the companion or counsellor of

[1] Sulaimán Shikoh, born in 1635, died while in prison in the fort of Gwalior about 1660.

[2] Rájá Jai Singh I., of Jaipur (Jeypore), commonly called *Mirza Rájá*; of the Rájáwat branch of the Kachhwáhas of Amber (Jaipur), a

his grandson. *Jesseingue* is at present one of the richest *Rajas* in *Hindoustan*, and perhaps the ablest man in the whole kingdom. The King gave him secret instructions to avoid, if possible, coming to an engagement, and to leave no method untried to induce *Sujah* to retrace his steps. 'Represent to my son,' he said, 'that not his duty alone, but also his policy, demand the reservation of his strength for a more justifiable and promising occasion: until my malady have terminated in death, or at least until the result of the united efforts of *Aureng-Zebe* and *Morad-Bakche* shall be ascertained.'

But all the efforts of *Jesseingue* to prevent a battle proved abortive. *Soliman-Chekouh*, on the one side, was full of military ardour, and ambitious of acquiring a great name; and, on the other, *Sultan Sujah* apprehended that if he delayed his march, *Aureng-Zebe* might overcome *Dara* and gain possession of the two capital cities, *Agra* and *Dehli*. Thus the two armies were no sooner in sight, than a heavy cannonade commenced; but I need not detain my readers by detailing the particulars of this action, especially as I shall have to describe others of greater consequence: it is sufficient to state that the onset was impetuous on both sides, and that after a warm struggle *Sultan Sujah* was obliged to give way, and at length to fly in confusion. It is certain that if *Jesseingue* and his bosom friend *Delil-kan*,[1] a *Patan* and an excellent soldier, had not purposely held back, the rout of the enemy would have been complete, and their commander probably made prisoner. But the *Raja* was too prudent to lay his hands on a Prince of the Blood, the son of his King; and he acted conformably to the *Mogol's* inten-

Rájpút clan of great antiquity and renown. This clan traces its origin to Dhola Raí, who is said to have founded the State of Amber in 967 A.D., the present Mahárájá of Jaipur, being the thirty-fifth from the Raí. Rájá Jai Singh I. died at Burhánpur on the 10th July 1667.

[1] Diler Khán, a Dáúdzai Afghán, and younger brother of Bahadur Khán, Rohila, an Amír of high rank. He died in 1683.

tions when he afforded *Sultan Sujah* the means of escape. Although the loss of the enemy was inconsiderable, yet as the field of battle and a few pieces of artillery remained in *Soliman-Chekouh's* possession, it was immediately reported at court that he had gained a decisive victory.[1] This affair, while it raised the reputation of *Soliman-Chekouh,* was injurious to that of *Sultan Sujah,* and the ardour of the *Persians* who favoured his cause was proportionably abated.

Soliman-Chekouh had been a few days employed in the pursuit of *Sujah,* when he received intelligence of the rapid and resolute march of *Aureng-Zebe* and *Morad-Bakche* on *Agra.* Aware of his father's want of conduct and prudence, and knowing that he was surrounded by secret enemies, he prudently determined to return to the capital, in the neighbourhood of which *Dara* would probably offer battle. Every one is of opinion that the young prince could not have adopted a wiser course; and that if he could have brought up his army in time, *Aureng-Zebe* would have gained no advantage, if indeed he had ventured to engage in so unequal a contest.

Nowithstanding the success which had attended the arms of *Soliman-Chekouh* at *Elabas* [2] (where the *Gemna* falls into the *Ganges*) affairs took a very different turn in the direction of *Agra.* The government were struck with amazement when they heard that *Aureng-Zebe* had crossed the river at *Brampour* and forced his way through all the difficult passes in the mountains, on the successful defence of which every reliance had been placed. A body of troops was hastily despatched to dispute the passage of the river of *Eugenes,*[3] while the main body of the army

[1] According to Kháfí Khán's account, the battle was fought near Benares in the month of December 1657.

[2] Ilahbas, a corruption of Ilahábás, the old name of Allahabad, and still used by the people to designate the capital of the North-West Provinces.

[3] Ujjain (Ujein), on the river Sipra, the ancient capital of Malwa, the Greenwich of the Hindoo geographers, as their first meridian

was preparing to move forward. To command this body of troops, two of the most skilful, and, in point of personal influence, two of the most powerful men, were selected. The name of the one was *Kasem-Kan,*[1] a soldier of first-rate reputation, sincerely attached to *Chah-Jehan,* but disliking *Dara:* he assumed the command very reluctantly, and only in obedience to the *Mogol.* The other was the Raja *Jessomseingue,*[2] who in importance and authority yielded not to *Jeisseingue.* He was son-in-law of the famous and powerful *Raja Rana,*[3] who lived in the reign of *Ekbar,* and was prince of the Rajas.

Dara addressed these two generals in the most affectionate terms, and presented them with costly gifts on their departure with the troops: but *Chah-Jehan* privately suggested the same measures of caution and forbearance, which were practised in the case of *Sultan Sujah.* The consequence was that messenger after messenger was sent to *Aureng-Zebe* to beg that he would retire; but while there appeared this indecision on one side, all was activity and resolution on the other: the messengers never returned, and the enemy unexpectedly crowned an eminence at a short distance from the river.[4]

passed through it; now one of the chief towns of the dominions of the Mahárájá Sindhia. Bernier refers to the District, not the town of Ujjain; 'the passage of the river' being, 'the ford of Akbarpúr,' of Kháfí Khán's account, which is still the Nerbudda crossing of the Great Deccan Road, about 16 miles due south of the old Fort of Mándú, and nearly 34 miles south-east of the military station of Mhow.

[1] Nawab Kasim Khán Jawiní, who held the rank of a commander of 5000.

[2] Rájá Jaswant Singh. See footnote 1, p. 7. On his death, in 1678, Alamgír attempted to force his children to become Moslems. This their attendants resisted, fighting valiantly when attacked by the Emperor's troops. They escaped safely to Jodhpur, but were compelled to take to the hills and woods. On the death of Alamgír in 1707, they regained their former possessions.

[3] The renowned Rana of Chitor (Chittour).

[4] The Nerbudda (Narbadá), the boundary of the Ujjain (*Eugenes* of Bernier) territory, about 70 miles to the south of the city of Ujjain.

It was summer, and the heat was intense;[1] the river therefore became fordable. *Kasem-Kan* and the *Raja* prepared for battle on perceiving, as they apprehended, a disposition on the part of *Aureng-Zebe* to force the river. But in point of fact, the whole of his army was not yet come up, and this was only a feint; for he feared that the enemy's troops might themselves cross the stream, cut him off from the water, attack him before the soldiers had recovered from their fatigue, and thus prevent him from taking up an advantageous position. It appears certain, indeed, that he was at this time totally incapable of opposing any effectual resistance, and that *Kasem-Kan* and the *Raja* might have obtained an easy victory. I was not present at this first encounter; but such was the opinion entertained by every spectator, especially by the *French* officers in *Aureng-Zebe's* artillery. The two commanders, however, were compelled by their secret orders quietly to take a position on the banks of the river, and to content themselves with disputing the passage.

His army having rested two or three days, *Aureng-Zebe* made the necessary dispositions for forcing the passage. Placing his artillery in a commanding position, he ordered the troops to move forward under cover of its fire. His progress was opposed by the cannon of the enemy, and the combat was at first maintained with great obstinacy. *Jessomseingue* displayed extraordinary valour, disputing every inch of ground with skill and pertinacity. With regard to *Kasem-Kan*, although it cannot be denied that he deserved the celebrity he had hitherto enjoyed, yet upon the present occasion he approved himself neither a dexterous general nor a courageous soldier: he was even suspected of treachery, and of having concealed in the sand, during the night that preceded the battle, the greater part of his ammunition, a few volleys having left the army without powder or ball. However this may be,

[1] The battle was fought on the 20th April 1658, 'near Dharmátpúr,' according to the *Álamgír-náma*.

the action was well supported, and the passage vigorously opposed. The assailants were much incommoded by rocks in the bed of the river; and the uncommon height of its banks, in many parts, rendered it extremely difficult to gain a footing on the other side. The impetuosity of *Morad-Bakche* at length overcame every impediment; he reached the opposite bank with his corps, and was quickly followed by the remainder of the army. It was then that *Kasem-Kan* ingloriously fled from the field, leaving *Jessomseingue* exposed to the most imminent peril. That undaunted *Raja* was beset on all sides by an overwhelming force, and saved only by the affecting devotion of his *Ragipous*,[1] the greater part of whom died at his feet. Fewer than six hundred of these brave men, whose number at the commencement of the action amounted to nearly eight thousand, survived the carnage of that dreadful day. With this faithful remnant, the *Raja* retired to his own territory, not considering it prudent to return to *Agra* on account of the great loss he had sustained.[2]

The word *Ragipous* signifies *Sons of Rajas*. These people are educated from one generation to another in the profession of arms. Parcels of land are assigned to them for their maintenance by the *Rajas* whose subjects they are, on condition that they shall appear in the field on the summons of their chieftain. They might be said to form a species of *Gentile* nobility, if the land were inalienable and descended to their children. From an early age they are accustomed to the use of opium, and I have sometimes been astonished to see the large quantity they swallow. On the day of battle they never fail to double the dose, and this drug so animates, or rather inebriates

[1] Rájpúts.

[2] Kháfí Khán in his account of the battle says :—'Every minute the dark ranks of the infidel Rájpúts were dispersed by the prowess of the followers of Islám. Dismay and great fear fell upon the heart of Jaswant, their leader, and he, far from acting like one of the renowned class of Rájás, turned his back upon the battle, and was content to bring upon himself everlasting infamy.'

them, that they rush into the thickest of the combat insensible of danger. If the *Raja* be himself a brave man, he need never entertain an apprehension of being deserted by his followers: they only require to be well led, for their minds are made up to die in his presence rather than abandon him to his enemies. It is an interesting sight to see them on the eve of a battle, with the fumes of opium in their heads, embrace and bid adieu to one another, as if certain of death. Who then can wonder that the *Great Mogol,* though a *Mahometan,* and as such an enemy to the *Gentiles,* always keeps in his service a large retinue of *Rajas,* treating them with the same consideration as his other *Omrahs,* and appointing them to important commands in his armies?[1]

I may here relate the disdainful reception experienced by the valiant *Jessomseingue* from his wife, a daughter of the house of Rana. When it was announced that he was approaching with his gallant band of about five hundred *Ragipous,* the melancholy remnant of nearly eight thousand, at the head of whom he had fought with noble intrepidity, quitting the field from necessity, but not with dishonour; instead of sending to congratulate the gallant soldier on his escape, and console him in his misfortune, she dryly commanded that the gates of the castle should be closed

[1] As the late Professor Blochmann has so ably demonstrated, in an article in *The Calcutta Review,* No. CIV. 1871 (*A chapter from Muhammadan history. The Hindú Rájás under the Mughal Government.*) India never became a thorough Muhammadan country. 'The invaders were few and the country was too large and too populous. The waves of immigration from Túrán were few and far between, and deposited on Indian soil adventurers, warriors, and learned men, rather than artisans and colonists. Hence the Muhammadans depended upon the Hindoos for labour of every kind, from architecture down to agriculture and the supply of servants. Many branches they had to learn from the Hindoos, as, for example, the cultivation of indigenous produce, irrigation, coinage, medicine, the building of houses, and weaving of stuffs suitable for the climate, the management of elephants, and so forth.' In course of time, as Bernier and many others record, the rulers had to depend on the Hindoos for recruiting their army.

against him. 'The man is covered with infamy,' she said, 'and he shall not enter within these walls. I disown him for my husband, and these eyes can never again behold him. No son-in-law of *Rana* can possess a soul so abject. He who is allied to his illustrious house must imitate the virtues of that great man: if he cannot vanquish he should die.' The next moment the temper of her mind took another turn. 'Prepare the funeral pile,' she exclaimed. 'The fire shall consume my body. I am deceived; my husband is certainly dead; it cannot possibly be otherwise:' and then again, transported with rage, she broke into the bitterest reproaches. In this humour she continued eight or nine days, refusing the whole of that time to see her husband. The arrival of her mother was attended, however, with a beneficial effect: she, in some measure, appeased and comforted her daughter, by solemnly promising, in the Raja's name, that as soon as he should be somewhat recovered from his fatigue, he would collect a second army, attack *Aureng-Zebe*, and fully retrieve his reputation.

This anecdote may serve as a specimen of the spirit which animates the women of this country. I might mention several instances of the same kind, having seen many wives burn themselves after the death of their husbands: but these are details which I reserve for another place; where I shall, at the same time, show the ascendency which prejudice, ancient habit, hope, the force of public opinion, and the principle of honour, have over the human mind.[1]

When *Dara* was made acquainted with the calamitous events that had occurred at *Eugenes*, the violence of his rage would have hurried him into a course of the most extravagant conduct, if he had not been restrained by the arguments and moderation of *Chah-Jehan*. That *Kasem-Kan*, had he been within his reach, would have paid the forfeit of his head, can scarcely be doubted; and *Emir*

[1] See pp. 306 *et seq.*

Jemla being regarded as the primary and principal cause of the present crisis (since it was he who supplied *Aureng-Zebe* with troops and money), *Dara* would have killed his son *Mahmet Emir-Kan* and compelled his wife and daughter to become prostitutes, had he not at length yielded to the suggestions of the King, who showed the extreme improbability of the *Emir's* concurrence in the measures of *Aureng-Zebe*. His judgment was too sound, he observed, to allow of his placing his family in jeopardy, for the sake of advancing the interests of a man for whom he could feel no warmth of friendship. On the contrary, it was sufficiently obvious that he had been himself deceived, and had fallen into the wiles of *Aureng-Zebe*.

The invaders, in the mean time, were flushed with success, impressed with an idea of their invincibility, and persuaded that there was no object, however difficult and stupendous, which they might not achieve. Still more to increase the confidence of his troops, *Aureng-Zebe* vaunted aloud that in *Dara's* army there were thirty thousand *Mogols* devoted to his service; and that this was not entirely an empty boast will soon be made apparent. *Morad-Bakche* felt impatient of delay, and expressed his eagerness to push forward; but his brother repressed this ardour, representing the necessity of some repose on the banks of the beautiful river[1] [Nerbudda], especially as it would afford an opportunity for corresponding with his friends, and ascertaining the situation of affairs. The advance on *Agra* was therefore slow and circumspect, exactly regulated by the information daily received.

Chah-Jehan was now reduced to a state of hopelessness and misery. He saw that his sons were not to be turned

[1] The Nerbudda (Narbadá) ranks second to the Ganges among the rivers of India in religious sanctity. In fact 'tis said that in the Samvat year 1951 (1895 A.D.) the sanctity of the Ganges will cease, while the purifying virtue of the Nerbudda will continue the same throughout all the ages of the world. This river, which well deserves the epithet of 'beautiful' applied to it by Bernier, then formed the boundary between Hindostan proper and the Deccan.

aside from their determination to enter the capital, and viewed with dismay the mighty preparation made by *Dara* for a decisive battle. He had a prescience of the terrible evils impending over his house, which he endeavoured by every expedient to avert. He was not in a situation, however, to resist the wishes of *Dara*, for he still continued to labour under the influence of disease, and was the servant rather than the sovereign of his eldest son. To that son he had long been compelled to resign all authority, and the military commanders, as well as the officers of the State, were instructed to yield implicit obedience to the orders of *Dara*. It is not surprising, therefore, that this Prince was enabled to assemble a numerous army, finer than perhaps had ever trod the plains of *Hindoustan*. The lowest calculation makes it amount to one hundred thousand horse, more than twenty thousand foot, and eighty pieces of cannon; besides an incredible number of camp-followers, and those *bazar* dealers,[1] so necessary for the support of an army in peace as well as in war, and who, I suspect, are often included by historians in the number of combatants, when they speak of immense armies of three or four hundred thousand men. Unquestionable it is, that the force under *Dara's* command was sufficient, in point of physical strength, to overwhelm two or three such armies as *Aureng-Zebe's*, whose utmost number could not exceed forty thousand men of all arms, and these harassed and nearly worn out by long marches under a vertical sun. Yet, notwithstanding this disparity of numbers, no one seemed to presage success to *Dara*; the only troops on whose fidelity he could depend being with the army under *Soliman-Chekouh*, and the principal *Omrahs* having manifested symptoms of disaffection to his interests. His friends, therefore, earnestly recommended him not to hazard an engagement. *Chah-Jehan* was most urgent on this point, offering, infirm as he

[1] The traders in the 'Regimental Bazaar' of a modern Indian cantonment or camp, so familiar to all Anglo-Indians.

was, to assume the chief command, and to face *Aureng-Zebe's* army. This scheme was admirably adapted to preserve peace, and to arrest the progress of that haughty prince: neither he nor *Morad-Bakche* would probably have felt disposed to fight against their father: or, if they had ventured upon such a step, their ruin must have been the consequence; for *Chah-Jehan* was popular among all the *Omrahs*, and the whole army, including the troops under the two brothers, was enthusiastically attached to his person.

FIG. 2.—The Emperor Sháh Jahán.

Failing in their attempt to prevent an appeal to the sword, *Dara's* friends exhausted every argument to dissuade him, at least, from acting with precipitancy, and to induce him to delay the battle until the arrival of *Soliman-Chekouh,* who was hastening to his assistance. This also was sound advice, the young Prince being generally beloved, and returning at the head of a victorious army, composed of soldiers, as I have before observed, attached to *Dara.* But he rejected this, as he had done the former proposition, and remained inflexible in his resolution to anticipate *Aureng-Zebe* and bring him immediately to action.

If indeed *Dara* could have commanded fortune, and controlled events, his own reputation and peculiar interest might have been promoted by such a procedure. These were the considerations that actuated him, and which he could not altogether conceal:—he was master of the King's person; in possession of his treasure, and enjoying undivided authority over the royal armies. *Sultan Sujah* was already half ruined; his other brothers were come, with a weak and worn-out army, voluntarily, as it were, to throw themselves into his hands. Once defeated, they would have no way of escape; he would then become absolute lord, attain the end of his labours, and ascend the throne without competition or difficulty. If he intrusted the management of the campaign to his father, an amicable accommodation would take place; his brothers would return quietly to their respective provinces; *Chah-Jehan,* whose health was evidently improving, would resume the reins of government, and affairs revert to their former state. If, again, he awaited the arrival of his son *Soliman-Chekouh,* the King might employ the interval in forming some design to his disadvantage, or enter into negotiation with *Aureng-Zebe* injurious to his interests; and, admitting that after the junction of his son's army, a battle were fought and gained, the part which he might have had in the success of the day would be denied him, and the honour of the achievement rest with *Soliman-Chekouh,* whose military reputation was already known and established. Then, who could tell the effect which the general applause might produce on his youthful and ardent mind, countenanced as he would be by his grandfather and many of the chief *Omrahs*? There was no saying how boundless his ambition might become, or how little it might be restrained by the affection and respect he owed to his father.

Such were the reasons which induced *Dara* to turn a deaf ear to the voice of prudence and friendship. He ordered the whole army to take the field, and presented himself before *Chah-Jehan,* then in the fortress of *Agra,* for the purpose of bidding him farewell. As his father embraced him, the unhappy old man shed tears; but addressing him in a grave and serious tone, he said, 'Well, my son, since you will have it your own way, may heaven bless your undertaking! but remember this—my injunction—if the battle be lost have a care how you come again into my presence!' Little impressed with these words, *Dara* took a hasty leave of the King, and marched his army to the river *Tchembel,*[1] about twenty leagues from *Agra,* where having fortified himself he waited with confidence the arrival of the enemy. But the quick-sighted and wily *Fakire,* who was everywhere provided with spies, fully aware of the difficulty of passing the river when thus defended, came indeed, and encamped sufficiently near to have his tents descried by *Dara,* but was at the same time intriguing with a *Raja* of the name of *Chempet,*[2] whom he gained over by presents and promises, and through whose territory he obtained permission to march his army for the purpose of reaching speedily that part of the river where it is fordable. *Chempet* even undertook to be his guide through forests and over mountains which perhaps were considered impracticable by *Dara*; and *Aureng-Zebe,* leaving his tents standing to deceive his brother, had crossed with his troops to the other side of the river[3] almost as soon as the enemy was apprised of his departure. In this emergency, *Dara* was compelled to abandon his fortifications, and pursue *Aureng-Zebe,* who advanced by rapid strides towards the river *Gemna,* on the banks of which he had time to intrench himself, refresh his men, and in his turn, await composedly the approach of the

[1] Chumbul, a river which rises near the military station of Mhow, one of the principal tributaries of the Jumna.

[2] Champat Ráí, a chief of the Bundelas.

[3] That is, the Chumbul.

enemy. The position chosen by him was five leagues distant from *Agra*; the name of the place which was formerly called *Samo :guer*,[1] is now *Fateabad*, that is to say the *Place of Victory*. *Dara* soon came up, and encamped also near the banks of the same river,[2] between *Agra* and the army of *Aureng-Zebe*.

The two armies remained in sight of each other three or four days without coming to an engagement. During this interval, *Chah-Jehan* sent letter upon letter to *Dara*, apprising him of *Soliman-Chekouh's* near approach, and entreating him to do nothing rashly or prematurely; but to draw closer to *Agra*, and select advantageous ground whereon to intrench his army until the arrival of his son. The only answer returned by *Dara* to these letters was, that three days should not elapse ere he brought *Aureng-Zebe* and *Morad-Bakche*, bound hands and feet, to his father, who might pass such judgment upon his rebellious sons as to him should seem meet. This answer despatched, he prepared for battle.

He placed the whole of his cannon in front, linked together by chains of iron, in order that no space might be left for the entrance of the enemy's cavalry. Immediately in the rear of the cannon, he ranged a line of light camels, on the forepart of whose bodies small pieces of ordnance, somewhat resembling swivels in our vessels, were fixed:[3] these the rider could charge and discharge at pleasure, without being obliged to dismount. Behind these camels was posted the most considerable part of the musketeers. The rest of the army consisted principally of cavalry, armed either with sabres, and those kind of half-pikes used by the *Ragipous*; or with sabres and bows-and-arrows; which latter weapon is generally used by the

[1] Samúgarh. [2] The Jumna.

[3] Camel swivel-guns, known by the name of *Zambúraq*, or 'Little Wasp,' also called *Shahín*, the name for the 'Royal Falcon.' Compare the falcon-beaked hammers of the 16th century and the old falcon and falconet pieces.

Mogols, that is (according to the present acceptation of the term *Mogol*) foreigners whose complexions are white, and who profess Mahometanism ; such as *Persians, Turks, Arabs*, and *Usbeks*.

The army was formed into three divisions. The command of the right wing, consisting of thirty thousand *Mogols*, was given to *Calil-ullah-Kan*, and the left wing was intrusted to *Rustám-Kan Dakny*, a brave and famous captain, conjointly with the Rajas *Chatresale*[1] and *Ramseingue Routlé*. *Calil-ullah* had been made *Bakchis*, or grand-master of the horse, in the stead of *Danechmend-Khan* (afterwards my *Agah*)[2] who resigned that situation because he knew that he had incurred *Dara's* displeasure by his solicitude to uphold the sole and unshackled authority of *Chah-Jehan*.

Aureng-Zebe and *Morad-Bakche* made a nearly similar disposition of their forces, excepting that among the troops of the *Omrahs*, stationed on either flank, a few pieces of field artillery were intermixed and concealed; a stratagem invented, it is said, by *Emir-Jemla*, and attended with some success. I am not aware that in this battle[3] recourse was had to any other artifice, unless it were that here and there were placed men who threw *bannes*,[4] which are a sort of grenade attached to a stick, and which were thrown, from various parts of the line, among the enemy's cavalry, and which produced the effect of terrifying the horses, and sometimes of killing the men.

It cannot be denied that the cavalry of this country manœuvre with much ease, and discharge their arrows with astonishing quickness; a horseman shooting six times before a musketeer can fire twice. They also pre-

[1] Rájás Chhattar or Sattar, Sál, and Rám Singh Rautela.

[2] Superior or Master, always used by Bernier in an affectionate sense when talking of Daníshmand Khán.

[3] For Kháfí Khán's account of this battle (in the *Muntakhabu-l Lubáb*), which was fought on the 28th May 1658, see pp. 220-226, vol. vii. of Sir H. M. Elliot's *History of India, as told by its own Historians*. Edited and continued by Professor John Dowson.

[4] The Hindostanee *bán*, a rocket.

serve excellent order, and keep in a compact body, especially when charging the enemy. But, after all, I do not think very highly of their proficiency in the art of war as compared with our well-equipped armies, for reasons which I shall mention in another part of this work.

The preparations I have described being completed, the artillery of both armies opened their fire, the invariable mode of commencing an engagement; and the arrows were already thick in the air, when suddenly there fell a shower of rain so violent as to interrupt the work of slaughter for a while. The weather had no sooner cleared than the sound of cannon was again heard, and *Dara* was at this time seen seated on a beautiful elephant of *Ceylon*, issuing his orders for a general onset; and, placing himself at the head of a numerous body of horse, advanced boldly toward the enemy's cannon. He was received with firmness, and soon surrounded by heaps of slain. And not only the body which he led to the attack, but those by which he was followed, were thrown into disorder. Still did he retain an admirable calmness, and evince his immoveable determination not to recede. He was observed on his elephant looking about him with an undaunted air, and marking the progress of the action. The troops were animated by his example, and the fugitives resumed their ranks; the charge was repeated, but he could not come up to the enemy before another volley carried death and dismay among the assailants: many took to flight; but the greater part seemed to have imbibed *Dara's* spirit, and followed their intrepid commander, until the cannon were forced, the iron chains disengaged, the enemy's camp entered, and the camels and infantry put completely to the rout. It was now that the cavalry of both armies coming in contact, the battle raged with the greatest fierceness. Showers of arrows obscured the air, *Dara* himself emptying his quiver: these weapons, however, produce but little effect, nine out of ten flying over the soldiers' heads, or falling short. The arrows discharged, the sword was drawn, and the contending squadrons fought hand to hand, both sides appearing to increase in obstinacy in proportion as the sword performed its murderous work. During the whole of this tremendous conflict, *Dara* afforded undeniable proofs of invincible courage, raising the voice of encouragement and command, and performing such feats of valour that he succeeded at length in overthrowing the enemy's cavalry, and compelling it to fly.

Aureng-Zebe, who was at no great distance, and mounted also on an elephant, endeavoured, but without success, to retrieve the disasters of the day. He attempted to make head against *Dara* with a strong body of his choicest cavalry; but it was likewise driven from the field in great confusion. Here I cannot avoid commending his bravery and resolution. He saw that nearly the whole of the army under his immediate command was defeated and put to flight; the number which remained unbroken and collected about his person not exceeding one thousand—I have been told it scarcely amounted to five hundred,—he found that *Dara,* notwithstanding the extreme ruggedness of the ground which separated them, evidently intended to rush upon his remaining little band; yet did he not betray the slightest symptom of fear, or even an inclination to retreat; but calling many of his principal officers by name, called aloud to them, *Delirané!*[1] (Courage, my old friends)—I am repeating his exact words—*Koda-hé*[2] (there *is* a God). *What hope can we find in flight? Know ye not where is our Decan? Koda-hé! Koda-hé!* And then, to remove all doubt of his resolution, and to show that he thought of nothing less than a retreat, he commanded (a strange extremity surely!) that chains should

[1] Dil í yáráná.

[2] *Khodah hai,* but the short, clipped utterance of one accustomed to the Deccanee accent is here reproduced exactly. A pleasant piece of evidence of the correctness and care with which Bernier wrote. His whole narrative is full of similar instances. See p. 76.

be fastened round the feet of his elephant; a command he would undoubtedly have seen obeyed, if all those who were about him had not given the strongest assurances of their unsubdued spirit and unshaken fidelity.

Dara all this time meditated an advance upon *Aureng-Zebe*, but was retarded by the difficulty of the ground and by the enemy's cavalry, which, though in disorder, still covered the hills and plains that intervened between the two commanders. Certainly he ought to have felt that without the destruction or capture of his brother, victory would be incomplete; nor should he have suffered any consideration to move him from his purpose of attacking *Aureng-Zebe*, now that he was so clearly incapable of offering effectual resistance. He had an easy opportunity to crush this formidable rival; but the circumstance I am about to relate distracted his attention, and saved *Aureng-Zebe* from the impending danger,

Dara perceived at this critical moment that his left wing was in disorder; and some one then brought him intelligence of the deaths of *Rustum-Kan* and *Chatresale*, and of the imminent peril into which *Ramseingue Routlé* was placed in consequence of having valiantly burst through the enemy, by whom he was, however, entirely surrounded. *Dara* then abandoned the idea of pushing toward *Aureng-Zebe*, and determined to fly to the succour of the left wing. After a great deal of hard fighting, *Dara's* presence turned the tide of fortune, and the enemy was driven back at all points; but the rout was not so complete as to leave him without occupation. Meanwhile *Ramseingue Routlé* was opposed to *Morad-Bakche*, and performing prodigies of valour. The *Raja* wounded the Prince, and approached so near as to cut some of his elephant's girths, hoping in that way to bring his antagonist to the earth; but the intrepidity and adroitness of *Morad-Bakche* did not permit him to accomplish his object. Though wounded and beset on all sides by the *Ragipous*, the Prince disdained to yield: he dealt his blows with terrible effect, throwing at the same time his shield over his son, a lad of seven or eight years of age, seated at his side; and discharged an arrow with so unerring an aim that the *Ramseingue Routlé* fell dead on the spot.[1]

It was not long before *Dara* was made acquainted with the serious loss he had sustained; and hearing also that *Morad-Bakche* was hemmed in by the *Ragipous,* rendered furious by the death of their master, he determined, notwithstanding every obstacle, to advance to the attack of that Prince; the only measure by which he could hope to repair the error committed in suffering *Aureng-Zebe* to escape: but even this step was rendered abortive by an act of treachery, which involved *Dara* in immediate and irretrievable ruin.

Calil-ullah-Kan, who commanded the right wing, consisting of thirty thousand *Mogols,* a force which alone was sufficient to destroy *Aureng-Zebe's* army, kept aloof from the engagement, while *Dara,* at the head of the left wing, fought with courage and success. The traitor pretended that his division was designed for a corps of reserve, and

[1] Kháfí Khán in his account of the battle tells us that 'At this moment Rájá Rám Singh, a man highly renowned among the Rájpúts for his bravery, wound a string of costly pearls round his head, and with his men clothed in yellow, as bent upon some desperate action, charged upon the elephant of Murád Bakhsh, and cried out defiantly, "What, do you contest the throne with Dárá Shukoh?" hurled his javelin against Murád Bakhsh. Then he cried out fiercely to the elephant-driver, "Make the elephant kneel down!" Murád Bakhsh, having warded off his assault, shot him in the forehead with an arrow and killed him. The Rájpúts who followed that daring fellow mostly fell dead around the feet of the Prince's elephant, and made the ground as yellow as a field of saffron.'

It was their practice to anoint their faces and hands with a preparation of turmeric, to show that they were come forth prepared to die. Occasionally they dressed in orange-coloured garments, emblematic of the followers of Mahadeo.

Prior to the onslaught of Rájá Rám Singh, it is recorded by Kháfí Khán that Murád Bakhsh, seeing that his elephant, on account of its being covered with arrow, spear, and battle-axe wounds, was likely to turn away, ordered a chain to be cast round its legs.

that he could not, consistently with his orders, move one step, or discharge a single arrow, until the last extremity: but the blackest perfidy was the cause of his inaction.

Some years prior to this period, *Calil-ullah* had suffered the indignity of having been shoebeaten[1] at the hands of *Dara*, and he considered the hour arrived when he might gratify the resentment which had never ceased to rankle in his bosom. His abstinence from all share in the battle did not, however, produce the mischief intended, *Dara* having proved victorious without the co-operation of the right wing. The traitor, therefore, had recourse to another expedient. He quitted his division, followed by a few persons, and riding with speed towards *Dara* precisely at the moment when that Prince was hastening to assist in the downfall of *Morad-Bakche*, he exclaimed, while yet at some distance, '*Mohbarek-bad, Hazaret, Salamet, Elhamd-ulellah*: May you be happy! May your Majesty enjoy health and reign in safety! Praise be to Allah, the victory is your own! But, my God! why are you still mounted on this lofty elephant? Have you not been sufficiently exposed to danger? If one of the numberless arrows, or balls, which have pierced your *howda*[2] had

[1] Tavernier (*Travels*, vol. i. p. 143) states that Sháh Jahán, when Prince Kurum, during the siege of Daulatábád, being offended at something that Azam Khán, one of the generals, had said, 'became so enraged that, sending at once for one of his *paposhes* or slippers, which they leave at the door, had him given five or six strokes with it on the head; this in INDIA is the highest affront, after which it is impossible for a man to show himself.'

[2] In the original, *dais*, which exactly describes the 'pad,' with a canopy, the war harness of the Mogul's elephants. Howdah (howda, more correctly) from the Arabic, *haudaj*, a camel litter, ought strictly speaking to be applied to the well-known framed seat used for State purposes, sporting, etc. (See note on next page.) For much curious information in this connection, consult the work by Christopher Petri, of Hartenfels, entitled, *Elephantographia curiosa, seu elephanti descriptio . . . multisque selectis observationibus physicis, medicis et jucundis historiis referta, cum figuris æneis . . . Erfordiæ . . .* 1715, 1 vol. quarto, which is rather a scarce book.

touched your person, who can imagine the dreadful situation to which we should be reduced? In God's name descend quickly and mount your horse; nothing now remains but to pursue the fugitives with vigour. I entreat your Majesty permit them not to escape.'

Had *Dara* considered the consequences of quitting the back of his elephant on which he had displayed so much valour, and served as a rallying-point to the army, he would have become master of the Empire; but the credulous Prince, duped by the artful obsequiousness of *Calil-ullah*, listened to his advice as though it had been sincere. He descended from the elephant, and mounted his horse; but a quarter of an hour had not elapsed when, suspecting the imposture, he inquired impatiently for *Calil-ullah-Kan*. The villain was not, however, within his reach: he inveighed vehemently against that officer, and threatened him with death; but *Dara's* rage was now impotent, and his menace incapable of being executed. The troops having missed their Prince, a rumour quickly spread that he was killed, and the army betrayed; an universal panic seized them; every man thought only of his own safety, and how to escape from the resentment of *Aureng-Zebe*. In a few minutes the army seemed disbanded, and (strange and sudden reverse!) the conqueror became the vanquished. *Aureng-Zebe* remained during a quarter of an hour steadily on his elephant, and was rewarded with the crown of *Hindoustan*: *Dara* left his own elephant a few minutes too soon, and was hurled from the pinnacle of glory, to be numbered among the most miserable of Princes:—so short-sighted is man, and so mighty are the consequences which sometimes flow from the most trivial incident.[1]

[1] Kháfí Khán states that after the death of Rustam Khán and Rájá Sattar Sál, Dárá became discouraged and knew not what to do. 'Just at this time a rocket struck the *howda* of his elephant. This alarmed and discouraged him so much that he dismounted in haste without even waiting to put on his slippers, and he then without arms mounted a horse. The sight of this ill-timed alarm, and of the empty *howda*, after he had changed his elephant for a horse, disheartened the soldiers. The

These immense armies frequently perform great feats; but when thrown into confusion it is impossible to restore them to discipline. They resemble an impetuous river which has burst its banks; and whose waters, unrestrained in their course, disperse over the surrounding country, while no means can be devised to arrest them in their career of desolation. I could never see these soldiers, destitute of order, and marching with the irregularity of a herd of animals, without reflecting upon the ease with which five-and-twenty thousand of our veterans from the army in *Flanders*, commanded by *Prince Condé*[1] or *Marshal Turenne*,[2] would overcome these armies, however numerous. I am no longer incredulous, or even astonished, when I read of the exploits of the ten thousand *Greeks*, or of the achievements of the fifty thousand *Macedonians* under *Alexander*, though opposed to six or seven hundred thousand men; if, indeed, it be true that the armies of *Darius* amounted to so many, and that the servants, and various other persons employed to procure provisions, were not comprehended in this number. By receiving the onset with their usual steadiness, the *French* troops would throw any *Indian* army into consternation; or they might, as *Alexander* did, direct their chief effort to a particular part of the line; and the success attending such a movement would fill the enemy with terror, and occasion an immediate and general dispersion.

Aureng-Zebe determined to derive every possible benefit from this unexpected and almost miraculous victory; and,

men lost heart in sympathy with their leader, and began to think of flight. Just at this time, as one of his attendants was girding him with a quiver, a cannon-ball carried off the man's right hand and he fell dead. The sight of this struck terror into the hearts of those around him; some of them dispersed, and others fled from the fatal field. Dárá, beholding the dispersion of his followers, and the repulse of his army, prizing life more than the hope of a crown, turned away and fled.'

[1] Louis de Bourbon, Prince of Condé, usually known as 'Condé the Great,' born 1621, died in 1681.

[2] Henri de la Tour d'Auvergne, Vicomte de Turenne, one of the great soldiers of France, was born in 1611, and died in 1675.

to ensure the attainment of the sole object of his desire, absolute dominion, resorted to every kind of unprincipled base intrigue. The perfidious *Calil-ullah-Kan* soon appeared in his presence, proffering his submission, and the services of whatever portion of the troops he might seduce from their first allegiance. The Prince thanked him, and loaded him with promises, but was cautious not to receive him in his own name. He carried him at once to *Morad-Bakche,* by whom the traitor was hailed, as may easily be imagined, with every profession of kindness. During this interview *Aureng-Zebe* addressed his brother as his acknowledged King and Sovereign, observing to *Calil-ullah-Kan* that it was *Morad-Bakche* alone who was qualified to wear the crown, and that the victory was gained only by the skilful conduct and irresistible valour of that Prince.[1]

Notwithstanding this semblance of fealty to his younger brother, *Aureng-Zebe* was actively employed day and night in writing to the *Omrahs,* whom he brought over gradually to his party. *Chah-hest-kan,*[2] his uncle, was unwearied in promoting the views of his nephew, and was indeed an invaluable coadjutor, being active, intelligent, and possessed of extensive influence. He had the reputation of writing the most insinuating letter, and using the most persuasive eloquence, of any man in *Hindoustan.* It is known that owing to some real or imaginary affront he greatly disliked *Dara,* and therefore embraced this opportunity of contributing to his downfall. *Aureng-Zebe* concealed under the garb of disinterestedness and purity of intention his raging passion for sovereignty. Everything that was done, the negotiations entered into, and the pro-

[1] It is stated by Kháfí Khán that the howdah which Murád Baksh used during the battle was stuck as thick with arrows as a porcupine with quills, so that the ground of it was not visible. Also that it was kept in the store-house in the fort of the capital (Delhi) as a curiosity, and as a memorial of the bravery of that descendant of the house of Timúr, remaining there till about 1713.

[2] Shaista Khán (see p. 13) was a son of the wazir Asaf Khán, and brother of Shah Jahán's wife, Mumtáz Mahál.

mises made, all was in *Morad-Bakche's* name: from him every command was to emanate, and he was to be regarded as the future King. *Aureng-Zebe* acted only as his lieutenant, as his zealous and dutiful subject; the turmoils of government were ill suited to the disposition of his mind; to live and die as a *Fakire* was his firm and inflexible resolution!

As for *Dara*, he was weighed down with dispondency and terror. He repaired with all diligence to *Agra*, but did not venture into his father's presence; for his last stern injunction,[1] 'Remember, *Dara*, if thou art defeated, never return to me,' still sounded in his ear. The good old man nevertheless sent a faithful eunuch in secret to condole with the unhappy Prince, to assure him of his unalterable affection, and of the grief into which he was plunged by the late disaster. 'But,' added the King, 'there is surely no reason for despair while an army under *Soliman-Chekouh* remains. For the present, I advise you to take the road to *Dehli*, where you will find a thousand horses in the royal stables; and the governor of the fort has my orders to furnish you with money and elephants. You should not withdraw to a greater distance than prudence may demand; I shall write frequently, and wish you to be within easy reach of my letters. I still think I possess the means of bringing *Aureng-Zebe* into my power, and of inflicting due chastisement upon him.' So utterly cast down, so absorbed in sorrow was *Dara*, that he could frame no answer to this affecting communication, or even transmit a formal acknowledgment of it to his father. He sent several messages to *Begum-Saheb*, and departed at midnight, with his wife, daughters, and his youngest son *Sepé-Chekouh*,[2] accompanied, and this is almost incredible, by not more than three or four hundred persons. Let

[1] See p. 46.

[2] Dárá Shikoh was married, when in his twentieth year, to the Princess Nádira, the daughter of his uncle, Sultán Parwez, by whom he had two sons, Sulaimán Shikoh and Sipihr Shikoh, who shared the ill-fortunes of their father, both dying in prison in the fort of Gwalior.

him pursue his melancholy way to Dehli, while we consider the deep policy and consummate address which marked the conduct of *Aureng-Zebe* at *Agra.*

One of his first measures was to gain over, or at least to sow the seeds of disunion, among the victorious troops commanded by *Soliman-Chekouh,* and thus destroy *Dara's* last hope of retrieving his fortunes. He, therefore, represented to the *Raja Jesseingue* and to *Delil-kan,* the principal officers in that army, the utter ruin of *Dara's* affairs. The formidable force on which he founded such confident hopes of success, observed *Aureng-Zebe,* after sustaining a total overthrow, had come over to his standard. *Dara* was now a fugitive, unattended by a single regiment, and must soon fall into his hands; and, with respect to *Chah-Jehan,* such was the state of his health, that no expectation could be entertained of his surviving many days. It was evident that they were engaged in a cause which was now desperate, and that a longer adherence to *Dara's* fallen fortune would be extremely imprudent. He counselled them to consult their best interests by joining his army, and bringing with them *Soliman-Chekouh,* whose person they might easily seize.

Jesseingue hesitated for some time as to the line of conduct he should pursue. He still feared *Chah-Jehan* and *Dara,* and dreaded the consequence of laying hands on a Royal Personage; a violence not likely to escape punishment, sooner or later, though that punishment should be inflicted by *Aureng-Zebe* himself. He was acquainted, too, with the high and undaunted spirit of *Soliman-Chekouh,* and could have no doubt that the Prince would die rather than submit to the loss of liberty.

At last this was what he determined upon. After having taken counsel with *Delil-kan* his great friend, and having renewed oaths of fealty to each other, it was decided between them that *Jesseingue* should straightway repair to *Soliman-Chekouh's* tent, show him the overtures made by *Aureng-Zebe,* and disclose frankly the whole state of his mind. 'I ought not to disguise from you,' he told the Prince, 'the danger of your situation: you can depend neither upon *Delil-kan*, or *Daoud-kan*,[1] nor upon any part of the troops; and, by advancing to the relief of your father, you may involve yourself in irretrievable ruin. In this emergency you cannot do better than seek refuge in the mountains of *Serenaguer*.[2] The *Raja* of that country will receive you kindly; his territory is inaccessible, and he can be in no dread of *Aureng-Zebe*. While in this secure retreat, you may calmly observe the progress of events, and descend from your mountains when a favourable occasion shall arise.'[3]

The young Prince could not fail to understand from this discourse that he had lost all authority both with the *Raja* and the troops; and that he should endanger the safety of his own person if he refused to relinquish the command: he yielded, therefore, to the sad necessity of the case, and proceeded toward the mountains. He was attended by a few affectionate friends, chiefly *Manseb-dars*[4] and *Saieds*, and others who considered themselves

[1] Probably Dáúd Khán, Kureshi, who became commander of 5000 in the reign of Alamgír. In the year 1670 he was appointed governor of Allahabad.

[2] Srínagar, in what is now the Garhwál District of the North-West Provinces, a wild mountain country along the valley of the Alaknanda River. Srínagar, the name of the principal village in the district, was in Bernier's time the capital of the Garhwál Rájás; it is now to a great extent deserted. Many writers and commentators have confounded this place with the Srínagar in Kashmir. The position of this (Garhwál) Srínagar, is shown with considerable accuracy, titled *Serenagher*, on the map of the *Mogol Empire* in the first edition, Paris, 1670, of *The History of the late Rebellion, etc.*, and titled *Serenagher montes*, on the map in the early Dutch edition, Amsterdam, 1672 (see the reproductions at pp. 238 and 454), and also in other editions.

[3] Sulaimán Shikoh was afterwards given up by the Rájá (called the Zamíndár of Srínagar in the *'Amal-i Sálih* of Muhammad Sálih Kambú) in 1670 to the officers of Aurangzeb. See p. 105.

[4] Mansabdárs, commanders, officers, from *mansab*, Pers. 'a command.'

bound to follow him. The bulk of the army remained with the *Raja* and *Delil-Kan,* who had the baseness to send a body of men to plunder the Prince's baggage. Among other booty, they seized an elephant laden with *Roupies*[1] of gold. Many of *Soliman-Chekouh's* attendants, discouraged by this disgraceful outrage, deserted him, and the peasantry, after spoiling them, even assassinated many of the Prince's followers. He made his way, however, to the mountains with his wife and family, and was received with the honours due to his rank ; the *Raja* of *Serenaguer*[2] assuring him he should be in perfect security while in his territory, and that he would assist him with all his forces. We must now resume the thread of our narrative, as it relates to what took place at *Agra.*

Three or four days after the battle of *Samonguer,*[3] *Aureng-Zebe* and *Morad-Bakche* presented themselves before the gate of the city, in a garden, about a league distant from the fortress. They then despatched a message to *Chah-Jehan,* by an eunuch in the confidence of *Aureng-Zebe,* and possessing all his address and deceit. This man saluted the aged Monarch in the name of his master, assured him of his undiminished respect and affection, and expressed his deep sorrow for the events which had recently taken place, events attributable to the inordinate ambition and sinister designs of *Dara.* He begged leave most sincerely to congratulate his august parent on the improvement which was manifesting itself in the state of his health, and declared that he was come to *Agra* only to receive and execute his commands.

Chah-Jehan affected to approve of his son's conduct, and expressed himself satisfied with these expressions of allegiance. He was, however, too well acquainted with his hypocrisy and love of power, to place any confidence

[1] Gold mohurs in fact, called 'Gold Roupies,' by many of the old travellers.

[2] Srínagar in Garhwál. See p. 92.

[3] Samúgarh, nine miles east of Agra. See p. 47.

in his protestations; yet, instead of acting with decision, showing himself to his people, and assembling his *Omrahs*, for which there was still time, he chose rather to try his own skill in artifice and dissimulation with *Aureng-Zebe*, who surpassed all men in both. It is not surprising, therefore, that the father fell into the snare which he had spread for his son. He sent a trusty eunuch to say how sensible he was not only of the improper behaviour of *Dara*, but also of his incapacity; to remind *Aureng-Zebe* of the peculiar tenderness he had ever borne him, and to request he would visit his affectionate father, that such arrangements might be concluded as the present distracted state of affairs rendered necessary. The cautious Prince likewise mistrusted *Chah-Jehan*; for he knew that *Begum-Saheb* quitted him neither night nor day; that he was completely under her control; that she had dictated the message, and that there were collected in the fortress several large and robust *Tartar* women, such as are employed in the seraglio, for the purpose of falling upon him with arms in their hands, as soon as he entered the fortress. *Aureng-Zebe* would not, therefore, venture within its walls; and though he repeatedly fixed the day for obeying his father's summons, he as often deferred it to the morrow. Meanwhile, he continued his secret machinations, and sounded the opinions of the most powerful *Omrahs*, until, having well digested his plans, the public all at once found to their astonishment that his son, *Sultan Mahmoud*, had taken possession of the fortress. This enterprising young man, having posted a number of men in the vicinity, entered the place on the plea of visiting the *Mogol* with a message from *Aureng-Zebe*, and fell suddenly on the guards stationed at the gate; he was quickly followed by his men, who overcame the unsuspecting garrison, and made themselves masters of the fortress.

If ever man was astonished, that man was *Chah-Jehan* when he perceived that he had fallen into the trap he had prepared for others, that he himself was a prisoner, and *Aureng-Zebe* in possession of the fort. It is said that the unhappy Monarch sent at once a message to *Sultan Mahmoud*, promising, on his crown and the *Koran*, to nominate him King, provided he served him faithfully in this conjuncture. 'Come to me,' added the *Mogol*, 'and lose not this opportunity of delivering your grandfather from prison; an act which will obtain for you the blessing of heaven, and a glorious name that shall never die.'

If *Sultan Mahmoud* had possessed sufficient daring to close with these proposals, it appears extremely probable that he might have supplanted his father. *Chah-Jehan's* influence was still powerful, and if he had been permitted to leave the citadel, and to assume the personal command of the troops, I have reason to believe that they would have acknowledged his authority, and the leading *Omrahs* remained faithful to his government. *Aureng-Zebe* would not himself have been bold or savage enough to fight against his own father in person, especially as he must have thought that he would have been abandoned by every one, possibly by *Morad-Bakche* himself.

It is the general opinion that *Sultan Mahmoud* committed the same error upon this occasion as his grandfather had done after the battle of *Samonguer* and flight of *Dara*. And, as I am again led to the subject, it is fair I should observe that there are several politicians who contend that, considering all the circumstances of his situation, the aged Monarch, after the battle and the defeat of *Dara*, adopted the most prudent course in remaining within the fortress, and endeavouring to overcome *Aureng-Zebe* by stratagem. It is the vulgar practice, these people say, to judge of the wisdom of every plan according to the event by which it is followed: the worst-digested schemes are frequently attended with success, and then they are applauded by all the world; and if, as there was reason to expect, the appearance of affection and goodwill toward *Aureng-Zebe*, assumed by *Chah-Jehan*, had enabled him to seize the person of that

Prince, he would be extolled for sagacity and wisdom, as much as he is now contemned for being, as is injuriously said, a mere driveller, guided by his *Begum*,[1] a woman whose passions blinded her understanding, and whose vanity led her to believe that *Aureng-Zebe* would hasten to visit her; in other words, that the bird would, of his own accord, fly into the cage. But to return to *Sultan Mahmoud.*—It is inconceivable, according to the politicians of this country, that he did not eagerly grasp at a sceptre which seemed to fall into his hands; especially when, by thus gratifying his ambition, he would have gained a reputation for tenderness and generosity. By restoring his grandfather to freedom this young Prince might have become the sovereign arbiter of affairs; whereas he is now probably destined to terminate his existence in *Goüaleor.*[2]

Few will believe that *Sultan Mahmoud* was restrained by a sense of duty to his father from acceding to the wishes of *Chah-Jehan*: it is more likely that he doubted the sincerity of the King's promises, and felt all the danger of disputing the crown with a man endued with the mental energy and imposing talents of *Aureng-Zebe.* Whatever were his motives, he disregarded the offers of the unhappy prisoner, and even refused to enter his apartments, alleging that he was not authorised to visit him, but had received positive orders not to return to his father without carrying away with him the keys of every gate in the fort, in order that *Aureng-Zebe* might come in perfect security for the purpose of kissing his Majesty's feet. For the space of nearly two days, *Chah-Jehan* could not persuade himself to surrender the keys; but observing that his people were gradually deserting him, especially the soldiers stationed at the little gate, and that he was no longer safe, he delivered the keys at length into the hands of *Sultan Mahmoud,* with an injunction to *Aureng-Zebe* to come to him without further delay, if he were wise,

[1] That is, his daughter, Begum Sáhib.

[2] See p. 83.

as he had secrets of the greatest moment to disclose. As may be well supposed *Aureng-Zebe* was too wary a man, and knew too much to commit such a glaring blunder, and so far from obeying the injunction, he immediately appointed his eunuch *Etbarkan* governor of the fortress, by whose orders *Chah-Jehan,* with *Begum-Saheb* and the whole of the women, were closely confined. Many of the gates were also walled up, and all intercourse between the *Mogol* and his friends was effectually prevented. He was not even permitted to leave his apartment without the knowledge of the Governor.

At this period *Aureng-Zebe* wrote a letter to his father which, before he sealed it, was shown to everybody. 'I cannot better explain my conduct,' observed the Prince, 'than by stating that while you professed extraordinary partiality for me, and expressed your displeasure at *Dara's* proceedings, I was informed, on indisputable authority, that you had sent him two elephants laden with golden *roupies.* Thus is he furnished with means to collect new armies, and to prolong this disastrous war; I, therefore, put it to you plainly whether I am not driven by his pertinacity to resort to measures which appear harsh and unnatural? Is he not, properly speaking, the cause of your imprisonment? and is it not owing to him that I have so long been deprived of the pleasure of throwing myself at your feet, and discharging the duties, and paying the attentions, you have a right to demand from an affectionate son? It only remains for me to beg that you will pardon what now seems strange in my conduct, and to recommend the exercise of patience under the temporary loss of liberty; for be assured that, as soon as *Dara* shall be rendered incapable of disturbing our repose, I shall fly to the citadel, and with my own hands open the doors of your prison.'

I have been told that *Chah-Jehan* did, in fact, send the elephants, with the *roupies* of gold,[1] to *Dara,* on the very

[1] See p. 60 text, and footnote [1].

night of his departure from *Dehli*, and that it was *Rauchenara-Begum* who communicated the information to *Aureng-Zebe.* That Princess also apprised him of the presence of the *Tartar* women, by whom it was intended he should be assailed when he entered the castle. It is even said that *Aureng-Zebe* intercepted some letters written by his father to *Dara.*

Many intelligent persons, however, deny the truth of these allegations, and contend that the letter, thus generally exhibited, was a mere invention to deceive the public, and to reconcile them to the outrageous measures of which the *Mogol's* adherents had so much right to complain. Be the truth what it may, it is certain that the close confinement of *Chah-Jehan* seemed the signal for nearly the whole body of *Omrahs* to pay their court to *Aureng-Zebe* and *Morad-Bakche.* I can indeed scarcely repress my indignation when I reflect that there was not a single movement, nor even a voice heard, in behalf of the aged and injured Monarch; although the *Omrahs*, who bowed the knee to his oppressors, were indebted to him for their rank and riches, having been, according to the custom of this court, raised by *Chah-Jehan* from a state of the lowest indigence, and many of them even redeemed from absolute slavery. A few there were, such as *Danech-mend-Kan* and some others, who espoused no party; but, with this small exception, every *Omrah* declared in favour of *Aureng-Zebe.*

It may, however, diminish our censure of this ungrateful conduct, if we call to mind that the *Omrahs* of *Hindoustan* cannot be proprietors of land, or enjoy an independent revenue, like the nobility of *France* and the other states of *Christendom.* Their income, as I said before,[1] consists exclusively of pensions which the King grants or takes away according to his own will or pleasure. When deprived of this pension, they sink at once into utter insignificance, and find it impossible even to borrow the smallest sum.

[1] See p. 5.

The combined Princes, having thus disposed of *Chah-Jehan*, and received the homage of the *Omrahs*, set out in pursuit of *Dara*. The royal treasury supplied their pecuniary wants, and *Chah-hest-Kan*, the uncle of *Aureng-Zebe*, was appointed governor of *Agra*.

When the day arrived for the departure of the army, *Morad-Bakche's* particular friends, and chief among them the eunuch *Chah-Abas*, employed every argument to induce him to remain with his own troops in the neighbourhood of *Agra* and *Dehli*. An excess of respect, and too smooth a tongue denoted, they said, a treacherous heart. They represented to him that being King, and universally acknowledged as such, even by *Aureng-Zebe* himself, it was his wisest policy not to remove from the neighbourhood of *Agra* or *Dehli*, but to let his brother go alone in pursuit of *Dara*. Had he been swayed by this prudent counsel, *Aureng-Zebe* would indeed have felt greatly embarrassed; but it made no impression upon his mind, and he continued to repose unreserved confidence in his brother's solemn promises, and in the oaths which they had mutually and repeatedly sworn on the *Koran*. The two brothers quitted *Agra* together, and took the road to *Dehli*.

When they halted at *Maturas*[1] four short journeys from *Agra*, the friends of *Morad-Bakche*, who had seen and heard enough to excite their suspicion, once more endeavoured to awaken his fears. They assured him that *Aureng-Zebe* entertained some evil design, and that some dreadful plot was certainly in progress. Of this, information had reached them from various quarters: he must, therefore, absolutely abstain from visiting his brother, at least for that day. Indeed it was advisable, they added, to anticipate, without delay, the meditated blow; for which purpose the Prince need only excuse himself, on the plea of indisposition, from visiting *Aureng-Zebe*, who would thus be induced to come to *Morad-Bakche* attended, as usual, with very few persons.

[1] Mathura (Muttra), on the right bank of the Jumna, about 30 miles above Agra.

But neither argument nor entreaty could remove the spell by which he appeared bound. The feigned and fulsome adulation of *Aureng-Zebe* had indeed enchanted the unhappy Prince; and, notwithstanding the strenuous efforts of his friends, he accepted an invitation from his brother for supper. The latter expected him, and had concerted his measures with *Mirkan* and three or four other of his minions. *Morad-Bakche* was greeted with even more external courtesy and respect than had been usual since *Aureng-Zebe* had marked him for his victim; tears of joy seemed to flow, and his brother wiped, with a gentle hand, the perspiration and dust from the face of the devoted and credulous Prince. During supper, the utmost good-humour and conviviality apparently prevailed; the conversation was enlivening and incessant, and at the end of the repast, a large quantity of the delicious wines of *Chiraz* and *Caboul* was introduced. *Aureng-Zebe* then rose softly, and with a countenance that beamed with affection and delight, said, 'I need not inform your Majesty of the serious turn of my mind, and that, as a *Mahometan*, I feel scruples which do not permit me to indulge in the pleasures of the table; but though I deem it my duty to retire, yet I leave you in excellent company. *Mirkan* and my other friends will entertain your Majesty.' An extravagant fondness for wine was among *Morad-Bakche's* foibles, and upon the present occasion, finding it peculiarly good, he drank to such excess that he became intoxicated, and fell into a deep sleep. This was precisely the effect which *Aureng-Zebe* intended the wine should produce. His servants were ordered to withdraw that their master might not be disturbed; and *Mirkan* took away both his sword and dagger.[1] It was not long before *Aureng-Zebe*

[1] In the original, 'son sabre et son jemder ou poignard.' A *jamdhar* (? from the Sanscrit *Yama-dhára* = 'death-bringer') was a short, broad dagger with the 'grip' at right angles to the blade, between side guards for the hand. Some had two points (*dú-likhána* = 'two scratcher,' from *likhna*, to write or scratch), others were triple-pointed

came to rouse him from his sleep. He entered the room, and pushing the Prince rudely with his feet, until he opened his eyes, uttered this short and insolent reprimand, 'Oh, shame and infamy! Thou a King and yet possessing so little discretion? What will the world now say of thee, and even of me? Let this wretched and drunken man be bound hand and foot, and removed there within, to sleep away his shame.' The command was no sooner given than executed; five or six soldiers rushed upon *Morad-Bakche,* and in spite of his cries and resistance, fetters and handcuffs were applied, and he was carried away. This violence could not be perpetrated without the knowledge of his immediate attendants; they wished to sound an alarm, and attempted to break into the apartment; but they were silenced and overawed by *Allah-Couly,* the chief officer in *Morad-Bakche's* artillery, who had long been corrupted by the gold of *Aureng-Zebe.* Some agitation soon began, however, to manifest itself among the troops; and to prevent the consequences of any sudden movement, emissaries were busily employed during

(*seh-likhána* = 'three scratcher'). Shaikh Abul Fazl, the Emperor Akbar's minister and friend, tells us (*Aín-i-Akbarí*) that 'All weapons for the use of His Majesty have names, and a proper rank is assigned to them. Thus there are thirty swords, one of which is daily sent to His Majesty's sleeping apartments. The old one is returned, and handed over to the servants outside the Harem, who keep it till its turn comes again. . . . Of *jámdhars* and . . . there are forty of each. Their turn recurs every week,' vol. i. p. 109, Professor Blochmann's *Translation,* Calcutta, 1873. For a great deal of invaluable information regarding Eastern swords and daggers, see *An Illustrated Handbook of Indian arms. . . By the Hon. Wilbraham Egerton, M.A., M.P. Published by order of the Secretary of State for India in Council,* London. William H. Allen & Co., 1880.

Catrou, quoting Manouchi, states that the sabre and dagger were taken away by Aurangzeb's grandson, Azam, son of Prince Muhammad, a boy of six years of age: 'Oramgzeb as if he intended his brother only a piece of pleasantry, while sleeping, promised his grandson a jewel if he could take away from the prince his sabre and his poignard without awaking him. The child acquitted himself very dexterously of the office, and conveyed the arms of Moradbax into the adjoining tent.'

the night in representing the occurrences in *Aureng-Zebe's* tent, as perfectly trifling and unimportant: they were present (they pretended), and *Morad-Bakche* having drunk to excess, had lost his self-possession, and made use of very intemperate language. There was no one upon whom he had not cast injurious reflections, and he had even loaded *Aureng-Zebe* himself with the foulest abuse. In short, he had grown so quarrelsome and ungovernable, that it became necessary to confine him apart: but in the morning, when recovered from his night's debauch, he would be again set at liberty. In the mean time, large bribes and larger promises were given to all the superior officers; the pay of the whole army was immediately augmented; and, as there were few who had not long foreseen the downfall of *Morad-Bakche*, it is not surprising that when the day dawned scarcely a trace of the late partial commotion existed. *Aureng-Zebe* felt that he might venture to shut his brother up in a covered *embary*,[1] a kind of closed litter in which women are carried on elephants; and in this manner the Prince was conveyed to Dehli, and incarcerated in the ancient citadel of *Selim-guer*,[2] which is situated in the middle of the river.

FIG. 3.—Prince Murád Bakhsh.

[1] For *amári*, a Persian word meaning a covered-in howdah, or litter.

[2] Salím-ghar, built by the Emperor Salím Sháh Súr, in the year 1546, and now in ruins.

The army submitted to this new order of things, with the exception of the eunuch *Chah-Abas,* who occasioned much trouble.[1] *Aureng-Zebe* received the troops lately under the command of *Morad-Bakche* into his service; and resumed the pursuit of *Dara,* who was advancing with the utmost expedition on *Lahor,* with the intention of fortifying himself in that city, and rendering it the rendezvous for his friends and adherents. But he was pressed so closely by his eager enemy, that he found it impossible to fortify that position: he, therefore, continued his retreat on the road to *Moultan*; but here again the vigour of his brother's movements disappointed any expectation he might have formed of maintaining that post. Nothing, indeed, could exceed the ardour and activity of *Aureng-Zebe.* Notwithstanding the great heat of the weather, his army marched day and night; and, with a view of encouraging the troops, he was often two or three leagues in advance, nearly unattended. Nor did he fare better than the private men: his meal consisted of dry bread and impure water, and his bed was the bare ground.

Dara is blamed by the statesmen of this country for not having taken the route to the kingdom of *Caboul* when he abandoned *Lahor.* He was strongly advised to adopt that course, and his reasons for refusing such sage counsel must always be enigmatical. The governor of *Caboul* was *Mohabet-kan,* one of the most ancient and powerful *Omrahs* of *Hindoustan,* who had never been on friendly terms with *Aureng-Zebe;* and there were assembled in that kingdom above ten thousand troops destined to act against the *Augans,*[2] the *Persians,* and the *Usbecs. Dara* was amply supplied with money, and there can be little doubt that the military force of that country and *Mohabet-kan* himself would willingly have espoused his cause. It should also be observed that in *Caboul, Dara* would have

[1] Catrou says that he was deported along with Murád Bakhsh.

[2] Afgháns, called by the old travellers, Auganes, and sometimes Agwans.

been on the borders of *Persia* and *Usbec,* from which countries he might have derived considerable support. He ought indeed to have recollected how *Houmayon* was restored to his kingdom by the power of the *Persians,* notwithstanding the opposition of *Zaher-kan,*[1] king of the *Patans,* by whom he had been expelled. But it was generally the fate of the unhappy *Dara* to undervalue the opinions of the wisest counsellors; and upon this occasion, instead of throwing himself into *Caboul,* he proceeded towards *Scimdy,*[2] and sought refuge in the fortress of *Tatabakar,* that strong and celebrated place situated in the middle of the river *Indus.*

When *Aureng-Zebe* knew the point on which *Dara* was directing his retreat, he felt it quite unnecessary to continue the pursuit. Having ascertained that *Caboul* was not within the plan of his brother's operations, his mind was relieved from any serious apprehension; and sending only seven or eight thousand men under the command of *Mir-baba,* his foster-brother, to watch the movements of *Dara,* he retraced his steps towards *Agra* with the same expedition he had used in the pursuit of his brother. His mind, indeed, was harassed by fears of what might happen in the capital during his absence: some of the powerful *Rajas,* such as *Jesseingue* or *Jessomseingue,* would, perhaps, he thought, release *Chah-Jehan* from prison; *Soliman-Chekouh,* and the *Raja* of *Serenaguer,* might descend as a torrent from their mountains; or, finally, *Sultan Sujah* would

[1] Sher Khán Súr, the son of the governor of Jaunpur, for some time in the service of Muhammad Lohání, king of Behar. He defeated the Emperor Humáyún in 1539 at Chaunsá in Behar, and in 1540 at Kanauj, and pursued him until he was driven beyond the Indus. Sher Khán then became the sovereign of Delhi, ascended the throne in 1542, under the title of Sher Sháh; and died in 1545. After an exile of fifteen years Hamáyún returned to India, and became a second time Emperor of Hindostan.

[2] Sind (Scinde). The fortress is at Bukkur on an island in the Indus between Sukkur and Rohri. Owing to its position it was a stronghold of great importance.

now probably venture to approach *Agra.* A slight incident now occurred, which, as it was occasioned by it, may serve to give an idea of *Aureng-Zebe's* precipitate mode of acting.

While on his return from *Moultan* to *Lahor,* and when marching with his accustomed rapidity, he was astonished to see the Raja *Jesseingue* at the head of four or five thousand well-appointed *Ragipous,* advancing towards him. *Aureng-Zebe* had, as usual, preceded his army; and being aware of the *Raja's* strong attachment to *Chah-Jehan,* it may easily be imagined that he considered his situation one of extreme peril. It was natural for him to conclude that *Jesseingue* would seize upon so happy an occasion and by a *coup d'état* at once rescue his venerated sovereign from the iniquitous thraldom under which he groaned, and inflict condign punishment upon the unfeeling son from whom he had experienced so much unprovoked outrage and cruelty. It is, indeed, conjectured that the *Raja* undertook this expedition with no other design than the capture of *Aureng-Zebe,* and there appears ground for the opinion from the fact of his having been met on the road leading from *Lahor* to *Moultan,* when the information just before received by the Prince left no doubt upon his mind that the *Raja* was still at *Dehli*; with such astonishing speed had he conducted this long march! But the self-possession of *Aureng-Zebe* and his decision of character carried him safely through the impending danger. He betrayed no symptom of agitation or alarm, but assuming a countenance expressive of pleasure at the sight of the *Raja,* rode directly toward him, making signs with his hand for him to hasten his pace, and calling out, '*Salamet bached Raja-gi! Salamet bached Baba-gi!*' Thus hailing him as 'My Lord *Raja*! My Lord Father!' When the *Raja* approached, he said: I cannot describe how impatiently I have waited to see you. The war is at an end: *Dara* is ruined and wanders alone. I have sent *Mir-Baba* after the fugitive; he cannot possibly escape.' He then took off his pearl necklace, and, as an act of the utmost courtesy and condescension, placed it round the neck of the *Raja*. 'My army is fatigued, I am anxious you should immediately proceed to *Lahor*, for I am apprehensive of some movement there. I appoint you Governor of the city, and commit all things to your hands. I shall soon join you; but before we part, I cannot avoid returning my thanks for your manner of disposing of *Soliman-Chekouh*. Where have you left *Delil-kan*? I shall know how to punish him. Hasten to *Lahor*. *Salamet Bachest*, Farewell!'

Dara, when arrived at *Tata-bakar*, nominated an eunuch distinguished for his intelligence and resolution, Governor of the fortress, and formed an excellent garrison of *Patans*, and *Sayeds*, and as gunners, a number of *Portuguese, English, French*, and *Germans*. These Europeans were employed in the artillery, and had been induced by his magnificent promises to enter into the Prince's service. In the event of his ascending the throne, it was intended to promote them to the rank of *Omrahs*, even although they were *Franks*. Depositing his treasure in the fortress, for he still possessed a large quantity of gold and silver, *Dara* pursued his march without delay along the banks of the *Indus* towards *Scimdy*, at the head of but two or three thousand men; and traversing with incredible speed the territories of the *Raja Katche*[1] soon reached the province of *Guzarate*, and presented himself before the gates of *Amed-Abad*. The Governor of the city was *Chah-Navaze-kan*,[2] the father-in-law of *Aureng-Zebe*, descended from the ancient Princes of *Machate*[3] [*Mascate*], a man of no military reputation, but

[1] Or as he is now called, the Rao of Cutch (Kachh).

[2] Sháhnawaz Khán was father-in-law to Murád Bakhsh also, and his daughter was in Ahmadabád when Dárá came there. It was through her entreaties that Sháhnawaz Khán was induced to espouse the cause of Dárá.

[3] Muscat (Máskat), the chief town of Omán in Arabia. This is interesting as it serves to support the statement in the *Ma-asíru-l Umará* of 'Abdu-r Razzak al Husainí, that Sháhnawaz Khán was a

accomplished, polite, and addicted to pleasure. The city of *Amed-Abad*[1] contained a strong garrison, and was in a condition to oppose a vigorous resistance; but whether from failure of courage in the governor, or from his having been taken by surprise, the gates were opened to *Dara* and he was received by *Chah-Navaze* with every mark of honour. It seems indeed that this man was so assiduous in paying court to *Dara*, that he succeeded in impressing his mind with an opinion of his devotedness and esteem; and although warned of his treacherous character, the deluded Prince had the imprudence to confide in the governor's professions, communicating to him the whole of his plans, and showing him the letters from the Raja *Jessomseingue*, and several other faithful adherents, who were making preparations to join him with all the forces they could muster.

Aureng-Zebe was equally surprised and perplexed when he heard that *Dara* was master of *Amed-Abad*. He knew that his pecuniary resources were still considerable, and he could entertain no doubt that not only his brother's friends, but malcontents from all parts, would flock around his standard. He was not insensible of the importance of following *Dara* in person and dislodging him from so advantageous a position: but at the same time he saw the danger of withdrawing so far from *Agra* and *Chah-Jehan*, and of marching his army into provinces

son of Mirza Rustam Kandahári, a great-grandson of Sháh Ismail, king of Persia. It is usually stated that he was the son of the wazir Asaph Khán, the Prime Minister of the Emperor Jahángír. For an account of 'the ancient Princes of Mascate' of Bernier's narrative, see the late Rev. George Percy Badger's *History of the Imâms and Seyyids of 'Omân. Translated from the original Arabic.* London. Hakluyt Society, 1871.

[1] Situated about 50 miles north of the head of the Gulf of Cambay and 310 miles from Bombay, on the banks of the Sábarmatái river, founded, in 1413, by Ahmad Sháh on the site of an ancient Hindoo city, and one of the most splendid towns of India during the 16th and 17th centuries.

which comprehended the territories of *Jesseingue, Jessomseingue,* and other powerful *Rajas.* His attention was also distracted by the rapid advance of *Sultan Sujah*—then near *Elabas*—with a powerful army, and by the preparations which he understood were being made by *Soliman-Chekouh* in conjunction with the Raja of *Serenaguer* to take an active part in the war. He was placed in a critical and intricate situation; but his best course, he thought, was to leave *Dara* for the present with *Chah-Navaze-kan,* and to march toward *Sultan Sujah,* who had already crossed the *Ganges* at *Elabas.*

Sultan Sujah encamped at a small village called *Kadjoüé,* a situation which on account of a large *talab,* or reservoir of water, was judiciously chosen.[1] There he determined to await the attack of *Aureng-Zebe,* who, on bringing up his army, took up a position on the banks of a small river, distant about a league and a half. Between the two armies was a spacious plain well adapted for them to engage. *Aureng-Zebe* felt impatient to finish the contest, and on the day after his arrival, leaving his baggage on the other side of the river, proceeded to the attack. The *Emir-Jemla,* erstwhile prisoner in the Decan, joined him on the morning of the action with the forces he could collect; the flight of the unhappy *Dara* having released his wife and children from captivity, and his own imprisonment being no longer necessary to the promotion of *Aureng-Zebe's* designs. The battle was warmly contested, aud the efforts of the assailants were almost incredible; but *Sultan Sujah* maintained his ground, repulsing every assault with great slaughter, and increasing *Aureng-Zebe's* embarrassment by steadily adhering to his

[1] 'Shujá's army rested by the tank of Khajwa or Kachhwa'—*Amal-i Sálih.* Now called Khajúa, about 30 miles to the west of Fatehpur-Haswa in the Allahabad District, between the Ganges and the Jumna. The battle was fought on the 5th January 1659. *Talab* is another form of the word *talao,* meaning an artificial pond, or tank as usually translated.

plan of not advancing into the plain. To defend the advantageous and well-fortified position he had selected was for the present his sole object, foreseeing that the heat of the weather would very soon compel his enemy to retreat to the river, and that it would then be the time to fall with effect upon his rear-guard. *Aureng-Zebe* was very sensible of the reasons which actuated his brother, and became the more intent on pressing forward. But a new and unexpected source of uneasiness now presented itself.

He was informed that the Raja *Jessomseingue,* who had, with apparent sincerity, entered into terms of amity, had fallen suddenly upon the rear-guard, routed and put it to flight, and that he was now employed in pillaging the baggage and treasure. The news soon spread; and as is common in *Asiatic* armies, the fears of the soldiers multiplied the danger. But *Aureng-Zebe* did not lose his presence of mind, and being aware that retreat would be ruinous to his hopes, he determined, as at the battle with *Dara,* not to recede, but await with firmness the progress of events. The disorder spread more and more among the troops, and *Sultan Sujah* availing himself of so unlooked-for an opportunity, commenced a furious attack. An arrow killed the man who guided *Aureng-Zebe's* elephant; the animal became unmanageable, and the danger growing more appalling, he was about to dismount, when *Emir-Jemla,* who was near him, and whose conduct the whole of this day excited the admiration of every beholder, ejaculated with a loud voice, *Decankou! Decankou!* (where is the Decan?)[1] and prevented him from accomplishing his fatal purpose. *Aureng-Zebe* was

[1] This war-cry was probably used somewhat tauntingly in the sense of 'Where are ye now, O men of the Deccan?' See p. 50, footnote[2]. This and the war-cries given at p. 50, may be taken as similar to the 'Doun the Gallow-gate, my lads' of Sir John Moore, to encourage a regiment in the Peninsula which had a number of Glasgow men in its ranks; or to the slogan, 'It 's a far cry to Loch Awe,' and that of the clan Grant, 'Stand fast, Craigellachie,' so nobly maintained of late by one of the clan at Thobal.

now to all appearance reduced to the last extremity: his situation seemed irremediable, and he was every moment expecting to fall into the enemy's hands. Yet such is the caprice of fortune, that he was in a few minutes crowned with victory; and *Sultan Sujah* was obliged, like *Dara* at the battle of *Samonguer*, to fly for his life.

Sultan Sujah owed his discomfiture to the same trifling circumstance as occasioned the defeat of his eldest brother,—that of descending from his elephant for the sake of more expeditiously following the retreating foe: but it may be doubted whether the man by whose advice he acted was influenced by an honest or a perfidious intention. *Allah-verdi-kan*,[1] one of his principal officers, earnestly entreated him to mount a horse, and it is remarkable that he made use of an artifice very similar to that of *Calil-ullah-kan* at the battle of *Samonguer*. He ran towards *Sultan Sujah*, and, when yet some way off, saluted him (as did *Calil-ullah-kan*), and then, joining his hands in the manner of fervent entreaty, he said: 'Why, my Prince, incur unnecessary risk on this exalted elephant? do you not see that the enemy is in complete disorder, and that it were an unpardonable fault not to pursue him with alacrity? Mount your horse, and you are King of the *Indies*.' As in the case of *Dara*, the sudden disappearance of the Prince from the view of the whole army induced a general idea that he was either killed or betrayed; the troops fell into disorder, and dispersed, without the possibility of restoring their ranks.[2]

[1] Aliwardí Khán, Governor of Patna, who espoused the cause of Sultán Shuják, whom he followed to Bengal, where he was killed in July 1659.

[2] See pp. 53, 54. Father Joseph Tieffenthaler, S.J., in the article on 'Cazua' (Khajúa) in his *Description of Hindustan*, Berlin, 1785, says that Prince Sujah's elephant fell into a pit (*Grube*, which may have been a dry well, not uncommon in those parts at the present day) and that then the Prince fled. Tieffenthaler also states that a fine serai ('caravanserai') at 'Cazua' was the one built by Aurangzeb to commemorate his victory. This fort-like serai, a walled garden (called

Jessomseingue, perceiving the strange turn that the action had taken, contented himself with securing the fruits of his plunder, and without loss of time returned to *Agra,* intending to continue his retreat thence to his own dominions. The rumour had already reached the capital that *Aureng-Zebe* had lost the battle; that he and *Emir-Jemla* were taken prisoners, and that *Sultan Sujah* was advancing at the head of his victorious army. *Chah-hest-kan,* Governor of the city, and the uncle of *Aureng-Zebe,* so fully believed the report, that when he saw *Jessomseingue,* of whose treason he had been apprised, approach the gate of the city, he grasped, in his despair, a cup of poison. He was prevented, however, from swallowing it by the promptitude of his women, who threw themselves upon him, and dashed the cup to the ground. Two days elapsed before the inhabitants of *Agra* were undeceived; and it is not doubted that the *Raja* would have succeeded in releasing *Chah-Jehan* from confinement had he acted with vigour and decision;—had he threatened with boldness, and promised with liberality: but as he was acquainted with the actual state of affairs, he would neither venture to prolong his stay in the capital, nor to undertake any daring enterprise: he merely marched through the town, and proceeded homeward, agreeably to his original intention.

Aureng-Zebe was full of inquietude as to the probable proceedings of *Jessomseingue,* and expected to hear of a revolution at *Agra.* He, therefore, scarcely followed *Sultan Sujah* in his retreat, but directed his rapid steps to the capital with the whole of his army. He soon learnt, however, that the troops whom he had just encountered, and who suffered little or no diminution of numbers in the

the Bádsháhi Bágh, or Royal Garden), and a masonry tank with an area of fourteen acres, still remain as a memorial of imperial magnificence. The serai has as many as 130 sets of vaulted rooms, three of which have been thrown into one to serve as a school. The square in the centre of the serai has an area of ten acres, and 223 acres in all are covered by these memorial works.

late action, were daily receiving considerable accession of strength from the different *Rajas* whose territories were situated on both sides of the *Ganges*, and who were induced to give their assistance on the strength of the reputation *Sultan Sujah* had for wealth and liberality. He found also that his brother was establishing himself in *Elabas*, that important and celebrated passage of the *Ganges*, and justly considered the key of *Bengale*.

Under these circumstances, it occurred to *Aureng-Zebe* that he had two persons near him very capable of rendering him assistance—his eldest son, and *Emir-Jemla*; but he knew that those who have rendered essential service to their Prince often become inflated with the idea that no recompence is too great for them. He already perceived that *Sultan Mahmoud* betrayed impatience of paternal control, and was continually presuming on the skill and prowess he had displayed in the capture of the citadel of *Agra*, whereby all the plans of *Chah-Jehan* had been baffled. In regard to the *Emir*, the Prince fully appreciated his transcendent talents, his conduct, and his courage; but these very excellencies filled him with apprehension and distrust: for the *Emir's* great riches, and the reputation he possessed of being the prime mover in all affairs of importance, and the most acute statesman in *India*, left no doubt on the mind of *Aureng-Zebe* that the expectations of this extraordinary man were as high as those of *Sultan Mahmoud*.

These considerations would have disconcerted an ordinary mind; but *Aureng-Zebe* knew how to remove these two personages to a distance from the court with so much address that neither the one nor the other felt any cause of complaint. He sent them at the head of a powerful army against *Sultan Sujah*, giving the *Emir* to understand not only that the valuable government of *Bengale* was intended for him during life, but that he should be succeeded therein by his son. He added that this was but one mark of the sense he entertained of his great services: when he had defeated *Sujah* he should be created *Mir-ul-omrah* [*Amír-ul-Umará*]; the first and most honourable title in *Hindoustan,* signifying Prince of the *Omrahs.*

To *Sultan Mahmoud* he addressed only these few words: 'Remember that you are the eldest of my children, and that you are going to fight your own battles. You have done much; and yet, properly speaking, you cannot be said to have done anything until the projects of *Sultan Sujah* be defeated, and you become master of his person: he is the most formidable of our adversaries.'

Aureng-Zebe then presented both the *Emir* and *Sultan Mahmoud* with the customary *seraphas,*[1] or rich vests, a few horses and elephants, superbly caparisoned, and contrived to retain at court his son's wife (the King of *Golkonda's* daughter) and *Emir-Jemla's* only son *Mahmet Emir-kan*; the former, because the presence of so distinguished a woman might embarrass the operations of the army; the latter, because he was partial to the youth, and wished to superintend his education: but he viewed them doubtless in the light of hostages for the fidelity of the two commanders.

Sultan Sujah was continually in dread that the Rajas of *Lower Bengale,* who had reason to complain of his exactions, would be excited to insurrection against his authority. He was, therefore, no sooner apprised of these arrangements than he broke up his camp at *Elabas,* and marched to *Benarés* and *Patna,* and afterwards to *Moguiere,*[2] a small town on the *Ganges,* commonly called the Key of the Kingdom of *Bengale,* forming a species of strait between the mountains and a forest which is contiguous to the town. He made this movement from an apprehension that it was meant to cut off his retreat, and that *Emir-*

[1] Sar-o-pá, from the Persian meaning from head to foot, *cap-à-pie,* a complete suit, or robe of honour.

[2] Monghyr, the fort described by Bernier, now contains the public offices, and the residences of the Europeans.

Jemla would cross the river either above or below *Elabas*. Intending to make a stand at *Moguiere*, he threw up fortifications, and cut a deep trench (which I saw some years afterwards)[1] extending from the town and the river to the mountains. In this strong position he resolved to wait the approach of his enemy, and dispute the passage of the *Ganges*. He was, however, greatly mortified when informed that the troops which were slowly descending the banks of the river were designed merely for a feint; that *Emir-Jemla* was not with them; but that having gained over the *Rajas* whose territories lay among the mountains, on the right of the river, he and *Sultan Mahmoud* were marching with the utmost speed across those mountains toward *Rage-Mehalle*[2] accompanied by the flower of the army, evidently with the object of shutting him out from *Bengale*. He was constrained, therefore, to abandon all the fortifications erected with so much care: yet notwithstanding that his march was much lengthened by the necessity of following the various bends of the *Ganges*, still he arrived at *Rage-Mehalle* some days before the Emir. Time was afforded him to throw up entrenchments; because, when the combined commanders perceived that *Sultan Sujah* could not be prevented from occupying *Rage-Mehalle*, they inclined on the left toward the *Ganges*, through almost impracticable paths, for the purpose of receiving the troops, heavy artillery and baggage, which were coming down the river. When this object was accomplished, they proceeded to the attack of *Sultan Sujah*, who defended his position during five or six days with considerable success; but perceiving that the ceaseless fire of the *Emir's* artillery ruined his fortifications, which consisted only of made earth, sand, and fascines,

[1] On the 31st December 1665, when travelling with Tavernier. —*Travels*, vol. i. p. 124.

[2] Rájmahál, Akbar's capital of Bengal, on the right bank of the Ganges. The Muhammadan city is now in ruins, extending for about four miles to the west of the modern city.

and that the approaching rains would render his position still less tenable, he withdrew under favour of the night, leaving behind him two larges pieces of ordnance. The fear of some ambuscade deterred the enemy from pursuing him that night, and before break of day the rain descended so violently that no idea could be entertained of quitting *Rage-Mehalle.* Happily for *Sultan Sujah,* the shower that fell so opportunely, was the commencement of those incessant and heavy rains with which the country is visited in the months of *July, August, September,* and *October.* They render the roads so difficult that no army can act offensively during their prevalence; and upon the present occasion the Emir was obliged to put his troops into winter-quarters at *Rage-Mehalle*; while *Sujah* remained at liberty to choose the place of his retreat, and to reinforce his army. A large number of *Portuguese* came to him from *Lower Bengale,* bringing with them several pieces of cannon. The great fertility of the soil attracts many *Europeans* to these parts, and it was *Sultan Sujah's* policy to encourage and conciliate the foreigners settled in this province. He particularly favoured the *Portuguese* Missionary Fathers, holding out a prospect of future wealth to them all, and promising to build churches wheresoever they might desire to have them erected. Indeed these people were capable of rendering the Prince essential service; the *Frankish* families residing in the kingdom of *Bengale,* whether half-caste[1] or of *Portuguese* birth, amounting to eight or nine thousand, at the lowest computation.

During the interval there arose a serious disagreement between *Sultan Mahmoud* and *Emir-Jemla.* The former aspired to the absolute and undivided command of the army, and behaved to the latter with studied insolence and contempt. He even allowed expressions to escape him that denoted a total disregard of the affection and respect due to his father; spoke openly of his achievement in the

[1] 'Mestic' in the original.

fortress of *Agra,* and boasted that it was to him *Aureng-Zebe* should feel indebted for his crown. He was at length informed of the anger he had excited in his father's breast; and fearing lest the Emir should receive orders to seize his person, he withdrew [from Rájmahál] attended by very few followers, and retiring towards *Sultan Sujah* made that Prince a tender of his services. But *Sujah,* suspecting this to be a device of *Aureng-Zebe* and of *Emir-Jemla* to entrap him, placed no confidence in his splendid promises, or in his oaths of undeviating constancy. He, therefore, intrusted him with no command of importance, and kept an eye upon his conduct. *Sultan Mahmoud* was soon disgusted with this treatment, and, after the absence of a few months, in despair of what might befall him, abandoned his new master, and ventured to appear in *Jemla's* presence. The Emir received him with some degree of courtesy, promising to intercede with *Aureng-Zebe* in his behalf, and persuade him to pardon this great transgression.

Many persons have told me that all this strange conduct of *Sultan Mamoud* was planned by *Aureng-Zebe,* who was very willing to see his son engage in any enterprise, however hazardous, which had for its object the ruin of *Sultan Sujah.* Whatever the event might be, he hoped to gain some specious pretext for having *Sultan Mahmoud* conveyed to a place of security. Accordingly, when informed of his son's return [to Rájmahál], feeling, or feigning to feel, the utmost indignation, he sent a letter, commanding him in peremptory terms to repair to *Dehli.* The unhappy Prince dared not disobey; but he had scarcely set foot on the opposite shore of the *Ganges,* when a company of armed men seized and forced him into an *embary*[1] as had been *Morad-Bakche,* he was then conducted to *Goüaleor* in which fortress he will probably end his days.[2]

[1] See p. 69 text, and footnote [1].

[2] Sultán Muhammad died on the 5th December 1676 in the fort of Gwalior, the Mogul state prison, and was buried at Delhi, near the Kuttub.

Having thus disposed of his eldest son, *Aureng-Zebe* advised his second son, *Sultan Mazum,* not to imitate the lofty and unyielding spirit of his brother. 'The art of reigning,' he told him, 'is so delicate, that a King's jealousy should be awakened by his very shadow. Be wise, or a fate similar to that which has befallen your brother awaits you. Indulge not the fatal delusion that *Aureng-Zebe* may be treated by his children as was *Jehan-Guyre* by his son *Chah-Jehan*; or that, like the latter, he will permit the sceptre to fall from his hand.'

FIG. 4.—Sultan Shujah.

Here, however, I may observe that, judging from the whole tenor of *Sultan Mazum's* conduct, his father has no reason to suspect him of any evil design: the most abject slave cannot be more tractable or obsequious; nor is it possible that the language and behaviour of the lowest menial should discover less of the workings of a discontented and ambitious mind. *Aureng-Zebe* never appeared more careless of power and dignity, or more devoted to the cause of religion and charity. There are many shrewd persons, however, who believe that the father's character is, in every respect, the archetype of the son's, and that the heart of *Sultan Mazum* is set upon sovereign authority,[1] of which we may have proof in due course; meanwhile let us pass on to other occurrences.

Whilst all these events were happening in *Bengale, Sultan Sujah* resisted, to the best of his ability, his skilful opponent, passed, as he judged it expedient, from one bank of the *Ganges* to the other, crossing and recrossing the rivers and water-courses with which this part of the country abounds. Meanwhile, *Aureng-Zebe* remained in the neighbourhood of *Agra*. At length, after having consigned *Morad-Bakche* to *Goüaleor*, he went to *Dehli*, where he began in good earnest, and undisguisedly, to assume all the acts, and exercise all the prerogatives, of a legitimate King. His attention was principally engaged in the formation of plans for expelling *Dara* from *Guzarate*; an object very near his heart, but, for the reasons already stated, difficult of accomplishment. Nevertheless, his extraordinary skill and continued good-fortune overcame every impediment.

Jessomseingue had no sooner returned to his own country than he employed the treasure plundered at the battle of *Kadjoüé* in raising a strong army. He then informed *Dara* that he would join him with all his forces on the road leading to *Agra*, on which city he advised him to march without delay. The Prince had himself contrived to assemble a large number of troops, though not perhaps of the choicest description: and being sanguine in his expectation that as he approached the capital, accompanied by this distinguished Raja, his friends would be encouraged to crowd around his standard, he quitted *Ahmed-Abad* and hastened

[1] Aurangzeb, at this time about forty-one years old, lived and reigned to the age of ninety, and was succeeded, in 1707, by his son, Sultán Mu'azzam, with the title of Sháh 'Álam Bahádur Sháh, who survived his father only five years.

to *Asmire*,[3] a city seven or eight days' journey from *Agra*. But *Jessomseingue* violated his promise. The Raja *Jesseingue* considering that the chances of war were decidedly in favour of *Aureng-Zebe* and that it was his best policy to conciliate that Prince, exercised his influence with *Jessomseingue* to deter him from espousing the cause of *Dara*. 'What can be your inducement,' he wrote to him, 'to endeavour to sustain the falling fortunes of this prince? Perseverance in such an undertaking must inevitably bring ruin upon you and your family, without advancing the interests of the wretched *Dara*. From *Aureng-Zebe* you will never obtain forgiveness. I, who am also a *Raja*, conjure you to spare the blood of the *Ragipous*. Do not buoy yourself up with the hope of drawing the other rajas to your party; for I have means to counteract any such attempt. This is a business which concerns all the *Indous* (that is to say all the *Gentiles*),[2] and you cannot be permitted to kindle a flame that would soon rage throughout the kingdom, and which no effort might be able to extingnish. If, on the other hand, you leave *Dara* to his own resources, *Aureng-Zebe* will bury all the past in oblivion; will not reclaim the money you obtained at *Kadjoüé*, but will at once nominate you to the government of *Guzarate*. You can easily appreciate the advantage of ruling a province so contiguous to your own territories: there you will remain in perfect quiet and security, and I hereby offer you my guarantee for the exact fulfilment of all I have mentioned.' To be brief, *Jessomseingue* was persuaded to remain at home, while *Aureng-Zebe* advanced with the whole of his army on *Asmire*, and encamped within view of *Dara*.

Who that reads this history can repress an emotion of

[1] Ajmere, about 230 miles to the south-west of Agra. The Emperors Jahángír and Sháh Jahán often resided there, and it was here that Sir Thomas Roe, the ambassador of James I. of England, was received by the Emperor Jahángír in December 1651.

[2] In the original, 'c'est à dire toute la Gentilité.'

pity for the misguided and betrayed *Dara*? He now discovered the bad faith of *Jessomseingue*; but it was too late to provide against its fatal consequences. Willingly would he have conducted the army back to *Amed-Abad*, but how could he hope to effect this desirable object in the midst of the hot season, and during the drought that then prevails; having a march of five-and-thirty days to accomplish through the territories of Rajas, friends or allies of *Jessomseingue*, and closely pressed by the eager *Aureng-Zebe* at the head of a fresh and numerous army? 'It is better,' he said, 'to die at once the death of a soldier; the contest is sadly unequal, but on this spot I must conquer or perish.' He did not, however, comprehend the full extent of his danger: treason was lurking where he least expected it; and he continued to confide in the perfidious *Chah-Navaze-kan*, who kept up a regular correspondence with *Aureng-Zebe*, putting him in possession of all *Dara's* designs. As a just retribution for his faithlessness, this man was slain in the battle, either by the hand of *Dara* himself, or, as is thought more probable, by the swords of persons in *Aureng-Zebe's* army, who, being the secret partisans of *Dara*, felt apprehensive that *Chah-Navaze-kan* would denounce them, and make mention of the letters they had been in the habit of writing to that Prince. But what now availed the death of the traitor? It was from the first moment of his taking possession of *Ahmedabad* that *Dara* ought to have listened to the sage advice of his best friends and treated *Chah-Navaze* with the contempt and distrust he merited.

The action commenced between nine and ten in the morning.[1] *Dara's* artillery, which was advantageously placed on a small eminence, made noise enough; but the pieces, it is supposed, were charged only with blank

[1] For Kháfí Khán's account of the defection of Rája Jaswant Singh and the battle (fought on the 12th and 13th March 1659 at Deorá, about six miles to the south of Ajmere), see Sir H. M. Elliot's *History*, etc., vol. vii. pp. 238-240.

cartridges, so widely was the treachery extended. It is unnecessary to enter into any particular detail of this battle, if battle it should be called; it was soon a complete rout. I shall simply state that the first shot was scarcely fired when *Jesseingue,* placing himself within sight of *Dara,* sent an officer to inform him that if he wished to avoid capture he must instantly quit the field. The poor Prince, seized with sudden fear and surprise, acted upon this advice, and flew with so much precipitation that he gave no directions concerning his baggage: indeed, considering the critical situation in which he was placed, he had reason to congratulate himself on being allowed time to secure his wife and family. It is certain that he was in the power of *Jesseingue,* and that it was to his forbearance he was indebted for his escape: but the *Raja,* aware of the danger that would attend any insult offered to a Prince of the blood, has upon all occasions shown respect to every branch of the Royal family.

The miserable and devoted *Dara,* whose only chance of preservation was to regain *Amed-Abad,* was constrained to pass through a long range of what might be considered hostile territory, destitute of tents and baggage. The country between *Asmire* and *Amed-Abad* consists almost entirely of territories belonging to Rajas. The Prince was accompanied by two thousand men at most; the heat was intolerable; and the *Koullys* followed him day and night, pillaging and assassinating so many of his soldiers that it became dangerous to separate even a few yards from the main body. These *Koullys* [1] are the peasantry of this part of the country, and are the greatest robbers,

[1] In Bernier's time, this was the term applied to dwellers in villages. The word is supposed to be derived from the Tamil *kūli,* meaning hire or wages; in modern times *Cooly.* For an interesting note on this subject, see Yule's *Glossary,* under the head 'Cooly.' There is a race of hill people, the Kolis, who are to be found in Guzerat, in the Konkan, and in the Deccan; and in the *Râs Mâlâ* the Koolees are spoken of as a tribe that lived near the Indus. In Blaeu's map of *The Empire of the Great Mogol,* published in 1655, territory to the north-

and altogether the most unprincipled people in the *Indies*. Notwithstanding every obstruction, *Dara* contrived to advance within a day's journey from *Amed-Abad*, expecting to enter the city on the following day, and to assemble an army; but the hopes of the vanquished and unfortunate are seldom realised.

The Governor whom he had left in the castle of *Amed-Abad*, alarmed by the menaces, or allured by the promises of *Aureng-Zebe*, had basely deserted the cause of his master; and sent a letter to *Dara* by which he desired him not to advance nearer to the city, whose gates were shut, and whose inhabitants were armed to oppose his entrance. I had now been three days with *Dara*, whom I met on the road by the strangest chance imaginable; and being destitute of any medical attendant, he compelled me to accompany him in the capacity of physician. The day preceding that on which he received the Governor's communication, he expressed his fear lest I should be murdered by the *Koullys*, and insisted upon my passing the night in the *Karavanserrak*, where he then was. The cords of the *kanates*, or screens, which concealed his wife and women (for he was without even a tent) were fastened to the wheels of the carriage, wherein I reposed. This may appear almost incredible to those who know how extremely jealous the great men of *Hindoustan* are of their wives, and I mention the circumstance as a proof of the low condition to which the fortunes of the Prince were reduced. It was at break of day that the Governor's message was delivered, and the shrieks of the females

west of Cambay is titled *Reino dos Collys*. Chardin, in his *Travels in Persia* (p. 479, vol. vii. of Langlés' edition, Paris 1811), tells us of a race of robbers in Persia whom he calls *Kaulys* or *qoülys*, and says of them that they were all arrant rogues and thieves, like the gipsies of his own country. In *The Pioneer Mail*, Allahabad, 19th August 1891, will be found (pp. 239-240) a long account of the recent doings in the Akola District of a 'Native Jack Sheppard,' one Rasjee Koli.

drew tears from every eye. We were all overwhelmed with confusion and dismay, gazing in speechless horror at each other, at a loss what plan to recommend, and ignorant of the fate which perhaps awaited us from hour to hour. We observed *Dara* stepping out, more dead than alive, speaking now to one, then to another; stopping and consulting even the commonest soldier. He saw consternation depicted in every countenance, and felt assured that he should be left without a single follower; but what was to become of him? whither must he go? to delay his departure was to accelerate his ruin.

During the time that I remained in this Prince's retinue, we marched, nearly without intermission, day and night; and so insupportable was the heat, and so suffocating the dust, that of the three large oxen of *Guzarate* which drew my carriage, one had died, another was in a dying state, and the third was unable to proceed from fatigue. *Dara* felt anxious to retain me in his service,[1] especially as one of his wives had a bad wound in her leg; yet neither his threats nor entreaties could procure for me a single

[1] Tavernier, who probably derived his information from Bernier himself, thus describes this incident: 'As he [Dárá] approached AHMADÁBÁD, Monsieur BERNIER, a French physician, who was on his way to AGRA to visit the Court of the GREAT MOGUL, and who is well known to all the world, as much by his personal merits as by the charming accounts of his travels, was of great assistance to one of the wives of this Prince who was attacked with erysipelas in one leg. DÁRÁ SHÁH, having learnt that an accomplished European physician was at hand, sent immediately for him, and Monsieur BERNIER went to his tent, where he saw this lady and examined into her ailment, for which he gave a remedy and quick relief. This poor Prince, being much pleased with Monsieur BERNIER, strongly pressed him to remain in his service, and he might have accepted the offer if DÁRÁ SHÁH had not received news the same night that the Governor whom he had left at AHMADÁBÁD had refused to allow his quarter-master to enter the town, and had declared for AURANGZEB. This compelled DÁRÁ SHÁH to decamp quickly in the darkness of the night, and take the road to SIND, fearing some new treachery, which he could not defend himself from in the unhappy condition in which he found himself.'—*Travels*, vol. i. p. 349.

horse, ox, or camel; so totally destitute of power and influence had he become! I remained behind, therefore, because of the absolute impossibility of continuing the journey, and could not but weep when I beheld the Prince depart with a force diminished to four or five hundred horsemen. There were also a couple of elephants laden, it was said, with gold and silver. *Dara*, I understood, intended to take the road to *Tatta-bakar*, and under all circumstances this was not perhaps an unwise selection. There was indeed only a choice of appalling difficulties, and I could not cherish the hope that the Prince would succeed in crossing the sandy desert which separated him from that *Fort*. In fact, nearly the whole of the men, and many of the women, did perish; some dying of thirst, hunger, or fatigue, while others were killed by the hands of the merciless *Koullys*. Happy would it have been for *Dara* had he not himself survived this perilous march! but he struggled through every obstacle, and reached the territory of the *Raja Katche*.[1]

The *Raja* received him with the utmost hospitality, promising to place the whole of his army at *Dara's* disposal, provided that Prince gave his daughter in marriage to his son.[2] But the intrigues of *Jesseingue* were as successful with this *Raja* as they had been with *Jessomseingue*; a change in his conduct was very soon perceptible, and *Dara*, having reason to apprehend that the barbarian had a design against his life, departed without a moment's hesitation for *Tata-bakar*.

I should, I fear, only tire my readers were I to enter upon a long narration of my own adventures with *Messieurs* the *Koullys*, or robbers; relating how I moved

[1] Kháfí Khán states that when Dárá was denied entry to Ahmadábád he went 'to Kari, two *kos* from the city and there sought assistance from Kánjí Kolí, one of the most notorious rebels and robbers of that country. Kánjí joined him and conducted him to the confines of Kachh.'

[2] This confirms in several details, Kháfí Khán's narrative. See Sir H. M. Elliot's *History*, vol. vii. p. 243.

their compassion, and by what means I preserved the little money which was about my person. I made a grand display of my professional skill; and my two servants, who experienced the same terror as myself, declared I was the most eminent physician in the world, and that *Dara's* soldiers had used me extremely ill, depriving me of everything valuable. It was fortunate for me that we succeeded in creating in these people an interest in my favour; for after detaining me seven or eight days, they attached a bullock to my carriage, and conducted me within view of the minarets of *Amed-Abad*. In this city I met with an *Omrah* who was proceeding to *Dehli*, and I travelled under his protection. On the road our eyes were too often offended with the sight of dead men, elephants, oxen, horses, and camels; the wrecks of poor *Dara's* army.

While *Dara* pursued his dreary way towards *Tata-bakar*, the war was still raging in *Bengale*; *Sultan Sujah* making much greater efforts than had been foreseen by his enemies. But the state of affairs in this quarter occasioned little inquietude to *Aureng-Zebe*, who knew how to appreciate the talents and conduct of *Emir-Jemla*; and the distance of *Bengale* from *Agra* lessened the immediate importance of the military operations in that country. A source of much greater anxiety was the vicinity of *Soliman-Chekouh*, and the apprehension which seemed generally to prevail that he and the *Raja* were about to descend with a hostile force from the mountains,[1] distant scarcely eight days' journey from Agra. This enemy *Aureng-Zebe* was too prudent to despise, and how to circumvent *Soliman-Chekouh* became now the chief object of his attention.

The most likely method of attaining that object was, he conceived, to negotiate with the *Raja* of *Serenaguer*, through the medium of *Jesseingue*: who accordingly wrote to him letter upon letter promising the most splendid remuneration if he delivered up *Soliman-Chekouh*, and threatening the severest punishment should he refuse to

[1] Of Srínagar, *i.e.* the Siwáliks. See p. 59. footnote [2].

comply. The *Raja* answered that the loss of his whole territory would affect him less than the idea that he had been guilty of so base and ungenerous an action. When it became evident that neither solicitation nor menace could move the *Raja* from the path of honour and rectitude, *Aureng-Zebe* marched his army to the foot of the mountains, and there employed an immense number of pioneers in levelling huge rocks and widening narrow ways: but the *Raja* laughed at these vain and puerile attempts to gain an ingress into his country; the mountains would have been inaccessible though assailed by the armies of four such countries as *Hindoustan*; so that after all this display of impotent resentment, the army was withdrawn.

Meanwhile *Dara* approached the fortress of *Tata-bakar*; and when only two or three days' journey from the place, he received intelligence (as I have been since informed by our *Frenchmen* and other *Franks* who formed part of the garrison) that *Mir-Baba*, by whom the fortress had been long besieged, had at length reduced it to the last extremity. Rice and meat sold for upwards of a crown[1] per pound,[2] and other necessaries in the same proportion. Still the Governor continued undaunted; making frequent and successful sorties, and in every respect approving himself a prudent, brave, and faithful soldier; opposing, with equal calmness and resolution, the vigorous assault of General *Mir-Baba*, and deriding both the threats and the promises of *Aureng-Zebe*.

That such was the praiseworthy conduct of the Governor I have been well assured by *Frenchmen*, our fellow-countrymen, and many other *Franks* who were his companions in arms. I have heard them say that when he received news of *Dara's* approach, he increased his liberal payments; and that the whole garrison would cheerfully have sacrificed themselves in an effort to drive the enemy

[1] *Ecu* in the original, worth 4s. 6d.

[2] *Livre* in the original, equivalent to 1lb. 1oz. $10\frac{1}{6}$ dr. av.

from the walls, and open a passage for the entrance of *Dara*; so well did this valiant commander understand how to gain the hearts of his soldiers. He had moreover so judiciously managed, by means of numerous and intelligent spies, whom he contrived, by various dexterous schemes, to introduce in *Mir-Baba's* camp, as to impose upon the besiegers a firm belief that *Dara* was coming up with a formidable body of troops for the purpose of raising the siege. These spies pretended they had themselves seen him and his army; and this stratagem produced all the effect which the governor anticipated; terror seized the enemy's troops, and no doubt was entertained that, if *Dara* had arrived at the time he was confidently expected, *Mir-Baba's* army would partly have disbanded, and partly joined the Prince's party.

But *Dara* seemed doomed never to succeed in any enterprise. Considering it impossible to raise the siege with his handful of men, he was at one time resolved to cross the river *Indus*, and make the best of his way to *Persia*; although that plan would likewise have been attended with nearly insurmountable obstacles: he would have had to traverse the lands of the *Patans*,[1] inconsiderable *Rajas* who acknowledge neither the authority of *Persia* nor of the *Mogol*; and a vast wilderness interposed in which he could not hope to find wholesome water. But his wife persuaded him to abandon the idea of penetrating into that kingdom, alleging a much weaker reason than those I have mentioned. If he persevered in his intention, he must make up his mind, she told him, to see both her and his daughter slaves of the *Persian* Monarch, an ignominy which no member of his family could possibly endure. She and *Dara* forgot, or seemed to forget, that the wife of *Houmayon*, when placed under similar circumstances, was subjected to no such indignity, but treated with great respect and kindness.[2]

[1] Here meaning the Afghâns, and their numerous clans.

[2] See p. 71.

While *Dara's* mind was in this state of perplexity and indecision, it occurred to him that he was at no considerable distance from *Gion-kan*,[1] a *Patan* of some power and note, whose life he had been twice the means of preserving, when condemned by *Chah-Jehan* to be thrown under the elephant's feet, as a punishment for various acts of rebellion. To *Gion-kan Dara* determined to proceed, hoping to obtain by his means forces to enable him to drive *Mir-Baba* from the walls of *Tata-bakar*. The plan he now proposed to himself was briefly this :—after raising the siege with the troops supplied by the *Patan*, he intended to proceed, with the treasure deposited in that city, to *Kandahar*, whence he might easily reach the kingdom of *Kaboul*. When in *Kaboul* he felt quite sanguine in the expectation that *Mohabet-kan* would zealously and unhesitatingly embrace his cause. It was to *Dara* this officer was indebted for the government of that country, and being possessed of great power and influence, and very popular in *Kaboul*, the Prince was not unreasonable in the hope that he would find in *Mohabet-kan* a sincere and efficacious ally. But *Dara's* family, agitated by dismal forebodings, employed every entreaty to prevent him from venturing in *Gion-kan's* presence. His wife, daughter, and his young son, *Sepe-Chekouh*, fell at his feet, endeavouring, with tears in their eyes, to turn him aside from his design. The *Patan*, they observed, was notoriously a robber and a rebel, and to place confidence in such a character was at once to rush headlong into destruction. There was no sufficient reason, they added, why he should be so pertinaciously bent upon raising the siege of *Tata-bakar*; the road to *Kaboul* might be safely pursued without

[1] The 'Mălik Jíwan Ayyúb, an Afghán' of the *'Álamgír-náma*; whose territory was Dádar, the chief town of the same name, being about 5 miles east of the Bolan Pass, and between Sibi and Rindli on the Bolan section of the Sind Pishin Ry., 'surrounded by bare and rocky hills, which render the heat in summer perhaps greater than that of any other place in the world in the same parallel [29° 28′ N.] of latitude.'

that operation, for *Mir-Baba* would scarcely abandon the siege for the sake of interrupting his march.

Dara, as if hurried away by his evil genius, could not perceive the force of these arguments; remarking, what indeed was the truth, that the journey to *Kaboul* would be full of difficulty and danger; and that he did not believe it possible he should be betrayed by a man bound to him by such strong ties of gratitude. He departed, notwithstanding every solicitation; and soon afforded an additional and melancholy proof that the wicked feel not the weight of obligations when their interests demand the sacrifice of their benefactors.

This robber, who imagined that *Dara* was attended by a large body of soldiers, received the Prince with apparent respect and cordiality, quartering his men upon the inhabitants, with particular injunctions to supply all their wants, and treat them as friends and brethren. But when *Gion-kan* ascertained that *Dara's* followers did not exceed two or three hundred men, he threw off all disguise. It is still doubtful whether he had been tampered with by *Aureng-Zebe*, or whether he were suddenly tempted to the commission of this monstrous crime.[1] The sight of a few mules laden with the gold, which *Dara* had saved from the hands of the robbers, by whom he had been constantly harassed, very probably excited his cupidity. Be

[1] Tavernier tells us that Dárá, on hearing of the death 'of one of his wives whom he loved most' from heat and thirst (see p. 103, footnote [2], for Kháfí Khán's account, which confirms Tavernier), was so overcome by this grief, although he had always appeared to be unmoved on all previous occasions of misfortune, that he refused all the consolation offered by his friends and put on garments of mourning. 'It was in this miserable costume that he entered the house of the traitor JUIN KHÁN, where, having laid himself down on a camp-bed to rest, a new subject of grief appeared on his awakening. JUIN KHÁN on attempting to seize SEPEHR SHEKO, the second son of DÁRÁ SHÁH, the young Prince, though but a child, resisted the traitor with courage, and having taken up his bow and arrow laid three men low on the ground. But being alone he was unable to resist the number of traitors, who secured the doors of the house, and did not allow any one of those who might

this as it may, the *Patan* having assembled, during the night, a considerable number of armed men, seized this gold, together with the women's jewels, and fell upon *Dara* and *Sepe-Chekouh*, killed the persons who attempted to defend them, and tied the Prince on the back of an elephant. The public executioner was ordered to sit behind, for the purpose of cutting off his head, upon the first appearance of resistance, either on his own part, or on that of any of his adherents; and in this degrading posture *Dara* was carried to the army before *Tata-bakar*, and delivered into the hands of General *Mir-Baba*. This officer then commanded the Traitor, *Gion-kan*, to proceed with his prisoner, first to *Lahor* and afterwards to *Dehli*.

When the unhappy Prince was brought to the gates of *Dehli*, it became a question with *Aureng-Zebe*, whether, in conducting him to the fortress of *Goüaleor*, he should be made to pass through the capital. It was the opinion of some courtiers that this was by all means to be avoided, because, not only would such an exhibition be derogatory to the royal family, but it might become the signal for revolt, and the rescue of *Dara* might be successfully attempted. Others maintained, on the contrary, that he ought to be seen by the whole city; that it was necessary to strike the people with terror and astonishment, and to impress their minds with an idea of the absolute and

have aided him to enter. DÁRÁ SHÁH, having been awakened by the noise which these cruel satellites made when seizing this little Prince, saw before his eyes his son, whom they brought in with his hands tied behind his back. The unhappy father, unable to doubt any longer the black treason of his host, could not restrain himself from launching these words against the traitor JUIN KHÁN: "*Finish, finish*," said he, "*ungrateful and infamous wretch that thou art, finish that which thou hast commenced; we are the victims of evil fortune and the unjust passion of* AURANGZEB, *but remember that I do not merit death except for having saved thy life, and remember that a Prince of the royal blood never had his hands tied behind his back.*" JUIN KHÁN, being to some extent moved by these words, ordered the little Prince to be released, and merely placed guards over DÁRÁ SHÁH and his son. —*Travels*, vol. i. pp. 351, 352.

irresistible power of *Aureng-Zebe*. It was also advisable, they added, to undeceive the *Omrahs* and the people, who still entertained doubts of *Dara's* captivity, and to extinguish at once the hopes of his secret partisans. *Aureng-Zebe* viewed the matter in the same light; the wretched prisoner was therefore secured on an elephant; his young son, *Sepe-Chekouh*, placed at his side, and behind them, instead of the executioner, was seated *Bhadur-Kan.*[1] This was not one of the majestic elephants of *Pegu* or *Ceylon*, which *Dara* had been in the habit of mounting, pompously caparisoned, the harness gilt, and trappings decorated with figured work; and carrying a beautifully painted howdah, inlaid with gold, and a magnificent canopy to shelter the Prince from the sun: *Dara* was now seen seated on a miserable and worn-out animal, covered with filth; he no longer wore the necklace of large pearls which distinguish the princes of *Hindoustan*, nor the rich turban and embroidered coat; he and his son were now habited in dirty cloth of the coarsest texture, and his sorry turban was wrapt round with a *Kachemire* shawl or scarf, resembling that worn by the meanest of the people.

Such was the appearance of *Dara* when led through the *Bazars* and every quarter of the city. I could not divest myself of the idea that some dreadful execution was about to take place, and felt surprise that government should have the hardihood to commit all these indignities upon a Prince confessedly popular among the lower orders, especially as I saw scarcely any armed force. The people had for some time inveighed bitterly against the unnatural conduct of *Aureng-Zebe*: the imprisonment of his father, of his son *Sultan Mahmoud*, and of his brother *Morad-Bakche*, filled every bosom with horror and disgust. The crowd assembled upon this disgraceful occasion was immense; and everywhere I observed the people weeping, and lamenting the fate of *Dara* in the most touching

[1] Bahádur Khán, one of Aurangzeb's officers, who had been sent from Ajmere in pursuit of Dárá.

language. I took my station in one of the most conspicuous parts of the city, in the midst of the largest bazar; was mounted on a good horse, and accompanied by two servants and two intimate friends. From every quarter I heard piercing and distressing shrieks, for the Indian people have a very tender heart; men, women, and children wailing as if some mighty calamity had happened to themselves. *Gion-kan* rode near the wretched *Dara*; and the abusive and indignant cries vociferated

FIG. 5.—Prince Dárá Shikoh and his son Sipihr Shikoh.

as the traitor moved along were absolutely deafening. I observed some *Fakires* and several poor people throw stones at the infamous *Patan*;[1] but not a single movement was made, no one offered to draw his sword, with a

[1] He received the title of Bakhtiyár Khán for this act of treachery. See Sir H. M. Elliot's *History*, vol. vii. pp. 245, 246 for Kháfí Khán's very vivid account of the indignation of the people against Malik Jíwan.

view of delivering the beloved and compassionated Prince. When this disgraceful procession had passed through every part of *Dehli,* the poor prisoner was shut up in one of his own gardens, called *Heider-Abad.*[1]

Aureng-Zebe was immediately made acquainted with the impression which this spectacle produced upon the public mind, the indignation manifested by the populace against the *Patan,* the threats held out to stone the perfidious man, and with the fears entertained of a general insurrection. A second council was consequently convened, and the question discussed, whether it were more expedient to conduct *Dara* to *Goüaleor,* agreeably to the original intention, or to put him to death without further delay. By some it was maintained that there was no reason for proceeding to extremities, and that the Prince might safely be taken to *Goüaleor,* provided he were attended with a strong escort: *Danech-Mend-kan,* although he and *Dara* had long been on bad terms, enforced this opinion with all his powers of argument: but it was ultimately decided that *Dara* should die, and that *Sepe-Chekouh* should be confined in *Goüaleor.* At this meeting *Rauchenara-Begum* betrayed all her enmity against her hapless brother, combating the arguments of *Danech-Mend,* and exciting *Aureng-Zebe* to this foul and unnatural murder. Her efforts were but too successfully seconded by *Kalil-ullah-kan* and *Chah-hest-kan,* both of them old enemies of *Dara*; and by *Takarrub-kan,* a wretched parasite recently raised to the rank of *Omrah,* and formerly a physician. He was originally distinguished by the appellation of *Hakim Daoud,* and had been compelled to fly from *Persia.*[2] This man rendered

[1] 'Khizrábád, in old Dehli,' in Kháfí Khán's account.

[2] Hákim (Doctor) Daoud was the principal medical attendant on Sháh Súfí I. the king of Persia who reigned from 1628-41, but by his intriguing conduct was obliged to fly to India, where he amassed great wealth, part of which he spent in building one of the principal mosques in Ispahan (the *Hákim Daoud Masjid*), where his family lived in great style on the money he remitted to them from Hindostan. Chardin says that he was called *Areb Can* in India, and that his end there was a

himself conspicuous in the council by his violent harangue. '*Dara* ought not to live,' he exclaimed; 'the safety of the State depends upon his immediate execution; and I feel the less reluctant to recommend his being put to death, because he has long since ceased to be a *Musulman*, and become a *Kafer*. If it be sinful to shed the blood of such a person, may the sin be visited upon my own head!' An imprecation which was not allowed to pass unregarded; for divine justice overtook this man in his career of wickedness: he was soon disgraced, declared infamous, and sentenced to a miserable death.

The charge of this atrocious murder[1] was intrusted to a slave of the name of *Nazer*, who had been educated by *Chah-Jehan*, but experienced some ill-treatment from *Dara*. The Prince, apprehensive that poison would be administered to him, was employed with *Sepe-Chekouh*

miserable one, his downfall being brought on by the failure of some of his political intrigues. See p. 462 of vol. vii. of *Voyages du Chevalier Chardin en Perse*, Paris 1811. Areb Can is probably intended for Tákurab Khán, as given by Bernier, as Chardin is not so correct in his transliteration as his friend Bernier.

[1] Catrou's account of this tragic scene, which he took from the narrative of Manouchi, the Venetian physician, who, as has been before stated (p. 6), had attached himself to the person and fortunes of Dárá, and was probably an eye-witness, is as follows:—'Dara was waiting in his prison the decision of his fate, when his son was taken from his arms, to be conveyed to the citadel of Gualier, the ordinary place of confinement for Princes. When the father found himself deprived of his son he rightly judged that it was time to think of preparing for death. The Christian sentiments, with which the Missionaries had endeavoured to inspire him, were revived in the closing hour of his life. He requested to be allowed a conversation with Father Busée, a Flemish Jesuit, who had formerly instructed him in our sacred Mysteries. All communication with the Europeans was denied him. In this universal desolation, the Prince sought for consolation in God. He was heard to say more than once: *Mahomet has destroyed me, Jesus Christ the son of the Eternal will save me.* A few hours before he was put to death Orangzeb caused a captious question to be put to his brother: "What would you have done to the Emperor," they said to him, "had he fallen into your hands as you have fallen into his?" "He is a rebel and a parricide," said Dara; "let him judge of the treat-

in boiling lentils, when *Nazer* and four other ruffians entered his apartment. 'My dear son,' he cried out, 'these men are come to murder us!' He then seized a small kitchen knife, the only weapon in his possession. One of the murderers having secured *Sepe-Chekouh*,[1] the rest fell upon *Dara*, threw him down, and while three of the assassins held him, *Nazer* decapitated his wretched victim. The head was instantly carried to *Aureng-Zebe*, who commanded that it should be placed in a dish, and that water should be brought. The blood was then washed from the face, and when it could no longer be doubted

ment he has merited by reflecting upon his crimes, and such deserts he would have received with the utmost rigour at my hands." This answer exasperated Orangzeb. He only now sought a minion who would have the barbarity to execute his orders. Nazar, one of the slaves of Cha-Jaham, whose occupation was that of a writer to the Emperors, offered himself for this cruel service. He proceeded to the spot where Dara was expecting the moment which was to terminate his miseries. He found the Prince in his apartment raising his eyes to heaven, and repeating these words: "*Mahamed mara micuchet è ben alla Mariam mi bachet*" [Mahammad ma-rá mikushad, ibn Allah Maryam mibáshaid, Pers.], which is, "Mahomet gives me death, and the Son of God [and Mary] will [are necessary to] save me." He had scarcely finished these words, when the executioner threw him to the earth and cut off his head. Such was the termination of the life of a Prince in whose character was blended such a mixture of virtues and defects as to render him more capable of taking the lead as a Mogol noble, than fit him for controlling the Empire. He died on the 22d of October in the year 1657 [*sic*], lamented by the people, and regretted even by those who had abandoned and betrayed him.'

It is probable that 1657 is a misprint for 1659. Kháfí Khán states that it was in September 1659 that the order was given for his execution, 'under a legal opinion of the lawyers, because he had apostatised from the law, had vilified religion, and had allied himself with heresy and infidelity.' The judicial murder may thus have been perpetrated on the 22d October as stated by Manouchi; on this point, however, there are many conflicting statements. See the late Professor Blochmann's paper on *The Capture and Death of Dárá Shikoh*, Jour. As. Soc. Bengal, pp. 274-279, vol. xxxix., 1870.

[1] Tavernier says, 'In the meantime SEPEHR SHEKO was drawn aside, and, whilst they amused him, a slave cut off DÁRÁ SHÁH's head.'—*Travels*, vol. i. p. 354.

that it was indeed the head of *Dara*, he shed tears, and said, '*Ah* [*Ai*] *Bed-bakt!* Ah wretched one! let this shocking sight no more offend my eyes, but take away the head, and let it be buried in *Houmayon's* tomb.'[1]

Dara's daughter was taken that same evening to the seraglio, but afterwards sent to *Chah-Jehan* and *Begum-Saheb*; who begged of *Aureng-Zebe* to commit the young Princess to their care. *Dara's* wife, foreseeing the calamities which awaited her and her husband, had already put a period to her existence, by swallowing poison at *Lahor*.[2] *Sepe-Chekouh* was immured in the

[1] Catrou (Manouchi) tells us that when Dárá's head was brought to Aurangzeb, 'he examined it with an air of satisfaction; he touched it with the point of his sword; he opened the closed eyes to observe a speck, that he might be convinced that another head had not been substituted in the place of the one he had ordered to be struck off.' Afterwards, following the counsel of Raushan Ará Begum, he caused it to be embalmed and conveyed to Sháh Jahán and enclosed in a box, to be offered to him in the name of Aurangzeb. Before the box was opened the old Emperor said, 'It is at least a consolation for an unhappy father to find that the usurper has not wholly forgotten me,' but when the packet was opened, and he beheld 'the head of the son so tenderly beloved, the good old man fell into a swoon. The Princess Begòm Saëb, always faithful to the cause of Dara, made the air resound with her cries. Nothing, indeed, could be more affecting than the melancholy and despair excited by so tragical a spectacle in the prison of Agra.'

[2] It is stated by Kháfí Khán, that Dárá's wife, Nádira Begum, died when with her husband in Malik Jíwan's territory, and that her body was sent to Lahore to be buried. 'When Dárá reached the land of this evil *zamíndár*, Malik Jíwan came out like the destroying angel to meet him. As a guest-murdering host he conducted Dárá home, and exerted himself to entertain him. During the two or three days that Dárá remained here, his wife Nádira Begam, daughter of Parwez [Sultan Parwez his uncle, second son of the Emperor Jáhángír. Dárá was married to Nádira in 1633, when he was twenty years of age, and she was the mother of Sulaimán Shikoh and Sipihr Shikoh], died of dysentery and vexation. Mountain after mountain of trouble thus pressed upon the heart of Dárá, grief was added to grief, sorrow to sorrow, so that his mind no longer retained its equilibrium. Without considering the consequences [the deceased had left a will desiring to be buried in Hindostan—'*Álamgír-náma*], he sent her corpse to

fortress of *Goüaleor*; and soon after these tragical events *Giön-kan* was summoned before the council, and then dismissed from *Dehli* with a few presents. He did not escape the fate, however, which he merited, being waylaid and assassinated in a forest, within a few leagues of his own territory. This barbarian had not sufficiently reflected, that though tyrants appear to countenance the blackest crimes while they conduce to their interest, or promote a favourite object, they yet hold the perpetrators in abhorrence, and will not scruple to punish them when they can no longer be rendered subservient to any iniquitous project.

In the mean time, the brave governor of *Tata-bakar* was compelled to surrender the place, an order for its immediate surrender, exacted from *Dara* himself, having been sent to the faithful eunuch; who insisted, however, on honourable terms of capitulation. The perfidious enemy, intending to violate every promise, readily assented to the conditions proposed, and *Mir-Baba* was admitted into the town.

The governor proceeded to *Lahor*, where he and the feeble remains of his intrepid garrison were miserably slaughtered by *Kalil-ullah-kan*, who commanded in that city. The reason for this atrocious act was, that although the eunuch professed his intention of visiting the King at *Dehli*, to gratify the desire expressed by *Aureng-Zebe* to converse with so brave a soldier, yet he really meditated a rapid march to *Serenaguer*, with all his followers, for the purpose of making common cause with *Soliman-Chekouh*. Among these followers (many of whom were *Franks*) he distributed money with a liberal hand.

Of *Dara's* family, there now remained only *Soliman-Chekouh*, whom it would not have been easy to draw from

Láhore in charge of Gul Muhammad to be buried there. He thus parted from one who had been faithful to him through his darkest troubles.' Sir H. M. Elliot's *History*, vol. vii. p. 244. See p. 69, note, for Tavernier's account.

Serenaguer, if the *Raja* had been faithful to his engagements. But the intrigues of *Jesseingue*, the promises and threats of *Aureng-Zebe*, the death of *Dara*, and the hostile preparations of the neighbouring Rajas, shook the resolution of this pusillanimous protector. *Soliman-Chekouh* felt that he was no longer in safety, and endeavoured to reach *Great Tibet*.[1] His route lay across the most dreary country, consisting of nothing but sterile and mountainous tracts. He was pursued by the Raja's son, overtaken and wounded; and being conveyed to *Dehli*, was shut up in *Selim-guer*, the fortress in which *Morad-Bakche* was imprisoned.[2]

Aureng-Zebe acted upon this occasion as he had done in the case of *Dara*. That *Soliman-Chekouh's* identity might be established, the King commanded that he should be brought into the presence of all the courtiers. I could not repress my curiosity, and witnessed the whole of this dismal scene. The fetters were taken from the Prince's feet before he entered the chamber wherein the *Omrahs* were assembled, but the chains, which were gilt,[3] remained about his hands. Many of the courtiers shed tears at the sight of this interesting young man, who was tall and extremely handsome. The principal ladies of the court

[1] The territory now known as Ladákh. [2] See p. 69.

[3] When Isaac Comnenus, king of Cyprus, surrendered to Richard I. Cœur de Lion, king of England, in May 1191, he begged that he might not be fettered with chains of iron. Richard accordingly ordered that his chains should be of silver in consideration of his royal birth. In the words of John Brompton, the compiler of old chronicles, who, in this instance, is confirmed by historians of accepted authority, *Et cum in manu et potestate regis omnia jam essent à rege solum petiit, ne in compedibus et manicis ferreis permitteret eum poni . . . Rex vero petitionem ejus audiens ait, Quia nobilis est et nolumus eum mori, sed ut vivat innoxius, cathenis argenteis astringatur.* Col. 1200. Catrou tells us that the 'fetters and handcuffs' with which Murád Bakhsh was secured (p. 68) were of silver, and that his brother (Aurangzeb) had caused them to be made a long time previously, 'and which he often showed to his son Mahamud, to keep him to his duty. As for the eunuch [Sháhbáz], he was secured without difficulty and loaded with iron fetters.'

had permission to be present, concealed behind a lattice-work, and were also greatly moved. *Aureng-Zebe,* too, affected to deplore the fate of his nephew, and spoke to him with apparent kindness. 'Be comforted,' the King told him; 'no harm shall befall you. You shall be treated with tenderness. God is great, and you should put your trust in him. *Dara,* your father, was not permitted to live only because he had become a *Kafer,* a man devoid of all religion.' Whereupon the Prince made the salaam, or sign of grateful acknowledgment, lowering his hands to the ground, and lifting them, as well as he was able, to his head, according to the custom of the country. He then told the King, with much self-possession, that if it were intended to give him the *poust* to drink, he begged he might be immediately put to death. *Aureng-Zebe* promised in a solemn manner, and in a loud voice, that this drink should most certainly not be administered, and that his mind might be perfectly easy. The Prince was then required to make a second salaam; and when a few questions had been put to him, by the King's desire, concerning the elephant laden with golden *roupies,* which had been taken from him during his retreat to *Serenaguer,* he was taken out of the chamber, and conducted on the following day to *Goüaleor,* with the others.

This *poust* is nothing but poppy-heads crushed, and allowed to soak for a night in water. This is the potion generally given to Princes confined in the fortress of *Goüaleor,* whose heads the Monarch is deterred by prudential reasons from taking off.[1] A large cup of this

[1] Johannes de Laet, at p. 40 of his book *De Imperio Magni Mogolis, sive India Vera,* Lugd. Bat. Elzevir, 1631, gives a very interesting description of the Mogul state prisons in Hindostan. In his account of the fort at Gwalior, he says: 'Above the fourth and highest gate stands the figure of an elephant skilfully cut out of stone. [This is the well-known *Hathipul,* or "Elephant's Gateway," and de Laet also describes, in a previous passage, the vast staircase leading to it, so familiar to all visitors to this celebrated fortress.] This gate is most sumptuously built of green and blue stone; on the top are

beverage is brought to them early in the morning, and they are not given anything to eat until it be swallowed; they would sooner let the prisoner die of hunger. This drink emaciates the wretched victims; who lose their strength and intellect by slow degrees, become torpid and senseless, and at length die. It is said that it was by this means, that *Sepe-Chekouh*, the grandchild of *Morad-Bakche* and *Soliman-Chekouh*, were sent out of the world.

Morad-Bakche was put to death in a more violent and open manner. Though in prison, he was yet very popular, and verses were continually composed in praise of his courage and conduct. *Aureng-Zebe*, therefore, did not deem it safe to make away with him in secret, by the *poust* as the others were; fearing that there would always

several gilded turrets that shine brilliantly. Here the Governor of the place dwells; and here also State prisoners are confined. The King is said to have three prisons of this kind. The second is at Rantipore [Ranthambhor or Rintimbur, the picturesque ancient rock-fortress in the Jeypore State, formerly a stronghold of the Rájá of Búndí who transferred it to the Emperor Akbar], forty coss from this place, whither the King sends those whom he has condemned to death. They are for the most part kept here for two months, after which the Governor brings them out, places them on the top of the wall, and having caused them to drink some milk, casts them down headlong on the rocks beneath. [*Praefectus arcis eos producit, et in fastigio muri constitutos et lacte potatos, praecipites agit in subjectas rupes*, thus in the original. The "milk" being a decoction of the milky juice of the poppy given to the prisoners to render them insensible. The *poust*, a slow poison (púsṭa, from *púst*, a poppy, also called *koknár*, which, like some of the preparations of *mudduk*, sold in the opium dens of Lucknow, had the effect of emaciating those who partook of it by taking away an appetite for solid food) of Bernier's description being reserved for members of the Royal family, as being a more secret death, free from the outward signs of laying violent hands upon one of the Blood Royal. See in this connection pp. 97, 100, and 180]. The third prison fortress is in the fort of Rotas [Rohtásgarh, about 30 miles south of the town of Sasseram, in Bengal, overlooking the junction of the Koel and Soane rivers, an ancient site, the top of the plateau, on which the remains of the fort stand, being 1490 feet above the level of the adjacent country], in the province of Bengal; whither are sent those who are condemned to imprisonment for life; they very seldom manage to escape.'

be some doubt whether he had been really put to death or not, and that this uncertainty might some day be used as a pretext for an uprising, the following charge, they say, was brought up against him.

At the period when *Morad-Bakche* was making extensive preparations for war, in his government of *Guzarate*, he put to death a certain *Sayed* at *Amed-Abad*, that he might obtain possession of his great wealth. The children of the murdered *Sayed* now presented themselves in open court, calling loudly for justice, and demanding the head of *Morad-Bakche*. No *Omrah* would venture to reprove or silence this procedure; both because the person whose innocent blood had been shed was a *Sayed*, or descendant of the prophet *Mahomet*, to whom unbounded veneration is due, and because it could not but be evident to every person that this was a mode designed by the King to rid himself of a dangerous rival under the cloak of justice. The demand of the sons[1] was granted, and without any other form of process, an order for the head of the murderer was given, with which they immediately repaired to *Goüaleor*.

There now existed only one member of his family who created anxiety or apprehension in the mind of *Aureng-Zebe*, and this was *Sultan Sujah*. Hitherto he had displayed much resolution and vigour, but now felt the necessity of yielding to the power and fortune of his

[1] Kháfí Khán's (who states that his father was one of Murád Bakhsh's confidential servants) account of this mock trial does not quite agree with Bernier's. He says that the eldest son refused to demand satisfaction for his father's death, but that the second son complied with the expressed wish of some of the Emperor's friends, viz., that the two sons of Alí Nákí, whom Murád Bakhsh had put to death, should bring a charge of murder against him. Also that after the death of Murád Bakhsh, Aurangzeb rewarded the eldest son for not enforcing his claim of blood. Catrou states that Aurangzeb compassed his brother's death by ordering some soldiers of his guard to proceed to Gwalior, and there sting him 'by one of those adders whose poison is quick and mortal.'

brother. Reinforcements continued to be sent to *Emir-Jemla,* until the Prince, encompassed on all sides, was compelled to fly for his personal safety to *Daké,*[1] which is the last town in *Bengale,* on the borders of the sea; and this ends the whole tragedy.

The Prince being destitute of ships to put to sea, and not knowing whither to fly for refuge, sent his eldest son, *Sultan Banque,* to the King of *Racan,* or *Mog,*[2] a *Gentile* or idolater, to ascertain if he would grant him a temporary asylum, and a passage to *Moka,* when the favourable season arrived;[3] it being his wish to proceed thence to *Meca,* and afterward take up his residence in *Turkey* or *Persia.* The King's answer was in the affirmative, and expressed in the kindest terms. *Sultan Banque* returned to *Daké* with a large number of *galeasses*[4] (as they call the half galleys of this King) manned by *Franks,* for so I would designate those fugitive *Portuguese,* and other wandering *Christians,* who had entered into the King's service, and whose chief occupation was to ravage this part of *Lower Bengale.* On board these vessels, *Sultan Sujah* embarked with his family, consisting of his wife, his three sons and his daughters. The King [of Arakan] gave them a tolerable reception, and supplied them with every necessary of life. Month after month passed; the favourable season arrived, but no mention was made of vessels to convey them to *Moka,* although *Sultan Sujah* required them on no other terms than the payment of the hire; for he yet wanted not *roupies* of gold and silver, or gems. He had indeed too great a plenty of them: his great wealth

[1] Dacca, on the Burígangá river, formerly the main stream of the Ganges.

[2] Arakan or Magh, the *Rakhang* of Kháfí Khán.

[3] 'La moisson du vent' in the original. Moisson is for the Arabic word *mausim,* a season, which the Portuguese corrupted into *monçao*; our *monsoon,* the French *mousson.*

[4] From the early Portuguese word *geluas,* which was the name for a kind of half-decked craft used on the shores of the Red Sea, called in Arabic *jalba,* from which is derived our English word *jolly-boat.*

being probably the cause of, or at least very much contributing to, his ruin. These barbarous kings are devoid of true generosity, and little restrained by any promises which they have made. Seldom guided by considerations of good faith, their present interest is the sole guide of their conduct, and they appear insensible of the mischief which may accrue to themselves from their perfidiousness and cruelty. To escape out of their hands, either you must have nothing to tempt their avarice, or you must be possessed of superior strength. It was in vain that *Sultan Sujah* evinced the utmost solicitude to depart for *Moka*; the King turned a deaf ear to his entreaties; became cool and uncivil, and reproached the Prince for not visiting him. I know not whether *Sultan Sujah* considered it beneath his dignity to associate with him, or whether he apprehended that his person would be seized, and his treasure plundered, if he ventured into the palace. *Emir-Jemla* had offered the King, in the name of *Aureng-Zebe,* large sums of money, and other considerable advantages, on condition of his delivering up the Prince. Though *Sultan Sujah* would not himself venture into the royal residence, yet he sent his son, *Sultan Banque,* who, as he approached the palace, bestowed *largesse* to the people, throwing among them half *roupies,* and also whole *roupies,* both of gold and silver; and, when he came before the King, presented him with various rich brocades and rare pieces of goldsmith's work, set with precious stones of great value; and apologising for the unavoidable absence of his father, who was indisposed, entreated the King to remember the vessel and the promise which he had made.

This visit proved as unavailing as every preceding effort to induce the barbarian to fulfil his engagements; and to add to the mortification and perplexity of the illustrious fugitive, the King, five or six days after this interview, made a formal demand of one of his daughters in marriage. *Sultan Sujah's* refusal to accede to this request exasperated him to such a degree that the Prince's situation became quite desperate. What then ought he to do? To remain inactive was only quietly to await destruction. The season for departure was passing away; it was therefore necessary to come to a decision of some kind. He meditated, at length, an enterprise which never was exceeded in extravagance, and which proves the hopelessness of the situation to which he was reduced.

Although the King of *Rakan* be a *Gentile*, yet there are many *Mahometans* mixed with the people, who have either chosen to retire among them, or have been enslaved by the *Portuguese* before mentioned, in their expeditions to the neighbouring coasts. *Sultan Sujah* secretly gained over these *Mahometans*, whom he joined with two or three hundred of his own people, the remnant of those who followed him from *Bengale*; and with this force resolved to surprise the house of the King, put his family to the sword, and make himself sovereign of the country. This bold attempt, which resembled more the enterprise of a desperado than that of a prudent man, had nevertheless a certain feasibility in it, as I was informed by several *Mahometans, Portuguese,* and *Hollanders,* who were then on the spot. But the day before the blow was to be struck, a discovery was made of the design, which altogether ruined the affairs of *Sultan Sujah,* and involved in it the destruction of his family.

The Prince endeavoured to escape into *Pegu*; a purpose scarcely possible to be effected, by reason of the vast mountains and forests that lay in the route; for there is not now, as formerly, a regular road in that direction. He was pursued and overtaken, within twenty-four hours after his flight: he defended himself with an obstinacy of courage such as might have been expected, and the number of barbarians that fell under his sword was incredible; but at length, overpowered by the increasing host of his assailants, he was compelled to give up the unequal combat. *Sultan Banque,* who had not advanced so far as his father, fought also like a lion, until covered with the blood of the wounds he received from the stones that had been showered upon him from all sides, he was seized, and carried away, with his two young brothers, his sisters, and his mother.

No other particulars, on which much dependence may be placed, are known of *Sultan Sujah.* It is said that he reached the hills, accompanied by an eunuch, a woman, and two other persons; that he received a wound on the head from a stone, which brought him to the ground; that the eunuch having bound up the Prince's head with his own turban he arose again, and escaped into the woods.

I have heard three or four totally different accounts of the fate of the Prince, from those even who were on the spot. Some assured me that he was found among the slain, though it was difficult to recognise his body; and I have seen a letter from a person at the head of the Factory which the Hollanders maintain in that region, mentioning the same thing. Great uncertainty prevails, however, upon the subject, which is the reason why we have had so many alarming rumours at *Dehli.* It was reported, at one time, that he was arrived at *Massipatam,*[1] and that

[1] Masulipatam, the modern rendering of the vernacular name Machhli-patnam or 'Fish Town,' the generally received etymology of the name, which, however, Colonel Yule considered erroneous. That distinguished historical-geographer held that the coast was the *Mæsolia* of the Greek geographers, and believed the name to be a relic of that word. Bernier's version of the name seems to me to support Colonel Yule's contention. It may, however, be intended for 'Machipatam,' a local, clipped, colloquial way of pronouncing the name; similar to '*Machhlīshahr*' for Machhlīshahr, a town in the Jaunpur District of the North-Western Provinces which is a modern name, meaning 'City of Fishes,' given to it owing to its liability to floods in the rainy season, its ancient name being Chiswá. The Dutch established a factory at Masulipatam about 1615, the English in 1622, the French in 1669, and the site of their factory, a patch of ground about three hundred yards square, is still claimed by France. Sterne's 'Eliza' was at one time a resident at Masulipatam, where her

the Kings of *Golkonda* and *Visapour* engaged to support his cause with all their forces. It was confidently said, at another period, that he had passed within sight of *Sourate*, with two ships flying red colours, with which he had been presented either by the King of *Pegu* or of *Siam*. Again, we were told that the Prince was in *Persia*; that he had been seen in *Schiras*, and soon afterwards in *Kandahar*, ready to invade the kingdom of *Caboul*. *Aureng-Zebe* once observed, perhaps by way of joke, that *Sultan Sujah* was become at last an *Agy*[1] or pilgrim; insinuating that he had visited *Meca*; and even at this day, there are a great many persons fully persuaded that he is returned to *Persia* from *Constantinople*, having obtained large supplies of money in that city. But in my opinion there never existed ground for any of these reports. I attach great importance to the letter from the *Dutch* gentleman, which states that the Prince was killed in his attempt to escape; and one of *Sultan Sujah's* eunuchs, with whom I travelled from *Bengale* to *Massipatam*, and his former commandant of artillery, now in the service of the King of *Golkonda*, both assured me that their master was dead, although they were reluctant to communicate any further information. The *French* merchants whom I saw at *Dehli*,[2] and who came direct from *Ispahan*, had never heard a syllable of *Sultan Sujah's* being in *Persia*. It seems

husband Mr. Daniel Draper was stationed in the service of the Honourable East India Company, and 'Eliza's Tree' was to be seen there, until it was unfortunately washed away in the cyclone of 1864. See *Round about Bombay*, by James Douglas, and Sir George Birdwood's article, illustrated, in *The Journal of Indian Art*, for January 1891, entitled 'Eliza Draper's Letter.'

[1] For Hájjí, the incorrect form used by Turks and Persians of the Arabic word *Hájj*, a pilgrim to Mecca.

[2] Although Bernier does not mention his name, I believe one of the French merchants to have been Tavernier, who had left Ispahan on the 24th February 1665, and travelling *viâ* Bandar Abbas reached Surat on the 5th May. He remained in Surat for some time, and travelling most probably by Burhánpur, Gwalior, and Agra, reached Jahánábád (Delhi) in September, where he halted for a few weeks. On

also that his sword and dagger were found soon after his defeat: and if he reached the woods, as some people pretend, it can scarcely be hoped that he escaped; as it is probable he must have fallen into the hands of robbers, or have become a prey to the tigers or elephants which very greatly infest the forests of that country.

But whatever doubts may be entertained of the fate of *Sultan Sujah,* there are none as to the catastrophe which befell his family.[1] When brought back, men, women, and children were all thrown into prison, and treated with the utmost harshness. Some time after, however, they were set at liberty, and used more kindly: the King then married the eldest Princess, and the Queen-mother evinced a strong desire to be united to *Sultan Banque.*

While these events were happening, some servants of *Sultan Banque* joined the *Mahometans,* of whom I have spoken, in a plot similar to the last. The indiscreet zeal of one of the conspirators, who was probably heated with wine, led to the discovery of the design on the day on which it was to be executed. In regard to this affair, too, I have heard a thousand different tales; and the only fact I can relate with confidence is, that the King felt so exasperated against the family of *Sujah* as to give orders for its total extermination. Even the Princess whom he had himself espoused, and who, it is said, was advanced in

the 10th November he was shown the Emperor's jewels, including the great Mogul diamond (see p. 22, footnote [4]). Shortly afterwards he left for Agra, and on the 25th November 1665 he, in company with Bernier, started for Bengal. Tavernier had with him a young nephew, son of his brother Maurice Tavernier, four attendants of different professions, and a surgeon.—*Travels,* Introduction to vol. i. and generally.

[1] Catrou states that 'the subjects of the King of Arracan invested on all sides the palace in which the Mogol Prince was residing. The unfortunate Cha-chuia found no longer any security but was compelled to fly to the forests. He made his escape to their depths, but these tigers pursued him; and after having massacred, without pity, his wives and his children, they deprived him of life on the 7th of February in the year 1658.'

pregnancy, was sacrificed according to his brutal mandate. *Sultan Banque* and his brothers were decapitated with gruesome-looking axes,[1] quite blunt, and the female members of this ill-fated family were closely confined in their apartments, and left to die of hunger.

In this manner terminated the war which the lust of domination had kindled among these four brothers. It lasted between five and six years; that is to say, from about the year 1655 to the year 1660 or 1661; and it left *Aureng-Zebe* the undisputed master of this mighty Empire.

[1] 'Avec de malheureuses haches toutes émoussées' in the original, probably intended to denote the well-known *dao* or hill-knife, which has a blade about eighteen inches long, narrow at the haft, square and broad at the top, pointless and sharpened on one side only, set in a handle of wood, a bamboo root being considered the best; a common weapon at the present day among the Arakan hill tribes, and others on the north-east frontier of India.

REMARKABLE

OCCURRENCES

Or an account of the most important events after the war, during five years or thereby, in the States of the Great Mogol.

THE war being ended, the *Tartars* of *Usbec* eagerly despatched ambassadors to *Aureng-Zebe.* These people had been witnesses of his conduct and valour in many battles, when in command of the corps which *Chah-Jehan* sent to the assistance of the *Kan* of *Samarcande,* then engaged in hostilities with him of *Balk*; and they had reason to apprehend that *Aureng-Zebe* did not forget the treachery of which they had been guilty when he was on the point of capturing *Balk,* the capital city of the enemy. Upon that occasion, the two *Kans* made up their differences, and united in one common effort to drive him back, lest he should seize upon both their territories, in the same manner as *Ekbar* had obtained possession of the kingdom of *Kachemire.* The *Usbec Tartars* were not ignorant of the occurrences which had taken place in *Hindoustan,* of the victories gained by *Aureng-Zebe,* and of the total discomfiture and death of the other competitors for the crown. They were aware that although *Chah-Jehan* still lived, yet his son was, in reality, the recognised and established King of the *Indies.* Whether, then, they dreaded his just resentment, or hoped, in their inbred avarice and sordidness, to obtain some considerable present, the two *Kans* sent ambassadors, with a proffer of their services, and with injunctions to perform the ceremony of the *Mobarek*: that is, to express in a solemn manner their wishes that his reign might be long and auspicious. *Aureng-Zebe* knew how to value an offer of service made at the conclusion of a war: he knew the fear of punishment, or the expectation of advantage, had induced the *Kans* to send their ambassadors. They were received, however, with due form and polite-

FIG. 6.—The Emperor Álamgir (Aurangzeb).

ness, and as I happened to be present at the audience, I can relate the particulars with accuracy.

The ambassadors, when at a distance, made the *Salam*, or *Indian* act of obeisance, placing the hand thrice upon the head, and as often dropping it down to the ground. They then approached so near that *Aureng-Zebe* might easily have taken the letters from their own hands; but this ceremony was performed by an *Omrah*: the letters were received and opened by him, and then presented to the King, who, after having perused the contents with a grave countenance, commanded that there should be given to each of the ambassadors a *Ser-apah* or vesture from head to foot; namely, a vest of brocade, a turban, and a sash or girdle, of embroidered silk. This done, the presents from the *Kans* were brought before the King, consisting of some boxes of *Lapis-lazuli* or the choicest *Azure*[1]; a few long-haired camels; several horses of great beauty, although the *Tartar* horses[2] are generally something better than merely beautiful: some camel-loads of fresh fruit, such as apples, pears, grapes, and melons; *Usbec* being the country which principally supplies *Dehli* with these fruits, which are there eaten all the winter, and many loads of dry fruit, as *Bokara* prunes,[3] apricots,

[1] Used, pounded up, by the calligraphers of Persia, Kashmir, and Delhi as the basis for that 'azure blue' colour, in their choice illuminated MSS., which is unsurpassable, and cannot even be approached by any modern artificial chemical substitute. Lapis-lazuli was largely used in the pietra dura work in the Táj; and these Tartar ambassadors may have been bringing some of it as a tribute or offering to the Mogul Court for this very purpose. This tomb, although finished in 1648 as far as the mere structure is concerned, was probably worked at for many years afterwards ('built by Titans, finished by jewellers'), as much of the exquisite detail of its decorations could not have been carried out in any other way. In a translation of a Persian MS., published at Lahore in 1869, at the Victoria Press, by Azeezoodeen, giving an account of the building of the Táj, particulars are given of the source of supply and cost of the various stones used. In this account lapis-lazuli is said to have been brought from Ceylon, but I believe that this mineral is never found there. We are also informed that 'most of these [stones] were received in lieu of tribute from different nations under the Emperor's rule, or were made presents voluntarily, or otherwise, by the different Rajahs and Nawabs.'

[2] 'The fine up-standing Turkoman horse' of the everyday Calcutta horse-dealers' sale-catalogues. Moorcroft's journey to Tibet, in 1819, was chiefly undertaken with the object of obtaining Turkoman horses of the choicest breed, which it was his great ambition to domesticate in India.

[3] The *Ali Bokharas* imported largely into India at the present day, and most excellent simply stewed, or in a tart.

kichmiches,[1] or raisins, apparently without stones, and two other kinds of raisins, black and white, extremely large and delicious.

Aureng-Zebe expressed himself well pleased with the liberality of the *Kans*; extolling in exaggerated strains the beauty and rareness of the fruits, horses, and camels; and when he had spoken a few words on the fertility of their country, and asked two or three questions concerning the College at *Samarcande*,[2] he desired the ambassadors to go and repose themselves, intimating that he should be happy to see them often.

They came away from the audience delighted with their reception, without any feeling of mortification on account of the salam *à l'Indien*, which certainly savours of servility, and not at all displeased that the King had refused to receive the letters from their own hands. If they had been required to kiss the ground, or to perform any act of still deeper humiliation, I verily believe they would have complied without a murmur. It should indeed be observed that it would have been unreasonable to insist upon saluting *Aureng-Zebe* according to the custom of their own

[1] *Kishmish*, the stoneless raisins of the modern dried-fruit sellers.

[2] The present city of Samarkand, at one time the capital of Timur, is but a wreck of its former self, but time brings round strange changes, and this Holy city may have a renascence. 'The central part of Samarkand is the Righistan, a square limited by the three *madrasahs* (colleges) of Ulug-beg, Shir-dar, and Tilla-kari; in its architectural symmetry and beauty this is rivalled only by some of the squares of Italian cities. . . . The college of Shir-dar (built in 1601) takes its name from the two lions, or rather tigers, figured on the top of its doorway, which is richly decorated with green, blue, red, and white enamelled bricks. It is the most spacious of the three, and 128 Mollahs inhabit its sixty-four apartments. The Tilla-kari ('dressed in gold') built in 1618, has fifty-six rooms. But the most renowned of the three madrasahs is that of Ulug-beg, built in 1420 or 1434, by Timur, the grandson of the great conqueror. It is smaller than the others, but it was to its school of mathematics and astronomy that Samarkand owed its wide renown in the fifteenth century.' P. A. K.[ROPOTKINE], *Encyc. Brit.* ninth ed. 1886.

country, or to expect that the letters would be delivered without the intervention of an *Omrah*: these privileges belong exclusively to *Persian* ambassadors; nor are they granted, even to them, without much hesitation and difficulty.

These people remained more than four months at *Dehli*, notwithstanding all their endeavours to obtain their *congé*. This long detention proved extremely injurious to their health; they and their suite sickened, and many of them died. It is doubtful whether they suffered more from the heat of *Hindoustan*, to which they are unaccustomed, or from the filthiness of their persons, and the insufficiency of their diet. There are probably no people more narrow-minded, sordid, or uncleanly, than the *Usbec Tartars*. The individuals who composed this embassy hoarded the money allowed them by *Aureng-Zebe* for their expenses, and lived on a miserable pittance, in a style quite unsuitable to their station. Yet they were dismissed with great form and parade. The King, in the presence of all his *Omrahs*, invested each of them with two rich *Serapahs*, and commanded that eight thousand *roupies* should be carried to their respective houses. He also sent by them, as presents to the two *Kans*, their masters, very handsome *Serapahs*, a large number of the richest and most exquisitely wrought brocades, a quantity of fine linens, *alachas*,[1] or silk stuffs

[1] Generally in pieces about five yards long, with a wavy line pattern running in the length on either side. The name *alchah* or *alácha*h, was also applied to any corded stuff. At p. 135 the markings of a zebra are compared to this fabric. Sivají, the Mahratta chief, in his portrait (Fig. 8), which was taken from life evidently by a Dutch artist, reproduced at p. 187 of this book, is therein depicted as clothed in *alchah*. In the words of Valentyn, 'we represent this Signior . . . from life, arrayed in a golden *alcha*, as well as a turban on his head' (Wy vertoonen dien Heer . . . na't leven, met een goude Alegia bekleed, en met zoo een tulbant op't hoofd.—*Beschryving*, p. 265). In this portrait the pattern of the fabric is well shown; and it was from authentic pictures such as these, the work of Indian artists as a rule, that our manufacturers, and those of other nations, took their first Oriental designs.

interwoven with gold and silver, a few carpets, and two daggers set with precious stones.

During their stay I paid them three visits, having been introduced as a physician by one of my friends, the son of an *Usbec*, who has amassed a fortune at this court. It was my design to collect such useful particulars concerning their country as they might be able to supply, but I found them ignorant beyond all conception. They were unacquainted even with the boundaries of *Usbec*, and could give no information respecting the *Tartars* who a few years ago subjugated *China*.[1] In short, I could elicit by my conversation with the ambassadors scarcely one new fact. Once I was desirous of dining with them, and as they were persons of very little ceremony, I did not find it difficult to be admitted at their table. The meal appeared to me very strange; it consisted only of horse-flesh. I contrived, however, to dine. There was a *ragoût* which I thought eatable, and I should have considered myself guilty of a breach of good manners if I had not praised a dish so pleasing to their palate. Not a word was uttered during dinner; my elegant hosts were fully employed in cramming their mouths with as much *pelau*[2] as they could contain; for with the use of spoons these people are unacquainted. But when their

[1] The first Tartar (correctly Tatar) conquest of China was in 1100. The invaders were afterwards expelled, but reconquered China in 1644, when Shun-chee, or, as it is sometimes written, Chun-chee, was declared Emperor. It is to this conquest that Bernier here refers, the Manchoo Tartar dynasty then established continuing to the present day.

[2] A corruption of the Persian word *palao*, that favourite dish among the Muhammadans in the East. Ovington, in *A Voyage to Suratt, in the Year* 1689, p. 397 (Lond. 1696), tells us that 'Palau, that is, Rice boiled so artificially, that every grain lies singly without being added together, with Spices intermixt, and a boil'd Fowl in the middle, is the most common *Indian* Dish; and a dumpoked Fowl, that is, boil'd with butter in any small Vessel, and stuft with Raisons and Almonds, is another.' 'Dumpoked' is meant for *dumpúkht*, from the Persian, meaning 'steam-cooked.' For achieving a dumpokht fowl to perfection, a *bain-marie* pan must be used.

stomachs were sated with the dainty repast, they recovered their speech, and would fain have persuaded me that the *Usbecs* surpass all other men in bodily strength, and that no nation equals them in the dexterous management of the bow. This observation was no sooner made than they called for bows and arrows, which were of a much larger size than those of *Hindoustan*, and offered to lay a wager that they would pierce an ox or a horse through and through. They proceeded to extol the strength and valour of their country-women, in comparison with whom the *Amazons* were soft and timorous. The tales they related of female feats were endless: one especially excited my wonder and admiration; would that I could relate it with genuine *Tartar* eloquence. It seems that when *Aureng-Zebe* was prosecuting the war in their country, a party of five-and-twenty or thirty horsemen entered a small village; and while employed in pillaging the houses, and binding the inhabitants, whom they intended to carry away as slaves, a good old woman said to them: 'Children, listen to my counsel, and cease to act in this mischievous manner. My daughter happens just now to be absent, but she will soon return. Withdraw from this place, if you are prudent; should she light upon you, you are undone.' They made contemptuous sport of the good lady, continuing to plunder the property, and to secure the persons, of individuals, until, having fully laden their beasts, they quitted the village, taking with them many of the inhabitants and the old woman herself. They had not gone half a league, however, before the aged mother, who never ceased to look behind, cried out in an ecstasy of joy, 'My daughter! My daughter!' Her person was indeed hid from view; but the extraordinary clouds of dust, and the loud trampling of a horse, left no doubt on the mind of the anxious parent, that her heroic child was at hand to rescue her and her friends from the power of their cruel enemies. Presently the Tartar maiden was seen mounted on a fiery steed, a bow and quiver hanging at her side; and, while yet at a considerable distance, she cried out that she was still willing to spare their lives, on condition that they restored the plunder, released their captives, and retired peaceably to their own country. The *Mogols* turned as deaf an ear to the words of the young heroine as to the entreaties of her aged parent; but were astonished when they saw her in a moment let fly three or four arrows, which brought to the ground the same number of men. They had instant recourse to their own bows, but the damsel was much beyond the reach of their arrows, and laughed at such impotent efforts to avenge the death of their companions. She continued to perform dreadful execution among them, with an accuracy of aim, and strength of arm, which was quite different to theirs; until having killed half of their number with arrows, she fell sword in hand upon the remainder, and cut them in pieces.[1]

The ambassadors from *Tartary* were still in *Dehli,* when *Aureng-Zebe* was seized with a dangerous illness.[2] He was frequently delirious from the violence of the fever, and his tongue became so palsied that he could scarcely articulate. The physicians despaired of his recovery, and it was generally believed he was dead, though the event was concealed by *Rauchenara-Begum* from interested motives. It was even rumoured that the Raja *Jessomseingue,* governor of *Guzarate,* was advancing to release *Chah-Jehan* from

[1] In the Dutch edition of Bernier, Amsterdam, 1672, at p. 10 of the section, *Remarkable Occurrences* (Bysondere Uytkomsten), there is a very quaint illustration to this passage. A copperplate engraving after a mere fancy sketch, in which the Tartar maiden is shown as dealing great execution among the ranks of the Moguls, their arrows falling short of her, a burning village indicated in the background. The consternation among the Moguls is very cleverly depicted, and the action of the Amazon's horse charging down on their ranks is exceedingly well expressed. See Bibliography, entry No. 5.

[2] The date of this illness varies in the various annals of the time. The date, 1662, given by Kháfí Khán, is generally accepted as correct.

captivity; that *Mohabet-kan,* who had at length acknowledged *Aureng-Zebe's* authority, had quitted the government of *Kaboul,* passed already through *Lahor,* and was rapidly marching on *Agra,* at the head of three or four thousand horse, with the same intention; and that the eunuch *Etbar-kan,* under whose custody the aged monarch was placed, felt impatient for the honour of opening the door of his prison.

On the one hand, *Sultan Mazum* intrigued with the *Omrahs,* and endeavoured by bribes and promises to attach them to his interest. He even went one night in disguise to the Raja *Jesseingue,* and entreated him, in the most respectful and humble language, to declare in his favour. On the other hand, a party formed by *Rauchenara-Begum* was supported by several *Omrahs* and *Feday-kan,*[1] grand master of the artillery, in behalf of the young Prince, *Sultan Ekbar,* the third son of *Aureng-Zebe,* a boy only seven or eight years of age.

It was pretended by both these parties, and believed by the people, that the sole object they had in view was to set *Chah-Jehan* at liberty; but this was merely for the sake of gaining popularity, and to save appearances, in case he should be liberated by *Etbar,* or by means of any secret intrigues on the part of other grandees. There was in fact scarcely a person of rank or influence who entertained the wish of seeing *Chah-Jehan* restored to the throne. With the exception, perhaps, of *Jessomseingue, Mohabet-kan,* and a few others who had hitherto refrained from acting flagrantly against him, there was no *Omrah* who had not basely abandoned the cause of the legitimate Monarch, and taken an active part in favour of *Aureng-Zebe.* They were aware that to open his prison door would be to unchain an enraged lion. The possibility of such an event appalled the courtiers, and no one dreaded

[1] Fidaí Khán, foster-brother to Aurangzeb. About 1676 he was honoured with the title of Azim Khán, and appointed Governor of Bengal, where he died in 1678.

it more than *Etbar*, who had behaved to his wretched victim with unnecessary rudeness and severity.

But *Aureng-Zebe*, notwithstanding his serious indisposition, continued to occupy his mind with the affairs of government, and the safe custody of his father. He earnestly advised *Sultan Mazum*, in the event of his death, to release the King from confinement; but he was constantly dictating letters to *Etbar-kan*, urging him to the faithful and rigid discharge of his duty; and on the fifth day of his illness, during the crisis of the disorder, he caused himself to be carried into the assembly of the *Omrahs*, for the purpose of undeceiving those who might believe he was dead, and of preventing a public tumult, or any accident by which *Chah-Jehan* might effect his escape. The same reasons induced him to visit that assembly on the seventh, ninth, and tenth days; and, what appears almost incredible, on the thirteenth day, when scarcely recovered from a swoon so deep and long that his death was generally reported, he sent for the Raja *Jesseingue*, and two or three of the principal *Omrahs*, for the purpose of verifying his existence. He then desired the attendants to raise him in the bed; called for paper and ink that he might write to *Etbar-kan*, and despatched a messenger for the *Great Seal*, which was placed under *Rauchenara-Begum's* care enclosed in a small bag, which was impressed with a signet which he always kept fastened to his arm;[1] wishing to satisfy himself that the Princess had not made use of this instrument to promote any sinister design. I was present when my *Agah* became acquainted with all these particulars, and heard him exclaim, 'What strength of mind! What invincible

[1] I have seen contemporary portraits of the Mogul Emperors, the work of Indian artists, in which is shown this counter-seal (not to be confounded with an amulet, which would be worn *on* the left arm), fastened underneath the right armpit. An engraving from such a portrait 'which was taken from a picture of his, drawn to the life' will be found between folios 346-7 of Edward Terry's *A Voyage to East India.* London, 1771; a reprint of the edition of 1655.

courage! Heaven reserve thee, *Aureng-Zebe*, for greater achievements! Thou art not yet destined to die.' And indeed after this fit the King improved gradually in health.

As soon as *Aureng-Zebe* became convalescent, he endeavoured to withdraw *Dara's* daughter from the hands of *Chah-Jehan* and *Begum-Saheb*, with the design of giving her in marriage to his third son, *Sultan Ekbar.* This is the son, whom, it is supposed, he intends for his successor, and such an alliance would strengthen *Ekbar's* authority and ensure his right to the throne. He is very young, but has several near and powerful relations at court, and being born of *Chah-Navaze-kan's* daughter, is descended from the ancient sovereigns of *Ma*[*s*]*chate*.[1] The mothers of *Sultan Mahmoud* and *Sultan Mazum* were only *Ragipoutnys*, or daughters of Rajas; for although these Kings are *Mahometans*, they do not scruple to marry into heathen families, when such a measure may promote their interests, or when they may thus obtain a beautiful wife.[2]

But *Aureng-Zebe* was frustrated in his intention. *Chah-Jehan* and *Begum-Saheb* rejected the proposition with disdain, and the young Princess herself manifested the utmost repugnance to the marriage. She remained inconsolable during many days from an apprehension that she might be forcibly taken away, declaring it was her

[1] See p. 73.

[2] In the *Ma-asir-i'Álamgírí* (Elliot, vol. vii. pp. 195, 196) it is stated that Muhammad Sultán the eldest, and Sultán Mu'azzam the second son, were both by the same mother, Nawab Baí; also that the mother of Muhammad Kám Bakhsh, the fifth and last son, was Baí Udaipuri; a statement which, if correct, hardly bears out the truth of the boast of the Udaipur family, that their house never gave a daughter to the Mogul zenana. Bernier has probably confused the eldest and the youngest son, although he correctly states that Aurangzeb had two Hindoo wives, daughters of Rajpúts, or Rajpútnís as he correctly calls them. Prince Muhammad Akbar was Aurangzeb's *fourth* son. His mother was a Muhammadan, the daughter of Sháhnáwaz Khán, and it was mainly on this account that Aurangzeb desired to make him his successor to the throne.

firm purpose to die by her own hand, rather than be united to the son of him who murdered her father.[1]

He was equally unsuccessful in his demand on *Chah-Jehan* for certain jewels, with which he was desirous of completing a piece of workmanship that he was adding to the celebrated throne, so universally the object of admiration.[2] The captive Monarch indignantly answered that *Aureng-Zebe* should be careful only to govern the kingdom with more wisdom and equity: he commanded him not to meddle with the throne; and declared that he would be no more plagued about these jewels, for that hammers were provided to beat them into powder the next time he should be importuned upon the subject.

The *Hollanders* would not be the last to present *Aureng-Zebe* with the *Mohbarec.* They determined to send an ambassador to him, and made choice of *Monsieur Adrican,*[3] chief of their factory at *Sourate.* This individual possesses integrity, abilities, and sound judgment; and as he does not disdain the advice offered by the wise and experienced, it is not surprising that he acquitted himself to the satisfaction of his countrymen. Although in his general deportment *Aureng-Zebe* be remarkably high and unbending, affects the appearance of a zealous *Mahometan,* and consequently despises *Franks* or *Christians,* yet upon the occasion of this embassy, his behaviour was most courteous and condescending. He even expressed a desire that *Monsieur Adrican,* after that gentleman had performed the *Indian* ceremony of the *Salaam,* should approach and salute him *à la Frank.* The King, it is true, received the

[1] See p. 166.

[2] The celebrated 'Peacock Throne,' see p. 269, which Sháh Jahán designed and caused to be made.

[3] Dirk van Adrichem, who was chief, or director, of the Dutch factory at Surat from 1662 to 1665. He succeeded in obtaining a 'concession' (*Firmaan, of gunst-brief* in the Dutch original), dated Delhi, 29th October 1662, from Aurangzeb, which conferred valuable privileges upon the Dutch in Bengal and Orissa.—Valentyn, *Beschryving,* p. 261.

letters through the medium of an *Omrah*, but this could not be considered a mark of disrespect, since he had done the same thing in regard to the letters brought by the *Usbec* ambassadors.

The preliminary observances being over, *Aureng-Zebe* intimated that the ambassador might produce his presents; at the same time investing him, and a few gentlemen in his suite, with a *Ser-Apah* of brocade. The presents consisted of a quantity of very fine broad cloths, scarlet and green; some large looking-glasses; and several articles of *Chinese* and *Japan* workmanship;[1] among which were a *paleky* and a *Tack-ravan*,[2] or travelling throne, of exquisite beauty, and much admired.

The *Great Mogol* is in the habit of detaining all ambassadors as long as can reasonably be done, from an idea that it is becoming his grandeur and power, to receive the homage of foreigners, and to number them among the attendants of his court. *Monsieur Adrican* was not dismissed, therefore, so expeditiously as he wished, though much sooner than the ambassadors from *Tartary*. His secretary died, and the other individuals in his retinue were falling sick, when *Aureng-Zebe* granted him permission to depart. On taking leave the King again presented him with a *Ser-Apah* of brocade for his own use, and another very rich one for the governor of *Batavia*,[3] together with a dagger set with jewels; the whole accompanied by a very gracious letter.

The chief aim of the *Hollanders* in this embassy was to ingratiate themselves with the *Mogol*, and to impart to

[1] I possess contemporary pictures, of Mogul court-life, by Indian artists, in which Japanese hangings and Chinese vases are very correctly and artistically shown.

[2] *Tukht-i-rawan*, from *tukht*, a seat or throne, and *rawan*, the present participle of the verb *rufteen*, to go, to move, to proceed. The tukht-i-rawan was carried on men's shoulders, and was used by royalty alone. See p. 370.

[3] Who was the chief of all the Dutch factories and possessions in the East Indies, the Governor-General of the Dutch Indies in fact.

him some knowledge of their nation, in order that a beneficial influence might thus be produced upon the minds of the governors of sea-ports, and other places, where they have established factories.[1] They hoped that those governors would be restrained from offering insult, and obstructing their commerce, by the consideration that they belonged to a powerful State, that they could obtain immediate access to the King of the *Indies* to induce him to listen to their complaints, and to redress their grievances. They endeavoured also to impress the government with an opinion that their traffic with *Hindoustan* was most advantageous to that kingdom; exhibiting a long list of articles purchased by their countrymen, from which they showed that the gold and silver brought by them every year into the *Indies* amounted to a considerable sum: but they kept out of sight the amount of those precious metals extracted by their constant importations of copper, lead, cinnamon, clove, nutmeg, pepper, aloes-wood, elephants, and other merchandise.[2]

It was about this period that one of the most distinguished *Omrahs* ventured to express to *Aureng-Zebe* his fears lest his incessant occupations should be productive of injury to his health, and even impair the soundness and vigour of his mind. The King, affecting not to hear, turned from his sage adviser, and advancing slowly toward another of the principal *Omrahs*, a man of good sense and literary acquirements, addressed him in the following terms. The speech was reported to me by the son of that *Omrah*, a young physician, and my intimate friend.

'There can surely be but one opinion among you learned men, as to the obligation imposed upon a sovereign, in seasons of difficulty and danger, to hazard his life, and, if

[1] The *farmán* (*lit.* an order, a 'patent' or commission) obtained by Dirk van Adrichem, see p. 127, footnote [3], is here very accurately summarised by Bernier.

[2] In this connection see Bernier's letter to Colbert, pp. 200 *et seq.*

necessary, to die sword in hand in defence of the people committed to his care. And yet this good and considerate man would fain persuade me that the public weal ought to cause me no solicitude; that, in devising means to promote it, I should never pass a sleepless night, nor spare a single day from the pursuit of some low and sensual gratification. According to him, I am to be swayed by considerations of my own bodily health, and chiefly to study what may best minister to my personal ease and enjoyment. No doubt he would have me abandon the government of this vast kingdom to some vizier: he seems not to consider that, being born the son of a King, and placed on a throne, I was sent into the world by Providence to live and labour, not for myself, but for others; that it is my duty not to think of my own happiness, except so far as it is inseparably connected with the happiness of my people. It is the repose and prosperity of my subjects that it behoves me to consult; nor are these to be sacrificed to anything besides the demands of justice, the maintenance of the royal authority, and the security of the State. This man cannot penetrate into the consequences of the inertness he recommends, and he is ignorant of the evils that attend upon delegated power. It was not without reason that our great *Sadi* emphatically exclaimed "Cease to be Kings! Oh, cease to be Kings! or determine that your dominions shall be governed only by yourselves." Go, tell thy friend, that if he be desirous of my applause, he must acquit himself well of the trust reposed in him; but let him have a care how he again obtrudes such counsel as it would be unworthy of a King to receive. Alas! we are sufficiently disposed by nature to seek ease and indulgence, we need no such officious counsellors. Our wives, too, are sure to assist us in treading the flowery path of rest and luxury.'

A melancholy circumstance happened at this time which excited a great deal of interest in *Dehli*, particularly in the *Seraglio*, and which proved the fallacy of an opinion entertained by myself, as well as by others, that he who is entirely deprived of virility cannot feel the passion of love.

Didar-Kan, one of the principal eunuchs of the *Seraglio,* had built a house, to which he sometimes resorted for entertainment, and where he often slept. He became enamoured of a beautiful woman, the sister of a neighbour, a *Gentile,*[1] and a scrivener by profession. An illicit intercourse continued for some time between them, without creating much suspicion. After all, it was but an eunuch, privileged to enter anywhere, and a woman!

The familiarity between the two lovers became at length so remarkable, that the neighbours began to suspect something, and chaffed the scrivener on the subject. He felt so stung by these taunts that he threatened to put both his sister and the eunuch to death if the suspicions of their guilt should be verified. Proof was not long wanting: they were one night discovered in the same bed, by the brother, who stabbed *Didar-Kan* through the body, and left his sister for dead.

Nothing could exceed the horror and indignation of the whole *Seraglio.* Women and eunuchs entered into a solemn league to kill the scrivener; but their machinations excited the displeasure of *Aureng-Zebe,* who contented himself by compelling the man to become a *Mahometan.*

It seems nevertheless to be the general opinion that he cannot long escape the power and malice of the eunuchs. Emasculation, say the *Indians,* produces a different effect upon men than upon the brute creation; it renders the

[1] In the original 'un Ecrivain Gentil,' or, in other words, a Hindoo writer or clerk. At this period the collection of the revenue, the keeping of the accounts, the conduct of the official correspondence of the Court was all in the hands of Hindoo clerks, well versed in Persian. As Professor Blochmann tells us in his *Calcutta Review* article already quoted (p. 40, footnote [1]), 'the Hindús from the 16th century took so zealously to Persian education, that, before another century had elapsed, they had fully come up to the Muhammadans in point of literary acquirements.'

latter gentle and tractable; but who is the eunuch, they ask, that is not vicious, arrogant and cruel? It is in vain to deny, however, that many among them are exceedingly faithful, generous, and brave.

Much about the same time, *Rauchenara-Begum* incurred the displeasure of *Aureng-Zebe*, the Princess having been suspected of admitting two men into the seraglio. As it was only suspicion, however, the King was soon reconciled to his sister. Nor did he exercise the same cruelty toward the two men, who were caught and dragged into his presence, as *Chah-Jehan* had done upon a similar occasion toward the unhappy gallant concealed in the cauldron.[1] I shall relate the whole story exactly as I heard it from the mouth of an old woman, a half-caste *Portuguese*,[2] who has been many years a slave in the seraglio, and possesses the privilege of going in and out at pleasure. From her I learnt that *Rauchenara-Begum*, after having for several days enjoyed the company of one of these young men, whom she kept hidden, committed him to the care of her female attendants, who promised to conduct their charge out of the *Seraglio* under cover of the night. But whether they were detected, or only dreaded a discovery, or whatever else was the reason, the women fled, and left the terrified youth to wander alone about the gardens: here he was found, and taken before *Aureng-Zebe*; who, when he had interrogated him very closely, without being able to draw any other confession of guilt from him than that he had scaled the walls, decided that he should be compelled to leave the seraglio in the same manner. But the eunuchs, it is probable, exceeded their master's instructions, for they threw the culprit from the top of the wall to the bottom. As for the second paramour, the old *Portuguese* informed me that he too was seen roving about the gardens, and that having told the King he had entered

[1] See p. 12.

[2] 'Une vieille Mestice de Portugais,' in the original; from *mestiço*, the Portuguese word for one of mixed parentage.

into the *Seraglio* by the regular gate, he was commanded to quit the place through that same gate. *Aureng-Zebe* determined, however, to inflict a severe and exemplary punishment upon the eunuchs; because it was essential, not only to the honour of his house, but even to his personal safety, that the entrance into the seraglio should be vigilantly guarded.

Some months after this occurrence five ambassadors arrived at *Dehli,* nearly at the same time. The first was from the Cherif[1] of *Meca,* and the presents that accompanied this embassage consisted of a small number of Arabian horses and a besom which had been used for sweeping out[2] the small chapel situated in the centre of the Great Mosque at *Meca*; a chapel held in great veneration by *Mahometans,* and called by them *Beit-Allah,* or the House of God. They believe this was the first temple dedicated to the true God, and that it was erected by *Abraham.*

The second ambassador was sent by the King of *Hyeman,* or Arabia Felix;[3] and the third by the Prince of *Bassora*; both of whom also brought presents of Arabian horses.

The two other ambassadors came from the King of *Ebeche,* or Ethiopia.[4]

Little or no respect was paid to the first three of these diplomatists. Their equipage was so miserable that every

[1] The Grand Shereef (from the Arabic *sharíf,* noble) of Mecca, who has control over the Holy Places, claims to be a lineal descendant of the Prophet Muhammad. The name of the present (1891) Grand Shereef is 'Aun ér-Rafiq, and he succeeded to this dignity in 1882.

[2] Similar to the small hand-brushes, generally made of leaves of the date-palm, used in the mosques of India for a like purpose. The 'small chapel' being the Ka'bah, or Cube-house, in which is placed the Black Stone, in the centre of 'The Sacred Mosque' (Masjidu 'l-Haram) at Mecca. The term *Baitu'llah* or 'House of God' is applied to the whole enclosure, although it more specially denotes the Ka'bah itself.

[3] Yemen, the territory of *al-Yamen,* to the south-east of Mecca.

[4] Abyssinia, see p. 2 text, and footnote [2].

one suspected they came merely for the sake of obtaining money in return for their presents, and of gaining still more considerable sums by means of the numerous horses, and different articles of merchandise, which they introduced into the kingdom free of all duty, as property belonging to ambassadors. With the produce of these horses and merchandise, they purchased the manufactures of *Hindoustan*, which they also claimed the privilege of taking out of the kingdom without payment of the impost charged on all commodities exported.

The embassy from the King of *Ethiopia* may deserve a little more consideration. He was well informed on the subject of the revolution in the *Indies*, and determined to spread his fame throughout this vast region by despatching an embassy that should be worthy of his great power and magnificence. The whispers of slander, indeed, if not rather the voice of truth, will have it that in sending these ambassadors this Monarch had an eye only to the valuable presents which might be received from the liberal hand of *Aureng-Zebe*.

Now let us examine the personnel of this admirable Embassy. He chose as his Envoys two personages who doubtless enjoyed the greatest distinction at court, and were best qualified to attain the important ends he had in view. One of these was a *Mahometan* merchant, whom I met a few years before at *Moka*, when on my way from *Egypt* up the *Red Sea*.[1] He had been sent thither by his august sovereign for the purpose of selling a large number of slaves, and of purchasing *Indian* goods with the money thus commendably obtained.

Such is the honourable traffic of this Great *Christian* King of *Africa* !

The other ambassador was an *Armenian* and Christian merchant ; born and married at *Alep* [Aleppo], and known in *Ethiopia* by the name of *Murat*.[2] I saw him also at *Moka*, where he not only accommodated me with half his apart-

[1] See p. 2.

[2] The *Chodja Moraad* of Valentyn.

ment, but gave me such advice as deterred me from visiting *Ethiopia*, as was observed at the commencement of this history.[1] *Murat* is likewise sent every year to *Moka* for the same object as the Mahometan merchant, and always takes with him the annual presents from his master to the English and Dutch *East-India* Companies, and conveys those which they give in return to *Gonder*.

The *African* Monarch, anxious that his ambassador should appear in a style suitable to the occasion, contributed liberally toward the expenses of the embassy. He presented them with thirty-two young slaves, boys and girls, to be sold at *Moka*; and the money raised by this happy expedient was to supply the expenses of the mission. A noble largess indeed! for let it be recollected that young slaves sell at *Moka*, one with another, at five-and-twenty or thirty crowns per head.[2] Besides these, the *Ethiopian* King sent to the *Great Mogol* twenty-five choice slaves, nine or ten of whom were of a tender age and in a state to be made eunuchs. This was, to be sure, an appropriate donation from a Christian to a Prince! but then the Christianity of the *Ethiopians* differs greatly from ours. The ambassadors also took charge of other presents for the *Great Mogol*; fifteen horses, esteemed equal to those of *Arabia*, and a small species of mule, whose skin I have seen: no tiger is so beautifully marked, and no *alachá*[3] of the *Indies*, or striped silken stuff, is more finely and variously streaked;[4] a couple of elephants' teeth, of a size so prodigious that it required, it seems, the utmost exertion of a strong man to lift either of them from the ground; and lastly, the horn of an ox, filled with civet, which was indeed enormously large, for I measured the

[1] See p. 2.

[2] *Écus*, or 'white crowns' as they were then called, worth 4s. 6d. each.

[3] See p. 120, footnote.

[4] A zebra, which is still considered a great curiosity in India, as evidenced by the admiring crowds to be seen round the specimen in the Calcutta Zoological Gardens.

mouth of it at *Dehly*, and found that it exceeded half a foot[1] in diameter.

The ambassadors, thus royally and munificently provided, departed from *Gonder*, the capital city of Ethiopia, situated in the province of *Dumbia*. They traversed a desolate country, and were more than two months travelling to *Beiloul*, an out-of-the-way seaport, near *Bab-el-Mandel* and opposite to *Moka*. For reasons, which I shall perhaps disclose in the course of my narrative, they dared not take the usual and caravan road from *Gonder* to *Arkiko*, a journey easily performed in forty days. From *Arkiko* it is necessary to pass over to the island of *Masouva*, where the *Grand Seigneur*[2] has a garrison.

While waiting at *Beiloul* for a *Moka* vessel to cross the *Red Sea*, the party were in want of many of the necessaries of life, and some of the slaves died.

On arriving at *Moka*, the ambassadors found that the market had been that year overstocked with slaves. The boys and girls, therefore, sold at a reduced price. As soon as their sale was effected, they pursued their voyage, embarking on board an Indian vessel bound to *Sourate*, where they arrived after a tolerable passage of five-and-twenty days. Several slaves, however, and many horses died; probably from want of proper nourishment, the funds of this pompous embassy being evidently insufficient to supply all its wants. The mule also died, but the skin was preserved.

They had not been many hours on shore at *Sourate* when a certain rebel of *Visapour*, named *Seva-Gi*,[3] entered the

[1] The French 'pied de Ville' most probably, equal to 12⅝ inches English.

[2] That is, the Sultan of Turkey.

[3] Sivají, the founder of the Marátha power, born 1627, died (on the 5th April according to Elphinstone, but the 1st June is the date given in Valentyn's narrative) 1680. Of him it has been well said by Elphinstone (*History of India*, p. 647, ed. of 1874), 'Though the son of a powerful chief, he had begun life as a daring and artful captain of banditti, had ripened into a skilful general and an able statesman, and

town, which he pillaged and burnt. The house of the ambassadors did not escape the general conflagration; and all their effects that they succeeded in rescuing from the flames, or the ravages of the enemy, were their credentials; a few slaves that *Seva-Gi* could not lay hold of, or whom he spared because they happened to be ill; their *Ethiopian* apparel, which he did not covet; the mule's skin, for which, I expect, he had no particular fancy; and the ox's horn that had already been emptied of its civet.

These exalted individuals spoke in exaggerated terms of their sad misfortunes; but it was insinuated by the malicious *Indians*, who witnessed their deplorable condition on landing—without decent clothing, destitute of money or bills of exchange, and half famished—that the two ambassadors were, in fact, lucky people, who ought to number the ransacking of *Sourate*[1] among the happiest events of their lives, since it saved them from the mortification of conducting their wretched presents as far as *Dehli*. *Seva-Gi*, the Indians said, had furnished these worthy representatives of the Ethiopian King with an admirable pretext for appearing like a couple of mendicants, and for soliciting the governor of *Sourate* to supply them with the means of living, and with money and carts to enable them to proceed to the capital. The attack upon *Sourate* had also covered their misdeeds, in disposing, for their own benefit, of the civet, and many of the slaves.

left a character which has never since been equalled or approached by any of his countrymen. The distracted state of the neighbouring countries presented openings by which an inferior leader might have profited; but it required a genius like his to avail himself as he did of the mistakes of Aurangzíb by kindling a zeal for religion and, through that, a national spirit among the Marattas. It was by these feelings that his government was upheld after it passed into feeble hands, and was kept together, in spite of numerous internal disorders, until it had established its supremacy over the greater part of India.'

[1] This took place in January 1664. The Dutch account of the sack, as given by Valentyn, confirms Bernier's narrative very remarkably.

My excellent friend Monsieur *Adrican,*[1] chief of the Dutch factory, gave *Murat,* the Armenian, a letter of introduction to me, which he delivered into my hands at *Dehli,* without being aware that I had been his guest at *Moka.*[2] It was an agreeable surprise to meet thus unexpectedly, after an absence of five or six years. I embraced my old friend with affection, and promised to render him all the service in my power. Yet, though my acquaintance among the courtiers was pretty extensive, I found it difficult to be useful to these empty-handed ambassadors. The mule's skin, and the ox's horn, wherein was kept arrack, or brandy extracted from raw sugar, of which they are excessively fond, constituted the whole of their presents; and the contempt which the absence of valuable presents would alone inspire was increased by their miserable appearance. They were seen about the streets without a *paleky,* clad in true *Bedouin* fashion, and followed by seven or eight bare-footed and bare-headed slaves, who had no raiment but a nasty strip of cloth passed between their buttocks, and the half of a ragged sheet over the left shoulder, which was carried under the right arm, in the manner of a summer cloak. Nor had the ambassadors any other carriage than a hired and broken-down cart; and they were without any horse except one belonging to our Missionary Father, and one of mine that they sometimes borrowed, and which they nearly killed.

In vain did I for a long time exert myself in behalf of these despised personages; they were regarded as beggars, and could excite no interest. One day, however, when closeted with my Agah *Danechmend-kan,* who is minister for foreign affairs, I expatiated so successfully upon the grandeur of the Ethiopian Monarch, that *Aureng-Zebe* was induced to grant the ambassadors an audience, and to receive their letters. He presented both with a *Ser-apah,* or vest of brocade, a silken and embroidered girdle, and a

[1] See p. 127. [2] See p. 134.

turban of the same materials and workmanship; gave orders for their maintenance, and at an audience, when the Emperor gave them their *congé,* which soon took place, he invested each with another *Ser-apah*, and made them a present of six thousand *roupies,* equal at present to nearly three thousand crowns:[1] but this money was unequally divided, the *Mahometan* receiving four thousand *roupies,* and *Murat,* because a Christian, only two thousand.

Aureng-Zebe sent by them, as presents to their royal master, an extremely rich *Ser-apah;* two large cornets, or trumpets, of silver gilt; two silver kettle-drums;[2] a poniard studded with rubies; and gold and silver *roupies* to the amount of about twenty thousand francs: hoping, as he kindly expressed it, that this last gift would be peculiarly acceptable, and considered a rarity; the King of *Ethiopia* not having any coined money in his country.

The *Mogol* was well aware that not one of these *roupies* would be taken out of *Hindoustan,* and that the ambassadors would employ them in the purchase of useful commodities. It turned out just as he foresaw. They bought spices, fine cotton cloths, for shirts for the King and Queen, and for the King's only legitimate son, who is to succeed to the throne, *alachas* or silken stuffs striped, some with gold and some with silver, for vests and summer trousers; English broadcloths, scarlet and green, for a couple of *abbs,*[3] or Arabian vests, for their King; and lastly, quantities of cloth less fine in their texture for several ladies of the *seraglio* and their children. All

[1] This agrees with Tavernier's value (2s. 3d.) of the rupee. See also p. 135, footnote [2], and p. 200, note.

[2] *Karanás,* trumpets with a bend, somewhat of the type of a cornet, and *nakárahs,* drums in shape like the modern kettle-drum, but beaten resting on the ground by a man who either stands or squats behind them, according to their size, were part of the insignia of Mogul royalty.

[3] *Abah,* the well-known short coat or vest. English broadcloths were highly esteemed at the Mogul court, and the early travellers make frequent mention of them. Also see the chapter (32 of the first book) in the *Aín-i-Akbarí,* in which details of their price are given.

these goods they were privileged, as ambassadors, to export without payment of duty.

Notwithstanding all my friendship for *Murat*, there were three reasons why I almost repented of having exercised my influence in his behalf. The first was, that after he had promised to sell me his boy for fifty *roupies*, he sent word he would not part with the boy for less than three hundred. I felt almost disposed to give him his price, that I might have it in my power to say a father had sold me his own child. The lad was remarkably well made, and his skin of the clearest black; the nose was not flat, nor the lips thick, as is commonly the case among the *Ethiopians*. I was certainly angry with *Murat* for having violated his engagement.

I had, in the next place, ascertained that my friend, as well as his *Mahometan* companion, had solemnly promised *Aureng-Zebe* to urge his King to permit the repair of a mosque in *Ethiopia*, which had been in ruins since the time of the Portuguese. The *Mogol* gave the ambassadors two thousand *roupies* in anticipation of this service. The mosque, erected as the mausoleum of a certain *Cheik*, or *derviche*, who left *Meca* for the purpose of propagating Mahometanism in *Ethiopia*, and had made great progress there, was demolished by the Portuguese, when they entered the country with troops from *Goa*, as allies of the lawful sovereign, who had embraced Christianity, and been driven from the throne by a *Mahometan* prince.

My third objection to *Murat's* conduct arose from the part he took in entreating *Aureng-Zebe*, in the name of the Ethiopian King, to send the latter an *Alcoran* and eight other books, with the names of which I am familiar, and which are of the first repute among the treatises written in defence of the *Mahometan* creed.

There seemed to me something extremely base and wicked in these proceedings, on the part of a Christian ambassador, acting in the name of a Christian King. They afforded but too satisfactory a confirmation of the account I had received at *Moka* of the low ebb to which Christianity is reduced in the kingdom of *Ethiopia*. Indeed, all the measures of its government, and the character of the people, savour strongly of *Mahometanism*, and it cannot be doubted that the number, even of nominal Christians, has been on the decline since the death of the King, who was maintained on the throne by the troops from *Goa*. Soon after that event, the *Portuguese*, in consequence of the intrigues of the Queen-mother, were either killed or driven out of the country. The Jesuit Patriarch, whom his countrymen had brought from *Goa*, was compelled to fly for his life.

During the stay of the ambassadors at *Dehli*, my *Agah*, ever eager in search of knowledge, invited them frequently to his house. He asked many questions concerning the condition of their country and the nature of its government; but his principal object was to obtain information respecting the source of the *Nile*, which they call *Abbabile*,[1] and concerning which they talked to us as so well ascertained that no one need question it. *Murat* and a *Mogol*, who travelled with him from *Ethiopia*, have visited the source, and the particulars given by them both are substantially the same as those I had learnt at *Moka*. They informed us that the *Nile* has its origin in the country of the *Agans*, rising from two bubbling and contiguous springs, which form a small lake of about thirty or forty paces in length; that the water running out of this lake is already a pretty considerable river; which continues, however, to increase in size by reason of the small tributary streams which, from here and there, flow into it. They added that the river went on in a circuitous course, forming, as it were, a large island; and that after falling from several steep rocks, it entered into a great lake wherein are several fertile islands, quantities of crocodiles, and, what would be much more remarkable, if true,

[1] 'The Father of waters.'

numbers of sea-calves which have no other means of ejecting their excrement than the mouth. This lake is in the country of *Dumbia,* three short stages from *Gonder,* and four or five from the source of the *Nile.* The river, they continued, when it leaves the great lake, is much augmented by the numerous rivers and torrents which fall into that lake, especially in the rainy season; which is as periodical as in the *Indies,* commencing towards the end of July. This, by the way, is an important consideration, and accounts for the overflowing of the *Nile.* From the lake just mentioned the river runs by *Sonnar,* the capital city of the King of *Fungi* (tributary to the King of *Ethiopia*), and continues its course until it reaches the plains of *Mesra* or *Egypt.*

The two ambassadors dilated more copiously than was agreeable either to my *Agah* or myself on the magnificence of their sovereign, and the strength of his army; but their travelling companion, the *Mogol,* never joined in these panegyrics, and told us, during their absence, that he had twice seen this army in the field, commanded by the King in person, and that it is impossible to conceive troops more wretched and worse disciplined.

The *Mogol* gave us a great deal of information about *Ethiopia,* the whole of which is noted in my journal, and may one day be given to the public. At present I shall content myself with noticing three or four facts related by *Murat,* and which, considering that they occurred in a Christian land, will be deemed sufficiently remarkable.

He said that in *Ethiopia* there are few men who do not keep several wives; nor was he ashamed to confess that he himself had two, besides the wife to whom he was legally married, and who resided in *Aleppo.* The *Ethiopian* women, he observed, do not hide themselves as in the *Indies* among the *Mahometans* and even the *Gentiles*; and nothing is more common than to see females of the lower ranks, whether single or married, bond or free, mingled together, day and night, in the same apartment; the whole of them perfectly unacquainted with those feelings of jealousy so prevalent in other nations. The women, or wives of grandees, are at no great pains to conceal their attachment to any handsome cavalier, whose house they enter without fear or scruple.

If I had visited *Ethiopia,* I should have been compelled, they told me, to marry. A few years ago, a wife was forced upon an *European,* a Padry,[1] who passed for a Greek physician; and it is curious enough that the woman whom they obliged him to wed was the same that he designed for one of his sons.

A man, eighty years of age, having presented to the King four-and-twenty sons, all of mature age, and able to carry arms, was asked by His Majesty whether those were the only children he could exhibit? The old gentleman answered that they were indeed the whole of the male part of his family, but that he was also the father of a few daughters. 'Out then from my presence, thou old calf!' was the King's rejoinder. 'I am astonished that instead of feeling shame, thou presumest to appear before me. Is there a lack of women in my dominions that thou, a man well stricken in years, canst boast of only two dozen sons?' The *Ethiopian* King himself has at least eighty children, who are met running about indiscriminately in all parts [qui couroient pêle mêle] of the *seraglio.* They are known by a round stick varnished, resembling a small mace, which the King had made for them, and which they carry about with great delight, as a sceptre, to distinguish them from those who are the children of certain slaves or other people of the *seraglio.*

Aureng-Zebe sent twice for the ambassadors. He hoped, like my *Agah,* to increase his stock of knowledge by their conversation; but his chief anxiety was to be made acquainted with the state of *Mahometanism* in their country. He expressed a desire to see the mule's skin, which somehow or other remained afterward in the

[1] A Roman priest, see p. 323, footnote [1].

fortress, in possession of the officers; much to my disappointment, for it was promised me in return for my good services, and I had counted upon one day presenting it to one of our *Virtuosi* in *Europe*. I strongly recommended the ambassadors to show the great horn to the King, as well as the skin: but this might have subjected them to the very embarrassing question: how it happened, that in the ransacking of *Sourate* they lost the civet, and yet retained the horn?

The *Ethiopian* embassy was still in *Dehli*, when *Aureng-Zebe* assembled his privy-council, together with the learned men of his court, for the purpose of selecting a suitable preceptor for his third son, *Sultan Ekbar*,[1] whom he designs for his successor. He evinced upon this occasion the utmost solicitude that this young Prince should receive such an education as might justify the hope of his becoming a great man. No person can be more alive than *Aureng-Zebe* to the necessity of storing the minds of Princes, destined to rule nations, with useful knowledge. As they surpass others in power and elevation, so ought they, he says, to be pre-eminent in wisdom and virtue. He is very sensible that the cause of the misery which afflicts the empires of *Asia*, of their misrule, and consequent decay, should be sought, and will be found, in the deficient and pernicious mode of instructing the children of their Kings. Intrusted from infancy to the care of women and eunuchs, slaves from *Russia, Circassia, Mingrelia, Gurgistan*,[2] or *Ethiopia*, whose minds are debased by the very nature of their occupation; servile and mean to superiors, proud and oppressive to dependants;—these Princes, when called to the throne, leave the walls of the *Seraglio* quite ignorant of the duties imposed upon them by their new situation. They appear on the stage of life, as if they came from another world, or emerged,

[1] Muhammad Akbar, his fourth son, but the third then alive, revolted against his father, and took refuge in Persia, where he died.

[2] Georgia.

for the first time, from a subterraneous cavern, astonished, like simpletons, at all around them. Either, like children, they are credulous in everything, and in dread of everything; or, with the obstinacy and heedlessness of folly, they are deaf to every sage counsel, and rash in every stupid enterprise. According to their natural temperament, or the first ideas impressed upon their minds, such Princes, on succeeding to a crown, affect to be dignified and grave, though it be easy to discern that gravity and dignity form no part of their character, that the appearance of those qualities is the effect of some ill-studied lesson, and that they are in fact only other names for savageness and vanity; or else they affect a childish politeness in their demeanour, childish because unnatural and constrained. Who, that is conversant with the history of *Asia*, can deny the faithfulness of this delineation? Have not her Sovereigns been blindly and brutally cruel,—cruel without judgment or mercy? Have they not been addicted to the mean and gross vice of drunkenness, and abandoned to an excessive and shameless luxury; ruining their bodily health, and impairing their understanding, in the society of concubines? Or, instead of attending to the concerns of the kingdom, have not their days been consumed in the pleasures of the chase? A pack of dogs will engage their thoughts and affection, although indifferent to the sufferings of so many poor people who, compelled to follow the unfeeling Monarch in the pursuit of game, are left to die of hunger, heat, cold, and fatigue. In a word, the Kings of *Asia* are constantly living in the indulgence of monstrous vices, those vices varying, indeed, as I said before, according to their natural propensities, or to the ideas early instilled into their minds. It is indeed a rare exception when the *Sovereign* is not profoundly ignorant of the domestic and political condition of his empire. The reins of government are often committed to the hands of some *Vizier*, who, that he many reign lord absolute, with security and without contradiction, considers it an essential part of his plan to encourage his master in all his low pursuits, and divert him from every avenue of knowledge. If the sceptre be not firmly grasped by the first minister, then the country is governed by the King's mother, originally a wretched slave, and by a set of eunuchs, persons who possess no enlarged and liberal views of policy, and who employ their time in barbarous intrigues; banishing, imprisoning, and strangling each other, and frequently the *Grandees* and the *Vizier* himself. Indeed, under their disgraceful domination, no man of any property is sure of his life for a single day.

When *Aureng-Zebe* had received the different embassies I have described, news at length reached the court that one from *Persia* had arrived on the frontier. The *Persian Omrahs,* and others of that nation, in the service of the *Mogol,* spread a report that affairs of the utmost moment brought the ambassador to *Hindoustan.* Intelligent persons, however, gave no credence to the rumour: the period for great events was gone by, and it was clear that the *Persians* had no other reason for saying their countryman was intrusted with an important commission, than a vain and overweening desire to exalt their nation. It was also pretended by the same individuals, that the *Omrah* appointed to meet the ambassador on the frontier, and to provide for his honourable treatment during his journey to the capital, was strictly enjoined to spare no pains to discover the principal object of the embassy. He was instructed, they said, to prepare, by degrees, the haughty *Persian* for the ceremony of the *Salam,* which was to be represented, as well as that of delivering all letters through the medium of a third person, as a custom that has invariably obtained from time immemorial. It is sufficiently evident, however, from what we witnessed, that these were idle tales, and that *Aureng-Zebe* is raised much above the necessity of recurring to such expedients.

On his entry into the capital, the ambassador was received with every demonstration of respect. The *Bazars* through which he passed were all newly decorated, and the cavalry lining both sides of the way extended beyond a league. Many *Omrahs*, accompanied with instruments of music, attended the procession, and a salute of artillery was fired upon his entering the gate of the fortress, or royal palace. *Aureng-Zebe* welcomed him with the greatest politeness; manifested no displeasure at his making the *salam* in the *Persian* manner, and unhesitatingly received from his hands the letters of which he was the bearer; raising them, in token of peculiar respect, nearly to the crown of his head. An eunuch having assisted him to unseal the letters, the King perused the contents with a serious and solemn countenance, and then commanded that the ambassador should be clad, in his presence, with a vest of brocade, a turban, and a silken sash, embroidered with gold and silver, called a *ser-apah*, as I have before explained. This part of the ceremony over, the *Persian* was informed that the moment was come for the display of his presents; which consisted of five-and-twenty horses, as beautiful as I ever beheld, with housings of embroidered brocade; twenty highly bred camels, that might have been mistakee for small elephants, such was their size and strength; a considerable number of cases[1] containing excellent rose-water, and another sort of distilled water called *Beidmichk*,[2] a cordial held in the highest estimation and very scarce; five or six carpets of extraordinary size and beauty; a few pieces of brocade extremely rich, wrought in small flowers,

[1] *Caisses* in the original. Rosewater and *bedmushk* were enclosed in glass bottles, holding about 2½ gallons each, called in Persian *karábas* (hence the English word *carboy*) covered with wicker-work. *Case* is therefore a better rendering than *box*, as used by former translators of these *Travels*.

[2] *Bédmushk*, a cordial still highly esteemed in Northern India, distilled from a species of willow, *béd* in Persian.

in so fine and delicate a style that I doubt if anything so elegant was ever seen in *Europe*; four *Damascus* cutlasses, and the same number of poniards, the whole covered with precious stones; and lastly, five or six sets of horse-furniture, which were particularly admired. The last were indeed very handsome and of superior richness; ornamented with superb embroidery and with small pearls, and very beautiful turquoises, of the old rock.[1]

It was remarked that *Aureng-Zebe* seemed unusually pleased with this splendid present; he examined every item minutely, noticed its elegance and rarity, and frequently extolled the munificence of the King of *Persia*. He assigned the ambassador a place among the principal *Omrahs*; and after speaking about his long and fatiguing journey, and several times expressing his desire to see him every day, he dismissed him.

He remained at *Dehli* four or five months, living sumptuously at *Aureng-Zebe's* expense, and partaking of

[1] In the original, 'de la vieille Roche,' which means that they were, so to speak, of the finest water. This phrase was used to denote those precious stones in general that exhibited more or less perfect crystalline forms, being considered more developed than those with amorphous forms. Tavernier's (*Travels*, vol. ii. pp. 103, 104) description of the turquoise is valuable, as elucidating Bernier's account of the presents. 'Turquoise is only found in PERSIA, and is obtained in two mines. The one, which is called "the old rock," is three days' journey from MESHED towards the north-west and near to a large town called NICHABOURG [Nishapur in Meshed is the classic locality for the true turquoise]; the other, which is called "the new," is five days' journey from it. Those of the new are of an inferior blue, tending to white, and are little esteemed, and one may purchase as many of them as he likes at small cost. But for many years the King of PERSIA has prohibited mining in the "old rock" for any one but himself, because having no gold workers in the country besides those who work in thread, who are ignorant of the art of enamelling on gold, and without knowledge of design and engraving, he uses for the decoration of swords, daggers, and other work, these turquoises of the old rock instead of enamel, which are cut and arranged in *patterns* like flowers and other figures which the (jewellers) make. This catches the eye and passes as a laborious work. It is wanting in design.'

the hospitality of the chief *Omrahs,* who invited him by turns to grand entertainments. When permitted to return to his country, the King again invested him with a rich *Ser-apah,* and put him in possession of other valuable gifts, reserving the presents intended for the *Persian* Monarch for the embassy that he determined to send, and which was very soon appointed.

Notwithstanding the strong and unequivocal marks of respect conferred by *Aureng-Zebe* upon this last ambassador, the Persians at the court of *Dehli* insinuated that the King of *Persia,* in his letters, reproached him keenly with the death of *Dara,* and the incarceration of *Chah-Jehan,* representing such actions as unworthy a brother, a son, and a faithful *Musulman.* He also, they said, reproved him for having assumed the name of *Alem-Guire,* or Conqueror of the World, and for causing it to be inscribed on the coins of *Hindoustan.* They went so far as to affirm that these words formed part of the letters: 'Since then thou art this *Alem-Guire,* Besm-Illah, in the name of God, I send thee a sword and horses. Let us now, therefore, confront each other.' This would indeed have been throwing down the gauntlet. I give the story as I received it: to contradict it is not in my power; easy as any person finds it in this court to come to the knowledge of every secret, provided he be acquainted with the language, possess good friends, and be as profuse of money as myself for the sake of gratifying his curiosity. But I cannot be easily persuaded that the King of *Persia* made use of the language ascribed to him: it would savour too much of empty bluster and menace, though it cannot be denied that the *Persians* are apt to assume a lofty tone when they wish to impress an idea of their power and influence. I rather incline to the opinion entertained by the best informed, that *Persia* is not in a condition to act aggressively against such an empire as *Hindoustan.* She will have enough to do to retain *Kan-daher,* in the direction of *Hindoustan,* and preserve the integrity of her frontier towards *Turkey*. The wealth and strength of that nation are accurately estimated. Her throne is not always filled by a *Chah-Abas*,[1] a Sovereign intrepid, enlightened, and politic; capable of turning every occurrence to his benefit, and of accomplishing great designs with small means. If her government meditate any enterprise against *Hindoustan*, and be animated, as is given out, by these sentiments of regard for *Chah-Jehan* and the *Musulman* faith, who can explain why, during the late civil wars, which lasted so long in *Hindoustan*, she remained a quiet and apparently an unconcerned spectator of the scene? She was unmoved by the entreaties of *Dara*, of *Chah-Jehan*, of *Sultan Sujah*, and perhaps of the Governor of *Caboul*; although she might, with a comparatively small army, and at an inconsiderable expense, have gained possession of the fairest part of *Hindoustan*, from the kingdom of *Caboul* to the banks of the *Indus*, and even beyond that river; thus constituting herself the arbitress of every dispute.

The King of *Persia's* letters, however, either contained some offensive expressions, or *Aureng-Zebe* took umbrage

1 Sháh 'Abbas I., surnamed the Great, who ascended the throne in 1588, and died in 1629. 'He was the first who made Isfahán the capital of Persia, was brave and active, and enlarged the boundaries of his dominions. He took conjointly with the English forces, in 1622, the island of Ormus, which had been in the possession of the Portuguese for 122 years.'—*Beale*. I have been told by learned natives of India that the Indian exclamation, Shahbash (Persian *Sháh-básh*), meaning, 'Well done!' 'Bravo!' 'REX FIAS,' takes its origin from the name of this Persian monarch, or as Ovington, in his *Voyage to Suratt in the Year* 1689 (London, 1696), p. 169, so quaintly puts it, 'The mighty Deeds and renown'd Exploits of *Schah Abbas*, the *Persian* Emperor, have likewise imprinted Eternal Characters of Fame and Honour upon his Name, which is now by vulgar use made the signification of any thing extraordinary or Miraculous; so that when any thing surpassing Excellent, or wonderful, is either done or spoken, the *Indians* presently say of it, *Schah-Abbas!*' Compare Horace,

> . . . At pueri ludentes, *Rex eris*, aiunt
> Si recte facies.
>
> 1 *Epist.* i. 59, 60.

at the conduct or language of the ambassador; because the King complained, two or three days after the embassy had quitted *Dehli,* that the horses presented in the name of the *Persian* Monarch had been hamstrung by order of the ambassador. He commanded, therefore, that he should be intercepted on the frontier, and deprived of all the *Indian* slaves he was taking away. It is certain that the number of these slaves was most unreasonable; he had purchased them extremely cheap on account of the famine, and it is also said that his servants had stolen a great many children.

Aureng-Zebe, during the stay of this embassy at *Dehli,* was careful to demean himself with strict propriety; unlike his father, *Chah-Jehan,* who, upon a similar occasion, either provoked the anger of the ambassador of the celebrated *Chah-Abas,* by an ill-timed haughtiness, or excited his contempt by an unbecoming familiarity.

A *Persian,* who wishes to indulge in any satirical merriment at the expense of the *Indians,* relates a few such anecdotes as the following.

When *Chah-Jehan* had made several fruitless attempts to subdue the arrogance of the ambassador, whom no arguments or caresses could induce to salute the *Great Mogol* according to the *Indian* mode, he devised this artifice to gain his end. He commanded that the grand entrance of the court leading to the *Am-Kas,* where he intended to receive the ambassador, should be closed, and the wicket only left open; a wicket so low that a man could not pass through without stooping, and holding down the head as is customary in doing reverence *à l'Indien.* *Chah-Jehan* hoped by this expedient to have it in his power to say that the ambassador, in approaching the royal presence, bowed the head even nearer to the ground than is usual in his court; but the proud and quick-sighted *Persian,* penetrating into the *Mogol's* design, entered the wicket with his back turned toward the

King. *Chah-Jehan*, vexed to see himself overcome by the ambassador's stratagem, said indignantly, '*Eh-bed-bakt* (Ah, wretch !)[1] didst thou imagine thou wast entering a stable of asses like thyself?' 'I did imagine it,' was the answer. 'Who, on going through such a door, can believe he is visiting any but asses?'

Another story is this:—*Chah-Jehan*, displeased with some rude and coarse answer made by the *Persian* ambassador, was provoked to say, '*Eh-bed-bakt* ! has then *Chah-Abas* no gentleman in his court that he sends me such a fool?' 'O, yes ! the court of my Sovereign abounds with men far more polite and accomplished than I am; but he adapts the Ambassador to the King.'

One day, *Chah-Jehan* having invited the ambassador to dine in his presence, and seeking, as usual, an occasion to discompose and vex him; while the *Persian* was busily employed in picking a great many bones, the King said coolly, '*Eh Eltchy-Gy* (Well, My Lord Ambassador), what shall the dogs eat?' '*Kichery*,' was the prompt answer; a favourite dish with *Chah-Jehan*, which he was then indulging in,—*Kichery* being a mess of vegetables, the general food of the common people.[2]

The *Mogol* inquiring what he thought of his new *Dehli*, then building, as compared to *Ispahan*; he answered aloud,

[1] Ill-conditioned or ill-bred fellow, literally.

[2] The dish 'kedgeree,' formerly a favourite dish in Anglo-Indian families, but now going somewhat out of fashion. The word is derived from the Hindoo *khichri*, a mess of rice cooked with ghee and dāl (*Cajanus Indicus*, Spreng.) and flavoured with a little spice, stewed onions, and the like. Ovington, *op. cit.*, p. 310, has the following pleasant description of this dish :—'*Kitcherie* is another Dish very common among them, made of *Dol*, that is, a small round Pea and Rice boiled together, and is very strengthening, tho' not very savoury. Of this the *European* Sailers feed in these parts once or twice a Week, and are forc'd at those times to a Pagan Abstinence from Flesh, which creates in them a perfect Dislike and utter Detestation to those *Bannian* Days, as they commonly call them.' Bannian is a rendering of the word *Banyan*, a Hindoo trader, *Bunya* being the familiar name among Anglo-Indians in Upper India for a grain-dealer.

and with an oath, '*Billah! billah!*[1] *Ispahan* cannot be compared to the dust of your *Dehli:*' which reply the King took as a high encomium upon his favourite city, though the ambassador intended it in sportive derision, the dust being intolerable in *Dehli.*

Lastly, the Persians gave out that their countryman, being pressed by *Chah-Jehan* to tell him candidly how he estimated the relative power of the Kings of *Hindoustan* and *Persia,* observed that he likened the Kings of the *Indies* to a full moon fifteen or sixteen days old, and those of *Persia* to a young moon of two or three days. This ingenious answer was at first very flattering to the *Great Mogol's* pride, but became a source of deep mortification when he had rightly interpreted the ambassador's meaning; which was, that the kingdom of *Hindoustan* is now on the decline, and that of *Persia* advancing, like the crescent moon, in splendour and magnitude.

Such are the witticisms so much vaunted by the Persians in the *Indies,* and which they seem never tired of repeating. For my part, I think a dignified gravity and respectful demeanour would better become an ambassador than the assumption of a supercilious and unbending carriage, or the indulgence of a taunting and sarcastic spirit. Even if he possessed no higher principle to regulate his conduct, it is surprising that *Chah-Abas's* ambassador was not constrained by common considerations of prudence; and how much he had to fear from the resentment of a despot, whom he foolishly and unnecessarily provoked, was seen by the danger he narrowly

[1] Colloquial for *Bi-'lláhi* equivalent to 'By God.' This word forms part of the expression so constantly on the lips of Moslems, *La haula wa lá quwwata illá bi-'lláhi 'l 'alíyi 'l-'azím,* 'There is no power and strength but in God, the High One, the Great.' The Prophet Muhammad ordered his followers to recite it very frequently, 'for these words are one of the treasures of Paradise. For there is no escape from God but with God. And God will open for the reciter thereof seventy doors of escape from evil, the least of which is poverty.' —*Mishkátu'l-Masabíh,* Book x. ch. ii.

escaped. *Chah-Jehan's* malignity grew so violent and undisguised that he addressed him only in the most opprobrious terms, and gave secret orders that when the ambassador entered a long and narrow street in the fortress, leading to the Hall of Assembly, an elephant *must*,[1] and in a very dangerous state, should be let loose upon him. A less active and courageous man must have been killed; but the Persian was so nimble in jumping out of his *paleky*, and, together with his attendants, so prompt and dexterous in shooting arrows into the elephant's trunk, that the animal was scared away.

It was at the time of the return of the Persian ambassadors that *Aureng-Zebe* accorded that memorable reception to his quondam teacher *Mullah Salé*.[2] It is an uncommonly good story. This old man had resided for several years near *Kaboul* in retirement on an estate presented to him by *Chah-Jehan*, when he was made acquainted with the termination of the civil war, and the complete success which had attended the ambitious projects of his former pupil. He hastened to *Dehli*, sanguine in his expectation of being immediately advanced to the rank of *Omrah*; and there was no person of influence, up to *Rauchenara-Begum*, whom he did not engage in his favour. Three months elapsed before *Aureng-Zebe* would even appear to know that such a person was within the purlieus of the court; but weary at last with seeing him constantly in his presence, the

[1] Thus I render 'qui étoient en humeur.'

[2] Mulla Shah, a native of Badakshán, was the *Murshid* or spiritual guide of Dárá Shikoh, and was highly respected by Sháh Jahán. He died in Kashmir about the year 1660. He may be the *Mullah Salé* of Bernier's narrative, and have taught Aurangzeb also. I possess a very fine contemporary portrait, by a Delhi artist, of Dárá's teacher, who was one of the disciples of Mián Sháh Mír of Lahore, after whom part of the area now occupied as the Cantonment of Mián Mír (Meean Meer), near the capital of the Punjab, was named; the Mián Sáhib's tomb, with a mosque and land attached, being included within its boundaries.

Mogol commanded that he should come to him in a secluded apartment, where only Hakim-ul-Mouluk *Danech-mend-kan*, and three or four other grandees, who pride themselves upon their accomplishments, were present. He then spoke in nearly the following words. I say nearly, because it is impossible to transcribe so long a discourse precisely in the terms in which it was delivered. Had I been present myself, instead of my *Agah*, from whom I received a report of the speech, I could not hope to be verbally correct. There can be no doubt, however, that what *Aureng-Zebe* said was substantially as follows:—'Pray what is your pleasure with me, *Mullah-gy*—[Mulla-Jí] Monsieur the Doctor?—Do you pretend that I ought to exalt you to the first honours of the State? Let us then examine your title to any mark of distinction. I do not deny you would possess such a title if you had filled my young mind with suitable instruction. Show me a well-educated youth, and I will say that it is doubtful who has the stronger claim to his gratitude, his father or his tutor. But what was the knowledge I derived under your tuition? You taught me that the whole of *Franguistan* [1] was no more than some inconsiderable island, of which the most powerful Monarch was formerly the King of *Portugal*, then he of *Holland*, and afterward the King of *England*. In regard to the other sovereigns of *Franguistan*, such as the King of *France* [2] and him of *Andalusia*, you told me they resembled our petty Rajas, and that the potentates of *Hindoustan* eclipsed the glory of all other kings; that they alone were *Humayons*, *Ekbars*, *Jehan-Guyres*, or *Chah-Jehans*; the Happy, the Great, the Conquerors of the World, and the Kings of the World; and that *Persia*, *Usbec*, *Kachguer*, *Tartary*, and *Catay*, [3]

[1] Europe. [2] França, in the original.

[3] Here *Catay* (Cathay) is used as if the name of a distinct country other than China, whereas Khitai was the name for *all* China, from *Khitan*, the dynasty that ruled its Northern Provinces for 200 years. See p. 427, footnote [4].

Pegu, Siam, China and *Matchine,*[1] trembled at the name of the Kings of the *Indies.* Admirable geographer! deeply read historian! Was it not incumbent upon my preceptor to make me acquainted with the distinguishing features of every nation of the earth; its resources and strength; its mode of warfare, its manners, religion, form of government, and wherein its interests principally consist; and, by a regular course of historical reading, to render me familiar with the origin of States, their progress and decline; the events, accidents, or errors, owing to which such great changes and mighty revolutions, have been effected? Far from having imparted to me a profound and comprehensive knowledge of the history of mankind, scarcely did I learn from you the names of my ancestors, the renowned founders of this empire. You kept me in total ignorance of their lives, of the events which preceded, and the extraordinary talents that enabled them to achieve, their extensive conquests. A familiarity with the languages of surrounding nations may be indispensable in a King; but you would teach me to read and write *Arabic*; doubtless conceiving that you placed me under an everlasting obligation for sacrificing so large a portion of time to the study of a language wherein no one can hope to become proficient without ten or twelve years of close application. Forgetting how many important subjects ought to be embraced in the education of a Prince, you acted as if it were chiefly necessary that he should possess great skill in grammar, and such knowledge as belongs to a Doctor of law; and thus did you waste the precious hours of my youth

[1] In the original 'Tchine et Matchine,' a rotund way of saying China. In olden times the more intelligent Muhammadans used the term *Máchín* (a contraction for *Máháchina*, 'Great China,' the ancient Hindoo name for China) when talking of the Chinese Empire. Chín Máchín, which occurs in many of the narratives of the old travellers, is, as Colonel Yule has pointed out (*Cathay and the Way Thither*), an instance of the use of a double assonant name, to express a single idea, a favourite Oriental practice; just as in Herodotus we have Crophi and Mophi, Thyni and Bithyni, and at the present day Thurn and Taxis.

in the dry, unprofitable, and never-ending task of learning words!'[1]

Such was the language in which *Aureng-Zebe* expressed his resentment; but some of the learned men, either wishing to flatter the Monarch and add energy to his speech, or actuated by jealousy of the *Mullah*, affirm that the King's reproof did not end here, but that, when he had spoken

[1] It is but seldom that an Emperor takes the world into his confidence, and proclaims aloud what he thinks of his schools and schoolmasters. Just this is what the Emperor Aurangzeb did in the speech reported by Bernier, and the utterances on the same subject made by the German Emperor at Berlin on the 4th December 1890, bear such a remarkable resemblance to those of the Mogul Emperor, constituting an interesting historical parallel, that it seems advisable to reproduce them here, from the report in *The Times* of the 5th December:—

BERLIN, *Dec.* 4.

To-day a special conference on educational reform in the higher schools and gymnasia of Prussia was opened, under the presidency of the Emperor himself in the Ministry of Public Worship. Herr von Gossler, the Minister, began by thanking the Emperor for the warm personal interest he displayed in such matters. The time had now come, he said, to consider whether Prussian schools were to continue on the same old classical path, or whether they should not now rather endeavour to adapt themselves to the spirit and practice and needs of modern life. All the learned professions were now filled to excess, and Germany was producing too many University men, for whom there seemed to be but scanty prospects in the growing struggle for existence.

The Emperor then followed with a long and well-thought-out address. He tabled a series of queries on the subject under discussion, and proceeded to argue at elaborate length that the gymnasia or higher public schools no longer answered the requirements of the nation and the necessities of the time. They produced crammed youths, but not men, wasting on Latin and classical lore the time which should be devoted to the German language and to German history—a knowledge which was of infinitely more value to a German than all the chronicles of antiquity. . . . He had himself sat on the various forms of a Gymnasium at Cassel, and knew all about their ways and methods, and the sooner these were mended the better it would be for every one. . . . Since 1870, the philologists, as *beati possidentes*, had been sitting enthroned in the gymnasia, devoting their attention more to increasing the book-learning of their pupils than to forming their characters and training them for the needs of practical life. This evil had gone so far that it could go no further. Much more stress was laid on cramming young men's heads with knowledge than on teaching them how to apply it.

He had frequently been described as a fanatical foe of the gymnasial system, but that was not so. He had an open eye to its crying defects, and of these perhaps the chief was its preposterous partiality for classical education. The basis of instruction in all such schools ought to be German, and their principal aim should be to turn out young Germans instead of youthful Greeks and Romans. They must courageously break with the mediæval and monkish habit of mumbling away at much Latin and a little Greek, and take to the German language as the basis of all their scholastic

for a short time on indifferent subjects, he resumed his discourse in this strain: 'Were you not aware that it is during the period of infancy, when the memory is commonly so retentive, that the mind may receive a thousand wise precepts, and be easily furnished with such valuable instruction as will elevate it with lofty conceptions, and render the individual capable of glorious deeds? Can we

studies. The same remark applied to history as to language. Preference should be given in all schools to German history, geographical and legendary. It was only when they knew all the ins and outs of their own house that they could afford to moon about in a museum. When he was at school the Great Elector was to him but a nebulous personage. As for the Seven Years' War, it lay outside the region of study altogether, and history ended with the French Revolution at the close of the last century. The Liberation wars, however, which were extremely important for the young, were not included, and it was only, thank God, by means of supplementary and very interesting lectures which he received from his private tutor, Dr. Hinzpeter, whom he was now glad to see before him, that he got to know anything at all about modern history. . . . His Majesty then proceeded to discuss what ought to be the relations between the classical and commercial education, even in the schools which had hitherto been devoted to one of these directions only, his remarks being listened to with the keenest interest, and regarded as a masterpiece of practical wisdom.—*Our Own Correspondent.*

The German Emperor's speech has naturally given rise to a great deal of discussion, and the opinions expressed by Scholars and Educational Experts all over Europe, as to his views on 'classical education differ very widely. As it will be my constant aim throughout *Constable's Oriental Miscellany* to impartially present both sides of any question on which there may be a difference of opinion among competent authorities, I now quote the opinions on the educational utility of the study of Greek, recently enunciated by a great Englishman (using this word in its widest signification), and one of the leading Educational Experts of the day.

On the 14th March 1891, Mr. Gladstone paid a visit to Eton, the school where, seventy years ago, he had been taught, and delivered a Saturday lecture to the boys now being educated there, on *The character and attributes of the goddess Artemis in the Iliad and Odyssey.*

At the conclusion of his lecture, Mr. Gladstone said (I quote from the report in *The Times* newspaper of the 16th March):—

When I was a boy I cared nothing at all about the Homeric gods. I did not enter into the subject until thirty or forty years afterwards, when, in a conversation with Dr. Pusey, who, like me, had been an Eton boy, he told me, having more sense and brains than I had, that he took the deepest interest and had the greatest curiosity about these Homeric gods. They are of the greatest interest, and you cannot really study the text of Homer without gathering fruits; and the more you study him the more you will be astonished at the multitude of lessons and the completeness of the picture which he gives you. There is a perfect encyclopædia of human character

repeat our prayers, or acquire a knowledge of law and of the sciences, only through the medium of *Arabic*? May not our devotions be offered up as acceptably, and solid information communicated as easily, in our mother tongue? You gave my father, *Chah-Jehan*, to understand that you instructed me in philosophy; and, indeed, I have a perfect remembrance of your having, during several years, harassed

and human experience in the poems of Homer, more complete in every detail than is elsewhere furnished to us of Achaian life. (The right hon. gentleman resumed his seat amid hearty cheers.)

The Rev. Dr. Hornby, the Provost of Eton College, then proposed a hearty vote of thanks to Mr. Gladstone for his kindness in coming among them, and the great honour he did to the present generation of his old school in thus addressing them in a lecture so full of matter for careful after-study, and also stated that it would be difficult, at once, to single out any special points for notice. The Provost then ended by saying:—

But I am sure we shall all have felt great pleasure and some comfort in knowing that a man so able, so laborious, so full of ideas as Mr. Gladstone, should still return in his leisure time to the old subjects which formed so large a portion of his school days. I hope I shall not be abusing his kindness by attributing to him an excessive educational conservatism which perhaps he would repudiate. But I cannot but think he intends to encourage us to hold fast to the old studies, as to which, though they cannot keep the exclusive place which was formerly theirs, we have Mr. Gladstone's authority for saying that there is no better foundation for the highest culture than the old Greek literature, and that in that literature there is nothing more healthy, more noble and splendid, than the early part of it, which Mr. Gladstone has done so much to illustrate and recommend to this generation. I propose a vote of thanks to Mr. Gladstone, to which, I am sure, you will accord a hearty reception. (Cheers.)

Mr. Gladstone, in thanking his audience for the manner in which he had been received, and telling them how refreshing it was for an old man to come back among young ones, standing more or less in the position he once stood himself, concluded with these words:—

'I have mentioned a subject which is of such profound and vast extent, that were I to allow myself to be tempted, it would lead me to make another infliction upon you, but I answer the Provost by saying he has understood me rightly. I have not the smallest desire that all boys should be put upon the bed of Procrustes, and either contracted or expanded to the possession of Greek and Latin, especially of Greek, culture. I may say it would probably be a case of expansion rather than contraction. But the object is to find right and sufficient openings for all characters and all capacities. But this, Mr. Provost, I say with confidence, that my conviction and experience of life leads me to the belief that if the purpose of education be to fit the human mind for the efficient performance of the greatest functions, the ancient culture, and, above all, Greek culture, is by far the best, the highest, the most lasting, and the most elastic instrument that can possibly be applied to it.' (Loud cheers.)

my brain with idle and foolish propositions, the solution of which yield no satisfaction to the mind—propositions that seldom enter into the business of life; wild and extravagant reveries conceived with great labour, and forgotten as soon as conceived; whose only effect is to fatigue and ruin the intellect, and to render a man headstrong and insufferable [*their Philosophy abounds with even more absurd and obscure notions than our own.*—Bernier]. O yes, you caused me to devote the most valuable years of my life to your favourite hypotheses, or systems, and when I left you, I could boast of no greater attainment in the sciences than the use of many obscure and uncouth terms, calculated to discourage, confound, and appal a youth of the most masculine understanding [*their Philosophers employ even more gibberish than ours do.*—Bernier]: terms invented to cover the vanity and ignorance of pretenders to philosophy; of men who, like yourself, would impose the belief that they transcend others of their species in wisdom, and that their dark and ambiguous jargon conceals many profound mysteries known only to themselves. If you had taught me that philosophy which adapts the mind to reason, and will not suffer it to rest satisfied with anything short of the most solid arguments; if you had inculcated lessons which elevate the soul and fortify it against the assaults of fortune, tending to produce that enviable equanimity which is neither insolently elated by prosperity, nor basely depressed by adversity; if you had made me acquainted with the nature of man; accustomed me always to refer to first principles, and given me a sublime and adequate conception of the universe, and of the order and regular motion of its parts;—if such, I say, had been the nature of the philosophy imbibed under your tuition, I should be more indebted to you than *Alexander* was to *Aristotle*, and should consider it my duty to bestow a very different reward on you than *Aristotle* received from that Prince. Answer me, sycophant, ought you not to have instructed me on one point at least, so essential to be known by a King; namely, on the reciprocal duties between the sovereign and his subjects? Ought you not also to have foreseen that I might, at some future period, be compelled to contend with my brothers, sword in hand, for the crown, and for my very existence? Such, as you must well know, has been the fate of the children of almost every King of *Hindoustan*. Did you ever instruct me in the art of war, how to besiege a town, or draw up an army in battle array? Happy for me that I consulted wiser heads than thine on these subjects! Go! withdraw to thy village. Henceforth let no person know either who thou art, or what is become of thee.'

At that time a slight disturbance arose against the astrologers, which I did not find unpleasing. The majority of *Asiatics* are so infatuated in favour of being guided by the signs of the heavens,[1] that, according to their phraseology, no circumstance can happen below, which is not written above. In every enterprise they consult their astrologers. When two armies have completed every preparation for battle, no consideration can induce the generals to commence the engagement until the *Sahet*[2] be performed; that is, until the propitious moment for attack be ascertained. In like manner no commanding officer is nominated, no marriage takes place, and no journey is undertaken, without consulting Monsieur the Astrologer. Their advice is considered absolutely necessary even on the most trifling occasions; as the proposed purchase of a slave, or the first wearing of new clothes. This silly superstition is so general an annoyance, and attended with such important and disagreeable consequences, that I am astonished it has continued so long: the astrologer is necessarily made acquainted with

[1] In the original *Astrologie Judiciaire*.

[2] More correctly *saiët*, from the Arabic *sa'id*, fortunate, propitious. See p. 244.

every transaction public and private, with every project common and extraordinary.

Now it happened that the *King's* principal astrologer fell into the water and was drowned. This melancholy accident caused a great sensation at court, and proved injurious to the reputation of these professors in divination. The man who had thus lost his life always performed the *Sahet* for the *King* and the *Omrahs*; and the people naturally wondered that an astrologer of such extensive experience, and who had for many years predicted happy incidents for others, should have been incapable of foreseeing the sad catastrophe by which he was himself overwhelmed. It was insinuated that in *Franguistan,* where the sciences flourish, professors in astrology are considered little better than cheats and jugglers, that it is there much doubted whether the science be founded on good and solid principles, and whether it be not used by designing men as a means of gaining access to the great, of making them feel their dependence, and their absolute need of these pretended soothsayers.

The astrologers were much displeased with these and similar observations, and particularly with the following anecdote, which was universally known and repeated:—*Chah-Abas,* the great King of *Persia,* having given orders that a small piece of ground within the seraglio should be prepared for a garden, the master-gardener intended to plant there several fruit-trees on a given day; but the astrologer, assuming an air of vast consequence, declared that unless the time of planting were regulated by the *Sahet,* it was impossible that the trees should thrive. *Chah-Abas* having acquiesced in the propriety of the remark, the astrologer took his instruments; turned over the pages of his books, made his calculations and concluded that, by reason of this or that conjunction of the planets, it was necessary to plant the trees before the expiration of another hour. The gardener, who thought of nothing less than an appeal to the stars, was absent when this wise determination was formed; but persons were soon procured to accomplish the work: holes were dug, and all the trees put into the ground, the King placing them himself, that it might be said they were all planted by the hand of *Chah-Abas.* The gardener, returning at his usual hour in the afternoon, was greatly surprised to see his labour anticipated; but observing that the trees were not ranged according to the order he had originally designed—that an apricot, for example, was placed in the soil intended for an apple-tree, and a pear-tree in that prepared for an almond—he pulled up the premature plantation, and laid down the trees for that night on the ground, covering the roots with earth. In an instant the astrologer was apprised of the gardener's proceedings, and he was equally expeditious in complaining to *Chah-Abas,* who, on his part, sent immediately for the culprit. 'How is it,' cried the Monarch indignantly, 'that you have presumed to tear up trees planted by my own hands; trees put into the ground after the solemn performance of the *Sahet?* We cannot now hope to repair the mischief. The stars had marked the hour for planting, and no fruit can henceforth grow in the garden.' The honest rustic had taken liberal potations of *Schiras* wine, and looking askance at the astrologer, observed after an oath or two, '*Billah, Billah,* an admirable *Sahet* certainly! thou augur of evil! Trees planted under thy direction at noon, are in the evening torn up by the roots!' *Chah-Abas,* hearing this unexpected piece of satirical drollery, laughed heartily, turned his back upon the astrologer, and walked away in silence.

I shall mention two other circumstances, although they happened during the reign of *Chah-Jehan.* The narration will be useful in showing that the barbarous and ancient custom obtains in this country, of the King's constituting himself sole heir of the property of those who die in his service.

Neik-nam-Kan was one of the most distinguished *Omrahs*

at court, and during forty or fifty years while he held important offices had amassed an immense treasure. This lord always viewed with disgust the odious and tyrannical custom above mentioned, a custom in consequence of which the widows of so many great *Omrahs* are plunged suddenly into a state of wretchedness and destitution, compelled to solicit the Monarch for a scanty pittance, while their sons are driven to the necessity of enlisting as private soldiers under the command of some *Omrah*. Finding his end approaching, the old man secretly distributed the whole of his treasure among distressed widows and poor cavaliers, and afterwards filled the coffers with old iron, bones, worn-out shoes, and tattered clothes. When he had securely closed and sealed them, he observed that those coffers contained property belonging exclusively to *Chah-Jehan*. On the death of *Neik-nam-Kan*, they were conveyed to the King, who happened to be sitting in durbar, and who, inflamed with eager cupidity, commanded them to be instantly opened in the presence of all his *Omrahs*. His disappointment and vexation may easily be conceived; he started abruptly from his seat and hurried from the hall.

The second is but the record of the ready wit of a woman. Some years after the death of a wealthy *banyane*,[1] or Gentile merchant, who had always been employed in the King's service, and, like the generality of his countrymen, had been a notorious usurer, the son became clamorous for a certain portion of the money. The widow refusing to comply with the young man's request, on account of his profligacy and extravagance, he had the baseness and folly to make *Chah-Jehan* acquainted with the real amount of the property left by his father, about two hundred thousand *crowns*. The *Mogol* immediately

[1] In Bernier's time *Banyan* was the name generally applied by foreigners too Hindo traders generally. It is now, at least in Bengal, the name for a native broker attached to a house of business. See p. 152, footnote [2].

summoned the old lady, and, in presence of the assembled *Omrahs*, commanded her to send him immediately one hundred thousand *roupies*, and to put her son in possession of fifty thousand. Having issued this peremptory injunction, he ordered the attendants to turn the widow out of the hall.

Although surprised by so sudden a request, and somewhat offended at being rudely forced from the chamber without an opportunity of assigning the reasons of her conduct, yet this courageous woman did not lose her presence of mind; she struggled with the servants, exclaiming that she had something further to divulge to the King. 'Let us hear what she has to say,' cried *Chah-Jehan*. '*Hazret-Salamet!* (Heaven preserve your Majesty!) It is not perhaps without some reason that my son claims the property of his father; he is our son, and consequently our heir. But I would humbly inquire what kinship there may have been between your Majesty and my deceased husband to warrant the demand of one hundred thousand *roupies*?' *Chah-Jehan* was so well pleased with this short and artless harangue, and so amused with the idea of a *banyane*, or Gentile tradesman, having been related to the Sovereign of the *Indies*, that he burst into a fit of laughter, and commanded that the widow should be left in the undisturbed enjoyment of the money of her deceased husband.

I shall not now relate all the more important events which took place, from the conclusion of the war in or about the year 1660, to the period of my departure, more than six years afterwards. I doubt not that the account would very much promote the object I had in view in recording some of them: namely, an acquaintance with the manners and genius of the *Mogols* and *Indians*, and I may, therefore, notice the whole of those events in another place. At present, however, I shall confine my narration to a few important circumstances which regard personages with whom my readers have become familiar; beginning with *Chah-Jehan*.

Although *Aureng-Zebe* kept his father closely confined in the fortress of *Agra* and neglected no precaution to prevent his escape, yet the deposed monarch was otherwise treated with indulgence and respect. He was permitted to occupy his former apartments, and to enjoy the society of *Begum-Saheb* and the whole of his female establishment, including the singing and dancing women, cooks, and others. In these respects no request was ever denied him; and as the old man became wondrously devout, certain *Mullahs* were allowed to enter his apartment and read the *Koran*. He possessed also the privilege of sending for all kinds of animals, horses of state, hawks of different kinds, and tame antelopes, which last were made to fight before him. Indeed, *Aureng-Zebe's* behaviour was throughout kind and respectful, and he paid attention to his aged parent in every possible way. He loaded him with presents, consulted him as an oracle, and the frequent letters of the son to the father were expressive of duty and submission. By these means *Chah-Jehan's* anger and haughtiness were at length subdued, insomuch that he frequently wrote to *Aureng-Zebe* on political affairs, sent *Dara's* daughter to him, and begged his acceptance of some of those precious stones, which he had threatened to grind to powder if again importuned to resign them.[1] He even granted to his rebellious son the paternal pardon and benediction which he had often with vehement importunity in vain solicited.[2]

It should not be inferred from what I have said, that *Chah-Jehan* was always soothed with compliant submission.

[1] See p. 127.

[2] See Elliot's *History*, vol. vii. pp. 251, 252, for Kháfí Khán's account of these transactions. Kháfí Khán states that 'many letters passed between the Emperor Sháh Jahán and Aurangzeb full of complaints and reproaches on one side, and of irritating excuses on the other.' The historian gives three letters from Aurangzeb *in extenso*, the third being an answer to one written by Sháh Jahán to Aurangzeb, pardoning his offences and sending some jewels and clothes, belonging to Dárá Shikoh which had been left in his palace.

I was convinced by one of *Aureng-Zebe's* letters, that he could address his father with energy and decision, when provoked by the arrogant and authoritative tone sometimes assumed by the aged monarch. I obtained a sight of a portion of the letter, which ran in these words:—'It is your wish that I should adhere rigidly to the old custom, and declare myself heir to every person who dies in my service. We have been accustomed, as soon as an *Omrah* or a rich merchant has ceased to breathe, nay sometimes before the vital spark has fled, to place seals on his coffers, to imprison and beat the servants or officers of his household, until they made a full disclosure of the whole property, even of the most inconsiderable jewel. This practice is advantageous, no doubt; but can we deny its injustice and cruelty? and should we not be rightly served if every *Omrah* acted as *Neik-nam-Kan*, and if like the Hindoo[1] merchant's widow, every woman concealed her wealth?

'I wish to avoid your censure, and cannot endure that you should form a wrong estimate of my character. My elevation to the throne has not, as you imagine, filled me with insolence and pride. You know by more than forty years' experience, how burthensome an ornament a crown is, and with how sad and aching a heart a monarch retires from the public gaze. Our great ancestor *Ekbar*, anxious that his successors should exercise their power with mildness, discretion and wisdom, recommended to their serious attention in the excellent memoirs left behind him, a fine characteristic of *Mir-Timur*. He recounts that on the day on which *Bajazet*[2] was made prisoner, when he was brought into the presence of *Timur*, the latter, after attentively fixing his eyes upon the haughty captive,

[1] *Indou* in the original.

[2] The 'popular' and time-honoured form of the name of the Turkish Sultan Baiazíd I., taken prisoner by Timúr Lang on the 21st July 1402, then confined in an iron cage and carried about in this manner with the conqueror's camp, till he died on the 8th March 1403.

laughed in his face. *Bajazet,* much offended at this rudeness, told the conqueror not to exult too extravagantly in his good fortune; "It is *God,*" said he, "who exalts or debases Kings, and though you are victorious to-day, you may be in chains to-morrow." "I am very sensible," answered *Timur,* "of the vanity and mutability of earthly possessions, and Heaven forbid that I should insult a fallen enemy. My laughter proceeded not from any wish to wound thy feelings, *Bajazet*; it escaped involuntarily, while I was indulging a series of ideas suggested by the uncomeliness of both our persons. I looked at thy countenance, rendered unsightly by the loss of an eye; and then considering that I am myself a miserable cripple, was led into a train of reflections, which provoked me to laughter. What can there be within the circle of a crown," I asked, "which ought to inspire Kings with inordinate self-esteem, since Heaven bestows the bauble upon such ill-favoured mortals?"

'You seem to think, that I ought to devote less time and attention to measures which I conceive essential to the consolidation and security of the kingdom, and that it would better become me to devise and execute plans of aggrandisement. I am indeed far from denying that conquests ought to distinguish the reign of a great Monarch, and that I should disgrace the blood of the great *Timur,* our honoured progenitor, if I did not seek to extend the bounds of my present territories. At the same time, I cannot be justly reproached with inglorious inaction, and you cannot with truth assert that my armies are unprofitably employed in the *Decan* and in *Bengale.* I wish you to recollect that the greatest conquerors are not always the greatest Kings. The nations of the earth have often been subjugated by mere uncivilised barbarians, and the most extensive conquests have in a few short years crumbled to pieces. He is the truly great King who makes it the chief business of his life to govern his subjects with equity,' and so forth. *The remainder of this letter did not fall into my hands.*

SECONDLY. I shall now say a few words regarding the celebrated *Emir-Jemla*, recur to some of the incidents wherein he was concerned after the termination of the civil war, and mention the manner in which he closed his brilliant career.

In effecting the subjugation of *Bengale* that great man did not behave to *Sultan Sujah* with the cruelty and breach of faith practised by *Gion-Kan,* that infamous *Patan,* towards *Dara,* or by the *Raja* of *Serenaguer* towards *Soliman-Chekouh.* He obtained possession of the country like a skilful captain, and disdaining any unworthy stratagem to secure *Sujah's* person, contented himself with driving the discomfited Prince to the sea, and compelling him to leave the kingdom.[1] *Emir-Jemla* then sent an eunuch to *Aureng-Zebe* with a letter, supplicating the King to permit his family to repair to *Bengale* under the eunuch's care. 'The war is happily at an end,' he said, 'and as I am enfeebled and broken down by age, you will not, you surely cannot, refuse me the consolation of passing the remainder of my days with my wife and children.' But *Aureng-Zebe* penetrated at once into the design of this expert politician; he knew that if his son *Mahmet Emir-kan* were permitted to visit *Bengale*, the father, *Jemla,* would aspire to the independent sovereignty of that kingdom, if indeed such an acquisition would have satisfied the pretensions of that extraordinary man. He was intelligent, enterprising, brave, and wealthy; at the head of a victorious army; beloved and feared by his soldiers, and in possession of the finest province in *Hindoustan.* The transactions in which he had been engaged in *Golkonda* proved his impatient and daring spirit, and directly to refuse compliance with his request would unquestionably have been attended with danger. *Aureng-Zebe* acted upon this occasion with his wonted prudence and address. He sent to the Emir his wife and daughter, together with his son's children; created him

[1] See p. 109.

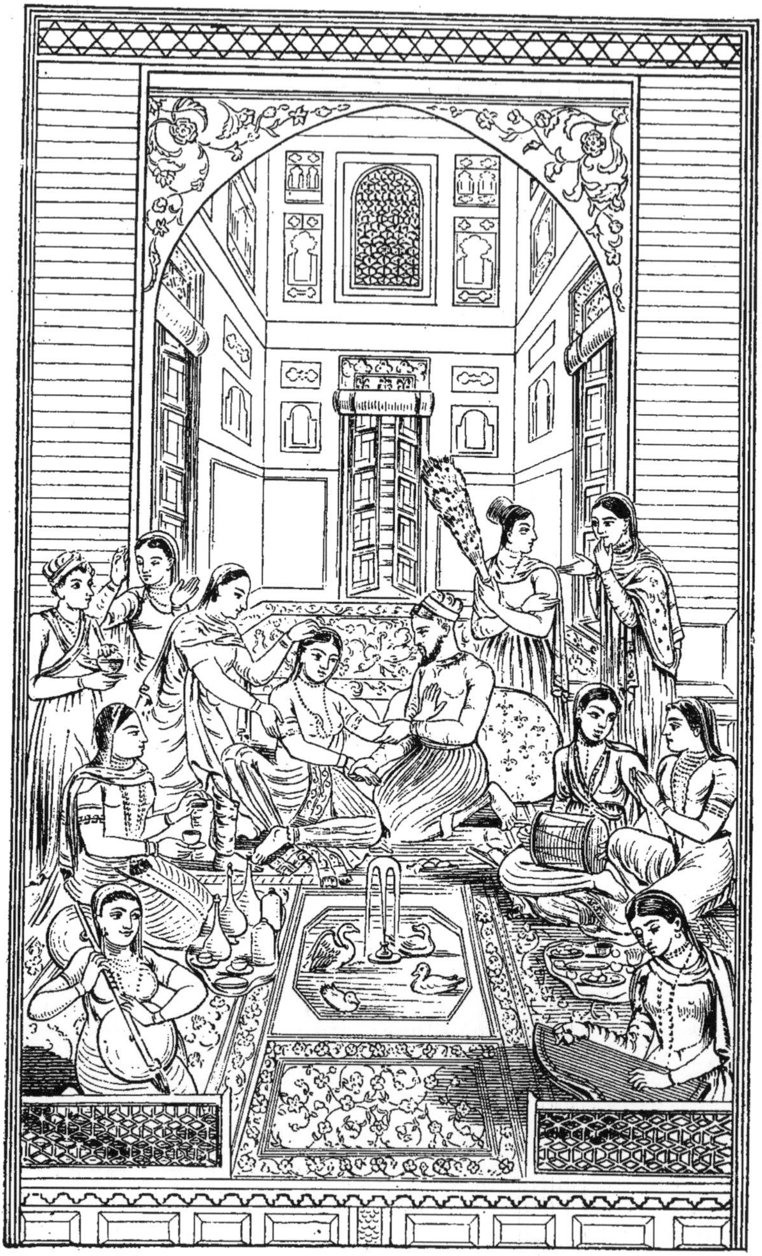

Fig. 7.—Amir Jumla amusing himself in his Zenana.

Mir-ul-omrah,[1] the highest rank that can be conferred by the King upon a favourite; and appointed the son, Mahmet Emir-Khan, *Grand Bakchis,*[2] or Grand Master of the Horse, the second or third situation in the state, which, however, confines the possessor to the court, rendering it difficult, if not impossible, for him to remain at a distance from the King's person. *Jemla* was also confirmed in the Government of *Bengale.*

Foiled in his object, the Emir felt that a second demand for his son could not be made without offending the King, and that his wisest course was to express gratitude for all these marks of royal favour.

Affairs had remained in this state nearly a twelvemonth, when the *Mogol* offered to *Jemla* the management of a war against the rich and powerful Raja of *Acham,*[3] whose territories lie north of *Daké,* on the Gulf of *Bengale. Aureng-Zebe* justly apprehended that an ambitious soldier could not long remain in a state of repose, and that, if disengaged from foreign war, he would seek occasion to excite internal commotions.

The Emir himself had been long meditating this enterprise, which he hoped would enable him to carry his arms to the confines of *China,* and secure to himself immortal fame. *Aureng-Zebe's* messenger found him perfectly prepared for the expedition. A powerful army was soon embarked at *Daké,*[4] on a river flowing from the dominions

[1] Amír-ul-Umará, the Amír of the Amírs, principal Amír.

[2] Mir Bakhshi, Commander-in-Chief; literally, principal paymaster (Bakhshi), as at that period commanding officers were at the same time paymasters, and collectors of the rents of the lands assigned to them for the payment of their contingents.

[3] Assam.

[4] Amír Jumla, in 1657, had made Dacca the capital of the Province of Bengal. This city is on the Buriganga River, formerly no doubt, as its name (*Old Ganges*) implies, the main stream of the Ganges. This river falls into the Megna, a branch of the Brahmaputra, the river referred to by Bernier. The expedition to conquer Assam started from Dacca in 1661.

about to be invaded, and Jemla and his troops ascended the stream in a north-east direction, until they reached a fortress named *Azo,* distant about one hundred leagues from *Daké,* which the Raja of *Acham* had wrested from a former Governor of *Bengale. Azo* was besieged and taken in less than a fortnight. The Emir then proceeded toward *Chamdara,* the key of the *Raja's* dominions, which he reached after a long march of eight-and-twenty days. Here a battle was fought to the *Raja's* disadvantage, who retired to *Guerguon,*[1] his capital city, forty leagues from *Chamdara*; but being closely and vigorously pressed by *Jemla,* he had not time to fortify himself in that place, and was therefore compelled to continue his retreat to the mountains of the kingdom of *Lassa. Chamdara* and *Guerguon* were given up to pillage. The latter contained an infinite booty for the captors. It is a large and well-built city, very commercial, and celebrated for the beauty of its women.

The progress of the invaders was checked by the rains which fell sooner than is customary, and which in this country are very heavy, inundating every spot of ground, with the exception of villages built on eminences. In the mean time, the *Raja* cleared the whole country, round the Emir's position, of cattle and every kind of provision, so that ere the rains ceased the army was reduced to great and urgent distress, notwithstanding the immense riches which it had accumulated. *Jemla* found it equally difficult to advance or to recede. The mountains in front presented impracticable barriers, while a retreat was prevented not only by the waters and deep mud, but also by the precaution taken by the *Raja* to break down the dike which forms the road to *Chamdara.* The *Emir,* therefore, was confined to his camp during the whole of the rainy season, and, on the return of dry weather, his men were so dispirited by their incessant fatigue and long privations, that he abandoned the idea of conquering

[1] Ghar-gánw of Kháfí Khán.

Acham. Under a less able commander, the army could not have hoped to reach *Bengale*: the want of provisions was severely felt; the mud, being still thick, greatly impeded the motions of the troops, and the *Raja* was active and indefatigable in pursuit; but *Jemla* conducted the movements of his army with his usual skill, and by his admirable retreat added greatly to his reputation. He returned laden with wealth.

The Emir, having improved the fortifications of *Azo*, left a strong garrison in that fortress, intending to renew, early in the following year, the invasion of *Acham*; but how far is it possible for the body, worn out by old age, to withstand the effects of fatigue? He, as well as others under his command, was not made of brass, and this illustrious man fell a victim to the dysentery which attacked the army soon after their arrival in *Bengale.*[1]

His death produced, as might be expected, a great sensation throughout the *Indies.* 'It is now,' observed many intelligent persons, 'that *Aureng-Zebe* is king of *Bengale.*' Though not insensible of his obligations of gratitude, the *Mogol* was perhaps not sorry to have lost a vicegerent whose power and mental resources had excited so much pain and uneasiness. 'You mourn,' he publicly said to *Mahmet Emir-kan,* 'you mourn the death of an affectionate parent, and I the loss of the most powerful and most dangerous of my friends.' He behaved, however, with the utmost kindness and liberality to *Mahmet*; assured the young man that in himself he should always find a second father; and instead of diminishing his pay, or seizing upon *Jemla's* treasures, *Aureng-Zebe* confirmed *Mahmet* in his office of *Bakchis,* increased his allowance by one thousand roupies per month, and constituted him sole heir to his father's property.

THIRDLY. I shall now bring before the notice of my

[1] He died on the 31st March 1663 at Khizarpúr in Kuch Behár.

readers *Aureng-Zebe's* uncle, *Chah-hestkan*,[1] who, as I have already said, contributed in an essential degree by his eloquence and intrigues to the exaltation of his nephew. He was appointed, as we have seen,[2] Governor of *Agra*, a short time before the battle of *Kadjoüé*, when *Aureng-Zebe* quitted the capital to meet *Sultan Sujah*. He was afterwards [3] nominated Governor of the *Decan*, and commander-in-chief of the forces in that province; and, upon *Emir-Jemla's* decease, was transferred to the government of *Bengale*,[4] appointed General of the army in that kingdom, and elevated to the rank of *Mir-ul-Omrah*, which had become vacant by the death of *Jemla*.

I owe it to his reputation to relate the important enterprise in which he was engaged, soon after his arrival in *Bengale*; an enterprise rendered the more interesting by the fact that it was never undertaken by his great predecessor, for reasons which remain unknown. The narrative will elucidate the past and present state of the kingdoms of *Bengale* and *Rakan*, which have hitherto been left in much obscurity, and will throw light on other circumstances which are deserving of attention.

To comprehend the nature of the expedition meditated by *Chah-hestkan*, and form a correct idea of the occurrences in the Gulf of *Bengale*, it should be mentioned that the Kingdom of *Rakan*, or *Mog*, has harboured during many years several *Portuguese* settlers, a great number of Christian slaves, or half-caste Portuguese, and other *Franks* collected from various parts of the world. That kingdom was the place of retreat for fugitives from *Goa*, *Ceylon*, *Cochin*, *Malacca*, and other settlements in the *Indies*, held formerly by the *Portuguese*; and no persons were better received than those who had deserted their monasteries, married two or three wives, or committed other great crimes. These people were Christians only in name; the lives led by them were most detestable, massacring or

[1] Shaista Khán, Amír-ul-Umará.

[2] See p. 66.

[3] In 1659.

[4] In 1666.

poisoning one another without compunction or remorse, and sometimes assassinating even their priests, who, to confess the truth, were too often no better than their murderers.

The King of *Rakan*, who lived in perpetual dread of the *Mogol*, kept these foreigners, as a species of advanced guard, for the protection of his frontier, permitting them to occupy a seaport called *Chatigon*,[1] and making them grants of land. As they were unawed and unrestrained by the government, it was not surprising that these renegades pursued no other trade than that of rapine and piracy. They scoured the neighbouring seas in light galleys, called *galleasses*, entered the numerous arms and branches of the *Ganges*, ravaged the islands of *Lower Bengale*, and, often penetrating forty or fifty leagues up the country, surprised and carried away the entire population of villages on market days, and at times when the inhabitants were assembled for the celebration of a marriage, or some other festival. The marauders made slaves of their unhappy captives, and burnt whatever could not be removed. It is owing to these repeated depredations that we see so many fine islands at the mouth of the *Ganges*, formerly thickly peopled, now entirely deserted by human beings, and become the desolate lairs of tigers and other wild beasts.[2]

Their treatment of the slaves thus obtained was most cruel; and they had the audacity to offer for sale, in the places which they had but recently ravaged, the aged people whom they could turn to no better account. It was usual to see young persons, who had saved themselves

[1] Chittagong, re-named in 1666 by the Moslems, *Islamabad*, commanding the mouth of the Megna, a port which played a very important part in the early history of European adventure in India.

[2] In Rennell's *Map of the Sunderbund and Baliagot Passages*, published in 1780, a note is entered across part of the territory referred to by Bernier: *Country depopulated by the Muggs*. Changes in the course of the Ganges had also much to do with the desertion of this tract of country.

by timely flight, endeavouring to-day to redeem the parent who had been made captive yesterday. Those who were not disabled by age the pirates either kept in their service, training them up to the love of robbery and practice of assassination, or sold to the *Portuguese* of *Goa, Ceylon, San Thomé,* and other places. Even the *Portuguese* of *Ogouli,*[1] in *Bengale,* purchased without scruple these wretched captives, and the horrid traffic was transacted in the vicinity of the island of *Galles,* near Cape *das Palmas.*[2] The pirates, by a mutual understanding, waited for the arrival of the *Portuguese,* who bought whole cargoes at a cheap rate; and it is lamentable to reflect that other Europeans, since the decline of the Portuguese power, have pursued the same flagitious commerce with these pirates, who boast, the infamous scoundrels, that they make more Christians in a twelvemonth than all the missionaries of the *Indies* do in ten years. A strange mode this of propagating our holy religion by the constant violation of its most sacred precepts, and by the open contempt and defiance of its most awful sanctions!

The *Portuguese* established themselves at *Ogouli* under the auspices of *Jehan-Guyre,* the grandfather of *Aureng-Zebe.* That Prince was free from all prejudice against Christians, and hoped to reap great benefit from their commerce. The new settlers also engaged to keep the Gulf of *Bengale* clear of pirates.

Chah-Jehan, a more rigid Mahometan than his father, visited the Portuguese at *Ogouli* with a terrible punishment. They provoked his displeasure by the encouragement afforded to the depredators of *Rakan,* and by their refusal to release the numerous slaves in their service, who had all of them been subjects of the *Mogol.* He first

[1] Húghlí, where the East India Company established a factory in 1640. Sháistá Khán's punitive expedition against the Arakan Rájá was undertaken in 1664-65.

[2] Now called Palmyras Point, the well-known headland on the Orissa coast.

exacted, by threats or persuasion, large sums of money from them, and when they refused to comply with his ultimate demands, he besieged and took possession of the town, and commanded that the whole population should be transferred as slaves to *Agra*.[1]

The misery of these people is unparalleled in the history of modern times: it nearly resembled the grievous captivity of *Babylon*; for even the children, priests, and monks shared the universal doom. The handsome women, as well married as single, became inmates of the *seraglio*; those of a more advanced age, or of inferior beauty, were distributed among the *Omrahs*; little children underwent the rite of circumcision, and were made pages; and the men of adult age, allured, for the most part, by fair promises, or terrified by the daily threat of throwing them under the feet of elephants, renounced the Christian faith. Some of the monks, however, remained faithful to their creed, and were conveyed to *Goa*, and other Portuguese settlements, by the kind exertions of the Jesuits and missionaries at *Agra*, who, notwithstanding all this calamity, continued in their dwelling, and were enabled to accomplish their benevolent purpose by the powerful aid of money, and the warm intercession of their friends.

Before the catastrophe at *Ogouli*, the missionaries had not escaped the resentment of *Chah-Jehan*: he ordered the large and handsome church at *Agra*, which, together with one at *Lahor*, had been erected during the reign of *Jehan-Guyre*, to be demolished. A high steeple stood upon this church, with a bell whose sound was heard in every part of the city.

Some time before the capture of *Ogouli*, the pirates

[1] This was in 1629-30, and other reasons than those given by Bernier led to the action taken by Sháh Jahán; such as the refusal of all aid to him, when in 1621, as Prince Khurram, he had revolted against his father, the Emperor Jahángír, and applied to the Portuguese at Húghlí for assistance in the shape of soldiers and munitions of war.

made a formal offer to the Viceroy of *Goa*, to deliver the whole kingdom of *Rakan* into his hands. *Bastian Consalve*[1] was then chief of the pirates, and so celebrated and powerful was he, that he married the King of *Rakan's* daughter. It is said that the Viceroy was too arrogant and envious to listen to this proposal, and felt unwilling that the King of *Portugal* should be indebted to a man of low origin for so important an acquisition. There was nothing, however, in the proposal to excite surprise; it was quite in keeping with the general conduct of the *Portuguese* in *Japan*, *Pegu*, *Ethiopia*, and other places. The decay of their power in the *Indies* is fairly ascribable to their misdeeds, and may be considered, as they candidly allow, a proof of the divine displeasure. Formerly their name was a tower of strength; all the *Indian* princes courted their friendship, and the *Portuguese* were distinguished for courage, generosity, zeal for religion, immensity of wealth, and the splendour of their exploits: but they were not then, like the *Portuguese* of the present day, addicted to every vice, and to every low and grovelling enjoyment.

The pirates, about the time of which I am speaking, made themselves masters of the island of *Sondiva*,[2] an

[1] Sebastian Gonzales Tibao, who had been a common sailor. According to Stewart (*History of Bengal*, Lond. 1813, p. 210), he married the Mugh's *sister* who had become a Christian, and this historian states that it was Anaporam, a brother of the King of Aracan, who, having been guilty of some misdemeanour when Governor of a province of that country, fled for refuge to Sundeep where he met Gonzales, whom he enlisted in his cause They invaded Aracan and were able to save the family of Anaporam and bring away a good deal of treasure. Anaporam then gave Gonzales a large sum of money and his sister in marriage, but shortly after that died, poisoned it is believed, and all his wealth fell into the hands of the pirate.

[2] Sundeep (Sandwíp), off the coast of Chittagong, at the mouth of the Meghna, and described by the Venetian traveller Cesare di Fedrici (*circa* 1565), as being one of the most fertile places in the country, and that such was the abundance of materials for shipbuilding in the neighbourhood that the Sultan of Constantinople found it cheaper to have his vessels built there than elsewhere.

advantageous post, commanding part of the mouth of the *Ganges*. On this spot, the notorious *Fra-Joan*, an *Augustine* monk, reigned, as a petty Sovereign, during many years; having contrived, God knows how, to rid himself of the Governor of the island.

These also are the identical freebooters who, as we have seen,[1] repaired in their *galleasses* to *Daka*, for the purpose of conveying *Sultan Sujah* to *Rakan*. They found means of opening some of his chests, and robbing him of many precious stones, which were offered secretly for sale in *Rakan* and disposed of for a mere trifle. The diamonds all got into the hands of the *Dutch* and others, who easily persuaded the ignorant thieves that the stones were soft, and that they would pay for them only according to their hardness.

I have said enough to give an idea of the trouble, vexation and expense, to which the *Mogol* was for many years exposed by the unjust and violent proceedings of the pirates established in *Rakan*. He had always been under the necessity of guarding the inlets of the kingdom of *Bengale*, of keeping large bodies of troops and a fleet of *galleasses* on the alert. All these precautions, however, did not prevent the ravaging of his territories; the pirates were become so bold and skilful that with four or five *galleasses* they would attack, and generally capture or destroy, fourteen or fifteen of the *Mogol's* galleys.

The deliverance of *Bengale* from the cruel and incessant devastations of these barbarians was the immediate object of the expedition contemplated by *Chah-hestkan* upon his appointment to the government of that Kingdom. But he had an ulterior design,—that of attacking the King of *Rakan*, and punishing him for his cruelty to *Sultan Sujah* and his family, *Aureng-Zebe* having determined to avenge the murder of those illustrious personages, and, by a signal example, to teach his neighbours, that Princes of the

[1] See pp. 58, 109.

Blood Royal, in all situations and under all circumstances, must be treated with humanity and reverence.[1]

Chah-hestkan has accomplished his first plan with consummate address. It was scarcely practicable to march an army from *Bengale* into the kingdom of *Rakan* owing to the great number of rivers and channels that intersect the frontiers; and the naval superiority of the pirates rendered it still more difficult to transport an invading force by sea. It therefore occurred to him to apply to the *Dutch* for their co-operation, and with this view he sent an envoy to *Batavia,* with power to negotiate, on certain conditions, with the general commandant of that colony, for the joint occupation of the kingdom of *Rakan*; in the same manner as *Chah-Abas* treated formerly with the English in regard to *Ormuz.*[2]

The Governor of *Batavia* was easily persuaded to enter into a scheme that offered an opportunity of still further depressing the *Portuguese* influence in the *Indies*, and from the success of which the Dutch company would derive important advantages. He despatched two ships of war to *Bengale* for the purpose of facilitating the conveyance of the *Mogol's* troops to *Chatigon*; but *Chah-hest*, in the meantime, had collected a large number of *galleasses* and other vessels of considerable tonnage, and threatened to overwhelm the pirates in irremediable ruin if they did not immediately submit to the *Mogol's* authority. '*Aureng-Zebe* is fixed in the resolution,' said he to them, 'of chastising the King of *Rakan,* and a Dutch fleet, too powerful to be resisted, is near at hand. If you are wise, your personal safety and the care of your families will now engross all your attention; you will quit the service of the

[1] See p. 106, footnote [1].

[2] The officers of Sháh Abbas, who looked with a covetous and resentful eye on the Portuguese occupation of Ormus, invoked the aid of the English Council at Surat, and on the 18th February 1622 the combined Persian and English forces laid siege to Ormus. The Portuguese, after a gallant resistance of five weeks, surrendered on the 1st May.

King of *Rakan*, and enter into that of *Aureng-Zebe*. In *Bengale* you shall have as much land allotted as you may deem necessary, and your pay shall be double that which you at present receive.'

The pirates about this period had assassinated one of the King of *Rakan's* principal officers, and it is not known whether they were more struck with terror by the punishment awaiting them for that crime, or moved by the promises and threats contained in *Chah-hest's* communication. Certain it is, however, that these unworthy *Portuguese* were one day seized with so strange a panic as to embark in forty or fifty *galleasses* and sail over to *Bengale*, and they adopted this measure with so much precipitation that they had scarcely time to take their families and valuable effects on board.

Chah-hestkan received these extraordinary visitors with open arms; gave them large sums of money; provided the women and children with excellent accommodation in the town of *Daka*,[1] and after he had thus gained their confidence, the pirates evinced an eagerness to act in concert with the *Mogol's* troops, shared in the attack and capture of *Sondiva*, which island had fallen into the hands of the King of *Rakan*, and accompanied the Indian army from *Sondiva* to *Chatigon*. Meanwhile the two Dutch ships of war made their appearance, and *Chah-hestkan* having thanked the commanders for their kind intentions, informed them that he had now no need of their services. I saw these vessels in *Bengale*, and was in company with the officers, who considered the Indian's thanks a poor compensation for the violation of his engagements. In regard to the Portuguese, *Chah-hest* treats them, not perhaps as he ought, but certainly as they deserve. He has drawn them from *Chatigon*; they and their families are in

[1] According to Stewart (*History of Bengal*, p. 299) at a place about twelve miles below Dacca, hence called *Feringhee Bazar*, where some of their descendants yet reside. The *Fringybazar* of Rennell's *Plan of the Environs of the City of Dacca*, published in 1780.

his power; an occasion for their services no longer exists; he considers it, therefore, quite unnecessary to fulfil a single promise. He suffers month after month to elapse without giving them any pay; declaring that they are traitors, in whom it is folly to confide; wretches who have basely betrayed the Prince whose salt they had eaten for many years.

In this manner has *Chah-hestkan* extinguished the power of these scoundrels in *Chatigon*;[1] who, as I have already said, had depopulated and ruined the whole of *Lower Bengale.* Time will show whether his enterprise against the King of *Rakan* will be crowned with similar success.[2]

FOURTHLY. Respecting the two sons of *Aureng-Zebe*, Sultan *Mahmoud* and Sultan *Mazum*, the former is still confined in *Goüaleor*; but, if we are to believe the general report, without being made to drink *poust*, the beverage usually given to the inmates of that fortress.[3] *Sultan Mazum* appears to comport himself with his accustomed prudence and moderation, although the transaction I am about to relate is perhaps an evidence that this Prince during the dangerous illness of his father had carried on secret intrigues, or that the displeasure of *Aureng-Zebe* was excited by some other circumstance unknown to the public. It may be, however, that, without any reference to the past, the King was only anxious to obtain authentic proof both of his son's obedience and of his courage, when he commanded him, in a full assembly of *Omrahs*, to kill a lion which had descended from the mountains and was then laying waste the surrounding country. The Grand Master of the Hunt[4] ventured to hope that *Sultan Mazum*

[1] For an exceedingly valuable account of the Feringhees of Chittagong and their present state, and what has led to their decline, see pp. 57, 89 of *The Calcutta Review*, vol. liii., 1871.

[2] The enterprise was eventually successful, and the Province of Aracan annexed to the Kingdom of Bengal.

[3] See p. 106, footnote [1].

[4] The *Mír Shikár*, an important officer at the Mogul Court, corresponding to our Chief Ranger of old days.

might be permitted to avail himself of those capacious nets which are ordinarily made use of in so perilous a chase.[1] 'He shall attack the lion without nets,' sternly replied the King. 'When I was Prince I thought not of such precautions.' An order given in so decisive a tone could not be disobeyed. The Prince declined not the fearful undertaking; he encountered and overcame the tremendous beast with the loss of only two or three men; some horses were mangled, and the wounded lion bounded on the head of the *Sultan's* elephant. Since this strange adventure, *Aureng-Zebe* has behaved to his son with the utmost affection, and has even raised him to the government of the *Decan.* It must be owned, however, that *Sultan Mazum* is so limited in authority[2] and circumscribed in pecuniary means, that he cannot occasion much uneasiness to his father.

FIFTHLY. The next personage I would recall to the recollection of my readers is *Mohabet-Kan*, the governor of *Kaboul.*[3] He was induced at length to resign the government of that province, and *Aureng-Zebe* generously refused to punish him, declaring that the life of such a soldier was invaluable, and that he deserved commendation for his fidelity to his benefactor *Chah-Jehan.* The King even nominated him Governor of *Guzarate* instead of *Jessomseingue,* who was sent to the seat of war in the *Decan.* It is true that a few costly presents may have disposed the *Mogol's* mind in *Mohabet's* favour; for besides what he gave to *Rauchenara-Begum,* he sent the King fifteen or sixteen thousand golden roupies and a considerable number of Persian horses and camels.[4]

The mention of *Kaboul* reminds me of the adjacent kingdom of *Kandahar,* at present tributary to *Persia*; to

[1] See pp. 378, 379.

[2] It was in 1663 that Prince Muhammad Muazzam was made Súbadar of the Deccan and given the command of the troops then being employed against Sivají.

[3] See p. 70.

[4] Mahábat Khán was the second son of the celebrated Mahábat Khán of Jahángír's reign, and is said to have died in 1674 when on his way from Kabul to the presence.

the subject of which I ought to devote one or two pages. Much ignorance prevails concerning that country, as well as on the political feeling which it creates between the governments of *Persia* and *Hindoustan.* The name of the capital is also *Kandahar,* which is the stronghold of this rich and fine kingdom. The desire of possessing the capital has been, for some ages, the cause of sanguinary wars between the *Mogols* and *Persians.* The great *Ekbar* wrested it from the latter,[1] and kept it during the remainder of his reign. *Chah-Abas* the celebrated King of Persia took the city from *Jehan-Guyre,*[2] the son of *Ekbar;* and the treachery of the Governor *Aly Merdankan*[3] delivered it into the hands of *Chah-Jehan* the son of *Jehan-Guyre. Aly Merdan* immediately placed himself under the protection of his new Sovereign; he had many enemies in his own country, and was too prudent to obey the summons of the Persian monarch, who called upon him to give an account of his government. *Kandahar* was again besieged and captured by the son of *Chah-Abas,*[4] and afterwards twice unsuccessfully attacked by *Chah-Jehan.* The first failure was owing to the bad conduct or the perfidy of the Persian *omrahs* in the *Great Mogol's* service, the most powerful noblemen of his court, and strongly attached to their native country. They betrayed a shameful lukewarmness during the siege, refusing to follow the Raja *Roup* who had already planted his stan-

[1] In 1594.

[2] In 1622.

[3] Ali Mardán Khán, a Persian, was governor of Kandahar under Sháh Safí, who it is said, treated him so cruelly that in despair he gave up the place in 1637 to Sháh Jahán, who received him well at Delhi, to which city he had returned. Ali Mardán Khán was a most capable administrator, and was at various times made Governor of Kabul and Kashmir, and has left behind him various monuments of his skill as a constructor of public works, notably the canal at Delhi, which bears his name, and, somewhat remodelled, is in use at the present day. It is said that he introduced the *Chenar* (Oriental plane-tree) into Kashmir. He died in 1657 when on his way to Kashmir, and was buried at Lahore.

[4] In 1648.

dard on the wall nearest to the mountain. *Aureng-Zebe's* jealousy occasioned the second failure. He would not storm the breach which the cannon of the Franks—*English, Portuguese, Germans,* and *French*—had rendered sufficiently practicable; because the enterprise had originated with *Dara,* at that time with his father in the city of *Kaboul,* and he felt unwilling that his brother should have the credit of so valuable an acquisition. *Chah-Jehan,* a few years before the late troubles, seemed on the point of besieging *Kandahar* for the third time, but was deterred from the enterprise by *Emir-Jemla,* who, as we have stated, advised the *Mogol* to send his army to the *Decan.*[1] *Aly Merdankan* seconded with great earnestness the *Emir's* arguments, and addressed the King in these extraordinary words:—'Your Majesty will never succeed in taking *Kandahar,* unless her gates be opened by such a traitor as myself; or unless you determine to exclude all *Persians* from the besieging army, and issue a proclamation promising entire freedom to the bazaars; that is, exempting them from the payment of any duty on provisions brought for the use of the army.' A few years ago *Aureng-Zebe,* following the example of his predecessors, made preparations for the attack of this celebrated city, being offended with the letter written by the King of *Persia,* or with the ungracious reception experienced by his ambassador, *Tarbiet-Kan,*[2] at the Persian court: but he heard of the King's death, and abandoned the project; feeling reluctant, as he pretended, to act with hostility against a child just seated on the throne; although *Chah-Soliman,* who succeeded his father, cannot, I think, be less than five-and-twenty years of age.

Sixthly. I would now say something of the warm par-

[1] See pp. 22, 23.

[2] Probably Shafí-ulláh Khán, who had had conferred upon him the title of Tarbiat Khán Barlas, a native of Persia who came to India and served under Sháh Jahán and Aurengzeb. He died at Jaunpur, of which he was Governor, in 1685.

tisans of *Aureng-Zebe,* most of whom have been promoted to situations of high trust and dignity. His uncle *Chah-hestkan* was made, as we have mentioned, Governor and Commander-in-chief in the *Decan*; subsequently this nobleman was made governor of *Bengale. Mir-Kan* obtained the government of *Kaboul*; *Kalilullah-Kan* that of *Lahor*; *Mir-baba,* of *Elabas*; *Laskerkan,* of *Patna*; and the son[1] of that *Allah-verdi-Kan,* whose advice cost *Sultan Sujah* the battle of *Kadjoüe,* was made Governor of *Scimdy. Fazelkan,* whose counsels and address had been essentially useful to *Aureng-Zebe,* was invested with the office of *Kane-saman,*[2] or Grand Chamberlain of the royal household. *Danechmend-Kan* was appointed Governor of *Dehli*; and, in consideration of his studious habits, and the time which he necessarily devotes to the affairs of the foreign department, he is exempted from the ancient ceremony of repairing twice a day to the assembly, for the purpose of saluting the King; the omission of which, subjects other *Omrahs* to a pecuniary penalty. To *Dianet-Kan, Aureng-Zebe* has intrusted the government of *Kachmire,* a little kingdom nearly inaccessible, and considered the terrestrial paradise of the *Indies. Ekbar* became possessed of that delightful country by stratagem. It boasts of authentic histories, in its own vernacular tongue, containing an interesting account of a long succession of ancient kings; sometimes so powerful as to have reduced to subjection the whole of *Hindoustan,* as far as the island of *Ceylon.* Of these histories *Jehan-Guyre* caused an abridgment to be made in the Persian language; and of this I procured a copy.—It is proper to mention in this place that *Aureng-Zebe* cashiered *Nejabatkan,* who greatly distinguished himself in the battles of *Samonguer* and *Kadjoüé*; but he seems

[1] Jafar Khán, appointed Subadar of Allahabad, where he died in 1669 (*Beale*).

[2] Properly Khanṣaman, a Persian word meaning a house steward. Now applied, in Northern India, to the chief table-servant and purveyor in Anglo-Indian households.

to have brought that disgrace upon himself by continually dwelling upon the services he had rendered the King. As to those infamous individuals, *Gionkan* and *Nazer*, the well-deserved fate of the former has been recounted; but what subsequently became of *Nazer* is not ascertained.

In regard to *Jessomseingue* and *Jesseingue*, there is some obscurity which I shall endeavour to clear up. A revolt had taken place, headed by a *gentile* of *Visapour*, who made himself master of several important fortresses and one or two seaports belonging to the King of that country. The name of this bold adventurer is *Seva-Gi*, or Lord Seva.[1] He is vigilant, enterprising, and wholly regardless of personal safety. *Chah-hestkan*, when in the *Decan*, found in him an enemy more formidable than the King of *Visapour* at the head of his whole army and joined by those *Rajas* who usually unite with that prince for their common defence. Some idea may be formed of *Seva-Gi's* intrepidity by his attempt to seize *Chah-hestkan's* person, together with all his treasures, in the midst of his troops, and surrounded by the walls of *Aureng-Abad*. Attended by a few soldiers he one night penetrated into *Chah-hestkan's* apartment, and would have succeeded in his object had he remained undetected a short time longer. *Chah-hest* was severely wounded, and his son was killed in the act of

FIG. 8.—Sivaji.

[1] See pp. 136-37 text, and footnote [3] on p. 135.

drawing his sword. *Seva-Gi* soon engaged in another daring expedition, which proved more successful. Placing himself at the head of two or three thousand men, the flower of his army, he silently withdrew from his camp, and pretended during the march to be a *Raja* going to the *Mogol's* court. When within a short distance of *Sourate*, he met the *Grand Provost* of the country,[1] on whom he imposed the belief that he intended to prosecute his journey without entering the town: but the plunder of that famous and wealthy port was the principal object of the expedition; he rushed into the place sword in hand, and remained nearly three days, torturing the population to compel a discovery of their concealed riches. Burning what he could not take away, *Seva-Gi* returned without the least opposition, laden with gold and silver to the amount of several millions; with pearls, silken stuffs, fine cloths, and a variety of other costly merchandise. A secret understanding, it was suspected, existed between *Jessomseingue* and *Seva-Gi*, and the former was supposed to have been accessory to the attempt on *Chah-hest* as well as the attack of *Sourate*. The Raja was therefore recalled from the *Decan*, but instead of going to *Dehli*, he returned to his own territories.

I forgot to mention that during the pillage of *Sourate*, *Seva-Gi*, the Holy *Seva-Gi*! respected the habitation of the Reverend Father *Ambrose*, the Capuchin missionary. 'The *Frankish* Padrys are good men,' he said, 'and shall not be molested.' He spared also the house of a deceased *Delale* or *Gentile* broker,[1] of the *Dutch*, because assured that he

[1] In the original 'grand Prevost de la campagne.' Valentyn calls him the 'Stadsvoogd' and says that they met at 'Utena, a village about one and a half miles from the town.' The official was most likely the Kotwāl or commandant of the fort, and this rendering agrees with Bernier's narrative (see p. 369) where he talks of the *Cotoüal, qui est comme le grand Prevost* (of the Mogul's camp).

[2] The appointment of Broker (Hindostanee *dálál*) was an exceedingly important one. Tavernier, in chapter xiv. of his *Travels*, vol. ii. pp. 33, 71, entitled 'Concerning the Methods to be observed for

had been very charitable while alive. The dwellings of the *English* and *Dutch* likewise escaped his visits, not in consequence of any reverential feeling on his part, but because those people had displayed a great deal of resolution, and defended themselves well. The *English* especially, assisted by the crews of their vessels, performed wonders, and saved not only their own houses but those of their neighbours.[1] The pertinacity of a Jew,

establishing a new Commercial Company in the EAST INDIES,' insists upon the importance of securing for this post the services of one 'who should be a native of the country, an idolater and not a Muhammadan, because all the workmen with whom he will have to do are idolaters. Good manners and probity are above all things necessary in order to acquire confidence at first among these people.'

Tavernier also gives some interesting details regarding the Dálál whose house was spared by Sivají (*Travels*, vol. ii. p. 204), where he tells us that 'in the month of January of the year 1661 the *Shroff* or money-changer of the Dutch Company, named MONDAS PAREK, died at SURAT. He was a rich man and very charitable, having bestowed much alms during his life on the Christians as well as on the idolaters; the Rev. Capuchin Fathers of SURAT living for a part of the year on the rice, butter, and vegetables which he sent them.

In the first English translation of this book, the passage about the *dálál* is translated as follows: 'He had also regard to the House of the Deceased *De Lale*,' a rendering which has been followed in other editions.

[1] Sir George Oxindon (thus he signed his name, as may be seen from records in the India Office, not Oxendon, or Oxendine, or Oxendin, or Oxenden, as frequently printed) was then Chief Factor or President, 'In whose time *Seva Gi* plunder'd *Surat*; but he defended himself and the Merchants so bravely, that he had a *Collat* or *Serpaw*, a Robe of Honour from Head to Foot, offered him from the *Great Mogul*, with an Abatement of Customs to Two and a half *per cent.* granted to the Company: for which his Masters, as a token of the high Sense they had of his Valour, presented him a Medal of Gold with this Device:

Non minor est virtus quam quaerere parta tueri.'

Fryer's *A New Account of East India and Persia*, London, 1698, p. 87.

Oxindon was appointed chief of the English Factory at Surat, on the 18th September 1662, and he died there on the 14th July 1669, aged fifty. His elaborate mausoleum forms the most prominent object in the old English cemetery at Surat.

a native of *Constantinople*, astonished everybody. *Seva-Gi* knew that he was in possession of most valuable rubies, which he intended to sell to *Aureng-Zebe*; but he persevered in stoutly denying the fact, although three times placed on his knees to receive the stroke of a sword flourished over his head. This conduct was worthy of a Jew, whose love of money generally exceeds his love of life.

Aureng-Zebe prevailed with *Jesseingue* to take the command of the army in the *Decan*, attended by *Sultan Mazum*, who, however, was not invested with any authority. The Raja's first operation was vigorously to attack *Seva-Gi's* principal fortress; but he had recourse, at the same time, to his favourite art, negotiation, which he brought to a favourable issue, as the place surrendered by capitulation long before it was reduced to extremity. *Seva-Gi* having consented to make common cause with the *Mogol* against *Visapour*, *Aureng-Zebe* proclaimed him a *Raja*, took him under his protection, and granted an *omrah's* pension to his son. Some time afterwards, the King meditating a war against *Persia*, wrote to *Seva-Gi* in such kind and flattering terms, and extolled his generosity, talents and conduct so highly, as to induce him to meet the *Mogol* at *Dehli*, *Jesseingue* having plighted his faith for the chieftain's security. *Chah-hestkan's* wife, a relation of *Aureng-Zebe's*, happened to be then at court, and never ceased to urge the arrest of a man who had killed her son, wounded her husband, and sacked *Sourate*.[1] The result was that *Seva-Gi*, observing that his tents were watched by three or four *omrahs*, effected his escape in disguise under favour of night. This circumstance caused great uneasiness in the palace, and *Jesseingue's* eldest son, being strongly suspected of having assisted *Seva-Gi* in his flight, was forbidden to appear at court. *Aureng-Zebe* felt, or

[1] Surat in those days being the place of embarkation of pilgrims to Mecca was looked upon as a sacred place by the Moslems of India. It was then sometimes called *Báb ul Makkah*, or the Gate of Mecca.

seemed to feel, equally irritated against the father and the son, and *Jesseingue,* apprehending that he might avail himself of this pretext to seize his territories, abandoned his command in the *Decan* and hastened to the defence of his dominions, but he died on his arrival at *Brampour.*[1] The kindness shown by the *Mogol* to the Raja's son,[2] when apprised of this melancholy event; his tender condolences, and the grant to him of the pension enjoyed by the father, confirm many persons in the opinion that *Seva-Gi* did not escape without the connivance of *Aureng-Zebe* himself. His presence at court must indeed have greatly embarrassed the King, since the hatred of the women was most fierce and rancorous against him: they considered him as a monster who had imbued his hands in the blood of friends and kinsmen.[3]

But here let us take a cursory review of the history of the *Decan,* a kingdom that, during more than forty years, has constantly been the theatre of war, and owing to which the *Mogol* is so frequently embroiled with the King of *Golkonda,* the King of *Visapour,* and several other less powerful sovereigns. The nature of the quarrels in that part of *Hindoustan* cannot be well understood while we remain ignorant of the chief occurrences and have only an imperfect knowledge of the condition of the Princes by whom the country is governed.

[1] Burhanpur. [2] Rám Singh.

[3] Fryer's account (*op. cit.* pp. 173, 174) of these transactions agrees with Bernier's narrative in many particulars, and with regard to Sivají's escape from Dehli (Agra according to Fryer), he says that Aurangzeb, 'desirous to try if by Kindness he could reclaim this famous Rebel, allures him to Court (Faith being plighted for his Safety), where shortly after, the Outcries of the Women in whose Kindred's Blood his hands were imbrued, made him shift for himself in an Hamper on a Porter's Back, which passed the Guards among many others, which were forced to be sent as *Piscashes*' [Peshcush, Persian *pesh-kash*, a present to a great man, etc.] 'to his Friends, as the manner is when under Confinement: With this Slight he got away (not without the *Mogul's* Privity), and 'tis believed will hardly venture to *Agra* again, unless better guarded.'

Two centuries have scarcely elapsed since the great peninsula of India, stretching from the Gulf of *Cambaye* on the west to the Gulf of *Bengale* near *Jagannate* on the east, and extending southerly to Cape *Comori*,[1] was, with the exception perhaps of a few mountainous tracts, under the domination of one arbitrary despot. The indiscretion of Raja, or King, *Ram-ras*, the last Prince under whom it was united, caused the dismemberment of this vast monarchy, and this is the reason why it is now divided among many sovereigns professing different religions. *Ram-ras* had three *Georgian* slaves in his service, whom he distinguished by every mark of favour, and at length nominated to the Government of three considerable districts. One was appointed governor of nearly the whole of the territory in the *Decan* which is now in the possession of the *Mogol*; *Daulet-Abad* was the capital of that government, which extended from *Bider*, *Paranda*[2] and *Sourate* as far as *Narbadar*. The territory now forming the kingdom of *Visapour* was the portion of the second favourite; and the third obtained the country comprehended in the present kingdom of *Golkonda*. These three slaves became extremely rich and powerful, and as they professed the *Mahometan* faith and declared themselves of the *Chyas* sect, which is that of the Persians, they received the countenance and support of a great number of *Mogols* in the service of *Ram-ras*. They could not, even if so disposed, have embraced the religion of the *Gentiles*, because the *gentiles* of *India* admit no stranger to the participation of their mysteries. A rebellion, in which the three *Georgian* slaves united, terminated in the murder of *Ram-ras*, after which they returned to their respective governments, and usurped the title of *Chah*, or King. *Ram-ras's* children, incapable of contending with these men, remained quietly in the country known

[1] The old and correct form for Comorin ; see p. 23, footnote [1].

[2] Purandhar, 20 miles south-east of Poona city, now a sanitarium for European troops.

commonly by the name of the *Karnateck*, and called on our maps *Bisnaguer*,[1] where their posterity are Rajas to this day. The remainder of the Peninsula was split at the same time into all those smaller states still existing, governed by *Rajas*, *Naïques*,[2] and other *Kinglets*. While the three *Slaves* and their successors preserved a good understanding with each other, they were able to defend their kingdoms, and to wage wars on a large scale against the *Mogols*; but when the seeds of jealousy were sown among them, and they chose to act as independent sovereigns who stood in no need of foreign assistance, they experienced the fatal effects of disunion. Thirty-five or forty years ago, the *Mogol*, availing himself of their differences, invaded the dominions of *Nejam-Chah*, or King Nejam, the fifth or sixth in succession from the first *Slave* and made himself master of the whole country.[3] *Nejam* died a prisoner in *Daulet-Abad*, his former capital.[4]

Since that period, the Kings of *Golkonda* have been preserved from invasion, not in consequence of their great strength, but of the employment given to the *Mogol* by the two sister kingdoms, and of the necessity he was under to capture their strong places, such as *Amber*, *Paranda*, *Bider* and others, before *Golkonda* could be prudently attacked. The safety of those Kings may also be ascribed to the wisdom of their policy. Possessing great wealth, they have always secretly supplied the monarch of *Visapour* with money, to enable him to defend his country; so that whenever the latter is threatened,

[1] Vijayanagar (Bijianuggur). The site of the ancient capital of this kingdom, whose ruins cover nine square miles, is Hampi in the Bellary District of the Madras Presidency, thirty-six miles north-west of Bellary.

[2] Naik, from the Sanskrit *náyaka*, a leader or chief. The name of a Telugu caste, whence the general name of these petty kings as *Trimul naik*, and so forth.

[3] Daulatabad was captured in 1632.

[4] It is stated in the *Bádsháh-náma* of Abdul Hamid Lahori, that Nizam Shah was confined in the fort of Gwalior.

the King of *Golkonda* invariably marches an army to the frontiers, to show the *Mogol* not only that preparations are made for internal defence, but that an ally is at hand to assist *Visapour,* if driven to extremity. It appears likewise that the government of *Golkonda* employs large sums as bribes to the generals of the *Mogol's* army, who therefore constantly give it as their opinion that *Visapour* ought to be attacked rather than *Golkonda,* on account of its greater proximity to *Daulet-Abad.* Indeed, after the convention concluded, as we have seen, between *Aureng-Zebe* and the present King of *Golkonda,* the former has no great inducement to march troops into that kingdom, which he probably considers as his own. It has been long tributary to the *Mogol,* to whom it presents annually a considerable quantity of hard cash, home-manufactured articles of exquisite workmanship, and elephants imported from *Pegu, Siam,* and *Ceylon.* There is now no fortress between *Daulet-Abad* and *Golkonda* capable of offering any resistance, and *Aureng-Zebe* feels confident, therefore, that a single campaign would suffice to conquer the country. In my own opinion, nothing has restrained him from attempting that conquest but the apprehension of having the *Decan* overrun by the King of *Visapour,* who knows that if he permits his neighbour to fall, his own destruction must be the necessary consequence.

From what I have said, some idea may be formed of the present state of the King of *Golkonda* in relation to the *Mogol.* There can be no doubt that his power is held by a most uncertain tenure. Since the nefarious transaction in *Golkonda,*[1] planned by *Emir-Jemla* and executed by *Aureng-Zebe,* the King has lost all mental energy, and has ceased to hold the reins of government. He never appears in public to give audience and administer justice according to the custom of the country; nor does he venture outside the walls of the fortress of *Golkonda.* Confusion and misrule are the natural and unavoidable

[1] See p. 16, *et seq.*

consequences of this state of things. The grandees, totally disregarding the commands of a Monarch for whom they no longer feel either affection or respect, exercise a disgusting tyranny; and the people, impatient to throw off the galling yoke, would gladly submit to the more equitable government of *Aureng-Zebe.*

I shall advert to five or six facts that prove the low state of degradation to which this wretched King is reduced.

First.—When I was at *Golkonda,* in the year 1667, an ambassador extraordinary arrived from *Aureng-Zebe,* for the purpose of declaring war, unless the King supplied the *Mogol* with ten thousand cavalry to act against *Visapour.* This force was not indeed granted; but, what pleased *Aureng-Zebe* still better, as much money was given as is considered sufficient for the maintenance of such a body of cavalry. The King paid extravagant honours to this ambassador and loaded him with valuable presents, both for himself and the *Mogol* his master.

Second.—*Aureng-Zebe's* ordinary ambassador at the court of *Golkonda* issues his commands, grants passports, menaces and ill-treats the people, and in short, speaks and acts with the uncontrolled authority of an absolute sovereign.

Third.—*Emir-Jemla's* son, *Mahmet-Emir-Kan,* although nothing more than one of *Aureng-Zebe's Omrahs,* is so much respected in *Golkonda,* and chiefly in *Maslipatam* [1] that the *taptapa,* his agent or broker, virtually acts as master of the port. He buys and sells, admits and clears out cargoes, free of every impost and without any person's intervention. So boundless was the father's influence formerly in this country, that it has descended to the son as a matter of right or necessity.

Fourth.—Sometimes the Dutch presume to lay an embargo on all the *Golkonda* merchant-vessels in the port, nor will they suffer them to depart until the King comply with their demands. I have known them even protest

[1] Masulipatam (Machlipatnam), see p. 112, footnote [1].

against the King because the Governor of *Maslipatam* prevented them from taking forcible possession of an English ship in the port, by arming the whole population, threatening to burn the Dutch factory, and to put all these insolent foreigners to the sword.

Fifth.—Another symptom of decay in this kingdom is the debased state of the current coin; which is extremely prejudicial to the commerce of the country.

Sixth.—A sixth instance I would adduce of the fallen power of the King of *Golkonda* is, that the Portuguese, wretched, poor, and despised as they are become, scruple not to menace him with war, and with the capture and pillage of *Maslipatam* and other towns if he refuse to cede *San Thomé*,[1] a place which these same Portuguese, a few years ago, voluntarily resigned into his hands to avoid the disgrace of yielding it to the superior power of the Dutch.

Many intelligent persons, however, assured me, when I was in *Golkonda*, that the King is by no means devoid of understanding; that this appearance of weakness and indecision and of indifference to the affairs of government is assumed for the purpose of deceiving his enemies; that he has a son concealed from the public eye, of an ardent and aspiring spirit, whom he intends to place on the throne at a favourable juncture, and then to violate his treaty with *Aureng-Zebe*. Leaving it to time to decide upon the soundness of these opinions, we shall proceed to say a few words about *Visapour*.

That country, though it has to contend frequently with the *Mogol*, still preserves the name of an independent kingdom. The truth is, that the generals employed against *Visapour*, like commanders employed in every other service, are delighted to be at the head of an army, ruling at a distance from the court with the authority of kings. They conduct every operation, therefore, with

[1] St. Thomas' Mount, which still contains several remains of the Portuguese settlement.

languor, and avail themselves of any pretext for the prolongation of war which is alike the source of their emolument and dignity. It is become a proverbial saying, that the *Decan* is the bread and support of the soldiers of *Hindoustan*.[1] It should also be observed, that the kingdom of *Visapour* abounds with almost impregnable fortresses in mountainous situations, and that the country on the side of the Great Mogol's territories is of a peculiarly difficult access, owing to the scarcity both of forage and of good wholesome water. The capital is extremely strong; situated in an arid and sterile soil, and pure and palatable water is found only within the gates.

Visapour, however, is verging toward dissolution. The *Mogol* has made himself master of *Paranda*,[2] the key of the kingdom; of *Bider*,[3] a strong and handsome town, and of other important places. The death of the King without male issue must also operate unfavourably on the future concerns of this country. The throne is filled by a young man, educated, and adopted as her son, by the Queen, sister of the King of *Golkonda*, who, by the by, has been ill requited for her kindness. She returned recently from *Mecca*, and experienced a cold and insulting reception; the young monarch pretending that her conduct on board the Dutch vessel which conveyed her to *Moka* was unbecoming both her sex and rank. It is even said that she was criminally connected with two or three of the crew, who abandoned the vessel at *Moka* for the purpose of accompanying the Queen to *Mecca*.

Seva-Gi, the *gentile* leader lately spoken of, profiting by the distracted state of the kingdom, has seized upon many strongholds, situated for the most part in the moun-

[1] Or, as Fryer puts it (p. 167), 'frustrated chiefly by the means of the Soldiery and great *Ombrahs*, who live Lazily and in Pay, whereupon they term *Duccan*, *The Bread of the Military Men*.'

[2] The fort was treacherously surrendered to the Mogul about the year 1635.

[3] Bidar was captured in 1653.

tains.[1] This man is exercising all the powers of an independent sovereign; laughs at the threats both of the *Mogol* and of the King at *Visapour*; makes frequent incursions, and ravages the country on every side, from *Sourate* to the gates of *Goa*. Yet it cannot be doubted that, notwithstanding the deep wounds which from time to time he inflicts upon *Visapour*, the kingdom finds in this daring chieftain a seasonable and powerful coadjutor. He distracts the attention of *Aureng-Zebe* by his bold and never-ceasing enterprises, and affords so much employment to the Indian armies, that the *Mogol* cannot find the opportunity of achieving the conquest of *Visapour*. How to put down *Seva-Gi* is become the object of chief importance. We have seen his success at *Sourate*; he afterwards captured the Portuguese settlement of *Bardes*, an island contiguous to *Goa*.

SEVENTHLY. It was after I had left Dehli, on my return [to France], that I heard, at *Golkonda*, of the death of *Chah-Jehan*,[2] and that *Aureng-Zebe* seemed much affected by the event, and discovered all the marks of grief which a son can express for the loss of his father. He set out immediately for *Agra*, where *Begum-Saheb* received him with distinguished honour. She hung the mosque with tapestries of rich brocades, and in the same manner decorated the place where the *Mogol* intended to alight before he entered the fortress. On arriving at the women's apart-

[1] ''Tis undeniable he hath taken and maintains against the *Moguls* Sixty odd strong Hills: But the Cause is, the *Moguls* are unacquainted with, and their Bodies unfit for such barren and uneasy Places; so that they rather chuse to desert than defend them: Whereby it is sufficiently evident SEVA GI is unable in the Plain to do anything but Rob, Spoil, and return with all the speed imaginable: And on that account it is *Aurengzeeb* calls him his Mountain-Rat, with which the greatest Systems of Monarchy in the World, though continued by an uninterrupted Descent of Imperial Ancestry, have ever been infested, finding it more hard to fight with Mountains than Men.'—Fryer, p. 171.

[2] He died on the 22d January 1666, and lies buried in the Taj, close by the grave of his wife, the 'Lady of the Taj.'

ment in the seraglio, the princess presented him with a large golden basin, full of precious stones—her own jewels, and those which belonged to *Chah-Jehan.* Moved by the magnificence of his reception, and the affectionate protestations of his sister, *Aureng-Zebe* forgave her former conduct and has since treated her with kindness and liberality.

I have now brought this history to a close. My readers have no doubt condemned the means by which the reigning *Mogol* attained the summit of power. These means were indeed unjust and cruel; but it is not perhaps fair to judge him by the rigid rules which we apply to the character of European princes. In our quarter of the globe, the succession to the crown is settled in favour of the eldest by wise and fixed laws; but in *Hindoustan* the right of governing is usually disputed by all the sons of the deceased monarch, each of whom is reduced to the cruel alternative of sacrificing his brothers, that he himself may reign, or of suffering his own life to be forfeited for the security and stability of the dominion of another. Yet even those who may maintain that the circumstances of country, birth and education afford no palliation of the conduct pursued by *Aureng-Zebe,* must admit that this Prince is endowed with a versatile and rare genius, that he is a consummate statesman, and a great King.

LETTER

TO MONSEIGNEUR

COLBERT

Concerning the Extent of Hindoustan, the Currency towards, and final absorption of gold and silver in that country; its Resources, Armies, the administration of Justice, and the principal Cause of the Decline of the States of Asia.

MY LORD,

In *Asia*, the great are never approached empty-handed. When I had the honour to kiss the garment of the great Mogol *Aureng-Zebe* (Ornament of the Throne), I presented him with eight *roupies*,[1] as a mark of respect; and I offered a knife-case, a fork and a pen-knife mounted in amber to the illustrious *Fazel-Kan* (The Accomplished Knight), a Minister charged with the weightiest concerns of the empire, on whose decision depended the amount of my salary as physician. Though I presume not, My Lord, to introduce new customs into *France*, yet I cannot be expected, so soon after my return from *Hindoustan*, to lose all remembrance of the practice just mentioned, and hope I shall be pardoned for hesitating to appear

[1] One roupie is worth about thirty sols.—*Bernier*. [Taking the sol as equal to 0.9 of a penny English, in 1670, one 'roupie' equalled 2s. 3d., which agrees with Tavernier's value.]

in the presence of a King who inspires me with very different feelings than did *Aureng-Zebe*; or before you, My Lord,[1] who deserve my respect much more than *Fazel-kan,* without some small offering, which may derive value from its novelty, if not from the hand that bestows it. The late revolution in *Hindoustan*, so full of extraordinary events, may be deemed worthy the attention of our great Monarch; and this letter, considering the importance of its matter, may not be unsuitable to the rank you bear in his Majesty's council. It seems, indeed, addressed with propriety to one whose measures have so admirably restored order in many departments which, before my departure from *France*, I feared were irremediably confused; to one who has evinced so much anxiety to make known to the ends of the earth the character of our sovereign, and of what the *French* people are capable in the execution of whatever you project for their benefit and glory.

It was in *Hindoustan*, My Lord, whither your fame extends, and from which country I am lately returned after an absence of twelve years, that I first became acquainted with the happiness of *France*, and with the share which you have had in promoting it, by your unwearied attention and brilliant abilities. This is a theme on which I could fondly dwell; but why should I expatiate on facts already and universally admitted, when my present purpose is to treat of those which are new and unknown? It will be more agreeable to you if I proceed, according to my promise, to furnish such materials as may enable your lordship to form some idea of the actual state of the *Indies*.

The maps of *Asia* point out the mighty extent of the *Great Mogol's* empire, known commonly by the name of the Indies, or *Hindoustan*. I have not measured it with mathematical exactness; but judging from the ordinary

[1] Jean Baptiste Colbert, born in 1619 and died in 1683, Finance Minister to Louis XIV. of France, who is the king referred to.

rate of travel, and considering that it is a journey of three months from the frontier of the kingdom of *Golkonda* to *Kazni*,[1] or rather beyond it, near to *Kandahar*, which is the first town in *Persia*, the distance between those two extreme points cannot be less than five hundred French leagues, or five times as far as from *Paris* to *Lyons*.

It is important to observe, that of this vast tract of country, a large portion is extremely fertile; the large kingdom of *Bengale*, for instance, surpassing *Egypt* itself, not only in the production of rice, corn, and other necessaries of life, but of innumerable articles of commerce which are not cultivated in *Egypt*; such as silks, cotton, and indigo. There are also many parts of the *Indies*, where the population is sufficiently abundant, and the land pretty well tilled; and where the artisan, although naturally indolent, is yet compelled by necessity or otherwise to employ himself in manufacturing carpets, brocades, embroideries, gold and silver cloths, and the various sorts of silk and cotton goods, which are used in the country or exported abroad.

It should not escape notice that gold and silver, after circulating in every other quarter of the globe, come at length to be swallowed up, lost in some measure, in *Hindoustan*. Of the quantity drawn from *America*, and dispersed among the different European states, a part finds its way, through various channels, to *Turkey*, for the payment of commodities imported from that country; and a part passes into *Persia*, by way of *Smyrna*, for the silks laden at that port. *Turkey* cannot dispense with the coffee,[2] which she receives from *Yemen*, or Arabia Felix; and the productions of the *Indies* are equally necessary to *Turkey*, *Yemen*, and *Persia*. Thus it happens that these countries are under the necessity of sending a portion of their gold and silver to *Moka*, on the Red Sea, near *Babel-mandel*; to *Bassora*, at the top of the *Persian Gulf*; and to *Bander Abassi* or *Gomeron*, near

[1] Ghazni.

[2] Cauvé in the original, from the Arabic *kahwa*, see p. 364, footnote [2].

Ormus; which gold and silver is exported to *Hindoustan* by the vessels that arrive every year, in the *mausem*, or the season of the winds, at those three celebrated ports, laden with goods from that country. Let it also be borne in mind that all the *Indian* vessels, whether they belong to the *Indians* themselves, or to the *Dutch*, or *English*, or *Portuguese*, which every year carry cargoes of merchandise from *Hindoustan* to *Pegu*, *Tanasseri*,[1] *Siam*, *Ceylon*, *Achem*,[2] *Macassar*, the *Maldives*, to *Mozambic*, and other places, bring back to *Hindoustan* from those countries a large quantity of the precious metals, which share the fate of those brought from *Moka*, *Bassora*, and *Bander-Abassi*. And in regard to the gold and silver which the Dutch draw from *Japan*, where there are mines, a part is, sooner or later, introduced into *Hindoustan*; and whatever is brought directly by sea, either from *Portugal* or from *France*, seldom leaves the country, returns being made in merchandise.

I am aware it may be said, that *Hindoustan* is in want of copper, cloves, nutmegs, cinnamon, elephants, and other things, with which she is supplied by the Dutch from *Japan*, the *Moluccas*, *Ceylon*, and *Europe*;—that she obtains lead from abroad, in part from *England*; broadcloths and other articles from *France*;—that she is in need of a considerable number of foreign horses, receiving annually more than five-and-twenty thousand from *Usbec*, a great many from *Persia* by way of *Kandahar*, and several from *Ethiopia*, *Arabia*, and *Persia*, by sea, through the ports of *Moka*, *Bassora*, and *Bander-Abassi*. It may also be observed that *Hindoustan* consumes an immense quantity of fresh fruit from *Samarkand*, *Bali*,[3] *Bocara*, and *Persia*; such as melons, apples, pears and grapes, eaten at *Dehli* and

[1] The ancient and correct form for Tenasserim, now the southern division of the Province of Lower Burmah.

[2] Acheen, the celebrated emporium at the north of the island of Sumatra.

[3] Thus in original; probably a misprint for *Balk* (Balkh).

purchased at a very high price nearly the whole winter; —and likewise dried fruit, such as almonds, pistachio and various other small nuts, plums, apricots, and raisins, which may be procured the whole year round;—that she imports a small sea-shell from the *Maldives*, used in *Bengale*, and other places, as a species of small money; ambergris from the *Maldives* and *Mozambic*; rhinoceros' horns, elephants' teeth, and slaves from *Ethiopia*; musk and porcelain from *China*, and pearls from *Beharen*,[1] and *Tutucoury*,[2] near *Ceylon*; and I know not what quantity of other similar wares, which she might well do without.

The importation of all these articles into *Hindoustan* does not, however, occasion the export of gold and silver; because the merchants who bring them find it advantageous to take back, in exchange, the productions of the country.

Supplying itself with articles of foreign growth or manufacture, does not, therefore, prevent *Hindoustan* from absorbing a large portion of the gold and silver of the world, admitted through a variety of channels, while there is scarcely an opening for its return.

It should also be borne in mind, that the *Great Mogol* constitutes himself heir of all the *Omrahs*, or lords, and likewise of the *Mansebdars*, or inferior lords, who are in his pay; and, what is of the utmost importance, that he is proprietor of every acre of land in the kingdom, excepting, perhaps, some houses and gardens which he sometimes permits his subjects to buy, sell, and otherwise dispose of, among themselves.

[1] The island of El-Bahrein, in the Persian Gulf, still the site of a great pearl-fishery. The name, literally the Two Seas, probably owes its origin to the notion that the Persian Gulf and the Sea of Omân meet there. It is used in the sense of τόπος διθάλασσος in Acts xxvii. 41, 'And falling into a place where two seas met, they ran the ship aground.'

[2] Tuticorin, the seaport in the Tinnevelli District, Madras Presidency, formerly in the hands of the Portuguese, then of the Dutch, has still a considerable foreign trade, the value of which ranks next to that of Madras, and the sixth in all India.

I think I have shown that the precious metals must abound in *Hindoustan,* although the country be destitute of mines; and that the *Great Mogol,* lord and master of the greater part, must necessarily be in the receipt of an immense revenue, and possess incalculable wealth.

But there are many circumstances to be considered, as forming a counterpoise to these riches.

First.—Of the vast tracts of country constituting the empire of *Hindoustan,* many are little more than sand, or barren mountains, badly cultivated, and thinly peopled; and even a considerable portion of the good land remains untilled from want of labourers; many of whom perish in consequence of the bad treatment they experience from the Governors. These poor people, when incapable of discharging the demands of their rapacious lords, are not only often deprived of the means of subsistence, but are bereft of their children, who are carried away as slaves. Thus it happens that many of the peasantry, driven to despair by so execrable a tyranny, abandon the country, and seek a more tolerable mode of existence, either in the towns, or camps; as bearers of burdens, carriers of water, or servants to horsemen. Sometimes they fly to the territories of a Raja, because there they find less oppression, and are allowed a greater degree of comfort.

Second.—The empire of the *Great Mogol* comprehends several nations, over which he is not absolute master. Most of them still retain their own peculiar chiefs or sovereigns, who obey the *Mogol* or pay him tribute only by compulsion. In many instances this tribute is of trifling amount; in others none is paid; and I shall adduce instances of nations which, instead of paying, receive tribute.

The petty sovereignties bordering the Persian frontiers, for example, seldom pay tribute either to the *Mogol* or to the King of *Persia.* Nor can the former be said to receive anything considerable from the *Balouches, Augans,* and other mountaineers, who indeed seem to feel nearly independent of him, as was proved by their conduct when the *Mogol* marched from *Ateck* on the Indus to *Kaboul*; for the purpose of besieging *Kandahar*.[1] By stopping the supply of water from the mountains, and preventing its descent into the fields contiguous to the public road, they completely arrested the army on its march, until the

FIG. 9.—'Gunga Din.'
''E would dot an' carry one,
Till the longest day was done,
An' 'e didn't seem to know the use o' fear.'

mountaineers received from the *Mogol* the presents which they had solicited in the way of alms.

The *Patans* also are an intractable race. They are Mahometans, who formerly inhabited a country in the vicinity of the *Ganges*, toward *Bengale*. Before the in-

[1] In 1651-52.

vasion of India by the *Mogols*, the *Patans* had rendered themselves formidable in several places. Their power was felt principally at *Dehli*,[1] many of the neighbouring *Rajas* being their tributaries. Even the menials and carriers of water belonging to that nation are high-spirited and warlike.[2] 'If it be not so, may I never ascend the throne of *Dehli*,' is the usual phraseology of a *Patan*, when wishing to enforce the truth of any assertion. They hold the *Indians*, both *Gentiles* and *Mogols*, in the utmost contempt; and, recollecting the consideration in which they were formerly held in *India*, they mortally hate the *Mogols*, by whom their fathers were dispossessed of great principalities, and driven to the mountains far from *Dehli* and *Agra*. In these mountains some *Patans* established themselves as petty sovereigns or *Rajas*; but without any great power.

The King of *Visapour*, so far from paying tribute to the *Mogol*, is engaged in perpetual war with him, and contrives to defend his dominions. He owes his preservation less to the strength of his arms than to many peculiar circumstances.[3] His kingdom is at a great distance from *Agra* and *Dehli*, the *Mogol's* usual places of residence; the capital city, called also *Visapour*,[4] is strong, and not easily accessible to an invading army, because of the bad water

[1] The Pathán Sultáns of Dehli may be said to have reigned from 1192-1554, somewhat more than three centuries and a half, during which time six dynasties, numbering in all forty kings, succeeded to the throne of Dehli. The boundaries of their Empire, at all times uncertain in extent, varying from the extreme limits of Eastern Bengal on one side to Kábul and Kandahár on the west, with Sind and the Southern Peninsula to complete the circle; occasionally reduced to a few districts around the capital and in one instance confined to the single spot enclosed within the walls of the metropolis itself. See Thomas's *Chronicles of the Pathán King of Dehli*, 1877.

[2] How true this is at the present day. The regimental *bihsthi* or water-carrier, generally a Pathán, is still a universal favourite, and his prowess has lately been sung in spirited verse by Rudyard Kipling in his barrack-room ballad of GUNGA DIN (*The Scots Observer*, 7th June 1890).

[3] See p. 196.

[4] Bijapúr.

and scarcity of forage in the surrounding country; and several *Rajas* for the sake of mutual security join him, when attacked, with their forces. The celebrated *Seva-Gi* not long ago made a seasonable diversion in his favour, by plundering and burning the rich seaport of *Sourate*.[1]

There is again the wealthy and powerful King of *Golkonda*, who secretly supplies the King of *Visapour* with money, and constantly keeps an army on the frontiers, with the double object of defending his own territories and aiding *Visapour* in the event of that country being closely pressed.

Similarly, among those not paying tribute may be numbered more than a hundred *Rajas*, or *Gentile* sovereigns of considerable strength, dispersed over the whole empire, some near and some at a distance from *Agra* and *Dehli*. Fifteen or sixteen of these *Rajas* are rich and formidable, particularly *Rana*,[2] formerly considered Emperor of the Rajas, and supposed to be descended from King Porus, *Jesseingue*[3] and *Jessomseingue*.[4] If these three chose to enter into an offensive league, they would prove dangerous opponents to the *Mogol*, each of them having at all times the means of taking the field with twenty thousand cavalry; better than any that could be opposed to them. These horsemen are called *Ragipous*, or sons of *Rajas*. Their military occupation, as I have stated elsewhere,[5] descends from father to son; and every man receives a grant of land on condition that he be always prepared to mount his horse and follow the *Raja*, whither he shall command. These men endure a great deal of fatigue, and require only discipline to become excellent soldiers.

Third.—It is material to remark that the *Great Mogol* is a Mahometan, of the sect of the *Sounnys*, who, believing with the Turks that Osman was the true successor of *Mahomet*, are distinguished by the name of *Osmanlys*. The

[1] See p. 188. [2] Rana Sanga or Sunka of Chittor.

[3] See p. 34 text, and footnote [2].

[4] See p. 37 text, and footnote [2]. [5] See p. 39.

majority of his courtiers, however, being Persians, are of the party known by the appellation of *Chias,* believers in the real succession of *Aly.* Moreover, the *Great Mogol* is a foreigner in *Hindoustan,* a descendant of *Tamerlan,* chief of those *Mogols* from *Tartary* who, about the year 1401, overran and conquered the *Indies.* Consequently he finds himself in an hostile country, or nearly so ; a country containing hundreds of *Gentiles* to one *Mogol,* or even to one *Mahometan.* To maintain himself in such a country, in the midst of domestic and powerful enemies, and to be always prepared against any hostile movement on the side of *Persia* or *Usbec,* he is under the necessity of keeping up numerous armies, even in the time of peace. These armies are composed either of natives, such as *Ragipous* and *Patans,* or of genuine *Mogols* and people who, though less esteemed, are called *Mogols* because white men, foreigners, and *Mahometans.* The court itself does not now consist, as originally, of real *Mogols* ; but is a medley of *Usbecs, Persians, Arabs,* and *Turks,* or descendants from all these people ; known, as I said before, by the general appellation of *Mogols.* It should be added, however, that children of the third and fourth generation, who have the brown complexion, and the languid manner of this country of their nativity, are held in much less respect than new comers, and are seldom invested with official situations : they consider themselves happy, if permitted to serve as private soldiers in the infantry or cavalry.—But it is time to give your lordship some idea of the armies of the *Great Mogol,* in order that you may judge, by the vast expenditure to which they subject him, what are really his effective means and resources.

I shall first speak of the native army,[1] which he must perforce entertain.

Under this head are comprehended the *ragipous* of *Jesseingue* and of *Jessomseingue* ; to whom, and to several other *Rajas,* the *Mogol* grants large sums for the service

[1] In the original, 'Milice du pais.'

of a certain number of their *ragipous,* to be kept always ready and at his disposal. *Rajas* bear an equal rank with the foreign and Mahometan *Omrahs,* whether employed in the army which the King retains at all times near his person, or in those stationed in the provinces. They are also generally subjected to the same regulations as the *Omrahs,* even to mounting guard; with this difference, however, that the *Rajas* never mount within a fortress, but invariably without the walls, under their own tents, not enduring the idea of being confined during four-and-twenty hours, and always refusing to enter any fortress unless well attended, and by men determined to sacrifice their lives for their leaders. This self-devotion has been sufficiently proved when attempts have been made to deal treacherously with a *Raja.*

There are many reasons why the *Mogol* is obliged to retain *Rajas* in his service.

First. Ragipous are not only excellent soldiers, but, as I have said, some *Rajas* can in any one day bring more than twenty thousand to the field.

Second. They are necessary to keep in check such *Rajas* as are not in the *Mogol's* pay; to reduce to submission those who take up arms rather than pay tribute, or refuse to join the army when summoned by the *Mogol.*

Third. It is the King's policy to foment jealousy and discord amongst the *Rajas,* and by caressing and favouring some more than others, he often succeeds, when desirous of doing so, in kindling wars among them.

Fourth. They are always at hand to be employed against the *Patans,* or against any rebellious *Omrah* or governor.

Fifth. Whenever the King of *Golkonda* withholds his tribute, or evinces an inclination to defend the King of *Visapour* or any neighbouring *Raja* whom the *Mogol* wishes to despoil or render tributary, *Rajas* are sent against him in preference to *Omrahs,* who being for the most part *Persians,* are not of the same religion as the *Mogol,* to wit *Sounnys,* but *Chias,* as are the Kings of *Persia* and *Golkonda.*

Sixth. The *Mogol* never finds the *Rajas* more useful than when he is engaged in hostility with the Persians. His *Omrahs,* as I have just remarked, are generally of that nation, and shudder at the idea of fighting against their natural King; especially because they acknowledge him as their *Imam,* their *Calife* or sovereign pontiff, and the descendant of *Aly,* to bear arms against whom they therefore consider a great crime.

The *Mogol* is also compelled to engage *Patans* in his service by reasons very similar to those I have assigned for employing *ragipous.*

In fine, he is reduced to the necessity of supporting those troops of foreigners, or *Mogols,* which we have noticed; and as they form the principal force of the kingdom, and are maintained at an incredible expense, a detailed description of this force may not be unacceptable.

These troops, both cavalry and infantry, may be considered under two heads: one part as always near the *Mogol's* person; the other, as dispersed in the several provinces. In regard to the cavalry retained near the King, I shall speak first of the *Omrahs,* then of the *Mansebdars,* next of the *Rouzindars*; and, last of all, of the common troopers. I shall then proceed to the infantry, and describe the musketeers and all the foot-men who serve in the artillery, saying a word in passing on the horse artillery.

It must not be imagined that the *Omrahs* or Lords of the *Mogol's* court are members of ancient families, as our nobility in *France.* The King being proprietor of all the lands in the empire, there can exist neither Dukedoms nor Marquisates; nor can any family be found possessed of wealth arising from a domain, and living upon its own patrimony. The courtiers are often not even descendants of *Omrahs,* because, the King being heir of all their possessions, no family can long maintain its distinction, but, after the *Omrah's* death, is soon extinguished, and the sons, or at least the grandsons, reduced generally, we might almost say, to beggary, and compelled to enlist as mere troopers in the cavalry of some *Omrah*. The King, however, usually bestows a small pension on the widow, and often on the family; and if the *Omrah's* life be sufficiently prolonged, he may obtain the advancement of his children by royal favour, particularly if their persons be well formed, and their complexions sufficiently fair to enable them to pass for genuine *Mogols*.[1] But this advancement through special favour proceeds slowly, for it is an almost invariable custom to pass gradually from small salaries, and inconsiderable offices, to situations of greater trust and emolument. The *Omrahs*, therefore, mostly consist of adventurers from different nations who entice one another to the court; and are generally persons of low descent, some having been originally slaves, and the majority being destitute of education. The *Mogol* raises them to dignities, or degrades them to obscurity, according to his own pleasure and caprice.

Some of the *Omrahs* have the title of *Hazary*, or lord of a thousand horse; some, of *Dou Hazary*, lord of two thousand horse; some, of *Penge*, lord of five thousand horse; some, of *Hecht*, lord of seven thousand horse; some, of *Deh Hazary*, lord of ten thousand horse; and sometimes an *Omrah* has the title of *Douazdeh Hazary*, lord of twelve thousand horse; as was the case with the King's eldest son. Their pay is proportionate, not to the number of men, but to the number of horses, and two horses are generally allowed to one trooper, in order that the service may be better performed; for in those hot countries it is usual to say that a soldier with a single horse has one foot on the ground. But let it not be supposed that an *Omrah* is expected to keep, or indeed that the King would pay for, such a body of horse as is implied by the titles of *Douazdeh* or *Hecht Hazary*; high-sounding names intended to impose on the credulous, and deceive *Foreigners*. The King himself regulates as well the effective number

[1] See pp. 3, 404.

that each *Omrah* is to maintain, as the nominal number which he need not keep, but which is also paid for, and usually forms the principal part of his salary. This salary is increased by the money that the *Omrah* retains out of every man's pay, and by what accrues from his false returns of the horses he is supposed to provide: all which renders the *Omrah's* income very considerable, particularly when he is so fortunate as to have some good *Jah-ghirs,* or suitable lands, assigned to him for the payment of his salary: for I perceived that the *Omrah* under whom I served, a *Penge-Hazary,* or lord of five thousand, whose quota was fixed at five hundred horses, had yet a balance over after the payment of all expenses, of nearly five thousand crowns a month, although, like all those who have no *Jah-ghirs,* he was a *Nagdy,*[1] that is to say, one who drew his pay in cash from the treasury. Notwithstanding these large incomes, I was acquainted with very few wealthy *Omrahs*; on the contrary, most of them are in embarrassed circumstances, and deeply in debt; not that they are ruined, like the nobility of other countries, by the extravagance of their table, but by the costly presents made to the King at certain annual festivals, and by their large establishments of wives, servants, camels, and horses.

The *Omrahs* in the provinces, in the armies, and at court, are very numerous; but it was not in my power to ascertain their number, which is not fixed. I never saw less than five-and-twenty to thirty at court, all of whom were in the receipt of the large incomes already mentioned, dependent for the amount upon their number of horses, from one to twelve thousand.

It is these *Omrahs* who attain to the highest honours and situations of the State,—at court, in the provinces, and in the armies; and who are, as they call themselves, the Pillars of the Empire. They maintain the splendour of the court, and are never seen out-of-doors but in the

[1] From the Persian word *naqd*, meaning silver, used in the sense of ready money.

most superb apparel; mounted sometimes on an elephant, sometimes on horseback, and not unfrequently in a *Paleky* attended by many of their cavalry, and by a large body of servants on foot, who take their station in front, and at either side, of their lord, not only to clear the way, but to flap the flies and brush off the dust with tails of peacocks; to carry the *picquedent*[1] or spitoon, water to allay the *Omrah's* thirst, and sometimes account-books, and other papers. Every *Omrah* at court is obliged, under a certain penalty, to repair twice a day to the assembly, for the purpose of paying his respects to the King, at ten or eleven o'clock in the morning, when he is there seated to dispense justice, and at six in the evening. An *Omrah* must also, in rotation, keep guard in the fortress once every week, during four-and-twenty hours. He sends thither his bed, carpet, and other furniture; the King supplying him with nothing but his meals. These are received with peculiar ceremony. Thrice the *Omrah* performs the *taslim*, or reverence, the face turned toward the royal apartment; first dropping the hand down to the ground, and then lifting it up to the head.[2]

Whenever the King takes an excursion in his *Paleky*, on an elephant, or in a *Tact-Ravan* (or travelling throne, carried upon the shoulders of eight men, who are cleverly relieved from time to time when on the march by eight others), all the *Omrahs* who are not prevented by illness, disabled by age, or exempted by a peculiar office, are bound to accompany him on horseback, exposed to the

[1] A capital transliteration of the Hindostanee word *pík-dán*, spit-box. The 'pigdaun' of modern Anglo-Indian colloquial. In another English translation of this book the word *picquedent* has been rendered 'tooth-pick,' a mistake that has been copied by others.

[2] 'The salutation called *taslím* consists in placing the back of the right hand on the ground, and then raising it gently till the person stands erect, when he puts the palm of his hand upon the crown of his head, which pleasing manner of saluting signifies that he is ready to give himself as an offering.'—*Aín-i-Akbari*, Blochmann's translation, vol. i. p. 158. See p. 258 text, and footnote [2].

inclemency of the weather and to suffocating clouds of dust. On every occasion the King is completely sheltered, whether taking the diversion of hunting, marching at the head of his troops, or making his progresses from one city to another. When, however, he confines his hunting to the neighbourhood of the city, visits his country house or repairs to the mosque, he sometimes dispenses with so large a retinue, and prefers being attended by such *Omrahs* only as are that day on guard.

Mansebdars[1] are horsemen with *manseb* pay, which is a peculiar pay, both honourable and considerable; not equal to that of the *Omrahs*, but much greater than the common pay. Hence they are looked on as petty *Omrahs*, and as being of the rank from which the *Omrahs* are taken. They acknowledge no other chief but the King, and have much the same duties imposed upon them as the *Omrahs*, to whom they would be equal if they had horsemen under them, as formerly was sometimes the case; but now they have only two, four, or six service horses, that is, such as bear the King's mark; and their pay is, in some instances, as low as one hundred and fifty *roupies* per month, and never exceeds seven hundred. Their number is not fixed,[2] but they are much more numerous than the *Omrahs*: besides those in the provinces and armies, there are never less than two or three hundred at court.

Rouzindars are also cavaliers, who receive their pay daily, as the word imports; but their pay is greater, in some instances, than that of many of the *mansebdars*. It is, however, of a different kind, and not thought so honourable, but the *Rouzindars* are not subject, like the Mansebdars, to the *Agenas*; that is, are not bound to take, at a valuation, carpets, and other pieces of furniture, that have

[1] *Mansab* means in Arabic and Persian an office, hence *Mansabdar* an officer, but the word was generally restricted to high officials.

[2] Akbar fixed the number of Mansabs at sixty-six, to correspond with the value of the letters in the name of Allah. See Blochmann's *Aïn*, vol. i. p. 327.

been used in the King's palace, and on which an unreasonable value is sometimes set. Their number is very great. They fill the inferior offices; many being clerks and under-clerks; while some are employed to affix the King's signet to *Barattes*,[1] or orders for the payment of money; and they scruple not to receive bribes for the quick issuing of these documents.

The common horsemen serve under the *Omrahs*: they are of two classes; the first consists of those who keep a pair of horses which the *Omrah* is bound to maintain for the King's service, and which bear the *Omrah's* mark on the thigh, and the second of those who keep only one horse. The former are the more esteemed, and receive the greater pay. The pay of the troopers depends, in a great measure,

[1] A *barát* corresponded somewhat to the modern cheque; it was a statement of account which contained details of the service or work for which it was issued, a pay order. It had to pass through many hands for 'countersignature' before being actually cashed. 'The receipts and expenditure of the Imperial workshops, the deposits and payments of salaries to the workmen (of whom some draw their pay on [military] descriptive rolls, and others according to the services performed by them, as the men engaged in the Imperial elephant and horse stables, and in the wagon department) are all made by *barats* (*Ain*, p. 262).

The Emperor Akbar who organised in a very thorough manner all the various departments of State, being desirous of avoiding delay, 'and from motives of kindness' ordered that certain classes of state papers, among others *baráts*, then all included in the term *sanad*, need not be placed before him personally. This practice appears from Bernier's statement to have been continued by succeeding Emperors, but apparently with not altogether satisfactory results.

At the present day the word *berat* is applied to certain documents of state in Turkey, and in *The Standard* newspaper, London, October 1st, 1890, we read with reference to the doings of Monsignor Senessi the Bulgarian Archbishop, in Macedonia, that . . . 'There can be little doubt, however, that, by the terms of his Berat, he is strictly within his right in visiting all villages where the Exarchist population is in marked majority, and in consecrating churches for them. Furthermore, besides the written authority, which might count for very little, he seems to enjoy if not the countenance, at least the tolerance of the Turkish authorities. . . .'

on the generosity of the *Omrah,* who may favour whom he pleases; although it is understood by the *Mogol* that he that keeps only one horse shall not receive less than five-and-twenty *roupies* a month, and on that footing he calculates his accounts with the *Omrahs.*[1]

The foot-soldiers receive the smallest pay; and, to be sure, the musketeers cut a sorry figure at the best of times, which may be said to be when squatting on the ground, and resting their muskets on a kind of wooden fork which hangs to them. Even then, they are terribly afraid of burning their eyes or their long beards, and above all lest some *Dgen,*[2] or evil spirit, should cause the bursting of their musket. Some have twenty *roupies* a month, some fifteen, some ten; but their artillerymen who receive great pay, particularly all the *Franguis* or Christians,—*Portuguese, English, Dutch, Germans,* and *French*; fugitives from *Goa,* and from the *Dutch* and *English* companies. Formerly, when the *Mogols* were little skilled in the management of artillery, the pay of the *Europeans* was more liberal, and there are still some remaining who receive two hundred *roupies* a month: but now the King admits them with difficulty into the service, and limits their pay to thirty-two *roupies.*

The artillery is of two sorts, the heavy and the light, or, as they call the latter, the artillery of the stirrup. With respect to the heavy artillery, I recollect that when the King, after his illness, went with his army to *Lahor* and *Kachemire* to pass the summer in that dear little 'paradise of the *Indies,*' it consisted of seventy pieces of cannon, mostly of brass, without reckoning from two to three hundred light camels, each of which carried a small field-piece of the size of a double musket, attached on the back of the

[1] In the time of the Emperor Akbar, a *yakaspah* (one horse) trooper was paid according to the kind of horse he maintained, and the amount varied from Rs. 30 per mensem for an Iráqí (Arabian) to Rs. 12 for a Janglah, or what would now be called a 'country bred.'

[2] The Arabic *jinn.*

animal, much in the same manner as swivels are fixed in our barks. I shall relate elsewhere this expedition to *Kachemire,* and describe how the King, during that long journey, amused himself almost every day, with the sports of the field, sometimes letting his birds of prey loose against cranes; sometimes hunting the *nilsgaus,* or grey oxen (a species of elk); another day hunting antelopes with tame leopards; and then indulging in the exclusively royal hunt of the lion.

The artillery of the stirrup, which also accompanied the *Mogol* in the journey to *Lahor* and *Kachemire,* appeared to me extremely well appointed. It consisted of fifty or sixty small field-pieces, all of brass; each piece mounted on a well-made and handsomely painted carriage, containing two ammunition chests, one behind and another in front, and ornamented with a variety of small red streamers. The carriage, with the driver, was drawn by two fine horses, and attended by a third horse, led by an assistant driver as a relay. The heavy artillery did not always follow the King, who was in the habit of diverging from the highroad, in search of hunting-ground, or for the purpose of keeping near the rivers and other waters. It could not move along difficult passes, or cross the bridges of boats thrown over the rivers. But the light artillery is always intended to be near the King's person and on that account takes the name of artillery of the stirrup. When he resumes his journey in the morning, and is disposed to shoot or hunt in game preserves, the avenues to which are guarded, it moves straight forward, and reaches with all possible speed the next place of encampment, where the royal tents and those of the principal *Omrahs* have been pitched since the preceding day. The guns are then ranged in front of the King's quarters, and by way of signal to the army, fire a volley the moment he arrives.

The army stationed in the provinces differs in nothing from that about the King's person, except in its superior numbers. In every district there are *Omrahs*, *Mansebdars*,

Rouzindars, common troopers, infantry and artillery. In the *Decan* alone the cavalry amounts to twenty or five-and-twenty, and sometimes to thirty thousand; a force not more than sufficient to overawe the powerful King of *Golkonda*, and to maintain the war against the King of *Visapour* and the *Rajas* who, for the sake of mutual protection, join their forces with his. The number of troops in the kingdom of *Kaboul*, which it is necessary to quarter in that country to guard against any hostile movement on the part of the *Persians*, *Augans*, *Balouchees*, and I know not how many other mountaineers, cannot be less than twelve or fifteen thousand. In the kingdom of *Kachemire* there are more than four thousand. In *Bengale*, so frequently the seat of war, the number is much greater; and as there is no province which can dispense with a military force, more or less numerous, according to its extent and particular situation, the total amount of troops in *Hindoustan* is almost incredible.

Leaving out of our present calculation the infantry, which is of small amount, and the number of horses, which is merely nominal, and is apt to deceive a superficial observer, I should think, with many persons well conversant with this matter, that the effective cavalry, commonly about the King's person, including that of the *Rajas* and *Patans*, amount to thirty-five or forty thousand; which, added to those in the provinces, forms a total of more than two hundred thousand horse.

I have said that the infantry was inconsiderable. I do not think that in the army immediately about the King, the number can exceed fifteen thousand, including musketeers, foot artillery, and generally, every person connected with that artillery. From this, an estimate may be formed of the number of infantry in the provinces. I cannot account for the prodigious amount of infantry with which some people swell the armies of the *Great Mogol*, otherwise than by supposing that with the fighting men, they confound servants, sutlers, tradesmen, and all those individuals belonging to *bazars*, or markets, who accompany the troops.[1] Including these followers, I can well conceive that the army immediately about the King's person, particularly when it is known that he intends to absent himself for some time from his capital, may amount to two, or even three hundred thousand infantry. This will not be deemed an extravagant computation, if we bear in mind the immense quantity of tents, kitchens, baggage, furniture, and even women, usually attendant on the army. For the conveyance of all these are again required many elephants, camels, oxen, horses, and porters. Your Lordship will bear in mind that, from the nature and government of this country, where the King is sole proprietor of all the land in the empire, a capital city, such as *Dehly* or *Agra*, derives its chief support from the presence of the army, and that the population is reduced to the necessity of following the *Mogol* whenever he undertakes a journey of long continuance.[2] Those cities resemble any place rather than *Paris*; they might more fitly be compared to a camp, if the lodgings and accommodations were not a little superior to those found in the tents of armies.

It is also important to remark the absolute necessity which exists of paying the whole of this army every two months, from the *omrah* to the private soldier; for the King's pay is their only means of sustenance. In *France*, when the exigencies of the times prevent the government from immediately discharging an arrear of debt, an officer, or even a private soldier, may contrive to live for some time by means of his own private income; but in the *Indies*, any unusual delay in the payment of the troops is sure to be attended with fatal consequences; after selling whatever trifling articles they may possess, the soldiers disband and die of hunger. Toward the close of the late civil war, I discovered a growing disposition in the

[1] In the time of the Emperor Akbar, porters, dâk runners or postmen, gladiators (*shamshérbaz*), wrestlers, palki bearers, and water-carriers, were all classed as infantry.

[2] See p. 381.

troopers to sell their horses, which they would, no doubt, soon have done if the war had been prolonged. And no wonder; for consider, My Lord, that it is difficult to find in the *Mogol's* army, a soldier who is not married, who has not wife, children, servants, and slaves, all depending upon him for support. I have known many persons lost in amazement while contemplating the number of persons, amounting to millions, who depend for support solely on the King's pay. Is it possible, they have asked, that any revenue can suffice for such incredible expenditure? seeming to forget the riches of the *Great Mogol,* and the peculiar manner in which *Hindoustan* is governed.

But I have not enumerated all the expenses incurred by the *Great Mogol.* He keeps in *Dehly* and *Agra* from two to three thousand fine horses, always at hand in case of emergency: eight or nine hundred elephants, and a large number of baggage horses, mules, and porters, intended to carry the numerous and capacious tents, with their fittings, his wives and women, furniture, kitchen apparatus, *Ganges'-water,*[1] and all the other articles neces-

[1] The Mogul Emperors were great connoisseurs in the matter of good water, and the following extract from the *Ain-i-Akbari,* vol. i. p. 55, regarding the department of state, the *Abdar Khanah,* which had to do with the supply and cooling of drinking water, also with the supply of ice, then brought in the form of frozen snow from the Himalayas, is interesting. 'His Majesty calls this source of life "the water of immortality," and has committed the care of this department to proper persons. He does not drink much but pays much attention to this matter. Both at home and on travels he drinks Ganges water. Some trustworthy persons are stationed on the banks of that river, who despatch the water in sealed jars. When the Court was at the capital Agra and in Futtepore-Seekree, the water came from the district of Sarun,[1] but now that his Majesty is in the Panjab, the water is brought from Hardwar. For the cooking of the food, rain water or water taken from the Jamnah and Chenab is used, mixed with a little Ganges water. On journeys and hunting parties his Majesty, from his predilection for good water, appoints experienced men as water-tasters.'

[1] Thus in printed translation; should be Soron, the well-known place on the Ganges south-west from Badaon, and the nearest point on that river from Agra.

sary for the camp, which the *Mogol* has always about him, as in his capital, things which are not considered necessary in our kingdoms in Europe.

Add to this, if you will, the enormous expenses of the *Seraglio*, where the consumption of fine cloths of gold, and brocades, silks, embroideries, pearls, musk, amber and sweet essences, is greater than can be conceived.

Thus, although the *Great Mogol* be in the receipt of an immense revenue, his expenditure being much in the same proportion, he cannot possess the vast surplus of wealth that most people seem to imagine. I admit that his income exceeds probably the joint revenues of the *Grand Seignior* and of the King of *Persia*; but if I were to call him a wealthy monarch, it would be in the sense that a treasurer is to be considered wealthy who pays with one hand the large sums which he receives with the other. I should call that King effectively rich who, without oppressing or impoverishing his people, possessed revenues sufficient to support the expenses of a numerous and magnificent court—to erect grand and useful edifices—to indulge a liberal and kind disposition—to maintain a military force for the defence of his dominions—and, besides all this, to reserve an accumulating fund that would provide against any unforeseen rupture with his neighbours, although it should prove of some years' duration. The Sovereign of the *Indies* is doubtless possessed of many of these advantages, but not to the degree generally supposed. What I have said on the subject of the great expenses to which he is unavoidably exposed, has perhaps inclined you to this opinion; and the two facts I am about to relate, of which I had an opportunity to ascertain the correctness, will convince your lordship that the pecuniary resources of the *Great Mogol* himself may be exaggerated.

First.—Toward the conclusion of the late war, *Aureng-Zebe* was perplexed how to pay and supply his armies, notwithstanding that the war had continued but five years, that the pay of the troops was less than usual, that, with the exception of *Bengale* where *Sultan Sujah* still held out, a profound tranquillity reigned in every part of *Hindoustan*, and that he had so lately appropriated to himself a large portion of the treasures of his father *Chah-Jehan.*

Second.—*Chah-Jehan*, who was a great economist, and reigned more than forty years without being involved in any great wars, never amassed six *kourours* of *roupies.*[1] But I do not include in this sum a great abundance of gold and silver articles, of various descriptions, curiously wrought, and covered with precious stones; or a prodigious quantity of pearls and gems of all kinds, of great size and value. I doubt whether any other Monarch possesses more of this species of wealth; a throne of the great *Mogol,* covered with pearls and diamonds, being alone valued, if my memory be correct, at three *kourours* of *roupies.* But all these precious stones, and valuable articles, are the spoils of ancient princes, *Patans* and *Rajas,* collected during a long course of years, and, increasing regularly under every reign, by presents which the *Omrahs* are compelled to make on certain annual festivals. The whole of this treasure is considered the property of the crown, which it is criminal to touch, and upon the security of which the King, in a time of pressing necessity, would find it extremely difficult to raise the smallest sum.

Before I conclude, I wish to explain how it happens that, although this Empire of the *Mogol* is such an abyss for gold and silver, as I said before, these precious metals are not in greater plenty here than elsewhere; on the contrary, the inhabitants have less the appearance of a moneyed people than those of many other parts of the globe.

In the first place, a large quantity is melted, re-melted, and wasted, in fabricating women's bracelets, both for

[1] I have already stated [see p. 200, footnote] that a *roupie* is worth about twenty-nine sols. One hundred thousand make a *lecque,* and one hundred lecques one *kourour.*—*Bernier.*

the hands and feet, chains, ear-rings, nose and finger rings, and a still larger quantity is consumed in manufacturing embroideries; *alachas*, or striped silken stuffs; *touras*,[1] or fringes of gold lace, worn on turbans; gold and silver cloths; scarfs, turbans, and brocades.[2] The quantity of these articles made in *India* is incredible. All the troops, from the *Omrah* to the man in the ranks, will wear gilt ornaments; nor will a private soldier refuse them to his wife and children, though the whole family should die of hunger; which indeed is a common occurrence.

In the second place, the *King*, as proprietor of the land, makes over a certain quantity to military men, as an equivalent for their pay; and this grant is called *jah-ghir*, or, as in Turkey, *timar*; the word *jah-ghir* signifying the spot from which to draw, or the place of salary. Similar grants are made to governors, in lieu of their salary, and also for the support of their troops, on condition that they pay a certain sum annually to the King out of any surplus revenue that the land may yield. The lands not so granted are retained by the King as the peculiar domains of his house, and are seldom, if ever, given in the way of *jah-ghir*; and upon these domains he keeps contractors,[3] who are also bound to pay him an annual rent.

[1] From the Persian word *turreh*, a lock of hair. Fringes, with which the ends of turban cloths are finished off.

[2] Recent travellers have remarked upon this 'abyss for gold and silver,' to use Bernier's forcible language, in the East generally, and in an interesting special article in *The Times* of March 13th, 1891, describing the cutting of the top-knot (a 'coming of age' ceremony) of the heir-apparent to the Crown of Siam which took place on the 19th of January, we read, *à propos* of the grand procession :—

> 'But a Siamese procession is in itself a marvel, compared with which the most ambitious Lord Mayor's Show is a very one-horse affair. The Royal crown alone worn by the King in his palanquin, would, if converted into pounds sterling, pay for a great many such shows. So would his jewelled uniform, and so would the crown of the small Prince. Many thousands of pounds' worth of pure gold is carried along on the belts and Court uniforms of the grandees; and an inventory of the other "properties" displayed would rather astonish a manager of stage processions in Europe.'

In this connection see Appendix IV.

[3] In the original, *Fermiers*.

The persons thus put in possession of the land, whether as *timariots*, governors, or contractors, have an authority almost absolute over the peasantry, and nearly as much over the artisans and merchants of the towns and villages within their district; and nothing can be imagined more cruel and oppressive than the manner in which it is exercised. There is no one before whom the injured peasant, artisan, or tradesman can pour out his just complaints; no great lords, parliaments, or judges of local courts, exist, as in *France*, to restrain the wickedness of those merciless oppressors, and the *Kadis*, or judges, are not invested with sufficient power to redress the wrongs of these unhappy people. This sad abuse of the royal authority may not be felt in the same degree near capital cities such as *Dehly* and *Agra*, or in the vicinity of large towns and seaports, because in those places acts of gross injustice cannot easily be concealed from the court.

This debasing state of slavery obstructs the progress of trade and influences the manners and mode of life of every individual. There can be little encouragement to engage in commercial pursuits, when the success with which they may be attended, instead of adding to the enjoyments of life, provokes the cupidity of a neighbouring tyrant possessing both power and inclination to deprive any man of the fruits of his industry. When wealth is acquired, as must sometimes be the case, the possessor, so far from living with increased comfort and assuming an air of independence, studies the means by which he may appear indigent: his dress, lodging, and furniture, continue to be mean, and he is careful, above all things, never to indulge in the pleasures of the table. In the meantime, his gold and silver remain buried at a great depth in the ground; agreeable to the general practice among the peasantry, artisans and merchants, whether *Mahometans* or *Gentiles*, but especially among the latter, who possess almost exclusively the trade and wealth of the country, and who believe that the money concealed during life will prove beneficial to them after death. A few individuals alone who derive their income from the King or from the *Omrahs*, or who are protected by a powerful patron, are at no pains to counterfeit poverty, but partake of the comforts and luxuries of life.

I have no doubt that this habit of secretly burying the precious metals, and thus withdrawing them from circulation, is the principal cause of their apparent scarcity in *Hindoustan*.

From what I have said, a question will naturally arise, whether it would not be more advantageous for the King as well as for the people, if the former ceased to be sole possessor of the land, and the right of private property[1] were recognised in the *Indies* as it is with us? I have carefully compared the condition of *European* states, where that right is acknowledged, with the condition of those countries where it is not known, and am persuaded that the absence of it among the people is injurious to the best interests of the Sovereign himself. We have seen how in the *Indies* the gold and silver disappear in consequence of the tyranny of Timariots, Governors, and Revenue contractors—a tyranny which even the monarch, if so disposed, has no means of controlling in provinces not contiguous to his capital—a tyranny often so excessive as to deprive the peasant and artisan of the necessaries of life, and leave them to die of misery and exhaustion—a tyranny owing to which those wretched people either have no children at all, or have them only to endure the agonies of starvation, and to die at a tender age—a tyranny, in fine, that drives the cultivator of the soil from his wretched home to some neighbouring state, in hopes of finding milder treatment, or to the army, where he becomes the servant of some trooper. As the ground is seldom tilled otherwise than by compulsion, and as no person is found willing and able to repair the ditches and canals for the conveyance of water, it happens that

[1] In the original, *ce Mien et ce Tien.*

the whole country is badly cultivated, and a great part rendered unproductive from the want of irrigation. The houses, too, are left in a dilapidated condition, there being few people who will either build new ones, or repair those which are tumbling down. The peasant cannot avoid asking himself this question: 'Why should I toil for a tyrant who may come to-morrow and lay his rapacious hands upon all I possess and value, without leaving me, if such should be his humour, the means to drag on my miserable existence?'—The Timariots, Governors, and Revenue contractors, on their part reason in this manner: 'Why should the neglected state of this land create uneasiness in our minds? and why should we expend our own money and time to render it fruitful? We may be deprived of it in a single moment, and our exertions would benefit neither ourselves nor our children. Let us draw from the soil all the money we can, though the peasant should starve or abscond, and we should leave it, when commanded to quit, a dreary wilderness.'

The facts I have mentioned are sufficient to account for the rapid decline of the *Asiatic* states. It is owing to this miserable system of government that most towns in *Hindoustan* are made up of earth, mud, and other wretched materials; that there is no city or town which, if it be not already ruined and deserted, does not bear evident marks of approaching decay. Without confining our remarks to so distant a kingdom, we may judge of the effects of despotic power unrelentingly exercised, by the present condition of *Mesopotamia, Anatolia, Palestine*, the once wonderful plains of *Antioch*, and so many other regions anciently well cultivated, fertile, and populous, but now desolate, and in many parts marshy, pestiferous, and unfit for human habitation. *Egypt* also exhibits a sad picture of an enslaved country. More than one-tenth part of that incomparable territory has been lost within the last eighty years, because no one will be at the expense of repairing the irrigation channels, and confining the *Nile* within its banks. The low lands are thus violently inundated, and covered with sand, which cannot be removed without much labour and expense. Can it excite wonder, that under these circumstances, the arts do not flourish here as they would do under a better government, or as they flourish in our happier *France*? No artist can be expected to give his mind to his calling in the midst of a people who are either wretchedly poor, or who, if rich, assume an appearance of poverty, and who regard not the beauty and excellence, but the cheapness of an article: a people whose grandees pay for a work of art considerably under its value, and according to their own caprice, and who do not hesitate to punish an importunate artist, or tradesman, with the *korrah*, that long and terrible whip hanging at every *Omrah's* gate. Is it not enough also to damp the ardour of any artist, when he feels that he can never hope to attain to any distinction; that he shall not be permitted to purchase either office or land for the benefit of himself and family; that he must at no time make it appear he is the owner of the most trifling sum; and that he may never venture to indulge in good fare, or to dress in fine apparel, lest he should create a suspicion of his possessing money?[1] The arts in the *Indies* would long ago have lost their beauty and delicacy, if the Monarch and principal *Omrahs* did not keep in their pay a number of artists who work in their houses,[2] teach the children, and are stimulated to exertion by the hope of reward and the fear of the *korrah*. The protection afforded by powerful patrons to rich merchants and tradesmen who pay the workmen rather higher wages, tends also to preserve the arts. I say rather

[1] In 1882 on the occasion of the formation of a Loan Collection of arts and manufactures in connection with an Agricultural Exhibition at Lucknow, many of the possessors of various ancient family jewels, amulets, and other works of art, were at first unwilling to lend them, lest by their doing so they should acquire the reputation of being wealthy and be assessed at a high rate for Income-tax.

[2] See p. 258 text, and footnote [3].

higher wages, for it should not be inferred from the goodness of the manufactures, that the workman is held in esteem, or arrives at a state of independence. Nothing but sheer necessity or blows from a cudgel keeps him employed; he never can become rich, and he feels it no trifling matter if he have the means of satisfying the cravings of hunger, and of covering his body with the coarsest raiment. If money be gained, it does not in any measure go into his pocket, but only serves to increase the wealth of the merchant who, in his turn, is not a little perplexed how to guard against some act of outrage and extortion on the part of his superiors.

A profound and universal ignorance is the natural consequence of such a state of society as I have endeavoured to describe. Is it possible to establish in *Hindoustan* academies and colleges properly endowed? Where shall we seek for founders? or, should they be found, where are the scholars? Where the individuals whose property is sufficient to support their children at college? or, if such individuals exist, who would venture to display so clear a proof of wealth? Lastly, if any persons should be tempted to commit this great imprudence, yet where are the benefices, the employments, the offices of trust and dignity, that require ability and science and are calculated to excite the emulation and the hopes of the young student?

Nor can the commerce of a country so governed be conducted with the activity and success that we witness in *Europe*; few are the men who will voluntarily endure labour and anxiety, and incur danger, for another person's benefit,—for a governor who may appropriate to his own use the profit of any speculation. Let that profit be ever so great, the man by whom it has been made must still wear the garb of indigence, and fare no better, in regard to eating and drinking, than his poorer neighbours. In cases, indeed, where the merchant is protected by a military man of rank, he may be induced to embark in commercial enterprises; but still he must be the slave of his patron, who will exact whatever terms he pleases as the price of his protection.

The *Great Mogol* cannot select for his service, princes, noblemen and gentlemen of opulent and ancient families; nor the sons of his citizens, merchants and manufacturers; men of education, possessing a high sense of propriety, affectionately attached to their Sovereign, ready to support, by acts of valour, the reputation of their family, and, as the occasion may arise, able and willing to maintain themselves, either at court or in the army, by means of their own patrimony; animated by the hope of better times, and satisfied with the approbation and smile of their Sovereign. Instead of men of this description, he is surrounded by slaves, ignorant and brutal; by parasites raised from the dregs of society; strangers to loyalty and patriotism; full of insufferable pride, and destitute of courage, of honour, and of decency.

The country is ruined by the necessity of defraying the enormous charges required to maintain the splendour of a numerous court, and to pay a large army maintained for the purpose of keeping the people in subjection. No adequate idea can be conveyed of the sufferings of that people. The cudgel and the whip compel them to incessant labour for the benefit of others; and driven to despair by every kind of cruel treatment, their revolt or their flight is only prevented by the presence of a military force.

The misery of this ill-fated country is increased by the practice which prevails too much at all times, but especially on the breaking out of an important war, of selling the different governments for immense sums in hard cash. Hence it naturally becomes the principal object of the individual thus appointed Governor, to obtain repayment of the purchase-money, which he borrowed as he could at a ruinous rate of interest. Indeed whether the government of a province has or has not been bought, the Governor, as well as the *timariot* and the farmer of the revenue, must find the means of making valuable presents, every year, to a *Visir*, a *Eunuch*, a lady of the *Seraglio*, and to any other person whose influence at court he considers indispensable. The Governor must also enforce the payment of the regular tribute to the King; and although he was originally a wretched slave, involved in debt, and without the smallest patrimony, he yet becomes a great and opulent lord.

Thus do ruin and desolation overspread the land. The provincial governors, as before observed, are so many petty tyrants, possessing a boundless authority; and as there is no one to whom the oppressed subject may appeal, he cannot hope for redress, let his injuries be ever so grievous or ever so frequently repeated.

It is true that the *Great Mogol* sends a *Vakea-Nevis* [1] to the various provinces; that is, persons whose business it is to communicate every event that takes place; but there is generally a disgraceful collusion between these officers and the governor, so that their presence seldom restrains the tyranny exercised over the unhappy people.

Governments also are not so often and so openly sold in *Hindoustan* as in *Turkey*. I say 'so openly,' because the costly presents, made occasionally by the governors, are nearly equivalent to purchase-money. The same persons, too, generally remain longer in their respective governments than in *Turkey*, and the people are gradually less oppressed by governors of some standing than when, indigent and greedy, they first take possession of their province. The tyranny of these men is also somewhat

[1] A corruption of the Persian word *Wáki'ahnawís*, a newswriter, an institution of the Emperor Akbar's. Fryer partly attributed Aurangzeb's non-success in the Deccan, although he had large armies there, to the false reports sent by his newswriters, stating:—'Notwithstanding all these formidable Numbers, while the Generals and *Vocanovices* consult to deceive the Emperor, on whom he depends for a true state of things, it can never be otherwise but that they must be misrepresented, when the Judgment he makes must be by a false Perspective.'

mitigated by the apprehension that the people, if used with excessive cruelty, may abandon the country, and seek an asylum in the territory of some *Raja*, as indeed happens very often.

In *Persia* likewise are governments neither so frequently nor so publicly sold as in *Turkey*; for it is not uncommon for the children of governors to succeed their fathers. The consequence of this better state of things is seen in the superior condition of the people, as compared to those of *Turkey*. The *Persians* also are more polite, and there are even instances of their devoting themselves to study.

Those three countries, *Turkey*, *Persia*, and *Hindoustan*, have no idea of the principle of *meum* and *tuum*, relatively to land or other real possessions; and having lost that respect for the right of property, which is the basis of all that is good and useful in the world, necessarily resemble each other in essential points: they fall into the same pernicious errors, and must, sooner or later, experience the natural consequences of those errors—tyranny, ruin, and misery.

How happy and thankful should we feel, My Lord, that in our quarter of the globe, Kings are not the sole proprietors of the soil! Were they so, we should seek in vain for countries well cultivated and populous, for well-built and opulent cities, for a polite, contented, and flourishing people. If this exclusive and baneful right prevailed, far different would be the real riches of the sovereigns of *Europe*, and the loyalty and fidelity with which they are served. They would soon reign over solitudes and deserts, over mendicants and barbarians.

Actuated by a blind and wicked ambition to be more absolute than is warranted by the laws of God and of nature, the Kings of *Asia* grasp at everything, until at length they lose everything; or, if they do not always find themselves without pecuniary resources, they are invariably disappointed in the expectation of acquiring the riches which they covet. If the same system of government existed with us, where, I must again ask, should we find Princes, Prelates, Nobles, opulent Citizens, and thriving Tradesmen, ingenious Artisans and Manufacturers? Where should we look for such cities as *Paris, Lyons, Toulouse, Rouen,* or, if you will, *London,* and so many others? Where should we see that infinite number of towns and villages; all those beautiful country houses, those fine plains, hills and valleys, cultivated with so much care, art and labour? and what would become of the ample revenues derived from so much industry, an industry beneficial alike to the sovereign and the subject? The reverse of this smiling picture would, alas! be exhibited. Our large towns would become uninhabitable in consequence of the unwholesome air, and fall into ruins without exciting in any person a thought of preventing or repairing the decay; our fertile hills would be abandoned, and the plains would be overrun with thorns and weeds, or covered with pestilential morasses. The excellent accommodation for travellers would disappear; the good inns, for example, between *Paris* and *Lyons,* would dwindle into ten or twelve wretched caravansaries, and travellers be reduced to the necessity of moving, like the *Gypsies,* with everything about them. The Eastern *Karavans-Serrah* resemble large barns, raised and paved all round, in the same manner as our *Pont-neuf.* Hundreds of human beings are seen in them, mingled with their horses, mules, and camels. In summer these buildings are hot and suffocating, and in winter nothing but the breath of so many animals prevents the inmates from dying of cold.

But there are countries, I shall be told, such for instance as the Grand *Seignior's* dominions, which we know better than any without going as far as the *Indies,* where the principle of *meum* and *tuum* is unknown, which not only preserve their existence, but maintain a great and increasing power.

An empire so prodigiously extensive as that of the Grand *Seignior,* comprising countries whose soil is so deep and excellent that even without due cultivation it will continue fertile for many years, cannot be otherwise than rich and powerful. Yet how insignificant is the wealth and strength of *Turkey* in comparison to its extent and natural advantages! Let us only suppose that country as populous and as carefully cultivated as it would become if the right of private property were recognised and acted upon, and we cannot doubt that it could raise and support armies as numerous and well-appointed as formerly: but even at *Constantinople* three months are now required to raise five or six thousand men. I have travelled through nearly every part of the empire, and witnessed how lamentably it is ruined and depopulated. Some support it undoubtedly derives from the *Christian slaves* brought from all quarters; but if that country continue many years under the present system of government, it must necessarily fall and perish from innate weakness, though, to all appearance, it is now preserved by that weakness itself; for there is no longer a governor, or any other person, possessed of pecuniary means to undertake the least enterprise, or who could find the men he would require to accomplish his purpose. Strange means of preservation! *Turkey* seems to owe its transient existence to the seeds of destruction in its own bosom! To remove the danger of commotion and put an end to all fears on that subject, nothing more appears necessary than the measure adopted by a *Brama*[1] of *Pegu*, who actually

[1] Thus in the original. Ferdinand Mendez Pinto, who travelled in Pegu about 1542-45, styles the then king of that country *Bramaa*. It is probable that Bernier uses the term to denote the Supreme King of Pegu, who in 1593 caused many of his most loyal officers to be put to death, and by other deeds of cruelty so alarmed his subjects that thousands abandoned the country and fled, which thus became depopulated and uncultivated. See chapter lxiii. of *The Voyages and Adventures of Ferdinand Mendez Pinto, a Portugal; During his travels for the space of one-and-twenty years in the Kingdoms of Ethiopia, China, . . Pegu . . London* 1663, which is entitled *That which the King of* Bramaa *did after his arrival at the city of* Pegu, *together with his besieging of* Savady.

caused the death of half the population by famine, converted the country into forests, and prevented for many years the tillage of the land. But all this did not suffice: even this plan was unsuccessful; a division of the kingdom took place, and *Ava*, the capital, was very lately on the point of being captured by a handful of fugitives from *China*.[1] We must confess, however, that there seems little probability of the total ruin and destruction of the *Turkish* empire in our day—it will be happy if we see nothing worse!—because the neighbouring states, so far from being able to attack it, are not in a condition to defend themselves effectually, without foreign aid, which remoteness and jealousy will always render tardy, inefficient, and liable to suspicion.

If it be observed that there is no reason why eastern states should not have the benefit of good laws, or why the people in the provinces may not complain of their grievances to a grand *Visir*, or to the King himself; I shall admit that they are not altogether destitute of good laws, which, if properly administered, would render *Asia* as eligible a residence as any other part of the world. But of what advantage are good laws when not observed, and when there is no possibility of enforcing their observance? Have not the provincial tyrants been nominated by the same grand *Visir* and by the same King, who alone have power to redress the people's wrongs? and is it not a fact that they have no means of appointing any but tyrants to rule over the provinces? either the *Visir* or the King has sold the place to the Governor. And even admitting that there existed a disposition to listen to a complaint, how is a poor peasant or a ruined artisan to defray the expenses of a journey to the capital, and to seek justice at one hundred and fifty or two hundred leagues from home? He would

[1] This happened in May 1659, and it is said that the repulse of the Chinese was mainly due to the skill and bravery of native Christian gunners, descendants of Portuguese captives.

be waylaid and murdered, as frequently happens, or sooner or later fall into the Governor's hands, and be at his mercy. Should he chance to reach the royal residence, he would find the friends of his oppressor busy in distorting the truth, and misrepresenting the whole affair to the King. In short, the Governor is absolute lord, in the strictest sense of the word. He is in his own person the intendant of justice, the parliament, the presidial court, and the assessor and receiver of the King's taxes. A *Persian,* in speaking of these greedy Governors, Timariots, and Farmers of Revenue, aptly describes them as men who extract oil out of sand. No income appears adequate to maintain them, with their crowds of harpies, women, children, and slaves.

If it be remarked that the lands which our Kings hold as domains are as well cultivated, and as thickly peopled as other lands, my answer is that there can be no analogy between a kingdom whose monarch is proprietor of a few domains, and a kingdom where the monarch possesses, in his own right, every acre of the soil. In *France* the laws are so reasonable, that the King is the first to obey them: his domains are held without the violation of any right; his farmers or stewards may be sued at law, and the aggrieved artisan or peasant is sure to find redress against injustice and oppression. But in eastern countries, the weak and the injured are without any refuge whatever; and the only law that decides all controversies is the cane and the caprice of a governor.

There certainly however, some may say, are some advantages peculiar to despotic governments: they have fewer lawyers, and fewer law-suits, and those few are more speedily decided. We cannot, indeed, too greatly admire the old Persian proverb, *Na-hac Kouta Better-Ez hac Deraz*:[1] 'Speedy injustice is preferable to tardy justice.' Protracted law-suits are, I admit, insupportable

[1] Or, as more correctly transliterated, *Ná-haqqi kūtah bihtar az haqqi diráz.*

evils in any state, and it is incumbent upon a Sovereign to provide a remedy against them. It is certain that no remedy would be so efficacious as the destruction of the right of private property. Do away with this *meum* and *tuum*, and the necessity for an infinite number of legal proceedings will at once cease, especially for those which are important, long, and intricate: the larger portion of magistrates employed by the King to administer justice to his subjects will also become useless, as will those swarms of attorneys and counsellors who live by judicial contests. But it is equally certain that the remedy would be infinitely worse than the disease, and that there is no estimating the misery that would afflict the country. Instead of magistrates on whose probity the monarch can depend, we should be at the mercy of such rulers as I have described. In *Asia*, if justice be ever administered, it is among the lower classes, among persons who, being equally poor, have no means of corrupting the judges, and of buying false witnesses; witnesses always to be had in great numbers, at a cheap rate, and never punished. I am speaking the language of several years' experience; my information was obtained from various quarters, and is the result of many careful inquiries among the natives, European merchants long settled in the country, ambassadors, consuls, and interpreters.[1] My testimony is, I know, at variance with the account given by most of our travellers. They happened, perhaps, in passing through a town, to see two poor men, the dregs of the people, in the presence of a *Kadi*. Our countryman may have seen them hurried out of court to receive, either the one or the other, if not both, hard blows on the soles of the feet, unless the parties were immediately dismissed with a '*Maybalé-Baba*,'[2] or a few soft words which the magistrate sometimes utters when he finds that no bribe can be

[1] *Truchemens* in the original, our 'dragoman.'

[2] Intended for *mubâ'eléh Baba*, 'Be at peace, my children,' equivalent to advising them to settle their case out of court.

expected. No doubt, this summary mode of proceeding excited the admiration of our travellers, and they returned to *France,* exclaiming, 'O, what an excellent and quick administration of justice! O, the upright *Kadis*! Models for the imitation of *French* magistrates!' not considering that if the party really in the wrong had possessed the means of putting a couple of crowns into the hands of the *Kadi* or his clerks, and of buying with the same sum two false witnesses, he would indisputably have gained his cause, or prolonged it as long as he pleased.

Yes, My Lord, to conclude briefly I must repeat it; take away the right of private property in land, and you introduce, as a sure and necessary consequence, tyranny, slavery, injustice, beggary and barbarism: the ground will cease to be cultivated and become a dreary wilderness; in a word, the road will be opened to the ruin of Kings and the destruction of Nations. It is the hope by which a man is animated, that he shall retain the fruits of his industry, and transmit them to his descendants, that forms the main foundation of everything excellent and beneficial in this sublunary state; and if we take a review of the different kingdoms in the world, we shall find that they prosper or decline according as this principle is acknowledged or contemned: in a word, it is the prevalence or neglect of this principle which changes and diversifies the face of the earth.

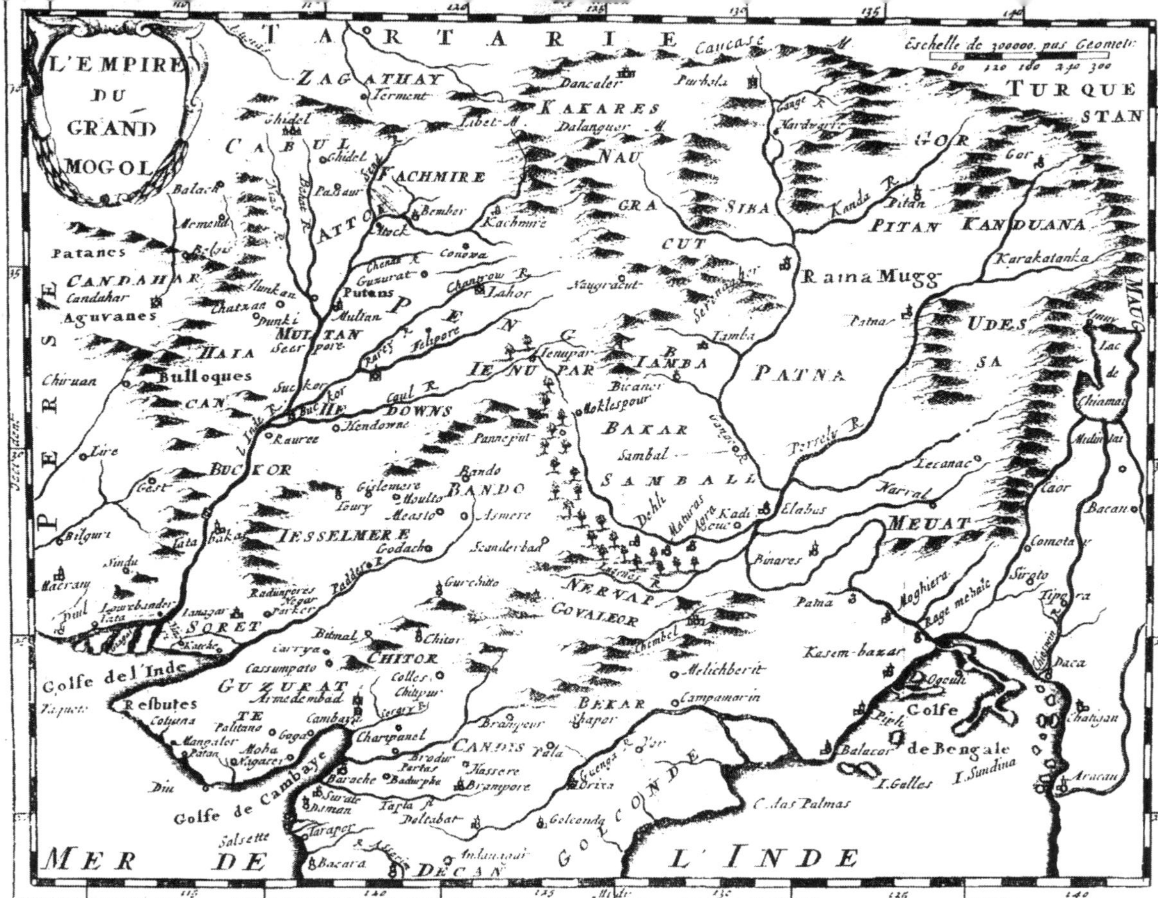
L'EMPIRE DU GRAND MOGOL
Eschelle de 300000. pas Geometr.
TARTARIE
TURQUESTAN
PERSE
CANDAHAR
CABUL
KACHMIRE
ATTOC
MULTAN
PENGAB
BUCKOR
IESSELMERE
BANDO
SAMBALL
BAKAR
PATNA
Raina Mugg
KANDUANA
PITAN
UDESSA
MEUAT
NERVAR
GOVALEOR
CHITOR
GUZURAT
SORET
CANDIS
BEKAR
GOLCONDE
DECAN
Golfe de l'Inde
Golfe de Cambaye
Golfe de Bengale
MER DE L'INDE

LETTER

TO MONSIEUR

DE LA

MOTHE LE VAYER

Written at Dehli the first of July 1663.

Containing a description of Dehli and Agra, the Capital Cities of the Empire of the Great Mogol, together with various details illustrative of the Court Life and the Civilisation of the Mogols and the People of the Indies.

MONSIEUR,

I know that your[1] first inquiries on my return to *France* will be respecting the capital cities of this empire. You will be anxious to learn if *Dehli* and *Agra* rival

[1] François de la Mothe le Vayer, 1588-1672, was a very voluminous and able writer on ethnological, geographical, and historical subjects. He succeeded his father Félix, who died on the 25th September 1625, in a parliamentary office, but soon abandoned law for letters. Bernier was one of his most intimate friends, and when he came to see him as he lay on his death-bed, almost his last utterance was the greeting, 'Eh bien! quelles nouvelles avez-vous du grand Mogol?' (Well! what news have you of the Great Mogul?)

Paris in beauty, extent, and number of inhabitants. I hasten, therefore, to gratify your curiosity upon these points, and I may perhaps intersperse a few other matters which you will not find altogether uninteresting.

In treating of the beauty of these towns, I must premise that I have sometimes been astonished to hear the contemptuous manner in which Europeans in the *Indies* speak of these and other places. They complain that the buildings are inferior in beauty to those of the Western world, forgetting that different climates require different styles of architecture; that what is useful and proper at *Paris*, *London*, or *Amsterdam*, would be entirely out of place at *Dehli*; insomuch that if it were possible for any one of those great capitals to change place with the metropolis of the *Indies*, it would become necessary to throw down the greater part of the city, and to rebuild it on a totally different plan. Without doubt, the cities of *Europe* may boast great beauties; these, however, are of an appropriate character, suited to a cold climate. Thus *Dehli* also may possess beauties adapted to a warm climate. The heat is so intense in *Hindoustan*, that no one, not even the King, wears stockings; the only cover for the feet being *babouches*,[1] or slippers, while the head is protected by a small turban, of the finest and most delicate materials. The other garments are proportionably light. During the summer season, it is scarcely possible to keep the hand on the wall of an apartment, or the head on a pillow. For more than six successive months, everybody lies in the open air without covering—the common people in the streets, the merchants and persons of condition sometimes in their courts or gardens, and sometimes on their terraces, which are first carefully watered. Now, only suppose the streets of *S. Jaques* or *S. Denis* transported hither, with their close houses and endless stories; would they be habitable? or would it be possible to sleep in them during the night, when the absence of wind

[1] *Paonposh*; literally *foot-cover.*

increases the heat almost to suffocation? Suppose one just returned on horseback, half dead with heat and dust, and drenched, as usual, in perspiration; and then imagine the luxury of squeezing up a narrow dark staircase to the fourth or fifth story, there to remain almost choked with heat. In the *Indies*, there is no such troublesome task to perform. You have only to swallow quickly a draught of fresh water, or lemonade; to undress; wash face, hands, and feet, and then immediately drop upon a sofa in some shady place, where one or two servants fan you with their great *panhas*[1] or fans. But I shall now endeavour to give you an accurate description of *Dehli*, that you may judge for yourselves how far it has a claim to the appellation of a beautiful city.

It is about forty years ago that *Chah-Jehan*, father of the present *Great Mogol*, *Aureng-Zebe*, conceived the design of immortalising his name by the erection of a city near the site of the ancient *Dehli*. This new capital he called after his own name, *Chah-Jehan-Abad*, or, for brevity, *Jehan-Abad*; that is to say, the colony of *Chah-Jehan*. Here he resolved to fix his court, alleging as the reason for its removal from *Agra*, that the excessive heat to which that city is exposed during summer rendered it unfit for the residence of a monarch. Owing to their being so near at hand, the ruins of old *Dehli* have served to build the new city, and in the *Indies* they scarce speak any more of *Dehli*, but only of *Jehan-Abad*; however, as the city of *Jehan-Abad* is not yet known to us, I intend to speak of it under the old name of *Dehli*, with which we are familiar.

Dehli, then, is an entirely new city, situated in a flat country, on the banks of the *Gemna*, a river which may be compared to the *Loire*, and built on one bank only in such a manner that it terminates in this place very much in the form of a crescent, having but one bridge of boats to cross to the country. Excepting the side where it is defended by the river, the city is encompassed by walls of brick.

[1] Thus in original; a misprint for *pankhas*.

The fortifications, however, are very incomplete, as there are neither ditches nor any other kind of additional defence, if we except flanking towers of antique shape, at intervals of about one hundred paces, and a bank of earth forming a platform behind the walls, four or five feet in thickness. Although these works encompass not only the city but the citadel, yet their extent is less than is generally supposed. I have accomplished the circuit with ease in the space of three hours, and notwithstanding I rode on horseback, I do not think my progress exceeded a league per hour. In this computation I do not however include the suburbs, which are considerable, comprising a long chain of buildings on the side of *Lahor*, the extensive remains of the old city, and three or four smaller suburbs. By these additions the extent of the city is so much increased that a straight line may be traced in it of more than a league and a half; and though I cannot undertake to define exactly the circumference, because these suburbs are interspersed with extensive gardens and open spaces, yet you must see that it is very great.

The citadel, which contains the *Mehalle* or *Seraglio*, and the other royal apartments of which I shall have occasion to speak hereafter, is round, or rather semicircular. It commands a prospect of the river, from which it is separated by a sandy space of considerable length and width. On these sands are exhibited the combats of elephants, and there the corps belonging to the *Omrahs* or lords, and those of the Rajas or *gentile* princes, pass in review before the Sovereign, who witnesses the spectacle from the windows of the palace. The walls of the citadel, as to their antique and round towers, resemble those of the city, but being partly of brick, and partly of a red stone which resembles marble, they have a better appearance. The walls of the fortress likewise excel those of the town in height, strength, and thickness, being capable of admitting small field-pieces, which are pointed toward the city. Except on the side of the river, the citadel is defended by a deep ditch faced with hewn stone, filled with water, and stocked with fish. Considerable as these works may appear, their real strength is by no means great, and in my opinion a battery of moderate force would soon level them with the ground.

Adjoining the ditch is a large garden, filled at all times with flowers and green shrubs, which, contrasted with the stupendous red walls, produce a beautiful effect.

Next to the garden is the great royal square, faced on one side by the gates of the fortress, and on the opposite side of which terminate the two most considerable streets of the city.

The tents of such *Rajas* as are in the King's pay, and whose weekly turn it is to mount guard, are pitched in this square; those petty sovereigns having an insuperable objection to be enclosed within walls.[1] The guard within the fortress is mounted by the *Omrahs* and *Mansebdars*.

In this place also at break of day they exercise the royal horses, which are kept in a spacious stable not far distant; and here the *Kobat-kan*, or grand Muster-master of the cavalry, examines carefully the horses of those who have been received into the service. If they are found to be *Turki* horses, that is, from *Turkistan* or *Tartary*,[2] and of a proper size and adequate strength, they are branded on the thigh with the King's mark and with the mark of the *Omrah* under whom the horseman is enlisted. This is well contrived, to prevent the loan of the same horses for different review days.[3]

Here too is held a *bazar* or market for an endless variety of things; which like the *Pont-neuf* at *Paris*, is the rendezvous for all sorts of mountebanks and jugglers. Hither, likewise, the astrologers resort, both *Mahometan* and *Gentile*. These wise doctors remain seated in the sun, on a dusty

[1] See p. 210.

[2] Called Turkí horses, and reckoned by Akbar as third class.

[3] Akbar introduced, or rather revived, very elaborate regulations for branding the royal horses. See *Ain*, vol. i. p. 139 *et seq.*

piece of carpet, handling some old mathematical instruments, and having open before them a large book which represents the signs of the zodiac. In this way they attract the attention of the passengers, and impose upon the people, by whom they are considered as so many infallible oracles. They tell a poor person his fortune for a *payssa* (which is worth about one sol); and after examining the hand and face of the applicant, turning over the leaves of the large book, and pretending to make certain calculations, these impostors decide upon the *Sahet*[1] or propitious moment of commencing the business he may have in hand. Silly women, wrapping themselves in a white cloth from head to foot, flock to the astrologers, whisper to them all the transactions of their lives, and disclose every secret with no more reserve than is practised by a scrupulous penitent in the presence of her confessor. The ignorant and infatuated people really believe that the stars have an influence which the astrologers can control.

The most ridiculous of these pretenders to divination was a half-caste *Portuguese*, a fugitive from *Goa*. This fellow sat on his carpet as gravely as the rest, and had many customers notwithstanding he could neither read nor write. His only instrument was an old mariner's compass,[2] and his books of astrology a couple of old Romish prayer-books in the *Portuguese* language, the pictures of which he pointed out as the signs of the *European* zodiac. *A tal Bestias, tal Astrologuo,*[3] he unblushingly observed to the Jesuit, the Reverend Father Buzé, who saw him at his work.

[1] Read *Saiët*, see p. 161.

[2] The Chinese used a modified form of the mariner's compass for purposes of divination from an early period. See p. 169 *et seq.* of a *Letter to Baron Humboldt, on the Invention of the Mariner's Compass, by M. J. Klaproth.* Paris, Dondey-Dupré, 1834. Other Oriental nations appear to have done the same.

[3] 'For such brutes, such an astrologer,' equivalent to *Like master, like man*, or the Hindostanee proverb, *Such a country, such a dress* (*Jaisa dhes waisae bhes*).

I am speaking only of the poor *bazar-astrologers*. Those who frequent the court of the grandees are considered by them eminent doctors, and become wealthy. The whole of *Asia* is degraded by the same superstition. Kings and nobles grant large salaries to these crafty diviners, and never engage in the most trifling transaction without consulting them. They read whatever is written in heaven; fix upon the *Sahet*, and solve every doubt by opening the *Koran*.

The two principal streets of the city, already mentioned as leading into the square, may be five-and-twenty or thirty ordinary paces in width. They run in a straight line nearly as far as the eye can reach; but the one leading to the *Lahor* gate is much the longer. In regard to houses the two streets are exactly alike. As in our *Place Royale*, there are arcades on both sides; with this difference, however, that they are only brick, and that the top serves for a terrace and has no additional building. They also differ from the *Place Royale* in not having an uninterrupted opening from one to the other, but are generally separated by partitions, in the spaces between which are open shops, where, during the day, artisans work, bankers sit for the despatch of their business, and merchants exhibit their wares. Within the arch is a small door, opening into a warehouse, in which these wares are deposited for the night.

The houses of the merchants are built over these warehouses, at the back of the arcades: they look handsome enough from the street, and appear tolerably commodious within; they are airy, at a distance from the dust, and communicate with the terrace-roofs over the shops, on which the inhabitants sleep at night; the houses, however, are not continued the whole length of the streets. A few, and only a few, other parts of the city have good houses raised on terraces, the buildings over the shops being often too low to be seen from the street. The rich merchants have their dwellings elsewhere, to which they retire after the hours of business.

There are five streets, not so long nor so straight as the two principal ones, but resembling them in every other respect. Of the numberless streets which cross each other, many have arcades; but having been built at different periods by individuals who paid no regard to symmetry, very few are so well built, so wide, or so straight as those I have described.

Amid these streets are dispersed the habitations of *Mansebdars*, or petty *Omrahs*, officers of justice, rich merchants, and others; many of which have a tolerable appearance. Very few are built entirely of brick or stone, and several are made only of clay and straw, yet they are airy and pleasant, most of them having courts and gardens, being commodious inside and containing good furniture. The thatched roof is supported by a layer of long, handsome, and strong canes, and the clay walls are covered with a fine white lime.

Intermixed with these different houses is an immense number of small ones, built of mud and thatched with straw, in which lodge the common troopers, and all that vast multitude of servants and camp-followers who follow the court and the army.

It is owing to these thatched cottages that *Dehli* is subject to such frequent conflagrations. More than sixty thousand roofs were consumed this last year by three fires, during the prevalence of certain impetuous winds which blow generally in summer. So rapid were the flames that several camels and horses were burnt. Many of the inmates of the seraglio also fell victims to the devouring element; for these poor women are so bashful and helpless that they can do nothing but hide their faces at the sight of strangers, and those who perished possessed not sufficient energy to fly from the danger.

It is because of these wretched mud and thatch houses that I always represent to myself *Dehli* as a collection of many villages, or as a military encampment with a few more conveniences than are usually found in such places. The dwellings of the *Omrahs,* though mostly situated on the banks of the river and in the suburbs, are yet scattered in every direction. In these hot countries a house is considered beautiful if it be capacious, and if the situation be airy and exposed on all sides to the wind, especially to the northern breezes. A good house has its courtyards, gardens, trees, basins of water, small *jets d'eau* in the hall or at the entrance, and handsome subterraneous apartments which are furnished with large fans, and on account of their coolness are fit places for repose from noon until four or five o'clock, when the air becomes suffocatingly warm. Instead of these cellars many persons prefer *Kas-kanays,*[1] that is, small and neat houses made of straw or odoriferous roots placed commonly in the middle of a parterre, so near to a reservoir of water that the servants may easily moisten the outside by means of water brought in skins. They consider that a house to be greatly admired ought to be situated in the middle of a large flower-garden, and should have four large divan-apartments raised the height of a man from the ground, and exposed to the four winds, so that the coolness may be felt from any quarter. Indeed, no handsome dwelling is ever seen without terraces on which the family may sleep during the night. They always open into a large chamber into which the bedstead is easily moved in case of rain, when thick clouds of dust arise, when the cold air is felt at break of day, or when it is found necessary to guard against those light but penetrating dews which frequently cause a numbness in the limbs and induce a species of paralysis.

The interior of a good house has the whole floor covered

[1] *Khaskhas,* the roots of a plant, *Andropogon muricatus* (Retz.), used for the well-known screens which are placed in the doorways of houses in India during the hot winds, and kept constantly wetted, so that the external air enters the house cool and fragrant. Rooms or *khanahs,* the *kanays* of Bernier, are sometimes made of these *khaskhas* mats.

with a cotton mattress four inches in thickness, over which a fine white cloth is spread during the summer, and a silk carpet in the winter. At the most conspicuous side of the chamber are one or two mattresses, with fine coverings quilted in the form of flowers and ornamented with delicate silk embroidery, interspersed with gold and silver. These are intended for the master of the house, or any person of quality who may happen to call. Each mattress has a large cushion of brocade to lean upon, and there are other cushions placed round the room, covered with brocade, velvet or flowered satin, for the rest of the company. Five or six feet from the floor, the sides of the room are full of niches, cut in a variety of shapes, tasteful and well proportioned, in which are seen porcelain vases and flower-pots. The ceiling is gilt and painted, but without pictures of man or beast, such representations being forbidden by the religion of the country.

This is a pretty fair description of a fine house in these parts, and as there are many in *Dehli* possessing all the properties above mentioned, I think it may be safely asserted, without disparagement to the towns in our quarter of the globe, that the capital of *Hindoustan* is not destitute of handsome buildings, although they bear no resemblance to those in *Europe.*

That which so much contributes to the beauty of European towns, the brilliant appearance of the shops, is wanting in *Dehli.* For though this city be the seat of a powerful and magnificent court, where an infinite quantity of the richest commodities is necessarily collected, yet there are no streets like ours of *S. Denis,* which has not perhaps its equal in any part of *Asia.* Here the costly merchandise is generally kept in warehouses, and the shops are seldom decked with rich or showy articles. For one that makes a display of beautiful and fine cloths, silk, and other stuffs striped with gold and silver, turbans embroidered with gold, and brocades, there are at least five-and-twenty where nothing is seen but pots of oil or butter, piles of baskets filled with rice, barley, chick-peas, wheat, and an endless variety of other grain and pulse, the ordinary aliment not only of the *Gentiles,* who never eat meat, but of the lower class of *Mahometans,* and a considerable portion of the military.

There is, indeed, a fruit-market that makes some show. It contains many shops which during the summer are well supplied with dry fruit from *Persia, Balk, Bokara,* and *Samarkande*; such as almonds, pistachios, and walnuts, raisins, prunes, and apricots; and in winter with excellent fresh grapes, black and white, brought from the same countries, wrapped in cotton;[1] pears and apples of three or four sorts, and those admirable melons which last the whole winter. These fruits are, however, very dear; a single melon selling for a crown and a half. But nothing is considered so great a treat: it forms the chief expense of the *Omrahs,* and I have frequently known my *Agah* spend twenty crowns on fruit for his breakfast.

In summer the melons of the country are cheap, but they are of an inferior kind: there are no means of procuring good ones but by sending to *Persia* for seed, and sowing it in ground prepared with extraordinary care, in the manner practised by the grandees. Good melons, however, are scarce, the soil being so little congenial that the seed degenerates after the first year.

Ambas,[2] or *Mangues,* are in season during two months in summer, and are plentiful and cheap; but those grown at *Dehli* are indifferent. The best come from *Bengale, Golkonda,* and *Goa,* and these are indeed excellent. I do not know any sweetmeat more agreeable.

[1] A common practice to the present day, the round wooden boxes filled with grapes imbedded in cotton wool arriving in India about November, brought by Afghan traders.

[2] *Am* or *Ambra* (from the Sanskrit *amra*), is the Northern Indian name for this well-known fruit. From the Tamil name, *mankay,* was derived the Portuguese *manga,* Anglicised as mangoe. The places named by Bernier are still renowned for the excellent quality of their mangoes.

Pateques,[1] or water-melons, are in great abundance nearly the whole year round; but those of *Dehli* are soft, without colour or sweetness. If this fruit be ever found good, it is among the wealthy people, who import the seed and cultivate it with much care and expense.

There are many confectioners' shops in the town, but the sweatmeats are badly made, and full of dust and flies.

Bakers also are numerous, but the ovens are unlike our own, and very defective. The bread, therefore, is neither well made nor properly baked. That sold in the Fort is tolerably good, and the *Omrahs* bake at home, so that their bread is much superior. In its composition they are not sparing of fresh butter, milk, and eggs; but though it be raised, it has a burnt taste, and is too much like cake, and never to be compared to the *Pain de Gonesse,*[2] and other delicious kinds, to be met with in *Paris.*

In the *bazars* there are shops where meat is sold roasted and dressed in a variety of ways. But there is no trusting to their dishes, composed, for aught I know, of the flesh of camels, horses, or perhaps oxen which have died of disease. Indeed no food can be considered wholesome which is not dressed at home.

Meat is sold in every part of the city; but instead of goats' flesh that of mutton is often palmed upon the buyer; an imposition which ought to be guarded against, because mutton and beef, but particularly the former, though not unpleasant to the taste, are heating, flatulent, and difficult of digestion.[3] Kid is the best food, but being

[1] *Pateca* is the word used by the Portuguese in India for a water melon (derived from the Arabic *al-battikh*), whence the French *pastèque.*

[2] So called from the small town of Gonesse, about 9½ miles to the north-east of Paris, in the midst of a fine agricultural country, now and anciently celebrated for its corn, flour, and bread. It was the head-quarters of the British army on the 2d July 1815.

[3] At the present time in Northern India the complaint of the Anglo-Indian housewife is that goats' flesh is palmed off upon the buyer as mutton.

rarely sold in quarters, it must be purchased alive, which is very inconvenient, as the meat will not keep from morning to night, and is generally lean and without flavour. The goats' flesh found in quarters at the butchers' shops is frequently that of the she-goat, which is lean and tough.

But it would be unreasonable in me to complain; because since I have been familiarised with the manners of the people, it seldom happens that I find fault either with my meat or my bread. I send my servant to the King's purveyors in the Fort, who are glad to sell wholesome food, which costs them very little, at the high price I am willing to pay. My *Agah* smiled when I remarked that I had been for years in the habit of living by stealth and artifice, and that the one hundred and fifty crowns which he gave me monthly would not otherwise keep me from starving, although in *France* I could for half a *roupie* eat every day as good meat as the King.

As to capons, there are none to be had; the people being tender-hearted toward animals of every description, men only excepted; these being wanted for their *Seraglios*. The markets, however, are amply supplied with fowls, tolerably good and cheap. Among others, there is a small hen, delicate and tender, which I call *Ethiopian*, the skin being quite black.[1]

Pigeons are exposed for sale, but not young ones, the *Indians* considering them too small, and saying that it would be cruel to deprive them of life at so tender an age.

[1] This is a curious instance of the acute observation of Bernier. It is, as he tells us, the *skin* of certain fowls that is black, not the flesh as asserted by other travellers. Linschoten relates of the fowls of Mozambique, which he visited in August 1583, remaining there for two weeks, that 'There are certain hennes that are so blacke both of feathers, flesh, and bones, that being sodden they seeme as black as inke; yet of very sweet taste, and are accounted better than the other; whereof some are likewise found in India, but not so many as in Mossambique.'—*Voyage to East Indies*, pp. 25, 26, vol. i. Hakluyt Soc. Ed., 1885.

There are partridges, which are smaller than ours, but being caught with nets, and brought alive from a distance, are not so good as fowls. The same thing may be remarked of ducks and hares, which are brought alive in crowded cages.

The people of this neighbourhood are indifferent fishermen; yet good fish may sometimes be bought, particularly two sorts, called *sing-ala* and *rau.*[1] The former resembles our pike; the latter our carp. When the weather is cold, the people will not fish at all if they can avoid it; for they have a much greater dread of cold than *Europeans* have of heat. Should any fish then happen to be seen in the market, it is immediately bought up by the eunuchs, who are particularly fond of it; why, I cannot tell. The *Omrahs* alone contrive to force the fishermen out at all times by means of the *korrah,* the long whip always suspended at their door.

You may judge from what I have said, whether a lover of good cheer ought to quit *Paris* for the sake of visiting *Dehli.* Unquestionably the great are in the enjoyment of everything; but it is by dint of the numbers in their service, by dint of the *korrah,* and by dint of money. In *Dehli* there is no middle state. A man must either be of the highest rank or live miserably. My pay is considerable, nor am I sparing of money; yet does it often happen that I have not wherewithal to satisfy the cravings of hunger, the *bazars* being so ill supplied, and frequently containing nothing but the refuse of the grandees. Wine, that essential part of every entertainment, can be obtained in none of the shops at *Dehli,* although it might be made from the native grape, were not the use of that liquor prohibited equally by the *Gentile* and *Mahometan* law. I drank some at *Amed-abad* and *Golkonda,* in Dutch and English houses, which was not ill-tasted. If wine be

[1] *Sing-ala* is the *singí* (*Silurus pungentissimus*, Buch.), and *rau* the well-known *rohú* (*Cyprinus denticulatus* Buch.), still considered the best ordinary river fish in Northern India.

sometimes found in the *Mogol* empire, it is either *Chiraz* or *Canary*. The former is sent by land from *Persia* to *Bander Abasy*, where it is embarked for *Sourate*, from which port it reaches *Dehli* in forty-six days. The *Canary* wine is brought by the *Dutch* to *Sourate*; but both these wines are so dear that, as we say at home, the taste is destroyed by the cost. A bottle containing about three *Paris* pints [1] cannot be purchased under six or seven crowns. The liquor peculiar to this country is *Arac*, a spirit drawn by distillation from unrefined sugar; the sale of which is also strictly forbidden, and none but *Christians* dare openly to drink it. *Arac* is a spirit as harsh and burning as that made from corn in *Poland*, and the use of it to the least excess occasions nervous and incurable disorders.[2] A wise man will here accustom himself to the pure and fine water, or to the excellent lemonade,[3] which costs little and may be drunk without injury. To say the truth, few persons in these hot climates feel a strong desire for wine, and I have no doubt that the happy ignorance which prevails of many distempers is fairly ascribable to the general habits of sobriety among the people, and to the profuse perspiration to which they are perpetually subject.[4] The gout, the

[1] About three imperial quarts, English.

[2] See p. 441.

[3] Made ordinarily of squeezed limes and water, the *nimbú* (lime) *paní* (water) of the present day. For those who could afford it, there were various sherbets; rose water and sugar being added to the juice of limes, pomegranates, and the like.

[4] Fryer, writing of the mortality among the English at Bombay and the parts adjacent, says: 'Notwithstanding this Mortality to the *English*, the Country People and naturalised *Portugals* live to a good Old Age, supposed to be the Reward of their Temperance; indulging themselves neither in Strong Drinks, nor devouring Flesh as we do. But I believe rather we are here, as Exotick Plants brought home to us, not agreeable to the Soil: For to the Lustier and Fresher, and oftentimes the Temperatest, the Clime more unkind; but to Old Men and Women it seems to be more suitable.'—*A new account of East India and Persia.* London, 1698, p. 69.

stone, complaints in the kidneys, catarrhs and quartan agues are nearly unknown; and persons who arrive in the country afflicted with any of these disorders, as was the case with me, soon experience a complete cure. Even the venereal disease, common as it is in *Hindoustan,* is not of so virulent a character, or attended with such injurious consequences, as in other parts of the world. But although there is a greater enjoyment of health, yet there is less vigour among the people than in our colder climates; and the feebleness and languor both of body and mind, consequent upon excessive heat, may be considered a species of unremitting malady, which attacks all persons indiscriminately, and among the rest Europeans not yet inured to the heat.

Workshops, occupied by skilful artisans, would be vainly sought for in *Dehli,* which has very little to boast of in that respect. This is not owing to any inability in the people to cultivate the arts, for there are ingenious men in every part of the *Indies.* Numerous are the instances of handsome pieces of workmanship made by persons destitute of tools, and who can scarcely be said to have received instruction from a master. Sometimes they imitate so perfectly articles of European manufacture that the difference between the original and copy can hardly be discerned. Among other things, the *Indians* make excellent muskets, and fowling-pieces, and such beautiful gold ornaments that it may be doubted if the exquisite workmanship of those articles can be exceeded by any European goldsmith. I have often admired the beauty, softness, and delicacy of their paintings and miniatures, and was particularly struck with the exploits of *Ekbar,* painted on a shield[1] by a celebrated artist, who

[1] In the *Times* newspaper of the 20th March 1891, will be found an interesting account of a shield, called the Ramayana shield, then just completed, the work of the premier Jeypore state workman, Ganga Baksh, Khati, who executed the work under the direction of Surgeon-Major T. H. Hendley, C.I.E., the Residency Surgeon, and Honorary

is said to have been seven years in completing the picture. I thought it a wonderful performance. The *Indian* painters are chiefly deficient in just proportions, and in the expression of the face; but these defects would soon be corrected if they possessed good masters, and were instructed in the rules of art.[1]

Want of genius, therefore, is not the reason why works of superior art are not exhibited in the capital. If the artists and manufacturers were encouraged, the useful and fine arts would flourish; but these unhappy men are contemned, treated with harshness, and inadequately remunerated for their labour. The rich will have every

Secretary, Jeypore Museum. On this shield the story of the Ramayana is told in a series of plaques, 'nearly all of which are faithful reproductions in relief, in silver-plated brass, of paintings by the most celebrated artists who flourished in Akbar's time.' It is further stated that Dr. Hendley has arranged for the production of two more large shields. One of these will be a companion to the Ramayana shield, the story of the Máhábárata being taken as the second great epic poem of the Hindoos. Here, again, the paintings of Akbar's time will be copied. The other shield will be known as the Ashwameda (horse sacrifice) shield, and will contain seven plaques, illustrating the sacrifice which Yudhishthira performed, an incident in the *Máhábárata*, the drawings being taken from Akbar's own copy of the *Razmnamah*, or Persian version of the great Hindoo epic. Jeypore will thus eventually possess three specimens of metal-work in relief unrivalled throughout India. In this connection, see p. 258, footnote [3].

[1] 'I have to notice that the observing of the figures of objects and the making of likeness of them, which are often looked upon as an idle occupation, are, for a well-regulated mind, a source of wisdom, and an antidote against the poison of ignorance. Bigoted followers of the letter of the law are hostile to the art of painting; but their eyes now see the truth. One day at a private party of friends, His Majesty [the Emperor Akbar], who had conferred on several the pleasure of drawing near him, remarked, "There are many that hate painting; but such men I dislike. It appears to me as if a painter had quite peculiar means of recognising God; for a painter in sketching anything that has life, and in devising its limbs, one after the other, must come to feel that he cannot bestow individuality upon his work, and is thus forced to think of God, the giver of life, and will thus increase in knowledge."'—*Áin*, vol. i. p. 108.

article at a cheap rate. When an *Omrah* or *Mansebdar* requires the services of an artisan, he sends to the *bazar* for him, employing force, if necessary, to make the poor man work; and after the task is finished, the unfeeling lord pays, not according to the value of the labour, but agreeably to his own standard of fair remuneration; the artisan having reason to congratulate himself if the *korrah* has not been given in part payment. How then can it be expected that any spirit of emulation should animate the artist or manufacturer? Instead of contending for a superiority of reputation, his only anxiety is to finish his work, and to earn the pittance that shall supply him with a piece of bread. The artists, therefore, who arrive at any eminence in their art are those only who are in the service of the King or of some powerful *Omrah*, and who work exclusively for their patron.

The citadel contains the *Seraglio* and other royal edifices; but you are not to imagine that they are such buildings as the *Louvre* or the *Escurial*.[1] The edifices in the Fort have nothing European in their structure; nor ought they, as I have already observed, to resemble the architecture of *France* and *Spain*. It is sufficient if they have that magnificence which is suited to the climate.

The entrance of the fortress presents nothing remarkable except two large elephants of stone, placed at either side of one of the principal gates. On one of the elephants is seated the statue of *Jemel*, the renowned Raja of *Chitor*; on the other is the statue of *Polta*, his brother. These are the brave heroes who, with their still braver mother,

[1] 'The palace at Delhi is, or rather was, the most magnificent palace in the East, perhaps in the world, and the only one, at least in India, which enables us to understand what the arrangements of a complete palace were when deliberately undertaken, and carried out in one uniform plan.'—Fergusson, *History of Indian Architecture*, edition of 1876. The harem and other private apartments of the palace alone covered more than twice the area of the Escurial, or, in fact, of any palace in Europe.

immortalised their names by the extraordinary resistance which they opposed to the celebrated *Ekbar*; who defended the towns besieged by that great Emperor with unshaken resolution; and who, at length reduced to extremity, devoted themselves to their country, and chose rather to perish with their mother in sallies against the enemy than submit to an insolent invader. It is owing to this extraordinary devotion on their part, that their enemies have thought them deserving of the statues here erected to their memory. These two large elephants, mounted by the two heroes, have an air of grandeur, and inspire me with an awe and respect which I cannot describe.[1]

After passing into the citadel through this gate, there is seen a long and spacious street,[2] divided in the midst by a canal of running water. The street has a long divan, or raised way, on both sides, in the manner of the *Pont-neuf*, five or six feet high and four broad. Bordering the divan are closed arcades, which run up the whole way in the form of gates. It is upon this long divan that all the collectors of market-dues and other petty officers exercise their functions without being incommoded by the horses and people that pass in the street below. The *Mansebdars* or inferior *Omrahs* mount guard on this raised way during the night. The water of the canal runs into the *Seraglio*, divides and intersects every part, and then falls into the ditches of the fortification. This water is brought from

[1] Rajas Jaimal and Pattá or Fatta. Chittor was besieged and taken by Akbar in 1568. For an interesting note on these statues, and a discussion of many vexed points in connection therewith, see Appendix A. of *A Handbook for Visitors to Delhi and its Neighbourhood*, H. G. Keene, M.L.A.S., Fourth edition: Calcutta; Thacker, Spink & Co., 1882.

The two figures are now in the Museum at Delhi, and one of the elephants is in the public gardens there. The other elephant seems to have totally disappeared. The statues themselves were discovered about 1863, buried among some rubbish inside the Fort.

[2] The well-known Chandni Chouk, or 'Silver Street.'

the river *Gemna* by means of a canal opened at a distance of five or six leagues above *Dehly*, and cut with great labour through fields and rocky ground.[1]

The other principal gate of the fortress also conducts to a long and tolerably wide street, which has a divan on both sides bordered by shops instead of arcades. Properly speaking, this street is a *bazar*, rendered very convenient in the summer and the rainy season by the long and high arched roof with which it is covered. Air and light are admitted by several large round apertures in the roof.

Besides these two streets, the citadel contains many smaller ones, both to the right and to the left, leading to the quarters where the *Omrahs* mount guard, during four-and-twenty hours, in regular rotation, once a week. The places where this duty is performed may be called splendid, the *Omrahs* making it a point to adorn them at their own expense. In general they are spacious divans or alcoves facing a flower-garden, embellished by small canals of running water, reservoirs, and fountains. The *Omrahs* on guard have their table supplied by the King. Every meal is sent ready dressed, and is received by them with all suitable ceremony, they three times performing the *taslim*, or salute of grateful acknowledgment, by turning the face toward the King's residence, and then raising the hand to the head and lowering it to the ground.[2]

There are, besides, many divans and tents in different parts of the fortress, which serve as offices for public business.

Large halls are seen in many places, called *Kar-kanays*[3]

[1] The canal was made by Ali Mardan Khan; see p. 184, footnote [3].

[2] 'Before taking leave, or presentation, or upon receiving a *mansab*, a jágír or a dress of honour, or an elephant, or a horse, the rule is to make three *taslíms*; but only one on all other occasions, when salaries are paid, or presents made.'—*Ain*, vol. i. p. 158. See p. 214, footnote [2].

[3] Kharkhanahs. In the palace of the Mahárájá of Benares, at Ramnagar, may still be seen excellent examples of such 'palace workshops,' which have served not a little to maintain a high standard of workmanship, or many of the specialities of the district. See p. 228.

or workshops for the artisans. In one hall embroiderers are busily employed, superintended by a master. In another you see the goldsmiths; in a third, painters; in a fourth, varnishers in lacquer-work; in a fifth, joiners, turners, tailors, and shoemakers; in a sixth, manufacturers of silk, brocade, and those fine muslins of which are made turbans, girdles with golden flowers, and drawers worn by females, so delicately fine as frequently to wear out in one night. This article of dress, which lasts only a few hours, may cost ten or twelve crowns, and even more, when beautifully embroidered with needlework.

The artisans repair every morning to their respective *Kar-kanays*, where they remain employed the whole day; and in the evening return to their homes. In this quiet and regular manner their time glides away; no one aspiring after any improvement in the condition of life wherein he happens to be born. The embroiderer brings up his son as an embroiderer, the son of a goldsmith becomes a goldsmith, and a physician of the city educates his son for a physician. No one marries but in his own trade or profession; and this custom is observed almost as rigidly by *Mahometans* as by the *Gentiles*, to whom it is expressly enjoined by their law. Many are the beautiful girls thus doomed to live singly, girls who might marry advantageously if their parents would connect them with a family less noble than their own.

I must not forget the *Am-Kas*,[1] to which you at length arrive, after passing the places just mentioned. This is really a noble edifice: it consists of a large square court of arcades, not unlike our *Place Royale*, with this difference, however, that the arcades of the *Am-Kas* have no buildings over them. Each arcade is separated by a wall, yet in such a manner that there is a small door to pass from one to the other. Over the grand gate, situated in the middle of one side of this court, is a capacious divan, quite open

[1] Am-Khas, place of audience. See p. 261.

on the side of the court, called the *Nagar-Kanay*.[1] In this place, which thence derives its name, are kept the trumpets, or rather the hautboys and cymbals, which play in concert at certain hours of the day and night. To the ears of an *European* recently arrived, this music sounds very strangely, for there are ten or twelve hautboys, and as many cymbals, which play together. One of the hautboys, called *Karna*, is a fathom and a half in length, and its lower aperture cannot be less than a foot. The cymbals of brass or iron are some of them at least a fathom in diameter. You may judge, therefore, of the roaring sound which issues from the *Nagar-Kanay*. On my first arrival it stunned me so as to be insupportable: but such is the power of habit that this same noise is now heard by me with pleasure; in the night, particularly, when in bed and afar, on my terrace this music sounds in my ears as solemn, grand, and melodious. This is not altogether to be wondered at, since it is played by persons instructed from infancy in the rules of melody, and possessing the skill of modulating and turning the harsh sounds of the hautboy and cymbal so as to produce a symphony far from disagreeable when heard at a certain distance. The *Nagar-Kanay* is placed in an elevated situation, and remote from the royal apartments, that the King may not be annoyed by the proximity of this music.

Opposite to the grand gate, which supports the *Nagar-Kanay*, as you cross the court, is a large and magnificent hall, decorated with several rows of pillars, which, as well as the ceiling, are all painted and overlaid with gold. The hall is raised considerably from the ground, and very airy, being open on the three sides that look into the court. In the centre of the wall that separates the hall from the

[1] *Nakárahkhanah*, from *nakárah* a drum, and *khanah* a room or turret chamber. The *nakárah* resembled a kettle-drum, and twenty pairs were used in the royal nákárahkhanah, of karranas, 'they never blow less than four' (*Ain*), and three pairs of cymbals, called *sanj*.

Seraglio, and higher from the floor than a man can reach, is a wide and lofty opening, or large window,[1] where the Monarch every day, about noon, sits upon his throne, with some of his sons at his right and left; while eunuchs standing about the royal person flap away the flies with peacocks' tails, agitate the air with large fans, or wait with undivided attention and profound humility to perform the different services allotted to each. Immediately under the throne is an enclosure, surrounded by silver rails, in which are assembled the whole body of *Omrahs,* the *Rajas,* and the *Ambassadors,* all standing, their eyes bent downward, and their hands crossed. At a greater distance from the throne are the *Mansebdars* or inferior *Omrahs,* also standing in the same posture of profound reverence. The remainder of the spacious room, and indeed the whole courtyard, is filled with persons of all ranks, high and low, rich and poor; because it is in this extensive hall that the King gives audience indiscriminately to all his subjects: hence it is called *Am-Kas,* or audience-chamber of high and low.

During the hour and a half, or two hours, that this ceremony continues, a certain number of the royal horses pass before the throne, that the King may see whether they are well used and in a proper condition. The elephants come next, their filthy hides having been well washed and painted as black as ink, with two large red streaks from the top of the head down to the trunk, where they meet. The elephants are covered with embroidered cloth; a couple of silver bells are suspended to the two ends of a massive silver chain placed over their back, and white cow-tails[2] from *Great Tibet,* of large value, hang from the ears like immense whiskers. Two small elephants, superbly caparisoned, walk close to these colossal creatures, like slaves appointed to their service.

[1] The celebrated *Jharokah,* still to be seen at Delhi.

[2] The tails of the Tibetan ox or yak, called chowries, still in common use in India.

As if proud of his gorgeous attire and of the magnificence that surrounds him, every elephant moves with a solemn and dignified step; and when in front of the throne, the driver, who is seated on his shoulder, pricks him with a pointed iron, animates and speaks to him, until the animal bends one knee, lifts his trunk on high and roars aloud, which the people consider as the elephant's mode of performing the *taslim* or usual reverence.

Other animals are next introduced;—tame antelopes, kept for the purpose of fighting with each other;[1] *Nilgaux*,[2] or grey oxen, that appear to me to be a species of elk; rhinoceroses; large *Bengale* buffaloes with prodigious horns which enable them to contend against lions and tigers; tame leopards, or panthers, employed in hunting antelopes; some of the fine sporting dogs from *Usbec*, of every kind, and each dog with a small red covering; lastly, every species of the birds of prey used in field sports for catching patridges, cranes, hares, and even, it is said, for hunting antelopes, on which they pounce with violence, beating their heads and blinding them with their wings and claws.[3]

Besides this procession of animals, the cavalry of one or two *Omrahs* frequently pass in review before the King; the horsemen being better dressed than usual, the horses furnished with iron armour, and decorated with an endless variety of fantastic trappings.

The King takes pleasure also in having the blades of cutlasses tried on dead sheep, brought before him without

[1] The Emperor Akbar was very fond of this sport, and in the *Ain* (pp. 218-222) will be found full details regarding the kinds of fighting deer, how they were fought, together with elaborate regulations as to the betting allowed on such encounters.

[2] Literally 'blue cows,' the Hindostanee name being *Nîlgau*. See page 364, footnote [3], also page 377.

[3] See the illustration of a Barkút eagle attacking a deer, from Atkinson's *Siberia*, at p. 385, vol. i. of Yule's *Marco Polo*, second ed., 1875, and the chapter (xviii. same vol.) on the animals and birds kept by the Kaan for the chase.

the entrails and neatly bound up. Young *Omrahs, Manseb-dars,* and *Gourze-berdars,*[1] or mace-bearers, exercise their skill, and put forth all their strength to cut through the four feet, which are fastened together, and the body of the sheep at one blow.

But all these things are so many interludes to more serious matters. The King not only reviews his cavalry with peculiar attention, but there is not, since the war has been ended, a single trooper or other soldier whom he has not inspected, and made himself personally acquainted with, increasing or reducing the pay of some, and dismissing others from the service. All the petitions held up in the crowd assembled in the *Am-Kas* are brought to the King and read in his hearing; and the persons concerned being ordered to approach are examined by the Monarch himself, who often redresses on the spot the wrongs of the aggrieved party. On another day of the week he devotes two hours to hear in private the petitions of ten persons selected from the lower orders, and presented to the King by a good and rich old man. Nor does he fail to attend the justice-chamber, called *Adalet-Kanay,* on another day of the week, attended by the two principal *Kadis,*[2] or chief justices. It is evident, therefore, that barbarous as we are apt to consider the sovereigns of *Asia,* they are not always unmindful of the justice that is due to their subjects.

What I have stated in the proceedings of the assembly of the *Am-Kas* appears sufficiently rational and even noble; but I must not conceal from you the base and disgusting adulation which is invariably witnessed there. Whenever a word escapes the lips of the King, if at all to the purpose, how trifling soever may be its import, it is immediately caught by the surrounding throng; and the chief *Omrahs,* extending their arms towards heaven, as if to receive some

[1] Gurz-burdar, from *gurz*, a Persian word, signifying a mace or war-club.

[2] Kádí, the Arabic word for a judge, colloquially Kází.

benediction, exclaim *Karamat! Karamat!* wonderful! wonderful! he has spoken wonders! Indeed there is no Mogol who does not know and does not glory in repeating this proverb in Persian verse:

> Aguer chah ronzra Goyed cheb est in
> Bubayed Gouft inck mah ou peruin.[1]
>
> [Should the King say that it is night at noon,
> Be sure to cry, Behold, I see the moon!]

The vice of flattery pervades all ranks. When a *Mogol*, for instance, has occasion for my services, he comes to tell me by way of preamble, and as matter of course, that I am the *Aristotalis*, the *Bocrate*, and the *Aboüysina-Ulzaman*,[2] the Aristotle, the Hippocrates, and the Avicenna of the age. At first I endeavoured to prevent this fulsome mode of address by assuring my visitors that I was very far from possessing the merit they seemed to imagine, and that no comparison ought to be made between such great men and me; but finding that my modesty only increased their praise, I determined to accustom my ears to their flattery as I had done to their music. I shall here relate an anecdote which I consider quite characteristic. A *Brahmen* Pendet or *Gentile* doctor, whom I introduced into my Agah's service, would fain pronounce this panegyric; and after comparing him to the greatest Conquerors the world has ever known, and making for the purpose of flattery a hundred nauseous and impertinent observations, he concluded his harangue in these words, uttered with all conceivable seriousness: 'When, my Lord, you place your foot in the stirrup, marching at the head of your cavalry, the earth trembles under your footsteps; the eight elephants, on whose heads it is borne, finding it impossible to support the extraordinary pressure.' The conclusion of this speech produced the effect that might be expected.

1 Agar Shah roza goyad shab ast ín,
Bebáyed guft inak mah u parwín.

2 *Bou-Alicenna ul-zaman.*

I could not avoid laughing, but I endeavoured, with a grave countenance, to tell my *Agah,* whose risibility was just as much excited, that it behoved him to be cautious how he mounted on horseback and created earthquakes, which often caused so much mischief. 'Yes, my friend,' he answered without hesitation, 'and that is the reason why I generally choose to be carried in a *Paleky.*'[1]

The grand hall of the *Am-Kas* opens into a more retired chamber, called the *Gosel-Kané,*[2] or the place to wash in. Few persons are permitted to enter this room, the court of which is not so large as that of the *Am-Kas.* The hall is, however, very handsome, spacious, gilt and painted, and raised four or five French feet from the pavement, like a large platform. It is in this place that the King, seated in a chair, his *Omrahs* standing around him, grants more private audiences to his officers, receives their reports, and deliberates on important affairs of state. Every *Omrah* incurs the same pecuniary penalty for omitting to attend this assembly in the evening as for failing to be present at the *Am-Kas* in the morning. The only grandee whose daily attendance is dispensed with is my Agah, *Danech-mend-Kan,* who enjoys this exemption in consequence of his being a man of letters, and of the time he necessarily devotes to his studies or to foreign affairs; but on Wednesdays, the day of the week on which he mounts guard, he attends in the same manner as other *Omrahs.* This custom of meeting twice a day is very ancient; and no *Omrah* can reasonably complain that it is binding, since the King seems to consider it as obligatory upon himself

[1] Sir William Jones quotes approvingly this passage from BERNIER in his dissertation on Eastern poetry, in that portion of chapter I., *Asiaticos ferè omnes Poeticae impensius esse deditos,* devoted to a consideration of Indian verse, p. 352, vol. ii. of the quarto edition of his works in six vols. London, 1799.

[2] *Ghusl khanah,* although strictly meaning a bath-room, was the name applied to the more private apartments in a Mogul palace.

as upon his courtiers to be present;[1] nothing but urgent business, or serious bodily affliction, preventing him from appearing at the two assemblies. In his late alarming illness *Aureng-Zebe* was carried every day to the one or the other, if not to both. He felt the necessity of showing himself at least once during the twenty-four hours; for his disorder was of so dangerous a character that his absence, though only for one day, might have thrown the whole kingdom into trouble and insurrection and caused the closing of every shop.[2]

Although the King, when seated in the hall of *Gosel-Kanay*, is engaged about such affairs as I have mentioned, yet the same state is maintained for the most part as in the *Am-Kas*; but being late in the day, and the adjoining court being small, the cavalry of the *Omrahs* does not pass in review. There is this peculiar ceremony in the evening assembly, that all the *Manseb-dars* who are on guard pass before the King to salute him with much form. Before them are borne with great ceremony that which they call the *Kours*,[3] to wit, many figures of silver, beautifully made, and mounted on large silver sticks: two of them represent large fish;[4] two others a horrible and fantastic animal called *Eiedeha*;[5] others are the figures of two lions;[6] others of

[1] 'His Majesty generally receives twice in the course of twenty-four hours, when people of all classes can satisfy their eyes and hearts with the light of his countenance.'—*Ain*, vol. i. p. 157. The first public appearance of the Emperor was called *Darsan*, from the Sanskrit *darçana*, sight, Greek δέρκομαι.

[2] See pp. 123-126.

[3] *Kur* was the name given to the collection of flags, arms, and other insignia of royalty.

[4] *Muhrattib-i-mahi*, or insignia of the fish, one of the ensigns of Mogul royalty

[5] *Azhdaha*, a dragon.

[6] 'The royal standard of the Great Mogul, which is a couchant lion shadowing part of the body of the sun.'—Terry's *Voyage to East India*. London, 1665.

two hands,[1] and others of scales;[2] and several more which I cannot here enumerate, to which the Indians attach a certain mystic meaning. Among the *Kours* and the *Mansebdars* are mixed many *Gourze-berdars,* or mace-bearers chosen for their tall and handsome persons, and whose business it is to preserve order in assemblies, and to carry the King's orders, and execute his commands with the utmost speed.

It would afford me pleasure to conduct you to the *Seraglio,* as I have introduced you into other parts of the fortress. But who is the traveller that can describe from ocular observation the interior of that building? I have sometimes gone into it when the King was absent from *Dehli,* and once pretty far I thought, for the purpose of giving my professional advice in the case of a great lady so extremely ill that she could not be moved to the outward gate, according to the customs observed upon similar occasions; but a *Kachemire* shawl covered my head, hanging like a large scarf down to my feet, and an eunuch led me by the hand, as if I had been a blind man. You must be content, therefore, with such a general description as I have received from some of the eunuchs. They inform me that the *Seraglio* contains beautiful apartments, separated, and more or less spacious and splendid, according to the rank and income of the females. Nearly every chamber has its reservoir of running water at the door; on every side are gardens, delightful alleys, shady retreats, streams, fountains, grottoes, deep excavations that afford shelter from the sun by day, lofty divans and terraces, on which to sleep coolly at night. Within the walls of this enchanting place, in fine, no oppressive or inconvenient heat is felt. The eunuchs speak with extravagant praise of a small tower, facing the river, which is covered with plates

[1] *Punja.*

[2] The symbol of a pair of scales, in gold and colours, can still be seen in the middle of the screen of marble tracery-work separating the Dívan-i-Khas from the private rooms in the palace at Delhi.

of gold, in the same manner as the two towers of *Agra*; and its apartments are decorated with gold and azure exquisite paintings and magnificent mirrors.[1]

Before taking our final leave of the fortress, I wish to recall your attention to the *Am-Kas,* which I am desirous to describe as I saw it during certain annual festivals; especially on the occasion of the rejoicings that took place after the termination of the war. Never did I witness a more extraordinary scene.

The King appeared seated upon his throne, at the end of the great hall, in the most magnificent attire. His vest was of white and delicately flowered satin, with a silk and gold embroidery of the finest texture. The turban, of gold cloth, had an aigrette whose base was composed of diamonds of an extraordinary size and value, besides an Oriental topaz,[2] which may be pronounced unparalleled, exhibiting a lustre like the sun. A necklace of immense pearls, suspended from his neck, reached to the stomach, in the same manner as many of the *Gentiles* wear their strings of beads. The throne was supported by six massy feet, said to be of solid gold, sprinkled over with rubies, emeralds, and diamonds. I cannot tell you with accuracy the number or value of this vast collection of precious stones, because no person may approach sufficiently near to reckon them, or judge of their water and clearness; but I can assure you that there is a confusion of diamonds, as well as other jewels, and that the throne, to the best of my recollection, is valued at four *Kourours* of *Roupies.* I observed elsewhere that a *Lecque* is one hundred thousand

[1] The *Khas Mahal,* still one of the wonders of the world, and visited by travellers from far and wide.

[2] This was probably the jewel shown to Tavernier, on the 2d November 1665 (*Travels*, vol. i. p. 400), and described by him as 'of very high colour, cut in eight panels.' He gives its weight as 158½ Florentine carats, or $152\frac{4}{25}$ English carats, and states that 'it was bought at Goa for the Great Mogul for the sum of 181,000 rupees or 271,500 *livres* [£20,412, 10s.] of our money.' It is figured by Tavernier.

roupies, and that a *Kourour* is a hundred *Lecques*; so that the throne is estimated at forty millions of *roupies*,[1] worth sixty millions of pounds [livres] or thereabouts. It was constructed by *Chah-Jehan*, the father of *Aureng-Zebe*, for the purpose of displaying the immense quantity of precious stones accumulated successively in the treasury from the spoils of ancient Rajas and *Patans*, and the annual presents to the Monarch, which every *Omrah* is bound to make on certain festivals. The construction and workmanship of the throne are not worthy of the materials; but two peacocks, covered with jewels and pearls, are well conceived and executed.[2] They were made by a workman of astonishing powers, a *Frenchman* by birth, named . . . . .[3] who, after defrauding several of the Princes of *Europe*, by means of false gems, which he fabricated with peculiar skill, sought refuge in the *Great Mogol's* court, where he made his fortune.

At the foot of the throne were assembled all the *Omrahs*, in splendid apparel, upon a platform surrounded by a silver railing, and covered by a spacious canopy of brocade with deep fringes of gold. The pillars of the hall were hung with brocades of a gold ground, and flowered satin canopies were raised over the whole expanse of the extensive apartment fastened with red silken cords, from which were suspended large tassels of silk and gold. The

[1] Which, at 2s. 3d. to the rupee, would amount to £4,500,000. Tavernier's *corrected* valuation was (see Appendix III.) £12,037,500.

[2] See Appendix III. p. 474, for Tavernier's account of this throne (*Travels*, vol. i. pp. 381-385) the remains of which, now in the Shah of Persia's possession in the Treasury at Teheran, have been valued at about £2,600,000 (S. G. W. Benjamin in the volume on 'Persia' in the *Story of the Nations* series); and truly styled, although but a mere wreck of the throne as seen by Tavernier and Bernier, 'the grandest object of sumptuary art ever devised by man.' The throne was part of the plunder which Nadir Shah took with him to Persia when he sacked Delhi in 1739.

[3] Bernier does not tell us his name, but Steuart, in his edition of part of this book, Calcutta, 1826 (see Bibliography, No. 18), gives it as La Grange. I have not been able to verify this.

floor was covered entirely with carpets of the richest silk, of immense length and breadth. A tent, called the *aspek*, was pitched outside, larger than the hall, to which it joined by the top. It spread over half the court, and was completely enclosed by a great balustrade, covered with plates of silver. Its supporters were pillars overlaid with silver, three of which were as thick and as high as the mast of a *barque*, the others smaller. The outside of this magnificent tent was red, and the inside lined with elegant *Maslipatam* chintzes,[1] figured expressly for that very purpose with flowers so natural and colours so vivid, that the tent seemed to be encompassed with real parterres.

As to the arcade galleries round the court, every *Omrah* had received orders to decorate one of them at his own expense, and there appeared a spirit of emulation who should best acquit himself to the Monarch's satisfaction. Consequently all the arcades and galleries were covered from top to bottom with brocade, and the pavement with rich carpets.

On the third day of the festival, the King, and after him several *Omrahs*,[2] were weighed with a great deal of ceremony in large scales, which, as well as the weights, are, they say, of solid gold. I recollect that all the courtiers expressed much joy when it was found that *Aureng-Zebe* weighed two pounds more than the year preceding.

Similar festivals are held every year, but never before were they celebrated with equal splendour and expense. It is thought that the principal inducement with the King for the extraordinary magnificence displayed on this occasion was to afford to the merchants an opportunity of disposing of the quantities of brocades, which the war had

[1] *Chittes* in the original, a corruption of the word *chīnt*, the Indian name, whence chintz. The best came from Masulipatam (Maslipatam) on the Madras coast. See p. 362.

[2] Many curious details concerning this ceremony are to be found in the *Ain*, vol. i. pp. 266, 267.

for four or five years prevented them from selling.[1] The expense incurred by the *Omrahs* was considerable, but a portion of it fell ultimately on the common troopers, whom the *Omrahs* obliged to purchase the brocades to be made up into vests.

An ancient custom attends these anniversary days of rejoicing, not at all agreeable to the *Omrahs*. They are expected to make a handsome present to the King, more or less valuable according to the amount of their pay.[2] Some of them, indeed, take that opportunity of presenting gifts of extraordinary magnificence, sometimes for the sake of an ostentatious display, sometimes to divert the King from instituting an inquiry into the exactions committed in their official situations or governments, and sometimes to gain the favour of the King, and by that means obtain an increase of salary. Some present fine pearls, diamonds, emeralds, or rubies; others offer vessels of gold set with precious stones; others again give a quantity of gold coins, each worth about a pistole and a half.[3] During a festival of this kind *Aureng-Zebe* having paid a visit to *Jafer-kan*,[4] not as his *Vizir* but as a kinsman, on the pretext that he wished to see a house which he lately erected, the *Vizir* made a present to the King of gold coins to the amount of one hundred thousand crowns, some handsome pearls, and a ruby, which was estimated at forty thousand crowns, but which *Chah-Jehan*, who understood better than any man the value of every kind of precious stone, dis-

[1] See p. 459.

[2] This payment was called *Pesh-kash*, and corresponded somewhat to the modern income-tax. See p. 191, footnote [3].

[3] A single *pistole* was worth about 16s. 9d., which would give about 25s. as the value of these coins. Or the double pistole, worth about £1, 13s. 3d. may be meant, in which case the coins referred to were probably specially minted gold mohurs prepared for the purpose.

[4] Jáfar Khán, entitled Umdat-ul-Mulk, was appointed Prime Minister by Aurangzeb (Alamgír) in 1662, and died in 1670 at Dehli. He was the son of Sádík Khán, a cousin of Núr Jahán's, who had married one of her sisters; hence his kinship to Aurangzeb.

covered[1] to be worth less than five hundred, to the great confusion of the principal jewellers, who in this instance had been completely deceived.[2]

A whimsical kind of fair[3] is sometimes held during these festivities in the *Mehale,* or royal seraglio: it is conducted by the handsomest and most engaging of the wives of the *Omrahs* and principal *Mansebdars.* The articles exhibited are beautiful brocades, rich embroideries of the newest fashion, turbans elegantly worked on cloth of gold, fine muslins worn by women of quality, and other articles of high price. These bewitching females act the part of traders, while the purchasers are the King, the *Begums* or Princesses, and other distinguished ladies of the *Seraglio.* If any *Omrah's* wife happens to have a handsome daughter, she never fails to accompany her mother, that she may be seen by the King and become known to the *Begums.* The charm of this fair is the most ludicrous manner in which the King makes his bargains, frequently disputing for the value of a penny. He pretends that the good lady cannot possibly be in earnest, that the article is much too dear, that it is not equal to that he can find elsewhere, and that positively he will give no more than such a price. The woman, on the other hand, endeavours to sell to the

[1] When the question was referred to him as an expert, by Aurangzeb, as we learn from Tavernier's narrative.

[2] Tavernier figures this ruby, and gives a full account of the incident narrated by Bernier, in his *Travels*, vol. ii. pp. 127, 128.

[3] 'On the third feast day of every month, His Majesty holds a large assembly, for the purpose of inquiring into the many wonderful things found in this world. The merchants of the age are eager to attend, and lay out articles from all countries. The people of His Majesty's harem come, and the women of other men also are invited, and buying and selling is quite general. His Majesty uses such days to select any articles which he wishes to buy, or to fix the prices of things, and thus add to his knowledge. The secrets of the Empire, the character of the people, the good and bad qualities of each office and workshop will then appear. His Majesty gives to such days the name of *Khusroz*, or the joyful day, as they are a source of much enjoyment.'—*Ain*, vol. i. pp. 276, 277.

best advantage, and when the King perseveres in offering what she considers too little money, high words frequently ensue, and she fearlessly tells him that he is a worthless trader,[1] a person ignorant of the value of merchandise; that her articles are too good for him, and that he had better go where he can suit himself better, and similar jocular expressions.[2] The *Begums* betray, if possible, a still greater anxiety to be served cheaply; high words are heard on every side, and the loud and scurrilous quarrels of the sellers and buyers create a complete farce. But sooner or later they agree upon the price, the Princesses, as well as the King, buy right and left, pay in ready money, and often slip out of their hands, as if by accident, a few gold instead of silver *roupies,* intended as a compliment to the fair merchant or her pretty daughter. The present is received in the same unconscious manner, and the whole ends amidst witty jests and good-humour.

Chah-Jehan was fond of the sex and introduced fairs at every festival, though not always to the satisfaction of some of the *Omrahs.*[3] He certainly transgressed the bounds of decency in admitting at those times into the seraglio singing and dancing girls called *Kenchens* (the gilded, the blooming), and in keeping them there for that purpose

[1] In the original, 'un Marchand de neige.'

[2] In the original, 'et ainsi de ces autres raisons de Dame Jeanne.' Similar badinage was indulged in at like fairs (*meena bazar*) held at Lucknow, during the reigns of some of the kings of Oudh, notably Nuseer-ood-deen Hyder and Wajid Ali.

[3] The orthodox Moslems at the Mogul Court were always opposed to these fairs. Badáoní, the fearless historian of Akbar's reign (*circa* 1596), who was bitterly opposed to the Emperor's religious policy, records of these fairs that, 'In order to direct another blow at the honour of our religion, His Majesty ordered that the stalls of the fancy bázárs, which are held on New Year's Day, should, for a stated time, be given up for the enjoyment of the Begums and the women of the harem, and also for any other married ladies. On such occasions, His Majesty spent much money; and the important affairs of harem people, marriage contracts, and betrothals of boys and girls, were arranged at such meetings."

the whole night; they were not indeed the prostitutes seen in bazaars, but those of a more private and respectable class, who attend the grand weddings of *Omrahs* and *Mansebdars*, for the purpose of singing and dancing. Most of these *Kenchens* are handsome and well dressed, and sing to perfection; and their limbs being extremely supple, they dance with wonderful agility, and are always correct in regard to time; after all, however, they were but common women. It was not enough for *Chah-Jehan* that the *Kenchens* visited the fairs; when they came to him on the Wednesdays to pay their reverence at the *Am-Kas*, according to an ancient custom, he often detained them the whole night, and amused himself with their antics and follies. *Aureng-Zebe* is more serious than his father; he forbids the *Kenchens* to enter the seraglio; but, complying with long established usage, does not object to their coming every Wednesday to the *Am-Kas*, where they make the *salam* from a certain distance, and then immediately retire.

While on the subject of festivals, fairs, and *Kenchens*, or *Kenchenys*, I am tempted to relate an ancedote of one of our countrymen, named *Bernard*. I agree with *Plutarch*, that trifling incidents ought not to be concealed, and that they often enable us to form more accurate opinions of the manners and genius of a people than events of great importance. Viewed in this light, the story, ridiculous as it is in itself, may be acceptable. *Bernard* resided at the court of *Jehan-Guyre*, during the latter years of that King's reign, and was reputed, with apparent justice, to be an excellent physician and a skilful surgeon. He enjoyed the favour of the *Mogol*, and became his companion at table, where they often drank together to excess.[1] The King

[1] Catrou says of Jáhángír that 'All the Franks in Agra, that is, all Europeans of whatsoever nation, were allowed free access to the palace. He continued drinking in their company till the return of day, and he abandoned himself especially to these midnight debaucheries at the season which the Mahomedans observe as a fast with the most scrupulous exactness.'

and his physician possessed congenial tastes; the former thought only of his pleasures, and left the management of public affairs to his wife, the celebrated *Nour-Mehale* or *Nour-Jehan-Begum*, a woman, he used to say, whose transcendent abilities rendered her competent to govern the Empire without the interference of her husband. *Bernard's* daily and regular pay was ten crowns [écus]; but this was greatly increased by his attendance on the high ladies of the *Seraglio* and on all the *Omrahs*, who seemed to vie with each other in making him the most liberal presents, not only because of the cures he effected, but on account of his influence at court. This man, however, disregarded the value of money; what he received with one hand he gave with the other; so that he was much beloved by everybody, especially by the *Kenchens*, on whom he lavished vast sums. Among the females of this description who nightly filled his house, was a young and beautiful damsel, remarkable for the elegance of her dancing, with whom our countryman fell violently in love; but the mother, apprehending that the girl would lose her health and bodily vigour with her virginity, never for a moment lost sight of her, and she resisted all the overtures and incessant solicitations of the court physician. While in despair of obtaining the object of his affections, *Jehan-Guyre*, at the *Am-Kas*, once offered him a present before all the *Omrahs* by way of remuneration for an extraordinary cure which he had effected in the seraglio. 'Your Majesty,' said *Bernard*, 'will not be offended if I refuse the gift so munificently offered, and implore that in lieu thereof your Majesty would bestow on me the young *Kencheny* now waiting with others of her company to make the customary *salam*.' The whole assembly smiled at this refusal of the present, and at a request so little likely to be granted, he being a *Christian* and the girl a *Mahometan* and a *Kencheny*; but *Jehan-Guyre*, who never felt any religious scruples, was thrown into a violent fit of laughter, and commanded the girl to be given to him, 'Lift her on the physician's shoulders,' he said, 'and let him carry the *Kenchen* away.' No sooner said than done. In the midst of a crowded assembly the girl was placed on *Bernard's* back, who withdrew triumphantly with his prize and took her to his house.

The festivals generally conclude with an amusement unknown in *Europe*—a combat between two elephants; which takes place in the presence of all the people on the

FIG. 10.—An elephant fight at Lucknow during the Nawabí.

sandy space near the river: the King, the principal ladies of the court, and the *Omrahs* viewing the spectacle from different apartments in the fortress.

A wall of earth is raised three or four feet wide and five or six high. The two ponderous beasts meet one another face to face, on opposite sides of the wall, each having a couple of riders, that the place of the man who sits on the shoulders, for the purpose of guiding the elephant with a large iron hook, may immediately be supplied if he should be thrown down. The riders animate the elephants either by soothing words, or by chiding them as cowards, and urge them on with their heels, until the poor creatures approach the wall and are brought to the attack. The shock is tremendous, and it appears surprising that they ever survive the dreadful wounds and blows inflicted with their teeth, their heads, and their trunks. There are frequent pauses during the fight; it is suspended and renewed; and the mud wall being at length thrown down, the stronger or more courageous elephant passes on and attacks his opponent, and, putting him to flight, pursues and fastens upon him with so much obstinacy, that the animals can be separated only by means of *cherkys*,[1] or fireworks, which are made to explode between them; for they are naturally timid, and have a particular dread of fire, which is the reason why elephants have been used with so very little advantage in armies since the use of fire-arms. The boldest come from *Ceylon*, but none are employed in war which have not been regularly trained, and accustomed for years to the discharge of muskets close to their heads, and the bursting of crackers between their legs.

The fight of these noble creatures is attended with much cruelty. It frequently happens that some of the riders are trodden underfoot, and killed on the spot, the elephant having always cunning enough to feel the importance of dismounting the rider of his adversary, whom he therefore endeavours to strike down with his trunk. So imminent is the danger considered, that on the day of combat the unhappy men take the same formal leave of their wives and children as if condemned to death. They are somewhat consoled by the reflection that if their lives should be preserved, and the King be pleased with their conduct, not only will their pay be augmented, but a sack of *Peyssas* (equal to fifty francs) will be presented to them

[1] *Charkhi* or wheel, catherine wheels on the end of a stick, a common firework in Northern India at the present day. For the mode of using them in elephant fights, see Fig. 10, opposite.

the moment they alight from the elephant.[1] They have also the satisfaction of knowing that in the event of their death the pay will be continued to their widows, and that their sons will be appointed to the same situation. The mischief with which this amusement is attended does not always terminate with the death of the rider: it often happens that some of the spectators are knocked down and trampled upon by the elephants, or by the crowd; for the rush is terrible when, to avoid the infuriated combatants, men and horses in confusion take to flight. The second time I witnessed this exhibition I owed my safety entirely to the goodness of my horse and the exertions of my two servants.

But it is time we should quit the fortress, and return to the city, where I omitted to describe two edifices worthy of notice.

The first is the principal *Mosquée*,[2] which is conspicuous at a great distance, being situated on the top of a rock in the centre of the town. The surface of the rock was previously levelled, and around it a space is cleared sufficiently large to form a handsome square, where four fine long streets terminate, opposite to the four sides of the *Mosquée*; one, opposite to the principal entrance, in front of the building; a second, at the back of the building; and

[1] 'Each elephant has his match appointed for fighting: some are always ready at the palace and engage when the order is given. When a fight is over if the combatants were *kháçah* [*i.e.* for the Emperor's own use] elephants, the *bhoís* [attendants, of which each elephant had three in the rutting season, at other times two] receive 250 *dáms* as a present; but if other elephants the *bhoís* got 200d.'—*Ain*, vol. i. p. 131. According to the latest investigations the dám in Akbar's time was an actual coin, twenty-five of which were equal to one paisa (pice = 1½ farthings). It was the custom to keep bags of 1000 *dams* at hand ready for distribution, as noted by Bernier.

[2] The Jamá Masjíd, of which Bernier's is one of the best descriptions ever written. It was begun in 1644, and finished in 1658, the same year that witnessed the deposition of its founder, the Emperor Sháh Jahán. Fergusson says of it (*History of Indian and Eastern Architecture*), that it is 'one of the few mosques, either in India or elsewhere, that is designed to produce a pleasing effect externally.'

the two others, to the gates that are in the middle of the two sides. The ascent to the three gates is by means of five-and-twenty or thirty steps of beautiful and large stones, which are continued the whole length of the front and sides. The back part is cased over, to the height of the rock, with large and handsome hewn stone, which hides its inequalities, and tends to give a noble appearance to the building. The three entrances, composed of marble, are magnificent, and their large doors are overlaid with finely wrought plates of copper. Above the principal gate, which greatly exceeds the others in grandeur of appearance, there are several small turrets of white marble that produce a fine effect; and at the back part of the *Mosquée* are seen three large domes, built also of white marble, within and without. The middle dome is much larger and loftier than the other two. The end of the *Mosquée* alone is covered: the space between the three domes and the principal entrance is without any roof; the extreme heat of the climate rendering such an opening absolutely necessary. The whole is paved with large slabs of marble. I grant that this building is not constructed according to those rules of architecture which we seem to think ought to be implicitly followed; yet I can perceive no fault that offends the taste; every part appears well contrived, properly executed, and correctly proportioned. I am satisfied that even in *Paris* a church erected after the model of this temple would be admired, were it only for its singular style of architecture, and its extraordinary appearance. With the exception of the three great domes, and the numerous turrets, which are all of white marble, the *Mosquée* is of a red colour, as if built with large slabs of red marble: although it consists of a species of stone, cut with great facility, but apt to peel off in flakes after a certain time.[1] The natives pretend that

[1] This is a marked characteristic of the red sandstone of Delhi, and it is not considered a good building material unless selected with great care.

the quarries from which it is taken reproduce the stone by degrees: this, if true, is very remarkable; but whether or not they rightly attribute it to the water which fills the quarries every year, I cannot decide.

The King repairs to this *Mosquée* every *Friday*, for the purpose of prayer, that day corresponding in *Mahometan* countries to our *Sunday*. The streets through which he passes are watered to lay the dust and temper the heat: two or three hundred musketeers form an avenue from the gate of the fortress, and as many more line both sides of a wide street leading directly to the mosque. The muskets of these soldiers are small but well finished, and have a sort of large scarlet covering with a little streamer on the top. Five or six horsemen, well mounted, are also ready at the fortress gate, and their duty is to clear the way for the King, keeping, however, at a considerable distance in advance, lest he should be incommoded by their dust. These preparations completed, his Majesty leaves the fortress, sometimes on an elephant, decorated with rich trappings, and a canopy supported by painted and gilt pillars; and sometimes in a throne gleaming with azure and gold, placed on a litter covered with scarlet or brocade, which eight chosen men, in handsome attire, carry on their shoulders. A body of *Omrahs* follow the King, some on horseback, and others in *Palekys*; and among the *Omrahs* are seen a great number of *Mansebdars*, and the bearers of silver maces, whom I have elsewhere described. I cannot say that this train resembles the pompous processions, or (which is a more appropriate term) the masquerades of the Grand *Seignior*, or the martial retinues of European Monarchs: its magnificence is of a different character; but it is not therefore the less royal.

The other edifice in *Dehly* to which I would draw your attention is what they call the *Karuansara* of the Princess,[1] because built by the celebrated *Begum-Saheb*, *Chah-Jehan's* eldest daughter, of whom I have so often

[1] The well-known *Begum Serai*.

spoken in my history of the late war. Not only this Princess, but all the *Omrahs* who wished to gain the favour of the old Monarch, embellished the new city at their own expense. The *Karuansara* is in the form of a large square with arcades, like our *Place Royale,* except that the arches are separated from each other by partitions, and have small chambers at their inner extremities. Above the arcades runs a gallery all round the building, into which open the same number of chambers as there are below. This place is the rendezvous of the rich *Persian, Usbek,* and other foreign merchants, who in general may be accommodated with empty chambers, in which they remain with perfect security, the gate being closed at night. If in *Paris* we had a score of similar structures, distributed in different parts of the city, strangers on their first arrival would be less embarrassed than at present to find a safe and reasonable lodging. They might remain in them a few days until they had seen their acquaintance, and looked out at leisure for more convenient apartments. Such places would become warehouses for all kinds of merchandise, and the general resort of foreign merchants.[1]

Before I quit the subject of *Dehli,* I will answer by anticipation a question which I am sensible you wish to ask, namely, What is the extent of the population of that city, and the number of its respectable inhabitants, as compared with the capital of *France?* When I consider that *Paris* consists of three or four cities piled upon one another, all of them containing numerous apartments, filled, for the most part, from top to bottom, that the streets are thronged with men and women, on foot and horseback; with carts, chaises, and coaches; and that there are very few large squares, courts, or gardens; reflecting, I say, upon all these facts, *Paris* appears to me the nursery of the world, and I can scarcely persuade myself that *Dehli* contains an equal number of people.

[1] But see p. 233, where Bernier does not pass such a favourable judgment on these buildings.

On the other hand, if we take a review of this metropolis of the *Indies*, and observe its vast extent and its numberless shops; if we recollect that, besides the *Omrahs*, the city never contains less than thirty-five thousand troopers, nearly all of whom have wives, children, and a great number of servants, who, as well as their masters, reside in separate houses; that there is no house, by whomsoever inhabited, which does not swarm with women and children; that during the hours when the abatement of the heat permits the inhabitants to walk abroad, the streets are crowded with people, although many of those streets are very wide, and, excepting a few carts, unincumbered with wheel carriages; if we take all these circumstances into consideration, we shall hesitate before we give a positive opinion in regard to the comparative population of *Paris* and *Dehli*; and I conclude, that if the number of souls be not as large in the latter city as in our own capital, it cannot be greatly less. As respects the better sort of people, there is a striking difference in favour of Paris, where seven or eight out of ten individuals seen in the streets are tolerably well clad, and have a certain air of respectability; but in *Dehli*, for two or three who wear decent apparel, there may always be reckoned seven or eight poor, ragged, and miserable beings, attracted to the capital by the army. I cannot deny, however, that I continually meet with persons neat and elegant in their dress, finely formed, well mounted, and properly attended. Nothing, for instance, can be conceived much more brilliant than the great square in front of the fortress at the hours when the *Omrahs, Rajas*, and *Mansebdars* repair to the citadel to mount guard, or attend the assembly of the *Am-Kas*. The *Mansebdars* flock thither from all parts, well mounted and equipped, and splendidly accompanied by four servants, two behind and two before, to clear the street for their masters. *Omrahs* and *Rajas* ride thither, some on horseback, some on majestic elephants; but the greater part are conveyed on the shoulders of six men, in rich *Palekys,* leaning against a thick cushion of brocade, and chewing their *bet-lé,* for the double purpose of sweetening their breath and reddening their lips. On one side of every *paleky* is seen a servant bearing the *piquedans,*[1] or spitoon of porcelain or silver; on the other side, two more servants fan the luxurious lord, and flap away the flies, or brush off the dust with a peacock's-tail fan; three or four footmen march in front to clear the way, and a chosen number of the best formed and best mounted horsemen follow in the rear.

The country in the neighbourhood of *Dehli* is extremely fertile. It produces corn, sugar, *anil* or *Indigo,*[2] rice, millet, and three or four other kinds of pulse, the food of the common people, in great abundance. Two leagues from the city, on the *Agra* road, in a place which the *Mahometans* call *Koia Kotub-eddine,*[3] is a very old edifice, formerly a *Deüra,* or Temple of idols, containing inscriptions written in characters different from those of any language spoken in the *Indies,* and so ancient that no one understands them.

In another direction, and at a distance of two or three leagues from *Dehli,* is the King's country house, called *Chah-limar,* a handsome and noble building, but not to be compared to *Fontainebleau, Saint Germain,* or *Versailles.*[4] I

[1] From the Hindi *pīk-dan,* very necessary in connection with betel-chewing. *Pīk* is properly the saliva caused by the lime and spices and the pán leaf used with the betel-nut. See p. 214, footnote [1].

[2] *Anil* was the old Portuguese name for indigo, from the Arabic *al-níl,* pronounced an-níl. *Níl* is the common name in India, from the Sanskrit *níla,* blue.

[3] By this Bernier may mean, Koh-i-Kutab-ud-din, or the hill or eminence of the Saint Kutab-ud-din Bakhtyárkákí, after whom the renowned Mosque and Minar are by some believed to have been named. As is well known, this mosque was built about 1200, and to some extent from the remains of ancient Hindoo and other temples.

[4] The Shahlamar gardens were begun about the fourth year of Sháh Jahán's reign, 1632, and Catrou states that their design was the invention of a Venetian.

assure you there are no such places in the vicinity of *Dehli*, nor seats such as *Saint Cloud, Chantilly, Meudon, Liancour, Vaux,* or *Ruelles,* or even the smaller country houses belonging to private gentlemen, citizens, or merchants; but this will create no surprise when it is considered that no subject can hold landed property in his own right. Between *Dehli* and *Agra,* a distance of fifty or sixty leagues, there are no fine towns such as travellers pass through in *France*; the whole road is cheerless and uninteresting; nothing is worthy observation but *Maturas,*[1] where an ancient and magnificent temple of idols is still to be seen; a few tolerably handsome caravansaries, a day's journey from each other; and a double row of trees [2] planted by order of *Jehan-Guyre,* and continued for one hundred and fifty leagues, with small pyramids or turrets,[3] erected from *kosse* to *kosse,* for the purpose of pointing out the different roads. Wells are also frequently met with, affording drink to travellers, and serving to water the young trees.

What I have said of *Dehli* may convey a correct idea of *Agra,* in regard at least to its situation on the *Gemna,* to the fortress or royal residence, and to most of its public buildings. But *Agra* having been a favourite and more frequent abode of the Kings of *Hindoustan* since the days of *Ekbar,* by whom it was built and named *Akber-abad,* it surpasses *Dehli* in extent, in the multitude of residences belonging to *Omrahs* and *Rajas,* and of the good stone or brick houses inhabited by private individuals, and in the number and conveniency of its *Karuans-Serrahs.* *Agra* has also to boast of two celebrated mausoleums, of which I shall speak by-and-by: it is, however, without walls, and inferior in some respects to the other capital; for not having been

[1] Mathura, considered by the Moguls one of the most fertile and agreeable situations in Hindoostan.

[2] Which form such a prominent feature in all the early maps of the Mogul Empire, and in some are continued from Dehli to Lahore.

[3] The kosā-minars, one or two of which are standing at the present day. Actual measurements between five pair of these kosā-minars, near Delhi, gave a mean of 2 miles, 4 fur., 158 yds. to the kos.

constructed after any settled design, it wants the uniform and wide streets that so eminently distinguish *Dehli.* Four or five of the streets, where trade is the principal occupation, are of great length and the houses tolerably good; nearly all the others are short, narrow, and irregular, and full of windings and corners: the consequence is that when the court is at *Agra* there is often a strange confusion. I believe I have stated the chief particulars wherein the two capitals differ; but I may add that *Agra* has more the appearance of a country town, especially when viewed from an eminence. The prospect it presents is rural, varied, and agreeable; for the grandees having always made it a point to plant trees in their gardens and courts for the sake of shade, the mansions of *Omrahs, Rajas,* and others are all interspersed with luxuriant and green foliage, in the midst of which the lofty stone houses of *Banyanes* or *Gentile* merchants have the appearance of old castles buried in forests. Such a landscape yields peculiar pleasure in a hot and parched country, where the eye seeks in verdure for refreshment and repose.

You need not quit *Paris,* however, to contemplate the finest, the most magnificent view in the world; for assuredly it may be found on the *Pont-neuf.* Place yourself on that bridge during the day, and what can be conceived more extraordinary than the throngs of people and carriages, the strange bustle, the various objects by which you are surrounded? Visit the same spot at night, and what, I fearlessly ask, can impress the mind like the scene you will witness? The innumerable windows of the lofty houses seen from the bridge exhibit their chastened and subdued lights, while the activity and bustle, observable in the day seem to suffer no diminution until midnight. There honest citizens and—what never happens in *Asia*—their handsome wives and daughters perambulate the streets, without apprehension of quagmires or of thieves; and to complete the picture, you see, in every direction, long lines of brilliant lamps, burning with equal constancy in foul and fair weather. Yes, my friend, when you are on the *Pont-neuf* at *Paris*, you may boldly aver, on my authority, that your eyes behold the grandest of all the artificial scenes in the world, excepting possibly some parts of *China* and *Japan*, which I have not visited. What will this view be, what will be its beauty, when the *Louvre* is completed![1] when the *Louvre*, which it was thought would never be seen but as a mere design and on paper, shall have actual existence in fact!

I have purposely introduced the word 'artificial'; because in speaking of fine prospects, according to the common acceptation of the term, we must always except that view of *Constantinople*, as viewed from the middle of the great strait opposite *Seraglio Point*. Never shall I forget the overpowering delight I experienced when first I beheld that vast, and, as it seemed to me, enchanted amphitheatre. The view of *Constantinople*, however, derives its chief beauty from nature; whereas in *Paris* everything, or nearly so, is artificial; which, to my mind, gives more interest to the view of the latter; because the work of man so displayed indicates the capital of a great empire, the seat of a mighty monarch. I may indeed say, without partiality, and after making every allowance for the beauty of *Dehli*, *Agra*, and *Constantinople*, that *Paris* is the finest, the richest, and altogether the first city in the world.

The *Jesuits* have a church in *Agra*, and a building which they call a college, where they privately instruct in the doctrines of our religion the children of five-and-twenty or thirty *Christian* families, collected, I know not how, in *Agra*, and induced to settle there by the kind and charitable aid which they receive from the *Jesuits*. This religious order was invited hither by *Ekbar* at the period when the power of the *Portuguese* in the *Indies* was at the highest; and that Prince not only gave them an annual income for

[1] The Louvre was not completed in accordance with the design referred to by Bernier until 1857, although portions of the work were completed in 1665 by Claude Perrault.

their maintenance, but permitted them to build churches in the capital cities of *Agra* and *Lahor*. The *Jesuits* found a still warmer patron in *Jehan-Guyre*, the son and successor of *Ekbar*; but they were sorely oppressed by *Chah-Jehan* the son of *Jehan-Guyre*, and father of the present King *Aureng-Zebe*. That Monarch deprived them of their pension, and destroyed the church at *Lahor* and the greater part of that of *Agra*, totally demolishing the steeple, which contained a clock heard in every part of the city.[1]

The good Fathers during the reign of *Jehan-Guyre* were sanguine in their expectation of the progress of Christianity in *Hindoustan*. It is certain that this Prince evinced the utmost contempt for the laws of the *Koran*, and expressed his admiration of the doctrines of our creed.[2] He permitted two of his nephews to embrace the Christian faith, and extended the same indulgence to *Mirza-Zulkarmin*, who had undergone the rite of circumcision and been brought up in the *Seraglio*. The pretext was that *Mirza* was born of Christian parents, his mother having been wife of a rich *Armenian*, and having been brought to the *Seraglio* by *Jehan-Guyre's* desire.

The *Jesuits* say that this King was so determined to countenance the Christian religion that he formed the bold project of clothing the whole court in *European* costume. The dresses were all prepared, when the King, having privately arrayed himself in his new attire, sent for one of his principal *Omrahs* whose opinion he required concerning the meditated change. The answer, however, was so

[1] See p. 177. Catrou states that it was Taj Mehál, the wife of Sháh Jahán, who was a principal instrument in exasperating the mind of the Emperor against the Christians in general, and particularly the Portuguese, who had given an asylum to two of her daughters converted to Christianity by the missionaries.

[2] 'His Majesty [*i.e.* Akbar] firmly believed in the truth of the Christian religion, and wishing to spread the doctrine of Jesus, ordered Prince Múrad [*i.e.* the second son of Akbar and brother of Jahángír (Salim)] to take a few lessons in Christianity by way of auspiciousness.'—*Ain*, vol. i. p. 182.

appalling that *Jehan-Guyre* abandoned his design and affected to pass the whole affair as a joke.[1]

They also maintain that when on his death-bed he expressed a wish to die a Christian, and sent for those holy men, but that the message was never delivered. Many, however, deny this to have been the case, and affirm that *Jehan-Guyre* died, as he had lived, destitute of all religion, and that he nourished to the last a scheme which he had formed, after the example of his father *Ekbar*, of declaring himself a prophet, and the founder of a new religion.

I am informed by a *Mahometan*, whose father belonged to *Jehan-Guyre's* household, that in one of that King's drunken frolics he sent for some of the most learned *Mullahs*, and for a *Florentine* priest, whom he named Father *Atech*,[2] in allusion to his fiery temper; and that the latter

[1] Catrou gives a different version of this story. According to his account Jáhángír, becoming impatient at the reproaches of the Moslem elders, who had admonished him that the use of certain meats was forbidden in the Koran, inquired of them 'in what religion the use of drink and food of every species without distinction was permitted.' The reply was in that of the Christian religion alone. "We must then," he rejoined, "all turn Christians." Let there be tailors brought to us, to converts our robes into close coats, and our turbans into hats. At these words the doctors trembled for their sect. Fear and interest made them hold a less severe language. They all declared that the sovereign was not bound by the precepts of the Koran; and that the Monarch might, without scruple, use whatever meats and drink were most agreeable to him.'

[2] *Atash* being the Persian for fire. Catrou gives a different version of this story. According to him it was Father Joseph D'Acosta, Superior of the Jesuits in Agra, that proposed to Jáhángír to carry out the ordeal. '"Let a large fire be lighted," said the Father, "and the chief of the Mahometan religion on one side enter it bearing the Alcoran, whilst on the other side I will cast myself into it, holding in my hand the Gospel. It will then be seen in whose favour Heaven will declare, whether for Jesus Christ or Mahomet." At these words the Emperor cast his eyes upon the Mahometan, who exhibited great symptoms of terror lest the challenge should be accepted. He took pity on the Moula, and refrained exacting him to serve a trial. As for the Jesuit, they caused him to change his name, and the Emperor no longer called him by any other than that of Father Ataxe, which means the Fire Father.'

having, by his command, delivered an harangue in which he exposed the falsehoods of the *Mahometan* imposture, and defended the truths of his own persuasion, *Jehan-Guyre* said that it was high time something should be done to decide the controversy between the *Jesuits* and *Mullahs*. 'Let a pit be dug,' he added, 'and a fire kindled. Father *Atech*, with the Gospel under his arm, and a *Mullah*, with the *Koran*, shall throw themselves into it, and I will embrace the religion of him whom the flames shall not consume.' Father *Atech* declared his willingness to undergo the ordeal, but the *Mullahs* manifested the utmost dread, and the King felt too much compassion both for the one and the other to persevere in the experiment.

Whatever credit this story may deserve, it is indisputable that the *Jesuits* during the whole of *Jehan-Guyre's* reign were honoured and respected at this court, and that they entertained what appeared a well-grounded hope of the progress of the Gospel in *Hindoustan*. Everything, however, which has occurred since the death of that Monarch, excepting perhaps the close intimacy between *Dara* and Father *Buzé*,[1] forbids us to indulge in any such expectation. But having entered insensibly upon the subject of missions, you will perhaps allow me to make a few observations, introductory to the long letter which I intend to write concerning that important topic.

The design, indeed, meets with my entire approbation; nor ought we to withhold the meed of praise from those excellent missionaries in this part of the world, especially the *Capuchins* and *Jesuits*, who meekly impart religious instruction to all descriptions of men, without any mixture of indiscreet and bigoted zeal. To Christians of every denomination, whether *Catholics*, *Greeks*, *Armenians*, *Nestorians*, *Jacobins*, or others, the demeanour of these good pastors is affectionate and charitable. They are the refuge and consolation of distressed strangers and travellers, and by their great learning and exemplary lives expose to

[1] See p. 6, also p. 101, footnote [1].

shame the ignorance and licentious habits of infidels. Some unhappily there are who disgrace the Christian profession by notoriously profligate conduct, and who ought, therefore, to be immured in their convents instead of being invested with the sacred character of missionaries. Their religion is a mere mummery, and so far from aiding the cause of *Christianity*, they become stumbling-blocks in the way of those whom they were sent to enlighten and reclaim; but these are merely the exceptions to a general rule which affect not the main argument. I am decidedly favourable to this establishment of missions, and the sending forth of learned and pious missionaries. They are absolutely necessary; and it is the honour as well as the peculiar prerogative of *Christians* to supply every part of the world with men bearing the same character and following the same benign object as did the Apostles. You are not, however, to conclude that I am so deluded by my love of missions as to expect the same mighty effects to be produced by the exertions of modern missionaries as attended the preaching of a single sermon in the days of the Apostles. I have had too much intercourse with infidels, and am become too well acquainted with the blindness of the human heart to believe we shall hear of the conversion, in one day, of two or three thousand men. I despair especially of much success among *Mahometan* Kings or *Mahometan* subjects. Having visited nearly all the missionary stations in the East, I speak the language of experience when I say, that whatever progress may be made among *Gentiles* by the instruction and alms of the missionaries, you will be disappointed if you suppose that in ten years one *Mahometan* will be converted to Christianity. True it is that *Mahometans* respect the religion of the *New Testament*: they never speak of *Jesus Christ* but with great veneration, or pronounce the word *Aysa*, which means Jesus, without adding *Azeret*,[1] or majesty. They even believe with us that he was miraculously begotten and

[1] Hazrat 'Isā.

born of a virgin mother, and that he is the *Kelum-Allah*[1] and the *Rouh-Allah,* the Word of God and the Spirit of God. It is in vain to hope, however, that they will renounce the religion wherein they were born, or be persuaded that *Mahomet* was a false prophet. The Christians of *Europe* ought nevertheless to assist the missionaries by every possible means: their prayers, power and wealth, ought to be employed in promoting the glory of their REDEEMER; but the expense of the missions should be borne by Europeans, for it would be impolitic to lay burthens on the people abroad; and much care should be had that want may not drive any missionary to acts of meanness. Missions ought not only to be liberally provided, but should be composed of persons of sufficient integrity, energy, and intelligence always to bear testimony to the truth, to seek with eagerness opportunities of doing good,—in a word, to labour with unwearied activity and unabated zeal in their Lord's vineyard whenever and wherever He may be pleased to give them an opening. But although it be the duty of every *Christian* State to act in this manner, yet there ought to be no delusion; credence ought not to be given to every idle tale, and the work of conversion, which in fact is full of difficulty, should not be represented as a matter of easy accomplishment. We do not adequately estimate the strong hold which the *Mahometan* superstition has over the minds of its votaries, to whom it permits the unrestrained indulgence of passions which the religion we require them to substitute in its stead declares must be subdued or regulated. *Mahometanism* is a pernicious code, established by force of arms, and still imposed upon mankind by the same brutal violence. To counteract its baneful progress, Christians must display the zeal, and use the means I have suggested, however clear it may be that this abominable imposture can be effectually destroyed only by the special and merciful interposition of Divine Providence. We may derive encourage-

[1] Kalamu'llāh, and Rūhu'llāh.

ment from the promising appearances lately witnessed in *China,* in *Japan,* and in the case of *Jehan-Guyre.* Missionaries have to contend, however, with another sad impediment—the irreverent behaviour of Christians in their churches, so dissonant from their belief of the peculiar presence of God upon their altars, and so different from the conduct of *Mahometans,* who never venture when engaged in the service of their mosques even to turn the head, much less to utter a monosyllable one to the other, but seem to have the mind impressed with profound and awful veneration.

The *Dutch* have a factory in *Agra,* in which they generally keep four or five persons. Formerly they carried on a good trade in that city by the sale of broadcloths, large and small looking-glasses, plain laces, gold and silver laces, and iron wares; likewise by the purchase of *anil* [1] or *Indigo,* gathered in the neighbourhood of *Agra,* particularly at *Bianes,*[2] two days' journey from the city, whither they go once every year, having a house in the place. The *Dutch* used also to make extensive purchases of cloths not only at *Jelapour,* but at *Laknau,*[3] a seven or eight days' journey from *Agra,* where they also have a house, and despatch a few factors every season. It seems, however, that the trade of this people is not now very lucrative, owing probably to the competition of the *Armenians,* or to the great distance between *Agra* and *Sourate.* Accidents continually befall their caravans, which, to avoid the bad roads and mountains in the direct road through *Goüaleor* and *Brampour,* travel by

[1] See p. 283, footnote [2].

[2] Biana, where there is still some indigo cultivation.

[3] The *Feringhi mahal,* or Franks' quarter, one of the divisions or wards of the city of Lucknow, is where this factory stood. The buildings were confiscated in the reign of Aurangzeb, and made over to a Moslem for a Madrissah or college. An enclosure now used as a place for washing the Moslem dead is pointed out as part of the old factory.

Jelapour, is most likely Jalálpur-Nahir, in the Fyzabad district of Oudh, about 52 miles to the south-east of Fyzabad, which is still a tolerably flourishing weaving town.

way of *Ahmed-abad,* over the territories of different *Rajas.* But whatever may be the discouragements, I do not believe the *Dutch* will follow the example of the *English,* and abandon their factory at *Agra*; because they still dispose of their spices to great advantage, and find it useful to have confidential persons near the court always ready to prefer a complaint against any governor, or other officer, who may have committed an act of injustice or tyranny in any of the *Dutch* establishments in *Bengale,* or at *Patna, Sourate,* or *Ahmed-abad.*

I shall finish this letter with a description of the two wonderful mausoleums which constitute the chief superiority of *Agra* over *Delhi.* One was erected by *Jehan-Guyre* in honour of his father *Ekbar*; and *Chah-Jehan* raised the other to the memory of his wife *Tage Mehale,* that extraordinary and celebrated beauty, of whom her husband was so enamoured that it is said he was constant to her during life, and at her death was so affected as nearly to follow her to the grave.

I shall pass *Ekbar's* monument[1] without further observation, because all its beauties are found in still greater perfection in that of *Tage Mehale,* which I shall now endeavour to describe.

On leaving *Agra,* toward the east, you enter a long, wide, or paved street, on a gentle ascent, having on one side a high and long wall, which forms the side of a square garden, of much greater extent than our *Place Royale,* and on the other side a row of new houses with arcades, resembling those of the principal streets in *Dehli,* which I have already described. After walking half the length of the wall, you find on the right, that is, on the side of the houses, a large gate, tolerably well made, which is the entrance of a *Karvan-Serrah,* and on the opposite side from

[1] Akbar's tomb at Secundra near Agra was commenced by himself, and it is believed by competent judges that he borrowed the design from a Buddhist model. It was finished by his son Jáhángír, and is quite unlike any other tomb built in India either before or since.

that of the wall is seen the magnificent gate of a spacious and square pavilion, forming the entrance into the garden, between two reservoirs, faced with hewn stone.

This pavilion is an oblong square, and built of a stone resembling red marble, but not so hard. The front seems to me longer, and much more grand in its construction, than that of *S. Louis*, in the rue *S. Antoine*, and it is equally lofty. The columns, the architraves and the cornices are, indeed, not formed according to the proportion of the five orders of architecture so strictly observed in *French* edifices. The building I am speaking of is of a different and peculiar kind; but not without something pleasing in its whimsical structure; and in my opinion it well deserves a place in our books of architecture. It consists almost wholly of arches upon arches, and galleries upon galleries, disposed and contrived in an hundred different ways. Nevertheless the edifice has a magnificent appearance, and is conceived and executed effectually. Nothing offends the eye; on the contrary, it is delighted with every part, and never tired with looking.[1] The last time I visited *Tage Mehale's*

[1] 'No building in India has been so often drawn and photographed as this, or more frequently described; but with all this it is almost impossible to convey an idea of it to those who have not seen it, not only because of its extreme delicacy and beauty of material employed in its construction, but from the complexity of its design. If the Taje were only the tomb itself, it might be described, but the platform on which it stands, with its tall minarets, is a work of art in itself. Beyond this are the two wings, one of which is a mosque, which anywhere else would be considered an important building. This group of buildings forms one side of a garden court 880 feet square, and beyond this again an outer court of the same width but only half the depth. This is entered by three gateways of its own, and contains in the centre of its inner wall the great gateway of the garden court, a worthy pendant to the Taje itself. Beautiful as it is in itself, the Taje would lose half its charm if it stood alone. It is the combination of so many beauties, and the perfect manner in which each is subordinate to the other, that makes up a whole which the world cannot match, and which never fails to impress even those who are most indifferent to the effects produced by architectural objects in general.'—Fergusson, *History of Indian Architecture*, 1876 ed.

mausoleum I was in the company of a French merchant,[1] who, as well as myself, thought that this extraordinary fabric could not be sufficiently admired. I did not venture to express my opinion, fearing that my taste might have become corrupted by my long residence in the *Indies*; and as my companion was come recently from *France*, it was quite a relief to my mind to hear him say that he had seen nothing in *Europe* so bold and majestic.

When you have entered a little way into the pavilion approaching toward the garden, you find yourself under a lofty cupola, surrounded above with galleries, and having two divans or platforms below, one on the right, the other on the left, both of them raised eight or ten French feet from the ground. Opposite to the entrance from the street is a large open arch, by which you enter a walk which divides nearly the whole of the garden into two equal parts.

This walk or terrace is wide enough to admit six coaches abreast; it is paved with large and hard square stones, raised about eight French feet above the garden; and divided the whole length by a canal faced with hewn stone and ornamented with fountains placed at certain intervals.

After advancing twenty-five or thirty paces on this terrace, it is worth while to turn round and view the back elevation of the pavilion, which, though not comparable to the front, is still very splendid, being lofty and of a similar style of architecture. On both sides of the pavilion, along the garden wall, is a long and wide gallery, raised like a terrace, and supported by a number of low columns placed near each other. Into this gallery the poor are admitted three times a week during the rainy season to receive the alms founded in perpetuity by *Chah-Jehan*.

Resuming the walk along the main terrace, you see before you at a distance a large dome, in which is the sepulchre, and to the right and left of that dome on a

[1] Probably Tavernier.

lower surface you observe several garden walks covered with trees and many parterres full of flowers.

When at the end of the principal walk or terrace, besides the dome that faces you, are discovered two large

FIG. 11.—The Empress Taj Mahál.

pavilions, one to the right, another to the left, both built with the same kind of stone, consequently of the same red colour as the first pavilion. These are spacious square edifices, the parts of which are raised over each other in the form of balconies and terraces; three arches leave openings which have the garden wall for a boundary, and you walk under these pavilions as if they were lofty and wide galleries. I shall not stop to speak of the interior ornaments of the two pavilions, because they scarcely differ in regard to the walls, ceiling, or pavement from the dome which I am going to describe. Between the end of the principal walk and this dome is an open and pretty large space, which I call a water-parterre, because the stones on which you walk,[1] cut and figured in various forms, represent the borders of box in our parterres. From the middle of this space you have a good view of the building which contains the tomb, and which we are now to examine.

This building is a vast dome of white marble nearly of the same height as the *Val De Grace*[2] of *Paris*, and encircled by a number of turrets, also of white marble, descending the one below the other in regular succession.

[1] They are of black and white marble in alternate rows, supposed to resemble rippling water.

[2] Above the façade of the church of the deaf and dumb asylum of Val-de-Grâce, designed by Fr. Mansart, and built in 1645-66, rises the famous dome, which is a reduced copy of that of St. Peter's at Rome, 133 feet high and 53 feet in diameter. The principal dome of the Taj is 80 feet high and 58 feet in diameter, and very much more gracefully proportioned, and with infinitely finer lines than the Val-de-Grâce dome, which can easily be verified by a comparison of photographs of the two structures. Tavernier (*Travels*, vol. i. p. 110, 111) was of the opinion that the dome of the Taj is scarcely less magnificent than that of the Val-de-Grâce, and adds that he witnessed the commencement and accomplishment of the building of the Taj, 'on which they have expended twenty-two years, during which twenty thousand men worked incessantly; this is sufficient to enable one to realise that the cost of it has been enormous. It is said that the scaffoldings alone cost more than the entire work, because, from want of wood, they had all to be made of brick, as well as the supports of the arches; this has entailed much labour and a heavy expenditure. Shah Jahán began to build his own tomb on the other side of the river, but the war which he had with his sons interrupted his plans, and Aurangzeb, who reigns at present, is not disposed to complete it.'

The whole fabric is supported by four great arches, three of which are quite open and the other closed up by the wall of an apartment with a gallery attached to it. There the *Koran* is continually read with apparent devotion in respectful memory of *Tage Mehale* by certain *Mullahs* kept in the mausoleum for that purpose. The centre of every arch is adorned with white marble slabs whereon are inscribed large *Arabian* characters in black marble, which produce a fine effect. The interior or concave part of the dome and generally the whole of the wall from top to bottom are faced with white marble: no part can be found that is not skilfully wrought, or that has not its peculiar beauty. Everywhere are seen the jasper, and *jachen*,[1] or jade, as well as other stones similar to those that enrich the walls of the *Grand Duke's* chapel at *Florence*, and several more of great value and rarity, set in an endless variety of modes, mixed and enchased in the slabs of marble which face the body of the wall. Even the squares of white and black marble which compose the pavement are inlaid with these precious stones in the most beautiful and delicate manner imaginable.

Under the dome is a small chamber, wherein is enclosed the tomb of *Tage Mehale*. It is opened with much ceremony once in a year, and once only; and as no Christian is admitted within, lest its sanctity should be profaned, I have not seen the interior, but I understand that nothing can be conceived more rich and magnificent.

It only remains to draw your attention to a walk or terrace, nearly five-and-twenty paces in breadth and rather more in height, which runs from the dome to the extremity of the garden. From this terrace are seen the *Gemna* flowing below, a large expanse of luxuriant gardens, a part of the city of *Agra*, the fortress, and all the fine residences of the *Omrahs* erected on the banks of the river. When I add that this terrace extends almost the whole length of one side of the garden, I leave you to

[1] *Yashm* is the Persian name for this mineral.

judge whether I had not sufficient ground for asserting that the mausoleum of *Tage Mehale* is an astonishing work. It is possible I may have imbibed an Indian taste; but I decidedly think that this monument deserves much more to be numbered among the wonders of the world than the pyramids of *Egypt,* those unshapen masses which when I had seen them twice yielded me no satisfaction, and which are nothing on the outside but heaps of large stones piled in the form of steps one upon another, while within there is very little that is creditable either to human skill or to human invention.

LETTER

TO MONSIEUR

CHAPELAIN,

DESPATCHED FROM CHIRAS IN PERSIA,
the 4th October 1667.

Describing the Superstitions, strange customs, and Doctrines of the Indous or Gentiles of Hindoustan;

From which it will be seen that there is no Doctrine too strange or too improbable for the Soul of man to conceive.

MONSIEUR,[1]

I have witnessed two solar eclipses which it is scarcely possible I should ever forget. The one I saw from *France* in the year 1654, the other from *Dehli* in the *Indies* in 1666. The sight of the first eclipse was impressed upon my mind by the childish credulity of the French people, and by their groundless and unreasonable alarm; an alarm so excessive that some brought drugs as

[1] Jean Chapelain (1594-1674), an excellent man but a poor poet. In 1662 he was employed by Colbert (see p. 201, footnote [1]) to draw up an account of contemporary men of letters to guide the King (Louis XIV.) in his distribution of pensions.

charms to defend themselves against the eclipse; some kept themselves closely shut up, and excluded all light either in carefully-barred apartments or in cellars; while thousands flocked to their respective churches; some apprehending and dreading a malign and dangerous influence; others believing that the last day was at hand, and that the eclipse was about to shake the foundations of the world. Such were the absurd notions entertained by our countrymen, notwithstanding the writings of *Gassendi*,[1] *Roberval*,[2] and other celebrated astronomers and philosophers, which clearly demonstrated that the eclipse was only similar to many others which had been productive of no mischief; that this obscuration of the sun was known and predicted, and was without any other peculiarity than what might be found in the reveries of ignorant or designing astrologers.

The eclipse of 1666 is also indelibly imprinted on my memory by the ridiculous errors and strange superstitions of the *Indians*. At the time fixed for its appearance I took my station on the terrace of my house, situated on the banks of the *Gemna*, when I saw both shores of the river, for nearly a league in length, covered with *Gentiles* or idolaters, who stood in the water up to the waist, their eyes riveted to the skies, watching the commencement of the eclipse, in order to plunge and wash themselves at the very instant. The little boys and girls were quite naked; the men had nothing but a scarf round their middle, and the married women and girls of six or seven years of age

[1] For some account of Pierre Gassendi (1592-1655), the European Agah, '*Friendly* Master,' of Bernier, see *Chronicle of Events*, etc., under date 24th October 1655.

[2] Gilles Personne de Roberval (1602-1675), the great French mathematician. Appointed to the chair of Philosophy in the Gervais College in 1631, and afterwards to the chair of Mathematics in the College of France: an appointment which he held until his death, although a condition of tenure of that Professorship was that the holder should propose questions for solution and resign in favour of any one who solved them better than himself.

were covered with a single cloth. Persons of rank or wealth, such as *Rajas* (*Gentile* sovereign princes, and generally courtiers in the service and pay of the King), *Serrafs*[1] or money-changers, bankers, jewellers, and other rich merchants, crossed from the opposite side of the river with their families, and pitching their tents fixed *kanates*[2] or screens in the water, within which they and their wives washed and performed the usual ceremonies without any exposure. No sooner did these idolaters perceive that the obscuration of the sun was begun than they all raised a loud cry, and plunged the whole body under water several times in quick succession; after which they stood in the river, lifted their eyes and hands toward the sun, muttered and prayed with seeming devotion, filling their hands from time to time with water, which they threw in the direction of the sun, bowing their heads very low, and moving and turning their arms and hands, sometimes one way, sometimes another. The deluded people continue to plunge, mutter, pray, and perform their silly tricks until the end of the eclipse. On retiring they threw pieces of silver at a great distance into the *Gemna,* and gave alms to the *Brahmens,* who failed not to be present at this absurd ceremony. I remarked that every individual on coming out of the water put on new clothes placed on the sand for that purpose, and that several of the most devout left their old garments as presents for the *Brahmens.*

In this manner did I observe from the roof of my house the solemnisation of the grand eclipse-festival, a festival which was kept with the same external observances in the *Indus,* in the *Ganges,* and in the other rivers and *Talabs* (or tanks of the *Indies*), but above all in that one at *Tanaiser,*[3] which contained on that occasion more than one

[1] The Arabic word *sarráf*, now modernised into shroff.

[2] The side walls of a tent.

[3] The sacred tank at Thaneswar, in the Umballa District, situated on the line of the old Mogul road to Lahore,—a very ancient place of Hindoo pilgrimage, being considered the centre of the 'Holy Land'

hundred and fifty thousand persons, assembled from all parts of the empire; its waters being considered on the day of an eclipse more holy and meritorious than those of any other.

The Great *Mogol,* though a *Mahometan,* permits these ancient and superstitious practices; not wishing, or not daring, to disturb the *Gentiles* in the free exercises of their religion. But the ceremony I have described is not performed until a certain number of *Brahmens,* as deputies from their fellows, have presented the King with a *lecque* of *roupies,* equal to about fifty thousand crowns; in return for which he begs their acceptance only of a few vests and an old elephant.

I shall now mention the wise and convincing reasons assigned for the festival of the eclipse, and for the rites with which it is attended.

We have, say they, our four *Beths*;[1] that is, our four books of law, sacred and divine writings given unto us by God himself, through the medium of *Brahma.* These books teach that a certain *Deüta,*[2] an incarnate divinity, extremely malignant and mischievous, very dark, very black, very impure, and very filthy (these are all their own expressions) takes possession of the Sun, which it blackens to the colour of ink, infects and obscures; that the Sun, which is also a *Deüta,* but of the most beneficent and perfect kind, is thrown into a state of the greatest uneasiness, and suffers a most cruel agony while in the power of and infected by this wicked and black being; that an endeavour to rescue the Sun from so miserable a con-

of Kurukshetra. During eclipses of the moon, the waters of all other tanks are believed to visit this tank, so that he who bathes in the assembled water obtains the concentrated merit of all possible ablutions. Thaneswar, which is now gradually falling into ruin, is one of the oldest and most famous towns in India connected with the legends of the *Máhábhárata* and the exploits of the Pándavas.

1 *Beids*, a corruption of *Vedas*, Divine knowledge.

2 *Deotah*, a corruption of *Devata*, 'Celestials,' most frequently the whole body of inferior gods.

dition becomes the duty of every person; that this important object can be attained only by means of prayers, ablutions, and alms; that those actions have an extraordinary merit during the festival of the eclipse, the alms then bestowed being a hundred times more valuable than alms given at any other time; and who is he, they ask, that would refuse to make a profit of cent per cent?

These, *Monsieur*, were the eclipses which I told you I could not easily forget, and they naturally lead me to speak of other wild extravagancies of the unhappy heathens, from which I shall leave you to draw whatever conclusions you please.

In the town of *Jagannat*,[1] situated on the Gulf of *Bengale*, and containing the famous temple of the idol of that name, a certain annual festival is held, which continues, if my memory fail not, for the space of eight or nine days. At this festival is collected an incredible concourse of people, as was the case anciently at the temple of *Hammon*, and as happens at present in the city of *Meca*. The number, I am told, sometimes exceeds one hundred and fifty thousand. A superb wooden machine is constructed, such as I have seen in several other parts of the *Indies*, with I know not how many grotesque figures, nearly resembling our monsters which we see depicted with two heads, being half man and half beast, gigantic and horrible heads, satyrs, apes, and devils. This machine is set on fourteen or sixteen wheels like those of a gun-carriage, and drawn or pushed along by the united exertions of fifty or sixty persons. The idol, *Jagannat*, placed conspicuously in the middle, richly attired, and gorgeously adorned, is thus conveyed from one temple to another.

The first day on which this idol is formally exhibited in the temple, the crowd is so immense, and the press so violent, that some of the pilgrims, fatigued and worn out in consequence of their long journey, are squeezed to

[1] In modern colloquial Juggernaut (a corruption of *Jaggannatha*, one of the forms of Krishna), near the town of Purí in Orissa.

death: the surrounding throng give them a thousand benedictions, and consider them highly favoured to die on such a holy occasion after travelling so great a distance. And while the chariot of hellish triumph pursues its solemn march, persons are found (it is no fiction which I recount) so blindly credulous and so full of wild notions as to throw themselves upon the ground in the way of its ponderous wheels, which pass over and crush to atoms the bodies of the wretched fanatics without exciting the horror or surprise of the spectators. No deed, according to their estimation, is so heroic or meritorious as this self-devotion: the victims believe that *Jagannat* will receive them as children, and recall them to life in a state of happiness and dignity.

The *Brahmens* encourage and promote these gross errors and superstitions to which they are indebted for their wealth and consequence. As persons attached and consecrated to important mysteries, they are held in general veneration, and enriched by the alms of the people. So wicked and detestable are their tricks and impostures that I required the full and clear evidence of them—which I obtained—ere I could believe that they had recourse to similar expedients. These knaves select a beautiful maiden to become (as they say, and as they induce these silly, ignorant people to believe) the bride of *Jagannat,* who accompanies the god to the temple with all the pomp and ceremony which I have noticed, where she remains the whole night, having been made to believe that *Jagannat* will come and lie with her. She is commanded to inquire of the god if the year will be fruitful, and what may be the processions, the festivals, the prayers, and the alms which he requires in return for his bounty. In the night one of these impostors enters the temple through a small back door, enjoys the unsuspecting damsel, makes her believe whatever may be deemed necessary, and the following morning when on her way to another temple, whither she is carried in that Triumphal Chariot, by the side of *Jagannat* her *Spouse,* she is desired by the *Brahmens* to state aloud to the people all she has heard from the lustful priest, as if every word had proceeded from the mouth of *Jagannat*. But let me relate follies of another kind.

In front of the chariot, and even in the *Deüras* or *Idol Temples*, public women during festival days dance and throw their bodies into a variety of indecent and preposterous attitudes, which the *Brahmens* deem quite consistent with the religion of the country. I have known females celebrated for beauty, and who were remarkably reserved in their general deportment, refuse valuable presents from *Mahometans, Christians,* and even *Gentile* foreigners, because they considered themselves dedicated to the ministry and to the ministers of the *Deüra*,[1] to the *Brahmens,* and to those *Fakires* who are commonly seated on ashes all round the temple, some quite naked with hideous hair, like, we may suppose, to that of *Megæra,* and in postures which I shall soon describe.

What has been said concerning women burning themselves will be confirmed by so many travellers that I suppose people will cease to be sceptical upon this melancholy fact. The accounts given of it have been certainly exaggerated, and the number of victims is less now than formerly; the *Mahometans,* by whom the country is governed, doing all in their power to suppress the barbarous custom. They do not, indeed, forbid it by a positive law, because it is a part of their policy to leave the idolatrous population, which is so much more numerous than their own, in the free exercise of its religion; but the practice is checked by indirect means. No woman can sacrifice herself without permission from the governor of the province in which she resides, and he never grants it until he shall have ascertained that she is not to be turned aside from her purpose: to accomplish this desirable end the governor reasons with the widow and makes her enticing promises; after which, if these methods fail, he sometimes sends her

[1] Hindostanee for a temple, a corruption of the Sanskrit, *Devala*, a temple.

among his women, that the effect of their remonstrances may be tried. Notwithstanding these obstacles, the number of self-immolations is still very considerable, particularly in the territories of the *Rajas*, where no *Mahometan* governors are appointed. But not to tire you with the history of every woman whom I have seen perish on the funeral pile, I shall advert to only two or three of those shocking spectacles at which I have been present; and first I shall give you some details concerning a female to whom I was sent for the purpose of diverting her from persevering in her dreadful intention.

One of my friends, named *Bendidas*,[1] Danechmend-kan's principal writer, died of a hectic fever for which I had attended him upwards of two years, and his wife immediately resolved to burn herself with the body of her husband. Her friends were in the service of my *Agah*, and being commanded by him to dissuade the widow from the commission of so frantic an act, they represented to her that although she had adopted a generous and commendable resolution, which would redound to the honour and conduce to the happiness of the family, yet she ought to consider that her children were of a tender age, that it would be cruel to abandon them, and that her anxiety for their welfare ought to exceed the affection she bore to the memory of her deceased husband. The infatuated creature attended not, however, to their reasoning, and I was requested to visit the widow as if by my *Agah's* desire, and in the capacity of an old friend of the family. I complied, and found on entering the apartment a regular witches' *Sabat* of seven or eight old hags, and another of four or five excited, wild, and aged *Brahmens* standing round the body, all of whom gave by turns a horrid yell, and beat their hands with violence. The widow was seated at the feet of her dead husband; her hair was dishevelled and her visage pale,

[1] The Muhamadanised form of Benidas, a common name among Hindoo 'writers' or clerks, who were largely employed, some of them in positions of considerable responsibility, by the Moguls.

but her eyes were tearless and sparkling with animation while she cried and screamed aloud like the rest of the company, and beat time with her hands to this horrible concert. The hurly-burly having subsided, I approached the hellish group, and addressed the woman in a gentle tone. 'I am come hither,' said I, 'by desire of *Danechmend-kan*, to inform you that he will settle a pension of two crowns per month on each of your two sons, provided you do not destroy your life, a life so necessary for their care and education. We have ways and means indeed to prevent your ascending the pile, and to punish those who encourage you in so unreasonable a resolution. All your relations wish you to live for the sake of your offspring, and you will not be reputed infamous as are the childless widows who possess not courage to burn themselves with their dead husbands.' I repeated these arguments several times without receiving any answer; but, at last, fixing a determined look on me, she said, 'Well, if I am prevented from burning myself, I will dash out my brains against a wall.' What a diabolical spirit has taken possession of you, thought I. 'Let it be so then,' I rejoined, with undissembled anger, 'but first take your children, wretched and unnatural mother! cut their throats, and consume them on the same pile; otherwise you will leave them to die of famine, for I shall return immediately to *Danechmend-kan* and annul their pensions.' These words, spoken with a loud and resolute voice, made the desired impression: without uttering a syllable, her head fell suddenly on her knees, and the greater part of the old women and *Brahmens* sneaked toward the door and left the room. I thought I might now safely leave the widow in the hands of her friends, who had accompanied me, and mounting my horse returned home. In the evening, when on my way to *Danechmend-kan* to inform him of what I had done, I met one of the relations who thanked me, and said that the body had been burnt without the widow, who had promised not to die by her own hands.

In regard to the women who actually burn themselves, I was present at so many of those shocking exhibitions that I could not persuade myself to attend any more, nor is it without a feeling of horror that I revert to the subject. I shall endeavour, nevertheless, to describe what passed before my eyes; but I cannot hope to give you an adequate conception of the fortitude displayed by these infatuated victims during the whole of the frightful tragedy: it must be seen to be believed.

When travelling from *Ahmed-abad* to *Agra*, through the territories of *Rajas*, and while the caravan halted under the shade of a banyan-tree[1] until the cool of the evening, news reached us that a widow was then on the point of burning herself with the body of her husband. I ran at once to the spot, and going to the edge of a large and nearly dry reservoir, observed at the bottom a deep pit filled with wood: the body of a dead man extended thereon; a woman seated upon the same pile; four or five *Brahmens* setting fire to it in every part; five middle-aged women, tolerably well dressed, holding one another by the hand, singing and dancing round the pit; and a great number of spectators of both sexes.

The pile, whereon large quantities of butter[2] and oil had been thrown, was soon enveloped in flames, and I saw the fire catch the woman's garments, which were impregnated with scented oil, mixed with sandalwood powder and saffron; but I could not perceive the slightest indication

[1] 'Bourgade' in the original, which I have ventured to take in this passage as intended for *Bargat*, the common name in Hindostan for a 'banyan'-tree, the *Ficus Indica*, L. A caravan would not halt even in a village (*bourgade*), especially when in a foreign territory; in the words of a previous translator, 'while the caravan halted *in a town* under the shade.' A famous banyan-tree near the town of Hardoi in Oudh is, or rather was, so extended (natural decay has, I believe, almost entirely destroyed it) that 'tis said that in 1858 two regiments of soldiers encamped under the shade of its branches. In various other parts of India other large 'banyan'-trees may be met with, quite capable of sheltering an ordinary caravan or camp.

[2] Ghee, which is clarified butter; see p. 438, footnote 4.

of pain or even uneasiness in the victim, and it was said that she pronounced with emphasis the words *five, two,* to signify that this being the fifth time she had burned herself with the same husband, there were wanted only two more similar sacrifices to render her perfect, according to the doctrine of the transmigration of souls: as if a certain reminiscence, or prophetic spirit, had been imparted to her at that moment of her dissolution.

But this was only the commencement of the infernal tragedy. I thought that the singing and dancing of the five women were nothing more than some unmeaning ceremony; great therefore was my astonishment when I saw that the flames having ignited the clothes of one of these females, she cast herself head-foremost into the pit. The horrid example was followed by another woman, as soon as the flames caught her person: the three women who remained then took hold of each other by the hand, resuming the dance with perfect composure; and after a short lapse of time, they also precipitated themselves, one after the other, into the fire.

I soon learnt the meaning of these multiplied sacrifices. The five women were slaves, and having witnessed the deep affliction of their mistress in consequence of the illness of her husband, whom she promised not to survive, they were so moved with compassion that they entered into an engagement to perish by the same flames that consumed their beloved mistress.

Many persons whom I then consulted on the subject would fain have persuaded me that an excess of affection was the cause why these women burn themselves with their deceased husbands; but I soon found that this abominable practice is the effect of early and deeply rooted prejudices. Every girl is taught by her mother that it is virtuous and laudable in a wife to mingle her ashes with those of her husband, and that no woman of honour will refuse compliance with the established custom. These opinions men have always inculcated as an easy mode of keeping wives in subjection, of securing their attention in times of sickness, and of deterring them from administering poison to their husbands.

But let us proceed to another of these dreadful scenes, not witnessed indeed by myself, but selected in preference to others at which I happened to be present on account of the remarkable incident by which it was distinguished. I have seen so many things which I should have pronounced incredible, that neither you nor I ought to reject the narrative in question merely because it contains something extraördinary. The story is in every person's mouth in the *Indies*, and is universally credited. Perhaps it has already reached you in *Europe*.

A woman, long engaged in love intrigues with a young *Mahometan*, her neighbour, by trade a tailor, and a player on the tambourine,[1] poisoned her husband, hoping that the young man would marry her. She then hastened to her lover, informed him of what she had done, and claiming the performance of his promise to take her to wife, urged the necessity of immediately flying, as had been previously projected, from the scene of their guilt; 'for,' added she, 'if there be the least delay, I shall be constrained by a common sense of decency to burn myself with the body of my dead spouse.' The young man, who foresaw that such a scheme would involve him in difficulty and danger, peremptorily refused, and the woman, without betraying the smallest emotion, went at the instant to her relations, informed them of the sudden death of her husband, and of her fixed resolution to die on the funeral pile. Pleased with so magnanimous an intention, and with the honour she was about to confer on the family, her friends prepare a pit, fill it with wood, lay the body upon the pile, and kindle the fire. These arrangements being completed, the woman makes the round of the pit for the purpose of embracing and bidding a last farewell to her

[1] Probably a *khunjuree*; a small tambourine played upon with the fingers.

kindred, among whom stood the young tailor, invited thither with other musicians to play on the tambourine according to the custom of the country. Approaching the lover as if she intended to take a last and tender adieu, the infuriated creature seized him with a firm grasp by the collar, drew him with irresistible force to the edge of the pit, and precipitated herself headlong, with the object of her resentment, into the midst of the raging fire.

As I was leaving *Sourate* for *Persia,* I witnessed the devotion and burning of another widow: several Englishmen and Dutchmen and Monsieur *Chardin*[1] of *Paris* were present. She was of the middle age, and by no means uncomely. I do not expect, with my limited powers of expression, to convey a full idea of the brutish boldness, or ferocious gaiety depicted on this woman's countenance; of her undaunted step; of the freedom from all perturbation with which she conversed, and permitted herself to be washed; of the look of confidence, or rather of insensibility which she cast upon us; of her easy air, free from dejection; of her lofty carriage, void of embarrassment, when she was examining her little cabin, composed of dry and thick millet straw, with an intermixture of small wood; when she entered into that cabin, sat down upon the funeral pile, placed her deceased husband's head in her

[1] Sir (then simply Monsieur) John Chardin, the celebrated traveller, was born at Paris in 1643, and died in London in 1713, and was buried in Westminster Abbey, where his monument bears the very appropriate inscription, *Nomen sibi fecit eundo.* His first journey was to Persia and India in 1665, and while there he received the patronage (his business was that of a jeweller) of Sháh Abbas II. He returned to Paris in 1670, and in 1671 he again set out for Persia and India, and in 1677 he returned to Europe by the Cape of Good Hope. A Protestant, the persecution going on in France led him to settle in London in 1681, where he was appointed Court Jeweller and knighted by Charles II. Chardin was in Surat in 1667 and in 1677, and it must have been in 1667 that Bernier met him there; as we know from the date of this letter to Monsieur Chapelain (see p. 300) that Bernier was in Sheraz in October 1667, after his return from India, *viâ* Surat, and, most probably, Bandar Abbassi.

lap, took up a torch, and with her own hand lighted the fire within, while I know not how many *Brahmens* were busily engaged in kindling it without. Well indeed may I despair of representing this whole scene with proper and genuine feeling, such as I experienced at the spectacle itself, or of painting it in colours sufficiently vivid. My recollection of it indeed is so distinct that it seems only a few days since the horrid reality passed before my eyes, and with pain I persuade myself that it was anything but a frightful dream.

It is true, however, that I have known some of these unhappy widows shrink at the sight of the piled wood; so as to leave no doubt on my mind that they would willingly have recanted, if recantation had been permitted by the merciless *Brahmens*; but those demons excite or astound the affrighted victims, and even thrust them into the fire. I was present when a poor young woman, who had fallen back five or six paces from the pit, was thus driven forward; and I saw another of these wretched beings struggling to leave the funeral pile when the fire increased around her person, but she was prevented from escaping by the long poles of the diabolical executioners.

But sometimes the devoted widows elude the vigilance of the murderous priests. I have been often in the company of a fair *Idolater*, who contrived to save her life by throwing herself upon the protection of the *scavengers*,[1] who assemble on these occasions in considerable numbers, when they learn that the intended victim is young and handsome, that her relations are of little note, and that she is to be accompanied by only a few of her acquaintance. Yet the woman whose courage fails at the sight of the horrid apparatus of death, and who avails herself of the presence of these men to avoid the impending sacrifice, cannot hope to pass her days in happiness, or to be treated with respect or affection. Never again can she live with

[1] Sweepers, *halal-khors*, who frequent burning ghâts (places for cremation) for various purposes at the present day.

the *Gentiles*: no individual of that nation will at any time, or under any circumstances, associate with a creature so degraded, who is accounted utterly infamous, and execrated because of the dishonour which her conduct has brought upon the religion of the country. Consequently she is ever afterwards exposed to the ill-treatment of her low and vulgar protectors. There is no *Mogol* who does not dread the consequences of contributing to the preservation of a woman devoted to the burning pile, or who will venture to afford an asylum to one who escapes from the fangs of the *Brahmens*; but many widows have been rescued by the *Portuguese*, in sea-ports where that people happened to be in superior strength. I need scarcely say how much my own indignation has been excited, and how ardently I have wished for opportunities to exterminate those cursed *Brahmens*.

At *Lahor* I saw a most beautiful young widow sacrificed, who could not, I think, have been more than twelve years of age. The poor little creature appeared more dead than alive when she approached the dreadful pit: the agony of her mind cannot be described; she trembled and wept bitterly; but three or four of the *Brahmens*, assisted by an old woman who held her under the arm, forced the unwilling victim toward the fatal spot, seated her on the wood, tied her hands and feet, lest she should run away, and in that situation the innocent creature was burnt alive. I found it difficult to repress my feelings and to prevent their bursting forth into clamorous and unavailing rage; but restrained by prudential considerations, I contented myself with silently lamenting the abominable superstition of these people, and applied to it the language of the poet, when speaking of *Iphigenia*, whom her father *Agamemnon* had offered in sacrifice to *Diana*:—

. . . quod contra saepius illa
religio peperit scelerosa atque impia facta
Aulide quo pacta *Triviai* virginis aram
Iphianassai turparunt sanguine foede

ductores *Danaum* delecti, prima virorum.

. . . .

tantum religio potuit suadere malorum.[1]

I have not yet mentioned all the barbarity and atrocity of these monsters. In some parts of the *Indies*, instead of burning the women who determine not to survive their husbands, the *Brahmens* bury them alive, by slow degrees, up to the throat; then two or three of them fall suddenly upon the victim, wring her neck, and when she has been effectually and completely choked, cover over the body with earth thrown upon it from successive baskets, and tread upon the head.

Most of the *Gentiles* burn their dead; but some partially broil the bodies with stubble, near the side of a river, and then precipitate them into the water from a high and steep bank.[2] I have attended these funeral rites on the *Ganges* several times, and observed flights of crows fluttering about the carcass, which becomes as much the prey of those birds as of the fish and crocodiles.

Some again carry a sick person, when at the point of death, to the river-side; place his feet in the water, let him sink gradually to the neck; and when it is supposed that he is about to expire, they immerse his whole body into the river, where they leave him, after violently clapping their hands, and crying out with great vehemence. The object of this ceremony (at which I have been present) is that the soul may be washed, on taking its flight, from

[1] This quotation (from Lucretius, *De Rerum Natura*, Book I. 82-102) has been thus rendered by H. A. J. Munro :—'Whereas on the contrary, often and often, that very religion has given birth to sinful and unholy deeds. Thus in Aulis the chosen chieftains of the Danai, foremost of men, foully polluted with Iphianassa's blood the altar of the Trivian maid. . . . So great the evils to which religion could prompt!' I have substituted the latest critical version, for the one given by Bernier, which he took from a Dutch edition of Lucretius.

[2] This is done by those too poor to afford the cost of an ordinary cremation.

all impurities which it may have contracted during its abode in the body. This absurd notion is not confined to the vulgar; I have heard it seriously defended by men of the highest reputation for learning.

Among the vast number, and endless variety of *Fakires*, or *Derviches*, and *Holy Men*, or *Gentile* hypocrites[1] of the *Indies*, many live in a sort of convent, governed by superiors, where vows of chastity, poverty, and submission are made. So strange is the life led by these votaries that I doubt whether my description of it will be credited. I allude particularly to the people called *Jauguis*,[2] a name which signifies 'united to God.' Numbers are seen, day and night, seated or lying on ashes, entirely naked; frequently under the large trees near *talabs*, or tanks of water, or in the galleries round the *Deüras*, or idol temples. Some have hair hanging down to the calf of the leg, twisted and entangled into knots, like the coat of our shaggy dogs, or rather like the hair of those afflicted with that *Polish* disease, which we call *la Plie*.[3] I have seen several who hold one, and some who hold both arms, perpetually lifted up above the head; the nails of their hands being twisted, and longer than half my little finger, with which I measured them. Their arms are as small and thin as the arms of persons who die in a decline, because in so forced and unnatural a position they receive not sufficient nourishment; nor can they be lowered so as to supply the mouth with food, the muscles having become contracted, and the articulations dry and stiff. Novices wait upon these fanatics, and pay them the utmost respect, as persons endowed with extraordinary sanctity. No *Fury* in the infernal regions can be conceived more

[1] In the original, 'ou Santons Gentils des Indes.' Santon originally meant a peculiar sect of Moslem devotee, but I have translated the word as meaning a hypocrite, in which sense it is used by Rabelais.

[2] Jogí, a corruption of *Yoga*, union or junction. Applied to those followers of the Yoga doctrine who are supposed to go about preaching the duty and necessity of religious retirement and meditation.

[3] The disease known as *Plica Polonica*.

horrible than the *Jauguis*, with their naked and black skin, long hair, spindle arms, long twisted nails, and fixed in the posture which I have mentioned.

I have often met, generally in the territory of some *Raja*, bands of these naked *Fakires*, hideous to behold. Some had their arms lifted up in the manner just described; the frightful hair of others either hung loosely or was tied and twisted round their heads; some carried a club like to *Hercules*; others had a dry and rough tiger skin thrown over their shoulders. In this trim I have seen them shamelessly walk, stark naked, through a large town, men, women, and girls looking at them without any more emotion than may be created when a hermit passes through our streets. Females would often bring them alms with much devotion, doubtless believing that they were holy personages, more chaste and discreet than other men.

I was for a long time disgusted with a celebrated *Fakire*, named *Sarmet*, who paraded the streets of *Dehli* as naked as when he came into the world. He despised equally the promises and the threats of *Aureng-Zebe*, and underwent at length the punishment of decapitation from his obstinate refusal to put on wearing apparel.

Several of these *Fakires* undertake long pilgrimages, not only naked, but laden with heavy iron chains, such as are put about the legs of elephants. I have seen others who in consequence of a particular vow stood upright, during seven or eight days, without once sitting or lying down, and without any other support than might be afforded by leaning forward against a cord for a few hours in the night; their legs in the meantime were swollen to the size of their thighs. Others again I have observed standing steadily, whole hours together, upon their hands, the head down, and the feet in the air. I might proceed to enumerate various other positions in which these unhappy men place their body, many of them so difficult and painful that they could not be imitated by our tumblers; and all this, let it be recollected, is performed from an assumed feeling of piety, of which there is not so much as the shadow in any part of the *Indies.*

I confess that this gross superstition filled me, on my first arrival in *Hindoustan,* with amazement. I knew not what to think of it. Sometimes I should have been disposed to consider the *Fakires* as remnants, if not as the founders, of the ancient and infamous sect of *Cynics,* could I have discovered anything in them but brutality and ignorance, and if they had not appeared to me vegetative rather than rational beings. At another time, I thought they might be honest though deluded enthusiasts, until I found that, in fact they were, in the widest sense of the word, destitute of piety. Again, I reflected that a life of vagrancy, idleness, and independence may have a powerful and attractive charm; or that the vanity which intermingles itself with every motive of human action, and which may be discovered as clearly through the tattered mantle of a *Diogenes* as under the comely garb of a *Plato,* was probably the secret spring that set so many strange engines in motion.

The *Fakires,* it is said, exercise painful austerities in the confident hope that they will be *Rajas* in their renascent state; or, if they do not become *Rajas*, that they shall be placed in a condition of life capable of more exquisite enjoyment than is experienced by those sovereign princes: but, as I have frequently observed to them, how can it be believed that men submit to a life of so much misery for the sake of a second state of existence, as short and uncertain as the first, and which cannot be expected to yield a much greater degree of happiness even to him who may be invested with the high dignity of *Rana,* or who may resemble *Jesseingue* or *Jessomseingue,* the two most powerful Rajas of the *Indies?* I am not to be so easily deceived, said I to them; either you are egregious fools, or you are actuated by some sinister views which you carefully hide from the world.

Some of the *Fakires* enjoy the reputation of being

peculiarly enlightened saints, perfect *Jauguis*, and really united to God. These are supposed to have entirely renounced the world, and like our hermits they live a secluded life in a remote garden, without ever visiting a town. When food is brought to them, they receive it: if none be offered to them it is concluded that the holy men can live without food, that they subsist by the favour of God, vouchsafed on account of previous long fasts and other religious mortifications. Frequently these pious *Jauguis* are absorbed in profound meditation. It is pretended, and one of the favoured saints himself assured me, that their souls are often rapt in an ecstasy of several hours' duration; that their external senses lose their functions; that the *Jauguis* are blessed with a sight of God, who appears as a light ineffably white and vivid, and that they experience transports of holy joy, and a contempt of temporal concerns which defy every power of description. My saintly informant added that he could at pleasure fall into such a trance as he described, and not one of the individuals who are in the habit of visiting the *Jauguis* doubts the reality of these vaunted ecstasies. It is possible that the imagination, distempered by continued fasts and uninterrupted solitude, may be brought into these illusions, or that the rapturous dreams of the *Fakires* may resemble the natural ecstasies into which *Cardan*[1] tells us he could fall whenever he pleased, especially as the *Fakires* practise some art in what they do, prescribing to themselves certain rules for the binding up of their senses by slow degrees. For example, they say that after having fasted several days upon bread and water, it is necessary to be alone in a sequestered spot, to fix the eyes most steadily toward heaven, and when they have been so riveted for some

[1] Girolamo Cardan, born at Pavia in 1501, died 1576, was famous as a mathematician, physician, and astrologer. He published his celebrated treatise on astrology in 1543, and in 1552 visited Scotland, as the medical adviser of Archbishop Hamilton of St. Andrews. Cardan, owing to the boldness of many of the theories which he enunciated, was involved in many disputes with his contemporaries.

time, to lower them gradually, and then point them both in such a manner that they shall look at one and the same time upon the tip of the nose, both sides of that feature being equally seen; and in this posture the saint must continue firm, the two sides of the nose in even proportions remaining constantly within sight until the bright luminary makes its appearance.

The trance, and the means of enjoying it, form the grand Mysticism of the sect of the *Jauguis*,[1] as well as that of the *Soufys*. I call it Mysticism [Mystere], because they keep these things secret among themselves, and I should not have made so many discoveries had it not been for the aid of the *Pendet*, or *Indou* Doctor whom *Danechmend-kan* kept in his pay, and who dared not conceal anything from his patron; my *Agah*, moreover, was already acquainted with the doctrines of the *Soufys*.[2]

I believe that extreme poverty, long fasts, and perpetual austerities count for something in the condition at which these men arrive. Our *Friars* and *Hermits* must not suppose that on these points they surpass the *Jauguis* or other *Asiatic* religionists. I can, for instances, appeal to

[1] In the original, 'le grand Mystere de la Cabale des Jauguis.'

[2] It would be difficult to give any better definition of Sufism than that by Mr. E. H. Whinfield, M.A., late B.C.S., in the Introduction (pp. 15, 16) to his edition of the *Masnavi-i Ma'navi, the Spiritual couplets, of Mulána Jalálu-'d-din Muhammad-i Rúmi*, London, Trübner, 1887. After explaining that the message of Muhammad, as revealed in the Koran, was eminently practical and not speculative, popular in language, and not meant to bear the strain of analysis, Mr. Whinfield relates how, after the death of Muhammad, the Faithful *did* philosophise, notwithstanding all the injunctions extant against such speculation as was then indulged in. Schoolmen arose who carried philosophy into divinity, and, in the light of the new learning, derived from Plato, Aristotle, and the speculations of the Christian sects, debated all the trite topics of Moslem theology. 'Parallel to this stream of scholasticism there ran another stream of mystical theosophy—derived in part from Plato, "the Attic Moses," but mainly from Christianity, as presented in the "spiritual Gospel" of St. John, and as expounded by the Christian Platonists and Gnostics. This second stream was Sufism.'

the lives and fasts of the *Armenians, Copts, Greeks, Nestorians, Jacobins,* and *Maronites*; compared to these people our European devotees are mere novices, though it must be confessed, from what I have myself experienced, that the pains of hunger are not so sensibly felt in the *Indies* as in our colder climates.

I have now to give an account of certain *Fakires* totally different from the *Saints* just described, but who also are extraordinary personages. They almost continually perambulate the country, make light of everything, affect to live without care, and to be possessed of most important secrets. The people imagine that these favoured beings are well acquainted with the art of making gold, and that they can prepare mercury in so admirable a manner that a grain or two swallowed every morning must restore a diseased body to vigorous health, and so strengthen the stomach that it may feed with avidity, and digest with ease. This is not all: when two of these good *Jauguis* meet, and can be excited to a spirit of emulation, they make such a display of the power of *Janguisism,* that it may well be doubted if *Simon Magus,* with all his sorceries, ever performed more surprising feats. They tell any person his thoughts, cause the branch of a tree to blossom and to bear fruit within an hour, hatch an egg in their bosom in less than fifteen minutes, producing whatever bird may be demanded, and make it fly about the room, and execute many other prodigies that need not be enumerated.

I regret that I cannot bear my testimony to the truth of all that people report of these conjurers. My *Agah* sent for one of these famous soothsayers, and promised to give him three hundred *roupies* (about an hundred and fifty crowns) if on the following day he would tell him, as he said he could do, what might then be passing in his mind, which he would previously write down in his presence to prevent any suspicion of unfair dealing on his own part. I engaged at the same time to present him with five-and-twenty *roupies* if he mentioned my thoughts; but the prophet did not again approach our house. On another occasion I was also disappointed in my expectation of the company of one of these egg-hatchers, to whom I had promised twenty *roupies*. Notwithstanding my diligence to pry into everything, I have never been so fortunate as to witness any marvellous performance; and whenever I happened to be present when a deed was done which excited the surprise of the spectators, it was generally my misfortune to examine and to question until I ascertained that the cause lay in some cheat or sleight of hand. I recollect detecting the gross deception of a fellow who pretended to find out, by the rolling of a cup, the person who had stolen my *Agah's* money.

But there are *Fakires* of a much more comely appearance than those whom we have been considering, and their lives and devotion seem less extravagant. They walk the streets barefooted and bareheaded, girt with a scarf which hangs down to the knee, and wearing a white cloth which passes under the right arm and goes over the left shoulder in the form of a mantle, but they are without any under garment: their persons, however, are always well washed, and they appear cleanly in every respect. In general they walk two and two with a very modest demeanour, holding in one hand a small and fair three-footed earthen pot with two handles: they do not beg from shop to shop like many other *Fakires*, but enter freely into the houses of the *Gentiles*, where they meet with a hearty welcome and an hospitable reception, their presence being esteemed a blessing to the family. Heaven defend him who accuses them of any offence, although everybody knows what takes place between the sanctified visitors and the women of the house: this, however, is considered the custom of the country, and their sanctity is not the less on that account. I do not indeed attach much importance to their transactions with the females of the house: such practices we know are not confined to the *Great Mogol's* dominions; but what appears truly ridiculous is their impertinent comparison of themselves with our own clergy in the *Indies*. I have sometimes derived much amusement from their weakness and vanity: I used to address them with great ceremony, and apparently with the most profound respect, after which they immediately observed to one another: 'The *Frangui* knows who we are; he has resided many years in the *Indies*, and is well aware that we are the *Padrys*[1] of the *Indous*.' But I dwell too long upon these heathen beggars, and shall proceed to notice the books of law and science.

Do not be surprised if, notwithstanding my ignorance of *Sanscrit*[2] (the language of the learned, and possibly that of the ancient *Brahmens*, as we may learn further on), I yet say something of books written in that tongue. My Agah, *Danechmend-kan*, partly from my solicitation and partly to gratify his own curiosity, took into his service one of the most celebrated *Pendets* in all the *Indies*, who had formerly belonged to the household of *Dara*,[3] the eldest son of the King *Chah-Jehan*; and not only was this

[1] The Portuguese word *Padre* was originally applied to Roman priests only. It is now the name given all over India to priests, clergymen, or ministers of all denominations, and is sometimes applied by natives to their own priests. *Lat Padre Sahib*, or the Lord Padre Sahib, is now the Indian name for a Christian bishop.

[2] 'Hanscrit' in the original, see p. 329, footnote [3].

[3] Dárá Shikoh, when Governor or Viceroy of Benares, in 1656, caused a Persian translation to be made from the Sanskrit text of the Upanishads ('the word that is not to be revealed'), which he called the Sarr-i-Asrár, or *Secret of Secrets*. This translation, which was made by a large staff of Benares Pandits, has been rendered into Latin by Anquetil-Duperron, and published by him at Paris, 1801, under the title of *Oupnekhat* (*id est, Secretum Tegendum*) *opus ipsa in India rarissimum*, etc. etc. His version is criticised in an article published in the second number (January 1803) of *The Edinburgh Review*, which I believe to have been written by Alexander Hamilton, 'a Scotchman who had been in India; . . . of excellent conversation and great knowledge of Oriental literature. He was afterwards professor of Sanscrit' [in the official lists he is designated *Professor of Hindû Literature* and History of Asia] 'in the East India College at

man my constant companion during a period of three years, but he also introduced me to the society of other learned *Pendets,* whom he attracted to the house. When weary of explaining to my *Agah* the recent discoveries of *Harveus* and *Pecquet* in anatomy, and of discoursing on the philosophy of *Gassendi* and *Descartes,*[1] which I translated to

Haileybury,' p. 141, vol. i. Cockburn's *Life of Lord Jeffrey*, Edin. 1852; also see p. 256, vol. i. of Lord Brougham's *Life and Times*, Edin. and Lond. 1871. In this critique pleasing testimony is borne to the great abilities of Prince Dárá Shikoh, as follows:—'If intolerance and fanaticism be the usual concomitants of Islamism (an assertion, we think, too generally expressed), the descendants of Tamerlane, who reigned in Hindûstan, furnish some remarkable exceptions to the received opinion. At the head of these illustrious personages we should, perhaps, place Dara Shecuh, the eldest son of the Emperor Shah Gehan. The attention which this Prince bestowed, investigating the antique dogmas of the Hindu theology, and the munificence with which he rewarded the learned Brahmans, whom he collected from all parts of the empire, furnished his brother Aurengzebe with a pretext to misrepresent his motives, and to alarm the zealous Moslems with the danger of an apostate succeeding to the throne. The melancholy catastrophe which ensued; the death of the unhappy Dara, with the long and brilliant reign of the successful hypocrite, who founded his greatness on the destruction of his brothers, are detailed in the page of history. If the sceptical philosopher be disposed to exclaim with the Roman Epicurean, 'Tanta Religio potuit suadere malorum,' we must state our conviction that ambition, not fanaticism, prompted the deed; though the steps by which he mounted the throne threw the rigid veil of superstition over the subsequent conduct of Aurengzebe, and gave that tone to his court.'

[1] William Harvey, born in 1578, and died in 1657. It was in 1616, the year of Shakespeare's death, that he began his course of lectures to the Royal College of Physicians in London, and formally announced his discovery of the circulation of the blood, which has rendered his name for ever famous.

Jean Pecquet, born at Dieppe, in France, in 1622, died in 1674. He studied medicine at Montpellier, where Bernier was also a student, and it was there that he prosecuted those investigations which led to his discoveries, in connection with the conversion of the chyle into blood, which have immortalised his name.

René Descartes, born at La Haye, Touraine, in France, in 1596, and died at Stockholm in 1650.

him in Persian (for this was my principal employment for five or six years) we had generally recourse to our *Pendet,* who, in his turn, was called upon to reason in his own manner, and to communicate his fables; these he related with all imaginable gravity without ever smiling; but at length we became disgusted both with his tales and childish arguments.

The *Hindous* then affirm that God, whom they call *Achar,* the Immovable or Immutable, has sent to them four books, to which they give the name of *Beths,* a word signifying science, because, according to them, these books comprehend all the sciences. The first of the books is named *Atherbabed*; the second *Zagerbed*; the third *Rek-bed*; and the fourth *Samabed.* These books enjoin that the people shall be divided, as in fact they are most effectually, into four tribes [Tribus]: first, the tribe of *Brahmens,* or interpreters of the law; secondly, the tribe of *Quetterys,* or warriors; thirdly, the tribe of *Bescué,* or merchants and tradesmen, commonly called *Banyanes*; and fourthly, the tribe of *Seydra,* or artisans and labourers. These different tribes are not permitted to intermarry, that is to say, a *Brahmen* is forbidden to marry a *Quettery,* and the same injunction holds good in regard to the other tribes.[1]

[1] Achara is well defined by Bernier, and this whole chapter is a good example of the careful manner in which he investigated such subjects. The word also means eternal beatitude, or exemption from further transmigration. His enumeration of the order of the Vedas does not correspond with that now generally adopted as the results of modern criticism, which assigns to the Rig-veda the greatest antiquity, after which the Yajur-veda, then the Sáma-veda, and places the Atharva-veda last, as the most recent of all. Bernier possessed a good knowledge of Persian, and as a rule his transliterations are excellent. In the enumeration of the theoretical divisions of Hindoo society, it is evident that he had to transliterate from the *vivâ voce* account given in Sanskrit or perhaps Hindí, by his Pandit, into Persian, then into French. Bernier's *Tribus* is a much more scientific term than our word 'caste,' or 'cast' as Elphinstone prefers to have it, a word derived from the Portuguese *Casta,* 'creed, race, or kind.' The modern renderings of these four divisions are, Bráhmans, Kshatt-

The *Gentiles* believe in a doctrine similar to that of the *Pythagoreans* with regard to the transmigration of souls, and hold it illegal to kill or eat any animal; an exception being made, however, in favour of a few of the second tribe, provided the flesh eaten be not that of the cow or peacock. For these two animals they feel a peculiar respect, particularly for the cow, imagining that it is by holding to a cow's tail they are to cross the river which separates this life from the next. Possibly their ancient legislators saw the shepherds of *Egypt* in a similar manner pass the river *Nile,* holding with the left hand the tail of a buffalo or ox, and carrying in the right a stick for the guidance of the animal; or this superior regard for the cow may more probably be owing to her extraordinary usefulness, as being the animal which supplies them with milk and butter [1] (a considerable part of their aliment), and which may be considered the source of husbandry, consequently the preserver of life itself. It ought likewise to be observed that owing to the great deficiency of pasture land in the *Indies* it is impossible to maintain large numbers of cattle; the whole therefore would soon disappear if animal food were eaten in anything like the proportion in which it is consumed in *France* and *England,* and the country would thus remain uncultivated. The heat is so intense, and the ground so parched, during eight months of the year, that the beasts of the field, ready to die of hunger, feed on every kind of filth like so many swine. It was on account of the scarcity of cattle that *Jehan-Guyre,* at the request of the *Brahmens,* issued an edict to forbid the killing of beasts of pasture for a certain number of years; and not long since they presented a similar petition

riyas, Vaisyas, and Súdras. There appears to be a slip in Bernier's transliteration of the name of the second tribe or class; Khátrí, a subdivision of the Vaisyas, is confounded with Kshattriyas, or, in its popular form, Chutree; although as a matter of fact some authorities hold that the Khátris are included in the second division.

[1] That is, ghee.

to *Aureng-Zebe,* offering to him a considerable sum of money to ensure his compliance.[1] They urged that the neglected and ruinous condition of many tracts of country during the last fifty or sixty years was attributable to the paucity and dearness of oxen.

Perhaps the first legislators in the *Indies* hoped that the interdiction of animal food would produce a beneficial effect upon the character of the people, and that they might be brought to exercise less cruelty toward one another when required by a positive precept to treat the brute creation with humanity. The doctrine of the transmigration of souls secured the kind treatment of animals, by leading to the belief that no animal can be killed or eaten without incurring the danger of killing or eating some ancestor, than which a more heinous crime cannot be committed. It may be also that the *Brahmens* were influenced by the consideration that in their climate the flesh of cows or oxen is neither savoury nor wholesome except for a short time during winter.

The *Beths* render it obligatory upon every *Gentile* to say his prayers with his face turned to the East thrice in the twenty-four hours: in the morning, at noon, and at night. The whole of his body must also be washed three times, or at least before every meal; and he is taught that it is more meritorious to perform his ablutions and to repeat his prayers in running than in stagnant water. Here again regard was probably had to what is not only proper but highly important in such a climate as that of *Hindoustan.* This, however, is found an inconvenient law to those who happen to live in cold countries, and I have met in my travels with some who placed their lives in imminent danger by a strict observance of that law, by plunging into the rivers or tanks within their reach, or if none were sufficiently near, by throwing large pots full of water over their heads. Sometimes I objected to their

[1] In recent years, similar action as regards petitioning the Supreme Government has been taken in India by influential Hindoos.

religion that it contained a law which it would not be possible to observe in cold climates during the winter season, which was, in my mind, a clear proof that it possessed no divine original, but was merely a system of human invention. Their answer was amusing enough. 'We pretend not,' they replied, 'that our law is of universal application. God intended it only for us, and this is the reason why we cannot receive a foreigner into our religion. We do not even say that yours is a false religion: it may be adapted to your wants and circumstances, God having, no doubt, appointed many different ways of going to heaven.' I found it impossible to convince them that the Christian faith was designed for the whole earth, and theirs was mere fable and gross fabrication.

The *Beths* teach that God having determined to create the world would not execute his purpose immediately, but first created three perfect beings; one was *Brahma*, a name which signifies penetrating into all things; the second, *Beschen*, that is, existing in all things; and the third *Mehahdeu*, or the mighty lord. By means of *Brahma* he created the world; by means of *Beschen* he upholds it; and by means of *Mehahdeu* he will destroy it.[1] It was *Brahma* who, by God's command, published the four *Beths*, and for this reason he is represented in some temples with four heads.

I have conversed with European missionaries who thought that the *Gentiles* have some idea of the mystery of the *Trinity*, and maintained that the *Beths* state in direct terms that the three beings, though three persons, are one God. This is a subject on which I have frequently heard

[1] Brahma was from the beginning considered as the Eternal Creative Power, the Holiest of the Holy, and he continued to be regarded as fulfilling the same function even after he had sunk into a subordinate position, and had come to be represented by the votaries of Vishnu and Mahadeva respectively as the mere creature and agent of one or other of these two gods.

the *Pendets* dilate, but they explain themselves so obscurely that I never could clearly comprehend their opinion.[1] I have heard some of them say that the beings in question are in reality three very perfect creatures, whom they call *Deütas,* without being able, however, properly to explain what they mean by this word *Deüta,* like our ancient idolaters, who could never, in my opinion, explain what they meant by the names *Genii* and *Numina,* which were probably equivalent to the *Deüta* of the *Indians.*[2] I have also discoursed with other *Pendets* distinguished for learning, who said that these three beings are really one and the same God, considered under three different characters, as the creator, upholder, and destroyer of all things; but they said nothing of three distinct persons in one only God.

I was acquainted with the Reverend Father *Roa,*[3] a

[1] 'I shall declare to thee that form composed of Hari and Hara (Vishnu and Mahadeva) combined, which is without beginning, middle or end, imperishable, undecaying. He who is Vishnu is Rudra: he who is Rudra is Pitámaha (Brahma); the substance is one, the gods are three: Rudra, Vishnu, and Pitámaha.'—Muir's *Original Sanskrit Texts,* vol. iv. p. 237.

[2] See p. 303.

[3] Thus in all the editions of Bernier's *Travels* known to the editor, intended for Father Heinrich Roth, S. J., attached to the Goa Mission. About 1650-1660 he journeyed from Goa to Agra, *viâ* Central India, and during these years studied Sanskrit and the doctrines of the Hindoo religion, in which he was ever afterwards regarded as the best authority of his time, and it is pleasant to find that even thus early, a German should attain such fame as a Sanskrit scholar. About 1665 he travelled from Agra to Rome, *viâ* Lahore, Multan, down the Indus to 'Sindi' [? Sind] at its mouth, thence by sea, *viâ* Surat, to Ormuz, and overland through Persia and Armenia to Smyrna and Rome. He there drew up for Father Kircher (see p. 332, footnote [1]), the five engraved plates published by him in his *China Illustrata.* The first four plates contain the alphabet and elements (in the Devanagri character) of Sanskrit, explained in Latin, and the fifth is Our Lord's Prayer and an Ave Maria, in Sanskrit and Latin, to serve as an exercise for beginners. In most of the early editions of Bernier, certainly in all of those published during his lifetime, Sanskrit is everywhere printed *Hanscrit.* This

Jesuit, a German by birth, and missionary at *Agra,* who had made great proficiency in the study of *Sanscrit.* He assured me that the books of the *Gentiles* not only state that there is one God in three persons, but that the second person has been nine times embodied in flesh.[1] He added that when he was at *Chiras,* on his return to *Rome,* a Carmelite Father in that city succeeded, with much address, in ascertaining that the following doctrines are held by the *Gentiles.* The second person in the Trinity has been, according to them, nine times incarnate in consequence of various evils in the world, from which he delivered mankind. The eighth incarnation was the most remarkable;[2] for they say that the world having been enthralled by the power of giants, it was rescued by the second person, incarnated and born of a virgin at midnight, the angels singing in the air, and the skies raining flowers that whole night.

peculiarity has arisen, I believe, in this wise. Father Roth doubtlessly acquired his *grounding* in Sanskrit from a Persian Munshí, who would call the language 'Sanskrit, or *Sahanskrít,*' the form used in the Persian texts of the *Ain,* which was written about 1599. We learn from Father Kircher (who by the way never uses the word Sanskrit in any form), in the text of the work cited above, that it was Father Roth who with his own hand drew out the originals of these plates. The first plate is headed *Elementa Lingua* [sic] *Hanskret,* the letters *Sa* having been omitted by the engraver, or 'dropped,' to use a technical term; because although he has begun the heading correctly as to position, the centre of the 'title' being axial with the body of the plate, the word *Hanskret* ends just too short by a space sufficient for two letters. This error was probably discovered too late to be satisfactorily remedied, and has misled many subsequent writers without special or technical knowledge; and in Yule's *Glossary* this form of the word is characterised as 'difficult to account for.' Hyde, the well-known Orientalist of the Oxford University, has, however (p. 264, vol. ii., *Syntagma Dissertationum quas olim Thomas Hyde separatim edidit.* Oxon. 1767. Edited by Gregory Sharpe), questioned the correctness of Father Kircher's *Hanskrit,* himself using the word 'Sanscreet' to denote the language of the Brahmins.

[1] *Avatar,* a descent, especially of a deity from heaven; an incarnation. Allusion is made by Bernier to the ten avatars of Vishnu.

[2] That of Vishnu as Krishna, in which he is supposed to have been completely incarnate, at Brindabun in the Mathura (Muttra) District.

This in some degree savours of Christianity, but here comes the fable again ; for it is added that this incarnate god began by killing a giant who flew in the air, and was so huge as to obscure the sun: his fall caused the whole earth to tremble, and by his weight he so penetrated it that he tumbled at once into hell. The incarnate deity, wounded in the side in the conflict with this mighty giant, fell also, but by his fall put his enemies to flight. He arose again, and after delivering the world ascended into heaven, and because of his wound, he is generally known by the appellation of 'The wounded in the side.' The tenth incarnation, say the *Gentiles,* will have for its object the emancipation of mankind from the tyranny of the *Mahometan,* and it will take place at the time when, according to our calculation, *Antichrist* is to appear; this is however but a popular tradition, not to be found in their sacred books.

They say also that the third person of the Trinity[1] has manifested himself to the world; the following story is related of him. The daughter of a certain king, when she had reached the age of puberty, was desired by her father to mention the person whom she felt disposed to marry, and having answered that she would be united to none but a divine being, the third person of the Trinity appeared in the same instant to the king in the form of fire. He presently apprised his daughter of this happy circumstance, and she without hesitation consented to the marriage. The divine personage, though still assuming a fiery appearance, was invited to the king's council, and finding that the privy counsellors opposed the match, he first set fire to their beards, and then burnt them together with the royal household, after which he married the princess. Ridiculous![2] In regard to the second person, the *Gentiles* say that his first incarnation was in the nature of a *Lion,* the second in that of a *Hog,* the third in that

[1] Mahadev or Śiva, the Destroyer and Creator.

[2] In the original, 'Contes de ma mère l'Oye.'

of a *Tortoise,* the fourth in that of a *Serpent,* the fifth in that of a dwarfish female *Brahmen* [Pygmee Brahmane], only a cubit in height, the sixth was in the form of a monstrous *Man-lion,* the seventh in that of a *Dragon,* the eighth as already described, the ninth in the nature of an *Ape,* and the tenth is to be in the person of a mighty *Cavalier.*

I entertain no doubt that the Reverend Father *Roa* derives from the *Beths* his knowledge of the doctrines held by the *Gentiles,* and that the account he gave me forms the basis of their mythology. I had written at considerable length upon this subject, sketched the figures of several of the gods or idols placed in their temples, and caused them to give me the characters of their language, *Sanscrit*; but finding that the principal matter of my manuscript is contained in the *China Illustrata* of Father *Kirker*[1] (who obtained much of his information when at *Rome* from Father *Roa*[2]), I deem it sufficient to recommend that book to your perusal. I must observe, however, that the word 'incarnation,' employed by the Reverend Father,[3] was new to me, having never seen it used in the same direct sense.

[1] Published at Amsterdam by Janszon in 1667, in which, between folios 162 and 163, will be found five full-page copperplate engravings, the first specimens of Sanskrit ever printed or engraved (as for a book) in Europe, or indeed anywhere. Athanasius Kircher, S. J., was born at Giessen near Fulda in 1602, and died at Rome in 1680. A man of immense literary activity, he was, *inter alia*, what we would now call Home Editorial Secretary of the annual reports sent to Europe by the Jesuit and other Roman missionaries. Kircher was also at one time Professor of Oriental Languages at Würtzburg. See p. 329, footnote [3].

[2] Father Roth supplied Kircher with all the information concerning Hindoo mythology contained in his *China Illustrata*, which will be found, illustrated with curious engravings after Indian drawings, at pp. 156-162 of that work.

[3] Kircher quotes Father Roth's own words as follows :—'Universim dicunt, secundam personam ex Trinitate novies jam incarnatam fuisse, et adhuc semel incarnatum est.'

Some *Pendets* explained their doctrine to me in this manner: formerly God appeared in the forms which are mentioned, and in those forms performed all the wonders which have been related. Other *Pendets* said that the souls of certain great men, whom we are wont to call heroes, had passed into the different bodies spoken of, and that they had become *Deüta*s; or, to speak in the phraseology of the idolaters of old, they had become powerful Divinities, *Numina*, *Genii*, and *Dæmons*; or, if you will, *Spirits* and *Fairies*; for I know not how else to render the word *Deüta*; but this second explanation comes much to the same thing as the first, inasmuch as the *Indous* believe that their souls are constituent parts of the deity.

Other *Pendets* again gave me a more refined interpretation. They said that the incarnations or apparitions mentioned in their books, having a mystic sense, and being intended to explain the various attributes of God, ought not to be understood literally. Some of the most learned of those *Doctors* frankly acknowledged to me that nothing can be conceived more fabulous than all the incarnations, and that they were only the invention of legislators for the sake of retaining the people in some sort of religion. On the supposition that our souls are portions of the deity, a doctrine common to all *Gentiles*, must not (observed the *Pendets*) the reality of those incarnations, instead of being made a mysterious part of religion, be exploded by sound philosophy? for, in respect of our souls, we are God, and therefore it would in fact be ourselves who had imposed upon ourselves a religious worship, and a belief in the transmigration of souls, in paradise, and in hell,—which would be absurd.

I am not less indebted to Messieurs *Henry Lor* and *Abraham Roger*[1] than to the Reverend Fathers *Kirker* and

[1] Henry Lord, the Anglican chaplain at Surat and author of (1) *A Display of two forraigne Sects in the East Indies*; (2) *A Discoverie of the Sect of the Banians*; (3) *The Religion of the Persees*. *Imprinted*

Roa. I had collected a vast number of particulars concerning the *Gentiles,* that I have since found in the books written by those gentlemen, and which I could not have arranged in the order which they have observed without great labour and difficulty. It is not necessary, therefore, that I could do more than touch briefly on the studies and the science of this people; which I shall do in a general and desultory manner.

The town of *Benares,* seated on the *Ganges,* in a beautiful situation, and in the midst of an extremely fine and rich country, may be considered the general school of the *Gentiles.* It is the Athens of India, whither resort the *Brahmens* and other devotees; who are the only persons who apply their minds to study. The town contains no colleges or regular classes, as in our universities, but resembles rather the schools of the ancients; the masters being dispersed over different parts of the town in private houses, and principally in the gardens of the suburbs, which the rich merchants permit them to occupy. Some of these masters have four disciples, others six or seven, and the most eminent may have twelve or fifteen; but this is the largest number. It is usual for the pupils to remain ten or twelve years under their respective preceptors, during which time the work of instruction proceeds but slowly; for the gene-

at London for Francis Constable, and are to be Sold at his Shoppe in Paule's Churchyard, at the signe of the Crane, 1630.

Abraham Roger, the first Dutch chaplain (1631-1641) at Pulicat, the earliest settlement of the Hollanders on the mainland in India; their fort, which they called Geldria, having been built in 1609. He returned home in 1647, and died at Gouda in 1649. His widow published her husband's work, which is in every way superior to Henry Lord's, as '*La Porte ouverte, pour parvenir à la connoissance du Paganisme Caché.* Amsterdam, Chez Jean Schipper, 1670.' The information contained in this book is very correct, as the author had it all at first-hand from a Brahman, whom he calls Padmanaba (*Padmanābha*), who knew Dutch, and who gave him a Dutch translation of Bhartrihari's *Satakas,* see p. 293 of Roger's book, the first published translation from Sanskrit into any European language.

rality of them are of an indolent disposition, owing, in a great measure, to their diet and the heat of the country. Feeling no spirit of emulation, and entertaining no hope that honours or emolument may be the reward of extraordinary attainments, as with us, the scholars pursue the studies slowly, and without much to distract their attention, while eating their *kichery*,[1] a mingled mess of vegetables supplied to them by the care of rich merchants of the place.

The first thing taught is the *Sanscrit*, a language known only to the *Pendets*, and totally different from that which is ordinarily spoken in *Hindoustan*. It is of the *Sanscrit* that Father *Kirker* has published an alphabet, which he received from Father *Roa*.[2] The name signifies 'pure language;' and because the *Gentiles* believe that the four sacred books given to them by God, through the medium of *Brahma*, were originally published in *Sanscrit*, they call it *the holy and divine language*. They pretend that it is as ancient as *Brahma* himself, whose age they reckon by *lecques*, or hundreds of thousands of years, but I could not rely upon this marvellous age. That it is extremely old, however, it is impossible to deny, the books of their religion, which are of unquestionable antiquity, being all written in *Sanscrit*. It has also its authors on philosophy, works on medicine written in verse, and many other kinds of books, with which a large hall at *Benares* is entirely filled.

When they have acquired a knowledge of Sanscrit, which to them is difficult, because without a really good grammar, they generally study the *Purane*,[3] which is an abridgment and interpretation of the *Beths*; those books being of great bulk, at least if they were the *Beths* which were shown to me at *Benares*. They are so scarce

[1] See p. 152, footnote [2]. [2] See p. 329, footnote [3].

[3] The Puránas, eighteen in number; and it is said that there are also eighteen Upa-Puráńas or minor Puránas, but many of them are not now procurable.

that my *Agah,* notwithstanding all his diligence, has not succeeded in purchasing a copy. The *Gentiles* indeed conceal them with much care, lest they should fall into the hands of the *Mahometans,* and be burnt, as frequently has happened.

After the *Purane,* some of the students apply their minds to philosophy, wherein they certainly make very little progress. I have already intimated that they are of a slow and indolent temper, and strangers to the excitement which the possibility of advancement in an honourable profession produces among the members of *European* universities.

Among the philosophers who have flourished in *Hindoustan* six bear a great name;[1] and from these have sprung the six sects, which cause much jealousy and dispute, the *Pendets* of each pretending that the doctrines of their particular sect are the soundest, and most in conformity to the *Beths.* A seventh sect has arisen, called *Bauté,*[2] which again is the parent of twelve others; but this sect is not so considerable as the former: its adherents are despised and hated, censured as irreligious and atheistical, and lead a life peculiar to themselves.

All their sacred books speak of first principles; but each in a manner totally different from the others. Some say that everything is composed of small bodies which are indivisible, not by reason of their solidity, hardness, and resistance, but because of their smallness; and upon this notion they build many other hypotheses, which have an affinity to the theories of *Democritus* and *Epicurus*; but their

[1] These schools of philosophy are: 1. The Nyáya, founded by Gautama; 2. The Vaiseshika, by Kanáda; 3. The Sánkhya, by Kapila; 4. The Yoga, by Patanjali; 5. The Mimánsá, by Jaimini; 6. The Vedanta, by Bádaráyana.

[2] Buddha, whose religion, Buddhism, although asserting itself from the first as an independent religion, may be fairly said to be in many respects a development of Brahmanism. This passage bears unmistakable signs of the Hindoo origin of the information regarding this creed recorded by Bernier.

opinions are expressed in so loose and indeterminate a manner that it is difficult to ascertain their meaning; and considering the extreme ignorance of the *Pendets*, those even reputed the most learned, it may be fairly doubted whether this vagueness be not rather attributable to the expounders than to the authors of the books.

Others say that everything is composed of matter and form, but not one of the doctors explains himself clearly about matter, and still less about form. They are so far intelligible, however, as to show me that they understand neither the one nor the other in the same manner as these terms are usually explained in our *Schools*, where we speak of educing form out of the power of matter; for they always take their examples from material objects, such as that of a vessel of soft clay, which a potter turns and forms into various shapes.

Some hold that all is composed of the four elements and out of nothing; yet they give not the least explanation concerning commingling and transmutation. And as to 'nothing,' which is nearly tantamount to our privation, they admit I know not how many sorts, which I imagine the *Pendets* neither comprehend themselves, nor can make intelligible to others.

Some maintain that light and darkness are the first principles, and in support of this opinion they make a thousand foolish and confused observations; alleging reasons disowned by true philosophy, and delivering long discourses which would suit the ear only of the vulgar and illiterate.

There are others again who admit privation as a principle, or rather the privations which they distinguish from nothing, and of which they make a long enumeration, so useless and unphilosophical that I can scarcely believe their authors would employ the pen about such trifling opinions, and that consequently it cannot be contained in their books.

Many, in fine, pretend that everything is the result of

fortuitous circumstances, and of these they also have a long, strange, and tedious catalogue, worthy only of an ignorant and low babbler.

In regard to all these principles, it is agreed by the *Pendets* that they are eternal. The production from nothing does not seem to have occurred to their mind, any more than to the mind of many of the ancient philosophers. There is one of the sages, however, who, they pretend, has said something on the subject.

On physic they have a great number of small books, which are rather collections of recipes than regular treatises. The most ancient and the most esteemed is written in verse. I shall observe, by the way, that their practice differs essentially from ours, and that it is grounded on the following acknowledged principles: a patient with a fever requires no great nourishment; the sovereign remedy for sickness is abstinence; nothing is worse for a sick body than meat broth, for it soon corrupts in the stomach of one afflicted with fever; a patient should be bled only on extraordinary occasions, and where the necessity is most obvious—as when there is reason to apprehend a brain fever, or when an inflammation of the chest, liver, or kidneys, has taken place.

Whether these modes of treatment be judicious, I leave to our learned physicians to decide; I shall only remark that they are successful in *Hindoustan*, and that the *Mogol* and *Mahometan* physicians, who follow the rules of *Avicenna* and *Averroes*, adopt them no less than do those of the *Gentiles*, especially in regard to abstinence from meat broth. The *Mogols*, it is true, are rather more given to the practice of bleeding than the *Gentiles*; for where they apprehend the inflammations just mentioned, they generally bleed once or twice, not in the trifling manner of the modern practitioners of *Goa*[1] and *Paris*, but

[1] The doctors of Goa were held in high esteem, and great honours, such as being allowed to have umbrellas carried over them, were paid to them. John Huyghen van Linschoten, who lived in Goa for five

copiously, like the ancients, taking eighteen or twenty ounces of blood, sometimes even to fainting; thus frequently subduing the disease at the commencement, according to the advice of *Galen*, and as I have witnessed in several cases.

It is not surprising that the *Gentiles* understand nothing of anatomy. They never open the body either of man or beast, and those in our household always ran away, with amazement and horror, whenever I opened a living goat or sheep for the purpose of explaining to my *Agah* the circulation of the blood, and showing him the vessels, discovered by *Pecquet*, through which the chyle is conveyed to the right ventricle of the heart.[1] Yet notwithstanding their profound ignorance of the subject, they affirm that the number of veins in the human body is five thousand, neither more nor less; just as if they had carefully reckoned them.

In regard to astronomy, the *Gentiles* have their tables, according to which they foretell eclipses, not perhaps with the minute exactness of *European* astronomers, but still with great accuracy. They reason, however, in the same ridiculous way on the lunar as on the solar eclipse, believing that the obscuration is caused by a black, filthy, and mischievous *Deüta*, named *Rach*,[2] who takes possession of the moon and fills her with infection. They also maintain, much on the same ground, that the moon is four

years, 1583-1588, says of them: 'There are in Goa many Heathen phisitions which observe their gravities with hats carried over them for the sunne, like the Portingales, which no other heathens doe, but [onely] Ambassadors, or some rich Marchants. These Heathen phisitions doe not onely cure there owne nations [and countriemen] but the Portingales also, for the Viceroy himselfe, the Archbishop, and all the Monkes and Friers doe put more trust in them then in their own countrimen, whereby they get great [store of] money, and are much honoured and estéemed.'—*Voyage to the East Indies*, Hakluyt Soc. ed. 1885, vol. i. p. 230.

[1] See p. 324.

[2] Rakshasas, literally giants, 'unknown creatures of darkness, to which superstition of all ages and races has attributed the evils that attend this life, and a malignant desire to injure mankind.'

hundred thousand coses, that is, above fifty thousand leagues, higher than the sun; that she is a luminous body, and that we receive from her a certain vital liquid secretion, which collects principally in the brain, and, descending thence as from its source into all the members of the body, enables them to exercise their respective functions. They believe likewise that the sun, moon, and stars are all so many *deiitas*; that the darkness of night is caused by the sun retiring behind the *Someire*,[1] an imaginary mountain placed in the centre of the earth, in form, like an inverted sugar loaf, and an altitude of I know not how many thousand leagues: so that they never enjoy the light of day but when the sun leaves the back of this mountain.

In geography they are equally uninstructed. They believe that the world is flat and triangular; that it is composed of seven distinct habitations, differing in beauty, perfection, and inhabitants, and that each is surrounded by its own peculiar sea; that one sea is of milk; another of sugar; a third of butter; a fourth of wine; and so on; so that sea and land occur alternately until you arrive at the seventh stage from the foot of the *Someire* mountain, which is in the centre. The first habitation, or that nearest to the *Someire*, is inhabited by *Deiitas* who are very perfect; the second has also *Deiitas* for inhabitants, but they are less perfect; and so it is with the rest, whose inhabitants are less and less perfect, until the seventh, which is our earth, inhabited by men infinitely less perfect than any of the *Deiitas*; and finally that the whole of this world is supported on the heads of a number of elephants, whose occasional motion is the cause of earthquakes.

If the renowned sciences of the ancient *Bragmanes* of the *Indies* consisted of all the extravagant follies which I have detailed, mankind have indeed been deceived in the

[1] By this is meant Su-meru, or the Golden Meru, the shape of which is variously described in the different Puránas, though all represent it as of enormous size and great beauty—the Olympus of the Hindoos

exalted opinion they have long entertained of their wisdom. I should find it difficult to persuade myself that such was the fact, did I not consider that the religion of the *Indians* has existed from time immemorial; that it is written in *Sanscrit*, as are likewise all their scientific books; that the *Sanscrit* has long become a dead language, understood only by the learned; and that its origin is unknown: all which proves a very great antiquity. I will now say a word or two on the worship of idols.

When going down the river *Ganges*, I passed through *Benares*, and called upon the chief of the *Pendets*, who resides in that celebrated seat of learning. He is a *Fakire* or *Devotee* so eminent for knowledge that *Chah-Jehan*, partly for that consideration, and partly to gratify the *Rajas*, granted him a pension of two thousand *roupies*, which is about one thousand *crowns*. He is a stout, well-made man, and his dress consists of a white silk scarf, tied about the waist, and hanging half way down the leg, and of another tolerably large scarf of red silk, which he wears as a cloak on his shoulders. I had often seen him in this scanty dress at *Dehli*, in the assembly of the *Omrahs* and before the *King*, and met him in the streets either on foot or in a *paleky*. During one year he was in the constant habit of visiting my *Agah*, to whom he paid his court in the hope that he would exercise his influence to obtain the pension of which *Aureng-Zebe*, anxious to appear a true *Musulman*, deprived him on coming to the throne. I formed consequently a close intimacy with this distinguished personage, with whom I had long and frequent conversations; and when I visited him at *Benares* he was most kind and attentive, giving me a collation in the university library,[1] to which

[1] Tavernier, when travelling from Agra to Bengal in 1665, on which journey he was accompanied by Bernier, was at Benares on the 11th, 12th, and 13th December of that year. He tells us (*Travels*, vol. ii. pp. 234, 235) that adjoining a great temple, 'on the side which faces the setting sun at midsummer, there is a house which serves as a

he invited the six most learned *Pendets* in the town. Finding myself in such excellent company, I determined to ascertain their opinion of the adoration of idols. I told them I was leaving the *Indies* scandalised at the prevalence of a worship which outraged common sense, and was totally unworthy such philosophers as I had then the honour of addressing. 'We have indeed in our temples,' said they, 'a great variety of images, such as that of *Brahma*, of *Mehadeu*,[1] of *Genich*,[2] and of *Gavani*,[3] who are the principal and the most perfect of the *Deüitas*, and we have many others esteemed less perfect. To all these images we pay great honour; prostrating our bodies, and presenting to them, with much ceremony, flowers, rice, scented oil, saffron and other similar articles. Yet do we not believe that these statues are themselves *Brahma* or *Bechen*;[4] but merely their images and representations. We show them deference only for the sake of the deity whom they represent, and when we pray it is not to the statue, but to that deity. Images are admitted in our temples, because we conceive that prayers are offered up with more devotion where there is something before the eyes that fixes the mind; but in fact we acknowledge that God alone is absolute, that He only is the omnipotent Lord.'

I have neither added to nor taken from the answer that the *Pendets* gave me; but I suspect it was so framed

college, which the *Raja* JAI SINGH, the most powerful of the idolatrous princes, who was then in the Empire of the GREAT MOGUL, has founded for the education of the youth of good families. I saw the children of this Prince, who were being educated there, and had as teachers several *Brahmins*, who taught them to read and write in a language which is reserved to the priests of the idols, and is very different from that spoken by the people.'

[1] Mahá-Deva, the great god, one of the names of Siva.

[2] Ganesh, the son of Siva and Parvati, the god of good luck.

[3] Probably a misprint for *Bavani*, meaning Bhawání, one of the names of the wife of Siva.

[4] Vishnu, the preserver and restorer

as to correspond with the tenets of *Christianity.* The observations made to me by other learned *Pendets* were totally different.

I then turned the conversation to the subject of chronology, and my company soon showed me a far higher antiquity than ours. They would not say that the world was without a beginning; but the great age they gave it sounded almost as if they had pronounced it eternal. Its duration, said they, is to be reckoned by four *Dgugues,* or distinct ages;[1] not ages composed, as with us, of an hundred years, but of one hundred *lecques,* that is to say, of an hundred times one hundred thousand years. I do not recollect exactly the number of years assigned to each *Dgugue,* but I know that the first, called *Sate-Dgugue,* continued during a period of five-and-twenty *lecques* of years; that the second, called *Trita,* lasted above twelve *lecques*; the third, called *Duapor,* subsisted, if I mistake not, eight *lecques* and sixty-four thousand years; and the fourth, called the *Kale-Dgugue,* is to continue I forget how many *lecques* of years. The first three, they said, and much of the fourth, are passed away, and the world will not endure so many ages as it has done, because it is destined to perish at the termination of the fourth *Dgugue,* when all things will return to their first principles. Having pressed the *Pendets* to tell me the exact age of the world, they tried their arithmetical skill over and over again; but finding that they were sadly perplexed, and even at variance as to the number of *lecques,* I satisfied myself with the general information that the world is astonishingly old. Whenever any of these learned *Brahmens* is urged to state the facts on which he grounds his belief of this vast antiquity, he entertains the inquirer with a set of ridiculous fables, and finishes by

[1] *Yugas* or ages, concerning the correct method of reckoning which there are many conflicting accounts. They are termed the Krita (same as the Sate, for *Satí,* of Bernier's enumeration), Tretá, Dwápara, and Kali Yuga.

asserting that it is so stated in their *Beths*, or *Books of the Laws*, which have been given to them by *Brahma*.

I then tried them on the nature of their *Deütas*, but their explanation was very confused. These Gods consist, they said, of three kinds, good, bad, and indifferent. Some of the learned believe that the *Deütas* are composed of fire, others that they are formed of light, and many are of opinion that they are *Biapek*;[1] a word of which I could obtain no clearer explication than that God is *Biapek*, that our soul is *Biapek*, and that whatever is *Biapek* is incorruptible and independent of time and place. There are *Pendets* again who, according to my learned host and his companions, pretend that *Deütas* are only portions of the divinity ; and lastly, others consider them as certain species of distinct divinities, dispersed over the surface of the globe.

I remember that I also questioned them on the nature of the *Lengue-cherire*,[2] which some of their authors admit ; but I could elicit no more from them than what I had long before learnt from our *Pendet* ; namely, that the seeds of plants, of trees, and of animals do not receive a new creation ; that they have existed, scattered abroad and intermixed with other matter, from the first creation of the world ; and that they are nothing more or less, not only in potentiality, as it is called, but in reality, than plants, trees and animals entirely perfect, but so minute that their separate parts only become visible when being brought to their proper place, and there receiving nourishment they develop and increase ; so that the seed of an apple- or pear-tree is a *Lengue-cherire*, a small

[1] For *vyâpaka* (Sanskrit), all-pervading.

[2] Linga, or spiritual body, of the *Bhagavad Gítá*, or Sacred Lay, the great Sanskrit philosophical poem. Bernier here alludes to the doctrine of the immortality of the soul and the transmigration of the soul, after the material body formed in the womb has been dissolved into its primary elements after death. The spiritual body (*linga*), formed of the finer elements of matter, then accompanies the soul in all its migrations, until the latter has attained to *nirvana*, or absorption into the Supreme Creator.

apple- or pear-tree, perfect in all its essential parts; and the seed of a horse, of an elephant, or of a man is a *Lengue-cherire,* a small horse, a small elephant or a small man, which requires only life and nourishment in order to its visibly assuming its proper form.

In conclusion, I shall explain to you the *Mysticism* of a Great *Sect* [1] which has latterly made great noise in *Hindoustan,* inasmuch as certain *Pendets* or *Gentile Doctors* had instilled it into the minds of *Dara* and *Sultan Sujah,* the elder sons of *Chah-Jehan.* [2]

You are doubtless acquainted with the doctrine of

[1] In the original, 'le mystere d'une grande Cabale.'

[2] Mirzá Muhammad Kazím, the historian, in his *Alamgír Náma,* which is a history of the first ten years of the reign of the Emperor Alamgír (Aurangzeb), written in 1688, treats of the heresy of Dárá Shikoh as follows:—

'Dárá Shukoh in his later days did not restrain himself to the free-thinking and heretical notions which he had adopted under the name of *Tasawwuf* (Sufism), but showed an inclination for the religion and institutions of the Hindús. He was constantly in the society of *Bráhmans, Jogis,* and *Sannyásís,* and he used to regard these worthless teachers of delusions as learned and true masters of wisdom. He considered their books, which they call *Bed,* as being the Word of God and revealed from Heaven, and he called them ancient and excellent books. He was under such delusion about this *Bed* that he collected *Brahmans* and *Sannyásís* from all parts of the country, and paying them great respect and attention, he employed them in translating the *Bed.* He spent all his time in this unholy work, and devoted all his attention to the contents of these wretched books. . . . Through these perverted opinions he had given up the prayers, fasting, and other obligations imposed by the law. . . . It became manifest that if Dárá Shukoh obtained the throne and established his power, the foundations of the faith would be in danger and the precepts of Islám would be changed for the rant of infidelity and Judaism.'—Elliot, *History of India,* vol. vii. page 179. For a definition of Sufism, which is and always has been looked upon as rank heresy by orthodox Moslems, see p. 320, footnote [2]. *Sannyásí* is the name in modern times for various sects of Hindoo religious mendicants who wander about and subsist upon alms; the '*naked Fakires*' described by Bernier (p. 317), of whom Sarmet was one. According to the laws of Manu, the life of a Brahman was divided into four stages, the fourth of which was that of a Sannyási. 'The religious mendicant

many of the ancient philosophers concerning that great life-giving principle of the world, of which they argue that we and all living creatures are so many parts: if we carefully examine the writings of *Plato* and *Aristotle*, we shall probably discover that they inclined towards this opinion. This is the almost universal doctrine of the *Gentile Pendets* of the *Indies*, and it is this same doctrine which is held by the sect of the *Soufys* and the greater part of the learned men of *Persia* at the present day, and which is set forth in Persian poetry in very exalted and emphatic language, in their *Goul-tchen-raz*,[1] or Garden of Mysteries. This was also the opinion of *Flud*,[2] whom

who, freed from all forms and observances, wanders about and subsists on alms, practising or striving for that condition of mind which, heedless of the flesh, is intent only upon the Deity and final absorption.'—Dowson, *Classical Dict. of Hindu Mythology*, London, 1879.

[1] The *Gulshan Raz*, or 'Mystic Rose Garden,' was composed in 717 A.H. (1317 A.D.) in answer to fifteen questions on the doctrines of the Sufis propounded by Amir Syad Hosaini, a celebrated Sufi of Khorásán. Hardly anything is known of the author, Muhammad Shabistari, further than that he was born at Shabistar, a village in Azarbaiján, and that he wrote this poem and died at Tabriz, the capital town of the same province, in 720 A.H. = 1320 A.D. 'To the European reader the *Gulshan Raz* is useful as being one of the clearest explanations of that peculiar phraseology which pervades Persian poetry, and without a clear understanding of which it is impossible to appreciate that poetry as it deserves. And it is also interesting as being one of the most articulate expressions of "Sufism," that remarkable phrase of Muhammadan religious thought which corresponds to the mysticism of European theology.' See the *Gulshan Raz of Najm ud din, otherwise called Sa'd ud din Mahmud, Shabistari Tabrizi*. Translated by E. H. Whinfield, M.A., of the Bengal Civil Service. Wyman and Co., Publishers, Hare Street, Calcutta, 1876.

[2] Robert Flud, or Fludd, Physician, healer by 'faith-natural,' and Rosicrucian, was born at Bearsted in Kent in 1574, and died in London, 1637. He is the chief English representative of that school of medical mystics who laid claim to the possession of the key to universal science, and his voluminous writings on things divine and human, attracted more attention abroad than in his own country. Gassendi's contribution to the controversy was his *Examen Philosophiae Fluddanae*, published in 1633, and an earlier treatise, published in 1631.

our great *Gassendy* has so ably refuted; and it is similar to the doctrines by which most of our alchymists have been hopelessly led astray. Now these *Sectaries* or *Indou Pendets,* so to speak, push the incongruities in question further than all these philosophers, and pretend that God, or that supreme being whom they call *Achar*[1] (immovable, unchangeable) has not only produced life from his own substance, but also generally everything material or corporeal in the universe, and that this production is not formed simply after the manner of efficient causes, but as a spider which produces a web from its own navel, and withdraws it at pleasure. The Creation then, say these visionary doctors, is nothing more than an extraction or extension of the individual substance of *God,* of those filaments which He draws from his own bowels; and, in like manner, destruction is merely the recalling of that divine substance and filaments into Himself; so that the last day of the world, which they call *maperlé* or *pralea,*[2] and in which they believe every being will be annihilated, will be the general recalling of those filaments which God had before drawn forth from Himself.—There is, therefore, say they, nothing real or substantial in that which we think we see, hear or smell, taste or touch; the whole of this world is, as it were, an illusory dream, inasmuch as all that variety which appears to our outward senses is but one only and the same thing, which is God Himself; in the same manner as all those different numbers, of ten, twenty, a hundred, a thousand, etc., are but the frequent repetition of the same unit.—But ask them some reason for this idea; beg them to explain how this extraction and reception of substance occurs, or to account for that apparent variety; or how it is that God not being corporeal

[1] See p. 325.

[2] Mahá-pralaya, or total dissolution of the universe at the end of a *kalpa* (a day and night of Brahmá, equal to 4,320,000,000 years) when the seven *lokas* (divisions of the universe) and their inhabitants, men, saints, gods, and Brahmá himself, are annihilated. Pralaya is a modified form of dissolution.

but *biapek*, as they allow, and incorruptible, He can be thus divided into so many portions of body and soul, they will answer you only with some fine similes :—That *God* is as an immense ocean in which many vessels of water are in continual motion; let these vessels go where they will, they always remain in the same ocean, in the same water; and if they should break, the water they contain would then be united to the whole, to that ocean of which they were but parts.—Or they will tell you that it is with *God* as with the light, which is the same everywhere, but causes the objects on which it falls to assume a hundred different appearances, according to the various colours or forms of the glasses through which it passes.—They will never attempt to satisfy you, I say, but with such comparisons as these, which bear no proportion with *God*, and which serve only to blind an ignorant people. In vain will you look for any solid answer. If one should reply that these vessels might float in a water similar to their own, but not in the same; and that the light all over the world is indeed similar, but not the same, and so on to other strong objections which may be made to their theory, they have recourse continually to the same similes, to fine words, or, in the case of the *Soufys*, to the beautiful poems of their *Goul-tchen-raz*.

Now, Sir, what think you? Had I not reason from all this great tissue of extravagant folly on which I have remarked; from that childish panic of which I have spoken above; from that superstitious piety and compassion toward the sun in order to deliver it from the malignant and dark *Deüta*; from that trickery of prayers, of ablutions, of dippings, and of alms, either cast into the river, or bestowed on *Brahmens*; from that mad and infernal hardihood of women to burn themselves with the body of those husbands whom frequently they have hated while alive; from those various and frantic practices of the *Fakires*; and lastly, from all that fabulous trash of their *Beths* and other books; was I not justified in taking as a motto to this letter,—the wretched fruit of so many voyages and so many reflections, a motto of which the modern satirist has so well known how to catch and convey the idea without so long a journey—'There are no opinions too extravagant and ridiculous to find reception in the mind of man'?

To conclude, you will do me a kindness by delivering *Monsieur Chapelle's*[1] letter into his own hands; it was he who first obtained for me that acquaintance with your intimate and illustrious friend, *Monsieur Gassendi*, which has since proved so advantageous to me. I am so much obliged to him for this favour that I cannot but love and remember him wherever my lot may be cast. I also feel myself under much obligation to you, and am bound to honour you all my life, not only on account of the partiality you have manifested toward me, but also for the valuable advice contained in your frequent letters, by which you have aided me during my journeys, and for your goodness in having sent me so disinterestedly and gratuitously a collection of books to the extremity of the world, whither my curiosity had led me; while those of whom I requested them, who might have been paid with money which I had left at *Marseilles*, and who in common politeness should have sent them, deserted me and laughed at my letters, looking on me as a lost man whom they were never more to see.

[1] The letter referred to, despatched, as was the present one, from Chiras, but on the 10th June 1668, *Concerning his intention of resuming his studies, on some points which relate to the doctrine of atoms, and to the nature of the human understanding*, is not printed in this present edition. It contains much curious matter, but nothing directly relating to Bernier's Indian experiences. Claude-Emmanuel Luillier Chapelle (1626-1645) was a natural son of François Luillier's, at whose house Gassendi was a frequent guest; struck by the talent of young Chapelle he gave him lessons in philosophy together with Molière and Bernier.

FIRST LETTER

TO MONSIEUR

DE MERVEILLES

Written at Dehli, the 14th December 1664,
Aureng-Zebe being about to set forth.

Concerning the March of Aureng-Zebe. His Army, with the horse Artillery which as a rule he retains as a body-guard. The State maintained by his principal Nobles. The causes of the badness of the water, and various other details worthy of note when travelling in the Indies.

MONSIEUR,

SINCE the time of *Aureng-Zebe's* recovery it had been constantly rumoured that he intended to visit *Lahor* and *Kachemire,* in order to benefit his health by change of air and avoid the approaching summer heat, from which a relapse might be apprehended. Many intelligent persons, it is true, could scarcely persuade themselves that the King would venture upon so long a journey while his father remained a prisoner in the citadel of *Agra.* Considerations of policy, however, have yielded to those of health; if in-deed this excursion may not rather be attributed to the arts and influence of *Rauchenara-Begum,* who has been long anxious to inhale a purer air than that of the *Seraglio,* and to appear in her turn amid a pompous and magnificent army, as her sister *Begum-Saheb* had done during the reign of *Chah-Jehan.*

The King left this city on the sixth of December, at three o'clock in the afternoon; a day and hour which, according to the astrologers of *Dehli,* cannot fail to prove propitious to long journeys. Having reached *Chah-limar,*

FIG. 12.—Raushan Ará Begum.

his country villa, which is about two leagues distant from the capital, he remained there six whole days in order to afford time for the preparations required by an expedition which was to last eighteen months. We hear to-day that he has set out with the intention of encamping on the *Lahor* road, and that after two days he will pursue his journey without further delay.

He is attended not only by the thirty-five thousand

cavalry which at all times compose his body-guard, and by infantry exceeding ten thousand in number, but likewise by the heavy artillery and the light or stirrup-artillery, so called because it is inseparable from the King's person, which the large pieces of ordnance must occasionally quit for the high roads, in order that they may proceed with greater facility. The heavy artillery consists of seventy pieces, mostly of brass. Many of these cannon are so ponderous that twenty yoke of oxen are necessary to draw them along; and some, when the road is steep or rugged require the aid of elephants, in addition to the oxen, to push the carriage-wheels with their heads and trunks. The stirrup-artillery is composed of fifty or sixty small field-pieces, all of brass; each mounted, as I have observed elsewhere, on a small carriage of neat construction and beautifully painted, decorated with a number of red streamers, and drawn by two handsome horses, driven by an artilleryman. There is always a third or relay horse, which is led by an assistant gunner. These field-pieces travel at a quick rate, so that they may be ranged in front of the royal tent in sufficient time to fire a volley as a signal to the troops of the *King's* arrival.

So large a retinue has given rise to a suspicion that instead of visiting *Kachemire*, we are destined to lay siege to the important city of *Kandahar*, which is situated equally on the frontiers of *Persia*, *Hindoustan* and *Usbec*. It is the capital of a fine and productive country, yielding a very considerable revenue; and the possession of it has consequently been at all times warmly contested between the Monarchs of *Persia* and *India*.

Whatever may be the destination of this formidable force, every person connected therewith must hasten to quit *Dehli*, however the urgency of his affairs may require his stay; and were I to delay my own departure I should find it difficult to overtake the army. Besides, my Navaab, or Agah, *Danech-mend-kan*, expects my arrival with much impatience. He can no more dispense with his philosophical studies in the afternoon than avoid devoting the morning to his weighty duties as Secretary of State for Foreign Affairs and Grand Master of the Horse. Astronomy, geography, and anatomy are his favourite pursuits, and he reads with avidity the works of *Gassendy* and *Descartes*.[1] I shall commence my journey this very night, after having finally arranged all my affairs, and supplied myself with much the same necessaries as if I were a cavalry officer of rank. As my pay is one hundred and fifty crowns per month, I am expected to keep two good *Turkoman* horses, and I also take with me a powerful *Persian* camel and driver, a groom for my horses, a cook and a servant to go before my horse with a flagon of water in his hand, according to the custom of the country. I am also provided with every useful article, such as a tent of moderate size, a carpet, a portable bed[2] made of four very strong but light canes, a pillow, a couple of coverlets, one of which, twice doubled, serves for a mattress, a *soufra*,[3] or round leathern table-cloth used at meals, some few napkins of dyed cloth, three small bags with culinary utensils which are all placed in a large bag, and this bag is again carried in a very capacious and strong double sack or net made of leathern thongs. This double sack likewise contains the provisions, linen, and wearing apparel, both of master and servants. I have taken care to lay in a stock of excellent rice for five or six days' consumption, of sweet biscuits flavoured with anise, of limes and sugar. Nor have I forgotten a linen bag with its small iron hook for the purpose of suspending and draining *days*, or curds; nothing being considered so refreshing in this country as

[1] See p. 324.

[2] In the original, *lit à sangles*, a camp-bed with ordinary webbing or tape (*newar* in Hindostanee), in common use at the present day, most useful for travelling in Kashmir.

[3] *Sufra*, sometimes made of cotton chintz. Leather ones, of the sambhur deer-skins are still made in the Gorakhpur district of Northern India.

lemonade and *days*.[1] All these things, as I said before, are packed in one large sack, which becomes so unwieldy that three or four men can with difficulty place it on the camel, although the animal kneels down close to it, and all that is required is to turn one of the sides of the sack over its back.

Not a single article which I have mentioned could conveniently be spared during so extended an excursion as the one in prospect. Here we cannot expect the comfortable lodgings and accommodations of our own country; a tent will be our only inn, and we must make up our minds to encamp and live after the fashion of *Arabs* and *Tartars*. Nor can we hope to supply our wants by pillage: in *Hindoustan* every acre of land is considered the property of the King, and the spoliation of a peasant would be a robbery committed upon the King's domain. In undertaking this long march it is consoling to reflect that we shall move in a northern direction, that it is the commencement of winter, and that the periodical rains have fallen. This is, indeed, the proper season for travelling in the *Indies*, the rains having ceased, and the heat and dust being no longer intolerable. I am also happy at the idea of not being any longer exposed to the danger of eating the bazar bread [2] of *Dehli*, which is often badly baked and full of sand and dust. I may hope, too,

[1] *Dhye*, the curdled milk so well known to all Anglo-Indians, somewhat resembling the *dicke milch* (thickened milk) of Northern Germany. Ovington, at p. 310 of *A voyage to Suratt in the year* 1689, Lond. 1696, describes it very correctly as follows: '*Dye* is a particular innocent kind of Diet, fed upon by the *Indians* for the most part about Noon. It is sweet Milk turn'd thick, mix'd with boil'd Rice and Sugar, and is very effectual against the Rage of Fever and of Fluxes, the prevailing Distempers of *India*. Early in the Morning, or late at Night, they seldom touch it, because they esteem it too cool for their Stomachs and Nocturnal Delights.'

[2] *Bazaar ka roti* is still at a discount in India. It is considered rather a reproach among the Moslems of Northern India to habitually eat 'bazaar-baked bread,' as implying that their families are too indolent, or for other reasons unable to provide good 'home-made' bread.

for better water than that of the capital, the impurities of which exceed my power of description; as it is accessible to all persons and animals, and the receptacle of every kind of filth. Fevers most difficult to cure are engendered by it, and worms are bred in the legs which produce violent inflammation, attended with much danger. If the patient leave *Dehli,* the worm is generally soon expelled, although there have been instances where it has continued in the system for a year or more. They are commonly of the size and length of the treble string of a violin, and might be easily mistaken for a sinew. In extracting them great caution should be used lest they break; the best way is to draw them out little by little, from day to day, gently winding them round a small twig of the size of a pin.[1]

It is a matter of considerable satisfaction to me to think that I shall not be exposed to any of these inconveniences and dangers, as my *Navaab* has with marked kindness ordered that a new loaf of his own household

[1] The Guinea-worm, a parasitic worm (*Filaria Medinensis*) inhabiting the subcutaneous cellular tissue, so called on account of their prevalence in Guinea as recounted in *Purchas.* Indian medical experts, foremost among whom is Sir William Moore, K.C.I.E., Q.H.P., of the Bombay Establishment, are of opinion that the 'fiery serpents' with which the children of Israel were afflicted were Guinea-worms. '5. And the people spake against God, and against Moses, Wherefore have ye brought us up out of Egypt to die in the wilderness? for *there is* no bread, neither *is there any* water; and our soul loatheth this light bread.' '6. And the Lord sent fiery serpents among the people, and they bit the people; and much people of Israel died.' (Numbers xxi.)

Thanks to the measures for introducing improved sanitation into India, one of the greatest benefits that British rule has conferred upon that country, 'there is a consensus of opinion that dysentery has become less severe in its nature and also less prevalent. Guinea-worm has been banished from localities where it was formerly endemic. Delhi-sore has become almost a memory of the past, as most opine from the use of good water.' See Sir William Moore's paper on *Sanitary Progress in India*, read at a special meeting for the consideration of questions relating to hygiene and demography in India, held at the London University, 13th August 1891.

bread, and a *sourai* of *Ganges* water (with which, like every person attached to the court, he has laden several camels)[1] should be presented to me every morning. A *sourai* is that tin flagon of water, covered with red cloth, which a servant carries before his master's horse. It commonly holds a quart, but mine is purposely made to contain two, a device which I hope may succeed. This flagon keeps the water very cool, provided the cloth which covers it be always moist. The servant who bears it in his hand should also continue in motion and agitate the air; or it should be exposed to the wind, which is usually done by putting the flagon on three neat little sticks arranged so that it may not touch the ground. The moisture of the cloth, the agitation of the air, or exposure to the wind, is absolutely necessary to keep the water fresh, as if this moisture, or rather the water which has been imbibed by the cloth, arrested the little bodies, or fiery particles, existing in the air at the same time that it affords a passage to the nitrous or other particles which impede motion in the water and produce cold, in the same manner as glass arrests water, and allows light to pass through it, in consequence of the contexture and particular disposition of the particles of glass, and the difference which exists between the minute particles of water and those of light. It is only in the field that this tin flagon is used. When at home, we put the water into jars made of a certain porous earth, which are covered with a wet cloth; and, if exposed to the wind, these jars keep the water much cooler than the flagon. The higher sort of people make use of saltpetre, whether in town or with the army. They pour the water, or any other liquid they may wish to cool, into a tin flagon, round and long-necked, as I have seen *English* glass bottles. The flagon is then stirred, for the space of seven or eight minutes, in water into which three or four handfuls of saltpetre have been thrown. The liquid thus

[1] See p. 221.

becomes very cold and is by no means unwholesome, as I apprehended, though at first it sometimes affects the bowels.[1]

But to what purpose am I indulging in scientific disquisitions when on the eve of departure, when my thoughts should be occupied with the burning sun to which I am about to be exposed, and which in the *Indies* it is sufficiently painful to endure at any season; with the daily packing, loading and unloading; with the never-ceasing instructions to servants; with the pitching and striking of my tent; with marches by day, and marches by night; in short, with the precarious and wandering life which for the ensuing eighteen months I am doomed to experience? Adieu, my *Friend*; I shall not fail to perform my promise, and to impart to you from time to time all our adventures. The army on this occasion will advance by easy marches: it will not be disquieted with the apprehension of an enemy, but move with the gorgeous magnificence peculiar to the Kings of *Hindoustan*. I shall therefore endeavour to note every interesting occurrence in order that I may communicate it as soon as we arrive at *Lahor*.

[1] 'Saltpetre, which in gunpowder produces the explosive heat, is used by his Majesty as a means for cooling water, and is thus a source of joy for great and small.'—*Ain*, p. 55.

SECOND LETTER

TO THE SAME

Written at Lahor, the 25th February 1665.

Aureng-Zebe having arrived there.

Concerning the extent, the magnificence, and the mode of ordering the Camp of the Great Mogol. The number of the Elephants, Camels, Mules, and Men-Porters necessary for its transport. The arrangement of the Bazars or Royal Markets, the quarters set apart for the Omrahs or Nobles, and the rest of the Army. The area occcupied by the Army when thus encamped. The various difficulties met with and how overcome. The measures taken to prevent robberies. The modes of travelling adopted by the King, the Princesses, and the rest of the Harem. The risks one encounters on approaching too near the Seraglio. The various kinds of Hunting enjoyed by the King, accompanied by all his Army. The number of persons accompanying the Army, and how they exist.

MONSIEUR,

THIS is indeed slow and solemn marching, what we here call *à la Mogole.* Lahor is little more than one hundred and twenty leagues or about fifteen days' journey from *Dehli,* and we have been nearly two months on the road. The King, it is true, together with the greater part of the army, diverged from the highway, in search of better ground for the sports of the field, and for the convenience of obtaining the water of the *Gemna*, which we had gone in search of to the right;[1] and we leisurely skirted its bank, hunting and shooting amid grass so high as almost to conceal our horsemen, but abounding in every kind of game. We are now in a good town, enjoying repose; and I cannot better employ my time than in committing to paper the various particulars which have engaged my mind since I quitted *Dehli*. Soon I hope to conduct you to *Kachemire*, and to show you one of the most beautiful countries in the world.

Whenever the King travels in military pomp he has always two private camps; that is to say, two separate bodies of tents. One of these camps being constantly a day in advance of the other, the King is sure to find at the end of every journey a camp fully prepared for his reception. It is for this reason that these separate bodies of tents are called *Peiche-kanés*[2] or houses which precede. The two *Peiche-kanés* are nearly equal, and to transport one of them the aid of more than sixty elephants, two hundred camels, one hundred mules, and one hundred men-porters is required.[3] The most bulky things are carried by the elephants, such as the large tents, with their heavy poles, which on account of their great length and weight are made so as to be taken down into three pieces. The smaller tents are borne by the camels, and the luggage and kitchen utensils by the mules. To the porters are confided the lighter and more valuable articles, as the porcelain used at the King's table, the painted and gilt beds, and those rich *Karguais*,[4] of which I shall speak hereafter.

[1] See p. 221, footnote [1].

[2] *Paish-khanah*, advance house or camp, the double set of tents which add so immensely to the comfort of 'camping' in India.

[3] 'Each encampment requires for its carriage 100 elephants, 500 camels, 400 carts, and 100 bearers.'—*Ain*, p. 47.

[4] Khargáhs, folding tents, some with one, others with two doors, and made in various ways.

One of the *Peiche-kanés* has no sooner reached the place intended for the new encampment than the *Grand Quarter-Master* selects some fine situation for the King's tents, paying, however, as much attention as possible to the exact symmetry of the whole camp. He then marks out a square, each side of which measures more than three hundred ordinary paces. A hundred pioneers presently clear and level this space, raising square platforms of earth on which they pitch the tents. The whole of this extensive square is then encompassed with *kanates*, or screens, seven or eight feet in height, secured by cords attached to pegs, and by poles fixed two by two in the ground, at every ten paces, one pole within and the other without, and each leaning upon the other. The *kanates* are made of strong cloth, lined with printed Indian calico, representing large vases of flowers.[1] The royal entrance, which is spacious and magnificent, is in the centre of one of the sides of the square, and the flowered calico of which it is composed, as well as that which lines the whole exterior face of this side of the square, is of much finer texture and richer than the rest.

The first and largest tent erected in the royal camp is named *Am-kas*; being the place where the King and all the nobility keep the *mokam*; that is, where they assemble at nine o'clock in the morning for the purpose of deliberating on affairs of state and of administering justice.[2] The Kings of *Hindoustan* seldom fail, even when in the field, to hold this assembly twice during the twenty-four hours, the same as when in the capital. The custom is regarded as a matter of law and duty, and the observance of it is rarely neglected.[3]

The second tent, little inferior in size and somewhat

[1] These *khanats* were technically called *gulálbár*, and were a series of folding screens, frames of wood covered with red cloth tied on with tape, and fastened together with leather straps. See *Aín*, p. 54.

[2] In the Emperor Akbar's camps this was a two-storied tent or pavilion.

[3] See p. 266.

further within the enclosure, is called the *gosle-kané*,[1] or the place for bathing. It is here that all the nobility meet every evening to pay their obeisance to the King, in the same manner as when the court is at *Dehli*. This evening assembly subjects the *Omrahs* to much inconvenience; but it is a grand and imposing spectacle in a dark night to behold, when standing at some distance, long rows of torches lighting these *Nobles*, through extended lanes of tents, to the *gosle-kané*, and attending them back again to their own quarters. These flambeaux, although not made of wax, like ours in *France*, burn a long time. They merely consist of a piece of iron hafted in a stick, and surrounded at the extremity with linen rags steeped in oil, which are renewed, as occasion requires, by the *masalchis*, or link boys, who carry the oil in long narrow-necked vessels of iron or brass.

Still deeper in the square is the third tent, smaller than those I have spoken of, called *Kaluet-kané*, the retired spot, or the place of the privy council. To this tent none but the principal ministers of state have access, and it is here that all the important concerns of the kingdom are transacted.

Advancing beyond the *Kaluet-kané*, you come to the King's private tents, which are surrounded by small *kanates*, of the height of a man, some lined with *Maslipatam* chintz, painted over with flowers of a hundred different kinds, and others with figured satin, decorated with deep silken fringes.

Adjoining the royal tents are those of the *Begums*, or Princesses, and of the great ladies and principal female attendants of the *Seraglio*. These tents are also enclosed on every side by rich *kanates*; and in the midst of them are the tents of the inferior female domestics and other women connected with the *Seraglio*, placed generally in much the same order, according to the offices of the respective occupants.

[1] The *ghusl-khána*, or bath-room, at that period the name given to the private apartment in the Mogul's palace. See p. 265, footnote 2.

The *Am-kas*, and the five or six other principal tents, are elevated above the rest, as well for the sake of keeping off the heat as that they may be distinguished at a distance. The outside is covered with a strong and coarse red cloth, ornamented with large and variegated stripes; but the inside is lined with beautiful hand-painted chintz, manufactured for the purpose at *Maslipatam*, the ornamentation of which is set off by rich figured satin of various colours, or embroideries of silk, silver, and gold, with deep and elegant fringes.[1] Cotton mats, three or four inches in thickness, are spread over the whole floor, and these again are covered with a splendid carpet, on which are placed large square brocade cushions to lean upon. The tents are supported by painted and gilt pillars.

In each of the two tents wherein the King and nobility meet for deliberation is erected a stage,[2] which is most sumptuously adorned, and the King gives audience under a spacious canopy of velvet or flowered silk. The other tents have similar canopies, and they also contain what are called *karguais* or cabinets, the little doors of which are secured with silver padlocks.[3] You may form some idea of them by picturing to yourself two small squares of our folding screens, the one placed on the other, and both tied round with a silken cord in such a manner that the extremities of the sides of the upper square incline towards each other so as to form a kind of dome. There is this difference, however, between the *karguais* and our screens, that all their sides are composed of very thin and light deal boards painted and gilt on the outside, and embellished around with gold and silk fringe. The inside is lined with scarlet, flowered satin, or brocade.

I believe that I have omitted nothing of consequence contained within the great square.

[1] 'The inside is ornamented with brocade and velvet, and the outside with scarlet sackcloth, tied to the walls with silk tape.'—*Ain*, p. 54.

[2] Such a stage or raised platform may still be seen in the ruins of Fathpúr Síkri, near Agra.

[3] See p. 359.

In describing what is to be seen without, I shall first notice two handsome tents on either side of the grand entrance, or royal gate.[1] Here is to be seen a small number of the choicest horses, saddled and superbly caparisoned, ready to be mounted upon any emergency, but intended rather for ceremony and parade.[2]

On both sides of the same royal gate are ranged the fifty or sixty small field-pieces of which the stirrup-artillery is composed, and which fire a salute when the King enters his tent, by which the army is apprised of his arrival.

A free space, as extensive as may be convenient or practicable, is always kept in front of the royal entrance, and at its extremity there is a large tent called *Nagar-kané*,[3] because it contains the trumpets and the cymbals.

Close to this tent is another of a large size, called *tchauky-kané*,[4] where the *Omrahs* in rotation mount guard for twenty-four hours, once every week. Most of them, however, order one of their own tents to be pitched in its immediate vicinity, where they find themselves more comfortable and are in greater privacy.

Within a short distance of the three other sides of the great square are the tents of officers and others appro-

[1] The grand entrance was usually at the eastern end of the camp enclosure.

[2] Among them were two horses for the Emperor's own use, also courier horses.

[3] Properly *Nakárah khánah*, the nakárah was a monster kettledrum. Some were as high as four feet, resting on the ground and played upon by one man with a pair of sticks. In each nakárah khánah, there were twenty pairs, more or less, of these instruments, together with trumpets and horns of various shapes, and cymbals (*sanj*) of which three pairs were used. See p. 260, footnote [1].

[4] *Chauki-khánah*, the first part of which has passed into English slang, as the name for a prison.

'From predilection and a desire to teach soldiers their duties, as also from a regard to general efficiency, His Majesty pays much attention to the guards. If any one is absent without having a proper excuse, or from laziness, he is fined one week's pay, or receives a suitable reprimand.'—*Ain*, p. 257.

priated to particular purposes, which, unless there be local impediments, are always placed in the same relative situation. Every one of these tents has its particular appellation, but the names are difficult of pronunciation, and as it is not within my scope to teach you the language of the country, it may suffice to state that in one of them are deposited the arms of the King; in a second the rich harnesses; and in a third the vests of brocade, which are the presents generally made by the King. The fruits, the sweetmeats, the *Ganges* water, the saltpetre with which it is cooled, and the *betlé*, are kept in four other tents. *Betlé* is the leaf (of which I have spoken elsewhere[1]) which, after it has undergone a certain preparation, is given as a mark of royal favour (like coffee[2] in Turkey), and which when masticated sweetens the breath and reddens the lips. There are fifteen or sixteen other tents which serve for kitchens and their appurtenances; and in the midst of all these are the tents of a great number of officers and eunuchs. There are, lastly, six others, of considerable length, for led horses; and other tents for choice elephants and for the animals employed in hunting; for the birds of prey that invariably accompany the court and are intended both for show, and for field sports; the dogs; the leopards for catching antelopes; the *nil-ghaux*, or grey oxen, which I believe to be a species of elk;[3] the lions and the rhinoceroses, brought merely for parade; the large *Bengale* buffaloes, which attack the lion; the tamed antelopes, frequently made to fight in the presence of the King.

The quarters of the Monarch are understood to compre-

[1] See p. 13.

[2] *Kauve* in the original, as previously used, spelt *cauvé*, by Bernier, see p. 202. In Arabic *kahwa*. Most of the early writers who mention this beverage employ similar derivatives, such as 'Caova,' 'Cahoa,' and 'Chaoua.'

[3] The Hindostanee name is *nílgau*, or 'blue cow,' and is the popular name of the well-known large antelope common over the greater portion of Northern India, the *Portax pictus* of Jerdon.

hend not only the great square, but the numerous tents situated without the square, to which I have just drawn your attention. Their position is always in the centre of the army, or as much so as the nature of the ground will admit. You will easily conceive that there is something very striking and magnificent in these royal quarters, and that this vast assemblage of red tents, placed in the centre of a numerous army, produces a brilliant effect when seen from some neighbouring eminence; especially if the country be open, and offer no obstruction to the usual and regular distribution of the troops.[1]

The first care of the Grand Quarter-master[2] is, as before remarked, to choose a suitable situation for the royal tents. The *Am-kas* is elevated above every other tent, because it is the landmark by which the order and disposition of the whole army is regulated. He then marks out the royal bazars, from which all the troops are supplied. The principal *bazar* is laid out in the form of a wide street, running through the whole extent of the army, now on ie right, then on the left of the *Am-kas*, and always as uch as possible in the direction of the next day's en-mpment. The other royal *bazars*, which are neither so r nor so spacious, generally cross this one, some on one ue and some on another side of the King's quarters. All f them are distinguished by extremely long poles [cannes ès-hautes] stuck in the ground at the distance of three ndred paces from each other, bearing red standards, d surmounted with the tails of the Great *Tibet* cows, vhich have the appearance of so many periwigs.[3]

The quarter-master then proceeds to plan the quarters for the *Omrahs*, that there may always be the same

[1] Bernier's minute description of an Imperial camp is very correct, as may be seen by referring to the plan of one, plate iv., in vol. i. of the late Professor Blochmann's translation of the *Aín-i-Akbarí*.

[2] 'Le grand Maréchal des Logis,' the *Mír-manzil* of the *Aín*.

[3] A somewhat similar practice obtains at the present day in many of the regimental bazaars in our cantonments in India.

'The tails of the Great Thibet cows' are the yak tails still largely

observance of regularity, and that each nobleman may be placed at his usual distance from the royal square, whether on the right or on the left, so that no individual may be permitted to change the place allotted to him, or which he expressed a wish to occupy before the commencement of the expedition.

The description I have given of the great square is, in many particulars, applicable to the quarters of the *Omrahs* and *Rajas*. In general they also have two *peiche-kanés,* with a square of *kanates* enclosing their principal tents and those of their wives. Outside this square are likewise pitched the tents of their officers and troopers, and there is a *bazar* in the form of a street, consisting of small tents belonging to the followers of the army, who supply it with forage, rice, butter, and other necessary articles of life. The *Omrahs* need not, therefore, always have recourse to the royal *bazars,* where indeed everything may be procured, almost the same as in the capital. A long pole is planted at both ends of each *bazar,* and distinguished by a particular standard, floating in the air, as high as those of the royal *bazars,* in order that the different quarters may be readily discerned from a distance.

The chief *Omrahs* and great *Rajas* pride themselves on the loftiness of their tents, which must not, however, be too conspicuous, lest the King perceive it and command that the tents be thrown down, as he did on our late march. For the same reason, the outside must not be entirely red, there being none but the royal tents that can be of that colour;[1] and as a mark of proper respect every tent has also to front the *Am-kas,* or quarters of the King.

The remainder of the ground, between the quarters of the Monarch, those of the *Omrahs,* and the *bazars,* is filled with the tents of *Mansebdars,* or inferior *Omrahs,* of

used in India by Rájás, Nawabs and others, as fly flappers, or, mounted with silver in the hands of running footmen, etc., as marks of dignity; see p. 261. The *cannes très hautes* of the original might be translated 'tall bamboos,' of which such flag-staffs are generally made at the present day.

[1] See p. 362.

tradespeople of every description, of civil officers and other persons, who for various reasons follow the army; and, last of all, the tents of those who serve in the light and heavy artillery. The tents are therefore very numerous, and cover a large extent of ground; though with respect both to their number and the space occupied by them very extravagant notions are formed. When the army halts in a fine and favourable country, which leaves it at liberty to adopt the well-understood rules and order of a circular encampment, I do not believe that this space measures more than two leagues, or perhaps two leagues and a half[1] in circumference, including here and there several spots of unoccupied ground. It should be mentioned, however, that the heavy artillery, which requires a great deal of room, is commonly a day or two in advance of the army.

What is said of the strange confusion that prevails in the camp, and of the alarm thereby occasioned to a new-comer, is also much exaggerated. A slight acquaintance with the method observed in the quartering of the troops will enable you to go, without much difficulty, from place to place as your business may require; the King's quarters, the tents and standards peculiar to every *Omrah*, and the ensigns and 'periwigs' of the royal *bazars*, which are all seen from a great distance, serving, after a little experience, for unerring guides.

Sometimes, indeed, notwithstanding all these precautions, there will be uncertainty and disorder, particularly on the arrival of the army at the place of encampment in the morning, when every one is actively employed in finding and establishing his own quarters. The dust that arises often obscures the marks I have mentioned, and it becomes impossible to distinguish the King's quarter,

[1] The '*lieuë*' of Bernier's narrative may be taken as 2½ miles. The actual *lieue de poste* of France was equal to 2 miles and 743 yards. Dr. Ball, in his edition of Travernier's *Travels*, takes the *coss* as equal to the French *lieue*. The *coss* (kōs) in Northern India measured in Bernier's time 2 miles, 4 furlongs, 158 yards. See p. 284, footnote [3].

the different *bazars*, or the tents of the several *Omrahs*. Your progress is besides liable to be impeded by the tents then pitching, and by the cords extended by inferior *Omrahs*, who have no *peiche-kanés*, and by *Mansebdars* to mark their respective boundaries, and to prevent not only the public path from passing through, but the fixing of any strange tent near their own, where their wives, if accompanying them, reside. A horde of their lusty varlets, with cudgels [1] in their hands, will not suffer these cords to be removed or lowered; you then naturally retrace your steps, and find that while you have been employed in unavailing efforts to pass at one end, your retreat has been cut off at the other. There is now no means of extricating your laden camels but by menace and entreaty; outrageous passion, and calm remonstrance; seeming as if you would proceed to blows, yet carefully abstaining from touching any one; promoting a violent quarrel between the servants of both parties, and afterward reconciling them for fear of the consequences, and in this way taking advantage of a favourable moment to pass your camels. But the greatest annoyance is perhaps in the evening when business calls you to any distance. This is the time when the common people cook their victuals with a fire made of cow and camel dung and green wood. The smoke of so many fires of this kind, when there is little wind, is highly offensive, and involves the atmosphere in total darkness. It was my fate to be overtaken three or four times by this wide-spreading vapour.[2] I inquired, but could not find my way: I turned and roamed about, ignorant whither I went. Once I was obliged to stop until the smoke dispersed, and the moon arose; and at another time I with difficulty reached the *aguacy-dié*, at the foot of which I passed the night with my horse and

[1] In the original *gros bâtons*, the well-known *chaukidars' lathi* (watchmen's bamboo club) of that and the present period.

[2] All those who have been out in camp in the cold weather in Northern India will be able to testify to the truth of this vivid picture of a common experience.

servant.[1] The *aguacy-dié* resembles a lofty mast of a ship, but is very slender, and takes down in three pieces. It is fixed toward the King's quarters, near the tent called *nagar-kané,* and during the night has a lighted lantern suspended from the top. This light is very useful, for it may be seen when every object is enveloped in impenetrable darkness. To this spot persons who lose their way resort, either to pass the night secure from all danger of robbers, or to resume their search after their own lodgings. The name *aguacy-dié* may be translated Light of Heaven, the lantern when at a distance appearing like a star.[2]

To prevent robberies every *Omrah* provides watchmen, who continually perambulate his particular quarters during the night, crying out *Kaber-dar!* or, Have a care! and there are guards posted round the whole army at every five hundred paces, who kindle fires, and also cry out *Kaber-dar!* Besides these precautions, the *Cotoüal,*[3] or Grand Provost, sends soldiers in every direction, who especially pervade the *bazars,* crying out and sounding a trumpet. Notwithstanding all these measures, robberies are often committed, and it is prudent to be always on the alert; not to rely too much on the vigilance of servants; and to repose at an early hour, so as to watch during the remainder of the night.

I will now proceed to describe the different modes of travelling adopted by the *Great Mogol* on these occasions.

1 The *sais* or groom, who in India on such occasions follows close behind his master.

2 The *Akásdiah,* from *ákás,* sky, and *diah,* lamp, was a great feature in the Imperial camp. 'In order to render the royal camp conspicuous to those who come from afar, His Majesty has caused to be erected in front of the Durbár a pole upwards of forty yards high, which is supported by sixteen ropes; and on the top of the pole is a large lantern which they call *Akásdiah.* Its light is seen from great distances, guides the soldiers to the Imperial camp, and helps them to find their tents. In former times, before the lamp was erected, the men had to suffer hardships from not being able to find the road.'—*Aín,* pp. 49-50.

3 See p. 188, footnote 1.

Most commonly he is carried on men's shoulders in a *tact-ravan*,[1] or field throne, wherein he sits. This *tact* is a species of magnificent tabernacle, with painted and gilt pillars and glass windows, that are kept shut when the weather is bad. The four poles of this litter are covered either with scarlet or brocade, and decorated with deep fringes of silk and gold. At the end of each pole are stationed two strong and handsomely dressed men, who are relieved by eight other men constantly in attendance. Sometimes the King rides on horseback, especially when the weather is favourable for hunting; and at other times he is carried by an elephant in a *mikdember*, or in a *hauze*, which is by far the most striking and splendid style of travelling, as nothing can surpass the richness and magnificence of the harness and trappings. The *mikdember* is a small house, or square wooden tower, gilt and painted;[2] and the *hauze*,[3] an oval chair with a canopy on pillars, also superbly decorated with colours and gold.

In every march the King is accompanied by a great number of *Omrahs* and *Rajas*, who follow him closely on horseback, placing themselves promiscuously in a body, without much method or regularity. On the morning of a journey, they assemble at break of day in the *Am-kas*, with the exception of those who may be exempted by age or the nature of their office. They find these marches very fatiguing, especially on hunting-days, being exposed like a private soldier to the sun and dust, frequently until three o'clock in the afternoon.

These luxurious lords move along very differently when not in the train of the King: neither dust nor sun then annoys them, but they are stretched, as on a bed, in a

[1] Tukht-i-rawan, see p. 128.

[2] 'They also put comfortable turrets on the backs of swift-paced elephants, which serve as a travelling sleeping apartment.'—*Ain*, p. 131.

[3] Similar to the modern howdah (a Hindostanee word modified from the Arabic *haudaj*), but with a canopy.

paleky, closed and covered or not as may be found more agreeable; sleeping at ease until they reach their tent, where they are sure to find an excellent dinner, the kitchen and every necessary article having been sent forward the preceding night, immediately after supper. The *Omrahs* are always surrounded by a number of well-mounted cavaliers, called *gourze-berdars,* because they carry a kind of club,[1] or silver mace. The King is also attended by many of them, who go before him, both on the right and on the left, together with a multitude of footmen. The *gourze-berdars* are picked, good-looking men, of fine figures, and are employed to convey orders and despatches. With great sticks in their hands they drive everybody before them, and keep the way clear for the King.

The *Cours* follow the Rajahs surrounded by a large number of players on cymbals and trumpets. The *Cours,* as I before observed,[2] consists of figures in silver, representing strange animals, hands, balances, fishes and other mystical objects, borne at the end of large silver poles.

A numerous body of *Mansebdars* or inferior *Omrahs* comes next, well mounted, and equipped with sword, quiver, and arrows.[3] This body is much more numerous than that of *Omrahs,* which follows the King; because not only the *Mansebdars* who are on duty are obliged to assemble at break of day near the royal tent, for the purpose of accompanying the King, but there are many who join the train in the hope of attracting notice and obtaining preferment.

The Princesses and great ladies of the *Seraglio* have also different modes of travelling. Some prefer *tchaudoules,*[4] which are borne on men's shoulders, and are not unlike the *tact-ravans.* They are gilt and painted and covered with magnificent silk nets of many colours, enriched with

[1] See p. 263, footnote [1].

[2] See p. 266. The *kur* corresponded in some respects to the colours of a regiment, it had a special guard assigned to it, and was saluted on various occasions.

[3] Bernier has omitted to mention the bow and shield which also formed part of their equipment.

[4] *Chaudols.*

embroidery, fringes, and beautiful tassels. Others travel in a stately and close *paleky*, gilt and covered, over which are also expanded similar silk nets. Some again use capacious litters, suspended between two powerful camels, or between two small elephants. It is in this style I have sometimes seen *Rauchenara-Begum* pursuing her journey, and have observed more than once in front of the litter, which was open, a young, well-dressed female slave, with a peacock's tail in her hand, brushing away the dust, and keeping off the flies from the Princess. The ladies are not unfrequently carried on the backs of elephants, which upon these occasions wear massive bells of silver, and are decked with costly trappings, curiously embroidered. These lovely and distinguished females, seated in *Mikdembers*, are thus elevated above the earth, like so many superior beings borne along through the middle region of the air. Each *Mikdember* contains eight women, four on a side: it is latticed and covered with a silken net, and yields not in richness and splendour to the *tchaudoule* or the *tact-ravan*.

I cannot avoid dwelling on this pompous procession of the *Seraglio*. It strongly arrested my attention during the late march, and I feel delight in recalling it to my memory. Stretch imagination to its utmost limits, and you can conceive no exhibition more grand and imposing than when *Rauchenara-Begum*, mounted on a stupendous *Pegu* elephant, and seated in a *Mikdember*,[1] blazing with gold and azure, is followed by five or six other elephants with *Mikdembers* nearly as resplendent as her own, and filled with ladies attached to her household. Close to the Princess are the chief eunuchs, richly adorned and finely mounted, each with a wand of office in his hand; and surrounding her elephant, a troop of female servants, *Tartars* and *Kachmerys*, fantastically attired and riding handsome pad-horses. Besides these attendants are several eunuchs on horseback, accompanied by a multitude of *Pagys*,[2] or

[1] For *meghdambhar*.

[2] The Portuguese word *peão*, from *pé*, foot, and meaning a footman,

lackeys on foot, with large canes, who advance a great way before the Princess, both to the right and to the left, for the purpose of clearing the road and driving before them every intruder. Immediately behind *Rauchenara-Begum's* retinue appears a principal lady of the court, mounted and attended much in the same manner as the Princess. This lady is followed by a third, she by a fourth, and so on, until fifteen or sixteen females of quality pass with a grandeur of appearance, equipage, and retinue more or less proportionate to their rank, pay, and office. There is something very impressive of state and royalty in the march of these sixty or more elephants; in their solemn and, as it were, measured steps; in the splendour of the *Mikdembers*, and the brilliant and innumerable followers in attendance: and if I had not regarded this display of magnificence with a sort of philosophical indifference, I should have been apt to be carried away by such flights of imagination as inspire most of the *Indian* poets, when they represent the elephants as conveying so many goddesses conçealed from the vulgar gaze.

Truly, it is with difficulty that these ladies can be approached, and they are almost inaccessible to the sight of man. Woe to any unlucky cavalier, however exalted in rank, who, meeting the procession, is found too near. Nothing can exceed the insolence of the tribes of eunuchs and footmen which he has to encounter, and they eagerly avail themselves of any such opportunity to beat a man in the most unmerciful manner. I shall not easily forget being once surprised in a similar situation, and how narrowly I escaped the cruel treatment that many cavaliers have experienced: but determined not to suffer myself to be beaten and perhaps maimed without a struggle, I drew my sword, and having fortunately a strong and spirited horse,

Angliçised into peon; also the Hindostanee word *piyàda*, also meaning a footman. Scoticé, *pedee* (Latin, *pedisequus*), a footboy: 'Wm. Gray, Pedee to one Smith in the Rebel Life Guards.'—*List of Rebels in* 1745, p. 275. Scot. Hist. Soc., 1890.

I was enabled to open a passage, sword in hand, through a host of assailants, and to dash across the rapid stream which was before me. It is indeed a proverbial observation in these armies that three things are to be carefully avoided: the first, getting among the choice and led horses, where kicking abounds; the second, intruding on the hunting ground; and the third, a too near approach to the ladies of the *Seraglio*. It is much worse, however, in *Persia*. I understand that in that country life itself is forfeited if a man be within sight even of the eunuchs, although he should be half a league distant from the women; and all the male inhabitants of the towns and villages through which the *Seraglio* is to pass must abandon their homes and fly to a considerable distance.

I shall now speak of the field sports of the King.[1] I

[1] 'Superficial, worldly observers see in killing an animal a sort of pleasure, and in their ignorance stride about, as if senseless, on the field of their passions. But deep inquirers see in hunting a means of acquisition of knowledge, and the temple of their worship derives from it a peculiar lustre. This is the case with His Majesty. He always makes hunting a means of increasing his knowledge, and besides, uses hunting parties as occasions to inquire, without having first given notice of his coming, into the condition of the people and the army. He travels *incognito*, and examines into matters referring to taxation, or to *Sayúrghál* lands, or to affairs connected with the household. He lifts up such as are oppressed, and punishes the oppressors. On account of these higher reasons His Majesty indulges in the chase, and shews himself quite enamoured of it. Short-sighted and shallow observers think that His Majesty has no other object in view but hunting; but the wise and experienced know that he pursues higher aims.' —*Ain*, p. 282. Sayúrghál lands were those which had been given for benevolent purposes of various kinds. One of the classes of men on whom they were bestowed were 'inquirers after wisdom, who have withdrawn from all worldly occupation, and make no difference between night and daytime in searching after true knowledge.'—*Ain*, p. 268. An early example of 'endowments for research,' in fact. Such lands were hereditary, and differed for this reason from *Jágír* lands, which were conferred for a specified time, and to which Bernier alludes at p. 213. Akbar, however, considerably interfered with these Sayúrghál lands, arbitrarily resuming many of them and increasing his domain lands to the ruin of many a family.

could never conceive how the *Great Mogol* could hunt with an army of one hundred thousand men; but there certainly is a sense in which he may be said to hunt with two hundred thousand, or with any number of which his army may consist.

In the neighbourhoods of *Agra* and *Dehli,* along the course of the *Gemna,* reaching to the mountains, and even on both sides of the road leading to *Lahor,* there is a large quantity of uncultivated land, covered either with copse wood or with grasses six feet high. All this land is guarded with the utmost vigilance; and excepting partridges, quails, and hares, which the natives catch with nets, no person, be he who he may, is permitted to disturb the game, which is consequently very abundant.

Whenever the Monarch is about to take the field, every gamekeeper [Gardes Chasses] near whose district the army is to pass is called upon to apprise the Grand Master of the Hunt of the various sorts of game under his particular charge, and of the places where they are in the greatest plenty. Sentries are then stationed at the different roads of that district, to guard the tract of ground selected, which extends sometimes four or five leagues; and while the army is on its march, on one side or the other, so as to avoid that tract, the King enters it with as many *Omrahs* and other persons as have liberty to do so, and enjoys, leisurely and uninterruptedly, the sports of the field, varying them according to the nature of the game.

I shall, in the first place, describe the manner in which they chase antelopes with tame leopards.[1]

[1] The cheetah or hunting leopard is still largely employed, chiefly in the Native States of India, for the sport described by Bernier. In the *Ain* there is a story told of how once, 'from the kindness shown by His Majesty, a deer made friendship with a leopard. They lived together and enjoyed each other's company. The most remarkable thing was this, that the leopard when let off against other deer would pounce upon them as any other leopard.'

The lynx, the Hindostanee name for which, from the Persian, is *sihá-gosh,* or 'black ear,' was also employed in the chase by the Mogul

I think that I have elsewhere told you that there are in the *Indies* large numbers of antelopes, very much resembling our fawns in shape; that they move generally in herds; and that every herd, which is never composed of more than five or six, is followed by a male, who is easily distinguished by his colour. When one of these little troops is discovered, the first step is to have it seen by the leopard, who is kept chained on a small car.[1] The sagacious and cunning animal does not, as might be expected, run at once towards the antelopes, but winds about, hides himself, crouches, and in this cautious manner approaches them unperceived, so as to give himself a fair chance of catching them with those five or six bounds, which the leopard is noted for making with incredible agility. If successful, he gluts himself with their blood, heart, and liver! but if he miss his prey, as frequently happens, he makes no other effort, but stands perfectly still. It would indeed be useless to contend with these animals in a fair race, for they run much more fleetly and much longer than the leopard. His keeper finds no great difficulty in securing him again on the car; he approaches him quietly,

Emperors. 'His Majesty is very fond of using this plucky little animal for hunting purposes. In former times it would attack a hare or a fox; but now it kills black buck.'—*Ain*, p. 290. Capt. Alexander Hamilton, in his *New Account of the East Indies*, Edinburgh, 1727, 2 vols. 8vo, gives (vol. i. p. 124) an exceedingly quaint and graphic description of this mode of hunting, as follows: 'Deer, Antelopes, Hares, and Foxes are their wild Game, which they hunt with Dogs, Leopards, and a small fierce Creature, called by them a *Shoegoose*. It is about the Size of a Fox, with long prickt Ears like an Hare, and a Face like a Cat, a gray Back and Sides, and Belly and Breast white. I believe they are rare, for I never saw more than one. When they are taken out to hunt an Horseman carries it behind him hood-winkt, and their Deer and Antelopes, being pretty familiar, will not start before horses come very near. He who carries the *Shoegoose*, takes off the Hood, and shews it the Game, which, with large swift Springs, it soon overtakes, and leaping on their Backs, and getting forward to the Shoulders, scratches their Eyes out, and gives the Hunters an easy prey.'

[1] Technically called a *suggur*.

caresses him, throws down a few pieces of flesh, and, covering his eyes, fastens his chain. During the march, one of these leopards very unexpectedly afforded us this amusement, to the no small consternation, however, of many of us. A troop of antelopes ran through the midst of the army, as was indeed the case every day; but these happened to pass very close to two leopards who were placed as usual on their car. One, whose eyes were not covered, made so violent an effort as to break his chain, and rush after the antelopes, but without catching any. Impeded, however, in their flight, turned and pursued on all sides, one of them could not avoid again approaching the leopard, who pounced upon and seized the poor animal, notwithstanding the crowds of camels and horses that were in his way, and contrary to the common opinion that the leopard never attacks the prey which he has once missed.

There is nothing very interesting in the mode of hunting the *nil-ghaux*, or grey oxen; which, as I before stated, are a species of elk.[1] They enclose them in great nets, which are drawn closer by degrees; and, when the space is reduced to a small compass, the King enters with his *Omrahs* and huntsmen, and the animal is killed with arrows, short spikes, swords, and musketoons. Sometimes these animals are slaughtered in such numbers that the King sends quarters of them as presents to all the *Omrahs*.

It is curious enough to observe the manner in which cranes are caught. Their courageous defence in the air against the birds of prey[2] affords much sport. Sometimes they kill their assailants; but from the slowness of their movements in wheeling round they are overcome as the number of their enemies increases.

[1] See p. 364. The nílgau has a heavy shambling pace, and at the present day it is not considered quite sportsmanlike to shoot them.

[2] Hawks, of which several kinds were used. 'His Majesty, from motives of generosity and from a wish to add splendour to his Court, is fond of hunting with falcons, though superficial observers think that merely hunting is his object.'—*Aín*, p. 294.

But of all the diversions of the field the hunting of the lion[1] is not only the most perilous, but is peculiarly royal; for, except by special permission, the King and Princes are the only persons who engage in the sport. As a preliminary step, an ass is tied near the spot where the gamekeepers have ascertained the lion retires. The wretched animal is soon devoured, and after so ample a meal the lion never seeks for other prey, but without molesting either oxen, sheep, or shepherds, goes in quest of water, and after quenching his thirst, returns to his former place of retirement. He sleeps until the next morning, when he finds and devours another ass, which the gamekeepers have brought to the same spot. In this way they contrive, during several days, to allure the lion and to attach him to one place; and when information is received of the King's approach, they fasten at the spot an ass where so many others have been sacrificed, down whose throat a large quantity of opium has been forced. This last meal is of course intended to produce a soporific effect upon the lion. The next operation is to spread, by means of the peasantry of the adjacent villages, large nets, made on purpose, which are gradually drawn closer, in the manner practised in hunting the *nil-ghaux*. Everything being in this state of preparation, the King appears on an elephant protected in places with thin plates of iron, and attended by the Grand Master of the Hunt, some *Omrahs* mounted on elephants, and a great number both of *gourze-berdars* on horseback and of gamekeepers on foot, armed with *half-pikes*. He immediately approaches the net on the outside, and fires at the lion with a large musketoon. The wounded animal makes a spring at the elephant, according to the invariable practice of lions, but is arrested by the net;[2] and the King continues to discharge his *musketoon*, until the lion is at length killed.

It happened, however, during the last hunt, that the

[1] Except in Kathiawar lions are very rarely met with in any part of India now.

[2] See pp. 182-183.

enraged animal leaped over the net, rushed upon a trooper whose horse he killed, and then effected his escape for a time. Being pursued by the huntsmen, he was at length found and again enclosed in nets. The whole army was on that occasion subjected to great inconveniencies and thrown into a considerable degree of confusion. We remained three or four days patrolling in a country intersected with torrents from the mountains, and covered with underwood, and long grass that nearly concealed the camels. No *bazars* had been formed and there were no towns or villages near the army. Happy those who during this scene of disorder could satisfy the cravings of hunger! Shall I explain the weighty reason of this long detention in such abominable quarters? You must know, then, that as it is considered a favourable omen when the King kills a lion, so is the escape of that animal portentous of infinite evil to the state. Accordingly, the termination of the hunt is attended with much grave ceremony. The King being seated in the general assembly of the *Omrahs*, the dead lion is brought before him, and when the carcass has been accurately measured and minutely examined, it is recorded in the royal archives that such a King on such a day slew a lion of such a size and of such a skin, whose teeth were of such a length, and whose claws were of such dimensions,[1] and so on down to the minutest details.

Let me just add a word on the subject of the opium given to the ass. One of the principal huntsmen assures me that it is a tale of the vulgar, and that the lion is suffi-

[1] The Emperor Akbar, who was a great sportsman, caused not only an account to be kept of the game he shot, but ordered that particulars of the guns used should also be recorded. Jáhángír inherited his father's love of sport, except that he never hunted elephants nor did he care for shooting waterfowl. In his *Memoirs* he gives many details of his hunting exploits, and tells us how he caused the officials of the Hunting Department to draw up a 'game book' embracing his life from the age of twelve to fifty. This list tells us that during these years he shot 17,167 head of game of all kinds, including 86 tigers, 41 sparrows, 3276 crows (!), and 10 alligators.

ciently disposed to sleep without it when he has eaten to satiety.

I observed that the great rivers are commonly without bridges. The army crossed them by means of two bridges of boats, constructed with tolerable skill, and placed between two or three hundred paces apart. Earth and straw mingled together are thrown upon the planking forming the footway, to prevent the cattle from slipping. The greatest confusion and danger occur at the extremities; for not only does the crowd and pressure occur most there, but when the approaches to the bridge are composed of soft moving earth, they become so broken up and so full of pits, that horses and laden oxen tumble upon one another into them, and the people pass over the struggling animals in the utmost disorder. The evil would be much increased if the army were under the necessity of crossing in one day; but the King generally fixes his camp about half a league from the bridges of boats, and suffers a day or two to elapse ere he passes to the opposite side of the river; when, pitching his tents within half a league from the bank, he again delays his departure so as to allow the army three days and nights at least to effect the passage.

As to the number of people, whether soldiers or others, which the camp contains, it is not easy to determine this accurately; so various are the opinions on this point. I may venture, however, to state generally that in this march there are at least one hundred thousand horsemen, and more than one hundred and fifty thousand animals, comprising horses, mules, and elephants; that besides these, there cannot be much less than fifty thousand camels, and nearly as many oxen or horses employed to carry the wives and children, the grain and other provisions belonging to the poor people connected with the bazars, who when they travel take with them, like our gipsies, the whole of their families, goods, and chattels. The servants in the army must be indeed numerous, since nothing is done without their assistance. I rank only with a two-horse cavalier, and yet I cannot possibly contrive with less than three men. Many are of opinion that the camp contains between three and four hundred thousand persons; some believe this estimate to be too small, while others consider it rather exaggerated. Accurately to determine the question, the people should be numbered. All I can confidently assert is that the multitude is prodigious and almost incredible. The whole population of *Dehli*, the capital city, is in fact collected in the camp, because deriving its employment and maintenance from the court and army, it has no alternative but to follow them in their march or to perish from want during their absence.[1]

You are no doubt at a loss to conceive how so vast a number both of men and animals can be maintained in the field. The best solution of the difficulty will be found in the temperance of the *Indians* and simple nature of their diet. Of the five-score thousand troopers not a tenth, no not a twentieth part, eat animal food; they are satisfied with their *kichery*, a mess of rice and other vegetables, over which, when cooked, they pour boiled butter.[2] It should be considered too that camels endure fatigue, hunger, and thirst in a surprising degree, live upon little, and eat any kind of food. At the end of every march, they are left to browse in the fields, where everything serves for fodder. It is important likewise to observe that the same tradesmen who supply the bazars in *Dehli* are compelled to furnish them in the camp; the shops of which they are composed being kept by the same persons whether in the capital or in the field.

These poor people are at great pains to procure forage: they rove about from village to village, and what they succeed in purchasing, they endeavour to sell in the army at an advanced price. It is a common practice with them to clear, with a sort of trowel, whole fields of a peculiar kind of grass, which having beaten and washed,

[1] See p. 220.

[2] Ghee, see p. 438.

they dispose of in the camp at a price sometimes very high and sometimes inadequately low.[1]

There is a curious fact respecting the King which I had almost forgotten to relate. He enters the camp sometimes on one side, sometimes on another; that is, he will to-day pass near the tents of certain *Omrahs* and to-morrow near the tents of others.[2] This variation of route is not, as you might suppose, accidental: the *Omrahs,* whom the Monarch honours by his vicinity, must leave their quarters to meet him, and must present His Majesty with a purse of more or less value; from twenty to fifty golden *roupies,* twenty being equal to about thirty *pistoles,* according to their liberality and the amount of their pay.

I shall say nothing of the towns and villages between *Dehli* and *Lahor*: I have in fact scarcely seen any of them. My *Agah's* station not being in the centre of the army, which often kept to the highroad, but in the front of the right wing, it was our custom to traverse fields and bye-paths during the night, guided by the stars; frequently mistaking our way, and marching five or six leagues, instead of three or four, the usual distance between two encampments, till daylight again set us right.

[1] The general practice at the present day throughout Northern India, 'the peculiar kind of grass' being the well-known *dúb* (*Cynodon Dactylon,* Royle). On account of its creeper-like stem, a *khurpa,* the trowel-like instrument of Bernier, is required to scrape it, as it were, from off the ground.

[2] 'The nobles are encamped without on all sides according to their rank. The guards for Thursday, Friday, and Saturday encamp in the centre; those for Sunday and Monday on the right; and those for Tuesday and Wednesday on the left.'—*Ain*, p. 48.

THIRD LETTER

TO THE SAME

Written at Lahor, the King being then about to depart for Kachemire.

Description of Lahor, the Capital of the Penje-ab, or Kingdom of the five Rivers.

MONSIEUR,

IT is not without reason that the kingdom of which *Lahor* is the capital is named the *Penje-ab,* or the Region of the Five Waters; because five rivers do really descend from the great mountains which enclose the kingdom of *Kachemire,* and, taking their course through this country, fall into the *Indus,* which empties itself into the ocean at *Scymdi,*[1] near the mouth of the *Persian* Gulf. Whether *Lahor* be the ancient *Bucefalos,* I do not pretend to determine. *Alexander* is here well known by the name of *Sekander Filifous,* or Alexander the son of Philip: concerning his horse, however, they know nothing. The river on which the city was built, one of the five, is as considerable as our *Loire,* and is much in want of a similar embankment as that on which the road is carried on the banks of the French river; for it is subject to inundations, which cause great injury and frequently change its bed: indeed within a few years the river has receded a full quarter of a league from *Lahor,* to the great inconvenience of the

[1] By this I believe Bernier to mean Sind, which was called Sinda by Fryer, the mouths of the Indus being situated in the Province of Sind.

inhabitants.[1] Unlike the buildings of *Dehli* and *Agra,* the houses here are very lofty; but, the court having resided during the last twenty years or more in one of those two cities, most of the houses in *Lahor* are in a runious state.[2] Indeed, many have been totally destroyed and have buried many of the inhabitants under their ruins, in consequence of the heavy rains which have prevailed of late years. There are still five or six considerable streets, two or three of which exceed a league in length; but not a few of the houses in them are tumbling to the ground.[3] The river having changed its bed, the King's palace is no longer seated on its banks.[4] This is a high and noble edifice, though very inferior to the palaces of *Dehli* or *Agra.* It is more than two months since we arrived in this city: we have waited for the melting of the snow on the mountains of *Kachemire* in order to obtain an easier passage into that country; our departure is finally fixed, however, for to-morrow, as the King quitted *Lahor* two days ago. I have provided myself with a nice small *Kachemire* tent, which I purchased yesterday, as I was advised to do the same as others, and to proceed no further with my old tent, which is rather large and heavy. It will be difficult, they tell me, to find room for all our tents among the mountains of *Kachemire,* which besides are impassable to camels; so that requiring porters for our baggage, the carriage of my old tent would be too expensive. Farewell!

[1] The old bed of the Ravee is well known to all who have visited Lahore, and it has been proposed in recent years to divert the present stream into its old channel again.

[2] See p. 459.

[3] The Emperor Jáhángír, Sháh Jahán's predecessor, frequently resided at Lahore, and after his time it began to decline in population.

[4] Brought about, it is said, by an embankment which Aurangzeb constructed to prevent inundations, but which had the effect of so deflecting the current as to cause the river to alter its course entirely.

FOURTH LETTER

TO THE SAME

Written from the Camp of the Army marching from Lahor to Kachemire, the fourth day of the March.

MONSIEUR,

I HOPED that, as I had survived the heat of *Moka* near the Straits of *Bab-el-mandel,* I should have nothing to fear from the burning rays of the sun in any part of the earth; but that hope has abandoned me since the army left *Lahor* four days ago. I am indeed no longer surprised that even the *Indians* themselves expressed much apprehension of the misery which awaited them during the eleven or twelve days' march of the army from *Lahor* to *Bember,*[1] which is situated at the entrance of the *Kachemire* mountains. I declare, without the least exaggeration, that I have been reduced by the intenseness of the heat to the last extremity; scarcely believing when I rose in the morning that I should outlive the day. This extraordinary heat is occasioned by the high mountains of *Kachemire*; for being to the north of our road, they intercept the cool breezes which would refresh us from that quarter, at the same time that they reflect the scorching sunbeams, and leave the whole country arid and suffocating. But why should I attempt to account philosophically for that which may kill me to-morrow?

[1] Bhimbar, where the remains of one of the rest-houses built for the camps of the Mogul Emperors is still used by travellers.

FIFTH LETTER

TO THE SAME

Written from the Camp of the Army marching from Lahor to Kachemire, the sixth day of the March.

MONSIEUR,

I YESTERDAY crossed one of the great rivers of India, called the *Tchenau*.[1] Its excellent water, with which the principal *Omrahs* are providing themselves, instead of the Ganges water that has hitherto supplied their wants, induces me to hope that the ascent of this river does not lead to the infernal regions, but that it may really conduct us to the kingdom of *Kachemire*, where they would make me believe we should be gladdened with the sight of ice and snow. Every day is found more insupportable than the preceding, and the further we advance the more does the heat increase. It is true that I crossed the bridge of boats at broad noonday, but I am not sure that my sufferings would have been less if I had remained stifling in my tent. My object was at least attained: I passed over this bridge quietly, while everybody else was resting and waiting to cross toward the close of the day, when the heat is less oppressive. Perhaps I owe my escape from some fatal accident to my prudence and foresight, for no passage of a river, since the army quitted *Dehli*, has been attended

[1] The Chínáb, which is nearly 72 miles from Lahore by Bernier's route. He had therefore marched at the rate of about 12 miles a day.

with such dreadful confusion.[1] The entrance at one extremity of the bridge into the first boat, and the going out from the last boat at the other extremity were rendered extremely difficult and dangerous on account of the loose moving sand which it was necessary to pass, and which giving way under the feet of such crowds of animals, was carried off by the current, and left considerable cavities, into which numbers of camels, oxen, and horses were thrown down, and trodden underfoot, while blows were dealt about without intermission. There are generally upon these occasions officers and troopers attached to *Omrahs,* who to clear the way for their masters and their baggage make an active use of their canes. My *Navaab* has lost one of his camels, with the iron oven it carried;[2] so that I fear I shall be reduced to the necessity of eating the *bazar* bread. Farewell!

[1] This is the largest river they had yet crossed, and the sandy approaches to the main stream were always, until a few years ago when the combined railway and road bridge was built, very tedious for travellers, whether mounted or on foot.

[2] Probably one of those portable ovens, made of sheet-iron, so familiar to all Anglo-Indians, called a *tandúr* in Hindostanee.

THE SIXTH LETTER

TO THE SAME

Written from the Camp of the Army, marching from Lahor to Kachemire, the eighth day of the March.

MONSIEUR,

ALAS, my dear Sir! what can induce an European to expose himself to such terrible heat, and to these harassing and perilous marches? It is too much curiosity; or rather it is gross folly and inconsiderate rashness. My life is placed in continual jeopardy. Out of evil, however, may arise some good. When at *Lahor* I was seized with a flux, accompanied by acute pains in my limbs, in consequence of having passed whole nights on a terrace in the open air, as is commonly done in *Dehli* without danger. My health was suffering; but since we have been on the march the violent perspirations, continued for eight or nine days, have dissipated my bad humours, and my parched and withered body is become a mere sieve, the quart of water, which I swallow at a draught, passing at the same moment through every one of my pores, even to my fingers' ends. I am sure that to-day I have drunk more than ten pints. Amid all our sufferings, it is a great consolation to be able to drink as much water as we please with impunity, provided it be of a good quality.

THE SEVENTH LETTER

TO THE SAME

Written from the Camp of the Army, marching from Lahor to Kachemire, on the morning of the tenth day of the March.

MONSIEUR,

THE sun is just but rising, yet the heat is insupportable. There is not a cloud to be seen nor a breath of air to be felt. My horses are exhausted; they have not seen a blade of green grass since we quitted *Lahor*. My Indian servants, notwithstanding their black, dry, and hard skin, are incapable of further exertion. The whole of my face, my feet, and my hands are flayed. My body too is entirely covered with small red blisters, which prick like needles.[1] Yesterday one of our poor troopers, who was without a tent, was found dead at the foot of a tree, whither he had crept for shelter. I feel as if I should myself expire before night. All my hopes are in four or five limes still remaining for lemonade, and in a little dry curd which I am about to drink diluted with water and with sugar.[2] Heaven bless you! the ink dries at the end of my pen, and the pen itself drops from my hand.

[1] Prickly heat, so familiar to most Anglo-Indians.

[2] See p. 354 text, and footnote [1].

THE EIGHTH LETTER

TO THE SAME

Written at Bember, the entrance to the Mountains of Kachemire, after having encamped near that place for two days.

A description of Bember, we change our carriage there for that adapted to Hill travelling, incredible number of Men-Porters, and the order of March that has to be observed for five days when going through the Mountain Passes.

MONSIEUR,

At length we have reached *Bember*, situated at the foot of a steep, black, and scorched mountain. We are encamped in the dry bed of a considerable torrent, upon pebbles and burning sands,[1]—a very furnace; and if a heavy shower had not fallen opportunely this morning, and I had not received from the mountains a seasonable supply of curdled milk, limes, and a fowl, I know not what would have become of your poor correspondent. But God be praised! the atmosphere is evidently cooler, my appetite is restored, my strength improved; and the first use I make of returning health is to resume my pen. You must

[1] In the higher part of the town of Bhimbar are the remains of the Sarai, a building about 300 feet square, where the Emperor and his personal staff used to camp. Down in the plain, close to where the present travellers' bungalow stands, was the camping ground in the sands and boulders of the Bhimbar river which there enters the plains, where the rest of the camp was pitched, as graphically described by Bernier.

now be made acquainted with new marches and fresh troubles.

Yesterday, at night, the King left these suffocating quarters. He was accompanied by *Rauchenara-Begum* and the other women of the Seraglio, the Raja *Ragnat,*[1] who acts as *Vizier,* and *Fazel-kan,* the High Steward: and last night the grand master of the hunt also left the camp, with some principal officers of the royal household, and several ladies of distinction. To-night it will be our turn to depart: besides my Navaab *Danechmend-kan's* family, the party will consist of *Mahmet-Emir-kan,* son of the celebrated *Emir Jemla,* of whom I have already spoken so much; of my excellent friend *Dianet-kan* and his two sons, and of several other *Omrahs, Rajas,* and *Mansebdars.* The other *Nobles* who are to visit *Kachemire* will depart each in his turn, to lessen the inconvenience and confusion that must attend the five days' journey between this place and *Kachemire,* through difficult and mountainous paths. The remainder of the court, such as *Feday-kan,*[2] the Grand Master of the Artillery, three or four principal *Rajas,* and a large number of *Omrahs,* will continue stationed as guards, in this town and neighbourhood, during three or four months, until the great heat be over, when the King will return. Some will pitch their tents on the banks of the *Tchenau,*[3] others will repair to the adjacent towns and villages, and the rest will be under the necessity of encamping in this burning *Bember.*

That a scarcity of provisions may not be produced in the small kingdom of *Kachemire,* the King will be followed by a very limited number of individuals. Of females he takes only ladies of the first rank, the intimate friends of *Rauchenara-Begum,* and those women whose services cannot easily be dispensed with. The *Omrahs* and military will also be as few as possible; and those *Lords* who have per-

[1] Rájá Raghunath. [2] See p. 124, footnote [1].

[3] Probably close to Gujrát, about 30 miles from Bhimbar to the south-east.

mission to attend the Monarch will be accompanied by no more than twenty-five troopers out of every hundred; not, however, to the exclusion of the immediate officers of their household. These regulations cannot be evaded, an *Omrah* being stationed at the pass of the mountains, who reckons every person one by one, and effectually prevents the ingress of that multitude of *Mansebdars* and other cavaliers who are eager to inhale the pure and refreshing air of *Kachemire,* as well as of all those petty tradesmen and inmates of the *bazars,* whose only object is to gain a livelihood.

The King has a few of the choicest elephants for his baggage and the women of the *Seraglio.* Though heavy and unwieldy, these animals are yet very sure-footed, feeling their way when the road is difficult and dangerous, and assuring themselves of the firm hold of one foot before they move another. The King has also a few mules; but his camels, which would be more useful, are all left behind, the mountains being too steep and craggy for their long stiff legs. Porters supply the place of camels; and you may judge of the immense number that will be employed if what they tell me be true, that the King alone has no fewer than six thousand. I must myself have three, although I left my large tent and a considerable quantity of luggage at *Lahor*: every person did the same, not excepting the *Omrahs* and the King himself; and yet it is calculated that there are at least fifteen thousand porters already collected in *Bember*; some sent by the Governor of *Kachemire* and by the neighbouring *Rajas,* and others who are come voluntarily in the expectation of earning a little money. A royal ordinance fixes their pay at ten crowns for every hundred pounds weight. It is computed that thirty thousand will be employed; an enormous number, when it is considered that the King and *Omrahs* have been sending forward baggage, and the tradespeople articles of every sort, for the last month.

THE NINTH LETTER

TO THE SAME

Written in Kachemire, the Terrestrial Paradise of the Indies, after a residence there of three months.

An accurate description of the Kingdom of Kachemire, the present state of the surrounding Mountains, and replies to five important questions put by a Friend.

MONSIEUR,

THE histories of the ancient Kings of *Kachemire* maintain that the whole of this country was in former times one vast lake, and that an outlet for the waters was opened by a certain pire, or aged saint, named *Kacheb*,[1] who miraculously cut the mountain of *Baramoulé*. This account is to be met with in the abridgment of the above-mentioned histories,[2]

[1] *Kacheb* or *Kashuf* is the Persian form for Kasyupa, son of Marichi, son of Brahma, the Rishi or sage by whom, according to Hindoo tradition, the passage in question was formed.

[2] By Haidar Malik, son of Hasan Malik B. Malik Muhammad Naji, Charvarah (also written *Chadvaṛaḥ*, a village near Srinagar) who was of a noble Kashmír family. The work in question, a history

made by order of *Jehan-Guyre,* which I am now translating from the *Persian.* I am certainly not disposed to deny that this region was once covered with water: the same thing is reported of *Thessaly* and of other countries; but I cannot easily persuade myself that the opening in question was the work of man, for the mountain is very extensive and very lofty. I rather imagine that the mountain sank into some subterraneous cavern, which was disclosed by a

Kashmír from the earliest times till its conquest by Akbar, is mainly abridged, as stated by its author, from the *Rajátarangini* ('The Ocean of Kings') of Kalhana, the Royal Chronicle of Kashmír; but the Hijra dates are substituted for those of the Hindoo era, and some additions have been made to it in the late period. The author in the preface says that he commenced the work in A.H. 1027=1617 A.D., in the twelfth year of Jáhángír's reign, but further on A.H. 1029=1619 A.D. is mentioned as the current year; and in a very complete MS. of this work in the British Museum (Addl. 16705) that came from the collection of William Yule, the father of the late Sir Henry Yule, an event of A.H. 1030=1620 A.D. is recorded. A portion of the *Rajátarangini*, which is the only piece of history in Sanskrit which has come down to us, and is believed to have been written in the 12th century A.D., was translated into Persian by command of the Sultan Zín-ul-'ábidín of Kashmír, who named this version the *Bahr-ul-asmár*, or 'The Sea of Tales.' In A.H. 1003=1594 A.D., the historian Abd-ul-Kadir, Al-Badáoní was ordered by the Emperor Akbar to complete the translation, and he tells us how, during the progress of this work, the Emperor 'called me into his private bed-chamber to the foot of the bed, and till the morning asked for stories out of each chapter, and then said: "Since the first volume of the *Bahr-ul-asmár* . . is in Archaic Persian, and difficult to understand, do you translate it afresh into ordinary language, and take care of the rough copy of the book which you have translated." I performed the *zamínbós* [kissing the ground] and heartily undertook the commission.' Pp. 415, 416 *Muntakhab-ut-tawarikh.* Bibl. Indica Ed.: translated by W. H. Lowe, M.A. Calcutta, 1889.

All Orientalists must rejoice to know that at last there is every prospect of their possessing a satisfactory edition of the *Rajátarangini*, as Dr. Aurel Stein, Principal of the Oriental College at Lahore, has lately been able to secure the *Codex Archetypus* of all extant Kashmír MSS. of that work, written in the 17th century. In the Address to the Reader prefixed to the first edition of his *Travels*, Bernier promised to undertake a translation of the Persian text of Haidar Malik.

violent earthquake, not uncommon in these countries.[1] If we are to believe the Arabs of those parts, the opening of *Bab-el-mandel* was effected in the same manner; and it is thus that entire towns and mountains have been engulphed in great lakes.

Kachemire, however, is no longer a lake, but a beautiful country, diversified with a great many low hills: about thirty leagues in length, and from ten to twelve in breadth. It is situated at the extremity of *Hindoustan,* to the north of *Lahor*; enclosed by the mountains at the foot of *Caucasus,*[2] those of the Kings of *Great Tibet* and *Little Tibet,*[3] and of the *Raja Gamon,*[4] who are its most immediate neighbours.

[1] Bernier's theory has a great deal in its favour. There are authentic records of several severe and destructive earthquakes in 1552, in 1680, and one on the 26th June 1828, on which occasion, according to Vigne, who visited Kashmír in 1835, 1200 houses were shaken down and 1000 persons killed. The worst earthquake of all was that of the 30th May 1885. The shock was felt over an area of about 130,000 square miles, and its effects were destructive, to a considerable degree, over an area of about 500 square miles. It has been estimated that 20,000 houses, 30,000 cattle, and 3000 human beings were destroyed. *The focus of destruction was near* Báramúla, where the Fort, the travellers' bungalow, and three-fourths of the houses in the town were totally wrecked.

[2] The name used by many of the ancient geographers for a supposed continuous range from West to East, through the whole of Asia, embracing the Taurus Mountains of Asia Minor, the Persian Elburz, the Hindú Kush, and the Himalayas.

[3] Great Tibet was the name then generally applied to what is now known as Ladakh, Little Tibet—a term still applied to Baltistan.

[4] Rájá of Jummoo, the Rajput Rájás whose seat of rule has been established in or near the existing town of Jummoo from a remote period, Hindoo historians say for 5000 years. It was the Mahárájá Gulab Singh of Jummoo who in 1846 was able to effect the consolidation of various states, including Kashmír, into one Kingdom, over which his descendants still rule. *Raja Gamon* has been identified by Drew (*The Jummoo and Kashmir Territories.* Lond. 1875) as the Astor Rájá, but it is difficult to concur in this identification, which, however, Mr. Drew does not put forward as an absolute fact. It is most likely that by a typographical error *Gamon* has been printed instead of *Gamou* in the various editions of Bernier's *Travels.*

The first mountains which surround it, I mean those nearest to the plains, are of moderate height, of the freshest verdure, decked with trees and covered with pasture land, on which cows, sheeps, goats, horses, and every kind of cattle is seen to graze. Game of various species is in great plenty,—partridges, hares, antelopes, and those animals which yield musk. Bees are also in vast abundance; and what may be considered very extraordinary in the *Indies,* there are, with few or no exceptions, neither serpents, tigers, bears, nor lions. These mountains may indeed be characterised not only as innocuous, but as flowing in rich exuberance with milk and honey.[1]

Beyond the mountains just described arise others of very considerable altitude, whose summits, at all times covered with snow, soar above the clouds and ordinary mist, and, like *Mount Olympus,* are constantly bright and serene.

From the sides of all these mountains gush forth innumerable springs and streams of water, which are conducted by means of embanked earthen channels even to the top of the numerous hillocks[2] in the valley; thereby enabling the inhabitants to irrigate their fields of rice. These waters, after separating into a thousand rivulets and producing a thousand cascades through this charming country, at length collect and form a beautiful river,[3] navigable for vessels as large as are borne on our *Seine.* It winds gently around the kingdom, and passing through the capital, bends its peaceful course toward *Baramoulé,* where it finds an outlet between two steep rocks, being then joined by several smaller rivers from the mountains, and dashing over pre-

[1] Bears are not at all uncommon in Kashmír at the present day, two varieties of the brown or red species and a black bear. Bees are still kept by most cottagers in circular holes in the walls of their huts, especially by those living in the eastern portion of the valley. Milk is 'a drug in the market,' and is excellent in quality.

[2] These table-lands, called *karewas*, are a great feature in the landscape. See p. 412, footnote.

[3] The Jhelum.

cipices it flows in the direction of Atek,[1] and joins the *Indus*.

The numberless streams which issue from the mountains maintain the valley and the hillocks in the most delightful verdure. The whole kingdom wears the appearance of a fertile and highly cultivated garden. Villages and hamlets are frequently seen through the luxuriant foliage. Meadows and vineyards, fields of rice, wheat, hemp, saffron, and many sorts of vegetables, among which are intermingled trenches filled with water, rivulets, canals, and several small lakes, vary the enchanting scene. The whole ground is enamelled with our European flowers and plants, and covered with our *apple, pear, plum, apricot,* and *walnut trees,* all bearing fruit in great abundance. The private gardens are full of *melons, pateques* or *water melons, water parsnips, red beet, radishes,* most of our potherbs, and others with which we are unacquainted.

The fruit is certainly inferior to our own, nor is it in such variety; but this I am satisfied is not attributable to the soil, but merely to the comparative ignorance of the gardeners, for they do not understand the culture and the grafting of trees as we do in *France*. I have eaten, however, a great deal of very excellent fruit during my residence in *Kachemire,* and should entertain no doubt of its arriving at the same degree of perfection as that of *Europe* if the people were more attentive to the planting and soil of the trees and introduced grafts from foreign countries.

The capital of *Kachemire* bears the same name as the kingdom.[2] It is without walls and is not less than three

[1] *Attock*. Bernier was probably misled. The Jhelum, which leaves the valley of Kashmír at Báramúla, falls into the *Chínáb* near Jhung, about 100 miles above Mooltan; the general direction is quite correct.

[2] Srínagar (or *Surjyanagar*, 'the city of the sun') is the ancient and the present name of the city. During the rule of the Muhammadans this Hindoo name was disused, but when the Sikhs conquered Kashmír in 1819 they restored the old Hindoo name, although some Muhammadans still talk of the capital as *Kashmír*, or *Kashur* in the Kashmírí language.

quarters of a league in length, and half a league in breadth. It is situated in a plain, distant about two leagues from the mountains, which seem to describe a semicircle, and is built on the banks of a fresh-water lake,[1] whose circumference is from four to five leagues. This lake is formed of live springs and of streams descending from the mountains, and communicates with the river, which runs through the town, by means of a canal sufficiently large to admit boats. In the town there are two wooden bridges thrown over the river;[2] and the houses, although for the most part of wood, are well built and consist of two or three stories. There is, however, plenty of very fine freestone in the country; some old buildings, and a great number of ancient idol-temples in ruins, are of stone; but wood is preferred on account of its cheapness, and the facility with which it is brought from the mountains by means of so many small rivers. Most of the houses along the banks of the river have little gardens, which produce a very pretty effect, especially in the spring and summer, when many parties of pleasure take place on the water. Indeed most houses in the city have also their gardens; and many have a canal, on which the owner keeps a pleasure-boat, thus communicating with the lake.

At one end of the town appears an isolated hill, with handsome houses on its declivity, each having a garden. Toward the summit are a *Mosque* and *Hermitage*, both good buildings; and the hill is crowned with a large quantity of fine trees. It forms altogether an agreeable object, and from its trees and gardens it is called, in the language of the country, *Haryperbet*[3] or the Verdant Mountain.

Opposite to this hill is seen another, on which is also

[1] The Dal lake.

[2] There are now (1891) seven bridges across the Jhelum in the city of Srínagar.

[3] Harí Parbat, on the top of which there is the fort built by the Emperor Akbar.

erected a small *Mosque* with a garden and an extremely ancient building, which bears evident marks of having been a temple for idols, although named *Tact-Souliman*,[1] the Throne of Solomon. The *Mahometans* pretend it was raised by that celebrated King when he visited *Kachemire*; but I doubt whether they could prove that this country was ever honoured with his presence.

The lake is full of islands, which are so many pleasure-grounds. They look beautiful and green in the midst of the water, being covered with fruit trees, and laid out with regular trellised walks. In general they are surrounded by the large-leafed aspen, planted at intervals of two feet. The largest of these trees may be clasped in a man's arms, but they are as high as the mast of a ship, and have only a tuft of branches at the top, like the palm-trees.

The declivities of the mountains beyond the lake are crowded with houses and flower-gardens. The air is healthful, and the situation considered most desirable: they abound with springs and streams of water, and command a delightful view of the lake, the islands, and the town.

The most beautiful of all these gardens is one belonging to the King, called *Chah-limar*.[2] The entrance from the lake is through a spacious canal, bordered with green turf, and running between two rows of poplars.[3] Its length is about five hundred paces, and it leads to a large summer-house placed in the middle of the garden. A second

[1] The Takht-i Suliman hill, on the top of which is a Buddhist temple, built by Jaloka, the son of Asoka, who reigned about 220 B.C. Part of it was turned into a mosque at the time of the first invasion of Kashmír by the Muhammadans, about 1015 A.D.

[2] The Shálamár (*Shála*, house or abode, and *már*, the name of the Hindoo goddess of love) gardens still retain many of the features described by Bernier. It was the Trianon of the Mogul Emperors.

[3] The remains of this entrance can still be traced in the shape of large blocks of masonry, as well as the stone embankment which formerly lined the canal throughout.

canal, still finer than the first, then conducts you to another summer-house, at the end of the garden. This canal is paved with large blocks of freestone, and its sloping sides are covered with the same. In the middle is a long row of fountains, fifteen paces asunder; besides which there are here and there large circular basins, or reservoirs, out of which arise other fountains, formed into a variety of shapes and figures.[1]

The summer-houses are placed in the midst of the canal, consequently surrounded by water, and between the two rows of large poplars planted on either side. They are built in the form of a dome, and encircled by a gallery, into which four doors open; two looking up, or down, the canal, and two leading to bridges that connect the buildings with both banks. The houses consist of a large room in the centre, and of four smaller apartments, one at each corner. The whole of the interior is painted and gilt, and on the walls of all the chambers are inscribed certain sentences, written in large and beautiful *Persian* characters.[2] The four doors are extremely valuable; being composed of large stones, and supported by two beautiful pillars. The doors and pillars were found in some of the idol temples demolished by *Chah-Jehan,* and it is impossible to estimate their value. I cannot describe the nature of the stone, but it is far superior to porphyry, or any species of marble.[3]

You have no doubt discovered before this time that I am charmed with *Kachemire.* In truth, the kingdom surpasses in beauty all that my warm imagination had anticipated. It is probably unequalled by any country of the same extent, and should be, as in former ages, the seat of sovereign authority, extending its dominion over all the

[1] The water for these fountains is obtained from a stream which rises in the hills behind the garden, and now on fête days the fountains are made to play, having been restored some years ago.

[2] Among others, the celebrated legend, 'If there be an Elysium on earth, it is this, it is this.'

[3] The material forming the pillars is believed to be a black and grey fossiliferous marble; the stone doors no longer exist.

circumjacent mountains, even as far as *Tartary* and over the whole of *Hindoustan*, to the island of *Ceylon*.[1] It is not indeed without reason that the *Mogols* call *Kachemire* the terrestrial paradise of the *Indies*, or that *Ekbar* was so unremitting in his efforts to wrest the sceptre from the hand of its native Princes. His son *Jehan-Guyre* became so enamoured of this little kingdom as to make it the place of his favourite abode, and he often declared that he would rather be deprived of every other province of his mighty empire than lose *Kachemire*.[2]

I was quite prepared to witness the emulous contest between the *Kachemiry* and the *Mogol* poets. We were no sooner arrived than *Aureng-Zebe* received from the bards of both nations poems in praise of this favoured land, which he accepted and rewarded with kindness. They were written in a strain of extravagant hyperbole. One of them, I remember, speaking of the surrounding mountains, observed that their extraordinary height had caused the skies to retire into the vaulted form which we see; that Nature had exhausted all her skill in the creation of this country, and rendered it inaccessible to the attack of hostile force; because, being the mistress of the kingdoms of the earth, it was wise to preserve her in perfect peace and security, that she might exercise universal dominion without the possibility of ever being subject to any. The poet went on to say that the summits of the higher and more distant mountains were clothed resplendently in white, and the minor and more contiguous preserved in perpetual verdure and embellished with stately trees, because it was meet that the mistress of the kingdoms of the earth should be crowned with a diadem whose top and

[1] Surely this may be considered as a very early argument in favour of locating the Supreme Government of India in the Hills.

[2] Jáhángír died on the 28th October 1627, at Changas Sarai (Chingiz Hatlí), the *Tinguesq hatelij* of Blaeu's map of *The Empire of the Great Mogul*, 1655, between Rájáorí and Naushahra, three marches from Bhimbar, when returning to Lahore.

rays were diamonds issuing from a base-work of emeralds. 'The poet' (I remarked to my Navaab *Danechmend-kan,* who wished me to relish these productions) 'might easily have amplified his subject. He could, with a pardonable licence, have included the neighbouring mountainous regions within the kingdom of *Kachemire,* since it is pretended that they were once tributary to it. I mean *Little Tibet,* the states of *Raja Gamon, Kachguer,* and *Serenaguer.*[1] He might then have gone on to say that the *Ganges,* the *Indus,* the *Chenau,* and the *Gemna,* issue from the kingdom of *Kachemire,* rivers which cannot yield in beauty and importance to the *Pison,* the *Gihon* or the two other rivers spoken of in *Genesis*; and that it may therefore be reasonably concluded that the Garden of *Eden* was planted in *Kachemire,* and not, according to the received opinion, in *Armenia.*'

The *Kachemirys* are celebrated for wit, and considered much more intelligent and ingenious than the *Indians.* In poetry and the sciences they are not inferior to the *Persians.* They are also very active and industrious. The workmanship and beauty of their *palekys,* bedsteads, trunks, inkstands, boxes, spoons, and various other things are quite remarkable, and articles of their manufacture are in use in every part of the *Indies.* They perfectly understand the art of varnishing, and are eminently skilful in closely imitating the beautiful veins of a certain wood, by inlaying with gold threads so delicately wrought that I never saw anything more elegant or perfect. But what may be considered peculiar to *Kachemire,* and the staple commodity, that which particularly promotes the trade of the country and fills it with wealth, is the prodigious quantity of shawls which they manufacture, and which gives occupation even to the little children. These shawls are

[1] By this Bernier means the Srínagar in British Garhwal, then known as part of Sirmúr (Sirmoor); not far from which place are the sources of the Ganges and the Jumna, Gangotri and Jamnotri. See p. 59.

about an ell and a half long, and an ell broad, ornamented at both ends with a sort of embroidery, made in the loom, a foot in width. The *Mogols* and *Indians*, women as well as men, wear them in winter round their heads, passing them over the left shoulder as a mantle. There are two sorts manufactured: one kind with the wool of the country, finer and more delicate than that of *Spain*; the other kind with the wool, or rather hair (called *touz* [1]) found on the breast of a species of wild goat which inhabits *Great Tibet*. The *touz* shawls are much more esteemed than those made with the native wool. I have seen some, made purposely for the *Omrahs*, which cost one hundred and fifty *roupies*; but I cannot learn that the others have ever sold for more than fifty. They are very apt, however, to be worm-eaten, unless frequently unfolded and aired. The fur of the beaver is not so soft and fine as the hair from these goats.

Great pains have been taken to manufacture similar shawls in *Patna*, *Agra*, and *Lahor*; but notwithstanding every possible care, they never have the delicate texture and softness of the *Kachemire* shawls, whose unrivalled excellence may be owing to certain properties in the water of that country.[2] The superior colours of the *Maslipatam chittes* or cloths, painted by the hand [peintes au pince

[1] *Tús*, the 'shawl goat.' By Article X. of the Treaty of the 16th March 1846, by which the British Government made over for ever, as an independent possession, the Kashmír territory to the Mahárájá Golab Singh of Jummoo, he bound himself and his heirs for ever to acknowledge the supremacy of the British Government, and in token of such supremacy to present annually to the British Government, 'one horse, twelve perfect shawl goats of approved breed (six males and six females), and three pair of Cashmere shawls.'

[2] The Moguls were very anxious to introduce shawl-weaving into Hindostan, while not neglecting to encourage the indigenous industry in Kashmír. The *Ain* contains some very valuable information on the subject of shawls, from which the following is an extract:—

'His Majesty improved this department [*i.e.* of the Shawls, Stuffs, etc.] in *four* ways. The improvement is visible, *first*, in the *Tús* shawls, which are made of the wool of an animal of that name; its

au], whose freshness seems to improve by washing, are also ascribed to the water peculiar to that town.

The people of *Kachemire* are proverbial for their clear complexions and fine forms. They are as well made as Europeans, and their faces have neither the *Tartar* flat nose nor the small pig-eyes that distinguish the natives of *Kacheguer,* and which generally mark those of *Great Tibet.* The women especially are very handsome; and it is from this country that nearly every individual, when first admitted to the court of the *Great Mogol,* selects wives or concubines, that his children may be whiter than the *Indians* and pass for genuine *Mogols.*[1] Unquestionably there must be beautiful women among the higher classes, if we may judge by those of the lower orders seen in the streets and in the shops. When at *Lahor* I had recourse to a little artifice, often practised by the *Mogols* to obtain a sight of these hidden treasures; the women of that town being the finest brunettes in all the *Indies,* and justly renowned for their fine and slender shapes. I followed the steps of some elephants, particularly one richly harnessed,

natural colours are black, white, and red [brown], but chiefly black. Sometimes the colour is a pure white. This kind of shawl is unrivalled for its lightness, warmth, and softness. People generally wear it without altering its natural colour; His Majesty has had it dyed. It is curious that it will not take a red dye.' [The second improvement was in the quality of the Alchahs (see p. 120), and the third in the gold and silver embroidered stuffs.] '*Fourthly*, an improvement was made in the width of all stuffs; His Majesty had the pieces made large enough to yield the making of a full dress.'

'. . . In former times shawls were often brought from Kashmír. People folded them in four folds, and wore them for a very long time. Now-a-days they are generally worn without folds, and merely thrown over the shoulder. His Majesty has commenced to wear them double, which looks very well. His Majesty encourages in every possible way the manufacture of shawls in Kashmír. In Láhór also there are more than a thousand workshops.'

[1] See pp. 3 and 212. Marco Polo bore testimony to the good looks of the *Kashmíris*, and said of the inhabitants of the country, 'The men are brown and lean, but the women, taking them as brunettes, are very beautiful.'

and was sure to be gratified with the sight I was in search of, because the ladies no sooner hear the tinkling of the silver bells suspended from both sides of the elephant than they all put their heads to the windows. This is a stratagem with which I often amused myself in *Kachemire*, until a more satisfactory method of seeing the fair sex was devised by an old pedagogue, well known in the town, with whom I read the *Persian* poets. I purchased a large quantity of sweetmeats, and accompanied him to more than fifteen houses, to which he had freedom of access. He pretended I was his kinsman lately arrived from *Persia*, rich and eager to marry. As soon as we entered a house, he distributed my sweetmeats among the children, and then everybody was sure to flock around us, the married women and the single girls, young and old, with the two-fold object of being seen and receiving a share of the present. The indulgence of my curiosity drew many *roupies* out of my purse; but it left no doubt on my mind that there are as handsome faces in *Kachemire* as in any part of *Europe*.

It remains only to speak of my journey through the mountains, from *Bember* to this place, with which I ought perhaps to have commenced my letter;—of the little excursions I have made in the country, and finally of all which it has been in my power to collect concerning the other mountainous tracts that encircle this kingdom.

In respect then to the route from *Bember* I was surprised to find myself on the very first night transported on a sudden from a torrid to a temperate zone: for we had no sooner scaled that frightful wall of the world, I mean the lofty, steep, black, and bare mountain of *Bember*, and begun the descent on the other side, than we breathed a pure, mild, and refreshing air. What surprised me still more was to find myself, as it were, transferred from the *Indies* to *Europe*; the mountains we were traversing being covered with every one of our plants and shrubs, save the hyssop, thyme, marjoram, and rosemary. I almost imagined myself in the mountains of *Auvergne*, in a forest of fir, oak, elm, and plane trees, and could not avoid feeling strongly the contrast between this scene and the burning fields of *Hindoustan*, which I had just quitted and where nothing of the kind is seen.

My attention was particularly arrested by a mountain, distant between one and two days from *Bember*, covered on both sides with plants.[1] The side facing the south, that is, looking toward *Hindoustan*, is full of *Indian* and *European* plants, mingled together; but the side exposed to the north is crowded exclusively with the vegetable productions of *Europe*. It would seem that one side participates equally of the air and temperature of *India* and *Europe*, and that the other feels only the milder climate of the latter quarter of the globe.[2]

I could not avoid admiring, in the course of our march, the successive generation and decay of trees. I saw hundreds plunged and plunging into abysses, down which man never ventured, piled dead one upon another and mouldering with time; while others were shooting out of the ground, and supplying the places of those that were no more. I observed also trees consumed by fire; but I am unable to say whether they were struck by lightning, or ignited by friction, when hot and impetuous winds agitate the trees against each other, or whether, as the natives pretend, trees when grown old and dry may ignite spontaneously.

The magnificent cascades between the rocks increase the beauty of the scene. There is one especially which I conceive has not its parallel. I observed it at a distance

[1] Bernier here refers to the Ratan Mountains, which may be looked upon as the first 'real mountains' met with on the Pír Panjàl route. The Ratan Pír Pass, 8200 feet above sea-level, lies between Thanna Mandi and Baramgalla, the fifth and sixth stages from Bhimbar.

[2] On ascending the Pass, the heat of the sun, which is still felt there, is delightfully tempered by the bracing air, while on the Baramgalla side of the mountain the temperature of the air will be found to be very much colder than anything the traveller has yet experienced on his march from the plains.

from the side of a high mountain. A torrent of water rolling impetuously through a long and gloomy channel, covered with trees, precipitates itself suddenly down a perpendicular rock of prodigious height, and the ear is stunned with the noise occasioned by the falling of these mighty waters. *Jehan-Guyre* erected on an adjacent rock, which was smoothed for the purpose, a large building from which the court might leisurely contemplate this stupendous work of Nature, which, as well as the trees before mentioned, bears marks of the highest antiquity, and is perhaps coeval with the creation of the world.[1]

A strange accident cast a gloom over these scenes and damped all our pleasure. The King was ascending the *Pire-penjale* mountains,[2] the highest of all the mountains, and from which a distant view of the kingdom of *Kachemire* is first obtained. He was followed by a long line of elephants, upon which sat the ladies in their *mikdembers* and *embarys.* The foremost, appalled, as is supposed, by the great length and acclivity of the path before him, stepped back upon the elephant that was moving on his track, who again pushed against the third elephant, the third against the fourth, and so on until fifteen of them, incapable of turning round or extricating themselves in a road so steep and narrow fell down the precipice. Happily for the women, the place where they fell was of no great height; only three or four were killed; but there were no means

[1] This is the well-known *Nur-i-chasm* (spring or stream of light) waterfall, which can be conveniently visited from Baramgalla. A recent description of this noble fall, formed by a huge cleft in a mass of rock, bears out Bernier's description very vividly. 'The upper course of the icy torrent which feeds this fall runs through a most lovely dell, down which the stream bounds from rock to rock, roaring and splashing along as if rejoicing at the prospect of the mighty leap before it, of nearly 70 feet.'

[2] The Pír Panjàl Pass is 11,400 feet above sea-level, some of the neighbouring peaks are upwards of 16,000 feet high. It is said that on clear days the minarets of Lahore, 130 miles distant as the crow flies, can be seen from the top of the Pír Panjàl Pass.

of saving any of the elephants. Whenever these animals fall under the tremendous burden usually placed upon their backs, they never rise again even on a good road. Two days afterward we passed that way,[1] and I observed that some of the poor elephants still moved their trunks. The army, which had been marching four days in single file through the mountains, was subjected to serious inconvenience by this disaster. The remainder of the day and the following night, were employed in rescuing the women and in saving other matters, and the troops were under the necessity of halting during the whole of that time. Nearly every man continued pent up in the same spot, for it was impossible, in many places, to advance or recede, and the thieving varlets of porters with the tents and provisions were not within reach. My usual good fortune, however, attended me; I contrived to clamber out of the line of march and find a spot whereon I and my horse slept pretty comfortably. The servant who followed me had a small quantity of bread, which we shared. It was here, I recollect, that in stirring some stones, we found a large black scorpion, which a young *Mogol* of my acquaintance took up and squeezed in his hand, then in the hand of my servant, and lastly in mine, without any of us being stung. This young cavalier pretended that he had charmed the scorpion, as he had charmed many others, with a passage from the *Koran*; 'but I will not,' added he, 'teach you that passage, because the occult power would then depart from me and rest with you, in the same manner as it left my teacher the moment he imparted the secret.'

While traversing this same mountain of *Pire-penjale*, where the elephants tumbled down, three things recalled my old philosophical speculations. The first was that we ex-

[1] The place where this accident happened is believed to be close to the summit of the Pír Panjàl Pass, about two miles on the Hindostan side, where there are still rather ugly zig-zags in the road. In the map of Kashmír in the 1672 Dutch edition, here reproduced, the site of this accident is very graphically shewn.

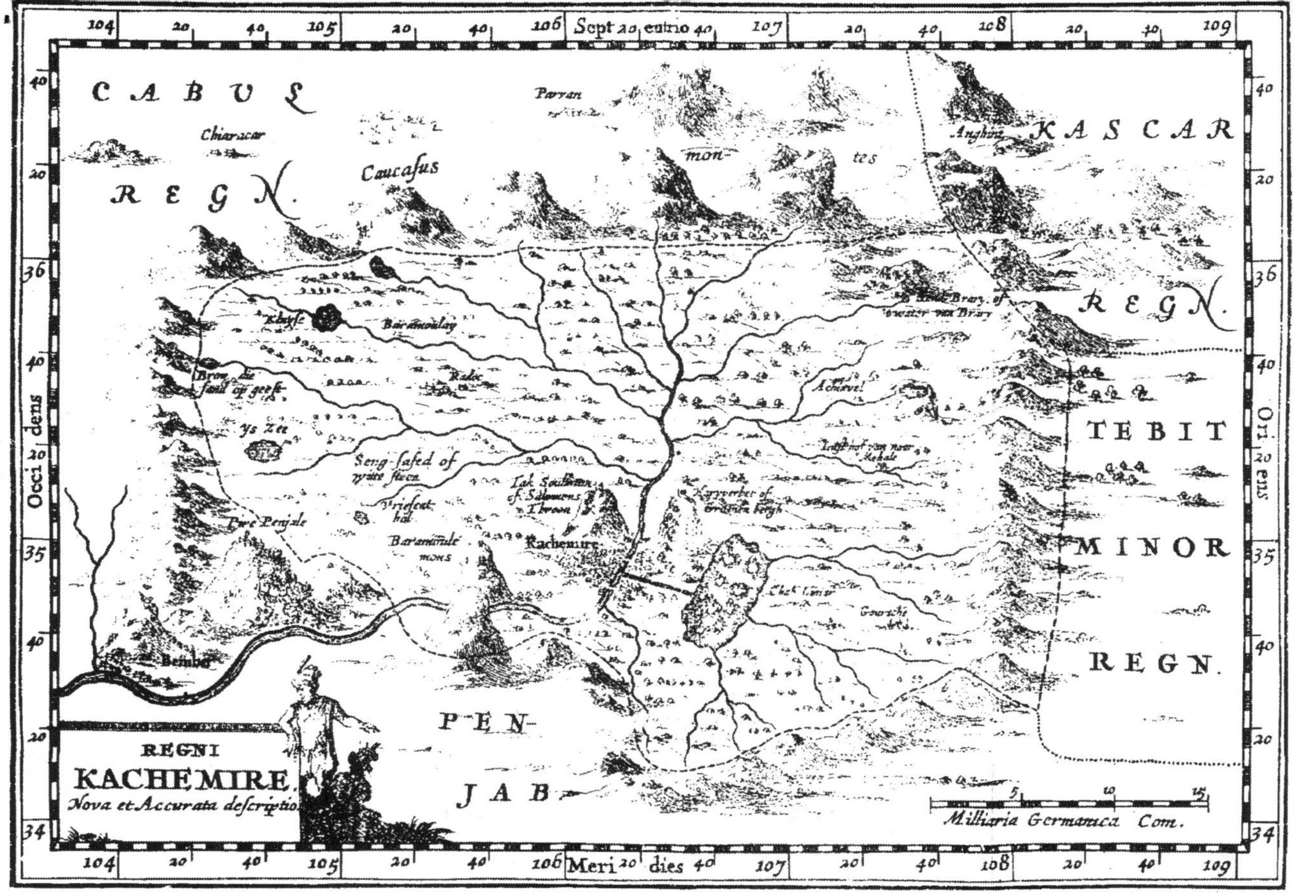
REGNI
KACHEMIRE
Nova et Accurata descriptio
CABUL
REGN.
KASCAR
REGN.
TEBIT
MINOR
REGN.
PEN
JAB
Caucasus
montes
Parran
Chiaracar
Kachemire
Milliaria Germanica Com.
Sept entrio
Meri dies
Occi dens
Ori ens

perienced the opposite seasons of summer and winter within the same hour. In ascending we were exposed to the intense heat of the sun, and perspired most profusely; but when we reached the summit, we found ourselves in the midst of frozen snow, through which a passage for the army had been recently cut; a small and congealed rain was falling, and the wind blew piercingly cold. The poor *Indians,* most of whom had never felt the severity of winter, and saw for the first time ice and snow, were in a state of great suffering and astonishment and fled with precipitation.

The second circumstance was, that within two hundred paces the wind blew from two opposite quarters. While climbing toward the summit it blew in my face, that is, from the north; but I no sooner began to descend on the other side than it blew on my back, that is, from the south; as if the vapours escaping from all sides, and rising to the summit of the mountain, had there condensed, and caused the wind; which, equally attracted by the warm exhausted air below, descended into the two opposite valleys.

The third extraordinary appearance was an aged hermit, who had resided on the top of this mountain ever since the time of *Jehan-Guyre.*[1] Of his religion everybody was ignorant; but it was said that he wrought miracles, caused strange thunders, and raised storms of wind, hail, snow, and rain.[2] His white and uncombed beard was extremely long

[1] This may have been the Fakir who is buried at the top of the Pass, and whose shrine is largely visited at the present day. The Kashmíris sometimes carry up their dead from long distances and bury them close by. At the present day, a Fakir is generally to be found close to an octagonal watch-tower at the top of the Pass, who supplies travellers with milk, water, and other necessaries. The Persian word *Pír* means an old man or saint, and it has always been the common practice for Fakirs or Pírs to establish themselves in such positions for the sake of contemplating the works of the Creator and of receiving the alms of travellers; hence the word Pír in Kashmír has now acquired the secondary meaning of a mountain pass. *Panjàl* being the name of the lofty range close by, the word Pír Panjàl may be translated as the Pass of the Great Range.

[2] Or as Marco Polo relates concerning the people of the kingdom of

and bushy; he had somewhat of the savage in his aspect, and was haughty in his manner of asking alms. He permitted the people to drink water out of some earthen cups placed in rows on a large stone, making signs with his hand that they should not stop, but hastily leave the summit of the mountain. The old man was also very angry with those who made a noise. After I had entered his cave, and softened his countenance by means of half a *roupie,* which I humbly put in his hand, he informed me that noise made there stirred up the most furious tempests imaginable. It was wise in *Aureng-Zêbe,* he added, to be guided by his advice, and to order the army to pass with stillness and expedition. His father, *Chah-Jehan,* always acted with the same prudence; but *Jehan-Guyre* having upon one occasion derided his counsel, and, notwithstanding his earnest remonstrance, having ordered the cymbals to be beaten and the trumpets to be sounded, narrowly escaped destruction.[1]

In regard to my excursions in different parts of this kingdom, I shall begin by informing you that we no sooner arrived in the city of *Kachemire* than my *Navaab, Danechmend-kan,* sent me to the further end of the country, three short journeys from the capital, that I might witness the 'wonders,' as they are called, of a certain fountain.[2]

Kashmír: 'They have an astonishing acquaintance with the devilries of enchantment, inasmuch as they make their idols to speak. They can also by their sorceries bring on changes of weather and produce darkness, and do a number of things so extraordinary that no one without seeing them would believe them.'

[1] At the present day the bands of pilgrims who visit the Holy Shrines, situated in the lofty mountains of Kashmír, refrain from chanting their hymns of praise when in the vicinity of banks of snow, as on several occasions the effect of such reverberations of sound has been to dislodge avalanches, which swept away to destruction many men and women.

[2] This is probably the sacred spring at Bawan or Mattan, about 40 miles to the south-east of Srínagar. The temple, dedicated to Vishnu, and the tank mentioned by Bernier, are still greatly resorted to by the Hindoos. The water from this spring finds its way into the Sandrahan

I was accompanied by a native, and escorted by one of my *Navaab's* troopers. The 'wonders' consist in this: in the month of May, when the melting of the snows has just taken place, this fountain, during the space of fifteen days, regularly flows and ebbs three times a day,—when the morning dawns, at noon, and at night. Its flow generally continues three quarters of an hour, and is sufficiently abundant to fill a square reservoir ten or twelve feet deep, and as many in length and breadth. After a lapse of fifteen days, the supply of water becomes less copious and regular, and at the expiration of a month the spring ceases to run, unless in the time of heavy and incessant rains, when it runs with the ebb and flow of other fountains. The *Gentiles* have a small temple on the side of the reservoir dedicated to *Brare,* one of their deities; and hence this spring is called *Send-brary,* or water of *Brare.* Pilgrims flock from all parts to this temple, for the purpose of bathing and purifying themselves in the sacred and miraculous water. Numberless fables are founded on the origin of this fountain, which, not having a shadow of truth, would be little entertaining in the recital. The five or six days that I remained in the vicinity of *Send-brary* were employed in endeavours to trace the cause of the 'wonder.' I paid considerable attention to the situation of the mountain, at whose foot is found this supernatural spring. With much labour and difficulty I reached the top, leaving no part unexplored, searching and prying at every step. I remarked that its length extends from north to south, and that though very near to other mountains, yet it is completely detached from any. Its form resembles an ass's back; the summit is of extreme length, but the greatest breadth is scarcely one hundred paces. One side of the mountain, which is covered with nothing but green grass, has an eastern aspect; but the sun, being intercepted by the opposite mountains, does not shine upon it before

river (*Send-brary* of Bernier?) which joins the Jhelum close to Islamabad, about 35 miles above Srínagar.

eight o'clock in the morning. The western side is covered with trees and bushes.[1]

Having made these observations, it occurred to me that this pretended wonder might be accounted for by the heat of the sun, combined with the peculiar situation and internal disposition of the mountain.

I supposed that the frozen waters, which during the winter, when the whole ground is covered with snow, had penetrated into the inner parts of that portion of the mountain exposed to the morning sun, became partially melted, that these waters running down, little by little, into certain beds of live rock, and being thence conveyed toward the spring, produced the flow at noon; that the sun quitting this part of the mountain (which then becomes cool) darts its vertical beams upon the summit, melting the congealed waters, which descend also by slow degrees, but through different channels, into the same beds of live rock, and are the cause of the flow at night; and finally, that the sun heating the western side of the mountain, similar effects are occasioned, and the morning flow is the consequence. That this last is slower than the others may be accounted for by the remoteness of the western side from the spring, by its being covered with wood, and therefore more sheltered from the sun, or simply by the coldness of the night. My reasoning may derive support from the fact of the water flowing most copiously during the first days, and that having gradually diminished in quantity it ceases to run altogether: as if the waters which had remained frozen in the earth were

[1] The spring at Bawan is situated under the northern side of the *karewa* (the Kashmíri name for a plateau of alluvial or lacustrine material) of Islamabad, which is a good specimen of the peculiar formation of the flat-topped type. Bernier has described it exactly, and it may be here stated that with reference to Bernier's remark about the irrigation of the karewas, or hillocks as he calls them (see p. 396), that extensive works in the shape of water channels have in recent years been carried out by the Kashmír Darbar (Government), with the object of bringing water from a higher level to the Islamabad karewa, the soil of which till then was arid and difficult of cultivation.

in greater plenty at the commencement than afterwards. It may be observed too, that even at the beginning the supply of water as to the quantity is very uncertain, and that the flow is sometimes greater at noon than at night or in the morning, or in the morning greater than at noon; because, as I conceive, some days are hotter than others, and because clouds, sometimes rendering the heat unequal, thus become the cause of inequality in the flow of water.

Returning from *Send-brary*, I turned a little from the high road for the sake of visiting *Achiavel*,[1] a country house formerly of the Kings of *Kachemire* and now of the *Great Mogol*. What principally constitutes the beauty of this place is a fountain, whose waters disperse themselves into a hundred canals round the house, which is no means unseemly, and throughout the gardens. The spring gushes out of the earth with violence, as if it issued from the bottom of some well, and the water is so abundant that it ought rather to be called a river than a fountain. It is excellent water, and cold as ice. The garden is very handsome, laid out in regular walks, and full of fruit-trees,—apple, pear, plum, apricot, and cherry. Jets-d'eau in various forms and fish-ponds are in great number, and there is a lofty cascade which in its fall takes the form and colour of a large sheet, thirty or forty paces in length, producing the finest effect imaginable; especially at night, when innumerable lamps, fixed in parts of the wall adapted for that purpose, are lighted under this sheet of water.

From *Achiavel* I proceeded to another royal garden,[2]

[1] Achibal, which is about five miles off the high road, was one of the favourite resorts of Núrmahal, and the Imperial gardens with their various fountains and pavilions are still a favourite resort of visitors to Kashmír, and are occasionally used by the Mahárájá, by whom they are maintained in good order.

[2] Vernag ('the powerful snake') about 11 miles from Achibal in a direct line. A very lovely place. The gardens described by Bernier were built by Jáhángír in 1612-1619, and it is said that they were designed and laid out by his wife Núrmahal. The 'pond' containing the sacred fish is now in charge of Brahmin priests, and is the head-water or source of the river Jhelum.

embellished much in the same manner. One of its ponds contains fish so tame that they approach upon being called, or when pieces of bread are thrown into the water. The largest have gold rings, with inscriptions, through the gills, placed there, it is said, by the celebrated *Nour-Mehalle*, the wife of *Jehan-Guyre*, grandfather to *Aureng-Zebe*.

Danechmend-kan seemed well satisfied with the account I brought of *Send-brary*, and wished me to undertake another journey, that I might bear my testimony to what he[1] called a *real miracle* [miracle assuré], such a miracle as would induce me to renounce my religion and become a *Musulman*. 'Hasten to *Baramoulay*,' said he; 'the distance is not greater than to *Send-brary*:[2] there you will see a *Mosque* which contains the tomb of a celebrated *Pire*,[3] or Holy *Derviche*, who though dead yet miraculously cures the sick and infirm. Perhaps you may deny the reality either of the disease or of the cure; but another miracle is wrought by the power of this holy man, which no person can see without acknowledging. There is a large round stone that the strongest man can scarcely raise from the ground, but which eleven men, after a prayer made to the saint, lift up with the tips of their eleven fingers with the same ease as they would move a piece of straw.' I was not sorry for another little excursion, and set out with both my former companions, the trooper and the native of the country. I found *Baramoulay* a rather pleasant place; the *Mosque* is a tolerable building and the *Saint's* tomb is richly adorned.[4] It was surrounded with a great number of people, engaged

[1] The Nawab desired to be able to explain satisfactorily the reason for the intermittent flow at Bawan, and thus refute, like a good Moslem, the fables of the Gentiles. Bernier's report having satisfied him, he appears to have resolved upon showing that however the Gentiles might invent stories the Moslem wonders were all genuine.

[2] The distance from Srínagar to Baramula, which is to the south-west, is about 32 miles by land.

[3] See p. 409, footnote [1].

[4] Or Ziarat (shrine), which is still to be seen, also the 'kitchen' mentioned by Bernier.

in acts of devotion, who said they were ill. Adjoining the *Mosque* is a kitchen, wherein I observed large boilers filled with meat and rice, which I conceived at once to be the magnet that draws the sick, and the miracle that cures them. On the other side of the mosque are the apartments and garden of the *Mullahs*, who pursue the even tenor of their way under the shadow of the *Pire's* miraculous sanctity. They are sufficiently zealous in celebrating his praises, but as I am always unhappy on similar occasions, he performed no miracle upon the sick while I remained there. As to the round and heavy stone that was to convert me, I noticed that eleven *Mullahs* formed themselves into a circle round it, but what with their long *cabayes*,[1] or vests, and the studied compactness of the circle, I had great difficulty to see the mode in which they held the stone. I watched narrowly, however, the whole of this cheating process, and although the *Mullahs* stoutly maintained that each person used only the tip of one finger, and that the stone felt as light as a feather, yet I could clearly discover that it was not raised from the ground without a great effort, and it seemed to me that the *Mullahs* made use of the thumb as well as of the forefinger. Still I mixed my voice with the cries of these impostors and bystanders, exclaiming *Karamet! Karamet!*—a miracle! a miracle! I then presented them with a *roupie*, and assuming a look of the deepest devotion, entreated that I might have for once the distinguished honour of being among the eleven who lifted the stone. The *Mullahs* were reluctant to comply with my request, but having presented them with a second *roupie*, and expressed my belief in the truth of the miracle, one of them gave up his place to me. No doubt they hoped that ten would be able, by an extraordinary effort, to lift the stone, although I contributed no other aid than the tip of my finger, and they expected to manage so adroitly that I should not discover the imposture. But they were much mortified to

[1] The *kabá* was a wadded coat or vest.

find that the stone, to which I persevered in applying the end of my finger only, was constantly inclining and falling towards me. I considered it prudent at last to hold it firmly with both my finger and thumb, when we succeeded, but with great difficulty, in raising it to the usual height. Observing that every person looked at me with an evil eye, not knowing what to think of me, and that I incurred the danger of being stoned, I continued to join in the cry of *Karamet!* and throwing down a third *roupie,* stole away from the crowd. Though I had taken no refreshment since my arrival, I did not hesitate to mount my horse directly, and to quit for ever the *Derviche* and his miracles. I availed myself of this opportunity to visit those celebrated rocks that form the outlet of all the waters of the kingdom, and to which I alluded at the commencement of this letter.

I was induced to quit the high road for the sake of approaching a large lake[1] that I saw at some distance. It is well stocked with fish, particularly eels, and covered with ducks, wild geese, and many other water-birds. The Governor comes hither in the winter, when these birds are in greatest plenty, to enjoy the sport of fowling. In the centre of the lake is an hermitage, with its little garden, which it is pretended floats miraculously upon the water. The hermit passes the whole of his life there; he never leaves the place. I shall not fill up this letter by recounting the thousand absurd tales reported of this hermitage, except it be the tradition that one of the ancient Kings of *Kachemire,* out of mere fancy, built it upon a number of thick beams fastened together.[2] The river which runs toward *Baramoulay* passes through the middle of this lake.

Leaving this lake, I went in search of a spring, con-

[1] The Wular (Woolar) Lake, through which the Jhelum flows.

[2] On the 22d September 1874, the editor of this volume was fortunate enough to discover, near the ruins of a mosque, on the Lanka Island in the Wular Lake, to which Bernier refers, a slab of black slate, on which there was a Persian inscription, a rubbing from which has been translated by Major H. S. Jarrett, B.S.C., as follows:—

sidered an object of curiosity.[1] It bubbles gently and rises with some force, bringing with it a certain quantity of very fine sand, which returns the way it came; after which the water becomes still a moment or two without ebullition and without bringing up sand, and then bubbles as before,

May this edifice be as firm as the foundations of the heavens,
May it be the most renowned ornament of the universe,
As long as the Monarch Zayn Ibád holds festival therein
May it be like the date of his own reign,—'happy.'

The numerical value of the letters in *khurram* (happy) is 847, which is the year of the Hijra it is intended to record, equivalent to A.D. 1443, 1444, during which Zayn-úl-Aábidín (the Zayn Ibád of the inscription, for both have the same meaning, viz., *Ornament of the Adorers*) ruled in Kashmír.

According to tradition, in the vicinity of the Wular Lake once stood a city of which the Rájá was Sudrasen. By reason of the enormity of his crimes the waters of the lake rose and drowned him and his subjects. It was said that during the winter months, at low water, the ruins of a submerged idol-temple might be seen rising from the lake. Zayn-úl-Aábidín constructed a spacious barge, which he sank in the lake, and upon which he laid a foundation of bricks and stones till it rose high enough to be level with the water. Upon this he erected a mosque and other buildings, and gave the islet the name of Lanka. The expense of the work was defrayed by the fortunate discovery of two idols of solid gold which had been brought up from the lake by divers. On the completion of Lanka the King ordered a great festival to be held, wherein large sums were distributed among the poor. Verses were written by the poets to commemorate this event, and among these the inscription under notice by Ahmad Allámah, Kashmíri, was engraved upon a stone and placed on the mosque. See pp. 54, 55, *Proc. As. Soc. Bengal* for 1880; also pp. 16-20 *Jour. As. Soc. Bengal*, Part I. 1880, *Notes on an inscription found upon a stone lying near the ruins of a Masjid on Lanka Island, Wular Lake, Kashmír. By Major H. S. Jarrett, B.S.C.*

Al-Badaoni alludes to the Lanka island in his *Muntakhab-ut-Tawarikh* as follows: 'Sultán Zain-ul-'ábidin, whose history has been written succinctly in my abridgment of the history of Kashmír' [see p. 393, footnote [2]] 'had a *jarib* of stones thrown into the water' [of the Lake], 'and built thereon a stone throne so lofty and grand that the like of it has not been seen in all the provinces of India.'—P. 398, Ed. *Bib. Indica As. Soc. Bengal*, 1889.

[1] The Wular Lake is partly fed by internal springs, and there are many noted springs in the neighbourhood.

and with the same effect; thus continuing its motion at irregular intervals. But the wonder, they say, consists in this, that the least noise made, either by speaking or knocking the feet against the ground, agitates the water and causes it to run and bubble in the manner described. I discovered, however, that its movements are influenced neither by speaking nor knocking, and that its action is the same whether you make a noise or are silent. As to the real cause of the water rising in this manner, I have not reflected sufficiently upon the subject to give you a satisfactory solution; unless it be that the sand by returning continues to obstruct the narrow channel of this small and weak spring, until the water thus opposed and closed in makes an effort to raise the sand and open a passage; or it may rather be, that the wind pent in the channel of the spring rises at intervals, as is the case in artificial springs.[1]

When we had sufficiently examined this fountain, we ascended the mountains, for the purpose of seeing an extensive lake,[2] in which there is ice, even in summer, which the winds heap up and disperse, as in a frozen sea. We

[1] It is very pleasant to trace in all Bernier's explanations of natural phenomena the influence of his greater master Gassendi, of whom it has been so well said that 'the clearness of his exposition and the manner in which he, like his great contemporary Bacon, urged the necessity and utility of experimental research were of inestimable service to the cause of science.'

[2] Probably the Gungabal Lake, about 15 miles to the north-east, as the crow flies, from the Wular Lake. A great festival is held here in August attended by pilgrims from all parts of the adjacent country. There are several lakes at Gungabal formed originally by the glaciers of the Haramuk Mountain, 16,903 feet high, and *Sang-i-safaīd*, the White Stone, may have been the Persian name given by the Moguls to these and the many other glaciers close by; or to limestone cliffs which are not far from the Gungabal lake. 'The grotto, full of wonderful congelations,' is probably the Amarnath cave where blocks of ice, stalagmites, formed by the dripping water from the roof, are worshipped, by the many Hindoos who resort here, as images of Shiva. Glaciers surround this place, which is considerably to the south-east of Gungabal.

then passed through a place called *Sengsafed,* that is to say, Whitestone, remarkable for producing in summer every kind of flower, the same as in a well-stored garden;[1] and for a circumstance said to have been observed from time immemorial, that when many persons visit this spot and make much noise and agitate the air, a heavy shower of rain invariably descends. Whether this be generally the case or not, there can be no doubt that a few years ago, when *Sengsafed* was visited by *Chah-Jehan,* the whole party was in danger of perishing in consequence of the violent and extraordinary rains which fell, although he had issued orders that no unnecessary noise should be made. This fact will remind you of the aged hermit's conversation with me on the summit of *Pire-penjale.*[2]

I was pursuing my journey to a grotto full of wonderful congelations, two days' journey from *Sengsafed,* when I received intelligence that my *Navaab* felt very impatient and uneasy on account of my long absence.

I regret that I can give you only imperfect and scanty information concerning the surrounding mountains. The subject has much occupied my thoughts since my arrival in this country; but I can meet with no congenial mind, with no person of observation and research, who possesses much knowledge of the matters about which I wish to be informed. What I have learnt I shall, however, communicate.

The merchants who every year travel from mountain to mountain to collect the fine wool with which shawls are manufactured, all agree in saying that between all the mountains still dependent upon *Kachemire* there are many fine stretches of country. Among these tracts there is one whose annual tribute is paid in leather and wool, and whose women are proverbial for beauty, chastity, and industry. Beyond this tract is another whose valleys are

[1] An oasis, not uncommon in the mountain chains of the West. A well-known example being the 'Jardin' of Mont Blanc.

[2] See p. 410.

delightful and plains fertile, abounding in corn, rice, apples, pears, apricots, excellent melons, and even grapes, with which good wine is made. The tribute of this tract is likewise paid in wool and leather,[1] and it sometimes happens that the inhabitants, trusting to the inaccessible nature of the country, refuse payment; but troops always contrive to penetrate, and reduce the people to submission. I learn also from the merchants, that in the more distant mountains, which have ceased to be tributary to *Kachemire,* there are other beautiful tracts and countries, where the inhabitants are white and well-formed, and remarkable for their attachment to their native land, which they seldom quit. Some of these people have no King, nor even, as far as can be discovered, any religion; though certain tribes abstain from fish, and consider it unclean.

I shall add what was related to me a few days ago by a fine old fellow, who married a descendant of the ancient kings of *Kachemire.* At the period when *Jehan-Guyre* was making a diligent search after all persons connected with the royal family, this old man effected his escape to the mountains last mentioned, accompanied by three domestics, scarcely knowing whither he was going. Wandering from place to place, he found himself at length in the midst of a small but beautiful district, where he was no sooner known than he experienced a cordial reception. The happy man was laden with presents, and in the evening the handsomest girls were presented by their parents, and he was entreated to make his choice from them, that the country might be honoured with his offspring. My friend proceeded to another district in the vicinity and was received with equal kindness and respect: the evening ceremony was different, however, in one particular; as

[1] Probably the goat-skins, tanned and coloured red, *láki,* for which there is still a great demand all over these hills, more particularly in Ladák, and Yarkand, where bright-coloured leathers are largely employed in the manufacture of boots, and for bridles and trappings of horses. See Cunningham's *Ladák.* London, 1854.

the husbands brought their wives,[1] not the fathers their daughters; observing that their neighbours were simpletons in having supplied him with the latter, because the children might not continue in their household, but must follow the footsteps of the daughters' future husbands.

Some few years since there existed great dissensions in the royal family of *Little Tibet*,[2] a country bordering on *Kachemire*. One of the pretenders to the crown having applied secretly to the Governor of this kingdom for assistance, the latter was commanded by *Chah-Jehan* to afford all the succour he might need. The Governor accordingly invaded *Little Tibet*, slew or put to flight the other competitors, and left this prince in undisputed possession of the throne, subject to an annual tribute of crystal, musk, and wool. Thus circumstanced, this petty King has not well been able to avoid paying his personal obeisance to *Aureng-Zebe*, bringing with him some of these articles as presents; but he is come with so wretched a retinue that I should never have taken him for a person of distinguished rank. My *Navaab* invited this personage to dinner, hoping to obtain some information concerning those mountainous regions. He informed us that his kingdom was bounded on the east by *Great Tibet*; that it was thirty or forty leagues in breadth; that he was very poor, notwithstanding the crystal, musk, and wool, which he had in small quantities; and that the opinion generally entertained of his possessing gold mines was quite erroneous.

[1] The system of polyandry, strictly confined to brothers, still prevails in Ladák. 'Each family of brothers has only one wife in common. The most usual number of husbands is two, but three, and even four husbands, are not uncommon. This system prevails, of course, only among the poorer classes, for the rich, as in all Eastern countries, generally have two or three wives, according to their circumstances. Polyandry is the principal check to the increase of population, and however revolting it may be to our feelings, it was a most politic measure for a poor country which does not produce sufficient food for its inhabitants.'—Cunningham's *Ladák*, p. 306. London, 1854.

[2] Or Baltistan, as it is now called.

The country, in certain parts,' he added, 'produces excellent fruit, particularly melons, but the winters are most severe, because of the deep snows.' The inhabitants heretofore were *Gentiles*, but the great majority have become *Mahometan*, as well as himself; of the sect of the *Chias*, which is that of all *Persia*.

He spoke also of the attempt made by *Chah-Jehan*, seventeen or eighteen years ago, to conquer *Great Tibet*, a country frequently invaded by the Kings of *Kachemire*.[1] The army, after a difficult march of sixteen days through the mountains, besieged and took a fortress, which threw the inhabitants into such consternation that the conquest of the kingdom would no doubt have been completed if the army had immediately crossed a certain celebrated and rapid river, and marched boldly to the capital city. The season, however, was advanced, and the governor of *Kachemire*, who commanded the troops, apprehending he might be overtaken by the snow, determined to retreat. He placed a garrison in the fortress just captured, intending to resume the invasion of the country early in the spring; but that garrison most strangely and unexpectedly evacuated the castle, either through fear of the enemy, or from want of provisions, and *Great Tibet* escaped the meditated attack that had been deferred to the next spring. That kingdom being threatened with war by *Aureng-Zebe*, the King despatched an ambassador when informed of the *Mogol's* arrival in *Kachemire*. The embassy was accompanied by various presents, the productions of the country; such as crystal, musk, a piece of jade,[2] and those valuable white tails taken from a species of cow peculiar to *Great Tibet*, which are attached by way of ornament to the ears of elephants.[3] The jade stone presented upon this occasion was of an extraordinary size, and therefore very precious.

[1] In 1638 when Ali Mardan Khan was Governor of Kashmír, *i.e.* about *twenty-seven* years before Bernier visited Kashmír.

[2] Jachen in the original, a corruption of *Yashm*, the Persian name for this mineral, see p. 298.

[3] See p. 251.

Jachen is in great estimation in the court of the *Mogol*: its colour is greenish, with white veins, and it is so hard as to be wrought only with diamond powder. Cups and vases are made of this stone. I have some of most exquisite workmanship, inlaid with strings of gold, and enriched with precious stones. The ambassador's train consisted of three or four *cavaliers*, and ten or twelve tall men, dried-up looking and lean, with very scanty beards like the *Chinese*, and common red caps,[1] such as our seamen wear. The

[1] The Red Cap sect of the Tibet Buddhists, called Dukpa or Shammar, in contradistinction to the Yellow Cap or Gelupka sect, the followers of the great reforming Lama, named Tsong-khapa, born in 1358, died 1419. He forbade clerical marriages, prohibited necromancy, and introduced the custom of frequent conferences among the Lamas. His reforms led to a schism in the Tibetan Church.

Bogle in his narrative of his mission to Tibet in 1774, pp. 179, 180 (edited by Clements R. Markham, C.B., F.R.S. London, 1876), gives an interesting account of an interview he had with a party of Red Caps, in April 1775, when on his return to Bengal: 'A blind man, with a young wife, came into the court and serenaded us. He played on the fiddle underhandwise; she sang; and both, assisted by a young boy, beat time hoppingly with their feet. The object of this compliment I fancy, it is needless to explain. Our musicians gave way to a parcel of mendicant priests. It may be necessary to state that there are two sets of clergy in Tibet, distinguished by, and classed under the names of, Yellow Caps and Red Caps. The Dalai and Teshu Lamas are at the head of the Yellow Caps; the Red Caps have their own Lamas and monasteries. In times of old there were violent disputes between them, in which the Yellow Caps got the victory, as well by the assistance of the Tartars as by their superior sanctity. But as I adhere to the tenets of this sect, and have acquired my knowledge of religion from its votaries, I will not here say much upon the subject lest it should be thought spiteful. I may be allowed, however, just to mention two things, which must convince every unprejudiced person of the wicked lives and false doctrines of the Red Caps. In the first place, many of the clergy marry; and in the next, they persist, in opposition to religion and common sense, in wearing Red Caps. The priests who now visited us were of the last sect. There might be about eight of them. Each held a staff in one hand and a rosary in the other. They formed into a circle, and began to chant their prayers, which, as I understood they were put up for my welfare, I was in no haste to interrupt. At length, to show them that however hostile to their principles I bore them no personal grudge, I dismissed them with a few small pieces of silver.'

remainder of the apparel was worthy of their head-gear. I rather think that four or five of these gentlemen wore swords, but the others followed the ambassador without staves or sticks. He entered into a negotiation with *Aureng-Zebe,* and promised on the part of his master that a *mosque* should be built in the capital, wherein prayers in the *Mahometan* form should be offered; that the coin should bear on one side the impress of *Aureng-Zebe*; and that the *Mogol* should receive an annual tribute. But no person doubts that this treaty will be totally disregarded as soon as *Aureng-Zebe* has quitted *Kachemire,* and that the King of *Great Tibet* will no more fulfil its stipulations than he did those of the treaty concluded between him and *Chah-Jehan.*

There was in the suite of the ambassador a physician, said to be from the kingdom of *Kassa,*[1] and of the *Lamy* or *Lama* tribe; a tribe which is the depositary of the law in *Lassa* as that of the *Brehmens* is in the *Indies,* with this difference, that the *Brehmens* of the *Indies* have no *Calife* or *Pontiff,* which these people have, who is not only recognised as such in the kingdom of *Lassa,* but throughout all *Tartary,* and is honoured and reverenced as a divine personage. The physician had a book of receipts which I could not persuade him to sell; the writing at a distance looked something like ours. We induced him to write down the alphabet, but he did this with so much difficulty, and his writing was so wretchedly bad in comparison with that in his book, that we pronounced him an ignoramus. He was an ardent believer in metempsychosis, and entertained us with wonderful tales. Among others, he mentioned that when his Grand *Lama* was very old and on the point of death, he assembled the council, and declared to them that his soul was going to pass into the body of an infant recently born. The child was nourished with tender care; and when he had attained his sixth or seventh year, a large

[1] Lhasa, the capital of the U province of Tibet.

quantity of household furniture and wearing apparel was placed before him, mixed up with his own, and he had the sagacity to discern which part was his own property, and which was not; a decisive proof, the physician observed, how true is the doctrine of the transmigration of souls. At first I thought the man was speaking in irony, but I soon discovered that he was perfectly serious. One day I went to see him at the ambassador's, taking a *Kachemirian* merchant acquainted with the language of *Tibet* with me as an interpreter, on the pretence that I desired to purchase certain stuffs which he had for sale, a species of felt about a foot wide; but the real object of the visit was to obtain information concerning those imperfectly known regions. But I learnt little or nothing new: he only said generally that *Great Tibet* would bear no comparison with his own country; that the latter was covered with snow more than five months in the year, and that it was frequently engaged in war with the *Tartars*; but which *Tartars* these were he could not say. At length I found that the time passed with this man was misspent, for he was incapable of answering any one of the numerous questions I intended to ask.

The following which I now relate is such a well-established fact that no one here doubts it, namely that it is not twenty years since caravans went annually from *Kachemire* to *Katay*.[1] They used to traverse the mountains of *Great Tibet*, enter *Tartary*, and reach *Katay* in about three months. It is an extremely difficult road, and there are impetuous torrents that can be crossed only by means of cords extended from rock to rock.[2] The caravans returned with *musk*, *China-wood* [bois de Chine],[3] *rhubarb* and

[1] See p. 427, footnote [4].

[2] This is an early mention of the rope suspension-bridges, *jholas*, which are common in Kashmír and Tibet, the ropes being made of hemp, or willow or birch twigs.

[3] Also known as China-root, used in the same way as sarsaparilla, to which species it belongs. It is held in great esteem at the present day in the native pharmacopœias of India and China.

mamiron,[1] a small root in great repute for the cure of bad eyes; and in returning through *Great Tibet* they further loaded themselves with the produce of that country, such as *musk, crystal, jade,* and especially with a quantity of very fine wool of two kinds, the first from the sheep of that country, and the latter which is known by the name of *touz*, and resembles, as already observed, the beaver, and should rather be called hair than wool. But since *Chah-Jehan's* irruption into *Great Tibet,* the King has not only interdicted the passage of caravans, but forbidden any person from *Kachemire* to enter his dominions. This is the reason why the caravans now take their departure from *Patna* on the *Ganges* so as to avoid his territories: they leave *Great Tibet* on the left and proceed directly to the kingdom of slaves, *Lassa*.[2]

In regard to the kingdom known here by the name of *Kacheguer,* which is in my opinion the same as our maps call *Kascar,* I shall relate all the information I have collected from merchants, natives of that country, who when they heard that *Aureng-Zebe* intended to visit *Kachemire,* brought into this kingdom for sale a great number of young slaves, girls and boys.

They say that *Kacheguer* lies to the east of *Kachemire* inclining somewhat to the northward;[3] that the shortest route from one kingdom to the other is through *Great Tibet,* but, that passage being now shut, they were under the necessity of taking the road of *Little Tibet.* The first town they passed in returning was *Gourtche*,[4] the last town de-

[1] Still, under the name of *Mamiran-i-Chini*, a popular drug in the bazaars of the Punjab. It is ground up with rose-water and then applied to the eyes.

[2] The route from Patna to Lhasa was through Napaul, and *viâ* the Kuti (Nialam) Pass to Shigatzé, and thence to Lhasa. From Lhasa there was a trade-route to Sining Fu on the Chinese frontier, north-east through Kokosai and the Charing Nor. This being the Patna-China route mentioned by Bernier on the next page.

[3] As a matter of fact the town of Kashgar is due north of Srínagar in Kashmír.

[4] Gurez or Gurais.

pendent upon *Kachemire,* and four days' journey from the city of *Kachemire*: from *Gourtche,* they were eight days in reaching *Eskerdou,*[1] the capital of *Little Tibet*; and in two days more they came to a small town called *Cheker,*[2] also within the territory of *Little Tibet,* and situated on a river celebrated for its medicinal waters. In fifteen days they came to a large forest, on the confines of *Little Tibet,* and in fifteen days more they arrived at *Kacheguer,* a small town which was formerly the royal residence, though now the King of *Kacheguer* resides at *Jourkend,*[3] a little more to the north, and ten days' journey from *Kacheguer.* These merchants added that the distance from the town of *Kacheguer* to *Katay*[4] is not more than a two months' voyage; that caravans go thither every year, which return laden with the articles I have enumerated, and proceed to *Persia* by way of *Usbek*; as there are others that go from *Katay* to *Patna,* in *Hindoustan.* They also informed me that the way from *Kacheguer* to *Katay* is through a small town, eight days' journey from *Coten,* and that *Coten*[5] is the last town on that side in the kingdom of *Kacheguer.* The road from *Kachemire* to *Kacheguer,* they said, is extremely bad, and among other difficult paths, there is the place where, in every season, you must go a quarter of a league over ice.[6]

[1] Skárdú, taken by the Mahárájá Gúláb Singh in 1840. *Viâ* Gurez, it is fourteen marches from Srínagar; the marches may have been longer in Bernier's time.

[2] Shigar, on the river of that name.

[3] Yarkand is to the south-east of the town of Kashgar.

[4] It is interesting to note Bernier's use of this word here. It is the name for China which would be used by his informants, the merchants from Kashgar, see p. 426, although he was probably under the impression, a very common one at his time, that Katay or Cathay was a country to the north of China. Father Martini, in his *Novus Atlas Sinensis* (1655), was one of the first to fully recognise its identity with China. See p. 155 text, and footnote [3].

[5] Khotan.

[6] This refers to a route from Skárdú to Yarkand, which crossed the Baltero Glacier, which now, owing to changes in the ice, is no longer passable.

This is all the information I could collect concerning these regions; it is certainly confused and scanty, but after all will be found tolerably complete considering the ignorance of these people, seldom able to give reasons for anything, and that I had also to deal with interpreters who experienced the utmost difficulty both in clearly stating my interrogatories, and in explaining satisfactorily the answers.[1]

Here I intended to close this letter, or rather this book, and take my leave of you until our return to *Dehli*; but my inclination for writing is still strong, and I enjoy some leisure. I shall endeavour, therefore, to answer the five questions which you put to me in your last letter, on behalf of the industrious and inquisitive *Monsieur Thevenot*,[2] who makes greater and more important discoveries in his study than others who circumnavigate the globe.

His first inquiry is, whether it be true that Jews have for a long period resided in the kingdom of *Kachemire*: whether they be in possession of the Holy Scriptures, and, if so, whether there be any discrepancy between their Old Testament and our own.

The second request is, that I should communicate whatever observations I may have made concerning the *Moisson*, or *Season* of the periodical rains in the *Indies*.

The third, that I make him acquainted with my remarks and opinions upon the singular regularity of the winds and currents in the seas of the *Indies*.

The fourth, whether the kingdom of *Bengale* be as fertile, rich, and beautiful as is commonly reported.

The fifth, that I give a decisive opinion on the old controversies as to the causes of the *Nile's* increase.

[1] Hence doubtless arose the errors in stating the relative bearings of Kashmír and Kashgar, and Kashgar, Yarkand.

[2] Melchisedec, the uncle of the *Traveller*, Jean de Thévenot (1633-1667), is the well-known *Publisher* of travels (Fol. Paris, 1663 *et seq.*), and was born about 1620, and died in 1692. He was the French Hakluyt and Purchas.

Answer to the first Inquiry, concerning the Jews.

I would be as much pleased as *Monsieur Thevenot* himself if *Jews* were found in these mountainous regions; I mean such *Jews* as he would no doubt desire to find,—*Jews* descended from the tribes transported by *Shalmaneser*: but you may assure that gentleman that although there seems ground for believing that some of them were formerly settled in these countries, yet the whole population is at present either *Gentile* or *Mahometan*. In *China*, indeed, there are probably people of that nation, for I have lately seen letters in the hands of our reverend Father the Jesuit of *Dehli*, written by a *German* Jesuit from *Pekin*, wherein he states that he had conversed with *Jews* in that city, who adhered to the forms of *Judaism* and retained the books of the Old Testament.[1] They were totally ignorant of

[1] The first settlement of the Jews in China is said to have taken place in the third century B.C. John de Marignolli, who was Papal Legate to the court of the Great Khan, and was in Peking (Cambalec) in 1341, states that he had many and glorious disputations with the Jews and other sectaries, and also made a great harvest of souls in that Empire.

The German Jesuit referred to was in all probability Father Johann Adam Schall, or Schaal as sometimes given, a German from Zell (Celle in Hanover), not Cologne, as has been stated by some writers. Father Schall was born in 1591, came to China in 1622, and died at Peking in 1666. He was a great mathematician, and was one of those 'followers of the doctrine of the Lord of Heaven' (*i.e.* Christians), who were appointed to reform the Chinese calendar, the calculations of which had fallen into disorder. This was by a special decree of the Emperor, and the work was duly finished 'by means of the new system of the Foreigners' in 1628. Father Schall was held in great esteem by the Emperor of China, who conferred upon him the Mandarin's button of the first grade, and as we know from independent Chinese sources the very great esteem in which this missionary from Je-rh-ma-ni (Germany) was held by all classes in the Chinese Empire, at Peking and elsewhere, it is quite likely that the Chinese Jews would ask him to rule over them. Schall was a constant contributor to Kircher's stores of learning, and his portrait in Chinese official dress will be found at p. 113 of *China Illustrata*, in which work a copy of the inscription tablets on the Jesuit church at Peking, built by Schall, is given at p. 107, from which we learn his birthplace as follows, . . PATER · JOANNES · ADAMUS SCHAL · A · ZELL · GERMANUS · . . .

the death of Jesus Christ and had expressed a wish to appoint the *Jesuit* their *Kakan*[1] if he would abstain from swine's flesh.

There are, however, many signs of *Judaism* to be found in this country. On entering the kingdom after crossing the *Pire-penjale* mountains, the inhabitants in the frontier villages struck me as resembling *Jews*. Their countenance and manner, and that indescribable peculiarity which enables a traveller to distinguish the inhabitants of different nations, all seemed to belong to that ancient people. You are not to ascribe what I say to mere fancy, the *Jewish* appearance of these villagers having been remarked by our *Jesuit Father*, and by several other *Europeans*, long before I visited *Kachemire*.

A second sign is the prevalence of the name of *Mousa*, which means *Moses*, among the inhabitants of this city, notwithstanding they are all *Mahometans*.

A third is the common tradition that *Solomon* visited this country, and that it was he who opened a passage for the waters by cutting the mountain of *Baramoulé*.

A fourth, the belief that *Moses* died in the city of *Kachemire*, and that his tomb is within a league of it.

And a fifth may be found in the generally received opinion that the small and extremely ancient edifice seen on one of the high hills was built by *Solomon*; and it is therefore called the *Throne of Solomon* to this day.[2]

You will see then, that I am not disposed to deny that Jews may have taken up their residence in *Kachemire*.[3]

[1] Khakan, or more properly Kháqán, the Χαγάνος of the Byzantine historians, the title of the Mogol Chingiz, and those who succeeded him on the throne of Northern China. The Great Caan of the early travellers.

[2] See p. 399.

[3] In recent times visitors to Kashmír seeing the names Rahimju, Lusju, Julju, etc., etc., common ones among the tradespeople who cater for foreign visitors in Srínagar, written up as Rahim Jew, Lus Jew, Jul Jew, have imagined that the bearers of these names were *Jews* by nationality!! The Jewish cast of features of many of the inhabitants of Kashmír is noticed by many modern travellers.

The purity of their law, after a lapse of ages, may have been corrupted, until, having long degenerated into idolatry, they were induced, like many other pagans, to adopt the creed of *Mahomet*.[1]

It is certain that many *Jews* are settled in *Persia*, at *Lar* and *Hyspan*; and in *Hindoustan*, towards *Goa* and *Cochin*.[2] I also learn that in *Ethiopia*, where they are very numerous, these people are remarkable for courage and military prowess; and if I am to believe two ambassadors from the *Ethiopian* King, lately at this court, there was a *Jew*, fifteen or sixteen years ago, grown so formidable, that he endeavoured to erect an independent kingdom in a certain small and mountainous district difficult of access.

Answer to the second Inquiry, concerning the Periodical Rains in the Indies.

The sun is so strong and oppressive in the *Indies* during the whole year, particularly during eight months, that the ground would be completely burnt, and rendered sterile and uninhabitable, if Providence did not kindly provide a remedy, and wisely ordain that in the month of July, when the heat is most intense, rains begin to fall, which continue three successive months. The temperature of

[1] The Moslem historian known as Albêrûnî, who was born in A.D. 973, says in his description of Kashmír, talking of the inhabitants: 'They are particularly anxious about the natural strength of their country, and therefore take always much care to keep a stronghold upon the entrances and roads leading into it. In consequence it is very difficult to have any commerce with them. In former times they used to allow one or two foreigners to enter their country, particularly Jews, but at present they do not allow any Hindú whom they do not know personally to enter, much less other people.'—P. 205, vol. i., English Ed. by Dr. Edward C. Sachau. London: Trübner, 1888.

[2] It is said that Jews settled in Cochin in the first year of the Christian era, and from copperplates still extant it is put beyond doubt that the Jewish church was firmly established there by the eighth century. There is a regular Jews' quarter in the town of Cochin.

the air thus becomes supportable, and the earth is rendered fruitful. These rains are not, however, so exactly regular as to descend undeviatingly on the same day or week. According to the observations I have made in various places, particularly in *Dehli,* where I resided a long time, they are never the same two years together. Sometimes they commence or terminate a fortnight or three weeks sooner or later, and one year they may be more abundant than another. I have even known two entire years pass without scarcely a drop of rain, and the consequences of that extraordinary drought were wide-spreading sickness and famine. It should be observed too that the rainy season is earlier or later, and more or less plentiful, in different countries, in proportion to their proximity or remoteness from one another. In *Bengale,* for instance, and along the coast of *Koromandel,* as far as the Island of *Ceylon,* the rains begin and end a month sooner than toward the coast of *Malabar;* and in *Bengale* they fall very violently for four months, in the course of which it sometimes pours during eight days and nights without the least intermission. In *Dehli* and *Agra,* however, the rains are neither so abundant nor of such long continuance; two or three days often elapsing without the slightest shower; and from dawn of day to nine or ten o'clock in the morning, it commonly rains very little, and sometimes not at all. It struck me very particularly that the rains come from different quarters in different countries. In the neighbourhood of *Dehli* they come from the east, where *Bengale* is situated; in the province of *Bengale* and on the coast of *Koromandel,* from the south; and on the coast of Malabar almost invariably from the west.

I have also remarked one thing, about which, indeed, there is a perfect agreement of opinion in these parts,—that accordingly as the heat of summer comes earlier or later, is more or less violent, or lasts a longer or shorter time, so the rains come sooner or later, are more or less abundant, and continue a longer or a shorter period.

From these observations I have been led to believe that the heat of the earth and the rarefaction of the air are the principal causes of these rains which they attract. The atmosphere of the circumjacent seas being colder, more condensed, and thicker, is filled with clouds drawn from the water by the great heat of the summer, and which, driven and agitated by the winds, discharge themselves naturally upon land, where the atmosphere is hotter, more rarefied, lighter, and less resisting than on the sea; and thus this discharge is more or less tardy and plentiful, according as the heat comes early or late, and is more or less intense.

It is also in accord with the observations contained in this dissertation to suppose that if the rains commence sooner on the coast of *Koromandel* than on the coast of *Malabar*, it is only because the summer is earlier; and that it is earlier may be owing to particular causes which it would not perhaps be difficult to ascertain if the country were properly examined. We know that according to the different situations of lands, in respect of seas or mountains, and in proportion as they are sandy, hilly, or covered with wood, summer is felt more or less early, and with greater or less violence.

Nor is it surprising that the rains come from different quarters; that on the coast of *Koromandel*, for example, they come from the south, and on the *Malabar* coast from the west; because it is apparently the nearest sea which sends the rain; and the sea nearest the *Koromandel* coast, and to which it is more immediately exposed, lies to the south; as the sea which washes the coast of *Malabar* is to the west, extending itself towards *Bab-el-mandel*, *Arabia*, and the *Persian* Gulf.

I have imagined, in fine, that although we see at *Dehli* the rainy clouds come from the east, yet their origin may be in the seas which lie to the south of that city: and being intercepted by some mountains or lands whose atmosphere is colder, more condensed and resisting, they are forced to turn aside and discharge themselves in a country where the air is more rarefied, and which consequently offers less resistance.

I had almost forgotten to notice another fact which fell under my observation while living in *Dehli*. There never falls any heavy rain until a great quantity of clouds have passed, during several days, to the westward; as if it were necessary that the expanse of atmosphere to the west of *Dehli* should be first filled with clouds, and that those clouds finding some impediment, such as air less hot and less rarefied, and therefore more condensed and more capable of resistance; or encountering other clouds and contrary winds, they become so thick, overcharged and heavy, as to burst and descend in rain; in the same manner as it happens when clouds are driven by the wind against some lofty mountain.

Answer to the third Inquiry, concerning the Regularity of the Currents of the Sea, and the Winds in the Indies.

As soon as the rains cease, which happens commonly about the beginning of October, the sea takes its course toward the South, and the cold North wind rises. This wind continues four or five months without any intermission. It blows the whole of this time with equal force, unattended with tempests, and always from the same quarter, excepting sometimes for a single day when it changes or lulls. After the expiration of this period, the winds blow for about two months without any regularity. This is called the intermediate season, or, as the *Dutch* have very correctly named it, the time of the doubtful and variable winds. These two months being passed, the sea resumes its course from the South to the North, and the South wind commences and continues to blow and the current continues to run four or five months from the same quarter. There then elapse about two months more, which constitute the other intermediate season. In these intervals Navigation is extremely difficult and perilous, but during the two seasons it is very easy, pleasant, and safe, excepting only the latter part of the South-wind season. It ought not, therefore, to excite your surprise that the *Indians,* who are a very timid people and ignorant of the art of navigation, undertake pretty long and important voyages; such as from *Bengale* to *Tanassery, Achem, Malacca, Siam,* and *Makascar,* or to *Maslipatam, Ceylon,* the *Maldives, Moka,* and *Bender-Abbassy.* They are of course very careful to avail themselves of the favourable Season for going and the favourable season for returning. It often happens, however, that they are detained beyond the proper time, overtaken by bad weather, and wrecked. This is indeed sometimes the case with *Europeans,* although they be far better Sea-men, bolder and more skilful, and the condition and equipment of whose vessels are so greatly superior. Of the two intermediate Seasons, the one which follows the South wind is without comparison the more dangerous, being much more subject to storms and sudden squalls. That wind, even during the season, is generally more impetuous and unequal than the North wind. I must not omit to notice in this place, that toward the end of the Season of the South-wind and during the rains, although there be a perfect calm out at sea, yet near the coasts, for a distance of fifteen or twenty leagues, the weather is extremely tempestuous. The captains of *European* and other vessels should consequently be careful to approach the coast of the *Indies,* that of *Surate* or *Maslipatam,* for instance, just after the termination of the rains; otherwise they incur great risk of being dashed on shore.

Such is the order of the seasons in the *Indies,* so far at least as my observations justify me in speaking upon the subject. I wish it were in my power to trace every effect to its true cause; but how is it possible to unravel these profound secrets of Nature! I have imagined, in the first place, that the air by which our Globe is surrounded ought to be considered one of its component parts, just as much as the waters of the sea and rivers; because both the one and the other gravitating on this globe, and tending to the same common centre, are in this manner united to our sphere. The Globe then is formed of three bodies,—air, water, and earth. *Secondly*, our Globe being suspended and balanced in that free and unresisting space wherein it pleased the Creator to place it, would be easily displaced if it came in contact with any unknown body. *Thirdly*, the sun, after having crossed the line, while moving toward one of the Poles, towards the Arctic Pole, for example, darting its beams that way, produces sufficient impression to depress in some measure the Arctic Pole, which is depressed more and more in proportion as the sun advances towards the Tropic; and in the same manner, the sun permits it again to rise gradually in proportion as it returns toward the *Equator*; until the same effect is produced by the power of its rays on the side of the *Antarctic* Pole.

Taking for granted the truth of these suppositions, and considering them conjointly with the diurnal motion of the earth, it is not without reason that the *Indians* affirm that the sun conducts and draws along with it both the sea and the wind; because, if it be true that, having passed the line on its way toward one of the Poles, the sun causes a change in the direction of the earth's axis and a depression of the Pole, it follows as a necessary consequence, that the other Pole is elevated, and that the sea and air, which are two fluid and heavy bodies, run in this declension. It is therefore correct to say, that the sun advancing toward one Pole causes on that side two great and regular currents,—the current of the sea and the current of the air, which latter constitutes the *Monsoon-wind*; as the sun is the cause of two opposite currents when it returns toward the other Pole.

Upon this theory it may, I think, be said that there are only two main and contrary flows [flux] of the sea, one from the *Northern* and the other from the *Southern* Pole; that if there existed a sea from one Pole to the other, which passed through *Europe*, we should there find these two currents regulated in every respect as in the *Indies*, and that the reason why this regularity is not general is that the seas are intercepted by lands, which obstruct, break, and diversify their course; in the same manner as some persons allege that the usual flux and reflux of the sea is prevented in those seas which, like the *Mediterranean*, stretch from East to West. According to this theory, it might also, in my opinion, be maintained that there are only two principal and opposite currents of air or wind, and that in regard to them the same regularity would reign generally, if the earth were also perfectly and generally smooth, and similar throughout.

Answer to the fourth Inquiry, as to the fertility, wealth and beauty of the Kingdom of Bengale.

Egypt has been represented in every age as the finest and most fruitful country in the world, and even our modern writers deny that there is any other land so peculiarly favoured by nature: but the knowledge I have acquired of *Bengale*, during two visits paid to that kingdom, inclines me to believe that the pre-eminence ascribed to *Egypt* is rather due to *Bengale*. The latter country produces rice in such abundance that it supplies not only the neighbouring but remote states. It is carried up the *Ganges* as far as *Patna*, and exported by sea to *Maslipatam* and many other ports on the coast of *Koromandel*. It is also sent to foreign kingdoms, principally to the island of *Ceylon* and the *Maldives*. *Bengale* abounds likewise in sugar, with which it supplies the kingdoms of *Golkonda* and the *Karnatic*, where very little is grown, *Arabia* and *Mesopotamia*, through the towns of *Moka* and *Bassora*, and even *Persia*, by way of *Bender-Abbasi*. *Bengale* likewise is celebrated for its sweetmeats, especially in places inhabited by *Portuguese*, who are skilful in the art of preparing them, and with whom they are an article of considerable trade. Among other fruits, they preserve large *citrons*, such as we have in *Europe*, a certain delicate root about the length of *sarsaparilla*, that common fruit of the *Indies* called *amba*,[1] another called *ananas*,[2] small *mirobolans*,[3] which are excellent, *limes*, and *ginger*.

Bengale, it is true, yields not so much wheat as *Egypt*; but if this be a defect, it is attributable to the inhabitants, who live a great deal more upon rice than the *Egyptians*, and seldom taste bread. Nevertheless, wheat is cultivated in sufficient quantity for the consumption of the country, and for the making of excellent and cheap sea-biscuits, with which the crews of *European* ships, *English*, *Dutch* and *Portuguese*, are supplied. The three or four sorts of vegetables which, together with rice and butter,[4] form the chief food of the common people, are purchased for the merest trifle, and for a single *roupie* twenty or more good fowls may be bought. Geese and ducks are proportionably cheap. There are also goats and sheep in abundance; and pigs are obtained at so low a price that the *Portuguese*, settled in the country, live almost entirely upon pork. This meat is salted at a cheap rate by the *Dutch* and *English*, for the supply of their vessels. Fish of every species, whether fresh or salt, is in the same profusion. In a word, *Bengale* abounds with every

[1] See p. 249.

[2] This is the name, from the Brazilian *nana* or *nanas*, of the pine-apple in every country where it has been introduced from its original habitat in America, except England. This fruit is now very common in many parts of India, especially in those places that were Portuguese settlements, or came under the influence of that people.

[3] Myrobalans, the general name then given to various dried fruits and kernels exported from India from a very remote period, and which had a high reputation in the mediæval pharmacopœia.

[4] That is, ghee, which is clarified butter. In preparing it, the butter is boiled until all the watery particles and curds have been thrown off by repeated skimmings. When the liquid is clear oil, it is poured into a vessel to cool, which it does in a granulated form, and if originally well boiled, will keep for years without taint.

necessary of life; and it is this abundance that has induced so many *Portuguese, Half-castes,*[1] and other *Christians,* driven from their different settlements by the *Dutch,* to seek an asylum in this fertile kingdom. The *Jesuits* and *Augustins,* who have large churches and are permitted the free and unmolested exercise of their religion, assured me that *Ogouli* alone contains from eight to nine thousand *Christians,* and that in other parts of the kingdom their number exceeded five-and-twenty thousand. The rich exuberance of the country, together with the beauty and amiable disposition of the native women, has given rise to a proverb in common use among the *Portuguese, English,* and *Dutch,* that the Kingdom of *Bengale* has a hundred gates open for entrance, but not one for departure.

In regard to valuable commodities of a nature to attract foreign merchants, I am acquainted with no country where so great a variety is found. Besides the sugar I have spoken of, and which may be placed in the list of valuable commodities, there is in *Bengale* such a quantity of cotton and silks, that the kingdom may be called the common storehouse for those two kinds of merchandise, not of *Hindoustan* or the Empire of the *Great Mogol* only, but of all the neighbouring kingdoms, and even of *Europe.* I have been sometimes amazed at the vast quantity of cotton cloths, of every sort, fine and coarse, white and coloured, which the *Hollanders* alone export to different places, especially to *Japan* and *Europe.* The *English,* the *Portuguese,* and the native merchants deal also in these articles to a considerable extent. The same may be said of the silks and silk stuffs of all sorts. It is not possible to conceive the quantity drawn every year from *Bengale* for the supply of the whole of the *Mogol Empire,* as far as *Lahor* and *Cabol,* and generally of all those foreign nations to which the cotton cloths are sent. The silks are not certainly so fine as those of *Persia, Syria, Sayd,*

[1] *Mestices,* in the original.

and *Barut*,[1] but they are of a much lower price; and I know from indisputable authority that, if they were well selected and wrought with care, they might be manufactured into most beautiful stuffs. The *Dutch* have sometimes seven or eight hundred natives employed in their silk factory at *Kassem-Bazar*, where, in like manner, the *English* and other merchants employ a proportionate number.

Bengale is also the principal emporium for *saltpetre*. A prodigious quantity is imported from *Patna*.[2] It is carried down the *Ganges* with great facility, and the *Dutch* and *English* send large cargoes to many parts of the *Indies*, and to *Europe*.

Lastly, it is from this fruitful kingdom, that the best *lac, opium, wax, civet, long pepper*, and various drugs are obtained; and *butter*,[3] which may appear to you an inconsiderable article, is in such plenty, that although it be a bulky article[4] to export, yet it is sent by sea to numberless places.

[1] Saida and Beirut (Beyrout), still great silk-producing places, on the shores of the Levant. Saida, close to the ancient site of Sidon, and Beirut about 25 miles to the north.

[2] One of the principal refineries of saltpetre was at Chuprah, about 25 miles from Patna, where the French, Dutch, and Portuguese had factories.

[3] Ghee, see p. 438. There is still a large export trade in this article, and the following table shows the quantity and value of ghee consigned from India, to foreign countries, from recent returns:

Three months, 1st April to 30th June.

	1889.	1890.	1891.
Quantity in lbs., .	469,581	611,254	530,543
Value in Rupees, .	1,69,905	2,26,940	2,00,117

[4] On account of the unwieldy nature of the large vessels made of dried skins (*kuppah* in Hindostanee), in which it was then exported. At the present time ghee is as a rule shipped in iron 'drums' or large tin canisters.

It is fair to acknowledge, however, that strangers seldom find the air salubrious, particularly near the sea. There was a great mortality among the *Dutch* and *English* when they first settled in *Bengale*; and I saw in *Balasor*[1] two very fine *English* vessels, which had remained in that port a twelvemonth in consequence of the war with *Holland*, and at the expiration of that period, were unable to put to sea, because the greater part of the crews had died. Both the *English* and *Dutch* now live with more caution and the mortality is diminished. The masters of vessels take care that their crews drink less punch;[2] nor do they permit them so frequently to visit the *Indian* women, or the dealers in *arac*[3] and *tobacco*. Good Vin de *Grave* or *Canary* and *Chiras* wines, taken in moderation, are found excellent preservatives against the effects of bad air, therefore I maintain that those who live carefully need not be sick, nor will the mortality be greater among them than with the rest of the world. *Bouleponge* is a drink composed of *arac*, a spirit distilled from molasses, mixed with lemon juice, water and nutmeg; it is pleasant enough to the taste, but most hurtful to body and health.

In describing the beauty of *Bengale*, it should be remarked that throughout a country extending nearly an hundred *leagues* in length, on both banks of the *Ganges*,

[1] The port of Balasor on the Orissa coast is still frequented by sloops from the Madras coast and Ceylon. In the Balasor District were several considerable ports in Bernier's time.

[2] 'Bouleponges' in the original. A curious combination of the name of the drink and the vessel in which it was brewed. *Bole-Ponjis containing the tale of the Bucaneer: A Bottle of Red Ink: The Decline and Fall of Ghosts, and other ingredients*, 2 vols. 8vo, was the name adopted in 1852 by H. Meredith Parker, a Bengal civilian well known in the Lower Provinces for his literary and dramatic tastes, as the title of a book which he wrote. *Bowle* is still the German name for punch, and the allied drinks.

[3] The Bengal arrack was held in great repute in those days. Ovington, in *A voyage to Suratt in the Year* 1686, Lond., 1696, says of it, '*Bengal* is a much stronger spirit than that of *Goa*, though both are made use of by the *Europeans* in making punch.

from *Raje-Mehale* to the sea, is an endless number of channels,[1] cut, in bygone ages, from that river with immense labour, for the conveyance of merchandise and of the water itself, which is reputed by the *Indians* to be superior to any in the world. These channels are lined on both sides with towns and villages, thickly peopled with *Gentiles*; and with extensive fields of *rice, sugar, corn,* three or four sorts of *vegetables, mustard, sesame* for oil, and small *mulberry-trees,* two or three feet in height, for the food of silk-worms. But the most striking and peculiar beauty of *Bengale* is the innumerable islands filling the vast space between the two banks of the *Ganges,* in some places six or seven days' journey asunder. These islands vary in size, but are all extremely fertile, surrounded with wood, and abounding in fruit-trees, and pine-apples, and covered with verdure; a thousand water-channels run through them, stretching beyond the sight, and resembling long walks arched with trees. Several of the islands, nearest to the sea, are now abandoned by the inhabitants,[2] who were exposed to the attacks and ravages of the *Arracan*[3] pirates, spoken of in another place. At present they are a dreary waste, wherein no living creature is seen except antelopes, hogs,[4] and wild fowls, that attract tigers,

[1] In the original *canaux,* from which it would almost appear that the artificial river embankments of Bengal led Bernier to believe that the rivers themselves were canals, the work of human agency in times past; although further on, at p. 453, he states that the periodical rains in Bengal obviate the necessity of cutting irrigation canals in that country, as has to be done in Egypt.

[2] Remains of houses and embankments have been found in isolated parts of this tract, called the Sundarbans; and various attempts, which have been to some extent successful in the northern portion, at reclaiming and cultivating the land have been made from time to time since the British acquired Bengal.

[3] In the original, 'Corsaires Franguys de Rakan;' see p. 175.

[4] Jungle fowl. In the original, *volaille devenus sauvages,* Bernier being apparently under the impression that the jungle fowl to be met with in the Sundarbans were descended from domestic poultry that escaped and became wild.

which sometimes swim from one island to another. In traversing the *Ganges* in small rowing boats, the usual mode of conveyance among these islands, it is in many places dangerous to land, and great care must be had that the boat, which during the night is fastened to a tree, be kept at some distance from the shore, for it constantly happens that some person or another falls a prey to tigers. These ferocious animals are very apt, it is said, to enter into the boat itself, while the people are asleep, and to carry away some victim, who, if we are to believe the boatmen of the country, generally happens to be the stoutest and fattest of the party.

I remember a nine days' voyage that I made from *Pipli* to *Ogouli*, among these islands and channels, which I cannot omit relating, as no day passed without some extraordinary accident or adventure. When my seven-oared *scallop* had conveyed us out of the river of *Pipli*,[1] and we had advanced three or four leagues at sea, along the coast, on our way to the islands and channels, we saw the sea covered with fish, apparently large *carp*, which were pursued by a great number of *dolphins*. I desired my men to row that way, and perceived that most of them were lying on their side as if they had been dead; some moved slowly along, and others seemed to be struggling and turning about as if stupefied. We caught four-and-twenty with our hands, and observed that out of the mouth of every one issued a bladder, like that of a *carp*, which was full of air and of a reddish colour at the end. I easily conceived that

[1] Pippli (*Pipilipatam* of Blaeu's map), at one time a very famous port, and the most important harbour on the Orissa coast, on the Subarnareka River, about 16 miles from its mouth, the earliest maritime settlement of the English in Bengal, founded in 1634, on the ruins of the Portuguese factory. Owing to changes in the course of the river not one stone now remains to mark the spot where the famous port once stood. It was probably here that Bernier saw the English vessels he mentions at p. 441. Subarnareka, about 12 miles from the mouth of the river, now a mere resort for fishing boats, was also at one time a considerable harbour of the Balasor district, after the decay of Pippli.

it was this bladder which prevented the fish from sinking, but could never understand why it thus protruded, unless it were that having been long and closely pursued by the *dolphins*, they made such violent efforts to escape, that the bladder swelled, became red, and was forced out of the mouth. I have recounted this circumstance to a hundred sailors, whom I found incredulous; with the exception, indeed, of a *Dutch* pilot, who informed me that, sailing in a large vessel along the coasts of *China*, his attention was arrested by a similar appearance, and that putting out their boat they caught, as we did, with only their hands, many of the fish.

The day following we arrived, at rather a late hour, among the islands; and having chosen a spot that appeared free from *tigers*, we landed and lighted a fire. I ordered a couple of fowls and some of the fish to be dressed, and we made an excellent supper. The fish was delicious. I then re-embarked, and ordered my men to row on till night. There would have been danger in losing our way in the dark among the different channels, and therefore we retired out of a main channel in search of a snug creek, where we passed the night; the boat being fastened to a thick branch of a tree, at a prudent distance from the shore. While keeping watch, I witnessed a *Phenomenon* of *Nature* such as I had twice observed at *Dehli*. I beheld a lunar rainbow, and awoke the whole of my company, who all expressed much surprise, especially two *Portuguese* pilots, whom I had received into the boat at the request of a friend. They declared that they had neither seen nor heard of such a rainbow.

The third day, we lost ourselves among the channels, and I know not how we should have recovered our right course, had we not met with some *Portuguese*, who were employed in making salt on one of the islands. This night again, our boat being under shelter in a small channel, my *Portuguese*, who were full of the strange appearance on the preceding night, and kept their eyes constantly fixed toward the heavens, roused me from my sleep and pointed out another rainbow as beautiful and as well defined as the last. You are not to imagine that I mistake a *halo* for an *iris*. I am familiar with the former, because during the rainy season at *Dehli*, there is scarcely a month in which a *halo* is not frequently seen round the moon. But they appear only when that luminary is very high above the horizon: I have observed them three and four nights successively, and sometimes I have seen them doubled. The *iris* of which I speak was not a circle about the *moon*, but was placed in an opposite direction, in the same relative position as a solar rainbow. Whenever I have seen a night *iris*, the moon has been at the west and the *iris* at the east. The moon was also nearly complete in its orb, because otherwise the beams of light would not, I conceive, be sufficiently powerful to form the rainbow; nor was the *iris* so white as the *halo*, but more strongly marked, and a variety of colours was even discernible. Thus you see that I am more happy than the ancients, who, according to *Aristotle*, had observed no lunar rainbows before his time.

In the evening of the fourth day we withdrew, as usual, out of the main channel to a place of security, and passed a most extraordinary night. Not a breath of wind was felt, and the air became so hot and suffocating that we could scarcely breathe. The bushes around us were so full of glow-worms that they seemed ignited; and fires resembling flames arose every moment to the great alarm of our sailors, who did not doubt that they were so many devils. Two of these luminous appearances were very remarkable. One was a great globe of fire, which continued longer than the time necessary to repeat a *Pater*, the other looked like a small tree all in flames, and lasted above a quarter of an hour.

The night of the fifth day was altogether dreadful and perilous. A storm arose so violent, that although we were, as we thought, in excellent shelter under trees, and our boat carefully fastened, yet our cable was broken, and we should have been driven into the main channel, there inevitably to perish, if I and my two *Portuguese* had not, by a sudden and spontaneous movement, entwined our arms round the branches of trees, which we held tightly for the space of two hours, while the tempest was raging with unabated force. No assistance was to be expected from my *Indian* boatmen, whose fears completely overcame them. Our situation while clinging for our lives to the trees was indeed most painful; the rain fell as if poured into the boat from buckets, and the lightning and thunder were so vivid and loud, and so near our heads, that we despaired of surviving this horrible night.[1]

Nothing, however, could be more pleasant than the remainder of the voyage. We arrived at *Ogouly* on the ninth day, and my eyes seemed never sated with gazing on the delightful country through which we passed. My trunk, however, and all my wearing-apparel were wet, the poultry dead, the fish spoilt, and the whole of my biscuits soaked with rain.

Answer to the fifth Inquiry, concerning the Periodical Rising of the Nile.

I know not whether my solution of this fifth question will be satisfactory; but I shall impart opinions formed after having been twice a witness of the increase, after having given to the subject the whole of my attention, and after making certain observations in the *Indies* which afford some facilities for the disquisition, which must have been wanting to the great man who has written so ingeniously and learnedly on this interesting topic, although he never saw *Egypt* but in his study.

[1] Bernier appears to have travelled from Pippli to Hooghly, not by the main channel of the river, but through minor channels. All those who are familiar with the nature of the Sundarban tracts will be able to testify to the vividness of the traveller's description of his journey.

I have already mentioned that while the two Ethiopian ambassadors were at *Dehli,* my Agah, *Danechmend-kan,* whose thirst for knowledge is incessant, invited them frequently to his house, and that I was always one of the party.[1] His object was to be made acquainted with the state of their country, and the nature of its government. Among other subjects, we spoke a great deal about the source of the *Nile,* which is called by them *Abbabile.* They spoke of its source as of a thing generally well known, and concerning which no one entertained any doubt. One of the ambassadors had even seen it, accompanied by a *Mogol* who had returned with him to *Hindoustan.* They told us that the source of the river *Nile* is in the country of the *Agaus*; that it gushes out of the earth by two large and bubbling springs near one another, and forming a small lake of about thirty or forty paces in length; that the river issuing from this lake is of considerable size, and that in its progress it receives many tributary waters, which swell it to an important stream. They went on to observe, that this stream pursues a winding course, and forms an extensive peninsula; and that after descending from several steep rocks, it falls into a large lake, in the country of *Dumbia,* only four or five days' journey from the source, and three short journeys from *Gonder,* the capital of *Ethiopia*; that having traversed this lake, the river leaves it, with the accession of all the waters which fall into the lake; passes through *Sonnar,* the chief city of the *Funges* or *Barberis,* tributaries to the King of *Ethiopia,* whence, tumbling among the *cataracts,* it pursues its way into the plains of *Messer,*[2] that is, *Egypt.*

When the ambassadors had furnished these particulars as to the source and course of the *Nile,* I wished to form some idea of the situation of the country where the source

[1] See p. 134 *et seq.*

[2] The Arabic *Misr,* meaning reddish-brown mud, or perhaps from the Hebrew *Mazor,* the fortified, referring to the natural strength of the country.

is found: I therefore inquired in what part of *Africa*, relatively to *Bab-el-mandel, Dumbia* is situated. But they could return no other answer than that it lay toward the *West.* I was surprised to hear this observation, especially from the *Mahometan* ambassador, who ought to be better informed than a Christian of the relative bearings of places, because all *Mahometans* are bound, when repeating their prayers, to look toward *Meca.* He also persisted in saying that *Dumbia* is situated to the west of *Bab-el-mandel*; so that the source of the river *Nile*, according to these ambassadors, is considerably to the north of the equator, and not to the south, where it is placed by *Ptolemy*, and in all our maps.

We inquired further of them when it rained in *Ethiopia*, and whether the rains were periodical in that country as in the *Indies.* They answered that it seldom or never rained along the coast of the *Red Sea*, from *Suaken, Arkiko*, and the island of *Masouva*, to *Bab-el-mandel*, any more than at *Moka*, in *Arabia Felix*, on the opposite shore of that sea. In the interior of the country, however, in the province of the *Agaus*, in *Dumbia*, and the circumjacent provinces, the rains were very heavy during the two hottest months of summer, those months when it also rains in the *Indies*, and exactly the time when, according to my computation, the increase of the *Nile* in *Egypt* takes place. They were quite aware, the ambassadors added, that the swelling of that river and the inundations of *Egypt* were caused by the rains of *Ethiopia*; and that the former country owed its fecundity to the slime conveyed and deposited thither by the *Nile.* It was from these circumstances, they observed, that the Kings of *Ethiopia* derived the right of exacting tribute from *Egypt*; and when that kingdom was subdued by the *Mahometans*, and its Christian population became oppressed and exposed to every indignity, the Ethiopian Monarch had thoughts of turning the course of the river toward the *Red Sea*, a measure which would have destroyed the fertility of *Egypt*, and consequently proved ruinous to the country: but the project appeared so gigantic, if not impracticable, that the attempt was never made to carry it into execution.[1]

All these particulars I had already been made acquainted with when at *Moka*, in the course of various conversations with ten or a dozen *Gonder* merchants, sent every year to that city by the King of *Ethiopia* for purposes of traffic

[1] This is a very curious version of the mediæval belief in Europe that the Abyssinian King, Prester John, received a large tribute from the Sultan of Egypt to prevent him from diverting the course of the Nile. Simon Sijoli, who travelled in the Levant in 1384, states that the tribute was a ball of gold with a cross upon it, worth 3000 golden bezants, and many other references to this subject could be quoted, for some of which see Yule's *Cathay and the Way Thither*, vol. ii. pp. 348-350. London. Printed for the Hakluyt Society, 1866. Ariosto alludes to the belief in his *Orlando Furioso*, Canto XXXIII. v. 106, as follows:—

> ''Tis said, the Sultan, Egypt's Sovereign,
> As subject to the King, does tribute pay;
> Since he the Nile is able to restrain
> From its right course, and elsewhere cause it stray
> And Cairo, thus afflicted, cause remain,
> With famine, and the parts that round it lay,
> Senapus named, by those his Empire own,
> We call him Presto, or else Prester John.'
>
> TEMPLE HENRY CROKER's Translation,
> London, 1755.

In our own time the feasibility of diverting the Nile into the Red Sea so as to 'put pressure on' Egypt has been several times mooted. In 1851 the late Dr. Beke forwarded to Lord Palmerston, then Secretary of State for Foreign Affairs, a copy of his *Memoir on the possibility of diverting the waters of the Nile so as to prevent the Irrigation of Egypt.*

In *The Times* newspaper of the 9th October 1888 will be found a letter from Sir Samuel W. Baker, in which he attributes the then abnormally low state of the Nile to some 'unexplained interference with the river,' one of the results in his opinion of the abandonment of the Soudan; and he goes on to reiterate his views as to the immense importance of the Soudan to Egypt, and the necessity for keeping a firm hand upon the basin of the Nile, 'As an enemy in possession of the Blue Nile, and the Atbara River could by throwing a dam across the empty bed . . . prevent the necessary flow towards Egypt. . . . I have seen a spot, about 230 miles from the mouth of the Atbara, where the river might be deflected without difficulty, and be forced to an eastern course towards the Red Sea.'

with the vessels from the *Indies*. The information is useful, as tending to demonstrate that the *Nile* increases only by means of the rains which fall near its source, and at a distance from *Egypt*. But I attach still greater importance to my own observations, made upon two separate occasions during the overflowing of that river, because they expose the fallacy of some popular opinions, and prove them to be merely vulgar and idle tales, the inventions of a people much given to superstition, and lost in astonishment at witnessing the increase of a river during the heat of summer, in a country where rain is unknown. I allude, among other conceits, to the notion that there is a certain determinate day on which the *Nile* begins its increase; that a particular dew, called the *Goute*, falls on this first day of the increase, which puts an end to the plague, no person dying of that disease when the *Goute* has begun to descend; and that the overflowing of the *Nile* is owing to particular and secret causes. I have discovered that this celebrated stream, like other rivers, swells and overflows in consequence of abundant rains, and that we are not to ascribe its increase to the fermentation of the nitrous soil of *Egypt*.[1]

I have seen it rise more than a foot, and become very turbid, nearly a month before the pretended determinate day of the increase.

I have remarked, in the time of its increase, and before the opening of the irrigation channels, that after the water had swollen during some days a foot or two, it decreased little by little, and then began to increase anew; and in this manner the river augmented or lessened, just

[1] The great cold in Western Tartary was attributed to the saltpetre in the soil. 'The saltpetre with which these countries abound may also contribute to this great cold, which is so violent that in digging the ground to three or four feet deep they take out clods quite frozen, as well as pieces of ice,' page 86 of *The History of the Tartar Conquerors of China. From the French of Père Pierre Joseph D'Orléans, S.J. Translated by the Earl of Ellesmere, with an Introduction by R. H. Major of the Brit. Mus.* London. Hakluyt Soc., 1854.

according as the rains did or did not fall near its source. The same thing is observable in our *Loire*; it increases or diminishes in proportion to the rains on the mountains whence that river flows.

Once, on my return from *Jerusalem,* I ascended the *Nile* from *Damietta* to *Cairo,* about a month before the day on which it is said that the *Goute* falls; and in the morning our clothes were soaked in consequence of the dew that had fallen during the night.

I supped with *M. de Bermon,* our vice-consul at *Rosetta,* eight or ten days after the fall of the *Goute.* Three of the party were that same evening seized with the plague, of whom two died on the eighth day; and the other patient, who happened to be *M. de Bermon* himself, would perhaps have fallen a victim to the disease if I had not ventured to prescribe a remedy, and lanced his abscess. I caught the infection, and but for the *butter of antimony,*[1] to which I had immediate recourse, it might have been seen in my case also that men die of the plague after the descent of the *Goute.* The emetic, taken at the commencement of the disorder, performed wonders, and I was not confined to the house more than three or four days. A *Bedouin* servant attended me; he endeavoured to keep up my spirits by swallowing, without a moment's hesitation, what remained of the soup I was taking; and being a predestinarian, he laughed at the idea of danger from the plague.

I am far from denying that this distemper is generally attended with less danger after the fall of the *Goute.* All I maintain is, that the decrease of danger should not be attributed to the *Goute.* In my opinion the mitigation of the disease is owing to the heat of the weather, then become intense, which opens the pores and expels the pestiferous and malignant humours that remained confined in the body.

Moreover I have carefully inquired of several *Rays,*[2] or

[1] Now called, sublimated muriate of antimony.

[2] Read *rāïs,* the Arabic for a captain of a boat, a pilot.

masters of boats, who have ascended the *Nile* to the extremity of the plains of *Egypt*, as far as the rocks and cataracts. They assured me that when the river overflows the Egyptian plains, the soil of which is represented as nitrous and fermentative, the *Nile* is greatly increased between the mountains of the cataracts, which it inundates in a surprising manner, although the soil upon those mountains is not apparently impregnated with nitre.

I was also very particular in making the necessary inquiries of the *Sonnar* negroes who repair to *Cairo* for employment, and whose country, tributary to the King of *Ethiopia*, is situated on the *Nile* among the mountainous tracts to the south of *Egypt*. These negroes all agreed in asserting, that at the time when the Nile inundates the plains of Egypt, it is swollen and impetuous in their own country, because of the rains which then fall, not only in their mountains, but higher up, in the region of *Habeche* or *Ethiopia*.

The observations made by me on the periodical rains of the *Indies*, which fall during the time that the *Nile* is increasing in *Egypt*, throw considerable light upon this subject, and will lead you to imagine that the *Indus*, the *Ganges*, and all the other rivers in this part of the globe are so many rivers *Nile*, and the countries contiguous to their mouths so many lands of *Egypt*. Such were the ideas which suggested themselves to my mind when in *Bengale*, and the following is, word for word, what I then wrote concerning this matter.

The numerous islands in the gulf of *Bengale*, at the mouth of the *Ganges*, which the course of ages has united together,[1] and at length has joined to the continent, recall

[1] Or, as so well described in *The Imperial Gazetteer of India*, 'The country' [*i.e.* the Sundarban district] 'is one vast alluvial plain, where the continual process of land-making has not yet ceased. It abounds in morasses and swamps now gradually filling up, and is intersected by large rivers and estuaries running from north to south. These are connected with each other by innumerable smaller channels; so that the whole tract is a tangled network of streams, rivers, and water-courses, enclosing a large number of islands of various shapes and sizes.'

to my mind the mouths of the river *Nile.* When in *Egypt* I remarked the same process of nature; and as it is often said, in the language of *Aristotle,* that *Egypt* is the workmanship of the *Nile,* so may it be observed that *Bengale* is the production of the *Ganges.* There is only this difference between the two rivers, that the *Ganges* being incomparably larger[1] than the *Nile,* it carries toward the sea a much greater quantity of earth; and thus forms a number of islands more numerous and larger than those of the *Nile.* The islands of the *Nile* too are destitute of trees; but those of the *Ganges* are all covered with them, owing to the four months of regular and excessive rains that fall in the midst of summer. These rains obviate the necessity of cutting canals in *Bengale,* as is done in Egypt, for the

[1] This statement, and in fact the entire passage, is a striking example of Bernier's wonderful powers of correct observation; the ordinary low water discharge of the Nile being 51,500 cubic feet per second, while that of the Ganges is 207,000; although the *length* of the stream of the Nile greatly exceeds that of the Ganges, the figures being 3370 and 1557 miles respectively. As has been so well and graphically stated by Sir W. W. Hunter in *The Imperial Gazetteer of India*:—

'After the lapse of twenty centuries, and the rise and fall of rival religions, veneration for the Ganges still figures as a chief article in the creed of modern Hinduism. . . . To bathe in the Ganges, especially at the great stated festivals, will wash away the stain of sin; and those who have thus purified themselves carry back bottles of the sacred water to their less fortunate relations. To die and be buried on the river bank is a passport to eternal bliss. Even to exclaim "Gangá, Gangá," at the distance of a hundred leagues, will atone for the sins committed during three previous lives.

'The river thus reverenced by the Hindus deserves their homage by reason of its exceptional utility for agriculture and navigation. None of the other rivers of India approach the Ganges in beneficence. The Brahmaputra and the Indus may have longer streams, as measured by the geographer, but the upper courses of both lie hidden within the unknown recesses of the Himálayas. Not one of the great rivers of central or Southern India is navigable in the proper sense of the term. The Ganges begins to distribute fertility as soon as it reaches the plains, within 200 miles of its sources; and at the same point it becomes in some sort navigable. Thenceforwards it rolls majestically down to the sea in a bountiful stream, which never becomes a mere destructive torrent in the rains, and never dwindles away in the hottest summer. If somewhat diminished by irrigation, its volume is forthwith restored by numerous great tributaries; and the wide area of its river-basin receives annually a sufficient rainfall to maintain the supply in every part. Embankments are in few places required to restrain its inundations, for the alluvial silt which it spills over its banks year by year affords to the fields a top-dressing of inexhaustible fertility. If one crop be drowned by the flood, the cultivator calculates that his second crop will abundantly requite him.'

purpose of irrigating and enriching the land. They could indeed be made with as much facility in the one country as in the other, the *Ganges* and other rivers of *Hindoustan* increasing, the same as the *Nile,* in summer in consequence of the rains which regularly fall at that season. There is this difference between the two countries: that in *Egypt* no rain is known, neither in summer nor scarcely at any other time, excepting occasionally in a small quantity toward the sea. It is only near the source of the *Nile,* in *Ethiopia,* that rain falls; whereas throughout the *Indies* it rains periodically in the countries through which the rivers flow. It should be observed, however, that this is not the case universally; for in the kingdom of *Scymdy,* toward the *Persian* Gulf, where the mouth of the *Indus* is situated, there are years during which no rain whatever falls, although the *Indus* be greatly swollen. The fields are then irrigated, as in *Egypt,* by means of *kalis,*[1] or artificial channels.

In regard to the wish expressed by *Monsieur Thevenot* that I should send you a detailed narration of my Adventures in the *Red Sea,* at *Suez, Tor, Mount Sinai, Gidda* (in that pretended holy land of Mahomet, half a day's journey from *Meca*), in the island of *Kamarane* and at *Louhaya,*[2] together with all the information which I obtained at *Moka* concerning the Kingdom of *Ethiopia,* and the best route for entering therein, it is my intention to gratify that wish when I have had time to put in order, God helping me, my *Papers.*

[1] *Khal,* the name in Bengal for an inlet of the sea or of a large river, a creek; the water being baled from the *khal,* and then distributed over the fields by means of small artificial channels.

[2] Kameran, now a British possession, off the coast of Arabia, in the same latitude as Annesley Bay in Abyssinia. Loheia, a town on the mainland of Arabia, about 20 miles to the north of the island of Kameran.

FINIS.

IMPERII MAGNI MOGOLIS Novissima Descriptio.
Oriens
Occidens
Meridies
TARTARIA
KASKAR REGN
KACHMIRE
TIBET MINOR
TIBET MAJOR
Rama Mug
Siba
Cabul
Attock REGN.
PENJE-AB
Candahar
REGNI Aguvanes
PERSICI PARS.
HAIA-Bulloques
CAN-Hed.
Buc-kor
Multan
Putans
Naugracut
Jamba
Ie-nupar
Owns
Bando
Iesselmere
Tatta
Scindy
Ranas
Chitor
Dehli
Agra
Sambal
Bikar
Govaleor
Patna
Udessa
LASSA
Necbal
Regn.
Tanchut Regn.
BENGALA
Berar
Ralbgouta
Candis
DECAN
Guzaratte
Cambaja
GOLCONDA
Golconda
Bengala
Chatigam
Benares
Ganges flu.
MARE ARABICUM.
SINUS GANGETICUS.
Golfo d'India

A MEMORANDUM *omitted to be included in my first Work, to complete the Map of Hindoustan, and make known the revenues of the Great Mogol.*

THE better to understand what follows it is necessary to know the signification of the following terms.

1. *Soubah,*[1] that is to say, Government and Province.
2. *Pragna,*[2] that is, the chief City, Burgh or Village which has many others subordinate to it, and where the Rents are paid to the King, who is the absolute Lord [*Seigneur*] of all the lands of his Empire.
3. *Serkar,*[3] that is the Exchequer of the King's income from all sources [Tresors du Roy].
4. *Kaziné,*[4] that is, Treasury.
5. *Roupie,*[5] the money of the Country, worth about thirty *sols*.

[1] *Súbah,* derived from the Arabic, originally a heap of money, or a granary, hence a Province.

[2] *Pargana,* a tract of country comprising the lands of many villages; there are several Parganas in a Zilla (or Shire), and several Zillas go to make up a Province.

[3] *Sirkar,* more familiarly 'circar,' as the 'Northern Circars.' The word literally means a chief, a superior; Bernier seems to use it in the sense of a sub-division of a Province in which a 'treasury' for rent collection was situated.

[4] *Khazána,* Bernier's rendering is the original meaning. It may also be translated as the public revenue, the land-tax or rent.

[5] Which is also Manouchi's and Tavernier's values, and makes the rupee then = 2s. 3d.; see page 200, footnote [1].

6. *Lecque,*[1] that is, one hundred thousand.
7. *Kourour,*[2] a hundred *Lecques.*

1. *Jehan-Abad* or *Dehli* is the first *Soubah*; it has sixteen *Serkars* dependent upon it, and two hundred and thirty *Pragnas.* It yields to the King in *Roupies*	[3] 1,95,25,000
2. *Agra,* otherwise called *Akber-abad,* is the second; it comprises fourteen *Serkars,* two hundred and sixteen *Pragnas,* and yields to the King	2,52,25,000
3. *Lahor* has fourteen *Serkars,* and three hundred and fourteen *Pragnas,* yielding to the King	2,46,95,000
4. *Hasmer,* which belongs to a *Raja,*[4] pays to the King a tribute of	2,19,70,000
5. *Gusarate,* of which the capital is *Ahmed-abad,* has nine *Serkars* and one hundred and ninety *Pragnas,* yielding to the King	1,33,95,000
6. The Kingdom of *Candahar* belongs to the King of *Persia,* but the *Pragnas* which still remain united to the Kingdom of the *Great Mogol* are fifteen, and yield him a rental of	19,92,500
Carry forward,	10,68,02,500

[1] Lack, from the Hindostanee *lakh* from the Sanskrit *laksha,* originally meaning a mark.

[2] Crore, from the Hindostanee *karor.* *Arb* is the name for 100 crores.

[3] For facility of reference the totals have been extended in this form, Bernier giving the figures in words only, which are difficult to add up.

[4] Ajmere, although nominally a province of the Mogul Empire in Bernier's time, was also to a great extent under the influence of the Rahtor Princes of Márwár. It was with the object of consolidating the Mogul power there, that Ajmere was made the capital of the Empire during several years of Jáhángír's reign.

Brought forward,	10,68,02,500
7. *Maloüa* comprises nine *Serkars,* one hundred and ninety *Pragnas,* yielding	91,62,500
8. *Patna,* or *Beara,* has eight *Serkars,* two hundred and forty-five *Pragnas,* yielding	95,80,000
9. *Elabas* has seventeen *Serkars,* two hundred and sixteen *Pragnas,* and yields	94,70,000
10. *Haoud* comprises five *Serkars,* one hundred and forty-nine *Pragnas,* yielding	68,30,000
11. *Moultan* has four *Serkars,* ninety-six *Pragnas,* and yields	1,18,40,500
12. *Jagannat,* in which is included *Bengale,*[1] has eleven *Serkars,* twelve *Pragnas,* and yields	72,70,000
13. *Kachemire* has five *Serkars,* forty-five *Pragnas,* and yields	(*sic*)[2] 3,50,000
14. *Caboul* has thirty-five *Pragnas,* yielding a rental of	32,72,500
15. *Tata*[3] has four *Serkars* and fifty-four *Pragnas,* yielding a rental of	23,20,000
16. *Aureng-abad,* formerly called *Daulet-abad,* has eight *Serkars,* seventy-nine *Pragnas,* and yields a rental of	1,72,27,500
17. *Varada*[4] comprises twenty *Serkars,* one hundred and ninety-one *Pragnas,* yielding	1,58,75,000
Carry forward,	20,00,00,500

[1] By *Jagannat* is meant Orissa, the Province in which is situated the celebrated Juggernaut (for Jagannáth) temple. A tax upon the offerings at that Hindoo shrine was probably very remunerative to the Moguls.

[2] Apparently a clerical error for 35,00,000. In a *Dastúr ul Amal* (Revenue Manual) of the third year of Aurangzeb, 1654-55, quoted by Thomas, in the work cited over leaf, the Revenue of Kashmír is given as Rs. 28,59,750.

[3] Sind.

[4] Berár.

Brought forward,	20,00,00,500
18. *Candeys,* of which the chief town is *Brampour,* has three *Serkars,* three hundred *Pragnas,* yielding	1,85,50,000
19. *Talengand,*[1] which marches on the Kingdom of *Golkonda,* in the direction of *Maslipatam,* has forty-three *Pragnas,* yielding a rental of	68,85,000
20 *Baganala,*[2] which borders the territory of the *Portuguese* and the mountain strongholds of *Seva-gi,* the *Raja* who plundered *Sourate,* has twelve *Serkars,* and eight *Pragnas,* and yields a rental of	5,00,000
TOTAL,	. 22,59,35,500

According to this Memorandum, which I do not believe to be very exact or credible, the Great Mogol has an annual revenue from his lands alone of more than two [sic] *Kouroures*[3] *of Roupies.*

NOTE on the foregoing *Memorandum.*

The late Mr. Edward Thomas, F.R.S., formerly in the service of the Honourable East India Company in Bengal, in his exceedingly valuable work, *The Revenue Resources of the Mughal Empire in India, from* A.D. 1593 *to* A.D. 1707 (London, Trübner, 1871) estimates the value of the above return very highly, although Bernier is apologetic for the table itself and expresses his distrust of the grand total, which he clearly considered to be far too large in amount. Mr. Thomas then goes on to say that 'so far from any excess in the grand total, I am disposed to impute a deficiency, especially in the complete omission of any

[1] Telingána.

[2] The cradle of the future Mahratta power ; 'Between the 20th and 21st degree N. latitude.'—*Rennell.*

[3] In the original, *plus de deux Kouroures,* the word *twenty* being omitted. This mistake has been copied by all Bernier's subsequent editors and translators, but see No. 5 of the *Bibliography.*

return for the Province of Bengal, and the manifest absence of a nought in the sum assigned for Kashmir.' I would venture, however, to point out that Bernier distinctly states (Item 12.) that the revenue from Bengal is included in that for 'Jagannat,' which I hold to be Orissa. Rs. 72,70,000 is certainly a comparatively small sum for the combined revenues, one of the Provinces, Bengal, being, according to Bernier's own showing (pp. 437-446) the richest in all the Indies ; but it should be borne in mind, that in his time Bengal had revolted, under Prince Shujah (see pp. 80 and 92), and it is not likely that the Emperor derived a large revenue from that Province during the period of rebellion. Bernier, however, does not tell us anything of the source from which he derived his figures, nor the exact period to which they refer, but as Mr. Thomas says 'they bear the stamp of a certain degree of authenticity, and allowing for deficiencies, they fairly fit in with the prior and subsequent returns.' It would be quite beyond the scope of the present publication to even attempt to deal tentatively with such an important subject as the revenues of Hindostan under the Moguls, but I believe that the following table, compiled from Mr. Thomas's masterly work, may be of considerable interest to many. It would be quite possible to explain the variations approximately, as due to the changing boundaries of the Empire at various periods, or to the agricultural advance or retrogression of the several Provinces, the result of famines or other causes. The effect of the residence of the Court upon the material prosperity of the favoured locality, as pointed out by Mr. Thomas, might also be learnt by an exhaustive analysis of the Provincial totals—the latter a factor of prosperity or otherwise, which Bernier with his keen insight has not failed to notice, as may be learnt from pp. 220, 271, 381 and 384 of this volume.

THE GROSS PROVINCIAL REVENUES OF THE MOGUL EMPIRE AT VARIOUS PERIODS.

PERIOD.	A.D. 1594. Akbar.	A.D. 1648. Sháh-Jahán.	A.D. 1654. Aurang-zeb.	? Some year between 1656-1667. BERNIER'S return.	Date uncertain, but held to be between 1667-1691. Official returns.	A.D. 1697. Aurang-zeb.	A.D. 1707. Aurang-zeb.
RUPEES.	14,19,09,576	22,00,00,000 (1)	26,74,39,702 (2)	22,59,35,500 (3)	35,64,14,308 (4)	38,62,46,802 (5)	30,17,96,859 (6)

Increases and decreases may then be accounted for, broadly as follows :—

1, 2. Increases due to gradual consolidation of Akbar's conquered Provinces.

3. Decrease accounted for by the effects of the Rebellion, the richest Province, Bengal, in partial revolt for several years.

4, 5. Returning prosperity, and conquests in the Deccan, adding new Provinces to the Empire.

6. The Mogul rule waning, the Marathás increasing in power, and incessantly harrying many of the Mogul Provinces, 'levying *chauth*[1] and *sardésmukhi*[2] with the alternative of fire and sword : cutting off the sources of revenue, and wearying out the disorganised armies of the Empire.' A. C. Lyall, *Berar Gazetteer*, Bombay, 1870, p. 122.

---

[1] A payment equal to one-fourth, hence the name, of the actual revenue collections of the State, demanded as the price for forbearing to ravage, blackmail in fact. In Robert Mabon's *Sketches Illustrative of Oriental Manners and Customs*, Calcutta, 1797, will be found (plate vi.) a very graphic illustration of the levying of *chauth*, entitled 'Mahratta Pendairees returning to camp after a plundering Excursion.'

[2] The proportion of ten per cent. exacted from the revenues of the Muhammadan territories of the Deccan, in addition to the *chauth*. It was originally claimed by Sivají as head *Desmukh* (a hereditary native officer who exercised the chief police and revenue authority over a district), whence the name.

Abstract of the King's Licence.

By the Favour and Licence of the King, dated the 25th April 1670, given at Paris and signed MASCLARAY: The *Sieur* BERNIER is permitted to print, sell and dispose of a book entitled *Memoirs by the Sieur Bernier on the Empire of the Great Mogol*, and this during the time and space of ten years; all persons of whatever rank and occupation they may be, are hereby forbidden to print, sell or otherwise dispose of any other editions than those of the said *Sieur* BERNIER, or others which he may authorise, under a penalty of a fine of three thousand *livres*, and other punishments which are set forth at length in the Letters of the said Licence.

The said *Sieur* Bernier has disposed of his Licence to Claude Barbin for his benefit, in terms of an agreement entered into between them.

Registered in the Book of the Society of Booksellers & Printers of Paris, the 13th August 1670. *Signed*, LOVIS SEVESTRE, *Syndic*.

APPENDICES

APPENDIX I.

Regarding Dryden's Tragedy of AURENG-ZEBE

Aureng-Zebe, A tragedy. Acted at the Royal Theatre. Written by John Dryden, Servant to his Majesty—is entered in the Stationers' Register on November 29th, 1675, and Malone is of opinion that it had probably been acted in the spring of that year. The *dramatis personæ* and plot are as follows, from which, and from what follows, will be seen what poetical licence the Author has taken with the text of the History he used :

THE OLD EMPEROUR [in love with Indamora].
AURENG-ZEBE, his son [in love with Indamora].
MORAT, his younger Son [son of Nourmahal].
ARIMANT, Governour of *Agra* [in love with Indamora].
DIANET, SOLYMAN AGAH, MIR BABA, ABBAS, ASAPH CHAWN, FAZEL CHAWN, — *Indian* Lords, or *Omrahs* of several Factions.
NOURMAHAL,[1] the Empress.
INDAMORA, a captive Queen [of Cassimere, in love with Aureng-Zebe].
MELESINDA, wife to *Morat*.
ZAYDA, favourite Slave to the Empress.

SCENE, *Agra*, in the year 1660.

The Emperour, who is 70 years of age, had been so ill that his death was expected--his four sons had taken up arms to contend for the Empire—Aureng-Zebe, who remains loyal to his Father, defeats

[1] Núr Mahál was the wife of the Emperor *Jahángir*, and died, aged 72, in 1645. Mumtáz Mahál was Sháh Jahán's wife, and she died in 1631, and is buried in the Taj. Many compilers of books of Indian History have confounded the one with the other. Dryden has of course availed himself of a poet's licence.

two of his brothers and enters Agra, but without his forces; the Emperour endeavours to persuade Aureng-Zebe to resign Indamora to him—he refuses—and the Emperour admits Morat and his troops into the City, Aureng-Zebe is placed in confinement—Morat falls in love with Indamora—Nourmahal makes love to Aureng-Zebe—he rejects her advances with horror—she, in revenge, summons her mutes and offers him a cup of poison—Morat enters and takes away the cup. This is a passage which most of the critics who have discussed this Tragedy, but apparently without any knowledge whatever of Bernier's book, have thought unworthy of its Author. I do not think, however, that, after a careful perusal of Bernier's narrative, their verdict will be generally concurred in, especially when it is borne in mind that Bernier's *entire work* formed the *leit motif*, nay a good deal more than that, of Dryden's drama. In support of this opinion, the passage in question, in Act IV., is here given :—

As he is going to drink, enter Morat, *attended.*

Mor. Make not such haste, you must my leisure stay :
Your Fate's deferr'd, you shall not die to-day.
[*Taking the Cup from him.*
Nour. What foolish pity has possess'd your mind,
To alter what your prudence once design'd ?[1]
Mor. What if I please to lengthen out his date
A day, and take a pride to cozen Fate?
Nour. 'Twill not be safe to let him live an hour.
Mor. I'll do't, to show my Arbitrary pow'r.
Nour. Fortune may take him from your hands again,
And you repent th' occasion lost in vain.
Mor. I smile at what your Female fear foresees ;
I'm in Fate's place, and dictate her Decrees.
Let Arimant be called.

Morat and his father quarrel—the Emperour reconciles himself to Aureng-Zebe—the latter defeats the forces of Morat—Nourmahal is going to stab Indamora, but is prevented by Morat—Morat dies of his wounds—Melesinda determines to burn herself on his funeral pile—Nourmahal poisons herself, and dies mad—the Emperour resigns Indamora to Aurenge-Zebe.

Dryden has of course taken great liberties with history, the manners and customs of the Indies, and so forth, but it is pleasing to see his keen appreciation of the genius of Bernier, which is well illustrated in a passage which will be found at the end of the Tragedy, Act V.,

[1] Compare Raushan Ará Begum's conduct towards her brother Dárá, when his fate was being decided, at p. 100.

where Morat's wife is about to become a *Suttee*. With this may be compared pp. 306-315 of Bernier's narrative :—

A Procession of Priests, Slaves following, and last, Melesinda *in white.*

Ind. Alas ! what means this pomp?
Aur. 'Tis the Procession of a Funeral Vow,
Which cruel Laws to *Indian* Wives allow,
When fatally their Virtue they approve ;
Chearful in flames, and Martyrs of their love.
Ind. Oh my foreboding heart ! th' event I fear ;
And see ! sad *Melesinda* does appear.
Mel. You wrong my love ; what grief do I betray?
This is the Triumph of my Nuptial day.
My better Nuptials ; which, in spight of Fate,
For ever joyn me to my dear *Morat.*
Now I am pleas'd ; my jealousies are o'er :
He's mine ; and I can lose him now no more.
Emp. Let no false show of Fame your reason blind.
Ind. You have no right to die ; he was not kind.
Mel. Had he been kind, I could no love have shown :
Each vulgar Virtue would as much have done.
My love was such, it needed no return ;
But could, though he supplied no fuel, burn.
Rich in it self, like Elemental fire,
Whose pureness does no Aliment require.
In vain you would bereave me of my Lord ;
For I will die : Die is too base a word ;
I'll seek his breast, and, kindling by his side,
Adorn'd with flames, I'll mount a glorious Bride.
[*Exit.*

Davies, in his *Dramatic Miscellanies,* London 1784, pp. 157-158 vol. iii., styles it Dryden's last and most perfect tragedy in ryme :—'In this play the passions are strongly depicted, the characters were discriminated, and the diction more familiar and dramatic than in any of his preceding pieces. . . . The Court greatly encouraged the play of Aureng-Zebe. The Author tells us, in his dedication, that Charles II. altered an incident in the plot, and pronounced it to be the best of all Dryden's tragedies.' It was revived in 1708, 1709, and 1721, when it was performed on the 11th December at Drury Lane.

Addison considered Aureng-Zebe's complaint of the vicissitudes and disappointments of life, Act iv. Scene I, the best lines in the play :—

Aur. When I consider Life, 'tis all a cheat ;
Yet, fool'd with hope, men favour the deceit ;

Trust on and think to-morrow will repay :
To morrow 's falser than the former day ;
Lies worse ; and, while it says, we shall be blest
With some new joys, cuts off what we possest.
Strange couzenage ! none would live past years again,
Yet all hope pleasure in what yet remain ;
And, from the dregs of life, think to receive
What the first sprightly running could not give.
I'm tired with waiting for the Chymick Gold,
Which fools us young, and beggars us when old.

Davies tells us that he had heard Dr. Johnson highly commend the full and pertinent answer given by Nourmahal :—

Nour. 'Tis not for nothing that we life pursue ;
It pays our hopes with something still that 's new :
Each day 's a Mistris, unenjoy'd before ;
Like Travellers, we 're pleas'd with seeing more.
Did you but know what joys your way attend,
You would not hurry to your journey's end.

As stated in our Preface, Dryden founded his play on the English translation, 1671-72, of Bernier's Travels, and even a cursory perusal of his Tragedy will show many passages which are mere paraphrases, so to speak, of Bernier's text—a remarkable instance being met with in Act 1. Scene i., where Arimant, Asaph Chawn, Fazel Chawn, and Solyman Agah are discussing the situation of affairs. In the course of their councils, they thus give their opinions as to the character of the Emperor's rebellious sons :—

Asaph. The name of Father hateful to him grows,
Which, for one Son, produces him three foes.
Fazel. *Darah*, the eldest, bears a generous mind ;
But to implacable revenge inclined.
Too openly does Love and hatred show ;
A bounteous Master, but a deadly foe.
Solym. From *Sujah's* valour I should much expect,
But he 's a *Bigot* of the *Persian* Sect,
And, by a Foreign Int'rest seeks to Reign,
Hopeless by Love the Sceptre to obtain.
Asaph. *Morat's* too insolent, too much a Brave,
His Courage to his Envy is a Slave.
What he attempts, if his endeavours fail
T' effect, he is resolved no other shall.
Arim. But *Aureng-Zebe*, by no strong passion sway'd,
Except his Love, more temp'rate is, and weigh'd :

This *Atlas* must our sinking State uphold ;
In Council cool, but in performance bold :
He sums their Virtues in himself alone,
And adds the greatest, of a Loyal Son :
His Father's Cause upon his Sword he wears,
And with his Arms, we hope, his fortune bears.
Solym. Two vast Rewards may well his courage move,
A parent's blessing, and a Mistris Love.
If he succeed, his recompense, we hear,
Must be the Captive Queen of *Cassimere*.

Which may be compared with pp. 6-11, of Bernier's text.

APPENDIX II.

On the identity of the 'Great Mogul's diamond' with the Koh-i-núr.

Catrou states that Mirza Mula (otherwise Mergi Mola) served for some time in the army of the Mogul (*i.e.* Sháh Jahán) and rose to high command, but that, disgusted with the contempt of Prince Dárá, he entered the service of the King of Golconda, by whom he was appointed 'superintendent over the customs and the traffic of the King.' Profiting by so advantageous a post, and trading on his own account, he soon amassed immense wealth, which at first he used to gain the good graces of his master, procuring for him as presents rarities from Europe, cabinets from China, and elephants from Ceylon. 'His magnificence caused him to be taken notice of at Court, and as soon as he became known, he attained to the first distinctions. What brought him into chief notice was an intrigue of gallantry, which he carried on in private with the mother of the King. She was a princess who still preserved her beauty, at a rather advanced period of life. The King's acquaintance with the irregular conduct of his mother served only to advance the fortunes of Mirza Mula. He was sent to a distance from the Court, that the queen-mother might be prevented from giving occasion to scandal ; and the government of the province of the Carnatic was bestowed upon him. The artful Persian knew how to turn his disgrace to his advantage. The diamond mine, which adds so much to the wealth of the kingdom of Golconda, was within the limits of his government. He consequently determined to make the best use of his time. He retained for his own use the largest and the most perfect of the diamonds. One, which he gave in the sequel to the Mogul Emperor, was unparalleled in its kind. It is still the admiration of all connoisseurs.'

Tavernier tells us that the Great Mogul's diamond was obtained by the Amir Jumla, from the Coulour (Kollúr) mine (*Travels*, English Trans. by V. Ball, vol. ii., p. 74). Dr. V. Ball, now Director of the Science and Art Museum, Dublin, but formerly of the Geological Survey of India, when in that country traced out by means of the routes given to it by Tavernier, who visited it personally, the position of this mine, which, known by its modern name Kollúr, is situated on the Kistna river in N. latitude 16° 42′ 30″, E. longitude 80° 5′, and on an old route from Masulipatam to Golconda (Haidarabad). This identification has since been further proved by the discovery of the remains of the old mining settlement at Kollúr.

The exact date of the discovery of the gem is not known, but about 1656 or 1657 it was presented, while still uncut, to Sháh Jáhan by Mir Jumla. It then weighed 756 English carats. Dr. Ball has shown that the carats used in his descriptions of stones by Tavernier were the Florentine, the lightest of all carats. Vide p. 17, footnote [3].

Tavernier was invited by Aurangzeb to see all his jewels, and among them the great diamond, which he was allowed to examine, make a drawing of, and weigh. He found it to weigh 268$\frac{1}{16}$ English carats. The loss in weight is thus explained by Tavernier (vol. i. p. 396):—'If this stone had been in Europe it would have been treated in a different manner, for some good pieces would have been taken from it, and it would have weighed more than it does, instead of which it has been all ground down. It was the *Sieur* HORTENSIO BORGIO, a Venetian, who cut it, for which he was badly rewarded, for when it was cut he was reproached with having spoilt the stone, which ought to have retained a greater weight; and instead of paying him for his work, the King fined him ten thousand rupees, and would have taken more if he had possessed it. If the *Sieur* HORTENSIO had understood his trade well, he would have been able to take a large piece from this stone without doing injury to the King, and without having had so much trouble grinding it; but he was not a very accomplished diamond cutter.' By this latter phrase, Dr. Ball, in opposition to a view held by Mr. King and others, is of opinion that Tavernier meant, not that Hortensio might have defrauded the Mogul by taking off a large piece, but that he might with advantage have cleaved the stone instead of grinding it; the pieces so cleaved would then have been the property of the Mogul, not the perquisite of Hortensio. This, after a careful examination of the original text, appears to me also to be the correct reading.

In 1739 the diamond was plundered from Aurangzeb's descendant,

Muhammad Sháh, by Nadir Sháh when he sacked Delhi, and carried it away, with an immense amount of other loot, to Persia. On first beholding it he is reported to have conferred upon it the title *Koh-i-núr* ('Mountain of Light,' or Lustre), a most suitable name for the stone described by Tavernier as 'a round "rose," very high at one side, of beautiful water, and a splendid stone.'

Dr. Ball then traces its history through the hands of Ahmed Sháh Durani in 1751, Sháh Zamán in 1793, Sháh Shujá in 1795, Ranjit Singh, in 1813, and, on the annexation of the Punjab in 1849, to the custody of the British Government, by whom it was sent — John Lawrence, afterwards Lord Lawrence, having been for a short time its custodian—to Her Majesty, Queen Victoria. It then weighed $186\frac{1}{16}$ carats English, and Dr. Ball ascribes the loss in weight, about 83 carats, to mutilation, to which it was subjected as he proves by the marks of cleavage apparent when it was received in England, and which took place, he believes, when in the possession of either Sháh Rukh, Shah Zamán, or Sháh Shujá, whose necessities may have caused them to have had pieces removed to furnish them with ready money.

In 1851 the *Koh-i-núr* was exhibited in the first great Exhibition, and in 1852 the re-cutting of the stone was intrusted by Her Majesty to the Messrs. Garrards, who employed Voorsanger, a diamond-cutter from M. Coster's *atelier* at Amsterdam. The actual cutting lasted thirty-eight days, and by it the weight was reduced to $106\frac{1}{16}$ carats. The cost of the cutting amounted to £8000.

APPENDIX III.

Tavernier's description of the Peacock Throne of the Great Mogul.

It should be stated that the GREAT MOGUL has seven magnificent thrones, one wholly covered with diamonds, the others with rubies, emeralds, or pearls.

The principal throne, which is placed in the hall of the first court, is nearly of the form and size of our camp-beds; that is to say, it is about 6 feet long and 4 wide. Upon the four feet, which are very massive, and from 20 to 25 inches high, are fixed the four bars which support the base of the throne, and upon these bars are ranged twelve columns, which sustain the canopy on three sides, there not being any on that which faces the court. Both the feet and the bars, which are more than 18 inches long, are covered with gold inlaid and enriched with numerous diamonds, rubies, and emeralds. In the middle of each bar there is a large *balass*[1] [*balet* in orig.] ruby, cut *en cabuchon*, with four emeralds round it, which form a square cross. Next in succession, from one side to the other along the length of the bars there are similar crosses, arranged so that in one the ruby is in the middle of four emeralds, and in another the emerald is in the middle and four *balass* rubies surround it. The emeralds are table-cut, and the intervals between the rubies and emeralds are covered with diamonds, the largest of which do not exceed 10 to 12 carats in weight, all being showy stones, but very flat. There are also in some parts pearls set in gold, and upon one of the longer sides of the throne there are four steps to ascend it. Of the three cushions or pillows which are upon the throne, that which is placed behind the King's back is large and round like one of our bolsters, and the two others that are placed at his sides are flat. There is to be seen, moreover, a sword suspended from this throne, a mace, a round shield, a bow and quiver with arrows; and all these weapons, as also the cushions and steps, both of this throne and the other six, are covered over with stones which match those with which each of the thrones is respectively enriched.

I counted the large *balass* rubies on the great throne, and there are about 108, all *cabuchons*, the least of which weighs 100 carats,[2] but there are some which weigh apparently 200 and more. As for the emeralds, there are plenty of good colour, but they have many flaws; the largest may weigh 60 carats and the least 30 carats. I counted about one hundred and sixteen (116); thus there are more emeralds than rubies.

The underside of the canopy is covered with diamonds and pearls, with a fringe of pearls all round, and above the canopy, which is a quadrangular-shaped dome, there is to be seen a peacock with elevated tail made of blue sapphires and other coloured stones, the body being of gold inlaid with precious stones, having a large ruby in front of the breast, from whence hangs a pear-shaped pearl of 50 carats or thereabouts, and of a somewhat yellow water. On both sides of the peacock there is a large bouquet of the same height as the bird, and consisting of many kinds of flowers made of gold inlaid with precious stones. On the side of the throne which is opposite the court there is to be seen a jewel consisting of a diamond of from 80 to 90 carats weight, with rubies and emeralds round it, and when the King is seated he has this jewel in full view. But that which in my opinion

1 A corruption of *Balakhshaf*, a popular form of *Badakhshaf*, because these rubies came from the famous mines on the Upper Oxus, in one of the districts subject to Badakhshán. A.C.

2 Rubies of good quality weighing 100 carats would be worth more than diamonds of equal weight, but it is probable that these were not perfect in every respect. V.B.

is the most costly thing about this magnificent throne is, that the twelve columns supporting the canopy are surrounded with beautiful rows of pearls, which are round and of fine water, and weigh from 6 to 10 carats each. At 4 feet distance from the throne there are fixed, on either side, two umbrellas, the sticks of which for 7 or 8 feet in height are covered with diamonds, rubies, and pearls. The umbrellas are of red velvet, and are embroidered and fringed all round with pearls.

This is what I have been able to observe regarding this famous throne, commenced by TAMERLANE and completed by SHÁH JAHÁN; and those who keep the accounts of the King's jewels, and of what this great work has cost, have assured me that it amounts to one hundred and seven thousand lakhs of rupees [*sic*] (*i.e.* 10,700,000,000), which amount to one hundred and sixty millions five hundred thousand *livres* of our money (*i.e.* 160,500,000).[1]

Behind this grand and magnificent throne there is placed a smaller one, which has the form of a bathing tub. It is of an oval shape of about 7 feet in length and 5 in breadth, and the outside is covered over with diamonds and pearls, but it has no canopy.—*Travels*, vol. i. pp. 381, 385.

APPENDIX IV.

Note on the letter to Monseigneur Colbert concerning the absorption of the precious metals in India.

Numberless writers have treated on the subject of the buried treasure of India, among others, Tavernier, who in his account of the *Belief of the Idolaters touching the Condition of the Soul of man after Death*, explains the reason for treasure being hoarded as follows:—

'There are some among them who are foolish enough to bury their treasures during their lifetime, as, for instance, nearly all the rich men of the kingdom of ASSAM, so that if they enter, after death, the body of any poor and miserable mendicant, they can have recourse to the money which they have buried in order to draw from it at necessity. This is the reason why so much gold and silver and so many precious stones are buried in INDIA, and an idolater must be poor indeed if he has not money buried in the earth.'—*Travels*, vol. ii. pp. 204, 205.

All recent authorities agree in stating that within the last fifty years

[1] As Dr. V. Ball has pointed out, there appears to be a clerical error here. The figure should be 107,000,000, namely one thousand and seventy *lakhs*, which at $\frac{3}{2}$ of a rupee to the *livre* would be equal to 160,500,000 *livres*, or £12,037,500, the rupee being 2s. 3d. and the *livre* 1s. 6d.

there has been an enormous increase to the amount of capital lying idle in India, in the shape of hoarded treasure and in the ornaments used by the people in all parts of that country, and one of the greatest of all Indian economic problems is the provision of means whereby the owners of this wealth could be induced to utilise part of it in such a way as would materially benefit themselves and others.

Mr. Clarmont J. Daniell, the well-known advocate for remonetising gold in India, estimates[1] that at the beginning of the year 1889 there was 'lying in India a stock of gold bullion wholly useless for commercial purposes, and increasing at the rate of nearly three millions annually, of the value of not less than £270,000,000 at the market, being probably two and a half times as great as all the gold money in circulation in the United Kingdom.'—P. 249, *op. cit.*

In 1886-87 the Indian Government was able to utilise for coining purposes 31,837,783 obsolete silver coins which had been buried in pits and wells in the palace of the Mahárájá Scindia, and were thus credited as part of the sum forming the Gwalior Durbar loan, yielding interest, instead of remaining useless as they had done for a very long period.

Bernier did not fail to observe the large consumption of gold and silver in India for the making of jewellery, and in other articles of personal adornment; see pp. 223, 224. Of late years such a use of the precious metals has largely increased, and reliable and convincing evidence of this, as regards the Punjab, may be found in a recent account of the gold and silver works of the Punjab,[2] compiled by Mr. E. D. Maclagan, B.C.S., who finds after careful investigation that the forty years' peace that Province has now enjoyed under British rule has brought about a threefold change in the goldsmiths' trade in that part of India, viz.: 'a decrease in the merely ostentatious class of work: an increase but a concentration of the better forms of ornament industry, and a large development of the simplest and coarsest kinds.'—*Para.* 12.

Mr. Maclagan concludes his very valuable and exhaustive Monograph as follows:—

THE FUTURE OF GOLD AND SILVER ORNAMENTS.—'The use of ornaments appears in this country so universal, and to most minds so excessive, that the subject has attracted some attention from a social point of view. The Punjábí is probably as profuse in ornamentation as the native of any other part of the plains of India; foreigners in this Province at any rate, such as Parsis, Bangális, and the like, are far

[1] *The Industrial Competition of Asia. An Inquiry into the Influence of Currency on the Commerce of the Empire in the East.* London. 1890.

[2] *Monograph on the Gold and Silver Works of the Punjab.* 1888-89. Published by Authority. Lahore. 1890.

more sparing than the native Punjábí in the ornamentation of themselves and their wives. The actual amount of potential wealth that the native locks up in jewellery is something beyond conception. Europeans in dealing with the subject are far more inclined to under- than to over-value the amount of ornaments which a native family, in whatever rank of life, possesses. And yet every day in large civil cases, in suits for dower, in dealing with wards' estates, in cases of elopements, thefts, burglaries, murders, and a thousand other ways, civil officers are constantly being confronted with this enormous mass of wealth lying in the coffers of the people. A competent authority guesses that in Amritsar city alone there are jewels to the value of two million pounds sterling. In Kulu the ornaments are estimated at a lakh-and-a-half; and the gold and silver attached to *deotas* [idols and their shrines] at three lakhs. The Jullundur estimate is four lakhs, which is probably below the mark; that of Montgomery—fifty lakhs—is possibly above it. In Jhelum two-fifths of the wealth of the district is said to be in ornaments. If we estimate the existing ornaments at twelve times the annual out-turn, those of the Gurgáon District must be valued at over ten lakhs. In Dera Ismail Khan, at five rupees to each woman, the ornaments of the district must exceed ten lakhs in value; and we should probably add two lakhs to this estimate for the ornaments in the families of the Nawábs and other Raises [Gentry]. In Kohát, again (probably one of the poorest districts of the Province in this respect), the estimate is taken at Rs. 800 for each Hindú family, and Rs. 10 for each Mussalmán family, and a lakh in aggregate for the Nawáb and other Raises; making a total for the district of seventy-five lakhs. This estimate is doubtless an exaggeration, but even a more exact calculation would probably surprise us in its results. These isolated instances will serve better than any formal estimate to show the extent to which the system is carried in the Province.

'The main evil which is laid at the door of this system is the loss of wealth. Another is the incentive to crime; in Dera Ismail Khan, for instance, it has been calculated that in one year, out of 968 cases of burglary, house-breaking, and dacoity, 824 were connected with jewellery. Advocates, therefore, of economic and social progress look forward to a diminution of the stock of ornaments in the country, and it is not improbable that under our rule such a diminution will take place. The steps taken to reduce marriage expenses will doubtless do something, though perhaps not very much, in the direction. The spread of English or Anglicised education will probably do more; for it is noticed that the classes so educated are on the whole simple in their habits in this respect. And if anything occurs to give a general impetus to commercial enterprise and mutual confidence, opening opportunities for investment, the use of ornaments may be extensively diminished. But any such changes can only be most gradual, and there are obstacles in their way. The "female vote" is one. The enormous respect for jewellery among the people as a criterion of respectability is another. And the distinctly agricultural, and the commercially unenterprising character of the class which mainly upholds the system is another. There is no fear, therefore, of the practice of ornamentation dying out; and the position of the *sunárs* [workers of gold or silver jewellery] appears a fairly assured one. European competition has as yet had little influence on the articles prepared for native custom. False jewellery, except in large towns or among the very poorest classes, is not largely sought after. The general character of the popular type of gold and silver work is rough and unfinished; it is more likely to improve than to deteriorate, and for its improvement it is at present being left to itself.'

Manouchi, the Venetian Doctor, from whose Memoirs I have frequently quoted, gives a very graphic picture of the buried treasures of the Emperor Sháh Jahán in the following words:—

'As the Emperor grew old, his passions changed with his years. Avarice took the place of prodigality. It may be said, that this passion equalled, or even surpassed, all his other vices. He rewarded the principal officers of his court and of the armies by permitting them to plunder the people with impunity, and as soon as the Omrhas [*sic*] had become enriched by their extortions, the Emperor seized on their wealth, and appropriated to himself the spoil. In order to preserve with greater security the immense wealth, which tributes and extortions augmented every year, he caused to be constructed, under his palace of Dely, two deep caves, supported by vast marble pillars. Piles of gold were stored in the one, and of silver in the other; and to render more difficult any attempt to convey away his treasure, he caused, of both metals, pieces to be made of so prodigious a size as to render them useless for the purposes of commerce [*i.e.* currency]. In these caves Cha-Jaham passed a great part of the day, under the pretence of enjoying their refreshing coolness; but, in reality, for the purpose of feasting his eyes on the prodigious wealth he had accumulated.'

At a meeting of the Asiatic Society of Bengal, held at Calcutta on the 3d January 1883, the Vice-President, the late Hon. Mr. Gibbs, C.S.I., C.I.E., F.R.G.S., exhibited a drawing and an estampage of a 'two hundred gold mohur piece' struck by the Emperor Sháh Jahan 'in the Palace of Shah Jehanabad' [Delhi, see my text, p. 241.] A.H. 1064 [A.D. 1653]. The drawing and estampage were sent by General Cunningham, who, in a note accompanying them, was of opinion that the coin was a piece used for the purpose of presentation to the Emperor by a Noble as a *nuzzer* (or ceremonial present from an inferior to a superior). Manouchi's account, which I believe has been hitherto overlooked, is, as will be seen, somewhat different. For a facsimile drawing of the two hundred gold mohur piece, intrinsically worth, probably, £450 sterling, see p. 3, *Proc. As. Soc. Bengal*, for 1883.

APPENDIX V.

Some particulars relating to Mr. H[enry] O[uldinburgh].

For a long time I was unable to discover the name of the Translator of the first English edition, 1671-1672, of Bernier's Travels, simply stated as H. O. on the title-page thereof. At last, when examining the 1684 edition, No. 10 of the Bibliography, I found out that it was Henry Ouldinburgh.

Other investigations followed, and at length I identified the translator as the first Secretary of the Royal Society. By the gracious permission of the President and Council of that Society I was permitted to examine the Oldenburg (for so he spells his name) MSS. in their possession, where in a letter-book—M. I., and indexed as 62—I found a transcript, 6 pp. folio, of the portion of the letter from M. de Monceaux, which is printed in the first volume of the History of the late Revolution, etc., London, 1671, as 'giving a character of the book here Englished, and its author,' and which I have reprinted at pp. xlix.-li. of my edition.

This transcript, in a contemporary hand, not that of Henry Oldenburg, however, is headed *Extraict d'une Lettre de | Monsieur De Monceaux | A Monsieur Oldenbourg Secretaire—De la societe Royale |* and is dated Paris, 26th July 1670, not 16th as printed in the London edition of 1671, an error which has been copied in all subsequent issues.

I am also permitted by the Council of the Royal Society to reprint the following biographical sketch of their first Secretary, which was compiled in 1860 by Charles Richard Welch, Assistant Secretary and Librarian, in connection with a descriptive catalogue of the portraits in the possession of the Society :—

Henry Oldenburg, F.R.S., Painted by John van Cleef, born at Bremen 1626, *died at Charlton, Kent*, 1676.

'Oldenburg descended from the Counts of Oldenburg in Westphalia, from whom he derived his name. He came to England as Consul for Bremen, and on losing that appointment undertook the education of Lord O'Brien. In 1656 he entered as student in the University of Oxford, and while there made the acquaintance of those philosophers who originated the Royal Society. On the incorporation of this

Institution Oldenburg was appointed Secretary. He performed the duties of his office with extraordinary zeal, carried on an extensive correspondence with learned foreigners, and published the Philosophical Transactions from 1664 to 1677, contributing largely to them himself. His constant epistolary communication with foreign *savants*, sometimes carried on under the anagrammatic name of Grubendol,[1] led to his being suspected of treasonable practices, and to his imprisonment in the Tower. He was, however, quickly liberated. His correspondence, so far as preserved, has been of the greatest importance in all questions relating to the scientific history of the time.

'Towards the close of his life he was much distressed by a controversy with Hooke respecting the mechanism of watches, which was terminated by the Council deciding in his favour. His portrait represents him holding a watch in his hand, probably in allusion to this controversy.'

For the following account of the Oldenburg portrait I am indebted to Mr. George Scharf, C.B., the Keeper and Secretary of the National Portrait Gallery, who, through his assistant Mr. L. G. Holland, caused it to be examined for the purpose, and whose description is as follows :—

'A life-sized figure, seen to the waist, turned to the right [spectator's], face seen in three-quarters to the left, his dark chestnut eyes look piercingly at the spectator, with a severe expression, thick aquiline nose, thin dark grey eyebrows, tanned complexion, fat cheeks and full neck, double, cloven chin, compressed thin lips and peculiar long scanty dark moustaches, which only cover the middle space between his nostrils and upper lip. His dark auburn hair is parted in the middle and hangs down in masses on each side to his shoulders. His dress is of sombre black, only relieved by a broad lie-down collar and cuffs of blue-grey. His right hand rests on a table holding a gold watch-case, the upper lid of which is open, by a handle ; while his left hand, displaying a ring on the little finger, is raised to his left breast. The shadows are very dark, and background plain dark brown.'

1 When examining the Oldenburg MSS. I chanced to find the following passage in the 'office copy' of a letter, dated London, June 30th, 1669, and addressed to Mr. George Cotton in Rome, concerning a philosophical correspondence :—'And I would desire that the Inscription of your Letters to mee may only run thus :—A Monsieur Monsr. Grubendol, à Londres : No more but soe, and all will come more safely to my hands, than if they were directed to my owne name.' A. C.

INDEX

INDEX